THE BIG BOOK OF

How to SayIt®

Relationships

includes the complete texts of

How to Say It® for Couples
by Dr. Paul Coleman
&
How to Say It® from the Heart
by Jack Griffin

Prentice
Hall Press

Prentice Hall Press
Published by The Berkley Publishing Group
A member of Penguin Group (USA) Inc.
375 Hudson Street
New York, New York 10014

Previously published as *How to Say It® for Couples,*
copyright 2002 by Dr. Paul Coleman and
How to Say It® from the Heart, copyright 2001 by Jack Griffin.

Special Markets ISBN: 978-0-7352-0440-9
Special Markets Edition: October 2008

Visit our website at www.penguin.com

Library of Congress Cataloging-in-Publication Data available upon request.

Printed in the United States of America

10 9 8 7 6 5 4 3 2 1

Contents

How to Say It® for Couples

PART FOUR

Compatible Lovers: Bridging the Differences in Personalities or Values 129

PART FIVE

The Touchiest of Subjects: Communicating About Sex and Affection 175

PART SIX

When Life Turns Upside Down: Meaningful Conversation During Adversity

PART SEVEN

Healing Words: Increasing Trust.

PART EIGHT

Soul Mates: Encouraging Dreams and Spiritual Longings 299

PART NINE

The Daily Grind: Handling Everyday Occurrences and Misunderstandings . . 325

How to Say It® from the Heart

PART ONE

PART 2

PART 5

for Couples

COMMUNICATING WITH TENDERNESS, OPENNESS AND HONESTY

Dr. Paul Coleman, Psy. D.
AUTHOR OF *How to Say It® to Your Kids*

Take the Test and Open the GIFTS

This book is about how to have meaningful conversation with your partner when the right words aren't obvious or don't come easily.

It offers an easy way for you to see your communication strengths and weaknesses and make *immediate* improvements where needed. It also reveals the fantastic new rules for healthy, effective, and meaningful conversation (the key ones form the mnemonic GIFTS and are described more fully in Chapters 1–6). They are few in number and easy to understand. Once you learn and apply them, you may discover that you enjoy your partner's company even more.

Of course, saying the right words in the right way is not all that is required for a happy, fulfilling relationship. If your partner says he or she loves you but never shows it, you won't feel loved. Timing is important, too. Asking, "Would you like spaghetti for dinner?" may seem like an innocent question. But if you ask it while making love, your partner might lose interest in both passion and pasta.

Still, the words you each use are enormously powerful. Frequently saying the wrong words will blunt and even kill relationship satisfaction. Very often, too, saying the right words settles conflicts, soothes feelings, and demonstrates caring and interest. On an average day, that's all most couples need to feel good.

Finally, this book is not about using ingenious phrases to manipulate a reluctant partner to agree with your point of view. (That's not a relationship, that's one-up-manship.) Anyone who repeatedly badgers or uses power tactics to force a partner to change will fail much of the time. Those strategies may work in the Army, but they won't make a bit of practical difference in your love life because the fundamental problem in such cases is not one of strategy but a lack of teamwork and mutual goodwill. Couples embroiled in stubborn standoffs, tugs of war, and repetitive arguments feel unappreciated, disrespected, and unloved—and those are reasons they remain stubborn.

But herein lies a paradox: If you use the ideas in this book to help you to understand your partner (and to speak in ways that help him or her to understand you), to decrease harsh exchanges, increase the amount of positive emotion in nonconflict situations, and make needed adjustments as soon as possible when conversations falter, you will probably possess *much more persuasive power*.

Ironically, when couples learn to talk in a way that demonstrates a desire to understand one another and seek common ground, and when they can show interest and add a dollop of humor, they often stop trying to change one another. Goodwill blossoms and positive changes automatically occur—and the changes that don't occur seem acceptable.

Take This Test!

This book is divided into nine parts. The first two parts are "New Power Rules for Great Conversation" and "The Communication Backpack." They reveal the most essential tools for effective communication and should be read first. Then you can read any of the chapters you wish in any order you wish, depending upon your current concerns or interests.

Is your current relationship generally satisfying or dissatisfying? How you answer that question will also determine how you use this book. Rate yourself according to the list below. Generally speaking, happier couples:

1. Experience five times as many positive interactions as negative. (The least happy couples have slightly more negative interactions than positive.)

    Happy_____ Unhappy_____

2. Give each other the benefit of the doubt when a partner is critical, cranky, hurtful, whiny, or a pain in the neck. (Unhappy couples doubt the benefits of their partner.)

    Happy_____ Unhappy_____

3. Will have some areas of recurring disagreement (the same ol' fight) but they are not locked in a deadly tug of war. (Unhappy couples insist on changing each other or defying each other's attempts to get them to change.)

    Happy_____ Unhappy_____

4. Find ways to spend time with each other even if they have crazy schedules. (Unhappy couples spend less time with each other and often look for ways to avoid being together.)

    Happy_____ Unhappy_____

5. Can get angry but their arguments tend to de-escalate. (Unhappy couples start an argument and it gets worse from there—or the discussion ends prematurely with one partner, usually the man, walking away or shutting down.)

    Happy_____ Unhappy_____

6. Are genuinely fond of one another. They are proud of each other's accomplishments, enjoy spending time together, and are devoted to bring out the best in their relationship and their family life.

    Happy_____ Unhappy_____

If you checked happy in four or more categories, your relationship is fairly strong. You should use this book as suggested in the first four goals below. If you checked unhappy three or more times, you will want to use this book according to all seven of the goals.

If your relationship is fairly satisfying, use this book to help you:

- **Discover** which of the ways lovers communicate that represent your talking strengths, and which of the ways you need to fine-tune.

- **Respond** more effectively to the repetitive, never-seem-to-ever-really-go-away disagreements in which even satisfied couples can get bogged down. (What couple hasn't disagreed about spending money, disciplining the kids, or how often to have sex?)

- **Identify** the hidden keys to successful communication (the GIFTS) so that you can consciously apply them when you and your partner inevitably reach communication gridlock over some topic.

- **Speak** the right words when you and your partner face an unexpected family crisis or tragedy such as a serious health problem, the loss of a loved one, or job loss. Even loving, well-intended partners don't always know the best words to speak during sad or scary times.

If you love your partner but your relationship has been strained and unsatisfying despite efforts to improve matters, you will want to use this book as described above *plus* you will absolutely need to follow these extra guidelines mentioned throughout the book:

- **Hang in there** when your new communication tools are still met with resistance. Hurt feelings and chronic misunderstandings will not evaporate the first few times you speak more effectively. Tips on how to achieve this are offered. Follow them.

- **Change** your negative and pessimistic inner talk that has interfered with your ability to accurately perceive the intent and meaning of your partner's words. (Many chapters include a section called "How to Say It to Yourself." Follow those guidelines closely.) For example, after a disheartening argument, a man might walk away thinking, "She's always so unreasonable. Why do I even bother talking?" Such self-talk interferes with reconciliation and will cause him to actually *misperceive* what his partner is saying the next time they argue. He'll hear criticism that isn't there or take her complaints personally when they are not always about him.

- **Make improvements** in *nonconflict* conversations before tackling any hot topics. It's good practice—and research shows—that when a couple can discuss relationship-neutral topics (events of the day, neighborhood news, etc.) regularly without sounding irritable, whiny, or uncooperative, their discussions about touchy subjects are likely to improve.

Give the GIFTS, Avoid the Gaffs

The GIFTS are perhaps *the most important* tools you can use to make your conversations both effective and gratifying. Without the GIFTS, your relationship will not be happy. With them, even couples with major issues to resolve stand a pretty good chance of overcoming them. I will mention them briefly now and point out the ways men and women differ in their use. They will be explained more fully later. Remembering to give the GIFTS (and avoid the *gaffs*) will transform difficult conversations into rewarding and intimate experiences.

- **G Gentle.** Try to begin discussions with a gentle touch. Keep your engines purring. (Roaring engines are a major gaff, especially at the outset of a conversation.) Anger is allowed but do your utmost to start the conversation less harshly. "I'm angry and want to talk about this . . ." is a gentler start-up than "I can't believe you ignored my parents the entire night! Don't you know how rude that was?"

  Men vs. Women: Research is clear that when it comes to making complaints, women are more likely to begin with their engines roaring instead of purring. (This is probably due to the fact that women can tolerate heightened emotions during discussions better than men can, and women anticipate men withdrawing from the discussion early—so their frustration shows right away.) Women must learn to start gently, and men must learn to hang in there when conversations get a bit intense.

- **I In-flight repairs.** Difficult conversations, by definition, can escalate into miserable arguments. "Repair" comments such as "I shouldn't have said that . . . I'm feeling overwhelmed, can we take a break and talk again in twenty minutes? . . . Please speak more softly . . . I may not be right . . . Can we begin again?" and others like them act as circuit breakers that keep emotional energy from exploding.

  Men vs. Women: Premature withdrawal from difficult conversations is a major gaff that most men make. Making in-flight repairs prevents that mistake. Repairs have a calming effect on both partners and enable men to have staying power.

- **F Find hidden concerns.** Many arguments are not what you are arguing about. Deeper issues of *Do you really love me? Am I important to you? Is this relationship fair?* can lie underneath. Ignoring these hidden issues is a gaff. Inquiring about such concerns may help you realize why your partner seems so irrationally upset about something that seems minor to you. He or she may really be upset about something unstated.

  Men vs. Women: A woman is more intuitive and can therefore detect underlying issues. Usually a better listener, a woman makes eye contact more than a man and often senses subtle variations in tone and timing of speech. She detects apparent contradictions between the speaker's words and nonverbal language and may adamantly accuse that despite what the man actually said, she knows exactly what he meant. (Men hate it when that happens.)

- **T Teamwork.** If you must "win" an argument, then the relationship loses and you have committed a major gaff. You are both on the same team, not adversaries. Unless you treat each other as such, nobody really wins. Teamwork implies a willingness to be influenced by your partner to some degree, to yield on certain points. No stubborn standoffs. Instead, find ways to say "That makes sense . . . I can understand why you feel that way . . . I'll go along with that . . . " Teamwork also means making time for one another during the day.

  Men vs. Women: If someone is refusing to yield on certain points and has a hard time admitting that his partner's view has some merit, that someone is usually the man. Women are more willing to compromise for the sake of the relationship whereas some men regard being right as more important than being friends.

- **S Supportive comments.** Reassure your spouse that you love him or her. Appreciate what was done right, don't make a gaff by just criticizing what you dislike. Let your partner know that you are proud of his or her accomplishments. If your partner is troubled or upset (especially if it's not about you), try to empathize.

  Men vs. Women: A woman has tremendous power in this area. A man flourishes when he believes that his wife has faith in him and is proud of his accomplishments. Especially if he is going through a rough time personally, a wife who says "I have faith in you" will boost his confidence (even if he initially scoffs at the remark). She doesn't necessarily need to help him explore his feelings. In fact, he might feel more vulnerable doing that. Men are supportive when they help a woman explore her feelings. Unfortunately, many men quickly get to "I'm sure it will all work out" as their attempt at support, and then try to change the subject.

The GIFTS in Action

Carl passed the bowl of pretzels to his two buddies and then cheered when his favorite football team scored a touchdown. The afternoon of camaraderie at his house had been underway for just about an hour when his wife suddenly appeared in the doorway. Karen scowled as she held the ice pack against their 5-year-old's forehead.

"He was crying in the bathroom," she said, her voice rising. "Didn't you hear him? You were supposed to watch him while I was at the store!"

Carl got up quickly and ushered his wife and son into the kitchen where they had some privacy.

"I swear he was fine a minute ago," he said. He patted his boy's arm. "He'll be fine. It's a small bump."

"That's not the point!" Karen said. *"And this isn't the first time you've been careless about watching him. What if he ran outside and into the street?"*

"But he didn't run outside and I wasn't careless," Carl said, trying to keep his voice down. *"I just looked away briefly. You knew I'd be watching TV with the guys. Why did you ask me to baby-sit?"*

Carl realized that Karen was upset but he was irritated, too. Couldn't she complain later? After his pals went home?

What, if anything, could Karen have said that would have made Carl *finally* take her seriously? What, if anything, could Carl have said that would have made Karen understand his point of view?

Karen and Carl's argument was predictable. Karen had often accused Carl of being lax in his care for their son and Carl accused Karen of being overprotective. Neither one was willing to see any merit to the other's position. Imagine if their discussion prior to the football game was more productive and went something like this:

KAREN: I was thinking I'd like to run to the mall this afternoon while you and the guys are watching the game. But I'd really rather not take Kyle.

CARL: No problem. I'll look after him.

KAREN: But I was also thinking about the argument we had the other day when I told you to be more observant when watching Kyle. Look, I know you are a good father. I just worry because Kyle is so active. He gets into everything.

CARL: He sure does. Boys will be boys.

KAREN: Yes, but do you see my point even a little bit?

CARL: Yes, I do. Kyle is a handful. You do watch him more closely than I do and there have been many times you've prevented him from getting hurt or breaking something. But he has skinned his knees on your watch, too.

KAREN: I know that. A parent can't be in all places at all times.

CARL: That's all I want you to understand. If Kyle hurts himself, it doesn't mean I neglected him.

KAREN: That's true, and I'll try not to be quick to judge you. But it would help a lot if you would at least not let him out of your sight whenever possible. You don't have to hover over him. Just be near enough to intervene.

CARL: Will do.

Had that conversation occurred, their boy, Kyle, might never have struck his forehead and the argument would never have taken place. Even if Kyle still managed to hurt himself, the odds are good that Karen would not have been so upset with Carl. What was magically different about their conversation? First, it began with a gentle touch (the G in GIFTS). Engines were purring, not roaring. Karen helped insure that by commenting that she knew Carl was a good father. Second, both Karen and Carl were able to admit that the other one had a valid point or two; in other words, they yielded on certain points and operated as a team (the T in GIFTS). No longer adversaries, they came up with a plan that was likely to help their situation. Karen and Carl used only *two* of the five GIFTS. But two was all they needed.

Get Into the Flow

Whether you are married, living together, or seriously dating someone, all relationship roads can get bumpy at times. But successful couples can break some of the old rules of communication without breaking their relationship because of two fundamental factors:

1. The communication rules they do follow while discussing areas of conflict are the few, most powerful rules that maintain their conversations in working order.

2. The couple has backup: a small but precious jewelry box containing an assortment of goodwill toward each other so that communication mishaps are easily corrected or forgiven. They also view each other's motivations as well intended, even when one of them is acting like a damn fool. This goodwill is demonstrated partly by shows of affection or thoughtful gestures. But according to research, this goodwill is strengthened significantly when the couple is able to carry out short (10 to 20 minutes) of meaningful conversation every day about nonrelationship issues. Thus, partners who can listen to each other's stories of how the day went without judging or criticizing or trying to fix anything (in other words, they show genuine interest and don't take a partner's upset personally), set the stage for handling relationship conflict well.

The best way to learn something new is to practice. If you practice the piano daily, you'll become an above-average piano player. If you lift weights four days a week, you'll double your strength over several months. It's the same way with communication skills. But such rehearsals can get cumbersome and strong feelings can interfere when you are emotionally involved with your partner. The fantastic thing about this book is that you are actually rehearsing by just reading the hundreds of examples provided. You will see in page after page the best ways to talk and eventually you'll slip into the "flow": the method of thinking and talking that makes for great communication. Soon, knowing "how to say it" best will become an instinctive part of your nature.

There is no greater intimacy in your relationship than that which is shared in meaningful conversation. Here is your chance to add to your intimacy and strengthen your love.

Paul Coleman

About the Author

Dr. Paul Coleman is a psychologist and author of eight books including *How to Say It® to Your Kids* and *25 Stupid Mistakes Couples Make*. He has appeared on national programs such as *Oprah* and the *Today* show, and on dozens of radio shows. He is happily married for twenty years and the father of three children.

Part One

The Super Six:
New Power Rules
for Great
Conversation

*H*ow you and your partner talk is usually more important than the topic you talk about. You can't be expected to cope with adversity, personality differences, or disagreements if your conversational skills are not up to par. Even nonconflict conversations (sharing feelings, discussing the day's events) can become strained when conversational know-how is less than optimal.

Part One is the most important part of the book. It will help you learn:

❯ To respond effectively when you or your partner get too critical or defensive.

❯ How it is that despite good intentions, you and your partner may misunderstand each other—and the power words that will correct the situation.

❯ How to get somewhere in a conversation that seems to be going nowhere.

❯ The *absolutely most vital and indispensable communication rules* such as starting conversations with your engines purring instead of roaring; and how to make "in-flight repairs" during the discussion.

You will also see how the conversations you have *with yourself* are helping or hurting the conversations you have with your partner, and you'll learn to change that self-talk when necessary.

If you find that some of the ideas suggested in the remaining sections of this book are not working as well as you'd like, reread this section on communication know-how. Your problem—and the solution—will be found here.

How to Start a Discussion Without Starting an Argument

1

Harry sits at the poolside of the hotel and watches his two children swim. He chats with the woman next to him, whose children are frolicking with Harry's brood.

"If you'd like to take a break," the woman says, "I can watch them for the next hour."

Harry is delighted. His wife, Cindy, is in their room and now they have a chance for some romance. It is difficult fanning the fires of passion in a hotel room with two kids.

Harry explains the situation to Cindy. "Now we have some time for ourselves," he says, lifting his eyebrows in a suggestive manner.

"You let a stranger watch our kids?" Cindy says.

Harry feels attacked. "Give me some credit for good judgment! She's a pleasant lady. Her kids are playing with ours and she offered to watch."

"I'd feel better if one of us went down to the pool," Cindy says. "I'll go."

"Some romantic vacation this turned out to be," Harry says. "Why can't you ever loosen up?"

Cindy glares at Harry. "Take a cold shower," she says. "For that matter, take one every day of the four we have left on this trip."

Mismatched expectation? Poor timing? Perhaps. But Harry's main tactical error occurred when he registered his complaint too harshly. Telling Cindy to loosen up was a hard jab. Cindy was no help when she insinuated he was neglecting their children by allowing them to be supervised by a stranger. Their conversation lasted all of 15 seconds but it was destined to deteriorate because it began with their engines roaring instead of purring.

The G in GIFTS stands for Gentle start-up. Instead of saying, "You let a stranger watch our kids?" Cindy might have softened her response. "I'd like some time alone with you, too. But I'm uneasy about a stranger supervising

3

our children. I'd like to introduce myself to her." Harry could have replied, "Maybe you should check the situation out. If you feel comfortable, come back up to our room. I'll be waiting . . . "

Have You Heard?

~ New findings suggest that the opening minutes of a disagreement will foretell whether it will boil over or simmer down. Harsh and jarring words lead to sparring whereas softer words succeed.

~ It is easier to make a complaint that isn't so attacking if you prepare your words ahead of time. If you are caught off guard and blurt out something harsh, apologize, take a minute to gather your thoughts, and try again.

~ Once the exchange becomes heated, each side feels unfairly attacked and will have a more difficult time showing understanding. (See Chapter 2 on how to de-escalate arguments.) Your best bet is to make your opening complaint easier to be heard. State your complaint as simply as possible and offer a suggestion that might fix the problem. Avoid rambling and avoid citing example after example of how your partner let you down. No name-calling, no sweeping generalizations.

~ Don't go to the opposite extreme and be so gentle that you sound meek and unsure of yourself. A complaint, done well, is a bit like giving someone a flu shot. It might pinch a little but that's all. If it goes well, it will inoculate you and your partner against a future, more serious argument.

~ The woman's role is key. Studies show that women tend to use more jarring remarks when stating a complaint than do men. Frequent harsh start-ups by women are associated with relationship decline and even divorce. (Women may have reason to be harsh. Men can be hard to engage in conversation and can get easily defensive.)

How to Say It

You can bark, but don't bite. Use praise to balance your concerns. Remember, your opening lines can steer you either into calm waters or the rapids.

- "We've had no time on this vacation for ourselves. I was really hoping we could use the time now to make love."

- "I know you are very busy. But it bothers me that the ceiling tiles are still sitting in the box unopened. My friend from college is visiting this weekend and I really want the ceiling fixed."

- "I get nervous and upset when you raise your voice to the kids. I know you're tired after a long day, but could you try smiling at them more? They love it when you get playful."

- "The credit card bills worry me. Can we discuss going on a budget?"

- "I really get frustrated when I come home from work and see the counter littered with dirty dishes. It would mean a lot to me if you could put them in the dishwasher right after you use them."

- "We visit your parents almost every weekend. As much as I like them, I get frustrated that we don't have much time together with just us and the kids. What are your thoughts?"

- "We haven't had a night out together in a long time. How about we make some plans?"

- "It bothers me that every morning we're in a rush and we both snap at the kids. I'd like mornings to be calmer. Got any ideas?"

How Not to Say It

Opening your remarks with personal attacks, a belligerent or uncompromising tone, name-calling, or use of inflammatory words can send the conversation into dangerous waters. Compare the harsh and jarring statements below with their gentler versions above.

- "What's wrong with you? Don't you have any interest in sex at all?"

  "That's just great. I'm hoping to make love but you can't let the kids out of your sight for a lousy thirty minutes. You're something else, you know that?"

- "You never do what I ask. How long have I been waiting for you to fix the damn ceiling?"

- "If you're going to yell at the kids so much, you're better off having nothing to do with them at all. Don't you care how they feel?"

- "You don't get it, do you? I'm not made of gold. You're going to spend us into bankruptcy."

- "Look at this mess? What have you done all night, watched television? You don't think of anybody around here except yourself."
- "I didn't marry your parents, I married *you*. Why do you always put them first and the rest of us second?"
- "If I ask you to take me out you'll probably find an excuse to say no. Why can't you take some interest in life and in me? You're so boring."
- "You're such a grouch in the morning, snapping at everybody just so you can get out the door a few minutes early. That's pretty self-centered, you know."

Don't make complaints while sounding weak and apologetic.

- "Sweetheart, I know you have a lot on your mind but sometimes, I mean, if you can find the time and I understand if you can't, but sometimes it would be nice if you could call me when you'll be running late. If it's not too inconvenient. But if you forget, I'll understand . . . "

Talking Point: A start-up with engines purring is no guarantee that your partner won't get defensive or uncooperative. But approaching the conversation by setting the proper tone has its advantages. If you and your partner are reasonably happy together, the discussion may get tense but will probably work out to your mutual satisfaction.

How to Make In-Flight Repairs and Deflate Anger

2

Handling conflict well is the hallmark of satisfied couples and enduring relationships. Couples mishandle their disagreements usually in one (or more) of three ways: Criticisms are harsh (causing defensiveness), old issues get reignited, or one person withdraws prematurely from the discussion. That "clash, rehash, and dash" approach fails miserably.

Even when conversations start out on the right path, however, breakdowns happen. Successful, happy couples manage conflict well not because they prevent it, but because they make the necessary repairs when communication inevitably breaks down.

The I in GIFTS stands for in-flight repairs. When a couple can make in-flight repairs during an argument, they develop an expanding faith that they are loved, cared about, respected, and possess the skills necessary to reverse directions when an argument is escalating. Living with someone who can fix conversational ruptures is like driving across country with a partner who is an auto mechanic. There is less to worry about.

Have You Heard?

 ⁓ Making in-flight repairs when conversations veer off-track is *the single most important tool you can have at your disposal.*

 ⁓ Withdrawing from conflict will not help the situation. However, a strategic retreat can help—especially if you are so physically agitated that all you can think about is fighting or fleeing. A good test: Take your pulse. As heart rates venture toward 80 beats per minute or higher, the ability to communicate effectively declines sharply.

~ Strategic retreats are brief timeouts (10–30 minutes) to help you relax and rehearse more effective communication techniques. Take your pulse before resuming the conversation. It should be near normal. A touch of humor (especially from the woman) can immediately lower a man's heart rate.

~ The person who tries to make an in-flight repair is only half of the team. According to esteemed researcher Dr. John Gottman (who has done extensive work helping couples learn to repair their conversations), the other partner must do his or her best to *accept* and respect the repair effort. It does no good if, as one person explained to me, "I'm trying to use Spackle but she keeps punching more holes in the wall."

How to Say It

Ask for help by making appropriate inquiries and offer noncritical opinions about how the conversational process has gone off-track:

- "May I start over? I think I came on too strong."
- "Can you speak more softly? I'm getting uptight and finding it hard to think."
- "Would you let me take a minute to get my thoughts together?"
- "May we take a break now? Let's start again in fifteen minutes."
- "This is what happens when the conversation starts to fall apart. Can we rewind this tape and start again?"
- "We agreed not to sound harsh or insulting. Can you rephrase what you just said?"
- "This is the point in our conversations where I have the most trouble. It would help me a lot if you could tell me what I've said that makes sense to you. Is there anything I've said that you can agree with?"
- "Can you bear with me? I'm not the best communicator, but I'm trying."
- "Did I just say something wrong? I didn't intend to."
- "Could we back up and try it again?"
- "Can you explain what you meant by that? I'm not sure I understand."

- "Can you say that again but a bit differently? I was getting upset."
- "What is the main thing you want me to understand that you don't think I understand yet?"
- "Can you please let me finish my thought? I promise I'll listen when it's your turn."

Find some merit to your partner's viewpoint and be encouraging.

- "I see your point about . . . "
- "From what you're telling me, you see my part of the problem as . . . "
- "Yes, I know I sound like I'm blaming you but I do realize that we both are contributing to the problem."
- "I know you ordinarily would give up now. I appreciate that you are hanging in there."
- "You're doing fine. I know you're angry but that's okay. I want to hear what you have to say."
- "Don't worry about getting every word right. I can be patient."

Apologize whenever you slip up.

- "I'm sorry. I shouldn't have said that."
- "I'm wrong."
- "Maybe I'm jumping to conclusions. I'm sorry. Repeat what you just said and this time I won't cut you off."
- "I'm getting defensive. That doesn't make it easy for you."

If you need to take a break or strategically retreat in order to relax, end the conversation with something positive and encouraging. A little humor can help.

- "That wasn't so bad. We handled things much better this time."
- "I liked it when you listened and didn't interrupt."
- "It meant a lot when you apologized for yelling. That showed me you really want us to work this out."
- (Smiling warmly but with irony) "This is kind of fun, right?"
- "When I started getting angry, you didn't return my fire. That was helpful."

- "When I asked you to lower your voice, you didn't debate me. You just spoke more softly. I appreciated that."
- "If you'd like, I'd be happy to rub your neck for a few minutes before we resume the discussion. I promise not to rub you the wrong way . . . Ha . . . ha . . . ha . . . "
- "We agreed ahead of time that we'd hug each other before the break. I'd like to do that now."

How Not to Say It

Anger has to be managed. It can exist but should ideally be expressed at low levels. The more furious a person gets, mutual escalation (or withdrawal) is likely. It is harder to deescalate an argument when anger is high than when it is moderate or low.

- "I don't care if I'm getting too loud. I'm really mad!" (When a partner tries to make an in-flight repair, such as "Please lower your voice," it is best to try to cooperate. If you find it hard, say something like: "I should lower my voice but I'm so frustrated right now! Just let me vent for a bit and I'll try to settle down, okay?")
- "I don't care how flooded you're feeling, I am not going to stop this discussion. We'll never get back to it if we stop." (*Better:* "I'd rather not stop now. Can you hang in there a little longer? If not, let's be sure we continue it within half an hour.")
- "This is getting nowhere. I'm out of here." (This is precisely the attitude that needs repairing. Take a break, focus on calming yourself and reminding yourself of your partner's better qualities, and return to the discussion soon. *Better:* "I need a break. Let me go for a walk or take a shower and I'll come right back.")

RED ALERT: Beware of "false" repair attempts: These *appear* to be recovery efforts but are really subtle ways to make the other person the bad guy:

- "You're getting angry. That's not helping right now." (Anger is impossible to eliminate. In fact, it is like nerve endings that cause us to feel physical pain—it hurts and we don't like it, but it is alerting us to something destructive. A partner's anger means that something destructive to the relationship needs to be worked out. See anger as a signpost, not a sin. *Better:* "You have a right to be angry and upset but please lower your voice.")

- "No, I won't repeat what I just said. If you still don't understand my point, you never will. Learn to listen." (*Better:* "I'm frustrated that I have to repeat myself. But I'm glad you asked me to instead of pretending to understand me.")

- "Maybe you should take a short break and calm down. You're starting to get snippy and defensive." (Here you get to be critical and cutting while sounding oh-so-practical and helpful. *Better:* "Is this a good time to take a break or do you want to continue a bit longer?")

- "Can you rephrase that? I get upset when your tone gets abusive and controlling." (Don't sound holier than thou.)

How to Say It to Yourself

What you tell yourself during the discussion and during the break (or after the discussion has ended) can add fuel to the fire or douse it. Self-talk that fuels resentment, righteous indignation, or an "I'm a victim" mentality must be challenged. (**Men are particularly likely to think that way after an argument!**) Instead, think about the good aspects of your partner and try to give him or her the benefit of the doubt.

- "She was upset and intense in part because the topic was important to her."
- "She was right when she said . . . "
- "I want to be understood and cared about, but so does he. I need to focus on achieving that."
- "I can show love and patience even if he is having trouble right now."
- "I'm grateful that she is trying to improve our communication. She really wants us to get along."
- "I know this isn't all his fault."
- "I can be sharp tongued. That hasn't helped."
- "I do love her. I can show that love more often during difficult conversations."

How Not to Say It to Yourself

After an argument (or during a timeout), you must eliminate the following kind of self-talk:

- "How can she say those things to me!" (*Better:* "People often say things they don't entirely mean when they are upset. Once I show her that I can listen and understand, she'll probably calm down.")

- "She's impossible to talk to. She'll never learn to speak more respectfully." (*Better:* "She doesn't always speak disrespectfully. If we try this new way to talk, there is a good chance our conversations will improve.")

- "I'm doing my best but she isn't." (*Better:* "It is a fact that people misjudge others more when they are angry or upset. Maybe she's trying harder than I realize. I can give her the benefit of the doubt.")

- "This is a waste of time. The best thing to do is avoid anything that might start an argument." (*Better:* "But I know I'll continue to resent it. Let me try to hang in there.")

- "How can he love me if he has so much to be critical about?" (*Better:* "I know he loves me. He has to learn to be less judgmental.")

Let's Talk

You can inflate or deflate an argument by your body language as much as by your verbal language. The most devastating nonverbal signals mock the speaker. Eye rolling or sighing aloud while shaking your head shows intolerance, even contempt, and suggests that you think your partner is stupid, disgusting, or hopeless. Finger or foot tapping may be a sign of nervousness but will come across as impatience. It is as if you are saying, "Hurry up and finish. I want to speak." Any melodramatic gesture that conveys "I can't believe you're saying such things!" also has a mocking, condescending quality.

When discussing an area of conflict or disagreement, it is best for you each to remain seated. Standing up during an argument increases the odds of loud exchanges and premature walkouts. Try not to cross your arms while listening or point your finger while talking. During particularly tense moment (or if you anticipate one), gently touch your partner's hand or shoulder. It conveys the attitude "I love you . . . I don't want to hurt you . . . I know this is hard . . . "

How to Find the Hidden Issues in Conversations

3

Jill's feet are sore. When her live-in partner of three years reaches over to rub them for her, she yanks them away and scowls. "You know I hate that," she says. Vince doesn't say a word. He just leans back on the couch, confused as to why she had such a strong, negative reaction to his offer.

The F in GIFTS stands for Find the hidden issue. One main reason conversations can be confusing and unsatisfying is because couples are sometimes having two conversations simultaneously: one about the overt topic and the other about the hidden, unstated topic. Without some sort of emotional Geiger counter to detect the hidden issue, the overt topic will never be resolved.

Jill didn't like having her feet rubbed—or so she said. But her hidden issue was that anytime Vince made some physical, affectionate overture, he tried to push for sex. By pulling away from his offer to rub her feet, she was really making a nonverbal (and unclear) statement about the resentment she felt. But Vince didn't understand that.

Have You Heard?

∼ Hidden issues are usually about the following: Am I loved and cared about by my partner? Is this relationship fair? Is my partner trustworthy? Does my partner show me love in ways that are meaningful to me? Am I respected?

∼ Clues that a hidden, unresolved issue exists include:

— Arguing about "little things."

— Frequent misunderstandings that result in comments like, "That's not what I meant!"

— An issue that was supposedly settled resurfaces.

— A partner gets harsh or defensive in response to something neutral or positive.

— Arguments where a partner uses sharp-edged words/phrases or words that are overdone or spoken in a harsh tone:

You make me sick.	*It's no use talking to you.*
I can't believe anything you say.	*Oh, give me a break.*
Bitch.	*That's ridiculous . . . nonsense . . .*
Bastard.	*You're being unfair.*
You always . . .	*You treat me like dirt.*
You never . . .	*You're cold . . . controlling . . .*
No!	*Stop that!*
What did I just tell you?	*Oh, never mind!*

How to Say It

- "I didn't get the response I thought I would. Did I say something wrong? Are you upset about something?"

- "Is it possible you're angry about more than what we're talking about?"

- "You seem to be in a cranky mood. Is something on your mind?"

- "It's hard for me to believe that you're upset about this. What else could be bothering you?"

- "I notice that every time I ask to rub your back, you pull away. What am I doing that you don't appreciate?"

If your partner responds:

- *"Nothing else is bothering me!"*
- *"Can't you keep to the topic at hand?"*

- *"Why are you looking for some problem that doesn't exist?"*
- *"If something else is bothering me, I'll tell you."*

You reply:

- *"I guess I said that because I often act the way you just did when I'm bothered about something."*
- *"Yes, we can go back to the topic. I'm just hoping you'll think about the possibility that something else is bothering you, too."*
- *"I suppose it seems like I'm looking for problems. I'm just trying to understand why you got so upset."*
- *"Thank you. If something is on your mind, I'd like to hear about it."*

If you have some hidden, unspoken issue, try to bring it to the surface.

- "Honey, I'm angry about something I shouldn't be that angry about. I think what's really bothering me is . . . "
- "The real issue is not where we go on vacation. What bothers me is that we always do what you want."
- "I'm annoyed right now because what you just said reminds me of . . . "
- "Maybe we keep misunderstanding each other because I'm not discussing what's really bothering me. What bothers me is . . . "
- "What bothers me about you is also something that bothered me about my father. Maybe I'm overreacting now. I need to think more about this."
- "I guess I'm feeling insecure. The last time I felt like that was my first year in college when . . . Maybe that has a lot to do with what I'm feeling now. Let me explore that."

How Not to Say It

- "I can't believe you're upset about that. Why do you make mountains out of molehills?" (Better to assume that an overreaction means that your partner has a hidden concern. Try gently to uncover it. If your partner balks, pull back and wait until the next time he or she overreacts.)
- "I don't *always* do that!" (If a partner accuses you of "always" or "never" doing something, it is probably an exaggeration. Rather than denying the

charge, use your partner's exaggeration as a clue that he or she has underlying concerns. "I disagree. I don't always do that but I have done that on occasion. It must really bother you.")

- "If you're going to lie or exaggerate, this discussion is over." (Hang in there. Most people with hidden issues will come on too strong. Ending the conversation won't bring out the hidden issue; it simply may stay hidden. *Better:* "Tell me more about why this bothers you. It seems to me that you are exaggerating, so maybe I'm missing something.")

How to Say It to Yourself

If you are complaining to yourself about your partner, your internal mutterings probably are about the deeper, underlying issue. Identify the issue and commit yourself to speaking up about it.

- "I don't want him to hug me because he'll take that as a sign to have sex. I hate it when he does that. But by pulling away from him when he tries to hug me, he probably doesn't realize why I'm annoyed. Then he may want to make love in order to feel reassured that everything's all right. I need to tell him what I'm thinking."

- "I'm arguing with her about a ten-dollar phone call. Why should that bother me? Can't she spend ten bucks to call her friend? Maybe what's bothering me is that I don't think she likes spending time with me. It makes more sense to ask her about that instead of making a jerk of myself by quibbling over ten dollars."

- "If he really loved me or cared about me, he would—wait, that's the problem. I'm arguing with him over little things because I'm worried about the big issue. Does he love me? To be fair, I should talk with him about that instead of sounding like a nag on all those smaller issues."

Talking Point: What bothers you may not be about your partner at all. It might be something about yourself or something from your past. Examine your feelings. Did you ever feel similarly before? With whom? What happened? Could you be oversensitive today because of that past experience? If so, discuss that with your partner.

How to Remain a Team and Slip Out of the "I'm Right/You're Wrong" Knot

4

Frank and Sheila have been dating for nearly a year. One day Sheila decides to buy a new car. She's already picked out the make and model. It is just a question of getting the best deal for her trade-in. By the time the afternoon is over, however, she wants to trade in Frank for a new boyfriend! He has accompanied her to the dealership and just as she is about to close the deal on a car, he grabs her hand and pulls her away. "That's too much money," Frank says to the salesperson. Sheila is furious. How could he do that? He makes her appear foolish. Frank is astonished by her reaction. The car is too expensive. She could probably get a better deal elsewhere. Besides, he is only looking out for her best interest.

"The price is just fine," Sheila counters. "You have no right to interfere."

"The price is too high," Frank says, exasperated that she wouldn't agree to an obvious fact. "If I pushed you out of the way of an oncoming train, I suppose that would be interfering too."

The T in GIFTS stands for Teamwork. Couples sometimes get into a heated debate about what is right and who is right. They act as adversaries, not teammates. One insists the other stop smoking for logical reasons. The other insists it is his or her right to smoke. One says the latest and fastest home computer is a must, while the other says they can purchase last year's fastest model and save a bundle. One says to invest in the stock market, the other prefers something less volatile. Differences of opinion are not the problem for these couples. The problem occurs when one uses intellect, experience, or clever verbal skills simply as a tool to get one's way. (A clever debater can always justify his point of view and try to get his way. But that's not friendship.) If you always need to be right in you're relationship, you're wrong.

Have You Heard?

～ Someone who needs to be right comes across as "I know better." Even if he or she does know better, that attitude is parental. (Over time, having sex with one's "parent" is a turnoff.)

～ Needing to be right can also show up as needing to make the other person wrong. This is often evident by disagreements that never need to happen in the first place. For example, you say, "You seem upset." The other person who needs to make you wrong will challenge the wording. "I'm not upset, I'm preoccupied." You say, "I heard it might rain today." He says, "Maybe, maybe not."

～ Often, right-versus-wrong sparring contests don't get resolved because the couple is arguing simultaneously about different issues. One is usually attending to the logic of the argument, while the other is feeling patronized or criticized and is responding to that. One argues intellectual "facts," while the other argues emotional "facts." (HE: "We can't afford Walt Disney World this year." SHE: "You've said that each of the last five years. Why can't you let the rest of us do what we want for a change?" If he continues to focus on economics and misses her point that she is feeling unfairly controlled, the argument will go nowhere.)

～ Disagreements are often about values. Should you spend money or save it? Should you discipline the kids this way or that way? Should you open Christmas presents on Christmas Eve or on Christmas day? There isn't a "right" answer.

～ Some clues that you and/or your partner compete over being right are:

— Someone always has to justify his or her actions.

— You argue about insignificant issues.

— He tells you that you are trying to control him by getting your way, but when he wants his way it is because his way makes sense.

— Your partner is allowed to make mistakes, but you are not.

— She tends to interrupt you. Her opinions matter more.

— If you get your way, your partner believes she "gave in" and that you should appreciate her sacrifice.

— There is no giving without feeling owed.

— There is no receiving without feeling entitled.

How to Say It

During nonconflict moments, mention how the two of you sometimes get into right-versus-wrong debates. (Anticipate your partner may disagree with that observation . . .)

- "Have you noticed how we sometimes debate over who is right? I'd like to change that. Otherwise, I'm afraid we'll get into a bad habit." (If your partner disagrees with that observation, say, "It's happening right now.")

- "The next time I notice we are locked in that battle, I'll call attention to it. Then I'll tell you what aspect of your point of view I agree with. Then you do the same for me."

- "Sometimes we have to decide which is more important: being right in a point of view or making sure we treat each other fairly. If one of us gets our way a lot, the other won't think it's fair."

Validate some of what your partner says, even if you disagree with certain aspects.

- "I agree with you. Smoking is harmful and I shouldn't do it."

- "A lot of people would agree with your view on investing. You're not wrong. But my view makes sense, too."

If you don't mind going along with your partner, but you resent the tendency to get his or her way, make fairness the issue.

- "Go and spend two thousand dollars on a stereo system if you want. It's not how I'd spend money, but I won't object. My real concern is not the stereo. My real concern is that if I wanted to spend two thousand dollars on a swimming pool, you'd not hear of it. I need to feel that our relationship is fair. It isn't, as far as I'm concerned."

- "I notice I'm arguing with you about whether we should get a fourth phone line or not. I really don't care one way or the other. What bothers me most is that when you feel you are right about something, you insist on getting your way. If I did that to you, I suspect you'd get angry and call me controlling."

- "Can we agree to disagree?"

- Negotiate. "In order to make the situation feel fair, I have an idea. Whenever we disagree and cannot find a way to compromise, we'll flip a coin to see who gets his or her way. Fairness will be insured."
- "Experts say that each partner should have more influence in areas most important to them or in areas they do most of the work in. Since I'm the one who keeps our yard looking nice, I'd like more say in what equipment to buy. Since you use the computer more than I do, you can have say over that. What do you think?"

If your partner responds to any of the above suggestions by saying:

- *"But my way really does make more sense!"*
- *"That's not the way I was raised."*
- *"You don't know what you're talking about!"*

You respond:

- *"I'm not saying it doesn't make sense. What I'm saying is that my way has merit, too. I need you to recognize that and I want each of us to find some middle ground when possible or to once in a while graciously go along with the other."*
- *"It's uncomfortable when we do things that differ from our traditions. But if I went along with everything you wanted, I'd be miserable. I'm asking for some give and take."*
- *"What bothers me most is your attitude toward me. That's why I debate you. I need you to respect my point of view even if you disagree."*

How Not to Say It

- "It makes absolutely no sense to do it your way . . . " (This is too dogmatic and disrespectful.)
- "That never happened! How could you say such a thing?" (You are challenging the person to defend his position. He will. *Better to say:* "I have a different memory of that event. Would you like to hear it?")
- "That's a lie!" (That's inflammatory.)

- "If you look at all the facts, you'll see that my way makes sense." (That sounds condescending. *Better:* "These are the facts as I see them. What do you think?")
- "I know better." (Then you must know that such an attitude will cause conflict.)
- "You're just being emotional. You're not looking at this logically." (Every time you say that, it is because the other person is upset. What she's upset most about is that you are stepping on her feelings and don't seem to care. *Better:* "You're upset about something. What don't I understand?")
- "The more logical viewpoint should win." (That's a self-serving argument. Getting along with a partner requires a willingness to *go along* with your partner, even when you disagree. Give up trying to be the master.)

Talking Point: Making changes in this area is not easy. The necessary first step is to come to an agreement that the two of you do, in fact, compete with one another. It might be useful to keep count of the many ways conversations become competitive. That can serve as a baseline figure so that you can determine later if improvements have been made.

How to Respond
Without Getting Defensive

5

Amanda wants to talk to Phil—again—about his tendency to ignore her family when they come by for a visit. A barbecue is planned for the upcoming weekend and she wants him to promise he'll act more friendly.

"I think you could do it for my sake," Amanda says. "It's just for a few hours. It won't kill you."

"Do it for your sake?" Phil volleys. "What about you doing something for my sake? I've asked you to stand up for me when your mother gets on her high horse, but you never do. You always want me to back down and take it."

"My mother doesn't get along with a lot of people. You take it so personally."

"And I don't have the right to do that, is that what you're saying?"

As in the previous chapter, **the T in GIFTS stands for Teamwork.** Failing to overcome defensiveness is one way of failing to be a team. If you learn to be less defensive, your conversations will inevitably improve.

Phil was defensive when he jabbed, "Do it for your sake?" and Amanda was defensive when she excused her mother's actions. Defensiveness happens in all relationships. It is a response to feeling attacked, blamed, misunderstood . . . or caught. True, people should stick up for themselves and their point of view when they are wrongly attacked. It also isn't necessarily terrible if people get angry during a conversation when they feel their partner isn't being considerate or fair. That's not the problem. The problem occurs when they refuse to see any merit at all to the other's position or only pay attention to comments they disagree with. In many cases there is a kernel of truth to an accusation or complaint, even if it is overstated or if some of the facts are wrong. Defensive people feel victimized; they see themselves as (fairly) innocent and well meaning and their partners as unfairly critical and mean-spirited. A defensive person tries to make excuses for objectionable actions by saying things like, "I forgot . . . I wasn't feeling well . . . It wasn't my problem . . . " But defensiveness becomes a problem in conversation because it gets in the way of listening and makes solutions harder to find.

You can reduce the odds your partner will get defensive if you state your concerns in a way that doesn't pin him or her against a wall. Starting a conversation gently with "engines purring" as discussed in the first chapter will reduce defensiveness. But what happens if the *middle* of the conversation gets heated? Then the defensive person must also work at becoming less defensive—even if his or her partner came on too strong with an accusation. The goal is to work together and find common ground—to be a team.

Imagine if Phil had responded less defensively: "You're right, it won't kill me to be nice to your family. I don't like having to ignore them any more than you do. I find it hard, however, when your mother gets critical. Is there any way you'd be willing to back me up if your mom gets out of line?

By saying "You're right," Phil acknowledged that Amanda had a point (a simple way to reduce defensiveness), but he also stated his concerns in a nonattacking way. Imagine if Amanda answered him this way: "It's impossible for me to stand up to my mother. I've tried and failed many times. You're much braver than I am in that area. I have a better idea. How about if you and I stay near each other a lot during the day. I promise I'll sit next to you and we'll hold hands a lot. You and me against the world?"

The tone now has changed considerably because Amanda and Phil are less defensive. Phil still might not have a delightful day with his in-laws, but chances are he won't resent Amanda when the day is over.

Have You Heard?

~ Women take the lead in making criticisms about the relationship, but men take the lead in being defensive. All couples will argue or disagree, and each partner will get defensive on occasion. The goal to eliminate defensiveness is an impossible one. But it must be minimized if the problems and disagreements are to get resolved or managed effectively. Women especially must learn to complain without making a personal attack.

∽ Common defensive maneuvers include: denying the charge ("That's not true!"); making excuses without accepting responsibility ("I was tired! . . . I was having a lousy day! . . . What else was I supposed to do?"); deflecting responsibility ("Me? What about YOU?"); or righteous indignance ("How could you say such a thing?").

∽ Without an ability and willingness to lower defensiveness, there can be no compromise, no mutual understanding, and no resolution of conflict.

∽ Reducing defensiveness means you are willing to go along with at least some of what your partner is saying. It means you are willing to find something with which you can agree. It may mean paying attention to the *spirit* of what your partner is saying, not necessarily to the precise words.

How to Say It

Find something to validate.

- "You have a point . . . "
- "You're right when you say . . . "
- "I agree with . . . "
- "This seems very important to you. You're not usually this concerned."
- "I know I'm not easy to live with at times."
- "It's true that . . . "
- "The part I agree with is . . . "
- "I might be wrong about that."
- "It's just my perception. I may not be right."
- "I'm not blaming you completely. I'm at fault, too."
- "We both made mistakes."

Make gentle inquiries:

- "Can you rephrase that? I'm getting angry."
- "Would you mind not sounding so harsh? I know you're upset, but I find it hard to listen when you come on too strong."
- "I've started getting defensive. Can you see any merit at all to anything I've said so far? It would help a lot if you could."

It's okay to give a strong, even angry opinion if your anger *matches* your partner's (a stronger reaction is riskier). However, soon into the conversation you need to use softer words that reveal a desire to find common ground. Here are snippets from the middle of two conversations. The dialogue has already escalated with engines roaring, but quickly downshifts to engines purring by lowering defensiveness.

SHE (engines roaring): "You annoy me."

HE (engines roaring): "You annoy me too. You jump down my throat without giving me a chance to explain." (Now she downshifts to engines purring): "Look, I can see why you're angry and maybe I did handle the situation poorly, but I'd like you to understand my position before you judge."

HE (engines roaring): *I* was the one who forgot? What about you? Where was it written that it was my job to remember the road map?

SHE (engines roaring): I asked you before we left if you had the map and you said yes! Or did you conveniently forget you said that?

HE (engines still roaring): And I also said I put it on top of the cooler which you were planning to carry to the car!

SHE (engines still roaring): How was I supposed to know to take the map? You said you wanted to look through it before we left!

HE (downshifting—engines purring): Maybe I didn't make it clear that I thought you would be bringing it to the car with the other stuff.

SHE (downshifting—engines purring): Right. I saw the map but I thought you planned on putting it in your pocket like you've done before. I should have asked just to be sure. A gas station will have a map. They're not that expensive.

HE (engines purring): Okay, sorry about the misunderstanding.

How Not to Say It

In all of the following comments, the speaker gets defensive and refuses to accept some responsibility for his or her actions. That never helps.

- "Why am I yelling? I'm yelling because you make me so furious sometimes!" (*Better:* "I yelled at you because I'm so frustrated. I shouldn't do that, but you're not easy to talk to either.")

- "If I don't sound friendly when you call me at the office, it's because you never consider that I might be busy!" (*Better:* "You're right, I probably don't sound friendly. I'm just real busy. May I call you back?")
- "I did not say anything wrong! You're just too sensitive!" (*Better:* "I didn't mean to sound harsh. May I rephrase it?")
- "If you'd give me a straight answer, I wouldn't have to interrogate you!" (*Better:* "You're right, this does sound like an interrogation. I can cut back, but I'd like you to give me a direct answer. Okay?")
- "If you'd wait until my show is over before you start yapping, I'd be able to listen to you better!" (*Better:* "I'd like to hear what you have to say. Can it wait a few minutes until my show is over?")
- "I may not be perfect but at least I try! You just sit there!" (*Better:* "This discussion is harder than I'd like it to be. How can we make it go easier?")
- "ME? What about YOU?" (*Better:* "You're right about that. I haven't been in a good mood lately either.")
- (A man invites friends over for a card game without telling his wife. She arrives home expecting dinner and finds a bunch of guys drinking beer around her dining room table. She takes her husband aside and expresses strong dissatisfaction. He responds defensively.) "Can't I have any friends over? . . . Why should I get your permission? . . . What's wrong with playing cards? . . ." (*Better:* "You're right, I should have touched base with you about this.")

Talking Point: Complaints and criticisms can cause a defensive response. However, complaints are valuable because they contain ingredients to the solution. For example, if your partner complains that you spend too much time on the computer instead of with him, the solution is to obviously find ways to spend more time together.

You can drastically reduce your defensiveness if you listen to a complaint and look for the implied solution. Instead of simply defending yourself ("I have a lot of work to do on the computer . . . You never want to do anything anyway . . . "), brainstorm possible solutions that were implied in the original complaint. For example, "It sounds like you want me to spend more time with you. Let's think of ways we could make that happen." Now the two of you are on the path toward effective problem solving and you won't spend energy needlessly debating each other.

How to Make Chitchat Charming

6

Dan walks into his house at the end of the day. His two young children trail behind him. He has just picked them up from day care. Marge, his wife, embraces her children and chats with them before calling out to her husband. "How was your day?"

Dan mutters something incomprehensible. He is often in a grumpy mood after work. Marge has come to expect that. At first she tried to be tolerant and understanding. He does have a long commute from the city. But recently she's been growing annoyed. I wish he'd grow up and learn to have a pleasant conversation. I'm only his wife, she thinks.

"Did we get any mail?" Dan calls out.

"Just junk mail," Marge answers.

"You mean the concert tickets still haven't arrived?"

"All we got was junk mail! Didn't I just say that? If the tickets had arrived, I'd have told you."

Marge hears Dan grumble again before he heads for the basement to his gym. Now she won't see him until dinner is half over.

The S in GIFTS stands for Supportive comments. Even happy couples in satisfying relationships can have moments like Dan and Marge. We're all entitled to an off day. But Dan and Marge's interaction revealed some key communication and relationship red flags. First, there wasn't an "I'm happy to see you!" greeting of any kind. Marge's willingness to ask how Dan's day went was a positive indicator. However, she had grown weary of Dan's grumping and his unwillingness to show interest in conversation. She was less willing to excuse his unfriendliness. Imagine if their conversation went like this:

DAN (first he kisses his wife): I had a lousy day. Most of it was spent in a meeting that was a complete waste of time while my real work piled up on my desk. I hope yours went better.

MARGE: Yeah, it did. Was anything about the meeting worthwhile?

DAN: They said profits were up, even though sales had barely inched forward. By the way, did the tickets come in the mail yet?

MARGE: No. All we got today was junk.

DAN (loudly, with obvious frustration): Damn, this day is not going well.

MARGE: Hang in there. Dinner will be ready soon.

DAN: I think I'll work out downstairs if it's okay with you. I need to blow off some steam. Call me when it's time to eat.

That conversation revealed that they were pleased to see each other. Marge showed real interest in Dan's day and he was willing to discuss it briefly even though he was irritable. When Dan spoke loudly ("Damn . . ."), Marge didn't scold him but simply changed the topic to a more pleasant one. In other words, they made many supportive comments. You had the sense that after the kids went to bed, Dan and Marge might cuddle on the couch and watch television, continue a friendly conversation, or make love.

Supportive comments are like the decorations that make a house into a home. They are often small but meaningful and add just the right touch to the situation. Supportive phrases include praise, encouragement, or simply acknowledging a person's right to feel a certain way.

Supportive comments aren't only used to de-escalate conflict. Research by Dr. John Gottman shows that the ability to have pleasant, interesting, supportive conversations during nonconflict moments improves the odds that later arguments will be less intense, less frequent, and more resolvable. The reverse is also true: The more negative a man is during nonconflict discussions (less humor, lack of interest, critical), then the more hostile the woman becomes later during a disagreement.

Have You Heard?

∾ How positively and supportively a couple talks during everyday conversation will depend, in part, on how positively they think about one another when they are apart. Take the time to think nice things about your partner when he or she is away.

〜 A supportive conversation is not one where emotions are always positive. Anger, hurt, or worry can certainly be expressed. But the couple shows interest and is able to add some pleasant emotion (humor, a smile) or show of affection. Belligerence is usually absent.

〜 Couples with little time together (ships passing in the night) inevitably get cranky and belligerent. Their conversations eventually become sharp and brittle, which make them withdraw further from one another.

〜 Many couples (especially dual-earner couples or couples who work different shifts) have precious little free time. But they make time for one another, even if it's only 15 minutes a day. They talk on the phone, they enjoy brief pillow talk even if one of them needs more sleep, they show affection whenever possible, and generally find time daily to talk about how each other is doing.

〜 You should know some of what your partner has planned for the day so you can inquire about it at day's end ("How did your dentist appointment go?")

How to Say It

The goal is to have simple, friendly, daily conversations about nonconflict issues and to make supportive comments. Inquire about the other person's day with genuine interest. Show affection. If your partner is particularly agitated or upset, try to view this as a sign that what's on his or her mind is important— not that he or she is being difficult.

- "Tell me about your day. I'd like to hear how it went."
- "How about I rub your neck and tell you about my day?"
- "You got a raise? Great! Tell me exactly what your boss said when she gave it to you."
- "Maybe after dinner I can make some coffee and you can tell me how your meeting went. I'd like to hear about it, but I don't have time now."
- "We don't talk about our day so much as we used to. I miss it."
- "I want to make touching base with you every day a priority. I get cranky when we don't connect."

Validate. Don't give advice until you've listened a while.

- "Sounds like you had a rough day."
- "Sounds like you'd rather not discuss it. If you change your mind, I'm interested."

If your partner is not showing interest in the conversation or is half-listening, say:

- "Is this not a good time to talk? You seem preoccupied."
- "I know you're probably listening, but I'd like your full attention. Thanks."
- "What could happen right now that would make you feel a little better?"

Chatting about the day's events is not the only topic worth discussing. Every couple or family enjoys looking forward to certain things such as birthdays, holidays, vacations, get-togethers, and so forth.

- "I went online today to look for possible vacation sites. You know what seemed interesting?"
- "I'd like to talk about what we should do for Anna's birthday party."

If you're in a bad mood when your partner wants to chat, try to be a bit gracious. It's okay to feel lousy. Just don't take it out on your partner.

- "This is not one of my best days. Bear with me. I just feel like hiding under a rock for awhile."
- "I'm sorry I'm acting like a grump. I just hate it when I miss the train. Now I have no time left to relax."

When you discuss a topic, don't just list facts. Mention how you feel about it or why it's important to you. According to author Daniel Wile in his book *After the Honeymoon*, that is more likely to grab a partner's interest than a tedious list of details.

- "That meeting was the best one I attended in years. The speakers were so motivating."
- "Wedding plans can get so complicated. I want so much for it all to go well and I'm worried we'll miss something."

If your partner is being particularly difficult and says things like:

- *"I'd rather be left alone, if you don't mind."*
- *"All you want to do is talk when I get home. Can't I just have a minute to myself?"*
- *"Does it look like I had a good day? Why would you even ask such a question?"*

You respond:

- *"If you're upset about something and would rather not talk, that's fine. Hopefully, you'll tell me later. But I'm on your side, remember."*
- *"Take whatever time you need."* (Then later, add) *"I don't mean to annoy you the minute you get home. Some days I need your help and I'm harried, too. Let's figure a way that we can improve this situation. It's better that we look forward to seeing each other at the end of the day."*
- *"I'm asking because I love you, even though you're not treating me well right now. Let me know when you might want to talk about it."*

How Not to Say It

Don't sound like you're half-interested or that you want the conversation over with. It's probably a brief discussion anyway. Hang in there.

- "Do we have to talk now?" (Of course you don't. But don't make it sound like an ordeal.)
- "Can't you see I'm busy?" (*Better:* "I'm busy right now, but I'll be finished soon. Is that okay?")
- "Can't we just have it quiet once in a while?" (*Better:* "It's important for us to talk. Sometimes, like right now, I just need to be quiet and relax. Okay?"

Don't give hasty advice or reassurances if your partner seems upset or emotional. It may seem like a nice thing, but it can make your partner think that you want the conversation ended or that you don't fully understand.

- "Tomorrow you'll feel better."
- "The driving always gets to you. I've told you before you should carpool."
- "It's not that big of a deal."

Don't criticize.

- "If you can't come home in a good mood, don't come home."
- "That's what you get for changing health plans. You'll have to get used to the new pediatrician."

Finally, don't chat when you're both standing up or doing other things. A talk in the kitchen while preparing dinner can be nice, but the distractions will be annoying if the topic is very important. Sit down or lie down together. The chat should not just be an exchange of information, but should also be an opportunity to relax with each other.

How to Say It to Yourself

Any negative, pessimistic self-talk about your everyday conversations with your partner should be challenged. Thoughts like "He bores me . . . I'd rather talk to my girlfriends . . . She never shuts up . . . She always complains about her job, I'm tired of hearing it . . . I'm not interested in his day . . . " will cause you two to drift apart.

- "Sometimes I don't feel like talking, but I know we should. It's important to her and it's an opportunity to connect and feel closer."
- "The book says that couples who can talk pleasantly to one another about everyday things and show interest in the conversation will talk more effectively when discussing problems. That's more of a reason to make sure we chat every day."
- "I'm in a lousy mood and I know when I walk in the door I'll have no time to myself and the house will be in chaos. But I want my family to be happy to see me. And I want to focus on being happy to see them, even if I am tired."
- "I know when we talk about our day she'll get distracted with the kids. I don't like it but I understand. If I'm patient and ask her if we can talk later when it's quiet, she'll agree."
- "He gets real cranky and is a pain sometimes when we try to talk. But I know he loves me and isn't always that way. He means well."
- "Sometimes he is boring. Maybe we haven't talked enough about what interests him."

- "Maybe I'm boring. Perhaps I should show more interest during our discussions."

Let's Talk

Numerous studies have repeatedly shown that happier couples think more positive thoughts about their relationship during interactions than do more distressed couples, and distressed couples think more negative thoughts about one another during interactions. (*Fact:* Those tendencies persist into second marriages. Changing one's spouse doesn't automatically change one's self-talk.)

Negative thoughts ("He's selfish . . . Why do I have to put up with this? . . . I can't stand her when she's like this . . . ") interfere with making improvements because behaviors that contradict negative beliefs (a partner acts with generosity) tend to be ignored or minimized while actions that confirm negative beliefs are focused on. After an argument or unpleasant interaction, men especially tend to rehearse negative thoughts. That has the effect of distorting memories so that negative beliefs are seen as true ("She did that on purpose!") and alternative, positive beliefs ("Maybe she didn't intend to be so thoughtless.") are discarded.

When you walk away from an argument (men especially take heed), search your brain for any negative beliefs that serve to maintain or add to your anger or distress. Take 15 to 20 minutes of calm relaxation (or, if very agitated, 5 minutes of aerobic exercise followed by 10 minutes of relaxation), and then replace negative beliefs with positive and realistic alternatives. Answering these questions can help you do that:

- "Even though I didn't like what happened, could my partner have meant well?"
- "What extenuating circumstances might account for her mood?"
- Did she have a legitimate gripe against me? Even a little bit?"
- "If I treated her the way she treated me, what reasons might I have given to justify my behavior? Do any of those reasons apply to her now?"
- "What qualities of her do I love, appreciate? Which would I miss if she weren't here?"

Part Two

Extra Supplies for Effective Conversation: The Communication Backpack

The GIFTS discussed in the first six chapters are among the most powerful, yet simple tools that you can use to make your conversations shine. If you take the time to learn and use those tools, you will undoubtedly have more successful dialogues with your partner and your relationship satisfaction will soar.

But even more help is available to help draw out those partners who prefer not to talk much or who end conversations sooner than is helpful. These additional tools will also improve your listening skills and help you to keep emotionally in touch with one another, even when conversations are brief.

Find what you need in the next six chapters and add them to the GIFTS. Your ability to communicate effectively will improve beyond your wildest dreams.

How to Solve Common Problems with Uncommon Effectiveness

7

Donna's mother has had hip-replacement surgery and is recuperating at home. Her father has phoned and it is obvious to Donna that her dad can't manage the aftercare as well as he'd hoped. Later, Donna speaks to her husband, Tom.

"I really need to visit her for a few hours every day. I can prepare their meals and help my mom with her personal care. Dad seems overwhelmed."

"But what about your job?" Tom asks. "And the kids? They have the science fair next week and have hardly started their projects."

"I haven't figured out the details," Donna says. "I may need you to take some time off. And you'll probably have to do a lot of the cooking. Fun, huh?"

"The kids like pizza," Tom says. "I can invite your dad over once in awhile."

"Pizza for dinner every night?"

"I was talking about breakfast," Tom laughs. "I'm thinking Chinese food for dinner."

Donna and Tom need to work out the details, but they are already near the finish line in solving this problem. It is obvious that they are on the same side and willing to make sacrifices. Tom's joke about pizza for breakfast is a clear indication that the problem will get handled—somehow. Their attitude is positive even though the situation is stressful.

But even Donna and Tom might have mishandled the situation had it occurred a year earlier. Then, Tom was working in a new job he didn't like after having been downsized by his former company. Their finances were tight, one of the kids had switched to middle school and was having a hard time adjusting, and Donna had been treated for both Lyme disease and bronchial pneumonia which put her out of commission for almost a month. Her mom's hip replacement might have put them over the edge.

Couples who love each other must tackle problems that inevitably come up from time to time. While some problems may be within the relationship (one partner doesn't help out so much, there is not enough lovemaking, and so forth), many stressors originate outside the relationship: an unexpected illness, a financial setback, a child in trouble at school, neighborhood problems, difficulties with a boss, and so on. The good news is that those problems are often temporary and solvable.

Have You Heard?

〜 Couples who report an increase in marital dissatisfaction often have experienced significant and stressful life events within the prior few months.

〜 Couples who relapsed within two years of relationship counseling were compared with couples who did not relapse. The relapsed couples experienced more negative life events than did the stable couples during the two years.

〜 The inability to resolve or manage "normal and expected" problems adds to relationship strain and reduces the odds that future problems will be successfully resolved.

〜 Every couple can identify several problems that have never been resolved. Strong personality differences or differences in values mean that some issues will knock on the couple's door every so often like an unwelcome relative during the holidays. Eradicating those problems is impossible and repeated attempts will only inflame the situation. (Read the chapters on dealing with personality differences for advice.) The best a couple can do is manage them.

〜 Offering emotional support (sincere listening, affection, sensitivity to your partner's point of view) has been shown to make a couple resilient when coping with life's hardships. Couples who offer emotional support suffer less emotional distress during a financial crisis than do couples who offer little support.

How to Say It

If the problem to be handled is not directly about the couple's relationship (illness, death of a family member, job disruption, child concern, and so forth), the ability to soothe and support one another emotionally is more important in reducing emotional distress than the specific details of how to tackle the problem. Emblazon this on your brain: FIRST SOOTHE, THEN SOLVE.

- "I'm sorry you lost your job. You must feel awful."
- "Let me give you a hug."
- "It's a bit overwhelming. We've had a lot hit us all of a sudden."
- "How are you feeling today? The problem is still on your mind, I bet."
- "You must be exhausted caring for your mom every day."

Offer encouragement.

- "I'm not sure how, but I have faith that we'll get through this."
- "This is a hard time, but I know it is temporary. We can hang in there."
- "We've been able to get through stressful times before."
- "This is our first major hurdle together. I'm glad we're partners."

Identifying the solutions is the next step but not always easy. Job loss means money may be tight, but old arguments about overspending might now resurface—resulting in a mix of problems. Put the animosities aside for the moment. Try to arrive at a small list of potential solutions to the current dilemma. The solutions must be reasonable and fair, and should not exploit one partner. Unhappy couples complain and blame, but stop short of coming up with practical ideas to solve certain problems.

- "Let's brainstorm possible solutions and not reject any out of hand. Ideally we'll find a solution that is reasonable and fair."
- "This is what I'm willing to do to fix this problem. What do you think about that?"
- Look for something you can agree with. "That makes sense . . . I agree with that . . . You're on to something . . . That idea has potential . . . I'm intrigued, tell me more . . . That's interesting . . . Let me think about that . . . "
- Negotiate. "I can take time off from work, but I need you to . . . "
- "That's not ideal for me, but it might work. I'm willing to give it a try."
- "I'd like to agree to that but I can't. I know it will backfire for me."
- "If we can't agree on which plan to implement, I'd be willing to flip a coin. How about you?"
- "I'll go along with your idea, but I want us to reevaluate it next week."

Touch base with one another as the solutions are implemented. Reassess the effectiveness of the solutions.

- "So far so good. What do you think?"
- "We might need to modify our agreement. I was having trouble with . . . "

How Not to Say It

Don't offer glib optimism at the expense of hearing out your partner's concerns. The following comments will likely cause your partner to argue with you, or to turn away thinking that you just don't understand.

- "I'm not worried about it. You shouldn't be, either."
- "You're getting too upset. It will all work out in the end."
- "Everybody goes through these things at some point. No sense making a big deal out of it."
- "We're not the only people on Earth with this problem, you know."
- "Let's just focus on pleasant things. No use thinking about what makes us miserable."

Don't latch on to a particular solution and be closed-minded about other options.

- "This is the only possible solution. You must go along with it." (Look for alternatives. If you each agree there are none, use a softer touch: "This seems to be all we can do right now. I know you don't like it. I appreciate you giving it your best.")
- "This idea is the best. It's a waste to talk about those other ideas." (Falling in love with a solution is common when anxiety is high. But flexibility and fairness is called for. *Better:* "I really like this idea. What do you think about trying it first?")
- "I'll figure it out myself. We don't see eye to eye." (Try to look for what is reasonable behind your partner's suggestions.)
- "We wouldn't have this problem if it wasn't for you . . . " (Even if you are correct, your job is to look for solutions. After solutions are agreed upon, you can bring up what's bothering you.)

Let's Talk

There is another approach worth trying, especially if problem-solving efforts get bogged down. One study showed that couples who chose to take a break from conversation and pray for help experienced a significant "softening" of their attitudes and language. Prayer seemed to cause a de-escalation of conflict and improved empathy between the partners. Furthermore, it seemed to help people switch their focus from "This is what you should do to change" to "This is what I should do to change." Prayer also seemed to facilitate a desire for reconciliation.

Over 90 percent of the U.S. population believe in God. For believers who are struggling to communicate effectively and resolve some problems, praying together during tense moments may bring about the miracle they are looking for.

How to Respond
When Past Mistakes
Are Thrown in Your Face

8

Ed and Eileen can handle most discussions pretty well. It becomes a problem, how-
ever, when Eileen—usually when she's very angry or feeling very misunderstood about
some issue—reminds Ed of the time he danced with a stripper at his best friend's bache-
lor party. Whenever she brings up that topic, their conversation spins out of control.

"Can't you forget the past?" Ed complains. "That was five years ago. It has nothing
to do with what we're discussing now!"

"I think it does," Eileen answers. "What bothers me is how you act like an imma-
ture teenager at times instead of a grown man. How can I forget that bachelor party when
you still act like you're seventeen years old?"

"Throwing it in my face every time you're upset with me, you call that mature?"

"If I partied all night with a male stripper, do you actually think you wouldn't have
a problem with that?"

"No, I wouldn't. I trust you. You should trust me."

"It's not about trust, Ed. It's about maturity. Aren't you listening?"

Many couples crash into a communication brick wall when one partner
brings up an old hurt that was, supposedly, put behind them. Women are more
apt to do this. Men respond predictably: with defensiveness and indignance
that their partner can't forgive and forget. What begins as a discussion about a
current problem rapidly escalates into a three-layer problem: the current topic,
the old topic, and anger that the old topic was raised.

Have You Heard?

〜 Old issues are brought up for two reasons: They are still unresolved and affecting one of the partners, or they symbolize a current problem and are mentioned to draw a parallel between what happened in the past and what is happening now. In the latter case, the intent should be to *clarify*, not *crucify*.

〜 Some old problems are particularly hard to put in the past (such as infidelity). Criticizing a partner to "Get over it!" shows insensitivity to the impact the problem had.

How to Say It

Validate the importance of the old issue your partner brings up, but suggest that you stick to the topic at hand.

- "You're right. I made a mistake before. Could we get back to what we were talking about and discuss the old issue later?"
- "If you really want to talk about that old topic, I will. But can we first finish the conversation we began?"
- "Are you bringing that up because our current problem is similar in some way? If so, tell me how it is similar and then let's focus more on the current problem."
- "It frustrates me to hear you bring that up. Can we discuss that after we finish this discussion?"
- "What has to happen for you to be able to let go of that issue? I'd like to know if I could do something that would help."
- "The fact that you bring that up must mean it's still important to you. Tell me what is still unresolved about it "
- "It bothers me that you bring that up because I don't like thinking it still hurts you. Does it still hurt? Or are you bringing it up to clarify your point of view?"
- "It worries me that we can't get past that issue."

How Not to Say It

- "If you're going to bring that up, we'll get nowhere." (Find out the reason it was brought up.)

- (With intense frustration or indignance) "Why are you talking about that now?" (You're really saying, "You have no right to do this!" Your partner, obviously, disagrees.)

- "You have no capacity to forgive." (You're making the situation worse. It's okay to be frustrated. It's not okay to get critical.)

- "I can forget the past. Why can't you?" (Again, you need to understand why it was raised. In many cases, old issues are not brought up as a personal attack but because what happened before was similar in some way to what is happening now. If it was meant as an attack, your best bet is to acknowledge that your partner is still angry, agree to discuss it later, and request that the current topic be addressed now.)

What do you say when you wish to bring up an old topic? If it is unresolved and still bothering you, don't bring it up during an argument about something else. It will clutter the conversation.

How to Say It

- "I've been thinking a lot about what happened when . . . I'm sure you've been hoping it was all in the past but I still need to discuss it further. Is now a good time?"

- "I thought I was over this, but I've realized recently that I'm not. It would help me if we could talk further about . . . "

If your partner responds:

- *"Let's not go there. We'll only argue."*
- *"We've talked about it a dozen times. One more time will only make us aggravated."*
- *"Okay, okay. But make it quick."*

You reply:

- *"I don't want to argue. It would help me now if you listened to my concerns and helped me figure out what we can do."*
- *"We have talked about it before and it hasn't helped. You're right about that. I'd like to discuss it differently today. Mostly, I need you to understand why it's been still bothering me."*
- *"I'm sure you'd rather not discuss it again. I don't blame you. But it's important that I feel I have your attention. It will take about ____ minutes. If now isn't a good time, we can talk tonight."*

If you bring up an old issue while discussing a current problem, do your best not to make it sound like you're throwing everything at him but the kitchen sink.

- "The problem we're having now reminds me of a problem we had before. I'm mentioning it—not to throw it in your face—but so you might understand why I'm so bothered by the current problem."

If your partner responds angrily or defensively, you reply:

- *"I don't want us to rehash that old problem. That's not why I brought it up. I brought it up because it might help to explain why I'm upset about the current problem."*
- *"You don't have to worry about that problem now. That problem isn't my concern. But it is similar in important ways to the problem we are discussing."*

How Not to Say It

- "I still haven't forgotten about . . . You owe me." (You need to find a way to put it past you once and for all. Rehashing it will aggravate your relationship. *Better:* "I'm still bothered about . . . I had hoped I'd be over it by now but I'm not. I guess what I need from you that would help me is . . . ")

- "What you did then was unforgivable. I'll never forget." (Forgiveness can be a difficult process. Sometimes people withhold forgiveness because they don't feel that the offending party really has demonstrated adequate understanding and remorse. If that is so for you, you may wish to say: "It would be easier for me to forgive if I really believed you understood the impact your actions had on me. Instead of defending your actions, I'd like it if you could show some genuine empathy and affection."

Let's Talk

Couples who have lingering resentments tend to bring up old hurts when arguing, making the conversation unwieldy and overwhelming. Ironically, this happens because of the buildup of many instances when a partner chose to *not* register a complaint in a noble effort to be bighearted. Having held his or her tongue in the past, a partner eventually feels entitled to complain. However, the conversation is cluttered with a backlog of unsettled hurts. The responding partner feels unfairly attacked, the conversation breaks down, the accuser goes away upset but with a resolve to keep silent about future, petty problems—only to eventually explode and the pattern of "clash, rehash, and dash" repeats itself.

A couple with a history of unsatisfying conversations should anticipate that their new attempts to improve communication will get sidetracked by a laundry list of old hurts. The best way to deal with this is to:

1. Try to have conversations that will offer a forum to deal explicitly with old hurts.
2. Observe when conversations of current problems get sidetracked. Gently veer the conversation back to the current problem with an agreement to talk later about the older issues that have also come up.
3. Realize that old hurts must be forgiven. That is made easier when the offender doesn't develop a "You should be over it by now" attitude but is instead understanding. It is easier to show understanding when the complainer doesn't use the old hurt as a weapon.

How to Encourage
More Conversation

9

Larry and Sally often have stilted, one-sided conversation. While driving through the countryside, Sally comments about the beauty of nature.

"Isn't that stretch of land gorgeous? It goes on for miles. I could stare at it for hours and never grow tired of it."

"Mm-hmm," Larry says flatly.

"No, really. Couldn't you imagine having a house on a hill overlooking all of this? Wouldn't it be magnificent."

"I guess."

"Is that all you can say?"

Larry sighs. "What would you like me to say?"

A lament for many, especially depressed wives, is "We don't talk." Even happier couples are often mismatched in the amount of talking each partner does. A perfect match isn't necessary for a couple to thrive. But too little conversation reduces intimacy, increases loneliness (at least for one partner), and increases the odds that conflicts will arise—which will cause the less-talkative partner to withdraw further from future conversations. A tug of war that begins with "Why won't you talk!" is a surefire way to add to conflict and withdrawal. How can a couple talk more often when one of them is disinclined?

Have You Heard?

~ It shouldn't be a surprise to learn that men speak fewer words and express fewer emotions than women. Biology plays a role in this, as does socialization. Studies show that parents use more emotional words when talking to daughters than to sons. Partners are wise not to take this difference so personally.

~ Sometimes, a woman who wants a man to talk more will be satisfied with simple acknowledgments that he is listening and interested in what she's saying (such as "That's interesting ... tell me more ... "). In those situations, men who can "pitch back" (give verbal or physical acknowledgment that he's listening) may improve relationship satisfaction without having to be an Olympic gold-medal conversationalist.

~ Generally, increasing the amount of conversation a couple has raises a woman's relationship satisfaction. But since men's satisfaction is less related to the amount of conversation, men have less of a need to converse. (They often have a greater need to make love.)

~ The partner who desires a bit more separateness than togetherness can often get that on his own. He simply has to make himself psychologically or physically unavailable. The partner who desires more closeness cannot get that on her own. She requires cooperation.

~ Mismanaged conflict increases the odds that one partner (most often the man) will withdraw from conversations—even positive or emotionally neutral conversations—because he anticipates an argument. Men become emotionally flooded during relationship conflicts and withdraw to reduce their physical distress. Women are less likely to become flooded and are more likely to express dissatisfaction—especially when their men have a habit of avoiding conversations. Thus, the pattern of woman complain/man withdraw is extremely common and predictive of relationship dissatisfaction.

~ In distressed relationships, women tend to respond negatively when men make even a mild complaint about them or the relationship. This causes men to withdraw more than they otherwise would—which makes the women more distressed. In fact, even if a man makes a neutral or positive comment, a woman who is unhappy with the relationship will respond negatively. (For example, the man says, "Looks like a nice day outside." The unhappy woman might reply, "So? What does that matter? You never want to go anywhere anyway.")

How to Say It

In very happy relationships, a direct (nonharsh) request for more conversation and a willingness to understand why your partner may not be too talkative will probably pay dividends.

- "It means so much to me when we have time to just talk and connect. I'd like to talk more than we do. What are your thoughts about that?"
- "Yesterday we sat on the porch and had a nice, simple conversation. That felt great. Can we talk like that more often?"
- "I've noticed that I usually enjoy chatting more than you. Do I have that right? Am I doing anything that makes it more uncomfortable for you to talk?" (His first response will be "No, you're doing nothing wrong" but later on he may have some different ideas. ("Now that I think about it, you do tend to go on and on about things. Sometimes I wish you could be more concise.") Don't respond negatively to those comments. If you disagree, better to say, "I never noticed that before.")
- "I'm frustrated that we don't talk as much as I'd like. What can we do about that?"
- "I'm getting angry. You seem occupied with so many things, but have less time for me." (If the relationship is satisfying, this remark will not be a problem. The listener may get defensive, but the conversation will likely stay on track.)

If you are upset about something not connected to your relationship and want to discuss it, preface your comments by stating what you want from your partner (for example, to give you advice or to simply listen and understand).

- "I need to talk about what happened at work today. I really don't want any advice, but I'd really like it if you could just listen." (A man's natural inclination is to solve his wife's problems and offer advice. If he is told ahead of time that he only needs to listen, he can relax.)

If your partner responds, "I don't feel like talking . . . I don't have anything to say . . . I really don't want to talk about work . . . ," see if he or she can acknowledge that talking more is generally a good idea. Then back off.

- "I guess you don't need to talk now if you don't want to. But I'm concerned that we don't talk as much as I'd like. I miss talking to you. I'm happy to let you be right now, but do you agree that we should spend more time in conversation?"

Get creative. Conversations while sitting across from each other at the dining room table may be too formal.

- "How about we talk for awhile in bed before we go to sleep? I'll be happy to massage your back."
- "You can rub my neck and tell me all about your day. Then I'll rub your feet and tell you all about mine."
- "How about we go for a brisk fifteen-minute walk?"

Your approach to increasing conversation must change if the relationship has been tense or there have been recent, unresolved arguments. Simple verbal requests to talk will meet with resistance. You must be willing to examine your role in why some conversations have derailed and own up to mistakes. If you and your partner are dissatisfied with the relationship, even beautifully phrased comments will be taken the wrong way.

- "I've just read how couples who haven't been getting along overreact to each other's comments and perceive things more negatively than they actually are. I don't want us to be that way. Do you think I've reacted too negatively to you? Do you think I misunderstand what you are trying to say?" If he responds by listing his complaints, try not to get defensive. Say, "I guess we are misunderstanding each other. I want us to learn to talk effectively so we don't needlessly hurt each other."
- "I am going to make up a rule for me to follow: Whenever I get upset with you, I'm going to presume I've misunderstood something you said or did. Will you help me with that?" If your partner replies with "That sounds like a lot of hogwash," you reply, "Perhaps. But I'd like to try anyway. I want us to get along better. Will you help me with that?"
- "We're caught in a merry-go-round. I get critical because I think you will withdraw from conversation, and you withdraw because I get critical. Can we try not to step on each other like that? I do love you, you know."

- "If I say something in a way that offends you, please do me a favor. Presume that my intention was good and give me a chance to explain myself." (If your partner replies with "That's hard to do," you respond, "Yes, I know. Probably because you are worried about my reaction. I'll do my best to stay calm.")

- "I have a problem. I just realized I'm less interested in having sex because I want more time for us to just talk and show affection." (If he replies: "Oh, so you will never make love until I talk, is that the game?" You respond: "I'm not saying that. I'm saying that my desire for sex is based in part on how well we get along and how close I feel to you. I feel closest when I know you won't shut me out. I'm asking for your help.")

- Most less-talkative partners want you to focus on all the other things they do for the relationship and to be content with that. For example, "What about all the things I do for you? I bought you the car you wanted, I landscaped our front yard, I let your sister live with us for two months while she was waiting for an apartment. Why can't you be satisfied with that?" You respond, "You are very considerate in those areas and I love you for it. But I'm lonely and I miss you. Looking at a beautifully landscaped yard is not the same as cuddling up to you and talking about our day. You underestimate how much chatting with you makes my day."

- Grab some old photos of the early days and hand them one at a time to your partner. Reminiscing can improve conversation if you keep your remarks pleasant. "There you are in the old station wagon. Remember the time we drove to Florida?"

If your partner does talk (he has to, eventually) and you don't like what he says, try to validate at least some of his comments. A nasty reply on your part will be his excuse for why he won't speak up more.

- "That isn't easy for me to hear, but I'm glad you said it."

- "I don't agree with your perception, but it means a lot that you decided to tell me."

- "It's hard to listen well when you say things I disagree with, but I'm trying. Bear with me."

How Not to Say It

When the relationship is already strained, don't give opinions that are sharply critical—however accurate they are. It won't help your cause.

- "You have no capacity for true intimacy, otherwise you'd talk more." (*His likely thought:* "To hell with you.")
- "How did you ever get this way?" (*His likely thought:* "You drove me to it.")
- "You're being passive–aggressive." (*His likely thought:* "You've been reading self-help books again.")
- "I don't care that you put in a new vinyl floor. That doesn't matter." (*His likely thought:* "You're telling me that the sacrifices I make don't count. I resent that.")

Don't criticize the nontalkative partner when he or she does open up.

- "It's about time you said something."
- "Finally! Look at all I had to go through just to have a two-minute conversation!"

How to Say It to Yourself

If the relationship has been less than satisfying, your self-talk about this issue will probably interfere with your progress. If you want your partner to talk more, say to yourself:

- "I'm not making the situation better by complaining. It's okay to be frustrated and hurt and angry, but if I criticize him now things will get worse. I'll focus on making the conversations we do have more pleasant and not be so quick to criticize."
- "I can probably compliment him more. That won't hurt and it might help me to appreciate him more than I do now."
- "To some extent I have to accept him the way he is. He may never talk as much as I'd like but he doesn't have to. If he could talk a little more often and show interest, I could live with that."

If your partner complains that you don't talk enough, say this to yourself:

- "I get angry because she's not accepting me the way I am. But I should also accept *her* way—which is to have more conversations. I can show acceptance by being willing to have more conversations once in a while."
- "I keep thinking that I'd talk more if she'd complain less. That's blaming her. She has a point. It's not unreasonable to want me to share more in conversation."
- "I'm just as responsible for this gridlock as she is. I can meet her halfway."

Talking Point: "I" statements are overrated. Phrasing complaints in terms of "I" (such as "I'm upset that we don't talk") as opposed to "You" ("You rarely want to talk to me") can soften an argument, but they are difficult to do in the heat of the moment. When a relationship is unsatisfying, perfectly phrased "I" statements have no effect. Finding something you can agree with about a partner's point of view makes more sense when you want the conversation to go more smoothly.

How to Check Out Assumptions

10

Michelle is frustrated that money is always tight. Her neighbors always seem to have money for extra items such as dinner at a restaurant, taking an aerobics class, a gym membership, a nicer car, or an annual vacation to some island. What are she and Rick doing wrong? She wants to talk to him about this, but she knows what he'll say: "We should be happy with what we've got . . . "

Michelle makes an assumption about what Rick will say. Perhaps she is right. But perhaps if she asks him his opinion anyway they might be able to have a useful conversation. Assumptions are often inaccurate (especially if there is disharmony in the relationship), but by failing to check them out, assumptions become self-fulfilling. If Michelle never asked Rick about how they could budget their money, she would always believe that he'd be uncooperative in that area.

Imagine that Michelle and Rick had the following conversation. See how hidden assumptions can make or break a conversation:

MICHELLE: I'd like to talk about our budget. It seems to me we should find a way to save more money.

RICK: (hidden assumption: *She's always complaining about my income. Doesn't she realize I'm working as hard as I can?*) I think you should just appreciate what we've got.

MICHELLE: (hidden assumption: *My opinion isn't important to him!*) You're not listening to me. Can't I have an opinion about how we budget our money?

RICK: (hidden assumption: *Nothing satisfies her.*) Sure you can have an opinion. But I'm working as hard as I can. Maybe you should appreciate that instead of criticizing me.

MICHELLE: I'm not criticizing you. I know you work hard.

RICK: (hidden assumption: *But I'm never good enough. Why won't she just come out and say it?*) Yeah, you sound real appreciative . . .

Now imagine if they checked out their assumptions:

MICHELLE: I'd like to talk about our budget. It seems to me that we should find a way to save more money.

RICK: Whenever you bring up money, I feel like you're criticizing me for not making enough. Is that true?

MICHELLE: Not at all! I know you work hard. I wish you didn't have to work as hard as you do. That's why I'm wondering if we're making some fundamental mistake in the way that we budget our money.

RICK: I don't know of any mistakes. Things are just expensive, that's all.

MICHELLE: But it would mean a lot to me if we could keep track of our expenses just to see where we might be wasting money. I want to believe that my opinions count.

RICK: Okay. If you think it's a good idea, we can give it a try.

That discussion immediately became friendly and constructive.

Have You Heard?

〜 The easiest time to make assumptions—and the time when assumptions are least likely to be valid—is during a tense discussion.

〜 A message is sent and the sender *automatically assumes* that the message sent was the message received. The receiver of the message interprets the meaning of the message and *automatically assumes* that the meaning received was the meaning sent. All it takes is for one assumption to be wrong—but still believed—and the conversation will get messed up.

∼ You know that you or your partner are making too many false assumptions when one of you frequently says:

That's not what I meant.	*You always think that, but it's not true.*
I didn't say that.	*You always think the worst.*
You're jumping to conclusions.	*You're not letting me explain.*
You don't understand.	*I know **exactly** what you meant.*
You're twisting my words.	*Don't tell me I heard wrong. I understood perfectly well.*

∼ In order to check out your assumptions, you must first be willing to admit (to yourself) that your assumptions might be incorrect.

∼ It is most important to check out assumptions that make you feel angry, hurt, or upset with your partner.

How to Say It

- "When you said XYZ, I took that to mean . . . Was I right?"
- "Are you telling me that you mean . . . ?"
- "I'm feeling aggravated by what you said. Let me be sure I understood you clearly . . . "
- "You look upset. Are you?"
- "You keep raising your voice. Are you mad at me or just upset about the situation?"
- "It bothered me when you . . . Was that what you intended?"
- "I didn't want to bring this up because I thought you'd get annoyed. But then I decided it's better to take a chance."
- "When I imagined talking to you about this, I thought you'd respond by saying XYZ. But I decided to ask anyway just in case I might be wrong."

How Not to Say It

- "That is not what you meant!" (Give your partner the benefit of the doubt. Some people mean one thing but have a hard time being clear. If they try to explain what they meant, don't disagree. Cut them some slack.)

- "You're impossible to talk to." (Determine what your assumptions are about what your partner just said, then check them out.)

- "Stop twisting my words. That was not what I meant!" (Be less harsh. *Better:* "Your interpretation is not accurate. What I meant was . . . ")

- "I know what you meant. You meant . . . Don't deny it!" (You seem more invested in being right than in having a constructive dialogue.)

How to Keep the Spark Alive by Staying Emotionally in Touch

11

Thus far, the rules and guidelines you've learned for effective conversation represent the fundamentals. They are similar to using the basic furniture and appliances you have in your house or apartment. Everyone needs a refrigerator, a stove, a couch or chair, a bed, a table and a lamp, and a telephone. But what makes a house a home? It's the little things—flowers, photographs, sentimental antiques, and familiar odds and ends. It's the various and subtle decorative items that make the house special and vibrant, that make you look forward to arriving there at the end of the day.

Your relationship with the person you're in love with is similar. Having technically precise conversations will mean little if the relationship is not decorated with small gestures of love and affection and gentle words of kindness and caring. In fact, the more fondness and devotion that is demonstrated in many small ways, the more likely that conversational errors will have minimal negative effect. Keeping emotionally in touch is one way to show fondness. It fills in the small spaces of the life you share and thereby provides a richness that would otherwise be lacking.

Have You Heard?

~ To be emotionally in touch with a partner requires a willingness to focus on subtle signs of emotion. Some partners ignore emotional cues. That's a mistake.

∼ It also requires knowledge of what your partner has planned for the day or the week so that you can make reasonable inferences as to what the person might be feeling. For example, "You had that big meeting today. Is that why you seem so preoccupied?"

∼ It requires a willingness to allow emotional expression. For some couples, certain feelings (especially anger or sadness) are disallowed, punished, or ignored.

∼ Learning to be emotionally in touch with your partner will not cause him or her to become excessively emotional. On the contrary, experiencing a genuine emotional connection helps a person to handle disappointments, losses, and letdowns and actually helps keep emotions on an even keel. It builds emotional *resilience*, not emotional roller-coaster rides.

∼ Staying emotionally in touch will automatically add to a feeling of intimacy. While some partners shy away from too much intimacy, these smaller gestures can create closeness without making the moment too intense or overwhelming. Furthermore, it will increase the odds that you and your partner will think more about each other during the day when you are apart.

∼ There may be gender differences. A man who is upset about something might not want to discuss it, at least not right away. It would be a mistake to insist he talk just so you can be emotionally in touch. Paradoxically, acknowledging and reaffirming his need to mull things over by himself *is being emotionally in touch*.

How to Say It

Pay attention to small indications of happiness, frustration, boredom, disappointment, excitement, and so on. Make inquiries that show interest. Back off (be friendly) if the responder shows little interest in your comment. A gentle, affectionate gesture can be nice. Men especially should approach a woman who seems upset and inquire what's wrong. Men typically avoid doing that because they fear they might be to blame for what's wrong or they presume (mistakenly) that the woman wants to mull things over by herself. A man may want time alone when he is upset. Give him the space he wants if he seems unresponsive to your inquiries.

- "Just thought I'd check in and see how you're doing."

- "Are you still thinking about . . . ?"
- "That phone call seemed to change your mood. Want to talk about it?"
- "Anything on your mind?"
- "You must be exhausted. Is there anything I can do for you?"
- "You had a long drive. What can I get for you?"
- "May I rub your back?"
- "May I pick something up at the store for you?"
- "I'll make you a cup of tea, then you can tell me what happened."
- "You don't have to talk about it if you don't want. I hope you feel better soon."
- "You must be relieved that your report is finished."
- "You really look like you're enjoying this vacation."
- "I didn't get a chance to see much of you before I left this morning, so I called to say hi."
- "I know I just saw you an hour ago but I wanted to call and tell you good luck on your test."

Offer compliments.

- "Thanks for calling me. It was a nice surprise."
- "I love the way you look in that shirt."
- "I love you."
- "I'm glad you're home."
- "I missed you."
- "You're still the sexiest woman (man) I know."
- "Hey, handsome!"
- "Hey, beautiful!"

If a woman replies to your inquiry with these comments:

- *"No, nothing is wrong."* (Yet she still seems upset.)
- *"You wouldn't understand."*
- *"It's not something I want to discuss."*

The man should respond:

- *"It looks to me like something is wrong. I'd really like to hear what's on your mind."* (Persist a bit. A woman who says nothing is wrong often is still hoping for your attention. If she insists that nothing is wrong, say: *"If you realize something is bothering you later on and you want to talk about it, I'm right here."*)
- *"Sometimes I don't understand. But I'd like to try. Tell me what's wrong."*
- *"I hope you change your mind. I'd like to find out what's troubling you."* (Sometimes a woman will say she doesn't want to discuss it because she thinks you don't want to discuss it. Reassure her that you do.)

If a man seems upset or preoccupied and you make inquiries, but he replies:

- *"No, nothing is wrong."*
- *"I'd rather figure it out by myself."*
- *"It's not something I want to discuss."*

The woman should reply:

- *"Okay. If you change your mind and want to talk about it, I'm here."* (Then she should drop it.)
- *"That's fine. I'm sure you'll make the right decision."* (Letting him know you have faith in him may actually draw him to you. If it doesn't, it's still smart to let him handle it alone. Don't take it as a rejection. He doesn't intend it that way.)
- *"Okay. Take your time."*

How Not to Say It

- "I know something is bothering you and I won't stop asking you about it until you tell me what it is." (You're coming on too strong. Show interest, but back off if you're not getting anywhere.)
- "Are you *still* upset (angry, crying, worried, sulking)?" (You're implying that it's wrong to feel that way.)
- "I can't talk to you if you're too emotional." (Talking will probably decrease your partner's emotionalism. Actually, *you're* probably too emo-

tional; otherwise, you could handle your partner's emotions. Breathe. Then listen to your partner.)

- "You should tell me more of what's bothering you. Don't make it superficial. I want to know your inner feelings." (Exploring inner feelings isn't necessary to keep emotionally in touch. If a partner doesn't want to explore his or her feelings any deeper, understanding and accepting that is in fact an emotional connection. *Better:* "You don't have to tell me more if you really don't want to. You're entitled to your innermost thoughts. But I'm here if there's more you want to add.")

How to Say It to Yourself

Encourage yourself to go the extra step and touch base with your partner when you might otherwise do nothing.

- "She doesn't seem quite herself. I should give her a hug and ask how she's doing."
- "She looks preoccupied. I know she spoke with her brother yesterday. I'll ask if everything is okay."
- "He looks like he wants to be left alone. Maybe something is on his mind or maybe he's just tired. I'll give him a kiss on the cheek and ask how his day went. If he doesn't seem too talkative, I won't press it. I'll just say that maybe he wants some time for himself."
- "I won't take it personally if he doesn't want to talk about it. Men like to mull things over by themselves."
- "I won't accept her words at face value if she says she doesn't want to talk about it. She may simply be assuming that *I* don't want to discuss it. I'll push a little, then back off if she insists."
- "I really like how she looks in that outfit. Maybe I should let her know that. I'm sure she'll be pleased."

How Not to Say It to Yourself

- "She looks upset about something. I won't say anything. She'll initiate the conversation if she wants to talk." (Don't presume that. You can make an inquiry and back away if she doesn't have much to say.)

- "I just saw her a couple of hours ago. There's no sense calling her on the phone."
- "He knows I love him. I don't have to keep saying it."
- "She knows I love her from all the things I do around the house. I don't need to use words or send flowers." (Are you sure? Many partners crave tender words and the occasional romantic gesture.)
- "Watching television together is fine. We're both busy during the week. We don't have the energy for anything more involved." (Again, are you sure? Ruts develop when a partner presumes the other is happy and content. Your partner may be lonely and bored. You need to ask to be sure.)

How to Listen
with Love

Tony acts like he is listening patiently while his live-in companion of two years, Marsha, complains about his lack of affection.

When Marsha stops talking, Tony looks up and asks, "Are you finished? May I talk now?" Just as he is about to utter his first word, Marsha interrupts him.

"You weren't listening to a thing I said, were you," she says.

"Of course I was," Tony answers. "You said I wasn't showing enough affection."

"Yes, I did say that but that wasn't all I said."

"Well, how do you expect me to remember everything you say when you go on and on like that?"

Next door, their neighbors are having a pleasant conversation when the husband tells his wife he'll be working late the following Friday.

"But next Friday we have tickets for the play."

"I thought that was the Friday after next," the husband says.

"No, I specifically told you it was next Friday. Weren't you listening?"

Most couples could make improvements in the listening department.

Have You Heard?

∾ Many couples offer each other too much advice or criticism and not enough affectionate comments or sincere listening. If couples tripled the amount of listening and offered one-third of the "I know better" advice, relationships would run more smoothly.

〜 From my book *25 Stupid Mistakes Couples Make,* poor listeners:

— Think they understand and yet they rarely do.

— Look for what's wrong or irrational about what's being said, instead of trying to understand.

— Sometimes try to make others feel better with pat advice. They don't really want to understand the other person's pain. They want to tell them why they shouldn't be feeling that way.

— Take offense at the first sign of conflict and stop trying to understand.

〜 According to Dr. Michael Nichols, in his remarkable book *The Lost Art of Listening,* "Couples who learn to listen to each other—with understanding and tolerance—often find that they don't need to change each other."

〜 People who don't feel listened to are lonelier for it.

〜 To listen well you must put aside your viewpoint and your need to be right and instead try to understand the other person as best as you can.

How to Say It

Use words that reveal that it matters to you what your partner has to say. Make supportive comments (the "S" in GIFTS).

- "That's interesting. What happened next?"
- "Tell me more."
- "May you repeat that? I didn't hear what you said."
- "I understand." (Be sincere.)
- "May I interrupt for a moment? You've said quite a bit and I want to be sure I understood it. Your main point is _____."
- "Uh-huh . . . Yes . . . Keep going . . . "

The hardest thing for a listener to do is to not get too defensive or angry when he or she doesn't like what's being said. It isn't fatal, but when that happens listening usually stops and arguments often begin. You don't have to be a living saint and respond with quiet gentleness when your partner is saying inflammatory things. But try to keep in mind that you eventually need to get back on the listening track.

When listening becomes difficult, say:

- "I want to keep listening but what you are saying is making me angry. Can we slow this down and take these points one at a time?"
- "I need to take a few minutes and calm down. What you are saying is upsetting."
- "Can you rephrase that? Can you say it with more respect?"
- "I need to respond now. Can you try to listen to me for a few minutes and not interrupt?"
- "It was hard listening to you because you said some things that I thought were unfair. But I did listen. Now I'd like to respond to what you said."

How Not to Say It

- "You shouldn't feel that way!" (But your partner *does* feel that way. You've stopped listening and you don't understand. *Better:* "I hear what you're saying but I do have another way of looking at the situation. Would you like to hear it?")
- "How can you say that?" (You've stopped listening and started judging.)
- "Yeah, yeah, I'm listening." (Don't make it sound like an ordeal. If your partner questions if you have been listening, say, "I'm doing the best I can. Keep going.")
- "When may I get a chance to talk?" (That comment suggests you stopped listening and simply *tolerated* the person speaking. If the other person has a tendency to talk too much, say, "May I respond to what you've said so far?")
- "You're wrong . . . That's not what happened . . . I don't believe you're saying this . . . You're being ridiculous . . . " (It's risky to jump in like this, so do it cautiously. Your partner will definitely believe that you are not hearing him or her out and will try to prove to you why *your* comments are wrong. Take a few deep breaths, wait for an opening, and ask if you may take a turn. It may not seem natural, but it will keep the conversation from getting out of hand. You may certainly disagree with your partner's viewpoints—just make sure you understand fully what your partner's viewpoints are.)
- When listening, don't make faces, don't roll your eyes, don't sigh in disgust, and don't groan.

Part Three

Everybody Say "Cheese": Situations Involving Family, Kids, and Friends

A happy couple may have eyes only for each other, but at some point they must turn their attention to the assortment of people—family and friends—who are a part of each other's world.

Family and friends add richness to life, but they can also be a source of strain. That strain can spill over into the couple's relationship, causing rifts, misunderstandings, and complaints such as "I married *you*, not *your* parents."

What if your partner dislikes your father, but you want to keep the peace? How do you best discuss that and not feel like you are taking sides?

How do you handle the holidays when you and your partner are being pulled in different directions trying to keep family and friends happy?

What if there are no divided loyalties, but the manner in which your new partner handles the kids is not the way you think is best?

How you talk to your partner about family, friends, and kids can help create a household of ill will or goodwill.

Celebrating Pregnancy

13

Clarissa and John stand by while waiting for the results of the early pregnancy test. Although they haven't specifically planned on getting pregnant, they have been open to the idea and stopped using birth control two months earlier. John isn't sure what he wants the results to show. Yes, he wants to become a father, but is now the best time? He begins thinking that even a delay of another six months might have allowed them to save more money for the baby. After all, Clarissa intends to take several months off from work after the baby is born and finances would be tight. Clarissa's thoughts are less practical and more sentimental. As soon as she stopped using birth control, she began anticipating motherhood and is now eager for it to begin. She'll be awfully disappointed if the test results are negative.

The color-coded results are getting clearer. Yes! She is pregnant! She jumps for joy and then hugs John as hard as she can. John's heart pounds inside his chest. He feels like he's just parachuted from a plane. There is no turning back now.

Have You Heard?

~ Even if a pregnancy was unexpected (half are unplanned), enthusiasm about it can pay dividends for the mother's and baby's emotional well being. An expectant father offers emotional support more effectively when his enthusiasm overrides his anxiety.

~ Stress experienced by an expectant mother during pregnancy (ill health, job loss, death of a family member, family problems, and so on) has been shown to significantly increase the likelihood of depression. However, if the woman's partner is aware of those stresses, he is more likely to offer emotional support and thereby offer a buffer against depression. Men who downplay or ignore the stresses their pregnant partners are facing unwittingly contribute to their partners' depression.

〜 Emotional support from a woman's intimate partner during pregnancy is more important than emotional support from other family members or friends.

〜 A woman who receives too little emotional support during pregnancy has a greater chance of becoming a less effective parent.

〜 Couples with a premarital pregnancy show the steepest decline in marital satisfaction after the first year of marriage. These young couples need extra support from each other and from their families.

How to Say It

If the pregnancy was planned, this is not a time to be low-keyed. Express excitement as often as possible and show interest in how your partner is handling the situation.

- "This is the most wonderful thing that has happened."
- "You'll be a terrific parent."
- "How does it feel to be six weeks' pregnant?"
- "How does it feel knowing you'll be a father (mother) in less than a month?"
- "It's fun watching your parents get so excited about the baby."
- "You look very pretty (sexy) in that new outfit."
- "Even though it's very early, have you thought about what the baby's room might look like?"

How Not to Say It

- "This is a lousy time to get pregnant." (If you can't be enthusiastic, at least offer reassurances that over time you will.)
- "Let's not get our hopes up. Miscarriages happen, you know." (True, but you and your partner should spend time celebrating, not worrying about what could go wrong. If you have experienced a miscarriage before and must express that concern, remain optimistic. *Better:* "This is what we've been waiting for! Let's remain hopeful that this pregnancy will work out.")

If anxieties about such things as money or housing arise, don't allow your fears to predominate the conversations. Express your concerns while making clear that the upcoming birth will be a wonderful event.

- "I can't help worrying about money, but I'm still glad this is happening."
- "Somehow we'll make it work."
- "I guess it's normal to be worried. But I'm excited, too."

If your partner says:

- *"I wish you'd act more happy about this!"*
- *"I wish you'd care about the finances as much as you do the pregnancy. Money will be tight, you know."*
- *"Why do I have to go with you to your doctor appointments?"*

You reply:

- *"You're right. I should show more excitement and I will try to do that. I guess I need us to talk about the things that worry me, too."*
- *"You're right. We do have to pay more attention to finances. But sometimes I just want to talk about the fun part of being pregnant and put aside our worries."*
- *"You won't have to go to all of them, but I want you there when they take the sonogram pictures and especially if we have any concerns. Plus I like the idea that we are starting to think of ourselves as a family."*

If the pregnancy was unplanned and you feel more scared and anxious than happy, it is okay to express those concerns. However, as long as the two of you intend to see the pregnancy through, it will be important to find ways to reassure one another that the fears will be temporary. More affection and touching can help make the two of you feel more connected.

How to Say It

- "I feel bad that our reaction to the pregnancy wasn't one of excitement. I guess it took us both by surprise. But I'm sure we'll feel better soon. Then we can really celebrate."

- "Being a parent (again) scares me. But I'm sure we'll both be thrilled by the time the baby is born. A year from now we'll wonder why we ever had any anxiety."
- "I wish I were more happy. Bear with me. I'll feel exhilarated soon. I just wasn't expecting this to happen."

How Not to Say It

- "This is your fault."
- "This is the worst thing that could ever happen." (No, it isn't. Put this in perspective.)

You Dislike Your Partner's Friends

14

"I don't like it when you go out with your girlfriends," Mark says to Rose. "Half of them are divorced. They're probably interested in going dancing or meeting men. You shouldn't go to places like that."

Rose tries not to overreact, but she is thinking that Mark is being a tad controlling. After all, he goes out with his friends—none of whom would qualify for the title of upstanding citizen of the month.

"I don't complain when you play golf with Rich. He's a swinging bachelor with a new woman on his arm every week. I'm sure you love hearing his stories of conquest."

"Rich is harmless. But your friend Terry isn't. I bet she fills your head with stories of how men are useless."

"No, she doesn't."

"Still, I wish you wouldn't see that much of her."

Without the proper discussion, Mark and Rose will make this issue a pebble in their shoe. Eventually, Rose might decline an invitation from her friends just to be loyal to Mark. Or Mark might turn down a golf outing with Rich. But they might feel resentful too. Sooner or later, however, Rose and Mark will feel entitled to go out with their friends because they never intended to stop their friendships, just reduce the frequency of the get-togethers. What will happen the next time Terry asks Rose to accompany her to a "girls night out"?

Have You Heard?

🗘 All else being equal, going out with friends is healthy. The real question is whether or not a friendship is displacing the romantic partnership.

🗘 If the primary relationship with your partner is satisfying, it's okay to make a complaint about a partner's friend but it's not okay to try to persuade your partner to cut back on that relationship. Your partner will probably defend his or her friends and you'll feel slighted.

🗘 If your relationship with your partner is somewhat dissatisfying, his or her friendships with others may be a false issue. The real issue may be that you feel neglected, unappreciated, or taken for granted. Or, you might worry that your partner is pulling away from you emotionally. Discuss ways your relationship can be enhanced without emphasizing time with friends.

🗘 Your partner should spend more pleasurable time with you than with friends. If that isn't happening, focus on how to spend more enjoyable time together rather than focus on how he or she should spend less time with a friend.

🗘 You may spend a lot of time with your partner. But if it is boring or uneventful, you may resent the fun time your partner has with friends. Improve the fun and romance in your life with your partner.

🗘 On average, men tend to draw distinctions between friendship with a spouse and friendship with a buddy. Women view friendships similarly, whether with their spouse or with their best friends. Thus, a woman who feels lonely for intimate discussions might think her husband is a great talker with his buddies, when in fact his conversations might be more superficial.

How to Say It

If your relationship is satisfying, state your opinion but don't make a big issue out of it. Your partner will have some degree of loyalty to a friend and may resent your opinion. You do not want to come off as demanding or in any way parental. Otherwise, you may win the battle but you will lose the war.

- "Just for the record, I'm not that impressed with Jim (or Mary). He's not the type of person with whom I could be close friends."

- "I know Sheila has been a lifelong friend. But I'm not that fond of her."
- "You're inviting Al to the party? Okay, I know he's your friend. I just wish he were more of an acquaintance."

If your partner responds:

- *"Nobody's asking you to be close friends."*
- *"Oh? How come?"*
- *"I wish you wouldn't be so judgmental."*

You reply:

- *"I'm sorry. I don't mean to sound critical of you. Obviously you care about him. He just bothers me a little, that's all."*
- *"It bothers me because . . . Maybe I shouldn't feel that way, but I do."*
- *"Sorry. I know she's your friend and I'm glad you like her. But that is how I feel."*

If your partner wants to debate you about the merits of his or her friend, you don't want to get into an "I'm right/You're wrong" banter. Better to acknowledge something positive about the friend and not drag out the discussion.

- "I'm not saying your friend is a horrible person. I just don't care that much for him. You're right, he is generous. I just don't care for his strange sense of humor."
- "I'm not saying you shouldn't be friends. I'm sure Jill is a terrific person in many ways. I just find her hard to take after ten minutes. Maybe it's just me."

If you insist that your partner end a friendship or drastically reduce time spent with a friend, then chances are it is not the friend who is the problem. Address your relationship concerns directly.

- "I don't like you spending time with Jack because he only likes to get drunk. But the more I think about it, Jack is not my concern. I don't like it that you want to have a six-pack every Friday night with Jack instead of spending it with your family."

- "I know I've complained about the time you spend with your friends. It's not the friends per se that bother me. Ever since we got married it feels to me that you still want to act like you're single. I feel left out. Can we figure out ways to change that?"

- "I guess what really worries me is that if you spend time with Terry at a bar, some guy is going to make a pass at you. I trust you, but I get uneasy thinking about that. Call me insecure or irrational. I guess I just need some reassurance that you'll be okay and safe."

If your partner gets extremely angry and defensive that you are objecting to a friend, there may be more going on than seems obvious. Maybe you hit a nerve because your partner senses he's been overdoing his friendship and he feels guilty. Maybe your partner is quick to feel controlled and resents any hint of being told what to do. Maybe your partner is just having a bad day, or perhaps you came across too harshly. The goal is to deescalate the argument and try to interject some positive emotion into the discussion.

- "May I start over? I didn't mean to sound so critical. I'm not saying you shouldn't be friends with _____. I do wish you spent more time at home, however. Can we discuss that?"

- "You're right when you say I shouldn't dictate who your friends can be. I'm not doing that. I do think your friend has a few qualities I don't admire and I don't feel wonderful when you spend time together."

- "Please hear me out. I don't think I made myself clear. I wasn't criticizing your friend so much as I was wishing that you and I got along as well as you and _____ get along."

- "I'm sure it would be fantastic if I liked your friend as much as you do. But I don't. Maybe in time I will."

How Not to Say It

- "How can you be friends with a person like that? What's wrong with you?" (Insulting your partner's judgment won't be appreciated.)

- "If you loved me you'd go along with my request and not see that friend of yours." (That's not fair. Anybody can precede any request with the words "If you really love me you will . . . " and it is always unfair. If you really loved your partner, you wouldn't phrase your requests that way.)

- "If it bothered you that I was spending time with someone you didn't like, I'd go along with your wishes. Why can't you do the same for me?" (How you would act is not necessarily the standard by which your partner should conform.)

- "We don't have any time for ourselves. Therefore, you shouldn't spend your free time with Tom. You married me, not him." (You are stating a proposed solution to a problem and insisting on that solution. Better to discuss the problem—in this case, not having enough time to spend together—and come up with several possible ways to fix it. Don't fall in love with one solution.)

You Aren't Fond of Your Partner's Children

15

Camille and Paulo have a hard time discussing the topic. Married for seven years, Camille's children from her first marriage are in their teens. Paulo is a caring stepfather, although his relationship with his stepchildren is occasionally strained. That is partly due to the fact that the older child has always been a bit of a troublemaker, testing Paulo's patience repeatedly. Now the couple have a new baby of their own and it is obvious to Camille that Paulo loves his biological child more than he loves his stepchildren. She understands why that could be but it upsets her nonetheless. Paulo feels uneasy about the situation but has to admit that he isn't always fond of his stepchildren, although he does love them and is devoted to them. It is a painful part of their relationship that never can be fully soothed.

Don and Dena have a different situation. Don is divorced and sees his kids every other weekend. Dena lives with Don and they are considering getting married. But Dena finds Don's children to be undisciplined and hard to warm up to. She tries her best but always prefers weekends alone with Don than weekends she has to share.

The feelings of a stepparent toward a child can be complicated. It is understood by most couples in a stepfamily situation that the biological parent will probably have stronger feelings of love for the child than will a stepparent, especially if the child was much older when the stepparent became part of the family. Still, that discrepancy in feelings can be a source of pain, guilt, or tension.

Have You Heard?

~ All else being equal, a remarried parent should put his or her children "first." That means that time with the new spouse should not come at the expense of time with one's children and that financial obligations towards one's children should be met. If a stepparent insists on being "first" in their spouse's life, either the marriage will fail or the parent's relationship with his or her children will suffer greatly.

~ Opinions of the stepparent's role in the family differ between adult and child. The adults see the stepparent as taking an active role in the family. Older children often prefer that the stepparent be a "friend." This difference may account for some strain.

~ On average, stepfathers tend to show a little less warmth toward children than do stepmothers. (It is also true that fathers in general show less warmth than do mothers.) These stepfathers, however, do take on a supervisory role with greater ease. Warmth is defined as offering hugs, kisses, playing games together, and searching for ways to have time alone together. Warmth toward the stepchildren is associated with more harmonious family functioning. Strains in a stepfamily occur when the stepparent disagrees with child-rearing methods, and when the children are caught in the middle of battles between their biological parents.

~ If a stepparent is getting along well with the kids, the marriage will be satisfying. If a stepparent is having trouble with the kids, he or she is likely to blame the biological parent in some way (ineffective discipline, siding with the kids against the stepparent, and so on) and the marriage will be more strained.

~ A stepparent doesn't have to love a stepchild so much as a biological parent does. However, the stepparent should be equally committed to that child.

How to Say It

Any complaint should focus on the child's behavior, *not* the child's character. You should be sensitive to the parent's wish to defend his or her child and not view that as close-mindedness. The parent wants the child to like you and you to like the child.

- Using the GIFTS is essential here. Preface your comments with remarks that gently set the stage. "May we talk about Adam and Sarah? I have some concerns and I'm not sure of the best way to deal with them."

- "May we set aside some time to discuss the kids? I'm not sure of the best way to deal with them at times and I really need your input."

- "Your children certainly have been through a lot in the past year. It hasn't been easy for you or them at times. I want to get along with them better but I'm having some trouble. May we talk about that?"

If your partner tries to gently minimize your concerns with comments like:

- *"You're doing fine."*

- *"Things will work out over time. Don't worry, it's a period of adjustment for us all . . . "*

- *"I know the kids like you. You don't have anything to be concerned about."*

You reply:

- *"I'm glad you're optimistic, but I'd still like to discuss it."*

- *"I'm happy you have faith in me. Still, I have some concerns that are not going away. I need to talk with you."*

- *"I'm glad the kids like me. But I'm having a hard time feeling comfortable with my role and I don't know the best way to handle the children sometimes. I really do need to discuss this with you for more than just a few minutes."*

After you have set the stage, be specific about your concerns.

- "There are times when the kids talk back to me and I don't know how to respond. I don't want to yell at them and make them dislike me, but I don't want to act like a pushover, either. Frankly, it's making it harder for me to warm up to them."

- "It really bothers me when Timmy acts that way. I know he's just a child and he has been through a lot. But his actions are hard for me to take sometimes."

- If your partner tries to end the discussion early by saying, *"I'll talk to the kids about it,"* you reply: "I appreciate that you want to address this. But maybe you and I need to figure out a way to respond to them when they act that way. I don't want them to think of me as the bad guy. I just want us to be clear about how we'll handle it when they act up."

If your partner gets angry or very defensive and says things like:

- *"I know the kids can be hard to manage but they are just kids! I expect you to be the adult!"*
- *"The kids are fine. Cut them some slack."*

Make in-flight repairs and reply:

- *"You're right. They are just children. But I'm playing a large role in their life now. I'm responsible for their well-being, too, but I don't have much power or authority. I'm asking for help on how to handle them when they act defiant and disrespectful."*
- *"I have cut them slack. I know that my presence in their lives is an adjustment for them. You're suggesting that matters will improve over time. Maybe you're right. But I'm concerned they might not. I'd like to discuss a strategy to help me when they act up and I'm feeling frustrated. Can you do that with me?"*

The more defensive the biological parent becomes—or the more he or she minimizes the stepparent's concerns—the stepparent-child problem will transform into a problem for the couple.

- "How well or how poorly I get along with your children will affect how well or how poorly we get along. You and I need to have some clear understanding of my role and clear guidelines on how I should handle the kids when they need to be disciplined. Otherwise, I'll get angry at you for not supporting me and you'll get angry at me for mishandling the situation."
- "When the kids disobey me, I find that I'm not so angry with them as I am with you. I'm angry because you've told me I should discipline the kids as I see fit, but when I do that you question my judgment. We need clear guidelines and we need to figure them out together."

If you do have a helpful discussion, the GIFTS approach includes making supportive comments.

- "Thanks for discussing this. It means a lot."
- "I'm glad we can work on this together as a team."

Let's Talk

A major study in 1999 examined stepfamilies that were not working out well. Three factors contributed to diminished family functioning:

1. *Competition from the nonresidential parent.* A biological parent who competes with the stepparent for the children's love and respect can add a tremendous strain in a household. It can be hard for adults to work together for the children's sake, especially when one of the biological parents felt betrayed by the marital breakup. But without some degree of cooperation and goodwill, the children may go through another family dissolution.

2. *The stepparent had a take-charge personality.* Stepparents are in a middle-management position. They have a great deal of responsibility but not the full authority. If the children or the parent does not accept their authority, a take-charge stepparent will step on toes. Stepparents should be consultants to discipline issues, not take-charge experts.

3. *Children do not recognize efforts by the stepparent to bond.* Many stepparents will do things they hope will be interpreted as kind or thoughtful. Packing a lunch, helping out with homework, driving a teen to a friend's house—all are nice. But if the child views those behaviors as "necessary" or "that's what any grown-up would do," they may not appreciate the effort.

The best advice for a stepparent who wants to bond with a child is to increase one-on-one time with the child and to do it so that the child recognizes it as a bonding attempt.

How Not to Say It

Any criticism of the child's character, as opposed to the child's behaviors, will likely generate defensiveness.

- "Your son is not easy to get along with." (This isn't a malicious comment but it characterizes the child on the whole in a negative way. *Better:* "I have a harder time getting along with your son when he acts this way . . .")
- "Your kids are brats!" (If you strongly feel this way, reconsider your relationship. There may be too much to overcome to make this potential new family a success.)

- "I can't wait until your daughter graduates from high school and leaves home. She's been nothing but a problem for us." (Again, while your point may have merit, the all-inclusive negative view of the child won't sit easily with your partner. *Better:* "As much as I care for Lisa, I think I'll be relieved when she leaves for college. I hope as she matures we can all get along better.")

- "I can't stand your kids when they act like that!" (You may be in over your head. Unless you can feel differently toward the children, the couple relationship may not last.)

Talking Point: If your emotional response to a stepchild is negative and extreme, it is likely that the issue is more than the child's behaviors per se. You may have issues with your partner that are showing up as stepparent–child issues or the child's actions are hitting a psychological sore spot that originates somewhere in your past.

Difficult In-Laws

16

"Your father did it again," Ben says to Alice. "I put the steaks on the barbecue and he told me I had no idea how to cook meat and he tried to grab the fork from my hand. I wouldn't let him have it. He said 'Have it your way' and then complained about our lawn. I can't take this anymore."

"You know he can be gruff. I just wish you wouldn't take it so personally."

"Well, I wish you wouldn't take it so lightly."

"What do you want me to do? That's the way my father is. He'll never change. You'll just have to take the high road and put up with it. Look, he's in his seventies. How many years does he have left?"

Grin and bear it. That's often the proposed solution when partner's tense up over in-laws. Sometimes that works, but the couple had better have a sturdy relationship. Often, partners feel that the other is not "sticking up for me" and they draw a line in the sand. "You have to choose who you're most loyal to— me or your parents!" That's when things can get sticky.

Have You Heard?

~ Conflicts with in-laws are more likely to occur when the adult child has some unresolved issues with the parent. Unresolved issues may push an adult into either an overly dependent relationship with parents or an overly distant relationship. Either way, when the couple and the parents all get together, complications can occur and the son- or daughter-in-law may pay the price.

∼ If your partner is too close to his or her parents, the parents may fear you will try to pull their child away from them. If your partner is too emotionally distant from them, they may blame you.

∼ If you don't want your parents to harbor bad feelings toward your partner, then don't complain to them about your partner. If you tell your partner bad things about your parents, be careful. Sharing of feelings is important to your relationship. But some people subconsciously want their partners to do the dirty work—that is, to express anger at the parents—and then they criticize their partners for doing what they set them up to do. It is hard for a partner who loves you to remain neutral when you have painted your parents in a negative light.

How to Say It

Many loving, fair-minded people hold this (often unstated) attitude: "It's okay for me to be critical of my family, but it's not okay for you to be so critical." Therefore, be cautious when complaining about an in-law. You may be walking on a land mine.

- "I know you feel loyal to your parents. Still, they mistreat me at times and I'm now in a bind. If I stand up to them, it might hurt you. If I don't, they will continue to mistreat me. Can we discuss this?"

- "I need to talk about your mother. I know you've asked me to cut her some slack but I'm having trouble doing that. I'd like to tell her off but I know that might just make things worse. But something needs to be done."

- "What phrases would you find acceptable that I could use when your father is rude to me?"

- "What should I say to your mother when she secretly gives the kids cookies after I've asked her repeatedly not to feed them sugar?"

- "I've tried to grin and bear it. But my resentment has grown so much that I no longer want to be around your parents—and I don't want to feel that way. Tolerating their behavior is no longer an option for me. It would help me a lot if we could come up with some plan."

Often, the couple disagrees on what to do. One person opts to stand up to the in-laws or limit involvement with them; the other suggests a more lenient approach. If the couple isn't careful, they can quickly develop into a battle of "If you loved me, you would do things my way." Avoid that. Try to see some merit in the other's position.

- "I can understand why you wouldn't want to start an argument with your parents. You're in an awful position. But something needs to be done. It seems we're damned if we do and damned if we don't."

- "I know you love me and I know you don't like the way your parents can treat me. I also know that it's hard to stand up to them and you've learned to ignore their criticisms over the years. I can ignore them, too. But only for awhile. Does that make sense?"

If it is your parents who are causing problems and you would like your partner to avoid making an issue out of matters, you are taking a risky (and probably a losing) position. Your partner needs to believe that you care about the impact your parents have on him or her. Defending your parents or minimizing what they've done is really a strategy of pretense: You are pretending that all will work out if the issues are avoided. That is unlikely. You should say:

- "You're right. My mom and dad can be difficult. I appreciate it when you try to rise above it but I know I can't expect you to tolerate it forever. I'm asking that you bear with me, however. I may not stand up to them as well as you'd like, at least not at first. This isn't easy for me. But I will try."

- "It won't change their ways if I stand up to them. They may be more cautious but they won't develop a better attitude. I need you to understand that some of what they do we'll have to accept. But I will talk to them and hopefully get them to back off a little."

If your partner says one of the two above comments, try to reply:

- "I understand they may not change completely. If I know that you are on my side on this and that we can speak up when necessary to your parents, maybe I'll be able to tolerate their actions a little more."

- "I'll try not to criticize you if I think you are too tame when you confront your folks. But I think you'll probably have to be willing to speak up to them more than once. Deal?"

How Not to Say It

Uncompromising stands are not helpful. The more extreme your reaction, the more defensive your partner will get and the less likely anything constructive will get done.

- "I'm never going to see your parents again!"
- "You should tell them that the next time they insult me, you will be out of their lives forever!"
- "If you loved me, you would defend me to the hilt." (That isn't fair.)
- "If you loved me, you'd put up with my parent's ways." (Ditto.)
- "I don't think I should have to defend you to my mother. This is between you and her." (If there is any truth to your partner's complaints about an in-law, you should defend your partner. If you believe your partner has inflamed the situation by treating your parent more harshly, say "You're right. My mom does mistreat you and I can't blame you for feeling angry. I can defend you and speak to my mother, but it will mean a lot to me if you can admit to the ways you have contributed to this problem and do your best to have a cease-fire.")
- "No wonder your family is messed up. Just look at how your parents act!" (You are getting off-track of the subject.)

Talking Point: As a rule of thumb, if your partner is mistreated or unfairly criticized by your parents, you should speak up on your partner's behalf. Your comments may or may not have an impact on your parents, but they will make a difference to your partner.

How to Say It to Yourself

Whether your in-laws are causing you problems, or whether it is your parents who are causing problems for your partner, your self-talk should not be about how you are being victimized or misunderstood. Rather, try to put yourself in your partner's shoes. Empathy can lead to a more cooperative dialogue between you and your partner.

- "It isn't easy for him to be in the middle between his mother and me. I can understand that he just may want to keep the peace and not confront her. He isn't being disloyal to me by thinking that way. He's just worried."

- "I know she's in an awful bind when my dad says harsh things to her. She wants to defend herself, yet she wants to keep the peace; she doesn't want to do anything that may cause permanent damage, and she wants to be sensitive to my feelings. That's a tough balancing act."

- "Yes, his parents always try to dictate how we should run our lives. But we didn't help matters when we relied on them early on to help us out financially and to baby-sit so often. In some ways we gave them a mixed message: 'We can't do this without you *and* treat us like adults and don't run our lives.'"

Let's Talk

Sometimes, a couple needs to learn to accept a parent's/in-law's difficult ways to some extent. How can they do that?

A good remedy is for the couple to make a private game out of a family get-together. For example, they might agree ahead of time to count the number of times a parent or in-law acts negatively. When the number reaches a certain amount, the couple will have earned enough "points" to go to a romantic dinner or movie together. That way, something positive always comes out of something negative.

Providing emotional support to an offended partner is important. But if confronting the parent gets nowhere, the couple can agree to have a passionate kiss in the presence of the parents anytime a parent does something offensive. No one else may be in on the "secret," but it allows the couple to have fun when ordinarily they would be angry and tense.

How to Happily Agree about Discipline

17

"I don't think he should go to the ballgame with his friends," Joe says, referring to his son Max. "I told him weeks ago to please clean out the garage and he has yet to do it. Maybe this will teach him a lesson."

Joe's wife, Maggie, disagrees. "But Max has been looking forward to the game for months. I think it's too harsh to tell him he can't go."

"You tend to go easy on him, don't you think? That's why he doesn't take us seriously when we tell him to do things. He knows he can count on you to be lenient."

Maggie sighs. "Sometimes I am lenient, but sometimes I do it to counteract you. You talk to him like you're a drill sergeant. I wish you wouldn't make big deals out of small things."

"My father was strict with me," Joe says. "I think it helped me in the long run."

Joe and Maggie are facing a logjam. Despite subdued tones, each one takes a jab at the other and neither seems willing to seek common ground. Maggie helps the situation when she agrees with Joe and says *"Sometimes I am lenient . . . ,"* but Joe doesn't follow her lead and admit that his strictness might be overdone. So Maggie calls him a drill sergeant and Joe defends himself by saying he is just like his father. The discussion is headed nowhere.

Every couple will disagree about the best ways to discipline a child or what the household rules should be. (How old should your teenager be when he or she starts to date? What is a realistic curfew? How many chores can an 8-year-old be expected to perform?) But satisfied couples usually discuss their ideas and make a decision without alienating one another. They look for common ground.

Have You Heard?

~ When a couple frequently disagrees about discipline or household rules, the children pay the price. Even if one spouse's ideas really are better and more effective, their usefulness will be undermined by the lack of teamwork.

~ If you agree to let your partner handle a situation differently from the way you'd prefer, make sure you: DON'T micromanage; DON'T say "I told you so!" if it doesn't work out; and DON'T hold a grudge because you didn't get your way. Instead: DO compliment your partner afterward; DO support your partner if he or she asks for assistance; and DO get used to the idea of cooperative parenting, not divisive parenting.

~ The key to effective discipline is "know your child." Don't get locked into a discipline method. A verbal reprimand can work for one child but not another.

Disagreeing about discipline is inevitable. But gridlock doesn't have to be. There are numerous possible reasons for gridlock:

1. At least one partner is dogmatic and uncompromising by nature.

2. The couple has drifted apart so that the mother (typically) is now over-involved with the kids to compensate for dissatisfaction in the marriage, and the father is overinvolved at work (and therefore underinvolved with family). This leads to a pattern where the mother thinks she knows what's best for the children and the father feels like a fifth wheel. He tries to assert his authority as a maneuver to get back into the family but is blocked by his partner.

3. The couple has the potential to cooperate but one or both is offended by the other's words or actions. Feeling insulted, they now take a more stubborn point of view on the issue being discussed. The hidden, unstated attitude of each is this: *"I resent what you said. So, in order to show respect for me and to prove you love me, you will have to agree with my point of view on this matter. I won't back down."*

4. They are really arguing about something else, but don't realize it. For example, if a parent feels unappreciated by his spouse, he may yell at the kids when he thinks that they, too, are taking him for granted. The issue is a marital one, but comes across as a parent–child problem.

How to Say It

Your child is what's most important—not winning the argument. Consider that your partner may have some valid points and that your child will be best served when parents act cooperatively with one another, not as adversaries or reluctant teammates. Be clear about your ideas but be open to new ones. Find something you can agree with (the T in GIFTS is for Teamwork). Don't automatically dismiss a partner's ideas.

- "I can see your point . . . That makes sense . . . I know what you mean . . . "
- "I hadn't thought of it that way before."

Show willingness to compromise.

- "I don't agree with you but I'm willing to try it your way."
- "I'm willing to try some of what you say. Could we agree to modify it, though, in this way . . . "
- "It seems very important to you that we do it your way. Why do you feel so strongly?"

If you are deadlocked, try to break the logjam.

- "We have reached an impasse. How about if I tell you what I think makes sense about your ideas, and you tell me what you think makes sense about my ideas."
- "We're at a standstill. Is there something about your point of view that you don't think I fully understand?"
- "The point I'm making that I need you to understand most is . . . "
- "The most important thing for me in this debate is . . . And the most important thing for you is . . . What solution can we come up with that will address both of our needs?"
- "Your idea makes sense in theory but we've tried it already and it doesn't seem to be as effective on our child. I'm suggesting we experiment with a different approach."

Look for hidden issues within the argument.

- "I'm worried that I don't have as much influence on our child as I should. Maybe that's why I'm so adamant about doing things my way."
- "I'm out of the loop when it comes to parenting. I feel like I have to defer to your judgment because you spend more time with the kids than I do. I want to be a more important part of their lives. Can you work with me on that?"
- "We've been worried about money (the upcoming surgery, the new job, and so on). Could that be contributing to our argument?"

How Not to Say It

- "I know what's best for our child since I'm with her more often." (You may be with the child more often and your ideas may be good, but that line of reasoning is self-serving. You simply don't want to give up power. Assuming your partner isn't proposing something dangerous for your child, you must be willing to give in on occasion and not be the "parenting expert." A *better* response when you really think you know what's best: "I've tried your idea before because it does make sense. But in my view it doesn't work so well with our child. Could we try it my way and reevaluate it later on?")
- "You're a woman. You don't understand what's best for a boy." (Don't pull rank. *Better:* "Your idea makes some sense. But I remember how it was for me as a boy. That's why I think my idea might be more effective. Would you mind going along with it?")
- "Okay, we'll do it your way. But don't expect me to be in a romantic mood anytime soon." (Don't punish your partner simply because you disagree on how best to deal with your child.)
- "You'll become like your father (mother) when it comes to parenting. You know how much I disagree with his (her) ways." (This is unfair. Your partner has a right to be an involved parent and your child deserves his or her involvement. You can express concerns but don't prevent your partner's involvement on the grounds that he or she will become a mirror image of his or her parent.)

Partner Is Too Gruff With the Kids

18

Jackie sits at the table with her son, helping him with his homework.
"You just answered this same question two minutes ago!" Jackie complains. "Don't tell me you've forgotten already!"
"But it's hard to remember all this stuff," Bobby replies.
Jackie sighs. "It's only hard because you're not paying attention. You never pay attention. How do you expect to do well on your test if you don't pay attention?"
Bobby doesn't respond.
"Okay," Jackie says, exasperated. "Let's go over this material again."

Jackie often speaks like that to her son. She's not a verbally abusive parent, she doesn't get belligerent, and she doesn't belittle her kids. But she often has an edge to her voice that her husband dislikes hearing. He has asked her to be more even-tempered, but their conversations about that get bogged down: He emphasizes what's wrong with her tone, and she says she wouldn't have to sound so harsh if her son would simply do his work. Around and around they go.

Have You Heard?

~ Partners who tend to have a gruff tone often do not hear themselves that way.

~ Partners accused of being too gruff and critical are often self-critical.

〜 Gruff-sounding parents need more fun time with the kids. They tend to restrict their activities to giving orders. They need to be more playful; otherwise, the kids view that parent like they view a school principal.

〜 Gruff-sounding parents often deny they were being harsh and blame the listener for being too sensitive. The better approach is to *restate, not debate:* The listener will point out when a comment was spoken too harshly (and not be harsh or cynical when pointing it out) and the speaker will immediately rephrase what he or she had said so that it is more respectful, more encouraging, and less critical.

〜 It can be helpful for the more gruff-spoken parent to anticipate likely scenarios before they happen and prepare his or her response. So, a father driving home from work may anticipate that the house will be messy, the kids will be fighting, or that his partner may be in a bad mood. He should figure out how he will act, emphasizing an attitude that shows he is happy to see the family, despite any chaos there might be.

〜 A person who successfully cuts back on critical parenting comments may not be given full appreciation. First, the other partner may feel that he *should* speak kindly anyway, so his successful efforts are not praised. Second, it is harder for the partner to take notice of the *absence* of a negative response. (By definition, it is something that *did not happen.*) Therefore, gruff-sounding parents must also try to increase the frequency of more positive words and tones: more praise, more laughter, more patience (when the children are testing one's patience), more affection, and more "I love you."

〜 Partners who speak gruffly to the kids almost always speak gruffly to their partners. Improving the tone in the marriage is also a necessary goal.

How to Say It

- "I just overheard your conversation with the kids. Maybe you meant well but it bothered me when you used such a gruff tone. Do you realize how you sound when you talk?"

- "You don't have to agree with me every time I say you sound too critical. But would you be willing anyway to change your tone at that moment and try to sound more gentle?"

- "Probably the hardest thing for me when I hear you being harsh is that I feel I have to protect our kids from you. I know you love them but I can't help wanting to rescue them from you sometimes."
- "What can I say or do that would help you in this?"
- "If I think you are being unnecessarily critical of the kids (or me), how can I call it to your attention so that you won't feel offended or angry with me?"
- "If there is something I do that offends you in some way, tell me about it. Maybe I can work on changing that while you work on speaking less gruffly."
- "I've noticed something that I need to speak up about. It bothers me a great deal and I can't ignore it. I know you love our kids but I think you speak too gruffly with them."

If your mate responds:

- *"No, I don't."*
- *"I do sometimes but so do you. Every parent does."*
- *"How else am I supposed to teach them that I'm upset with them?"*
- *"You always find fault with me. Nothing I do is ever right."*

You reply:

- *"I don't think I can prove it to you because I honestly think you don't hear yourself the way I do. But I'm asking that you take my concern seriously. If you don't think you are being gruff, would you be willing anyway to speak to the kids more gently? I'll be happy to give you feedback."*
- *"Every parent does speak roughly, you're right. But I see you speaking that way very often. For example, you were getting impatient and he was getting frustrated with you when you were helping Steve with his homework. I feel distant from you when you talk like that. I don't want to feel that way. Can we figure out a way to deal with this?"*
- *"I know it is important for us to teach our kids so they will learn. But I'm concerned that what they are learning is that you aren't the person to confide in about problems. I would feel better about this if I heard you say*

encouraging things to them a lot more often than you now do. Do you agree with anything I've said so far?"

- *"Really? Maybe both of us don't always realize how we come across to others. How about I work on my fault-finding tendencies and you work on reducing your gruffness?"*

How Not to Say It

- "I won't tolerate any critical tone from you." (Besides showing a critical tone yourself, you are expecting perfection.)
- "Yes, you have made some progress but that's not good enough." (Encourage your partner's efforts, don't discourage them.)
- "I'm not going to give you pats on the back just for treating our kids the way you should."
- "You are a lousy parent."
- "It's about time you spoke to them nicely!" (*Better:* "I overheard what you said to the kids and I really liked how you said it.")

Let's Talk

Be on the lookout for a common pattern:

1. You regularly have to repeat yourself four or five times to get your kids to listen.
2. You ask your partner to intervene and get the kids to behave.
3. Your partner feels like the "bad guy" and resents having to do your dirty work.

In the book *How to Say It to Your Kids!* I discuss how parents in this situation have trained their children to tune them out until one parent starts screaming. Parents do not need to repeat themselves more than once if they are willing to get their kids moving to do what needs to get done. (*"I asked you ten minutes ago to clean your room. Now we'll all go to your room together and I'll tell you what you need to do. Let's go."*) Yelling is not necessary, just firmness. It also eliminates your partner having to jump in and be the bad guy.

Partner Is Overinvolved/ Underinvolved in Children's Lives

19

Greg and Helen have been married for 35 years. They have three grown daughters. Greg loves to see his daughters, but he gets annoyed when Helen feels the need to call them almost daily. He thinks Helen is too involved in their daughters' lives and wishes she'd cut back on the unnecessary calls. He also feels neglected by Helen.

Hank and Julie have been married for 8 years. Julie wishes Hank would spend more time playing with their two children. Hank does the essentials—he'll prepare their breakfast or help them get dressed or watch them when they're at play. But he won't go the extra mile. He won't come up with games to play with them; he won't take them on excursions. He gives them the minimal daily allowance of his time. Julie wants him to do more.

Have You Heard?

~ Parents are more than caretakers. Still, overinvolvement isn't necessarily best for children. Overinvolved parents are less involved elsewhere. Usually what suffers most is the couple's relationship.

~ Overinvolved parents tend to make the children unnecessarily dependent on them. Such children may act younger than their age; they may ask for help when they are capable of doing things themselves.

~ Overinvolvement with the children is a sign that the marriage may be strained or that emotional distance has developed between the partners. A strained relationship can prompt one parent to compensate by getting even more involved with the kids, which in turn adds additional strain to a marriage.

~ Underinvolved parents don't have a good balance of warmth/affection and firmness. They lean too much in one direction. On the other hand, some can be extremely playful with the kids but act almost like children themselves. This can prompt the other parent to say, "I don't have a spouse, I have another kid!" Underinvolved parents are usually less informed about the details of their children's lives.

~ An underinvolved parent is usually overinvolved elsewhere. Typically, he or she is overinvolved with work or school (or both) and has little energy during free time to expend on the children besides meeting their basic needs. The longer this continues, the other parent has to get more involved with the children to make up for the other parent's absence. This leads to less quality couple time. Eventually, the parent who is underinvolved with the kids is on the periphery of the family, on the outside looking in, with less influence over the goings on than he or she should be.

~ Working mothers during the 1990s added about 12 hours a week to their jobs. These moms did their best to minimize the time taken from their children. Consequently, almost all of those extra work hours came at the expense of the couples' relationships.

~ Infants and toddlers require a tremendous amount of time from parents. A couple's time together invariably drops when children are quite young. Typically, women (even working women) still end up doing more of the childcare and housework than the men. If men took on more of those responsibilities, they would have less free time for themselves but would find that their partners have more free time for romantic interludes.

How to Say It

Complaining that a partner is under- or overinvolved with the kids is risky. The partner is likely to defend his or her level of involvement as either due to extenuating circumstances ("I work long hours") or as desirable ("The kids need me"). Honestly evaluate how your partner's ways with the children affect you. Then make *that* the issue.

- "I wish you'd spend more time with the kids. Not only do they need that, but also it frees me up to get some other things done. Otherwise, I'm always busy and have little time left over for just the two of us."

- "I like it that you spend time with our kids. But the problem is that I have little time with you. How can we increase the amount of time we have together?"

- "How we spend our time seems out of balance. There is little time for us anymore. What changes could we make to correct that?"

Be prepared for a defensive response and be prepared to look at the merit of that response. If your partner says:

- *"If you'd help out more, then I would have more time for you!"*

- *"You never seem interested in doing anything when I do have time, so I spend more of it with our children."*

You reply:

- *"I do help out, but maybe I'm not doing what you need most. What can I do that would help?"*

- *"You're right. Maybe I'm in a rut. All I know is that I'd like us to do more together. Can we try that?"*

How Not to Say It

- "You don't spend enough time with the children. You don't care about them." (*Better:* "I think the children do better when you spend more time with them. They miss you.")

- "If you loved me, you'd make time for me." (*Better:* "You don't seem to have any energy for me anymore. I'm worried about that.")

- "I can't do more with the kids because I have too much work to do . . . I've been extremely busy . . . I do what I can . . . " (These factors may be true but you sound as if you don't care about the impact your reduced involvement is having on the family. *Better:* "You're right. I've been very busy at work but I should try to do more with the kids. Can you help me figure out some ways?")

- "You criticize me every time I try to do more with the kids. Why should I bother?" (*Better:* "You seem to want to oversee things when I do get involved. I'd like time with the kids where I'm in charge so that you can do other things.")

Let's Talk

This issue contains subtle factors that can wreak havoc with potential solutions. For example, a parent who is overinvolved with the kids might suggest that the other parent get more involved. "If you did that, then I could have time for other things." But when the other parent tries to interact more with the children, the first parent criticizes that involvement. ("You're not doing that right . . . No, no it's done this way!") This "I know better" attitude has to change.

However, the less involved parent may purposely do things with the kids that are provocative. He might play games with them but afterward leave the room a mess. He might take them for a walk but later track mud into the house and ignore it. He might make them lunches but it's always a peanut butter sandwich. He'll help them with homework but be so impatient with them that his partner wishes he hadn't bothered. This is likely to provoke criticism from his partner and he may use her criticism as an excuse to give up trying.

Genuine cooperation is what's called for. Children do best with active involvement from each parent. An overinvolved parent must pull away a little and not nitpick. The less active parent must do more with the kids, but be mindful that a true parent can have fun with the kids and teach them proper behavior at the same time.

Thoughtful Attention After the First Baby Arrives

20

The Smiths and the Joneses are neighbors. Each of the women became pregnant around the same time and both couples are eagerly anticipating the births of their first children. The ladies have much to discuss as the weeks march on while the men discuss what it will be like becoming a father.

Both men take an extra interest in their wives' welfare during the pregnancies. The couples take classes together in natural childbirth. Everyone is excited as the delivery dates approach and everyone knows they can count on one another for emotional support after the babies are born.

Now a year has passed. The couples are entrenched in parenthood. The predictable small crises occur, such as a baby's first cold, but all is working out fine. Well, sort of. Actually, the Smiths are doing very well. They are both understandably tired and have less time for one another, but their relationship is more satisfying than it ever has been. Jim keeps a small photo of his wife and son on his desk. It is the one he loves where his wife is sitting on the floor in front of the washing machine dressed in sweats and looking a little worn but holding up their baby. Life is wonderful.

Home life is different for the Joneses. Marital conflict has increased. Pleasant moments together are in very short supply. Lovemaking is a distant memory. Even touching each other seems to happen only when they accidentally brush up against each other in the kitchen.

Both couples had been happy during the pregnancy. But what needs to happen for the Joneses to feel happier?

Have You Heard?

〜 Studies repeatedly show that, on average, marital happiness declines modestly after the birth of a baby for 40–67 percent of couples—mostly due to the added stress a new baby brings. Still, many new parents maintain their pre-baby level of happiness while as many as 18 percent of these couples increase their happiness.

〜 Despite the average dip in happiness, childless couples are twice as likely to divorce as couples with children. Part of that is explained by parents being willing to make their weak marriage stronger for the sake of their children.

〜 Reduction in relationship happiness is higher for women. The main reason for that seems to be division of labor: Women take on more responsibilities for housework and child-care than do men. Women not only resent that, but they also have little energy to devote to their husbands. Husbands resent that. Thus, conflict begins.

〜 Women who hold traditional views of a mother's role may actually increase their satisfaction even if they are doing more of the work. Women who place a high priority on their careers are most likely to be less happy with the unfair division of labor.

〜 Men who tend to be more critical of their wives even before the first pregnancy and who do not demonstrate regular shows of caring and fondness are most likely to trigger a large drop in marital satisfaction after the birth of the first baby.

How to Say It (Man)

On average, how a man treats a woman before, during, and immediately after a pregnancy will have the most impact on relationship quality. After the birth, men must show support, love, and be as involved as possible in child-care and household tasks.

- "It's my turn to leave work early and take the baby to the pediatrician."
- "Don't worry if you don't have time to do the grocery shopping. I can do it later."
- "Why don't you call your girlfriend and go to a movie tonight. The baby and I will be fine."

- "You're such a great mother."
- "I appreciate all that you do."
- "I was thinking about you all day today. I'm sure glad you're part of my life."
- "Sleep in tomorrow morning. I'll get up with the baby."
- "Somehow you're sexier now than you ever were."
- "Have I told you how happy I am that we're a family?"
- "Let me rub your back. You've had a long day."

How Not to Say It (Man)

- "What did you do all day? The house is a mess." (Clean it yourself. You have no idea how much work an infant requires. If a messy house really bothers you, say "I guess it's hard to get the cleaning done. Would you like me to clean up or would you like me to watch the baby?")
- "The only thing I needed you to do was go to the Post Office for me, and you couldn't even do that." (*Better:* "You didn't make it to the Post Office? You must have been really busy. No problem.")
- "It's about time you got home. Where've you been? The baby has been crying ever since you left." (*Better:* "I've had a hard time trying to settle the baby down. I'm glad you're home. Any suggestions on what I can do?")
- "The baby is your responsibility." (Fatherhood does not cease with impregnation. It begins.)
- "I just walked in the house for Pete's sake! Don't start giving me orders when I haven't even taken off my coat. I've had just as rough a day as you have." (The sentiment is understandable but more empathy is called for. *Better:* "I'm sure you're exhausted. I'm willing to take over but I need a little time to readjust. Is that okay?")
- "Other women can manage all the work. What's wrong with you? You're probably just disorganized." (That's a self-serving comment. *Better:* "This is new to both of us. If you're too busy and tired, then something is wrong. Let's figure out a new strategy.")

How to Say It (Woman)

Women may need to clarify their expectations about responsibilities for housework and child-care. Unspoken expectations often go unmet. Overtired, many women have a diminished interest in romance, affection, or sex. Tender overtures toward their partner can ease the situation.

- "I'd like to talk about how we're going to manage the housework now that the baby is here. Fun, huh?"
- "You work very hard all day. Still, when you get home from work I'll need you to share in the responsibilities. Let's discuss that."
- "I know I haven't been interested in making love. I appreciate it that you're so understanding. How about we plan on time together later this week?"
- "I thought I could manage the house responsibilities better, but I've underestimated how much time the baby takes up. We need to discuss new ways to get the chores done."
- "I know I haven't had much time for you lately. But I do love you."
- "I know you just got home and need time to settle in, but I've reached my limit for stress today. I need you to take the baby so I can take a shower and relax a bit. Thanks."

How Not to Say It (Woman)

- "I'm tired and I'm not interested in sex. Can't you understand that?" (You're probably feeling a little guilty for your diminished interest in sex. A gentler approach helps. *Better:* "I don't blame you for being frustrated. I wish I had more energy for sex too. Maybe we can find a way to spend some time together.")
- "If you want more sex, do more housework." (*Better:* "I need you to do more housework. I'm too busy as it is. If we can find ways to free up some time for me, I know I'll have more energy for sex.")
- "The baby deserves all my attention. You should realize that." (The couple relationship needs attention too. *Better:* "I know we don't have so much time for each other. Let's find small ways to connect. I miss you.")

- "I know you just got home from work but I've had the baby all day. Here, he's all yours." (Flexibility and sympathy will help. *Better:* "I'm glad you're home. I'm exhausted. I really need you to take over. Would you like some time to freshen up first?")

- "Other husbands help out more than you do." (*Better:* "I still feel that the division of labor is unfair and I'm beginning to get resentful. We need to make different arrangements.")

Talking Point: As a rule of thumb, housework and child-care responsibilities should be equally shared once the working parent(s) arrives home. A woman views her partner's willingness to do his share of the child-care as a demonstration of caring for *her*.

Your New Partner Wants You to Relocate Away from Your Children

Hal and Mary have been married for two years. It is Hal's second marriage. He has three children, ranging in age from 10 to 16. The kids live with their mom. Mary had turned down a job promotion with her company a year earlier because the couple would have had to relocate about 500 miles away. Hal said that was too far from his children. Now Mary is offered another promotion. This time the city they'd have to move to is a 3-hour drive away. Mary feels it is Hal's turn to make a sacrifice.

Hal isn't sure what to do. His kids are getting older now. Would it really be a problem for them if he moves farther away? Would Mary understand if he tells her he wants to remain close by?

Have You Heard?

～ Divorce has an adverse effect on children. Sometimes the effect is small. Usually it takes a few years before emotional or behavioral side effects of divorce are lessened. However, recent studies suggest that negative effects often show up in adulthood.

～ The negative impact of divorce on children can be lessened if two things happen: The noncustodial parent (usually the father) has regular involvement in the children's lives; and the parents cooperate with parenting issues while treating each other with civility. This happens in a minority of cases.

～ Fathers are usually regularly involved with their children for the first few years after the divorce. But only half see their children more than five times a year. Typically, fathers reduce their involvement after they remarry and espe-cially if they start another family. Noncustodial mothers usually see their chil-dren more often than do noncustodial fathers.

~ Divorced fathers should live close by their children. That makes it easier to have spontaneous or quick visits especially when the children get older and can make more decisions for themselves.

How to Say It

Divorced parents should remain devoted to their children and explain that devotion to their new partners. A new partner should have no illusions as to the nature and extent of that involvement.

- "I love you but I am committed to my children. Their welfare has to come first for me. If you want me, you'll have to accept that."
- "How can we make our relationship satisfying for you, knowing that I cannot leave my children?"
- "What could happen in our relationship that might compensate for your not taking that promotion?"
- "You deserve that promotion and I wish you could accept it. I just wouldn't be doing the right thing if I left my children behind."
- "You're right, that job promotion would be great for you. Ordinarily I'd go along with you, but I can't leave my kids."

If your partner says:

- *"You can still see them every other weekend."*
- *"They are getting older and can get by with seeing you less often."*
- *"You have a commitment to me, too."*

You reply:

- *"That isn't a lot of time to see them. Besides, they'll live so far away it will quickly become too difficult to make the trip regularly. It simply isn't realis-tic for me to move that far from them."*
- *"I am their father and they are still children. They do need me and I need them."*

- *"My commitment to them takes precedence. I'm sorry, but that's how it must be."*

How Not to Say It

- "If you go, you'll have to do it without me." (This is insensitive. Your partner will make a sacrifice by staying. Show understanding of that sacrifice. *Better:* "I can't blame you for asking. I know it would mean a lot to you if we did relocate. But I can't go, not if it means I'll see my children less often.")

- "We've had this discussion before. There's no need to have it again." (Shutting down the conversation isn't necessary. You can maintain your viewpoint while at the same time hear your partner's wishes. Otherwise, resentment can build.)

- "Okay, let's move. My kids will adjust to not seeing me. Besides, I need to think about my happiness for a change." (If you are willing to sacrifice your children, your partner has reason to doubt your commitment to the marriage, too.)

How to Happily Agree
about Holiday Traditions

"But we always go to my parents' house for Thanksgiving," Joan says. "It's a tradition."

"I know that," her husband, Ken, says. "But I'd like us to start our own tradition. Besides, we'll be seeing them over Hanukkah."

"But the kids expect us to go to their grandparents' house on Thanksgiving. That's what Thanksgiving means to them."

"Well, we can invite your parents here this year, then the kids won't miss out."

"It won't feel the same," Joan says.

"Why do we always have to do things your way?"

Randy and Sarah have a slightly different problem. He is a Christian and wants to put up a small manger scene in his home. It is the same manger scene his parents' had displayed when he was a boy. Randy's wife, Sarah, is Jewish. While the idea of a Christmas tree is acceptable, a manger scene in her home makes her uncomfortable, particularly since her family will be visiting. How should they handle the "December dilemma"?

Holidays can have profound meaning for many people. Doing away with old customs—or starting brand new ones—isn't always easy, especially when there is pressure from family members to conform to tradition.

Have You Heard?

~ Couples in interfaith marriages may have a particularly awkward time during holidays and holy days. Ideally, each partner would want to honor the other's traditions and beliefs in some way, without doing away with their own.

~ One study showed that in two out of three Jewish–Christian marriages, the children are raised in both faiths or neither faith. The study suggested that children are best served by having a clear religious identity.

How to Say It

State clearly what you would like without putting down your partner's traditions. Explain why some customs have special meaning for you.

- "I'd like to have the kids open some gifts on Christmas Eve instead of waiting for Christmas morning. Maybe they can open the gifts from their grandparents on Christmas Eve. I always did that as a child and it meant a lot."

- "I'd like to have Thanksgiving dinner at our house. Maybe we can have it next year at your sister's house."

- "The manger scene is important to me. How about if I limit the number of days we display it. For example, I could put it up a few days before Christmas and take it down the day after Christmas."

If your partner gets argumentative or resists going along with your ideas, you reply:

- *"Whatever we decide to do this year, one of us may want it to be different next year. What matters most is that we agree on ideas that seem fair. Does that make sense?"*

- *"I don't want you to abandon your traditions for mine. Your traditions are important. But mine are important to me. I'm searching for ways we both can get what we want."*

- *"I'm willing to be very flexible. But I need you to be flexible, too."*

- *"Here is a list of the traditions I'm used to. Which of these can you imagine going along with?"*

- *"We agreed to raise the children according to your religion. That's fine. But I feel more like a spectator than a member of the family. Having a few of my own traditions will help me feel more connected."*

Even if you aren't so excited about your partner's traditions, find something positive to say about them. It will mean a lot to your partner and may help you to appreciate customs you wouldn't ordinarily follow.

- "I can see why that has a lot of meaning for you."
- "That is my favorite part of your custom."
- "One of the nice things about the Passover Seder is . . . "
- "I think the children really like that custom."

Show gratitude.

- "Thanks for being open to my ideas. That means a lot."
- "I'm so glad I married you. You are so considerate of my needs."

How Not to Say It

- "But I've been doing it this way all my life!" (Your partner's traditions are also important. Incorporating your partner's traditions into your life may actually be something you truly learn to appreciate.)
- "My parents would never understand!" (Don't hide behind your parents. You have an obligation to honor your partner's beliefs just as he or she has an obligation to honor yours.)
- "Okay, if it's going to lead to an argument, we'll do it your way." (You may resent it later on. *Better:* "I'm willing to do it your way for now, but I'm not happy with it. We need to come up with a better plan next time.")
- "Thanks for finally showing some flexibility." (If your partner accommodates to your wishes, express sincere gratitude. Don't minimize your partner's effort to compromise.)
- "We can raise the children according to both religions. Then they can make up their own minds." (This isn't wise. It is important to show respect for the dual heritage, but provide your children with a clear, unambiguous religious identity.)

Partner Reveals Intimate Matters in Public

23

Kerry and Lee sit at the banquet table with most of Lee's co-workers. The dinner dishes have been cleared away and dessert is being served. A few of the diners seated near Lee remark about the newlywed couple at the other end of the table. They are clearly in love and not shy about showing affection in public.

Lee speaks up. "Whatever that woman ordered for dinner, I wish Kerry would start eating it." He turns to Kerry, sporting a huge grin. But Kerry's face is bright red, her expression one of humiliation. She is not amused.

Gina and Ben are trying to conceive a child and are following their physician's guidelines for couples with infertility difficulties. Gina often speaks to her mom about their day-to-day experiences. Ben's mother-in-law knows all about his low sperm count and the couple's rigid schedule of lovemaking. Gina feels less stressed after getting off the phone with her mother. Ben feels like he is an unwilling subject of a television documentary.

Have You Heard?

~ Revealing private intimacies in public puts your partner in a predicament. If he or she tries to appear unaffected, you might continue saying things that are inappropriate. But your partner may have difficulty getting you to stop without drawing public attention to his or her displeasure.

~ If you ever have misgivings about discussing a private matter in public, trust those instincts. Find out first if your partner would have a problem if the matter were discussed publicly.

~ The better the intimacy and communication a couple possesses, the more they will be able to gauge the appropriateness of bringing up a topic in public.

112

The less the intimacy and the poorer the communication, the odds are increased that private matters will be publicized.

~ If you raise a personal issue in public, that is a clue that you may not feel comfortable raising the issue privately. Or, it means you might want to get public support for your opinion.

How to Say It

If your partner takes you by surprise and reveals an embarrassing private issue in a public setting, find a firm but gracious way to tell him or her to keep quiet. A bit of humor can help.

- (Smiling broadly) "If you think I'm going to talk about that now, you're crazy."
- "Sweetheart, this isn't the Newlywed Game. Now is not the time or place to bring that up."
- "Keep talking. I want to see how big a hole you can dig for yourself."
- "Dear, did you eat something unusual today? It seems to have scrambled your common sense."

If your partner doesn't get the message, you will have no choice but to be firmer. You may be embarrassed doing so but the odds are good that others will view your partner as the fool, not you. If your partner responds:

- *"There's nothing wrong with talking about this. What's the big deal?"*
- *"We're among friends. They don't mind."*
- *"You're too sensitive."*

You reply:

- *"I would have preferred that you and I discussed this ahead of time. Please change the subject."*
- *"But I mind. Please don't talk about this now."*
- *"Maybe I am. But I'm asking you not to talk about this."*

Make your objections known if your partner has a habit of revealing relationship intimacies to friends or family on the phone or in situations where you're not present.

- "I don't like it when you tell your mother about arguments you and I have had. I'd like us to agree not to divulge information that's embarrassing or personal unless we decide ahead of time to do that."

- "I'm more of a private person. I know you don't feel embarrassed about revealing personal things to friends, but I do. Would you mind asking me ahead of time if certain personal topics are okay to make public?"

- "I just heard you criticize my mother to your friends. That really bothers me. I know my mother can be difficult, but I didn't like hearing what you said. I don't think you'd appreciate it if I criticized your mother. Can you stop doing that?"

Your partner may disagree with you. There is a large gray area where you might think information is too personal or inappropriate, but your partner does not. It doesn't help to get adamant and dogmatic. Try to find some merit to your partner's point of view. Often, that's all it takes if there is already goodwill between you.

- "I can see why you might talk about that with others. A lot of people would reveal that kind of personal information. I'd prefer we keep it as private as possible, though. Okay?"

- "You've always told your parents about your personal life. That's fine. But it bothers me when you tell them nitty-gritty details of *our* personal life. Can you see my point?"

- "I'm sure there are some things about you or our relationship that you wouldn't want me to mention in public. Well, there are things I don't want mentioned either."

How Not to Say It

Unless your partner has a track record of divulging private information, don't be too hard on your partner if he or she blurts out something you think should have been left unstated. Sharp criticisms are unnecessary.

- "I can't believe you said that in front of everybody! Don't you realize how inappropriate that was?"

- "Don't you have any common sense?"

- "Never bring up anything personal like that again!" (You are making two mistakes. First, you're being too dogmatic. You are basically claiming that your partner has no room to disagree. Second, you are vague. What is "personal"? Try to be more specific. *Better:* "I really don't like it when you discuss our sex life in front of others. I don't see a reason for it. Would you agree not to do that?")

If you are the one who is talking about private matters in public and your partner doesn't like it, you may get defensive at first. Try to see the merit to your spouse's point of view.

How to Say It

- "I didn't realize you'd be bothered by my bringing that up. I won't do it again."
- "I don't want to bring things up that would embarrass you. But I really don't understand why that particular topic should be kept private. Help me to understand."
- "You're right. I shouldn't have teased you like that in public."

How Not to Say It

- "Oh, and I suppose you've never said anything improper in public." (That's not the point. Your partner was embarrassed by what you said and wants you to stop.)
- "I can say what I want. They're my friends, too." (*Better:* "Since we were with friends, I didn't think you'd mind.")
- "You're overreacting." (You are dismissing your partner's complaint and belittling him or her. *Better:* "I wouldn't have minded it if you said those things about me, so it never occurred to me that you would mind. But now that I know, I won't say those things again in public. Sorry.")
- "All right, all right, I won't say that kind of thing anymore. Okay?" (Your underlying message is not "I was wrong" but "You're such a complainer! You're too sensitive!" Your partner won't appreciate the attitude. Admit that your brain had taken a holiday and that it was wrong to do what you did. Be sincere when you apologize.)

Spouse Is Overinvolved/ Underinvolved with His or Her Family of Origin

24

Abby has a very close and warm relationship with her parents. She is married to Will who is emotionally distant from his parents. At first, Will enjoyed the company of Abby's family. But Will now resents Abby's involvement with her folks. He accuses her of being "too close" to them and she counters by saying he doesn't know what a truly close family is. Abby tries to see her parents less often, but she resents it. Eventually, she refuses to bend to Will's demand. Will tries to understand when Abby does see her parents, but he resents it. Eventually, any involvement she has with her family feels like a slap in his face.

Have You Heard?

∼ A close relationship with one's parents is wonderful. Too much closeness usually comes at the expense of the couple's intimacy and time together.

∼ If your partner is emotionally distant from his or her parents, your partner may have difficulty trusting, and may easily get jealous or possessive. Consequently, any closeness you have with your family may eventually threaten your partner.

∼ If one's parents have a history of being verbally or physically abusive, or if a parent has sexually molested you or some other child, you should limit your contact with them. Your children should not be alone with them unless supervised.

∼ Even if you have a very good reason for staying away from your parents, you probably have unresolved issues with them. Those issues may show up in your marriage as you overreact to your partner when he or she pushes a hot button.

∽ Even if you have a good reason for staying very involved with your parents, you must put your marriage at the top of the list. Overinvolvement with parents almost always means underinvolvement with a spouse. You may be drawn to your parents precisely because you and your partner aren't getting along. But doing so diminishes the possibility of marital intimacy even further.

There is no clear formula for defining "too close" or "too distant." However, the following guidelines might help.

A relationship with one's parents (or siblings) is probably too close if:

∽ You discuss your marital issues with them far more often than you discuss them with your partner.

∽ Your parents are allowed to drop by unannounced at any time, instead of calling ahead at least some of the time.

∽ You resent time you spend with your partner's family if it takes time away from you and your parents.

∽ It is a sign of disloyalty to want to spend more time with your partner.

∽ You cannot say no to your parents without feeling very guilty.

∽ You'd rather spend time with your parents than your partner.

∽ Your parents have much say over how your children are raised.

A relationship with one's parents is probably too distant if:

∽ You rarely see them or talk to them.

∽ They are unaware of important events in your life (serious illnesses, job changes, and so on).

∽ You would give up an opportunity to see them for practically any reason.

How to Say It

Even if you don't like your partner's degree of involvement with his or her family, operate as a team. Try to find something on which you can agree.

- "You're right. Your parents have helped us out a lot over the years. They've always been there when we've needed them."

- "I agree. It's more comforting when your parents take care of our kids than if we hire a baby-sitter."
- "There's no doubt that your parents have treated you very unfairly over the years."
- "I can't blame you for wanting little to do with your family."

If you want to see some changes in this area, you'll have more leverage if you address how your partner's connection to his or her family affects you or the children.

- "I know you enjoy your parents' company. But I'm concerned that we have little time for ourselves. I'd like to spend more time as a couple. Any ideas?"
- "I know you don't like spending time with your family. But our children do enjoy seeing their grandparents and their cousins. I'm wondering if we can find a way to see them more often than we do, but not make you feel lousy in the process."
- "This isn't about your family per se. It's about us. Specifically, I feel like a stranger in my own home and I think your parents have more say over our life than I do. I want us to work together more effectively."

If your partner responds:

- *"My parents have always been there for me. It would be disloyal to turn my back on them."*
- *"I get more satisfaction being with my family than I do with you. You don't like to talk or do anything. You're always working or busy with some project."*
- *"I don't want to see my parents. If you want to visit them and take the kids along, that's up to you."*

You reply:

- *"I would never ask you to turn your back on them. I guess what I'm asking for is more time for you and me and more time with just our family. I don't feel we're connecting as a couple. I miss that."*
- *"I do work a lot, I know. Maybe I haven't made spending time together a priority. But I want to. How about if we make some plans so that once a month or so we take a day trip together? I'm open to any ideas."*

- *"I'm willing to take the kids to see your parents some of the time. I'm asking you to consider coming along on occasion. On those visits we don't have to stay very long. I know it isn't easy being with them and I love you. If you really can't go with us, I'll accept that."*

Focus on possible solutions.

- "If your parents call and invite us over, I'd really like it if you would check with me first before automatically saying yes. It's not that you have to ask my permission. I just want to feel I have some say."

- "Sometimes I'd like you to say no to your parents and instead tell them that you'd like to spend time alone with me."

- "If we really aren't busy, I don't mind agreeing to visit your parents. But some Sundays I'd just like to stay home and relax with you. Is that possible?"

- "If we can argue less and do more things together, I probably wouldn't mind it if you saw your parents often."

- "I understand why you don't want to see your parents. The problem is that they call here and ask what's wrong and I don't know what to say. I don't want to speak for you, but I don't want to put them off. Is it okay if I tell them to call back when you are home?"

How Not to Say It

- "Don't talk to me about how I'm too close to my family. You don't know what closeness really is." (This suggests that you are overinvolved with your parents because your marriage has been unsatisfying. *Better:* "Yes, I do see my family a great deal. My concern is that if I pulled back I'd get depressed because you and I don't spend time together. Let's discuss how to improve our marriage and the amount of time I spend with my family might automatically lessen.")

- "It's immoral to always avoid your family." (Honoring one's father and mother is not always easy, especially if one's parents had been abusive or neglectful. Don't criticize your partner. Try to first understand. *Better:* "I don't blame you for feeling the way you do. Still, I just wish there was a way to put aside some differences even a little.")

- "You obviously care more about your parents than you do me!" (The sentiment is understandable, especially if you have felt neglected by your partner. But this comment will invite defensiveness or criticism. *Better:* "I guess what really worries me [hurts, scares me] is that your relationship with your parents is much stronger than your relationship with me. I want us to mean more to one another than we do.")

Needing Time for Yourself

25

"My life is my job, coming home to the family at night, and scrambling to get chores done," Andrea says to her husband. "I have no time for myself. At least you get to play golf."

"Wait a minute," Steve says "You make it sound like all I do is relax and enjoy myself. I work hard. I just make time for some recreation. You could do that, too."

"What did you say when I wanted to visit my sister for the weekend? You said, 'What am I supposed to do with the kids? How am I going to get any work done?' Thanks for your enthusiasm, Steve."

"I never told you that you couldn't go."

"No, you just made it sound like I was being selfish. You tell me to find hobbies or go have fun, but you never make it possible for me to do those things."

"You don't make it easy for me, either. Yes, I play golf once in a while. But I had to leave at the fifteenth hole last time when I looked at my watch. It was getting late and I knew you'd be furious if I walked in the door twenty minutes later than I was supposed to."

Parents today are busier than ever. Especially when each partner is employed, there is little time left over to pursue personal hobbies. Instead, there are kids to raise, soccer practices to drive to, chores to get done, and a marriage to sustain. Finding time for personal recreation often means taking time away from other areas—and that's where the disagreements begin.

Have You Heard?

〰 For the busiest of families, couple-time gets sacrificed the most often. That is one reason why personal hobbies may be resented. A partner thinks "You have time for the gym but you have no time for me!"

〰 Often, one partner is the silent sufferer. He or she will want to develop a hobby or go out more with friends but feels guilty doing so. Resentment builds when they see their partner take some personal recreation time without any apparent guilt. It's a kind of class warfare that says "If I can't have fun, you can't have fun either."

〰 If this is a common area of conflict, then you are simply too busy. You will need to reexamine your schedule and do away with some low-priority activities in order to carve out some time for yourself and for each other. Simplify your life.

〰 In one-quarter of all two-income households, the spouses work different shifts. They have less time together, poorer health, less sleep, and less leisure time. Their rate of divorce is slightly higher than the national average.

How to Say It

- "I know we both are very busy, but I need to carve out some time for myself. I haven't had time to read or exercise or see friends. Maybe you could use more time, too. Can we try to figure out a way to make that happen?"
- "I'm overtired and overstressed. One reason is that I have little time for recreation. Can we come up with a plan so that we both have more time for fun?"

If your partner responds:

- *"You have enough time for play. I'm the one who never has any time for myself!"*
- *"And what am I supposed to do while you play? You think I'm not stressed?"*
- *"You're hardly home as it is. Now you'll never be home."*

You reply:

- *"I know you don't have time for yourself. Maybe I have more free time than you do, but it's still not enough. I'm wondering if we can reprioritize our life and free up some time so that we can each relax more. I'm willing to work with you on this."*
- *"I don't expect you to work harder just so I have free time. I want to find out what I can do to have some time for myself but in a way that's fair. I'm willing to make sacrifices so you can have free time too."*
- *"You're right. I am very busy. Something has to change. Can we review my schedule and figure out ways I can be more available at home but also have a little free time once in awhile?"*

If your partner wants to visit a friend, go out with folks from work, start a hobby, or even get away for a day or two alone, try to encourage it. The quality of your time together will not improve if your partner resents you. Every person needs some alone time and recreation time. A little of that here or there (with no guilt) can go a long way toward improving family satisfaction.

- "You want to play golf more often? I know you enjoy it but I also know I rarely see you as it is. I'm happy to work with you on this but could we also find ways to spend more time together?"
- "I can understand why you'd like to visit your sister for a few days. Let's figure out when would be the best time."
- "I think in the past I've not made it easy for you to go out and have some fun. I'd like to be more supportive."

After your partner comes back from some recreational time, be happy to see him or her. Don't spoil your partner's fun by stating what an awful time you had while he or she was away.

- "Well, it was a little rough while you were gone but I managed just fine. Did you have a good time? Great!"
- "Tell me about your trip (night out, bowling game, dance lesson ...). I'm glad you enjoyed yourself."
- "Don't worry about the kids and me. You deserve time for yourself."

How Not to Say It

- "I've never told you that you couldn't go out! Don't blame me because you never make time for yourself." (Your partner isn't making time for him- or herself but is instead trying to please you or make your life easier. *Better:* "I'd like you to have more time for yourself, too. Maybe I haven't made it easy for you to do that. Let's devise a plan so that can happen.")

- "Okay (loud sigh). You can go out with your friends. Do whatever the heck you want." (Don't lay on a guilt trip. If you have a legitimate reason that your partner should give up his or her plans, state it. You're entitled to fairness too, but don't go along with the request half-heartedly. It detracts from goodwill.)

- "Wednesday is my golf day. You know that. I shouldn't have to cancel it." (Good for you that you can have regular time for play. Now take the high road and show flexibility. Which is more sacred? Your marriage or tee time?)

Cherishing One Another When the Nest Is Empty

26

Meg stares out the kitchen window holding her cup of morning coffee. Meg and Tom's youngest child left home for college yesterday. She will be back for the holidays and summer vacation, of course, and her bedroom will be waiting for her. The nest isn't technically empty, but for all practical purposes it is. The couple is embarking on a new phase of their lives. So much of the energy that had been focused on the children now has to be focused elsewhere—on each other and on pursuing some long-ignored individual goals.

Tom walks up behind Meg and puts his arm around her. "I know what you're thinking," he says. "I miss her, too."

Meg clutches her husband's hand and squeezes his fingers. She is glad they have each other.

Have You Heard?

∼ Most couples handle the transition to empty nest very well. It is often a time where couple satisfaction rises. Men especially report this to be a happy time in their lives since they have usually achieved some degree of financial stability and the day-to-day concerns of parenting have receded.

∼ Seventy-two percent of women at mid-life report they are either happy or very happy. That is especially true if they have a satisfying relationship and future goals.

∼ It is a nice idea to plan a trip or some special event together. Marking this new phase of your lives can help you adjust better.

~ Couples with a weak relationship run a risk of breaking up while making the transition to an empty nest. It is vitally important for couples to keep their relationships thriving before the kids leave home so they will be better equipped to handle this period of their lives.

How to Say It

Regardless of the ups and downs you and your family experienced through the years, find something tender and positive to say to your partner. After all, you did raise children together and you each felt the array of emotions that parenthood and building a family life brings.

- "We have a lot to be proud of."
- "You've done a wonderful job as mom (dad). Our kids are so lucky to have you."
- "We did a good job, overall, wouldn't you say?"
- "There's nobody else I'd rather spend the rest of my life with than you."
- "You've been such an amazing parent. I can't wait to see you as a grandmother (grandfather)."
- "How did our kids get so lucky to have you as their parent?"

Make sure you allow the bittersweet feelings to be expressed. Don't be so quick to make a sad partner feel better with upbeat quips or you'll run the risk of causing him or her to simply withhold feelings and withdraw from you.

- "I don't blame you for crying. It's hard to see the kids go."
- "I feel the same way."
- "You're still sentimental after all these years. That's one of the reasons I fell in love with you."
- "What's the hardest part of this for you?"
- "I thought it would be easier for me when this day came, but I was wrong."
- "It's so strange. The house seems so much quieter."

- "I guess our parents must have felt a lot of what we are feeling now."

It is okay to counter your partner's negative feelings with optimistic forecasts. Just be sure you have taken the time to allow the sadder feelings to be expressed unhindered.

- "I'm sad, too. I suppose that's normal. But when I look around I see that most people in our situation adjust well over time. So will we."
- "You're right. It is hard to just let go of the past and look forward to the future. But I know that other parents really learn to enjoy relating to their children as adults and they get excited about the prospect of being grandparents."
- "This is a bittersweet time. But one of the sweet aspects is that you get to take those art courses you've always wanted to take."
- "What would you hope will be happening in our lives a year from now? What can we do to make that happen?"
- "Maybe we can talk to our parents (a neighbor, a friend, a relative) and find out how they coped when the kids left home."

If your partner says:

- *"In some ways I feel like my life is over."*
- *"I wish I'd been a better parent. Now it's too late."*
- *"I feel so old."*

You reply:

- *"That concerns me. I know our job of raising children is over but we still have many years left. Help me to understand what you mean."*
- *"No parent is perfect. What makes you say that? Are there things you could do differently now, even though the kids are older? I bet if you spoke to the kids about this, they would have a different view."*
- *"We certainly are older. But we have many, many great years left. And I'm so happy to be spending them with you."*

How Not to Say It

- "You knew this day would come. Why are you taking it so hard?"
- "This is part of life. You have to learn to deal with it."
- "There's no reason to get this upset." (Evidently there is. Perhaps you should try to understand those reasons instead of minimizing them. *Better:* "You're taking this harder than I thought you would. What troubles you the most?")
- "You're making a big deal out of this." (Don't miss the opportunity to connect to your partner. Be understanding and show some empathy. Don't criticize your partner's feelings.)
- "You seem unaffected by our last child getting married. Don't you have any feelings? Don't you care?" (Your partner is probably handling his or her emotions differently from you. *Better:* "You don't show your emotions easily. What are you feeling now that our daughter has married?")

Compatible Lovers:
Bridging the
Differences in
Personalities
or Values

Talkative or untalkative? Life of the party or lump on a log? Spender or saver? Our personality styles and core values don't usually change that quickly, if at all. That's why repeated efforts to get a partner to alter them accounts for so much marital tension and unhappiness. Personality differences can be tinkered with, improved upon, whittled down, or managed—but they usually can't be erased, overhauled, or completely and forever resolved.

The good news is they don't have to be.

Ironically, learning to accept these differences (not grudgingly) can promote goodwill and actually make it easier for a partner to modify some of his or her behaviors.

Over one-quarter of respondents in a 1996 study reported that they recently had—or were about to have—a nervous breakdown. The most frequently mentioned reasons were divorce, separation, marital strain, and troubles with the opposite sex. The wrong approach to dealing with differences in values and personality often accounts for much relationship difficulty.

Don't Make This Mistake: Confusing Chronic with Temporary Problems

It would be silly to expect that once you cleaned your house it would never get dirty again. Dust, grime, and clutter are *chronic, repetitive problems.* Someone who likes a spotless house will just have to get used to cleaning it very often. Well, personality differences between you and your partner will also recur. They will never be swept away completely. The problem with personality differences is not that they show up every so often like dust on a tabletop. The problem is that couples often fight about them *as if they shouldn't be there at all.* They accuse each other and say things like:

"You talk too much. Why can't you relax and keep quiet?"

"You don't talk enough. What's wrong with you?"

"You should save as much money as you can, not spend it as soon as you get it."

"You like to party and socialize too much."

Couples trapped in "Here we go again!" conflicts get caught up in "I'm right, you're wrong!" attitudes and insist that the other person change a core value or personality style. Like a naive resident of Buffalo, New York who thinks snow is an infrequent phenomenon, they don't recognize that some differences are so ingrained that they must recur and can never be done away with completely.

Managing a chronic problem as if it is (or should be) a temporary problem will always result in frustration, exasperation, and relationship complications.

Couples should learn how to live with personality differences, not "fix" them. Two tactics that are bound to fail boil down to two: Grin and bear it until you can't stand it anymore; or try to cajole, persuade, coax, harass, or otherwise pressure a partner to change. When these efforts fail, partners don't consider that their approach is wrong. They see their partners as stubborn or controlling and their relationship as flawed.

The Real Problem

A husband who doesn't like to talk much (a personality style) may withdraw further if his wife berates him periodically for not being talkative. Now that he's become even more close-mouthed, his wife feels increasingly aggravated and eventually berates him yet again. *It is the bad feelings that occur from mismanaged differences that are the real problems.* If a couple deals with their differences showing some interest, humor, and acceptance, the personality differences make less of a difference and each partner is usually more willing to go out of his or her way for the sake of the other.

The following section in this book will help you deal more effectively with the inevitable personality differences in your relationship. It will also help you cope with differences in values. The key points you need to remember are:

1. These problems, like snow in Buffalo, will recur. Insisting that they should be solved once and for all is unrealistic.

2. Yes, you might find a more compatible partner than the one you now have but don't be fooled: You will be trading one set of personality differences for another.

3. Research shows that displaying strong, negative emotions when dealing with differences is what makes the situation miserable. Learning to find some positive value to your differences and showing occasional humor during these repetitive conflicts will go a long way toward neutralizing them.

4. The qualities of your partner that make you batty were probably at one time charming, attractive, or at least tolerable. Remember that.

5. Abusive behaviors should not be tolerated.

6. The key rules to remember when discussing personality or value differences:

   - Never berate your partner or go for the jugular.

   - Don't expect your partner to show empathy (deep, emotional understanding of your viewpoint). You are from different worlds on the issue that divides you.

   - Instead, each of you should try to find some aspect of the other's viewpoint you can agree with—even a little agreement would help.

   - Make supportive comments when your partner is frustrated with you.

   - Reach a temporary agreement about how to handle the current situation, knowing you will be divided again in the future.

The "Accept Me as I Am" Conversation 27

Harry is ready to throw down the gauntlet. He and Marjorie have repeatedly argued about his lack of interest in socializing with friends. Now he is about to fire his last weapon: "Why can't you just accept me for who I am?"

Marjorie wants to scream. "Because I think you're being stubborn. You could at least try to socialize more often."

"You don't get it," Harry says. "It's not a question of trying. It's a question of who I am. You won't accept me and that's the problem."

Harry is partially right. Marjorie has become very insistent of late and seems to have no concern for his wishes. But Marjorie is right too. Harry is being stubborn. He doesn't have to enjoy going out with friends. But couldn't he manage to accompany her once in awhile for her sake?

What each one fails to realize is how often the other has tried, or was willing to try, to be more cooperative. Marjorie never knew (how could she? Harry never spoke up about it) of the times Harry felt bad for being a stick in the mud. In fact, if she had asked him nicely this last time, he'd have been willing to say yes to the outing with friends.

But Harry never appreciated just how often Marjorie kept quiet about her wishes to go out. If he realized that, he'd understand that she was cooperating with his wishes much more often than he cooperated with hers. But when she finally does get around to asking, she almost makes it a demand because she feels she has sacrificed enough and is now entitled to his cooperation. When he doesn't give it, she feels righteously angry. Then he feels disrespected. No wonder they can't find common ground.

Have You Heard?

~ The cry "Accept me as I am" is a sign of exasperation. It means "I don't know how to talk to you about this anymore, so why don't you drop it?" It also means, "I might be willing to talk if you'd just show some respect and understanding."

~ "Accept me as I am" is a sentiment that makes sense. It is also a cop-out. It is a refusal to find a way to cooperate while blaming the other person for being intolerant.

~ The cry "I shouldn't have to accept that part of you. It's unacceptable!" is another sign of exasperation. It means "I'm tired of being disrespected and misunderstood. I've tolerated your unacceptable ways and now you have to change them!"

~ "I shouldn't have to accept that part of you. It's unacceptable!" also makes some sense. It, too, is a cop-out (unless there is abuse—abuse should not be tolerated). It is an easy way to blame a partner when what's needed is honest recognition by each side that the other is not being completely unreasonable.

~ Compromise may help. But sometimes one of you needs to have it your way. If he wants to vacation by the shore and you want to go to the mountains, vacationing in the farm belt is a lousy compromise.

How to Say It

You need to do three things if your partner cries "Accept me as I am!" First, remember all the usual ways you respond to such claims. Second, stop using them. Three, try some of the following statements.

- "You're right, I'm not accepting your personality the way I'd like to." (This is not only true, it is conciliatory. It will get your partner's attention and begin to make it easier for him or her to want to see your point of view. If this is a long-standing disagreement, however, don't expect one sweet phrase to undo years of stubborn standoffs.)

- "You have a point. I shouldn't expect you to feel exactly as I do about this."

- "You're right, and I don't want you to feel that I don't accept you. I'm just frustrated that we haven't found a better way to work this out."

- "Even though we don't see eye to eye on discipline, I can see that we do agree we want our children to be well-behaved. We just have a different approach on how to achieve that goal."

Now, the temptation will be to resume old communication patterns and convince your partner that he or she is wrong and you are right. **Resist that temptation!**

- "Maybe what upsets you the most is not that I want you to do some things differently, but that I'm telling you you're wrong to disagree. Do I have that right?"
- "What I'd really like is to find a way to accept each other's wishes—and sometimes go along with them—without feeling resentful or unappreciated. Does that seem like a good idea?"
- "We've placed ourselves in a really fine mess. For me to accept you as you are, I'll have to give up some things I want. Then I'll feel that you aren't accepting me. Somehow, we have to be willing to cooperate enough so that neither of us feels mistreated. Any ideas?"

If you have been the one claiming "Accept me as I am!" and your partner says any of the above, show goodwill.

- "I appreciate you saying that."
- "It's nice to hear that. I know I can be difficult to get along with."
- "Well, I don't make your life easy either."
- "I'd like to find common ground too."
- "I'm willing to find a way out of this. I'm frustrated too."

An important part of any recurring conflict is to try to explain the symbolic importance of your viewpoint. Dr. John Gottman at the University of Washington calls this the "dream within the conflict." People often have deep, important reasons for what they do—reasons for which they might not be fully aware. Uncovering those reasons can help soften your feelings. For example, at the opening of this chapter, Marjorie was frustrated that Harry never liked to socialize. Imagine if Harry had said:

> *"I know it bothers you and I can't blame you for that. But when I was growing up my dad always took center stage. He had to be noticed, had to be*

heard. I often felt embarrassed by that. It's important to me not to stand out in a crowd. I'm not good at making small talk and I feel uneasy talking about myself. I guess that's why I don't have much fun at parties. I'm willing to go more often, but please accept that I won't be a chatterbox."

Marjorie might think Harry is overreacting to his past, but she'd probably have more sympathy for his point of view. That's what's needed to break the deadlock.

- "I'll tell you what. I promise not to interrupt or challenge you if you would take a minute and tell me why it's so important that I accept your viewpoint on this issue. I'm guessing that your viewpoint is important because it has something to do with strong feelings you've had in the past about a similar event."

- "Does this situation remind you of any past event in your life that you felt strongly about?"

- "Let me tell you about a story in my life. It will help explain why I feel the way I do. My parents didn't get along when I was young. My main sense of pleasure came from being with friends. So now I want us to socialize because it gives me such a sense of well being. I'm wrong to criticize you for being a homebody. But I want you to understand why it's important for me to be with friends."

- "It makes you feel good to stay at home. It makes me feel good to go out. I'd like to honor your dream and I'd like you to honor mine. Can we find a way to do this more often than we have?"

How Not to Say It

- "We'll never see eye to eye on this so let's move on to another topic." (You don't have to see eye to eye in order to manage this dilemma. You each must be willing to *yield* more to the other's wishes than you have so far. You won't win by force. You will win when your partner wants to go along with your wishes—at least this time. What will make your partner want to do that? If you are willing to go along with his or her wishes once in a while without having a bad attitude.)

- "You knew what you were getting when you married me. Don't expect me to change now." (Admitting personality flaws *and* trying to correct them is a sign of good character.)

- "Your values on this issue are different from mine. You'll just have to get used to that idea." (True. Acceptance will be important, but don't shut down communication. You still have to resolve your current dilemma despite your differences. Try to understand each other, not challenge each other. With an "engines purring" approach, a softer touch might bring about cooperation, despite differing viewpoints.)

How to Say It to Yourself

If you hear yourself claiming "Accept me as I am!" you also need to change some private thoughts that have fueled your frustration.

- "I want to be accepted but I need to accept her ways, too. That means I can't have it my way all the time."

- "It can't be easy to accept my ways when I know they can be irritating. I can bend a little."

- "Sometimes I can be stubborn. When I resent that she's not accepting me, I dig in my heels. That isn't helpful."

- "Sometimes when I say I want acceptance, what I really want is to have things go my way. The fair thing for me to do is be more flexible."

If your partner claims you don't accept him or her, be sure your self-talk isn't counterproductive.

- "If he's upset, there is something he wants me to understand that I don't understand."

- "If I tell him he's wrong to act the way he acts, he gets defensive. I need to remind him that he's not wrong. I just want more flexibility from him."

- "The more upset she is, the less she's feeling appreciated for all she does. I need to remind her that I do appreciate her."

Rigid versus Flexible Personalities

28

Lenny has no problem doing his share of housework. The problem is he doesn't do it exactly the way Lori wants him to do it. For example, Lenny might throw in a load of laundry at seven in the morning and have no problem tossing it in the dryer when he gets home from work at six. Lori calls that lazy. "He's really leaving it for me to do," she complains. "He should do the laundry when he has time to finish the job." Laundry is the tip of the iceberg. Lenny lets dirty dishes sit overnight. Lori can't relax until the kitchen is spotless. When they go on vacation, Lori takes hours devising a detailed itinerary. Lenny likes to wing it. He finds her need for structure confining. She finds his laid-back "I'll get to it sooner or later" attitude irresponsible.

Ellis works two jobs. His wife stays home with the school-age kids. On weekends he resents having to help out with chores. He believes he works hard all week and that Sandra has plenty of time when the kids are at school to get her work done. "I have my responsibilities, she has hers. It's not my job to bail her out if she isn't organized."

Often, our weaknesses are our strengths stretched to an unhealthy limit. It's good to be organized and to have a sense of duty. It's unhealthy to be so rigid that your relationships suffer and your ability to sit back and relax is compromised. It's good to be somewhat laid-back so pressures from the world won't always grind you down. But it's unhealthy to be lackadaisical or so ill prepared that others have to pick up the slack for you.

Have You Heard?

∼ Research shows that women do more of the "emotional work" in the family, in addition to their more obvious responsibilities. Men tend to overlook the

138

value of emotional work, which is defined as caring for the emotional well being of the children and the emotionally expressive side of the marriage.

~ The more rigid you are, you risk coming across as a critical "parent" to your partner. A rigid person has an "I know better" attitude which whittles down a partner's patience and esteem.

How to Say It

There is no way around this issue if relationship satisfaction is the goal. Each partner must bend a little. It is not a question of which way is the right way or the more efficient way. It is a question of give and take.

If your partner tends to be regimented and inflexible, say:

- "This is an area where we are two very different people. Sometimes your method works well for us, especially when we need things organized. But sometimes, my method works."
- "I could never do things your way all of the time. Neither do I expect you to do things my way all the time. We need to find a way to go along with each other once in a while without having a bad attitude. Do you agree?"
- "Some days I really appreciate it that you can be so driven and organized. Are there any times when you appreciate my approach?"
- "I know you don't agree with my way of doing this, but would you mind going along with it anyway for now? Thanks."
- Try to use humor whenever your personality styles clash. "Well, here we are again. The odd couple, Felix and Oscar. How should we handle it this time?"
- "Yes, I know I left the beds unmade and you don't like that. I did promise I would make them. I know it can be frustrating when I promise something and then delay getting around to it."

If you have a more regimented personality style, you say:

- "I'm in one of my more anxious moods right now. Bear with me."
- "I know it isn't easy going along with everything I say. I can be difficult at times."

- "I know you don't agree with my way of doing this, but would you mind going along with it anyway? I appreciate it."
- "What's one way I could change this so that you would find it easier to accept?"
- "What frustrates you the most about the way I do things? Can we figure out a way to make it less frustrating?"

Have a conversation where you try to uncover the emotional importance of your "flexible" or "rigid" style. Look for the underlying dream or wish.

- "I guess when everything in the house is orderly and in its place, I feel more at peace. My dream is that on some days I could count on everyone to chip in and really try to get his or her work done in an orderly way. I wish you and the kids had a whistle while you work attitude. The fun side of my personality has a hard time showing up when I feel like everything around me is in disarray."
- "I really value putting time with the kids—or time to relax—ahead of chores. I know that I have responsibilities and that chores need to get done. But it seemed to me that when growing up I always missed out on playtime with my parents because they were always working or cleaning up something. They'd get impatient just being with me and they always wanted me out of their way so they could accomplish some other chore. I promised myself I'd never be that way."

How Not to Say It

- "If you can't do it the right way (my way), don't do it at all." (*Better:* "Look, I know we don't see eye to eye on this. But for now I'd really appreciate it if you did it my way. I won't always need you to do it this way.")
- "I refuse to get as regimented as you. I like a more relaxed style and don't intend to change it." (You are rigid in your desire to be flexible. *Better:* "I can go along with your way once in a while. But I find it stressful, not relaxing. As long as you can understand that I'm not wrong to feel the way I do, I can work with you on this.")

- "It makes more sense to do it this way." (Logic alone isn't likely to win the debate. *Better:* "I know that your way works better for you and my way works better for me. Neither of us is wrong. Still, every once in awhile it would help if one of us just went along with the other's wishes without a debate. Okay?")

The Rejection-Sensitive Partner

"I left you a message," Gail says to her boyfriend, Ned. "Why didn't you return my call?"

"The message didn't sound urgent," Ned says. "You only called to say hello. I didn't think you expected me to call back."

"Does a call have to be urgent for you to return it?"

"No, but—"

"It wouldn't have taken much of your time, you know. A simple ten-second message on my answering machine would have sufficed."

"You're taking this very personally," Ned explains.

"Maybe I should. Maybe you're not so interested in this relationship as I thought you were."

"That's not fair!" Ned says.

"Hey, you were the one who didn't return the call," Gail continues. "If I rejected you that way, you wouldn't like it."

Ned is puzzled. He is also getting aggravated. It seems to him that Gail analyzes every small thing he does. She questions his love for her on numerous occasions, forcing him to go out of his way to prove his devotion. He resents being tested like that. In fact, he is starting to wonder if the relationship is worth it after all.

Gail is highly *rejection sensitive*. She expects rejection and therefore perceives ambiguous situations (such as not having a phone call returned) as evidence of rejection. She then blames Ned or finds fault with him. He says she is overreacting. He is right.

Have You Heard?

~ Rejection-sensitive people overreact to slights and perceive ambiguous situations as evidence of rejection when alternative explanations are possible.

~ People whose needs were not met sensitively and consistently as children are more apt to become rejection sensitive.

~ Rejection-sensitive people create a self-fulfilling prophecy. They act in ways that are more likely to elicit rejection than do nonrejection-sensitive people.

~ Rejection-sensitive people tend to ingratiate themselves. This may charm a partner initially but become tiresome later on.

~ Men who are rejection sensitive often don't want their wives going out alone and they easily get jealous. Women who are rejection sensitive create arguments where there need not be any and accuse their partners (unfairly) of being uncaring. They also act cold and distant after feeling rejected.

~ In a study of dating couples, 40 percent of couples with a rejection-sensitive partner had broken up within a year, compared with 15 percent of couples where partners were low in rejection sensitivity.

How to Say It

If you are rejection sensitive, it will take some time before you can feel more secure. However, you must change the way you act; otherwise, you risk losing the relationship.

- "I have a tendency to feel insecure when there is no need to. This is my problem, not yours. If I feel that you are slighting me, I'll try to work it out on my own. Thanks for understanding."

- "Here I go again, feeling insecure. Hang in there. I'll get over it."

- "I know I seem preoccupied. I took it personally when you didn't want to go out this weekend. I was wrong to do that. I have a tendency to feel insecure when I shouldn't. I'm working on it."

- "I was upset when you went out with your friends at work, especially since there were men there. I accused you of not caring about me. I was wrong and I'm sorry. In fact, I want you to be with friends from work—

even if some of them are guys—because I need to learn to feel more secure."

Talking Point: If you are insecure, you may want a lot of reassurance from your partner that he (she) loves you and is devoted to you. But be careful. If your anxiety and insecurity is only lessened by reassurance, you can become addicted to reassuring words. You will hunt for reassurance and nothing else will do. Your goal is to soothe and reassure *yourself* without requiring that constantly from your partner.

How Not to Say It

- "If you loved me you would . . ."
- "If you had left *me* a message to call you back, *I* would have . . . If you had asked *me* for a favor, *I* would have done it without hesitation . . . Since you didn't do this, you must not care." (*Better:* "I was hurt when you turned down my request for a favor because I never would have turned you down. However, you were not being unreasonable. I get insecure and sometimes have unfair expectations. I'm working on changing that.")
- "You didn't say much to me when you got home. I know what that means . . ." (Don't read minds. You will err on the side of seeing rejection when there is none. *Better:* "You didn't say much when you got home. Is there anything the matter?" If your partner says no, you're better off accepting that. If your partner has a history of saying nothing is wrong only to complain later that something is wrong, you can add: "I'm glad nothing is the matter. If there was, I'd want you to tell me.")
- "I know rejection when I see it." (Actually, you don't.)

How to Say It

If your partner is rejection sensitive and has been trying to control you or accuse you of not caring, you respond:

- "I try to reassure you, but I can only do so much of that. I know you feel insecure, but I am not the one making you feel that way. It's okay to tell me you're feeling insecure, but don't ask for reassurances. Thanks."

- "When you doubt my caring, it makes me question if this relationship can work."
- "I'm beginning to resent having to constantly prove my love. I don't want to feel that way. It would mean a lot to me if you could recognize this problem as your insecurity, not my lack of devotion."
- "You're feeling insecure again, I can tell. I'd be happy to listen to you as long as you don't find fault with me."
- "This is a problem I can't fix for you, only you can."
- Praise healthier functioning. "When I cancelled our date this weekend, I expected you to get angry and insecure. But you weren't. That meant a lot to me."

How Not to Say It

- "For Pete's sake, can't you stop being so insecure?" (The relationship may be unraveling. You have a right to be aggravated. *Better:* "I know you get anxious very easily about our relationship. I want to understand but it is hard. I get angry when you unfairly accuse me of not caring about you.")
- "Oh, you poor thing. Of course I love you!" (Be careful. Reassurance is often a temporary fix. Your partner may grow addicted to reassurance and you will grow weary of his or her insatiable need for comfort. *Better:* "We agreed that I wouldn't offer you reassurances in this situation. It's important for you to resolve your feelings yourself.")

How to Say It to Yourself

If you are a highly rejection-sensitive person, you need to challenge your anxious thoughts and replace them with more reassuring ones.

- "Just because I *feel* anxious and mistrusting doesn't mean I have reason to. I often overreact in these situations and I am doing so now."
- "If I were more secure, how might I interpret what happened? How can I give my partner the benefit of the doubt?"
- "I can talk to three or four trusted friends and see if they think I am overreacting. My own judgment isn't the best in these situations."

- "I must remember not to act impulsively when I get insecure and anxious. I must also not obsess about what could be going wrong. Instead, I should remind myself of the many ways my partner has shown love and devotion."

- "Even if he did slight me, everyone is entitled to an off day. He has been busy (preoccupied, fatigued, and so on)."

- "My need for love is too strong. I am smothering him. I don't have to ask for reassurance. I can learn to lower my anxiety without making him prove his devotion."

Spenders versus Savers

30

Another package arrives from the television shopping network. Lou is furious. He can't understand why his wife, Denise, just has to purchase items they truly don't need. And she never asks him about it. She just goes ahead and orders what she wants. When she arrives home he doesn't know whether to argue with her or give her the cold shoulder.

Denise is caught in the slow lane while driving home so she has plenty of time to think. She anticipates that the package will have arrived in the mail today, a package Lou will complain is too expensive and unnecessary. She is tired of his interrogations. Every expense has to be explained and justified. Yet it is perfectly acceptable whenever he wants to buy something for himself. It is a double standard. She stopped asking him his opinion about buying something because his answer is always the same: No. Well, she'll weather this storm and all future storms. They should both be used to it by now.

Have You Heard?

~ About 75 percent of couples argue about money.

~ The main disagreement is on discretionary income. Should it be saved or spent? And spent on what?

~ Repetitive arguments about spending are no longer about spending. Those arguments are about control and who exerts it.

~ Partners should have some private, discretionary spending. You shouldn't have to get permission to buy a new pair of jeans or a CD or have lunch at a restaurant with a friend. However, bigger ticket items or items that would affect both partners (a new television, furniture, and investments) should be a joint decision.

〜 In a marriage, the person who makes more money should not have final say over how the money is spent. Decisions should be considered joint. If a couple is living together but unmarried, it is common for expenses to be shared but for accounts to be kept separate.

〜 Cohabiting (unmarried) couples have to negotiate rules about money. If the roof leaks, who has to pay for it? The owner of the house? Both? If you go on vacation and take your partner's children along, who pays their fare? The parent only?

〜 Money inherited by a spouse during the course of the marriage should be considered as belonging to that spouse. He or she should have final say over how it is spent.

〜 Commonly, if one partner is in charge of the money, the other is in charge of sex.

How to Say It

If this personality difference has led to frequent disagreements, any attempt to outlogic, outwit, or outlast a partner is ill-advised. Basic personality differences must be accepted (like snow in Buffalo, New York), not eradicated. Disagreements can be managed effectively with respect and mutual give and take.

- "I guess what would help me is to agree on a minimum amount of money we will try to save each month. That way, I don't have to quibble about other expenses as long as I know a certain amount is being saved."

- "You're right, this isn't a necessary expense. I'd like us to have it, but I can get along without it."

- "You're right, it would be nice to own that. It isn't necessary to own, but it would be nice. Okay, let's go for it."

- "I just realized that no matter how much we argue, we always manage to save a certain amount of money each year and we always manage to spend a certain amount. Our arguing doesn't really accomplish much when you look at it that way."

- "I know I can be a pain about not spending money. I guess what I need you to understand is that I get worried when our savings are low. I feel more at peace knowing we have some money in savings that won't be wiped out the first time we have an emergency. I wish you'd appreciate how much our financial future concerns me."

- "I know I tend to spend money easily. What I want you to understand is that I do think about our bills and I do hold back from buying many things. I work hard, too, and I don't like feeling unnecessarily deprived. I want to enjoy our income, not just store it away."

- "You're not wrong for wanting to spend money and I'm not wrong for wanting to save more. What could I do so that your needs can be met and mine can be met without the hassle of arguing?"

- "A more expensive car is nice but unnecessary. How about if we find ways to cut back on other expenses for awhile and put that extra money toward the expensive car? We could cut out fast-food and restaurants except for once a month and save money there. We could get books at the library instead of the bookstore. We could cut back on long-distance calls. Does any of this sound workable?"

If an argument starts anyway, make some in-flight repairs.

- "I just noticed that we're having another unwinnable argument. I don't want us to do that. Let me tell you what I think makes sense about your viewpoint. Maybe from there we can reach some compromise."

- "I'm sorry. I just started arguing again when I know that this is a topic we'll never truly see eye to eye on. It is important that you get your way on this issue sometimes and it's important for me to get my way. I'm willing to see things your way this time."

- "I might be wrong about this. I know I can get hard headed at times, especially when it comes to money."

- "I agree with part of what you've said."

- "Can we take a break and let me clear my thoughts? I promise I'll continue this in half an hour."

How Not to Say It

- "It's too expensive. Case closed." (That attitude creates resentment. Your partner will get back at you in some other way—perhaps in the bedroom. *Better:* "It really seems too expensive to me. Can we find a way to cut back on some other expenses to help pay for it?")

- "I'm buying it anyway. Case closed." (Same as above.)

- "Life is meant to be lived! If we do things your way, we'll be richer but won't enjoy any of the money!" (This philosophical viewpoint won't wash. Your partner feels just as strongly about saving for the future as you do about living for the moment. Emotion fuels these differences more than logic.)

- "I refuse to discuss this anymore." (Maybe you could use a break if you're getting too emotional. But don't walk away from the discussion just because you don't agree. The goal is to learn how to cooperate with each other. *Better:* "I'm frustrated that this is getting nowhere. Is there something I could do that would make it easier for you to compromise or to go along with my way of thinking?")

Partner Not Ambitious Enough/Too Ambitious

31

Abby and Ben are engaged to be married after dating for the past two years. But Abby has a concern. Ben had planned to return to college and earn his degree, but now he seems content to continue working on a job that has no real future.

"I can use the money," Ben explains. "Money will be tight if I return to school."

"But my problem," Abby says, "is that you don't seem to have any ambition. How do you expect to provide for a family? You always spoke about having a career. What happened to that?"

"I still hope to have a career," Ben says. "But it bothers me that you seem so concerned about my ambition. I thought you wanted to marry me for me, not for my potential income."

"That's not fair," Abby says. "I'm marrying you because I love you. But I do have an expectation that you will work hard to provide for your family as best you can. Skipping college won't achieve that."

Is Abby right to expect that Ben should finish his college education? Or should she let him work at a job of his choosing, even if his income is not up to her standards?

Have You Heard?

⟿ Generally, socioeconomic status (or potential status) and ambitiousness are important factors for women when selecting a partner. Physical attractiveness, personality, or intelligence are not as critical. Women are not gold seekers. They simply want to make sure their children will be adequately provided for.

〜 Men are usually concerned if their partners are too ambitious. Husbands of working wives have a slightly higher risk for depression and diminished self-esteem. The reason for this seems to be that men (especially between the ages of 35 and 50) seem to require more emotional support from their wives, which is less available when wives work.

〜 Ambitiousness has its upside and downside. Ambitious people usually have less time for family involvement. However, lack of ambition may lead to a life that is not so gratifying as it might be.

How to Say It

If your partner has an ambitious dream, encourage it. Yes, the details of how to achieve the dream *and* have a satisfying family life do need to be worked out. But you don't want to douse the fires of your partner's dream. He or she may always hold it against you.

- "I think it's great that you want to go back to school and change careers. It worries me how to achieve that and pay all of our bills, but let's find a way."
- "If you want to earn extra money starting your own business, that's okay with me. I just want to make sure you have enough time for me, too. We'll figure a way to make it work."
- "You have it in you to be whatever you want to be."
- "If you really want something that bad, I'll support you on it."
- "I really want to support you on that ambition. It's obviously important to you. But it would mean I'd have to give up my dream of having you around more, especially while the kids are young. Can we find a way to honor both of our dreams?"
- "If you change careers the way you want to, your income will drop. I'm willing to contend with that, but I want to have a plan. I don't want us to suddenly be cash poor."

How Not to Say It

- "You can't be serious! You'll never be able to do that."
- "If that's what you want, fine. But don't expect me to support you on that." (You're better off discussing your concerns instead of killing off

your partner's hopes. *Better:* "That idea scares me a bit because it clashes with my hopes and dreams. But let's talk about it more. Maybe it will sound better over time.")

- "You should be content with what you already have!" (*Better:* "I'm wondering if you are unhappy with our life together.")

If your partner is not ambitious enough for your desired standard of living and you are unmarried, you may want to reconsider whether you'd truly be happy with this person. He or she may not be lacking in ambition, but simply content to live his or her life in a manner you find unappealing.

How to Say It

- "I need to believe that you will work hard to provide adequately for our future children. Your current attitude about work makes me doubtful."
- "Our obligation is to love one another. Out of love, I expect you will do your best to provide a good income, and I will do my best to appreciate your hard work. But I need to know you are trying."
- "If we're arguing about your ambition and we're not married, maybe I should reconsider if this relationship will be for the best."

How Not to Say It

- "If you tell me that you'll be more ambitious as soon as we have children or want to buy a house, I'll believe you." (Don't be foolish. Maturity and devotion should be evident now, not several years from now.)
- "I can't be with you unless you make a big salary." (If that's how you feel, the relationship may not stand the test of time. Your partner should be devoted to you and be conscientious about providing as good an income as possible. But some very good people may simply not make a lot of money.)

If your partner is an underachiever who is capable of more success, he or she probably thinks in black–white, all-or-nothing ways. Underachievers believe that unless they can be perfect, they are a failure. They criticize themselves for stumbling or for not succeeding quickly enough, and convince themselves they don't have what it takes. They make excuses why they can't get a better job or go back to college or get a promotion. It is difficult to get this person to change his or her perspective. In fact, underachievers are good at getting others to criticize them so that they have a justification to say that nobody understands them. The goal, then, is to empathize and to try to understand without jumping in to fix them.

How to Say It

If your partner is expressing doubts about his or her ability, try to empathize with the emotion and don't automatically challenge your partner's negative views.

- "The idea of going back to school seems a bit overwhelming right now."
- "You've never felt so confident about your abilities as others have of your abilities."
- "It must be frustrating when you'd like to be more successful and find it's not easy."
- "I notice that you often tend to criticize your abilities right at the point when you need to persevere."
- "It seems to you that everyone else is more successful and that you can't achieve what you want."
- "I guess I have more faith in you than you do."

How Not to Say It

- "You'll never achieve anything if you're so self-critical!"
- "You're such a pessimist!"
- "You want to fail!"
- "You don't love me."
- "You're a lousy role model."

Spouse Too Emotional/ Unemotional

32

Patricia and Vince are driving home after a 4-day sightseeing trip with their children and grandchildren. Patricia was overwhelmed by the architecture of Washington, D.C. She just loved the buzz of the city, the museums, and the sense of history. An unexpected rush of patriotism welled up inside her when she viewed the White House. She is one big waterfall of emotions and relishes the memories that are still very alive for her.

But Vince's memory of the last four days are superceded by thoughts about his overgrown lawn that needs mowing. When Patricia wants to once again talk about the fun they had with the grandkids, Vince just nods. He isn't really listening. In fact, he thinks Patricia is getting too carried away. Her emotionality annoys him—and his lack of emotions annoys her.

"If I can't share my feelings with the man I married," Patricia exclaims, "what's the use of having you around? Experiencing life to the fullest is what living is all about! Oh, you just don't get it."

Vince's words are crisp, brimming with logic, and undercut with anger that he tries to keep under control. "I am not like you," he says. "Just because I don't get as emotional as you do doesn't mean I'm wrong. You get carried away. You overreact to everything. I don't want to be like that." They don't speak another word the rest of the ride home.

Have You Heard?

~ Most couples are out of sync when it comes to emotional expression.

~ People who wish their partners would talk more usually want them to express more emotion. They might be content to have fewer words spoken if the words uttered conveyed emotions as well as thoughts.

~ Couples who wish their partners would talk less usually want them to be less emotional. They might be content to hear more words as long as those words were not emotionally laden or demanding an emotional response.

~ The less emotional partner sees emotions as problems to be solved. He or she views emotional expression as a sign of loss of control. Anger is usually the one emotion he or she allows to surface because it doesn't automatically feel like a sign of weakness.

~ If you are married, keep this in mind: You were attracted to your partner's way of dealing with emotions. Probably, his or her way represents parts of yourself that you pushed away and didn't want to acknowledge. If you are emotional, you are pushing aside the part of your personality that can be colder or unfeeling, and criticizing him or her instead. If you are unemotional, you are pushing away your own feelings and enticing your partner to express that emotional side for you. Then you nail your partner for being that way.

How to Say It

Stop trying to make an emotional partner less emotional or an unemotional partner more emotional. Stop punishing your partner with verbal attacks (or nonverbal attacks such as giving the cold shoulder) just because he or she is not on the same emotional wavelength as you.

If you are the less emotional partner and your partner is very frustrated with you, you will need to express more emotion than you have. But you can learn to do so in a manner that feels comfortable.

- "I'm sure it does bother you that I can seem so unaffected by things. If I reacted with emotions the way you do, I would feel out of control. Being out of control is a bit scary to me."

- "Sometimes I can't get to the feeling because I'm so focused on being judged by you for not having a feeling. If you can back off and not tell me I'm wrong or neurotic for not showing emotions, I'll work on trying to express my feelings more. Deal?"

- Find the deeper meaning or dream behind your wish to be less emotional. "I remember I had to fend for myself emotionally when I was younger. My parents were good but they were very busy. Dad always worked. Mom was busy with the younger kids. I think I learned that if I had a problem I'd take care of it myself. Talking about it got me nowhere. If I talk now about my problems, it makes me feel like I'm inadequate, that I can't handle it myself."

If your partner responds:

- *"But it's healthy to talk about your feelings."*
- *"You shouldn't have to deal alone with your problems. You should talk them over with me. Don't shut me out."*
- *"There is no intimacy if you won't talk about your feelings."*

You reply:

- *"It's also healthy to exercise and not smoke. But doing the healthy thing isn't always easy. I want you to understand that it's hard for me to express feelings. I will try to express them more. But I need you to not judge me."*
- *"I don't intend to shut you out and I feel bad that you take it that way. I've gotten into the habit of believing that asking for help is a sign of weakness. I don't like feeling weak."* (By admitting you have vulnerabilities, your partner will respond positively.)
- *"But I need to not feel judged. I need to feel respected and appreciated for all I do. That might make it easier to express myself."*

Find moments to express a simple feeling about little things. The most basic emotions are mad, sad, glad, and nervous.

- "I'm excited about seeing our son play ball."
- "I really enjoyed that movie."
- "It's sad that Millie and Tom are getting a divorce."
- "The meeting tomorrow makes me nervous."
- "Those autumn colors are really beautiful. It's very peaceful here."

Talking Point: An underemotional partner is often nonresponsive to his partner in hopes that she will get the message and become less emotional. In fact, the opposite happens: She becomes more hurt, more frustrated, and feels more disconnected, so she responds with heightened emotionality.

The overemotional partner hopes her intense feelings will prod her partner to express his feelings. In fact, the opposite happens: He becomes more agitated and overwhelmed, so he pushes those feelings down and responds with even less emotion than he otherwise might have.

How Not to Say It

- "Emotions just get in the way."

- "You're getting too emotional." (Don't make her wrong for being that way. *Better:* "Your emotions are a bit overwhelming for me right now. Could you talk more calmly and I'll try to hang in there with you.")

- "That's nice . . . Yes, I had a good time . . . Yes, I liked that meal . . . " (All these phrases express very blunted, colorless emotions. These are opportunities to practice being more expressive, especially if the issue is not a divisive one between you and your partner. *Better:* "Wow, that painting is really nice. It's beautiful. It's something I could look at often and really enjoy . . . I had a great time. I particularly like it when . . . That meal was delicious. And the company was good, too.")

- "I love you." (This phrase is wonderful if said with sincerity. However, less emotional people say it infrequently and say it with little depth. *Better:* "I love you so much . . . You mean everything to me . . . I'm so glad I found you.")

If you tend to be emotional and your partner is not, criticizing him or her won't work.

How to Say It

- "I know I get frustrated with you for not being emotional. I'm sure that annoys you because you probably have good reasons for being that way. I'm hoping that once in awhile you might tell me more about your feelings, however. That's when I feel closest to you."

- "Here I go again, wishing you could express some emotions. I guess I'm feeling disconnected right now and want to feel connected."

- "I know we'll never be a perfect match when it comes to expressing emotion. But what I want you to understand is that my emotional life is a huge part of who I am. I could no more do away with it than I could do away with my arm. When I can express myself emotionally and have that be appreciated, and when you can express emotions back to me even a little bit—that's when I'm at my best. I don't want to be at my best when I'm with others. I want it with you."

- "Here we are again, having this discussion about how emotional each one of us should be. This will come up again. How do you want to handle it today?"

How Not to Say It

- "It's about time you expressed some emotion. Why couldn't you have done that before?" (Don't criticize him the moment he does what you want. *Better:* "Thanks for talking about how you felt. That meant a lot to me.")
- "You have no soul. Don't you care about anything?" (Of course he cares. He'll dismiss that comment as objective proof that your emotionality blinds you to common sense. *Better:* "It helps when I know how you feel about something because I'll know if it matters to you.")
- "Do you like this? . . . Are you having fun? . . . Would you like to come back here again? . . . " (Don't ask questions that can be answered with one word. *Better:* "What are your thoughts about this?")
- "What do you feel about . . . " (If your partner gets uneasy expressing emotions, asking a "feeling" question may prompt him or her to get close-mouthed. Instead, ask a thinking question. "What are your thoughts about . . . What do think is best about . . . What did you hope to do with the grandkids today?" Thinking questions are more likely to elicit more informative answers—and a feeling answer may slip in, too.)

How to Say It to Yourself

Self-talk regarding this issue can do great damage or great good. Any self-talk that berates a partner will keep the two of you entrenched in a no-win tug of war. If you tend to express few emotions, say to yourself:

- "She's right. I could be more expressive. Sometimes I know I have feelings and I know I could mention them but I don't. That isn't fair to her."

- "One reason I married her was because I appreciated her emotionality. I love the way she can be sentimental. But I fight her on those very same things. I need to remind her that those are some of the reasons I fell in love with her."

- "My use of logic makes her more emotional. If I want her to be less intense, I need to convey my emotions once in a while."

- "If she were as unemotional as I, we wouldn't have as much fun and life would not be nearly so interesting."

- "I know I can be more emotional with others at times. She is the most important person in my life and deserves more from me."

- "If I truly wanted her to be less emotional, I wouldn't be as cold and unresponsive as I have been. My approach has only made her more emotional. Maybe I want her to be emotional but I just can't admit it to myself."

If you are the emotional partner, say to yourself:

- "One reason I fell in love with him was because he is solid and steady. I can rely on him to be a good provider. Sometimes the fact that he is unemotional helps me. He is my anchor when I get carried away."

- "If we were both as emotional as I am, we would probably have made some poor decisions."

- "I know my emotions can be intense and overwhelming. That's not fair to him."

- "As much as I want him to be more verbal and emotional, I don't want to lose sight of all that he does for me in other ways."

- "I shouldn't get as intense as I do. It only pushes him away and achieves the opposite of what I say I want."

You Like to Be On Time and Partner Is Always Late

33

Elliot paces the kitchen floor. He has half a mind to leave for the dinner reception without his wife, Lindsay. Elliot hates to be late, he thinks it is rude. He prides himself on his timeliness and efficiency. Sure, people can get delayed once in awhile. But Lindsay is never on time. He's complained in the past, but nothing has helped. The fact that she doesn't seem to take his concern seriously bothers him more than her lateness. Isn't he important enough to her? Don't his concerns matter?

Lindsay rushes down the stairway with a hairbrush in her hand.

"Have you seen my purse?" she asks.

"We're late as it is. You don't need a purse. C'mon, let's go."

"Of course I need my purse! It has my makeup in it." Elliot watches as his wife scurries into the bathroom.

"I'm leaving in three minutes," he says, "with or without you."

Have You Heard?

~ An often-heard complaint by women who are accused of always running late is this: "I wouldn't be so late if you would help me with the kids! You only worry about getting yourself ready. I have to make sure the kids are taken care of (dressed, fed, bathed, etc.) as well as take care of myself."

~ If strong differences in personality or values exist, this problem will never get completely resolved once and for all. Name-calling and intolerance will inflame the situation and your partner may become more inflexible.

~ If this is a long-standing bone of contention, it is no longer lateness that is the issue. Each side may be thinking "If he (she) really cared about me, he

161

(she) would . . . " It will be necessary, then, to find ways to show tolerance so that this issue doesn't boil over into a bigger issue.

How to Say It

Plan ahead.

- "Tomorrow night is the awards banquet. It is very important to me that we get there in plenty of time. Is there something I can do that will insure that we get there no later than six-thirty?"
- "Friday we're supposed to meet Dave and Bev for dinner. But I'll have little time to get ready after I get home from work. You should plan on us being fifteen minutes late. Do you want me to call Bev and Dave and tell them?"
- "I know I keep promising that I'll be home from work right at six o'clock. But that's only if traffic isn't slow and if I don't get any last-minute phone calls. Maybe you should just expect me by six-thirty and if I'm home before that, great."

Show some understanding.

- "We're supposed to leave in half an hour, but I can tell I won't be ready by then. I'm sorry. I know it annoys you when we're not on time."
- "I can see that you are rushing around because you know it bothers me when we are late. I appreciate you doing that. But if we're a few minutes late today, so be it."
- "I'm running late. It's really okay if we take separate cars. I know you hate being late and I hate making you late."
- "Look, I can see that you won't be ready on time and I always feel lousy when I have to tell you to hurry up. Would you mind if we took separate cars tonight? That way you don't have to rush and I won't get frustrated."

Discuss the issue when you both aren't in a hurry to get somewhere.

- "Can we talk about what happened yesterday? I want to find a way to deal with this issue of being on time."
- "We made it on time to the movies yesterday, but I hated that we were both in lousy moods trying to race around beforehand. I don't want to

make this an issue every time we go out. Any ideas how we can deal with this better?"

Example of a successful dialogue:

SHE: What bothers me the most is that I sometimes wonder if you care about me.

HE: Well, that goes for me, too. I know you like being on time but sometimes it feels like that's more important to you than I am.

SHE: How do you think I feel? You don't take my concerns seriously. You know I want to be on time and yet you manage to be late almost always.

HE: That's not fair. You see me rush around. I wouldn't be doing that if I didn't care.

SHE: Okay, you're right. Maybe I shouldn't have said that. But the fact remains we're late more often than we are on time. And you get mad at me for being annoyed by that.

HE: I get mad because I don't think you understand that I really am trying my hardest to be on time. But it takes me longer to get ready and I don't always have the luxury of starting early so I can take my time.

SHE: I don't think you understand that nine times out of ten I try to be patient and understanding.

HE: Okay. So what should we do? No matter what plan we come up with, there will always be exceptions. I have to accept that you like to be on time and you have to accept that I won't always be on time. Can we do that without holding a grudge?

SHE: I guess so. Maybe if I know we can be on time for some events—the ones most important to me—I won't mind if we're late for other things.

HE: That sounds good. But please understand that unforeseen circumstances might make the best plans fall through at the last minute.

SHE: I know that.

That conversation was not filled with sweet words. At times they were accusatory and each felt like more of a victim. But each one was able to admit that the other had a point. Each one was able to deescalate the tension by making in-flight repairs (such as " . . . I shouldn't have said that.") and they arrived at a plan that held promise. Goodwill was evident, despite moments when anger and irritation erupted. Successful dialogues don't have to be sugary sweet. There needs to be some gentleness, some ability to admit mistakes or acknowledge another's viewpoint, and a willingness to be influenced by a partner instead of stubbornly refusing to budge on an issue.

How Not to Say It

- "Why are you so irresponsible? There's absolutely no reason why you can't be on time!" (There could be reasons that have nothing to do with her efficiency. She may have too many responsibilities to take care of before she can get ready—such as preparing a meal for the kids, getting them dressed, and so on. If so, you should assist where needed. You're entitled to be frustrated, but you need to accept that this issue will come up again. *Better:* "It happens a lot that we're late and that makes me upset. Is there something I could do to help us be on time more often?")

- "It's no big deal if we're a few minutes late. Why do you always have to be so precise?" (*Better:* "I know it's important to you that we get there on time. I wish that was always possible but it isn't realistic. I'm willing to try to work harder at this, but I need you to be tolerant when we aren't on time.")

- "If you're not ready in five minutes, I'm leaving without you." (Taking separate cars is fine if you've discussed it ahead of time. Punishing your partner by leaving without her won't help. If she is on time, the car ride to wherever you are going won't be fun if you had just threatened her minutes before.)

- "Being five minutes late is just the same as being an hour late."

- "You should be understanding when I'm late." (He won't understand. However, tolerance is possible.)

Partner Is Boring

34

"We don't do anything fun anymore," Rich complains. "Our life is boring."

"Who has time to do anything?" Sally answers. "We have two children, we each have a job. What would you like to do, assuming we could find the time?"

Rich shrugs his shoulders. "I don't know. But that's a problem, too. A few years ago we would just get up and do something. We never had to think about it. Now everything is planned and none of it is very thrilling."

"We're not in college anymore, Rich. We do have responsibilities."

"But I think that attitude is wrong. Sure we have responsibilities. But can't we have fun, too? Life should be more exciting."

"I'm not bored," Sally says. "I have plenty to do."

Rich isn't sure what to say next. Sally seems content to busy herself with life's mundane chores and activities. Going to an occasional movie is her idea of a thrilling night out. Sally is boring—and that worries him. Could he spend the rest of his life with someone who shows such little passion and excitement?

Have You Heard?

∽ Boredom occurs in all relationships at various times. The longer you live with someone, the less novelty there is. However, a boredom rut is like putting on an extra 10 pounds: It's a sign you have been neglectful and it's an opportunity to make some changes.

∽ Chronic boredom can have serious consequences. In a study of people who divorced during the 1980s, boredom was the number-two reason cited for splitting up. Unmet emotional needs was number one; high-conflict was number three.

~ Depression and fatigue can contribute to boredom.

~ People who score high on measures of boredom proneness also tend to score high on measures of anger.

~ People who enjoy sensation-seeking or risk-taking activities can become easily bored by activities that a more laid-back person would find entertaining.

Let's Talk

Must couples have shared interests to stay happy? The answer is no. Many happy couples remain happy even if they have no common interests. However, spending time together is important. No couple can remain highly satisfied with the relationship if they spend little time together.

Boredom does diminish relationship satisfaction. But research suggests that satisfaction can be given a significant boost if the couple occasionally finds some activity to do together that is both different and exciting. An activity that causes them to laugh out loud or make their hearts pound with excitement can increase bonding. For some couples, a trip to an amusement park can have this effect if they really get a thrill out of some of the rides. Attending a play or a concert may seem pleasant but mundane for some couples; for others, it may be a spine-tingling adventure. Weekend getaways, even day trips, might do the trick if the activity is out of the ordinary for that couple (white-water rafting; sailing with friends; taking horse-riding lessons; and so on). Physical exertion often adds to the sense of excitement but it isn't necessary. What's called for is creativity, a willingness to try something new, and a desire to laugh.

As one man once told me, "Every once in a while a couple needs to have a hoot together." It is sound advice.

How to Say It

- "It's happening again. I'd like us to have fun this weekend and you want to stay home. Any chance of compromising?" (This has the advantage of a gentle start-up and emphasizes teamwork.)

- "I'd really like for us to plan an evening out. Something that would be fun. I enjoy looking forward to times like that. I know you don't always enjoy going out, but can we do this once in a while anyway? I'll make all the baby-sitting arrangements." (Supportive comments such as "I know you don't always enjoy going out . . ." make it easier to find common ground.)

Don't make boredom the issue. Talk about how you miss the connection with your partner.

- "It's not fun that I want—it's having fun with you."
- "I do stay home quite a bit and can enjoy that. But I need to have some excitement, too. More important, I want to do something fun together."

If your partner responds:

- *"You always have to be busy. Why can't you learn to appreciate staying at home?"*
- *"I'm not boring. You just can't be happy with the small things of life."*
- *"Why did you marry me if we're so different?"* (Someone who asks this question is feeling insecure and needs reassurance that the marriage is on solid ground despite differences.)

You reply:

- *"I do enjoy being home, but sometimes I find it boring. I'd really like to understand what worries you about this."*
- *"That's not fair. You and I just have different tastes. I'm willing to compromise. What can I do so you will feel better about all this?"*
- *"I have no intention of leaving you. I just want to find a way to make life more interesting and less boring. I'm open to suggestions."*

If the discussion seems to be going nowhere, don't use more force or try to be more persuasive. Make in-flight repairs instead.

- "Can we start over? We seem to be spinning our wheels."
- "I'm trying to talk you into something you don't like, and you're trying to talk me out of something I do like. We're not being very understanding."
- "I don't mind handling it your way this time, but we'll face this issue again. Maybe we need to come up with a plan that takes that into consideration."
- Look for hidden issues. "Maybe I'm wrong, but sometimes I get the impression that in order to prove my love for you, I'm not supposed to want to do anything but stay home and spend a quiet night together. What do you think?"
- "Sometimes I worry that you're depressed. Could that be true?"

- Discuss the dream behind your viewpoint. "When I think of the ideal marriage I think of two people who can have a fantastic time doing things together. Then going home and relaxing becomes a sort of hideaway from the world. I want a marriage to be fun, not just a serious responsibility."

- "I guess my dream is different. I always imagined that the ideal marriage was one where the couple just enjoyed each other's company, even if there was nothing to do. The ideal couple wouldn't need some outside excitement to stir their passion."

- "Okay, we see things differently. How can we honor each other's dreams?"

- "Even though I wasn't looking forward to this weekend, I had a nice time." (Show appreciation for your partner's preferences. It adds warmth and increases intimacy, which was probably what you wanted all along.)

Talking Point: If you are more of a homebody, surprise your partner with plans to do something more fun. Knowing you can initiate such plans will make him feel he doesn't always have to be the pushy one. If you crave more fun and excitement, tell your partner ahead of time that you want to spend quiet time at home—and then really aim to enjoy that quiet time with her. When she trusts you can enjoy her company, she won't feel so threatened by your desire to do more exciting activities.

How Not to Say It

- "If you don't want to have any fun, I'll find someone who will." (Never make threats of this type. It undermines trust.) *Better:* "I know I could go out with my friends if you don't want to come along, but I'd prefer you came with me.")

- "Can't you be content with home life?" (You're really wondering if your partner is content with you. But you are putting him in a bind by suggesting that he prove his contentment by giving up his desire for more exciting activities. *Better:* "I know you crave excitement. I guess I just need to know that staying home with your family is something you can really treasure, too.")

- "You know how I feel. Stop trying to force the issue." (You must find a way to compromise.)

Partner Is Too Shy

35

"I'd like you to meet my fiancée," Angeline says to her boss. She has just arrived at the dinner party with Lowell. They are to be married in six months. Lowell smiles at Angeline's boss but has a hard time with the small talk. He watches the two of them carry on the conversation and wishes he felt at ease meeting people. When the boss moves on to greet other guests, Angeline gives Lowell a curious look.

"You really seemed uncomfortable," she says.

"Small talk isn't my forte," Lowell says.

"It doesn't take much," she says. "Just ask a question or two, or even comment about the weather if you have to. That's better than saying nothing at all."

Lowell doesn't know what to do. He isn't an extrovert by nature. Sure he could carry on an interesting conversation but only if he knows the other person very well. Will Angeline be able to accept that?

Have You Heard?

〜 Introverts can learn to be a bit more sociable. However, it is not their nature to be an outspoken life of the party.

〜 Many shy people are more accurately described as "slow to warm up." Once they are familiar with a group of people, they can be more talkative.

〜 Shy people tend to marry later than non-shy people. Delaying marriage is associated with greater marriage success.

〜 For unmarried adults, shy men have a greater burden than shy women. Men are still expected to initiate opposite-sex encounters.

〜 While shy people do not talk so much in a group setting, they do not leave much of a negative impression. They just think they do.

〜 Shy people are very self-critical during social interactions.

How to Say It

If your partner is shy and you wish he or she were more socially at ease, you need to accept that trait and not try to change it. You owe it to your partner and yourself to emphasize those qualities you love and cherish. Keep in mind that there is probably something appealing to you about your partner's shyness.

- "I know these small get-togethers with my friends aren't that appealing to you, so I appreciate it when you accompany me."
- "I still like your company even though you don't find a lot to say."
- Show some empathy. "I know that when my family visits I'll probably spend some time chatting with my mother. That means you'll have to entertain Dad. I know that makes you uncomfortable. Maybe you could give me a sign when you'd like me to join you."

If you are shy, you cannot expect your partner to give up social events or to stand by your side at all times during gatherings with friends or family. In order for your partner to accept your personality, you'll have to accept your partner's. Mutual give and take is the only way around this issue.

- "Don't worry about me. I'll be fine. Feel free to talk to those people without me."
- "I'd prefer not go to your office holiday party. But I know you enjoy it, so I'll be happy to do that for you."
- "I wish I were more comfortable in social settings. I know you'd like it if I were more outgoing. But we always find a way to make it through."
- "We're a well-oiled team. You talk, I listen."
- "I guess I'd like you to understand that I am probably more hard on myself for being shy than anybody else would ever be. I often judge myself harshly. If I could simply change my personality I would. Knowing you can love me anyway, despite my shyness, makes me feel wonderful."

If this issue has somehow become divisive, then you are probably locked in an "accept me as I am" argument. Reread Chapter 27 for more help.

- "I could try to make more of an effort to go along with your wishes if I believed that you could accept my personality rather than criticize it. We each need to show some flexibility and some acceptance."

- "I guess what's bothering me is there are many times I turn down invitations because I know you'd rather not go. So when I do accept an invitation I feel entitled to go and I think you should be willing to go, too. Maybe it would help if I told you about those times I said no to an invitation. That way you'd know that I do try to compromise and respect your wishes."

How Not to Say It

- "Everyone thinks there is something wrong with you." (This is not only mean, it is also incorrect. Most people do not look down on shy people. In fact, a shy person is rarely loud or obnoxious and may be thought of as a nice person.)

- "There's no reason to be shy. You know everyone there." (Shyness is not a trait easily changed by logic. Otherwise, most shy people would be extroverts.)

- "It's not that I'm so shy, you're just too outspoken. You always have to be the center of attention." (Any kind of "I'm right, you're wrong" argument won't accomplish anything.)

- "This is who I am. There's nothing more to say about it." (*Better:* "I know my personality frustrates you at times. I'm doing the best I can but I know I can't act the way you'd like me to. Why do you think it troubles you so much?")

Appreciating and Praising Your Partner's Personality

36

Leslie's husband, Ted, is not much of a talker. Neither does he show a lot of affection. He is a devoted father and works very hard to provide his family with a comfortable house and a few amenities. At a neighborhood barbecue, Leslie glances at Ted while she is chatting with her friends and smiles. He notices but does not acknowledge her (or is that a slight smile?). Some of her friends wonder what she sees in Ted. He is a decent guy, definitely on the quiet side, and emotionally reserved. Leslie overflows with sentiment and displays affection easily. Don't their personality differences cause havoc? How could they fully appreciate those differences?

Have You Heard?

~ There are pluses and minuses to any personality style. Your personality style is flawed and not suited for certain situations. But it comes in handy in other situations.

~ It's possible to see the value in your partner's irritating ways. Don't pretend his or her faults are just fine, but don't pretend they are always problematic, either. You chose this person. Chances are good that something about his or her personality attracted you, even though it can be irritating at times.

~ Often, a person's personality weaknesses are simply their strengths that have been stretched too far. For example, a very sentimental person can show compassion easily and is capable of great empathy. But she can also get hurt easily. An emotionally reserved person is often practical and an anchor during life's storms. However, he can be detached and not always see the beauty of life. Hard workers can get grumpy if they push themselves to overwork. Savers can be thrifty but not always appreciate the joy of splurging once in a while. Very active people love to keep busy but can't relax. Learning to celebrate your partner's personality involves emphasizing the benefits of that personality style rather than emphasizing the drawbacks.

How to Say It

Compliments are always appreciated. Think about the benefits to your partner's personality and mention them. Don't worry that you will be reinforcing traits that have a downside. When your partner feels appreciated, he or she will be more willing to do things your way more often, even if it goes against his or her personality.

- "I'm glad you're good at talking to people. I have a hard time keeping conversations going."
- "Sometimes my emotions get in the way of my objectivity. I really rely on your ability to keep your emotions in check."
- "You like to be organized, planful, and on time for things. Those qualities are very helpful at times, especially when we're planning for vacations."
- "I complain sometimes that you get too emotional, but I married you because I love that about you, too."
- "You take such an interest in crafts for the kids. That amazes me. I have practically no interest in that area. I'm glad you do."
- "Your fastidiousness about a clean house has its benefits. I'm always proud of the way the house looks when we have people over."
- "I'd miss it if you weren't so . . . "
- "If you were a perfect match to my personality, our life would be boring."
- "It's nice that our child has developed that same trait as you."
- "It's good that the kids see us managing and appreciating our differences."
- "You can put up with my ways, I can certainly accept your ways."
- "You're a slob, but I love you."

How Not to Say It

Grim tolerance should be avoided.

- "I don't know what I ever saw in you."
- "I shouldn't have to put up with someone who is always late."
- "If you loved me, you wouldn't be that way."
- "I have no choice but to put up with your ways."

Part Five

The Touchiest
of Subjects:
Communicating
about Sex
and Affection

Some couples have no problem talking dirty to each other but they can't talk sex. Perhaps that is because people's early sexual encounters were rarely preceded by a discussion about what was to happen next. Couples on their way to having sex paid attention to nonverbal cues and body language and gave their consent to sex by saying nothing. They simply went along with what was happening. (That remains the number-one method of assenting to sex.) Since a partner's ego might be intimately tied to his or her sex life, talking can seem risky. The wrong word can cause a lot of psychological hurt.

Your sex life is vitally important to your relationship. Don't kid yourself about that. It is the only method of deeply connecting to one another not used in your other important relationships (I sincerely hope). When the relationship is very satisfying, the importance of the sex life diminishes because so many other facets of the relationship work well. But if the sexual connection isn't working the way you want it to, it looms large in the scheme of things. That's when talking about sex becomes as important as doing it.

Does good communication lead to better sex? Yes. But more precisely, good communication leads to improved relationship satisfaction, which leads to better sex. One study showed that engaged couples who reported good, open communication had the highest sexual satisfaction one year after marriage. If the men were able to make empathic comments before they were married, their wives showed the highest sexual fulfillment a year later.

In a study of 600 women between the ages of 30 and 50, the women who enjoyed good communication with their partners about sex had higher self-esteem and were less dependent than women who did not enjoy such good conversation. The good communicators also had more frequent sex.

Discussions about sex (or affection) become most essential when sexual concerns emerge. Failure to talk about these concerns may perpetuate them. Defensiveness and avoidance are the hallmark responses when couples discuss the touchy issue of sex. The way around it is to remember the GIFTS: Proceed *gently,* make *in-flight* repairs, *find* underlying concerns, remain a *team,* and offer *supportive* comments whenever you can.

Low Sexual Desire

37

"I don't need to see a doctor," Hal says to his wife as he slips into bed. "I don't have a problem. I've just had a lot on my mind."

Jean sits up. "You've had a lot on your mind for four months," she says. "Do you know how long it's been since we made love?"

"What about last Saturday?" Hal says.

"I said 'made love,' not 'go through the motions.' I had to practically drag you to bed and you weren't very enthusiastic." Hal sighs and faces away from her. Jean continues, "Look, I'm not complaining. I'm worried, and it bothers me that you're ignoring this problem."

"I told you, Jean. I don't have a problem. You seem to be the one who is bothered by this, not me."

Hal is one of the growing numbers of men who experience low sexual desire. It used to be more of a problem for women, but since men have started sharing household chores and child-rearing responsibilities, more men utter "Not tonight, dear" than ever before.

Have You Heard?

~ There is no clear-cut definition of low sexual desire. What's normal for some people may be abnormal for others. Generally, people who seek help for this problem report less frequency of sex, less desire for sex, fewer sexual fantasies, and lower sexual arousal.

~ Sixty-five percent of people who seek a sex therapist report this problem. Of these, 40 percent also report arousal or orgasmic difficulties.

∿ The prevalence is from 15–65 percent. Most couples experience a drop in sexual desire from time to time. It is not necessarily a problem. If it persists, a medical exam is a good idea and possibly a visit to a qualified sex therapist.

∿ In one study, 44 percent of women reported diminished sexual desire three months after giving birth. After nine months, 35 percent of women still reported low desire.

∿ Three reasons for low sexual desire predominate.

— *Medical.* Antihypertensive drugs, sedatives, glaucoma or pain medications, phenothiazines, hormonal fluctuations, as well as other medicines and medical conditions such as diabetes or cancer can contribute to this problem.

— *Personal.* Depression is a major cause, especially for women. Commonly, people with even a low-grade depression suffer a drop in sexual desire. Stress and fatigue are very common factors. Anyone with *lifelong* problems with desire may also have been traumatized as a child. Men with sexual-arousal problems often develop lower sexual desire as a defense against having to perform.

— *Interpersonal.* Relationship difficulties can wreak havoc with desire. Lack of frequent, tender affection and limited time for a couple to spend together unstressed by daily hassles can be a factor. Men can separate sex from relationship problems and are less likely to have lower desire when their marriage is troubled.

∿ As desire falls so does that person's efforts to show affection. That is because affection is often interpreted by the high-desire partner as a request to have sex—something that the low-desire partner wishes to avoid.

∿ Women with low desire may have lost touch with their feminine side. They may have stopped dressing in sexy or attractive clothing; they may care little about their hairstyle, and may have less time to spend with close female friends. Romantic movies or novels are not a cure but can help nudge their desire.

∿ Men with low desire may be out of touch with their masculine side. Spending time with male buddies, or watching or engaging in competitive sports can be rejuvenating.

How to Say It

Regardless of the cause, the partner with low sexual desire feels a mixture of emotions—usually anxiety, anger, sadness, and guilt. The best initial approach is one of kind concern. Expect defensiveness. Be prepared to make in-flight repairs as these discussions aren't easy for either party.

- "We don't make love nearly as much as we used to. Can we talk about that?"
- "I can't help but notice how often you pull back when I want to make love. At first I thought you were just tired or stressed out. Now I'm worried there is more to it. Please tell me what's going on."

If your partner responds with:

- *"There is no problem."*
- *"Is sex the only thing you care about?"*
- *"Do we have to talk about this now?"*

You reply:

- *"Maybe there isn't a problem. I hope not, anyway. But the fact remains we rarely make love much anymore and I'm starting to feel worried (annoyed). I can't make you talk to me, but I'd like to think you'll fill me in soon on what's going on."*
- *"Sex is not the only thing I care about. But it is one way we get close and shut out the rest of the world. I miss it."*
- *"We don't have to talk now. But I will want to talk about it tomorrow. Is that a deal?"*

Your partner may come up with accusatory answers. Try to listen without interrupting, even if you think the accusations are unfair. Women, more than men, lose sexual interest when their relationship is floundering or when they don't feel particularly connected to their partner. If your partner says the following:

- *"Why should I want sex after the way you've been treating me?"*
- *"You haven't been that enthusiastic, either. It's no wonder I've lost interest."*

- "*Don't you realize all the stress I've been under? I guess not; otherwise, you wouldn't be making such stupid comments.*"

Make some supportive comment. You reply:

- "*You're right. Maybe I haven't been the nicest person. Maybe I'm frustrated, too. Can we figure out a way to put things back together?*"
- "*I hadn't realized I wasn't enthusiastic. It always meant a lot to me. I'm willing to show more excitement, but I still wonder if there's more to this problem.*"
- "*Stress can make anybody lose their interest in sex. But this has gone on so long that it's interfering with our closeness. What needs to happen to improve the situation?*"

Many people with low desire "go through the motions" but feel inadequate that they cannot be more enthusiastic. Then they avoid sex, at least in part, to avoid feelings of inadequacy. Once you and your partner have an opportunity to make love, show enthusiasm for his or her willingness to get close and be less concerned about the degree of passion.

- "I love being close with you like this. You mean everything to me."
- "This was wonderful. I was looking forward to it all day."
- "I promise I won't presume that everything is fine now. I won't expect more sex. But I hope we can have some affectionate time together at least."

The one with low desire often avoids the topic of sex. That's a mistake. While it isn't easy, that person should try to initiate a discussion about his or her desire difficulties:

- "I really want to feel more sexual. I just don't and I can't explain why. I do love you."
- "I haven't lost my attraction to you. But I've lost my desire. I don't think about sex, I don't fantasize. I really want to feel differently."
- "I know that part of the problem is that I avoid affection for fear you will interpret it as an invitation to have sex. How about we try to show a lot more affection for awhile without it leading to sex?"

Let's Talk

Let's Talk—No, Let's Go for a Fast Walk!

Research suggests that 20 minutes of intense aerobic exercise can improve physiological sexual arousal in women with low desire. In one study, groups of women with low desire were placed into one of two groups. The first group watched a short, uninteresting movie followed by an erotic film. The second group engaged in 20 minutes of exercise before they viewed the erotic movie. Vaginal blood volume (which is an indication of sexual arousal) was significantly elevated in women who exercised prior to watching the erotic film. Interestingly, these women were not subjectively aware of being aroused.

Knowing that they can indeed become sexually aroused may help some women with low desire. Physical exercise may be one element to improve sexual functioning.

How Not to Say It

- "How do you think it makes me feel when you don't want sex?" (Your partner already knows she has lost interest in sex and she feels lousy about that. If you approach your partner with criticism or harshness, make an in-flight repair. "I'm sorry. I shouldn't have spoken to you that way. I guess I'm just worried that you don't care about me and I miss making love. Can we talk about this?")

- "Snap out of it." (Most people want to have a healthy interest in sex. If they could snap out of it, they would.)

- "Is this what I have to look forward to the rest of my life?" (Your frustration is understandable. But this kind of arguing won't get you what you want.)

- "There's something wrong with you." (There is something wrong, yes. It might be medical or personal or interpersonal. The tone here is accusatory, however, and not conducive to sexual passion. *Better:* "If there is something wrong with you or with our relationship, I want to fix it. I love you. Let's figure out what's wrong.")

- "Just have sex anyway." (*Better:* "I'm hoping if you go along with sex you won't find it so unappealing, even if it isn't all that exciting.")

How to Playfully and Lovingly Turn Down Sex

38

Eli crawls into bed and wonders if his wife, Peggy, would be interested in lovemaking. He knows it has been a long day for each of them and Peggy is tired—still he is in the mood.

He feels awkward about asking her outright. He prefers instead to simply caress her and hope she will get the message.

When Peggy climbs in next to him, she can tell that Eli wants sex. His pattern is familiar. She knows she won't have sex that night but she feels awkward telling him no. It seems a bit callous. Instead, she prefers to act nonresponsive and hopes he will get the message.

Eli gives up after 10 minutes. But he has a difficult time falling asleep. Is she attracted to him? Is sex still interesting to her? Is he doomed to having sex less often than he'd prefer? Is he overreacting?

Have You Heard?

~ A partner typically assents to having sex using nonverbal means. That makes things complicated when one wants to turn down sex without being open and direct. The lack of a clearly stated "Not tonight, sweetheart" can therefore be misinterpreted as a sign of possible interest.

~ The desire to spare a partner's feelings often makes it hard to speak openly about not wanting sex. Ironically, that lack of openness can cause a partner to overanalyze and misinterpret a partner's nonresponsiveness as lack of caring.

~ Fatigue is the number-one reason for not being in the mood. Don't automatically take it personally if your partner would rather relax than make love.

~> Married sex is far and away the most satisfying, according to research. However, married couples (especially when they have young children) must often make do with less than optimal conditions. If the frequency of lovemaking is declining due to fatigue and little time alone together, a couple can still communicate their sexual passion in other ways. Shows of nonsexual affection (especially by the man) increase sexual desire in the woman. Sexual affection (playful grabs) can be fun, as are "quickies" or peeking into the shower. Such actions convey the attitude "I'm attracted to you" which is always important.

How to Say It

If your relationship is very satisfying, you can sometimes get away with vague and indirect messages that say "No thanks" to sex. Your partner is not likely to take it as rejection. However, a clear statement is best. If the two of you have been disconnected lately, perhaps overworked and preoccupied with other matters, or if there has been some recent arguments or disagreements, any unclear nonverbal message may get misinterpreted. Your best bet is to be open and direct but once in a while make some playful, sexual gesture that shows you find your partner appealing even if the time is not right for sex.

- (After giving a passionate kiss) "I love you so much. I'm simply too tired. Please understand."
- (After a playful grab) "I love you but I'm not in the mood right now. Would you mind if we waited?"
- "You really turn me on but I've simply got too much on my mind."
- "I'd really like to make love but I'm just not in the mood. How about tomorrow night?" (*Important:* If you suggest an alternate time, make sure you follow through. Don't wait for your partner to initiate. Take the lead and show enthusiasm.)
- "I know it has been awhile since we've made love. Tonight just isn't a good time. Let's make a date for this weekend, okay?"
- "I'd love to have sex but I'm too tired. Would you mind giving me a full body massage instead? You'll have to control yourself, lover boy. Do you think you can do that?"
- "I'm really tired. Can you be satisfied with five minutes of kissing and groping? We can finish it up tomorrow."

- "I fantasize about us making love during the day but by the time we go to bed I'm too tired (not in the mood, preoccupied, and so on). Can we find some time earlier in the evening once in a while?"

How Not to Say It

- "Is sex all you ever think about?" (If you've been turning down sex recently, then that *is* all your partner might be thinking about. That comment suggests that you are irritated with your partner, perhaps about nonsexual matters. Or, you feel guilty for not being in the mood and criticize your partner instead. *Better:* "I want to have sex with you but I'm upset about some things. Can we clear them up?")
- "Can't you see that I'm exhausted?" (You are expecting your partner to read between the lines. That isn't always easy to do. Besides, you have probably had sex before when you were exhausted so your partner may not be getting a clear message unless you speak up.)
- Say nothing. Instead you just lie there and hope he gets the message. (You are better off giving him or her a kiss and showing affection, then gently saying that tonight isn't a good night for sex.)
- "Sex with you is not all that exciting." (If that is how you feel, the time to say that is when you and your partner can discuss it more fully. It is also a harsh comment that your partner will not soon forget. If sex is not exciting, you have an obligation to tell your partner what turns you on and to do so in a way that shows enthusiasm, not criticism. *Better:* "I think we're in a sexual rut. I love you and miss some of the passion we used to have. What could I do that would make sex more exciting for you?")

If you want sex but are unsure that your partner does, a more open and direct comment may be less frustrating than giving him or her nonverbal signals. If you know your partner may have reasons to be uninterested, you can acknowledge those reasons.

How to Say It

- "I know it's late, but would you like to make love?"
- "I'd really like to make love tonight. But I know you are tired. I can wait. What do you think?"

- "I'm in the mood. If you're not, would you mind if I rubbed your back for awhile? I promise I won't get carried away."
- Plan ahead. "We haven't made love in awhile. Could we plan on tonight?"
- "I've been fantasizing all day about making love with you. Any chance we could find the time?"

How Not to Say It

- "I don't care how tired you are. It's been days." (If you can say this playfully and with humor, and if you can stop pursuing if your partner clearly is not interested, this approach might change the mood. If you say this line with no concern for your partner's feelings, your selfishness is probably a huge problem in your relationship.)
- "You don't care about me." (If you are feeling rejected, don't make a blanket accusation. Besides, if you act like a victim and your partner gives in, will you really be satisfied? Probably not. *Better:* "It's hard for me not to take this personally. Is something wrong?" If the answer is no, inquire about when would be a good time to make love.)
- "What's wrong with you?" (Don't accuse.)

How to Say It to Yourself

- "If she's not in the mood, I'll tell her that I miss making love. I'll find out if we can plan on some other time."
- "If she's not in the mood, I'll suggest I rub her back. I'll tell her I won't take it any further than that but I just want to have a physical connection."
- "If I think she's avoiding me, I'll tell her that I'd like her to initiate sex more often."
- "It's not good to avoid sex that often, even if there are legitimate reasons. As a couple we need to have that time together. Maybe I can talk to him about how to improve the situation."
- "Saying yes to sex when I'm not in the mood isn't being a phony. It's perfectly okay to have sex more for my partner's benefit than mine. It's a way to show love. But in order to say yes when I'm not in the mood, I have to be sure I can freely say no on occasion, too."

- "The best way to have a satisfying love life is to discuss our preferences and cooperate. Giving him nonverbal signals isn't fair."

How Not to Say It to Yourself

The following comments to yourself suggest that relationship problems exist or you and your partner are in a subtle tug of war over sex:

- "She'd better be in the mood tonight."
- "She's taking a long time in the bathroom. She's avoiding me like she usually does."
- "I'll just ignore her when she comes to bed. Then she can see how it feels to be rejected."
- "I know he'll want sex later on. Maybe if I find an interesting movie to watch he'll take the hint that I'm not in the mood."
- "Saying yes to sex when I'm not in the mood is being phony."
- "If I say yes to sex tonight, he'll expect to have it more often."

Discussing Sexual History and Safe Sex

Sheryl and Rick have been dating for three months. Sheryl really likes Rick. She has dated many men but no one seemed to affect her the way he does. She knows quite a bit about his background, his interests, his future goals and dreams. And she knows he was engaged two years earlier, although that relationship ended before the wedding plans got very far. She presumes he'd had sex with his fiancée. She also presumes he'd had sex with other women. Just how many she could only guess.

She also knows that at some point their relationship will turn sexual. The smart thing to do is to ask him some blunt questions. Has he had unprotected sex? Did he ever have a sexually transmitted disease? Did he ever get a girl pregnant?

The idea of asking those questions makes her shudder. How embarrassing! How unromantic! Then she realizes that he is well educated. Wouldn't a smart guy like Rick have taken all the right precautions?

Have You Heard?

~ In a study of 600 unmarried adults ranging in age from 20 to 69, those people with the most formal education had a higher risk of contracting AIDS than did less educated people. Increased education led to more liberal attitudes about sex, which led to greater sexual promiscuity.

~ One in six Americans have had a sexually transmitted disease at some point in their lives. The number of STDs contracted in a given year by women is equal to the number of women who get pregnant.

~ Women are more likely to have had a sexual disease in their lives than men. That is because it is easier for a man to infect a woman than it is for a woman to infect a man.

~ The best predictor that you will contract a sexual disease is having had many sex partners (and an infrequent use of condoms). A man with two to four lifetime sex partners has about a 3-percent chance of contracting a bacterial or viral sexual disease. A woman with two to four partners has a 5-percent chance. The odds rise to approximately 30 percent if there were 20 sexual partners. Unlike bacterial diseases, viral diseases cannot be cured.

~ One study showed that a person who has had three sexual partners in a year is extremely likely (67 percent) to have had a one-night stand—which automatically carries a higher risk of contracting a sexual disease.

~ Single people who want to have sex will use deceptive means to attain that goal. The most common lie is "I love you . . . I care so much about you . . . " College males frequently express such a sentiment when they want sex.

~ On average, the number of *reported* sexual partners over one's lifetime is 10.5 for men and 3.3 for women. (But who are these men having all the sex with if not women?) The likelihood is that men overstate the number of sex partners to researchers while women understate their number of partners.

~ Dating partners in college often inquire about a partner's past sexual history. But the reason for their questions is more to assess if their date has the potential for a lasting relationship (the more previous partners, the less likely this relationship will last) than to assess disease risk.

~ In one study of women on a college campus, 38 percent reported having had one to four incidents of a sexually transmitted disease (chlamydia), 21 percent reported two or more sex partners in the past six months, 12 percent used condoms, and only 31 percent discussed their own or their partner's sexual history before having sex.

~ History of drug abuse is associated with a history of promiscuity for either sex.

~ Low attachment to one's parents is associated with increased promiscuity.

~ Unprotected sex is more likely when alcohol has been ingested.

How to Say It

This conversation should not happen in the middle of a passionate encounter. It should be discussed in a nonsexual context. The ideal time is when you are aware that your relationship may soon become sexual. The problem with any discussion you may have is knowing what to believe. People will lie about their sexual history if they are embarrassed or fear that you will be turned off. Still, not having the conversation is risky. Be very careful about who you have sex with, keep that number to a minimum, and use a condom. (Condom use does not guarantee safe sex but "safer" sex. The safest sex is abstinence.)

- "This is not an easy topic, but it's important to me that we discuss our sexual histories. Do you agree?" (If the answer is no, say no to sex.)
- "You mean a lot to me. Before our relationship goes any further, I need to find out more about your sexual history."
- "I'm falling in love with you. This is embarrassing and a little scary to bring up, but you should know that I do have herpes. I take medication which controls the outbreaks, but unprotected sex carries a risk."
- "I really want to make love with you someday. But I'm scared about the risk of disease. Would you be willing to have a blood test?"
- "I can understand your concerns. If it will make you feel better, I'd be happy to get tested. I don't want you to have to worry."
- "You mentioned that you and your ex-wife had a lousy love life. Maybe this seems a bit personal but I'd like to know what made it lousy for you. If possible, I don't want us to make the same mistakes."
- "What's the most number of people you've had sex with in any year?" (This answer is revealing. People who have sex with many partners are probably having sex with people who have also had many partners. The risk of infection rises.)
- "No condom, no sex."
- "I don't want to have sex until I get married. Can you live with that?" (Couples who delay sex until marriage have the most successful marriages.)

How Not to Say It

- "We've been dating so long I think I know you very well. You don't have to tell me any details. I trust you." (In today's world, that's naive.)
- "You don't have to tell me your history. You're entitled to privacy. We'll just use a condom." (Will you always use a condom with this person? If not, have a more serious discussion.)

- "Before we have sex, is there anything about you I should know?" (That's a bit weak. You sound more interested in having sex than in taking reasonable precautions. Good luck. You'll need it.)

- "If this is making you uncomfortable, we can talk about it some other time." (Talk about it now. Delaying the conversation may mean you'll never have it.)

Mismatched Desire

40

Gil and Karen have been happily married for ten years and have two children. They bought a house about six years ago. They are like the average couple in most ways. Their incomes are moderate, their savings account is low, and they eat out about once a week. And, oh yes, when it comes to sex, Gil would like to have it more often than Karen does.

Karen enjoys having sex. Gil would readily admit that Karen participates with enthusiasm and imagination. Except she could get by with having sex two or three times a month. Gil prefers two or three times a week. Their mismatched desire has led to a number of mild rifts, although they don't stay angry for long. But occasionally things get more tense than they'd like. Gil will push harder for sex and Karen will resist. He'll think she's being cold and stubborn; she'll think he's being selfish and demanding. Sometimes Karen uses humor. "Take a cold shower," she'll say with a smile.

Gil never laughs at that remark.

Have You Heard?

∿ Mismatched desire is the most common sexual complaint.

∿ Mismatched desire does not mean one partner has very low desire. Each could have normal desire but one may desire sex much more frequently than his or her partner.

∿ In a study of 100 educated couples, average age 33, 50 percent of the men and 77 percent of the women reported occasional lack of interest in sex. It is common for partners not to be in perfect sync when it comes to sexual desire.

~ About 37 percent of couples have sex a few times a month. One-quarter of couples have sex two or three times a week. About 16 percent have sex a few times a year.

~ Despite popular myths about being young and single, about 36 percent of men ages 18 to 24 either had no sex at all in the past year or had sex only a few times.

~ Married couples report the most satisfying sex. Even when the frequency is less than desirable (frequency of having sex does decline with age), couples report that having sex makes them feel cared for and loved.

~ For women over 40, engaging in acts of "sexual abandon" with their partner makes them feel more attractive.

~ The partner who is more interested in sex may underestimate how much his or her partner enjoys sex. A man can tap into his wife's sexual energy, for example, if he shows more affection, consideration, and talks to her more often.

How to Say It

If you prefer having sex more (or less) often than your partner, and this difference has held up over the years, it is unlikely the two of you will get in sync. This problem intensifies when you each try to force one another (through verbal persuasion, anger, pouting, emotional withdrawal, and so on) to match your level of desire. Making your partner "wrong" to feel the way he or she does won't help.

To improve the situation, focus on achieving three goals:

1. Discover what environmental or relationship factors (fatigue, overwork, lack of romance, insufficient thoughtfulness or kindness, and so on) might be contributing to mismatched desire and make adjustments where possible.

2. Give in graciously once in awhile. Have sex when you don't necessarily feel like it (have a "quickie"; take a shower together) or go along with not having sex when you want it (maybe cuddling or shows of affection would be an acceptable alternative). Also, learn how to say no to sex without offending your partner. (See Chapter 38.)

3. Accept (not grudgingly) that a difference in desire will always exist to some degree. If you can learn to talk about this difference in a lighthearted manner, the issue will not be toxic or cause unnecessary tension.

Find out your partner's preferences.

- "On average, how often would you like to make love?"
- "On average, how often would you like to get sexual without it necessarily turning into intercourse?"
- "On average, how many shows of affection per day would seem about right? . . . If we were affectionate about three times a day (kissing, hugging, stroking, and so on), would that be too infrequent or about right?" (If the amount of affection you typically offer is less than desirable, increasing affection may increase the frequency of sex.)

If you prefer sex less often, make sure you initiate sex once in awhile. If your partner knows he or she can count on that, he or she will probably be able to pursue sex less often.

- "I know we made love already this weekend, but I'm eager to do it again. Pick the place and time."
- "I like it when you initiate making love too. It takes the pressure off me and it makes me feel desired."
- "I know I desire sex less often than you do. But I desire more romance. You seem to desire less romance but more sex. Maybe increasing romance will help. Want to give it a try?"
- "If you were to be more romantic, I would want you to . . . "

Use humor or lighthearted comments when it's clear that you are out of sync with one another sexually. Poke fun at yourself if possible.

- "Not tonight? Okay, I'm sure I'll survive. Just barely, but I'll make it. It won't be easy but I'm a real trooper about this . . . "
- "Again? You want sex again? We just had sex last Christmas Eve . . . "
- "Dear, I know it's not my birthday but could we have a romp in the hay?"
- "I'm going to bed to have sex. Care to join me?"

How Not to Say It

- "I'm ready for sex, why not you? What's wrong with you?" (Don't criticize. Mismatched desire is common. *Better:* "I'd love to have sex. Any way I could interest you tonight?" If the answer is no, accept defeat gracefully as often as possible.)

- "Sex is all you ever think about." (A person who is thirsty thinks about getting a drink. Learn the art of a gentle turndown.)

- "If I'd known you'd want sex this frequently (infrequently), I'd have married someone else." (If you're frustrated, don't be mean. *Better:* "I guess I'm just frustrated. But I do love you.")

- "The more you push, the more I'll say no." Or, "The more you keep saying no, the more I'm going to keep asking." (This means you are in a tug of war. What's missing is some empathy and a willingness to go along [good heartedly] with your partner's wishes once in awhile. *Better:* "You keep pushing and I keep saying no. This is frustrating for both of us. I enjoy making love but sometimes I feel pressured and that turns me off. What I'd really like is more affection. I think that would help my desire.")

Fun and Positive
Sexual Coaching

41

Claudia has a few minutes left in bed before she has to get ready for work. She and Matt have just made love, each having awoken only about 10 minutes earlier. She knows that 10 minutes of sex first thing in the morning (when she is usually half-asleep) isn't the greatest. But the problem is that much of their sex life is becoming, well, boring. It is bland, predictable, often done as an afterthought. Is something wrong? Is this what life after 30 is all about? Is this the best she can expect from now on?

She glances up at Matt who is walking toward the bathroom. He doesn't even look at her. His focus is elsewhere. Whatever happened to those lingering after-glow moments? In the past, he'd have glanced her way and raced back to bed—jumping on top of her— just for a minute more of fondling and affection. Not now. She can practically read his mind. He just had sex, now he wants coffee. Good grief! But what is more horrifying is that she can practically taste her first cup of coffee too. In fact, it is much more appealing than sex!

Have You Heard?

~ Sex is *very exciting* for *both* partners about 40 percent of the time.

~ It is very fulfilling for one partner about 30 percent of the time, but somewhat less so for the other partner.

~ About one in five times a couple has sex, one partner is more passive and seems to be participating simply for the sake of the other.

~ Most partners could stand a little coaching. What *seems* to be stimulating may not be, and more stimulating techniques may be inadvertently overlooked.

～ A satisfying sex life does not require elaborate techniques or use of equipment. According to a national survey, the vast majority of couples find tried-and-true intercourse as the most satisfying and most used method. Slightly over 20 percent of people reported participating in oral sex during their last sexual encounter. Still, coaching helps with such details as intensity of caressing or rubbing, speed and number of thrusts, and so on.

～ Couples make sex more interesting using effective but fairly predictable methods: varying the sexual position, use of lotions, making love in unique places, adding romance to the scene (candles, music, a bed and breakfast, and so on), lingering foreplay, and sexy talk.

～ Purposely *not* reaching orgasm during sex can help a couple appreciate other aspects of the sexual experience. Sensual teasing can be tantalizing and exquisitely enjoyable even though orgasm doesn't occur. It teaches a couple to explore new methods and not rely on orgasm as the ultimate sexual outcome.

How to Say It

This topic is best discussed with an optimistic, upbeat attitude. A serious, formal conversation can make the issue seem more dire than it really is.

- "You have to undress me first. Slowly."
- "Anywhere but the bedroom . . . "
- "I'm in the mood for something a little different . . . "
- "What would you like me to do? Just name it . . . "
- "I think I'm in a sexual rut. Let's plan something a bit different for next time."
- "Sometime this weekend I want to make love outdoors! We'll have to find the right time and place. After all, we don't want to get arrested!"
- "Sex, yes. But no intercourse for the next hour. Let's see what else we can do, lover . . . "
- "A little slower (faster). Oh, that's perfect."

If your partner overreacts and takes offense or seems hurt and says things like:

- *"Aren't you happy with our sex life?"*
- *"Am I boring you?"*

- *"I'm not that creative. What's wrong with the same old stuff?"*
- *"You mean I've been doing it wrong all this time?"*

You reply:

- *"Yes, I'm happy. But I think we're in a small rut. Can we finish this conversation naked?"*
- *"No, I'm boring me. I want to spice things up once in awhile. Remember how we couldn't wait to get our hands on each other? A little more playfulness and romance and we'll be back there again."*
- *"I love hot fudge sundaes, but not all the time. You don't have to be creative, at least not now. I'll come up with an idea or two and let's see what happens. Are you game?"*
- *"You've been wonderful. I've just discovered that I like it even more when you do it this way."*

How Not to Say It

- "I shouldn't have to tell you what turns a man (woman) on." (Say that and you'll wound your partner for a long time. Besides, not everybody reacts the same to certain types of stimulation.)
- "We have a serious problem. Our sex life is absolutely boring." (Too harsh and serious. Ease up a little. Better yet, next time you have sex, *show* some innovation instead of talking about it. Your partner will get the message.)
- "Do other couples have as lousy sex as we do?"
- "My ex-wife was more interesting in bed than you are." (I hope you enjoy sleeping on the couch.)

Talking Point: A partner might suggest sexual acts or methods that you find unappealing (use of sex toys) or perhaps disgusting or immoral (anal sex, group sex). Even oral sex, while widely practiced, is something that about a quarter of the population never experiences. You are not wrong for saying no, especially if the act is offensive to you. But you still have an obligation to yourself and your partner to make sex romantic and mutually pleasurable. Find ways to be creative without compromising your values.

Magical Affection

42

"I just wish you would show more affection," Lillian says. "I don't think that's asking for too much!"

"How many times do I have to tell you that I wasn't raised that way," her husband, Ed, says. "Can't you just accept that?"

"No, I can't." You used to show more affection. I'm not asking for the world. Why is it that you manage to grab my breasts every morning before you leave for work but you can't put your arm around me and hug me goodbye?"

"Okay, I won't touch you at all if that's what you want."

"That's not what I meant and you know it. I just want more affection and tenderness. Why is that so impossible?"

"Because that's the way I am. Period. I don't know what else to say."

Lillian and Ed have a problem many couples share. Mismatched desire for affection is almost as common as mismatched desire for sex. The wrong approach is to stubbornly resist any influence from your partner. Give and take is required.

Have You Heard?

~ Feeling cherished is perhaps the most important attitude a couple can create for one another. Affection (especially nonsexual) is an important and magical component of cherishing.

~ Relationships die less from conflict than from failure to meet emotional needs. Inadequate shows of affection can corrode a couple's commitment.

∽ People who aren't touched enough by others are lonelier for it.

∽ Women usually require more affection and tenderness to feel sexual.

∽ Men who show less (nonsexual) affection probably will get less sex. Desiring more sex, these men might show more sexual affection. But the sexual affection will not be perceived as loving and tender but as self-serving. So the woman will further withhold sex.

∽ Couples with the happiest and most playful sex lives show the most affection.

How to Say It

- "I feel disconnected from you during the day if we don't have a chance to hug and kiss in the morning. Let's make sure we find the time for that."
- "It means so much to me when we cuddle. I miss it when it's not there."
- "Let's make a goal: We'll each hug or kiss each other at least four times during the day. Deal?"
- "Let's try to hold hands in the mall, at least part of the time. I love doing that."
- "I know you feel uncomfortable showing affection in public. I'll be tolerant of that if you would show more affection at home."
- "The more you hold me like this, the more I fantasize during the day about making love to you."

If your partner responds:

- "*You're asking me to do something unnatural. I wasn't raised that way.*"
- "*Why don't you appreciate all the other ways I show my love for you?*"
- "*You're asking me to be phony. I can't act like that.*"

You respond:

- "*I understand you weren't raised to show affection and I understand it doesn't come easily for you. But I'm telling you that I don't just want affection, I require it. I'll have to accept less affection from you than I'd like, but to be fair you'll need to give more affection than you'd like.*"

- *"I do appreciate the other things you do. Maybe I should show more appreciation. But that doesn't change the fact that I really need more affection. We need to find a way to make this work better."*
- *"I'm asking you to give me something I need."*

If this conversation starts to escalate into an argument or break down into a frustrating standoff, remember the GIFTS. Speak gently, make in-flight repairs, find hidden issues, be a team instead of adversaries, and make supportive comments that include some giving in. Verbal persuasion, punitive measures, or one-sided submission will not resolve this issue if it has been a major difference between you over the years.

- "We're starting to go in circles. I don't want to do that. What could I say or do that would make it easier for us to find some middle ground?"
- "All I know is that unless we find some middle ground, one or both of us will routinely be unhappy about this issue. I'm willing to compromise. Can you?"
- "I can be more open to sexual affection. That can be fun. But you need to be more willing to show (and receive) nonsexual affection."
- "I agree with you that you need more affection. I guess I'm concerned that if I give it more often, you'll want more and more."
- "I agree that giving affection is not your way. But I'm afraid that if I simply tolerate it I'll grow lonely and disconnected from you. What I'm asking for is a few displays of affection a day. That's all."

How Not to Say It

- "I'm not going to change. You'll have to accept my way on this." (It is essential for marital satisfaction that partners accept influence from each other. Stubbornness—especially by the man—has been shown to predict relationship decline. *Better:* "Okay. I'll work with you on this, but bear with me. It's not my nature to do this.")
- "It's about time. Why can't you hug me like that more often?" (*Better:* "That was great. Just the way I wanted it.")
- "Why did you marry me when you knew I wasn't that affectionate?" (Showing affection is a small act with huge payoffs. Work at making affection a normal part of your relationship.)

Romantic Sex During Pregnancy

43

Maria is in her eighth month of her first pregnancy. She is feeling as large as a house and eager to give birth. She is at the stage where no sleeping position is comfortable. Her husband, Kent, is supportive. He always asks what he can do to help and seems patient that their sex life is not nearly as frequent as their pre-pregnancy days. But she has hidden concerns. Does he really find her all that attractive? Will she ever get her old figure back? She tries to remember Kent's comments the last time they made love. He'd said with a smile that it was like making love to a whole different woman given that her breasts had ballooned "from the size of peaches to the size of grapefruits." Was that supposed to make her feel good?

Have You Heard?

~ Frequency of sexual intercourse changes during pregnancy. On average, women show a slight decline in interest during the first trimester and a sharp decline during the last trimester.

~ About 90 percent of couples still have intercourse during the fifth month of pregnancy. The second trimester is a time when most couples are happier and less anxious about the pregnancy.

~ The average couple resumes sexual relations about two months postpartum. Women who breastfeed are likely to have less interest in sex for many months after giving birth.

~ Sexual intercourse during pregnancy does not harm the developing fetus.

~ Physical affection is important during pregnancy especially since sexual activity will probably decline somewhat.

How to Say It

Now is the time to discuss questions or concerns that might pop up. It is also a good time to remind each other of the devotion you have.

- "I can't wait to be a parent. I'm sure you'll be a wonderful parent, too."
- "You're still gorgeous!"
- "I'm glad you like my new breasts. But remember, you'll have to share them soon."
- "Even though we're not having sex so often, let's make sure we have time every day just to lie down together."
- "What excites you most about becoming a parent?"
- "I think I need to hear some reassurances that you still think I'm attractive."
- "I guess it feels a little strange making love to a pregnant woman."
- "If you're not in the mood for sex but I am, what would you like me to do?"
- "It's okay if you're not in the mood. How about I rub your back instead?"
- "You're going to be a great mom (dad)."
- "I've been looking forward all day to our romantic evening."

How Not to Say It

- "I'll be glad when you can lose weight and get your old figure back." (Try to enjoy your wife's new body and appreciate that her physical changes are for the sole purpose of bringing a new life into the world—your child. *Better:* "I love you just the way you are. But if I gain forty pounds, you have to love me just the same as you do now. Deal?"
- "You don't want to have sex? Is this what I have to look forward to now that you're pregnant?" (Hormonal fluctuations during pregnancy can wreak havoc with sexual desire. Now is the time to be Mr. Understanding. *Better:* "I'd really like to make love right now. If you're not in the mood, we can do something else. Would you like a massage instead?")
- "I can't help how I feel. I'm hormonal. Just get used to it." (Try to show a bit more understanding. Also, you are teaching him to stop taking any initiative as he'll wait to get a signal from you on how to behave. That can lead to misunderstandings. *Better:* "I'm hormonal and my desires and moods really fluctuate. Thanks for being patient and understanding. Despite my moods, I really need you to be tender and affectionate.")

When You Don't Want the Relationship to Become Sexual—Yet

Emily and Les have been dating for six months. Les is divorced. His first marriage lasted a few years and had been considered a mistake from practically the beginning. Now he seems to have his life in order as a high school math teacher. Emily sells real estate. She is particular about the man of her dreams. She tends to end relationships fairly soon when she realizes that the man she is dating will not become her permanent partner. Emily is impressed with Les right from the start. Within a few months she has fallen in love. The only divisive issue is sex. She wants to wait—perhaps until her wedding day—or at least until they are engaged and well on their way toward an unbreakable commitment. Les understands, or so he says, but makes occasional lighthearted comments about her refusal to have sex. The comments have a slight edge to them. Emily knows he is frustrated but she feels strongly about her beliefs.

Have You Heard?

～ If you wish to delay having sex, be very clear what you mean by that. Is anything other than intercourse acceptable? If you think heavy petting is allowable but intercourse is not, your partner may misinterpret your actions as an invitation to have sex unless your statements leave no room for doubt.

～ According to a scientific survey, delaying sex for *at least a year* in a relationship gives you the best odds of future marriage. Fifty-five percent of couples who eventually married waited a year or more before having sex—"reflecting in part the choice among many couples to abstain from sex until marriage"; only 10 percent of couples who had sex within the first month of dating ended up married.

~ The reverse is true for cohabiting couples. About 36 percent had sex within a month of living together and after a year or more all but 16 percent had sex.

~ The divorce rate for cohabiting couples who eventually married was nearly twice that of non-cohabiting couples who married. The divorce rate when at least one partner was a virgin at the time of marriage was *less than half* the average divorce rate for couples who were not virgins at the time of the wedding.

~ In a study about men's attitudes, a "quality" relationship involved honesty and delaying sexual relations. "Quantity" relationships involved tactics where men used direct threats or psychological pressure to get their partners to have sex earlier in the relationship. (Does your man think of you as "quality" or "quantity"?)

~ In a survey of female college students, those who lost their virginity during their college years had intercourse the first time because they either felt they were in love or they felt psychologically pressured. Looking back, a majority of the women surveyed regretted losing their virginity when they did.

~ When 700 university students were given various descriptions of fictitious people, those people whose sexual activity was described as "low" were rated as most desirable as friends or marriage partners. People described as moderately or highly sexually active were desired as dates, but not as friends or potential marriage partners.

How to Say It

If you wish to delay sex but have some misgivings, don't wait until a passionate moment occurs before you state your views. You may get swept away by the moment. Better to have a discussion when reason is stronger than emotion.

- "I'm very attracted to you but I want to wait before we have a sexual relationship."
- "You are very important to me and I love you. But I firmly believe it is best that I wait before becoming sexual with you."
- "It's important to me that we not have sex until we are clearly committed to one another."
- "We've only known each other for _____. It's much too soon for me to have sex."

If your friend says:

- *"But we love each other."*
- *"You're being old-fashioned."*
- *"I've waited long enough."*

You reply:

- *"Yes, we do love each other. But that's not a good enough reason to make love. When we are fully committed to one another, we can have this discussion again."*
- *"I'm telling you what my values are. They are very important to me. I think if you love me, you can be patient."*
- *"You'll have to wait longer. If that is a problem for you, maybe we should rethink our relationship."*

If you have had sex with your friend but believe you made a mistake and you want to wait before you have sex again, say (during a nonpassionate moment):

- "Even though I care about you and find you attractive, making love has pushed our relationship along too fast. I want us to get to know each other a lot better before we have sex again."
- "I made a mistake and I don't want to repeat it. Are you willing to help me with that?"
- "I'm asking you not to make any sexual advances until I tell you clearly that I am ready. Don't mistake heavy kissing or petting for wanting to have sex."
- "If you insist on pressuring me to have sex, I won't see you anymore. I feel that strongly about it."

How Not to Say It

Don't use tentative words. Be clear and firm.

- "I'm really dying to have sex with you but we should probably wait. What do you think?"
- "I don't think it's a good idea." (That comment invites a debate. If you don't want a debate, be clearer. *Better:* "I'm not going to have sex with you. Sorry.")

- "We better not have sex. You might feel differently about me if we do." (If your friend wants to have sex, he will assure you that his feelings for you will never change. Don't define reasons why he shouldn't have sex. State reasons why you won't have sex. *Better:* "It's not the right time for me in this relationship. I'm going to wait.")

Erectile Problems

45

Rudy has experienced erectile difficulties for the past month. It took him by surprise the first time it happened. He tried to laugh it off but in fact it bothered him. When he and his wife began making love a few days later, he was unable to stay aroused. Now he is very worried.

His wife, Linda, asks if he'd been under any extra stress recently.

"No," Rudy says, "everything is the same as usual."

"Well, there must be a reason," Linda persists.

"If there is I have no idea what it could be," Rudy replies. Now he is annoyed. He really doesn't want to discuss it. Linda senses that and tries to be reassuring.

"It's nothing to worry about. Let's just cuddle for awhile."

Rudy gets out of bed. "I'm not in the mood," he says.

Have You Heard?

〜 About 10 percent of men report having had severe erectile difficulties in the past year. Up to 25 percent have milder difficulties.

〜 There are many possible causes of erection problems. Heart disease, diabetes, a low amount of HDL ("good" cholesterol), hypertension, and other medical conditions may be a factor. Medications for those conditions and other physical disorders can also contribute to the problem. Stress or anxious preoccupations can distract a man from the sexual encounter and cause changes in arousal.

〜 If a man has no history of arousal problems, any current difficulty in that area may be due to stress. Unresolved relationship issues could be lurking, but not necessarily. The parasympathetic nervous system—which is in charge of sexual arousal—shuts down when a person is stressed or anxious.

↷ The initial cause for an erection problem may not be what is maintaining the problem. Worries about sexual performance can make a man unable to relax during sex and therefore be unable to get an erection, even if the initial cause is no longer relevant.

↷ Many men falsely believe that if they do not maintain their arousal for the duration of a sexual encounter, then a problem exists. In fact, men who are very comfortable with their partners, who participate in longer lovemaking sessions, and who take time to focus on sensual foreplay instead of intercourse may not stay aroused at all times. Intimate moments that are tender but not passionate may cause a normal fluctuation in arousal.

↷ If the female partner has an enthusiastic attitude toward nonintercourse forms of sexual stimulation, a man with erectile problems may feel less pressure to have an erection. His anxiety thus reduced, his ability to get and maintain an erection can improve.

↷ Among older men, more active and direct stimulation of the penis by his partner may be necessary to improve arousal. While some changes in arousal occur in older men, erectile problems severe enough to be called a "disorder" are not inevitable and are not considered to be a typical part of the aging process.

↷ Couples with very good communication skills seem to have improved outcome in treatment of arousal problems compared with couples with poorer communication skills.

↷ It is premature (and often a mistake) for any person to conclude that erectile difficulties must automatically be a sign of disinterest in one's partner.

How to Say It

A man who is experiencing arousal difficulties for the first time—and who is troubled by it—is usually focusing too much on the questions "Will it happen again? and How am I doing now?" Such self-scrutiny only adds to the anxiety and serves as a distraction to the sexual experience, possibly helping to create a self-fulfilling prophecy. The female partner should not ask questions of concern that only serve to spotlight a man's worries. The best attitude for the woman is one of delight in being with her partner and of being excited about the man's ability to stimulate her regardless of his degree of arousal.

- "What I'd really love for you to do right now is take your hand and ... "
- "I'm really in the mood for a full body massage that lasts at least twenty minutes. I love it when you give me massages."
- "You can be worried if you want to but I also get turned on by you when we can just be playful."
- "Take whatever time you want to deal with your concern. I'm yours for life."
- "There are many ways you turn me on during sex. Intercourse is just one way. Let me show you the other ways."
- "I'm still going to give you hugs and kisses during the day because I love feeling you next to me."

If the man seems to avoid sex so as to avoid feeling embarrassed by his difficulty getting an erection, say:

- "We don't have to have intercourse. But I want you next to me. I can fall happily asleep just feeling your body and you feeling mine."
- "Guess what, lover? Avoiding sex will probably just make you more worried. I don't give a darn about your erection right now. I just want you next to me. Your fingers have always turned me on."
- "I've watched you get undressed hundreds of times and your relaxed body turns me on. I've peeked at you in the shower or as you step out of the shower. I love the way you look with and without an erection."

If the man does discuss things that may be bothering him about his life—such as job stress, frustration over job performance or income, fatigue, and so on— give brief, reassuring comments that show you care. Don't suggest solutions to his problems.

- "I can understand why that problem at work is upsetting. I'm sure you'll figure out what to do. What ideas have you had so far?"
- "You work so hard. No wonder you're exhausted."
- "Money is tight, yes. But you work hard and are dedicated to providing for your family. That's one reason I love you so much."

- "I have faith that you'll find a way to deal with the things that stress you out. I have confidence in you."

How Not to Say It

- "This is obviously a problem. I think you should talk to me about it." (He worries about what you think. The more concerned you seem to be, the more concerned he'll get—and that will aggravate his difficulty. *Better:* "If you want to discuss it, you can. But I'm not worried.")
- "What's wrong? Is it me?" (Don't take it personally. While relationship issues may be a factor, they often aren't.)
- "Oh, you poor thing. This must be awfully upsetting." (Don't get dramatic. *Better:* "I understand from articles I've read that most men have this happen to them and that it is usually a temporary problem.")

How to Say It to Yourself

Men can worsen the situation by saying unreasonable things to themselves. Such false beliefs must be challenged repeatedly.

- *False Belief:* "If I can't have a perfect erection every time, I'm a failure."
- *Correct Belief:* "It's not at all unusual for a man to have occasional changes in arousal."
- *False Belief:* "My wife can't enjoy sex if I can't get hard."
- *Correct Belief:* "Of course she can enjoy sex. There are many ways I can please her."
- *False Belief:* "She says she doesn't mind but I don't believe her."
- *Correct Belief.* "We disagree on many things so it's possible that she views this situation differently too. Just because it bothers me it doesn't have to bother her. She doesn't like the size of her breasts but I never minded."
- *False Belief:* "If it happened before, it will happen again the next time."
- *Correct Belief:* "Stress and worry can play a part in this. But even if it happened last time, it doesn't have to happen again. My best plan is to enjoy

having relaxing sex and not bother with intercourse. Chances are I'll relax and things will work out better."

- *False Belief:* "If I avoid sex, I don't have to feel so embarrassed."
- *Correct Belief:* "If I avoid sex, I'll never discover that this doesn't have to be a problem and that things can improve. If I avoid sex, then intimacy will diminish between my wife and me. The best thing to do is give and receive lots of affection and take the focus off of intercourse for awhile. There are many ways to sexually please each other."

Let's Talk

If erectile problems persist, a common culprit is the man's own anxiety about having to perform. Fearing failure, he concentrates less on sex and more on the moment-to-moment status of his penis. Not a good idea. A useful technique for many couples is called Sensate Focus. It occurs over many sessions of having sex. The goal is to experience longer, relaxing, sensual pleasures without having intercourse. When the demand for intercourse is removed and many of these sessions occur, a man often shifts his focus from his penis to his partner and normal sexual arousal eventually returns spontaneously.

Briefly, sensate focus can occur in four stages.

- *Stage One:* The couple is naked. The man caresses his partner's body—first her back, then her front—gently for at least half an hour. There is to be no touching of the breast or genitals. She can tell him what feels good and which areas to stroke more lightly or with more pressure. When the man is finished, the woman should now caress him. This stage should take place over several sessions.

- *Stage Two:* The same as stage one except touching of the breasts, nipples, and genitals is allowed. Orgasm is avoided, however.

- *Stage Three:* Same as stage two but now penetration is allowed but no movement or thrusting.

- *Stage Four:* As above, but now intercourse is fully allowed.

Many couples learn to relax and get playful during these exercises, which increases the likelihood that the man will experience spontaneous erections. It is a good idea not to attempt intercourse too soon, despite an unexpected ability to do so.

PMS

46

"Watch out, I'm PMS-ing," Maria says to Kyle.

Kyle knows to take cover. Maria's PMS symptoms tend to be severe. Not only do they make her miserable, but they often make Kyle's life difficult, too. Sometimes Maria will joke about it, but often the issue is serious. Kyle understands the problem intellectually but it annoys him. It especially bothers him that Maria does not seem to have any sympathy for how her irritability affects him. But Maria feels that Kyle doesn't truly understand what she is experiencing. He still expects her to put on a sweet disposition through sheer willpower despite her hormonal rages and cramps that could paralyze a city.

Have You Heard?

~ Premenstrual mood changes had a negative affect on the personal relationships of up to 45 percent of women.

~ Women most likely to suffer from PMS have careers and child-care responsibilities. Women who report fewest symptoms are stay-at-home moms by choice.

~ The higher the PMS distress, the higher the reported marital distress.

~ Many couples have satisfying relationships until the late luteal phase of the woman's cycle (when premenstrual symptoms emerge). Then marital satisfaction dips.

~ Some men discredit their partner's legitimate complaints when they think she is simply PMS-ing.

~ Some women use their PMS symptoms as the excuse they need to make complaints they otherwise would keep quiet about.

How to Say It (Men)

Thoughtfulness and understanding will go a long way toward keeping the relationship on an even keel.

- "Sorry you're not feeling well. What can I do to make your day easier?"
- "How about you take the afternoon off and I'll watch the kids."
- "It must be lousy for you to feel this way."
- "Looks like you have a full schedule tomorrow. Let me do something that will lighten the load."

How Not to Say It (Men)

- "It's not my problem."
- "I know you feel miserable. But why do you have to make everybody else miserable too?" (*Better:* "I know it's hard for you this time of the month. What can I do?")
- "I'm not going to listen to you when you get this way. Talk to me in a few days when you feel better." (She may be more agitated than usual, but the content of her message may be legitimate. *Better:* "It's hard for me to talk to you about this when you're in this mood. Please try to be a bit calmer and I'll try to listen.")
- "I hate it when you get like this." (She does too. *Better:* "This is no fun for either of us. What can I do to help?")

Want to boost marital satisfaction even if PMS symptoms have wreaked havoc with your relationship? There is a simple solution. Make a list of your main bothersome symptoms. Then, each day, you *and your partner* must rate the severity of each symptom. Do this daily for three months.

In a study where this was done, there was a significant increase in marital and sexual satisfaction, problem solving, and empathy. Each partner was more sensitive to the other's perspective. Able to predict when certain days would be difficult, the couples learned to postpone certain disagreements until the PMS symptoms subsided.

How to Say It (Women)

- "I'm starting to have PMS. Bear with me."
- "It would really help me in the next few days if you would . . . "
- "Don't take it personally if I get irritable."
- "Even though I have PMS, the issue I'm complaining about is still legitimate to me."
- "Thanks for being so understanding."

How Not to Say It (Women)

- "It has always bugged me whenever you . . . " (If you have a complaint about a recurrent problem, you're more likely to make headway on that issue when you are not having symptoms. *Better:* "I'm upset with you about this right now. But let's talk about it in a few days when I feel better.")
- "I don't care how *you* feel. How do you think *I* feel?" (Marital discord can increase during PMS days. A little sympathy can soften the hard edges. *Better:* "I guess we both feel rotten about this.")

You Dislike Aspects of Your Partner's Appearance

47

Al thinks his wife, Amy, has put on too much weight. He wants to say something but he doesn't want to hurt her feelings. He's tried to ignore her weight gain—he's put on weight himself the past several years—but the fact remains he just finds her less attractive. Should he tell her?

Phyllis has been living with Tom for two years. He started wearing glasses six months ago. She has hinted that he might consider wearing contact lenses instead. But she hasn't had the heart to tell him that she really dislikes how he looks in glasses. She mentions her concerns to her friends. Some tell her she should be glad she has no other problems in the relationship. But a few tell her that physical attractiveness plays a role in relationship satisfaction. If she's unhappy with his appearance, she should tell him so.

Physical appearance can't be ignored. Whether it's gray hair or no hair at all, plump thighs or love handles, flabby stomachs or bags under the eyes, skin conditions or sagging breasts, our bodies change over time. Many of these changes can be accepted. But what if your partner's appearance is now unappealing?

Have You Heard?

∼ The majority of Americans are dissatisfied in some way with their bodies.

∼ Physical attraction is typically an important quality in the early stages of a relationship. But couples only remain together if they are compatible on psychological factors.

∼ Partners in a highly committed relationship will often rate the appeal of other attractive people as still less appealing than their partners.

Special Considerations

Telling your partner that you dislike something about his or her appearance is tricky. People want to feel that, despite their physical imperfections, at least their partner loves them and finds them appealing. A criticism about one's appearance can burst that bubble and it might be hard to forget. Perhaps the most important factors when considering whether or not to make a comment about appearance are these:

1. *How satisfying is the relationship?* The happier the relationship and the more devoted partners are to each other, unflattering comments about one's physical appearance—however troubling to hear—may be handled well.

2. *Is the physical feature easily changed?* If so, a criticism will probably be viewed as inoffensive. Features such as hair color, clothing style, and facial hair can be changed with little fanfare. However, one's weight is not necessarily easy to change. Even if a spouse is able to lose weight, keeping weight off is difficult. (Studies show that 95 percent of weight loss is eventually regained within five years.) Similarly, a man's baldness or hair loss could be corrected surgically or with a hair replacement system, but such procedures are costly and may be impractical. Wrinkles, scars, certain skin conditions, and so on can be modified but are unlikely to be eradicated. Criticizing such things puts a partner in a helpless position.

Guidelines

Given the above two considerations, there are four possible situations that might occur:

1. *Satisfying relationship/physical appearance easily changed.* Here it is fine to comment on your partner's appearance. Of course, a gentle approach is always advisable.

2. *Satisfying relationship/physical appearance difficult to change.* Learning to accept these changes is the better alternative. If you know that your partner is displeased with those aspects of him- or herself, you can offer encouragement if attempts are made to correct those aspects. For example, say, "Hey, you've lost three pounds this week. Good for you! Your exercising is paying off."

3. *Unsatisfying relationship/physical appearance easily changed.* Making comments under these conditions could work to your advantage or could blow up in your face. A gentle, encouraging comment such as "You really look particularly attractive when you color the gray in your hair" might be interpreted favorably. However, partners unhappy with their relationship are notorious for interpreting positive comments in a negative light. Caution is required.

4. *Unsatisfying relationship/physical appearance difficult to change.* Don't say a word. You will only make your relationship worse.

How to Say It

Keep in mind the GIFTS. In particular, use a gentle approach, make supportive comments, and be ready to make any in-flight repairs that may be necessary.

Satisfying Relationship/Physical Appearance Easily Changed

- "I know you like that hairstyle but it isn't one of my favorites. I find you most attractive with your previous style."
- "I don't think that outfit does you any justice."
- "I know you like that mustache but I prefer you clean shaven. Your mustache tickles my face."
- "I guess I prefer you with longer hair. Would you mind growing it out?"

Satisfying Relationship/Physical Appearance Difficult to Change

- "I've noticed that your clothes are getting tighter. How about we go on a diet together? I know I should improve my eating habits."
- "Sweetheart, I've been reluctant to bring this up but I've noticed you've put on a lot of extra weight. I guess I'm hoping you've been thinking about a new diet or exercise program."
- "That skin condition seems to be getting worse. Have you thought about talking to a doctor?"

If your partner seems a bit hurt or offended and says things like:

- *"You think I'm fat."*

- *"Don't you think I've noticed already! I can't help how I look! I've tried to fix it but nothing works."*
- *"I suppose you don't find me attractive anymore."*
- *"Who asked you?"*

You respond:

- *"I think you're beautiful and sexy even though I wish you were a bit thinner. But I also think you'd like to lose weight, too."*
- *"I'm sorry. I didn't want to offend you. I love you the way you are. But I still think you might want to make a few changes."*
- *"I find you very attractive. Maybe I'm just resisting the fact that we're both getting older. If you think I'm out of line for bringing this up, I won't speak of it again. But if you'd like some help, I'd be happy to assist."*
- *"You're right. I'm sorry. I was just making an observation and I probably shouldn't have."*

Unsatisfying Relationship/Physical Appearance Easily Changed

- "If you don't mind my saying, I think you look a lot more sexy with a different hair color."
- "Of the two shirts you showed me, I think the blue one brings out the color of your eyes better."
- "You can wear glasses if you like, but I think you look even more attractive with contact lenses."

How Not to Say It

- "You look very old."
- "Everybody will laugh at you looking like that."
- "You'd better wear more frumpy clothes to hide that body."
- "You embarrass me."
- "I don't find you attractive at all when you look like that."
- "Why can't you look like ____?"

- "You've lost your looks."
- "You're not sexy like you used to be."

Talking Point: If your partner wants to lose weight (or gain weight), be a cheerleader. Offer encouragement and try to spend some time perhaps exercising together. Ask about your partner's progress and don't sabotage any diet by encouraging him or her to eat something forbidden.

Any criticism of your partner's physical appearance can sting a little. The hurt will be less if you ordinarily show a lot of caring gestures and loving remarks. Don't forget affection. Someone who is unhappy with his or her body needs affection. If your partner pulls away from affection out of unhappiness, let your partner know you find him or her appealing and that touching and holding him or her is important to you.

Sexual Difficulties When a Medical Problem Exists

48

Carl receives hormonal therapy for prostate cancer. One result is a difficulty in becoming sexually aroused. He and his wife understand the reasons for the problem, but Carl avoids physical intimacy with his wife to avoid his embarrassment.

Helen has severe diabetes. Due to restricted blood flow to the vagina, lubrication has diminished during menopause. Consequently, sexual intercourse becomes uncomfortable. Her choice is to limit sexual contact with her husband.

Fred is taking a popular antidepressant. One side effect for him is difficulty in reaching an orgasm.

Sandra injured her back in a car accident. She suffers chronic low back pain as a result. Her range of motion is also impaired. Her desire for sex is reduced and her enjoyment of sex is also diminished. Her husband understands but he isn't happy.

Have You Heard?

~ Many people with medical conditions are not fully informed about the effects on their sex life. Consequently, reduced functioning may be misinterpreted as willful lack of effort.

~ Reduced sexual functioning due to medical conditions is sometimes worsened by mistaken beliefs. Common mistaken beliefs include:

— Intercourse is the only normal method of sex.
— Orgasm reached through manual or oral manipulation is less effective than through intercourse.
— Sexual activity can worsen a heart condition.

~ When sexual activity must necessarily decrease, shows of tenderness and affection should increase. Otherwise, feelings of closeness can diminish.

~ Sometimes a person with a chronic medical condition acts more helpless or dependent than is necessary. While a partner may necessarily take on a care-taking role to some extent, overuse of that role is not advisable. It can detract from the desire for sexual intimacy.

How to Say It

The goals of the couple when their sexual relationship is impaired by a medical condition are multifold: Educate themselves on what is sexually feasible and what are the acceptable alternatives to their past sexual methods; increase affection; improve communication about sexual desires and concerns; and change their unrealistic or irrational beliefs about sexual functioning.

- "The doctor gave me some information to read about sexual side effects of my treatment. Let's review this together."
- "Let's make a list of questions I can ask my doctor at my next visit."
- "I want to be sexual with you but my desire for sex has changed. Bear with me. We'll figure out a way to make this work for both of us."
- "I've noticed that you'd prefer to avoid sex instead of altering our habits. I want to find different ways to be sexually close to you."
- "It's okay to touch me there. I'll let you know if it gets uncomfortable."
- "I'd prefer it if you didn't try so hard to get me aroused. I get frustrated when it doesn't happen. Let's just caress each other and let what happens happen."
- "Intercourse is nice but there are other things I like, too. Let's focus on them."
- "I feel uncomfortable discussing sex with you, but I know it's for the best."
- "Thanks for telling me how you feel. It's important to me."
- "I know I'm probably avoiding sex with you. I don't want to do that. I just haven't adjusted to the changes we have to make."
- "You're still the sexiest person I know, and the only one I want."

- "I've always found your body massages so satisfying. Let's do that now."
- "I know that your back bothers you (or you're recovering from surgery), but I think you should try to do as much for yourself as you can. I'm willing to help, but you need to be as independent as possible." (In the immediate days or weeks after the onset of an illness or surgery, the ill partner may need a lot of extra care from a partner. However, if the condition becomes chronic, it is in the patient's best interest to function as independently as possible. A partner should not routinely offer help when the person could help him- or herself.)

How Not to Say It

- "If we can't have intercourse, what's the point?" (You may be disheartened, but don't avoid every form of sex. You and your partner need the intimacy and closeness that comes from it.)
- "I don't feel like a man anymore." (Sexual functioning is just one facet of who you are. Inability to enjoy sex or to perform as well as you'd like does not stop you from pleasing your partner and being pleased. Give it time and be open to the possibilities. Your partner misses you.)
- "You could enjoy sex if you tried." (That's not necessarily true. Medical limitations are real. Any psychological factors that may be impairing sexual drive or performance might be alleviated if there is more supportive comments and shows of affection.)
- "We don't have to have sex if you don't want to." (Don't give up. Sexual relations are not done merely for physical satisfaction. It helps maintain emotional closeness. *Better:* "I know you don't want to have sex. But I know we can still be sexual and I want to be sexual with you. Let's give this time and find other ways to enjoy sex with each other.")
- "I'm not interested in sex anymore. Get used to it." (Your frustration can be overcome in time if you realize that sexual connection is important and need not be limited to your preferred methods. *Better:* "I don't feel like having sex but I know it's important for us. Just be patient if my heart isn't in it yet.")

When Life Turns Upside Down: Meaningful Conversation During Adversity

Mary and Jim always wanted to have children. But years of infertility have strained their relationship. Yet it isn't the infertility alone that causes problems, it is their difficulty talking about their situation. Many couples emerge from their deep disappointment about infertility with their relationship enhanced. One factor that can make the crucial difference is their communication skills.

Florence and Ted had a satisfying relationship until chronic and severe rheumatoid arthritis crippled Florence. As Ted is required to be more and more of a caretaker for his wife, his ability to cope with the situation is strengthened by their conversational skills. When stress is chronic and unrelenting, the right words can make the difference between a relationship breakthrough or a relationship breakdown.

Every couple, if they spend enough time together, will eventually experience some sort of personal or family adversity. Death of a loved one, financial loss, and serious illness are among the most common. (Contrary to conventional wisdom, the majority of persons suffering a chronic illness are *under* age 65.) Tragedies and crises almost always affect a couple's relationship: *It* will either strengthen it or weaken it. Illness can affect one's responsibilities as well as one's moods and self-esteem. Since adversity will strike at some point, couples can benefit from knowing which communication strategies are most helpful to their relationship.

Special considerations:

1. When a chronically ill person improves, it is not uncommon for the partner to verbalize more critical comments. Instead of displaying relief, a tired and worried partner may start to vent frustrations (or seek more attention) that were not vented when the partner was more ill.

2. A person with a chronic illness or coping with a permanent loss can vary in his or her ability to function, often from day to day. Thus, the partner's actions that are considered supportive and helpful on one day may be viewed as inadequate or too pampering the next day.

3. Not all support is helpful, regardless of the intent. Some ill partners resent the loss of independence and resist support. Some want assis-

tance but are not given the kind of support they need. The perfect fit of giving and receiving the right kind and amount of support is aided by effective communication and flexible personality styles.

4. During stress, a person's preferred method of coping is intensified. Thus, someone who needs companionship and dialogue will want more of that, but someone who prefers solitude will want more of that. That can put some couples in a no-win situation. But solutions are possible.

Generally, the weaker a relationship, the greater the likelihood that adversity will spur a rise in dissatisfaction. All couples, therefore, must do all they can to have a strong, satisfying relationship. In many ways, a strong relationship is powerful immunity to the negative affects of adversity. Just like a healthy diet and regular exercise can improve a person's resistance to disease and injury, a healthy marriage can be a buffer against the storms of life.

Coping with
Chronic Pain

49

Rob was injured in a construction accident. After surgery and 18 months of unemployment, he is finally placed on disability. Melissa, his wife, has a professional career and two children from her first marriage. Rob is able to look after the 4-year-old during the day while the older child is at school. But Rob suffers from chronic pain and is not able to move around with ease. He can perform a limited number of house chores, such as dusting and pushing a vacuum cleaner, but he is not able to do much bending or any strenuous labor. Melissa is overstressed as a result. She is responsible for the financial welfare of the family as well as most home chores. Adding to her frustration is the fact that Rob is often depressed. He'll sit on the couch when she arrives home and barely participate in family activities.

Have You Heard?

~ About one-third of American adults suffer from chronic pain.

~ People with chronic pain are depressed three times more often than people not in chronic pain. Partners are more likely to become depressed as well.

~ Partners should be educated about the nature of the pain/disability and taught how to respond to a partner's distress. Generally, it is a mistake to be oversolicitous. Persons in pain need to do as much for themselves as possible. Nonverbal pain signals (grimacing, sighing, holding a hand to one's head, use of heating pads, and so on) are best ignored (or attended to infrequently) by the partner. Instead, partners should be responsive when their partner engages in well behaviors such as taking on appropriate responsibilities, physical exercise, relaxation, and so on.

How to Say It

If your partner has chronic pain, respond to reasonable efforts at independent functioning:

- "You did a great job in the garden today. It looks beautiful."
- "Your swimming exercises are paying off."
- "It was great having you go with us to the movies."
- "If you need to take a break and do a relaxation exercise, go right ahead."
- "It was nice taking a walk together."

It is okay to express your own frustrations, but do so in a nonblaming way.

- "I just feel overwhelmed sometimes. This isn't easy for either of us."
- "Thanks for being a sounding board. Even though you have pain, it's nice to talk with you about my frustrations."
- "Every once in awhile I need to vent. I'm not blaming you for your pain condition. It's just hard for us. But I feel closer to you knowing we can discuss our situation openly."
- "It's easier for me to accept this situation when I know we can discuss it openly from time to time."

How Not to Say It

- "You're exaggerating just to get attention." (If your partner needs attention, it means you are probably too critical of her pain or you are ignoring her when she is managing her pain well. *Better:* "I feel helpless when you're in pain.")
- "Just relax. I'll take care of things. What can I get you?" (This is too solicitous. It is essential that your partner do as much as possible for himself. *Better:* "I can do this for you but it's best that you do it yourself whenever possible.")
- "It's all in your head." (No, it isn't.)
- "Everybody has pain. Why can't you learn to live with it?" (Not everyone has chronic pain. Don't minimize the problem. *Better:* "Since pain is invisible, I sometimes forget what you must be feeling.")

If you are the one with chronic pain, keep complaints about it to a minimum (but don't stuff your feelings). Better to emphasize what you're doing that is positive and constructive than to emphasize what hurts.

How to Say It

- "Yes, I had a lot of pain today but I managed to get some things done anyway."
- "It was nice to get out with some friends today."
- "I had a great morning, much better than usual."
- "It hasn't been a good day. I'm sure I'll feel better soon."
- "As much as I'd like to go out, this isn't a good time."

If you need some support, it's okay to ask for it. Be matter of fact. Don't whine.

- "I just need a sounding board for awhile. It hasn't been one of my better days."
- "I appreciate it when you listen to my complaints. I know it is hard for you, too."
- "How about you listen to my frustrations for a few minutes, then I'll rub your back and I can listen to *your* frustrations."

How Not to Say It

- "You can't possibly understand what it's like for me." (You may be correct. But you're basically saying it isn't any use for your partner to even try to understand. He or she may withdraw. *Better:* "Thanks for listening. Now tell me about your day.")
- "I know you keep saying you love me but I worry that you might leave me. After all, I'm not the easiest person to live with. I need to hear again how you feel." (That sounds desperate and insecure. Spend your energy doing all that you can do for yourself. Ask your partner—not to repeatedly reassure you of his or her love—but to be responsive when you are able to function for yourself.)

- "I'll never get better." (It may seem that way, but better is also a state of mind. Optimism is a sense that it can work out for the best and that you can handle what life dishes out. It doesn't mean you'll get everything you want.)

- "I need your support." (Be clear what you mean by support. Your partner shouldn't do for you what you could do for yourself. Your partner shouldn't have to listen to *daily* complaints. Your partner shouldn't have to keep his frustrations to himself. A supportive partner will help you when you really need it, will listen to your frustrations from time to time, will encourage you to do more for yourself, and will spend time with you in enjoyable activities.)

Cancer

Millie is one of the nearly 180,000 American women who has been diagnosed with breast cancer this year. The days and weeks following her diagnosis and surgery are especially frightening for her family. As the months progress, she and her husband feel less frantic and more optimistic. Still, they both are scared. As much as they try to keep their lives normal for the sake of their children, their lives feel far from routine. Chemotherapy weakens Millie. Her responsibilities diminish and her husband does his best to pick up the slack. There is less time for relaxation, practically no time for leisure pursuits. Housework needs to be done, bills need to be paid, and the kids still need help with their homework.
The family is under strain. What can they do?

Have You Heard?

~ The 5-year survival rate for breast and prostate cancers is just under 80 percent.

~ Studies show that one week after a diagnosis of cancer has been made, 50 percent of couples have not yet discussed their emotional reactions because they fear upsetting one another or they don't know how to begin such a dialogue.

~ Almost half of all breast cancer survivors and 70 percent of prostate cancer survivors have some reduction in sexual desire or functioning. Radiation in the treatment of gynecological cancers can kill vaginal cells, thereby diminishing lubrication and making intercourse slightly uncomfortable. But a satisfying sex life is still possible.

〜 Two types of support are needed: emotional and practical. Many men feel more comfortable offering practical support to their ill wives (driving them to appointments, helping out more with chores, and so on). However, emotional support is usually more desired by people with cancer. Just listening and expressing one's devotion is a powerful show of support.

〜 Couples with the most satisfying relationships before cancer strikes seem to be less distressed during treatment than couples whose relationships were less satisfying.

〜 Even loving partners can respond negatively as the course of the illness wears on. Feeling helpless and scared, partners sometimes avoid the cancer patients, or even criticize them for not doing all they can to improve.

〜 Couples in a satisfying marriage are also more likely to seek emotional support from friends and relatives, thereby enhancing their coping ability.

How to Say It

Supportive comments (the S in GIFTS) are most needed.

- "I'm scared . . . I'm worried . . . You must be very frightened . . . I'm in a state of shock . . . How have you been handling the news?" Don't hesitate to express your feelings. Don't hesitate to encourage your partner to express his or her feelings.

- "Even though I am the one with cancer, I worry about you, too." (Make sure the partner gets chances to talk.)

- "I'm glad you can talk to your friends, too. Any support we can get is good."

- "So how have things been for you today?" (Discussions should be ongoing, not a one-time-only deal.)

- "Sometimes I don't want to say what's on my mind because I worry I'll just upset you. But my guess is that we both have the same fears. We might as well talk about them together rather than thinking about them alone."

- "Sometimes I feel helpless. When I get that way I start giving you advice and try to make you feel optimistic. It doesn't mean I don't want to listen to you. It means I want to do something that will help. It's okay to kick me if you want me to just shut up and listen."

- "Just talking together and knowing you can listen to my concerns helps me a great deal."
- "You've told me that you feel less manly (womanly) right now. But I want you to know I love you no matter what."
- "You seem to be preoccupied. How about I rub your back and you tell me what's going on? If you'd rather have time for yourself, I understand. You need that, too."
- "Let's join a support group. We'll learn more about cancer and how to cope with it." (This is a marvelous idea. Any active coping on the part of the patient and partner reduces overall distress. "Avoidant" coping has been shown to have negative effects.)

How Not to Say It

- "Don't worry about me. I can handle this." (Trying to help your partner not to worry is impossible. You're better off discussing how you each feel from time to time.)
- "You have to be tough. With the right attitude you can beat this thing." (You are correct that the person with cancer has to have a fighting spirit. But don't express this sentiment just because your partner is feeling particularly worried or discouraged. Feeling scared is normal. Validation of that can help your partner to feel better. Also, cancer is not purely affected by one's mind. It is a real physical disease that affects many people despite the "right" attitude.)
- "You must always be optimistic. I don't want to hear any negative thoughts." (Hear your partner out, acknowledge the validity of the fears, and gently offer a more optimistic way of looking at things. *Better:* " I know how you feel. I worry, too. But I'm also optimistic that things can work out eventually. I'm glad we can talk about how we feel.")
- "I know you don't feel well but you have to push yourself. Don't give in to the medication." (Chemotherapy and radiation can be draining. Don't underestimate the severity of your partner's illness or the intense effects of the treatment.)

How to Say It to Yourself

- "Despite the surgery, I am still an attractive, sexual, and loving person."
- "People with my form of cancer have survived and been cured."
- "I can take some time now to really appreciate all the gifts God has given me."
- "There is a purpose to my life."
- "I can seek joy in the small things."
- "It's normal to feel scared and pessimistic once in awhile. It's normal to have good days, too."

Infertility

51

Janice and Mike have been trying unsuccessfully to get pregnant for over a year. They've grown more and more disheartened with each passing month. When they have a meeting with Janice's doctor, they are informed that they are one of two million married couples grappling with infertility. The doctor reassures them that that pregnancy is possible. But a swirl of issues now have to be faced. Do they want to consider treatment? Should they continue on their own for awhile? Could they imagine using a sperm donor if that becomes necessary?

The options and the medical terms being discussed overwhelm Mike. When he and Janice arrive home, Mike is only clear about one thing: If they don't have a child, he can live with that. Janice is shocked. She thought he was eager to be a father. She isn't ready to give up on motherhood without doing everything she can. Even if she can't conceive, what about adoption? Their ability to communicate never seems more important than now.

Have You Heard?

⁓ Infertility is defined as an inability to conceive a child after one year of trying, or the inability to carry a child to full term.

⁓ Some estimates reveal that about half of all couples designated as infertile will eventually succeed at pregnancy.

⁓ Statistically, women seem to take the lead in pursuing infertility treatments. Becoming pregnant is more important to them than it is to their partners.

⁓ Sometimes, in an effort to determine the reason for the problem, partners must disclose information to one another about their sexual history they would otherwise have not chosen to share (past pregnancies, incidents of sexually transmitted diseases, and so on). Tolerance and understanding helps.

~ While stressful, infertility does not automatically reduce a couple's relationship satisfaction. In fact, many such couples improve marital closeness during this time.

~ Relationship satisfaction is likely to be maintained the more the couple is in agreement on what steps to take regarding their infertility problem. However, couples often experience increased marital strain or depression if their treatment extends to a third year.

How to Say It

If there is a difference of opinion on whether to seek treatment, to adopt, or to keep trying without treatment, a gentle approach with in-flight repairs can keep the discussion from getting out of hand. Initially, each partner might be overwhelmed or confused.

- "You're right. We both want the same thing—to have a child. I'm just unsure of the best way to go about it. Treatment can be expensive."
- "Let's list all the things we agree on. We probably agree on more things than we disagree."
- "I can't blame you for not being enthusiastic about using a sperm donor."
- "I'm sorry for getting so upset with you. I'm just frustrated. We need to keep talking and I don't want to push you away by my strong feelings."
- "I avoid talking about this because I just think we'll end up disagreeing. But we obviously have to be a team on this decision; otherwise, we both lose."
- "I can accept the decision to go ahead with medical treatment, but I'm not enthusiastic. I'll cooperate, but please understand if I am not as hyped up as you are."
- "We have a long road ahead of us. Let's stay friends."

Find ways to offer support whenever possible.

- "Hi, partner. How was your day?"
- "We'll get through this. We're a team, remember?"

- "Somehow, someway, we'll be parents. We just don't know how or when."
- "Some days I'm not easy to live with. Thanks for putting up with me."
- "Somewhere there's a child who will be lucky to have you as a mother."
- "Tonight we're scheduled to make love. Be there on time. I don't want to start without you."
- "We've spent a lot of time and money on the fertility treatment. I know you worry about the finances. Thanks so much for your willingness to do this anyway."

As time marches on and the infertility remains a problem, the couple has more decisions to face.

- "Should we tell our parents (or friends)? I want some support from others but I know this is also very personal for both of us. Is there somebody you would like to tell whom you haven't yet?"
- "Can our lives still be meaningful even if we don't conceive a child?"
- "If we use a sperm donor, should we tell our parents?" (You have nothing to be ashamed about. However, you are entitled to your privacy if you wish.)
- "We've been trying various treatments unsuccessfully for years. Even though there is always new technology, at one point do we accept our situation and resume living a more normal life?"

How Not to Say It

- "I know I said we could adopt if all else failed. But I changed my mind." (Don't be inflexible. Couples struggling with infertility go on emotional roller coasters. Understanding, sympathy, and flexibility are needed. *Better:* "I know I said we could adopt, but I'm not enthusiastic about that now. I guess I'm just disappointed we couldn't conceive a child of our own. I'm sure I'll feel more upbeat soon.")
- "It's your fault we can't have kids of our own." (No, it isn't. The problem is best approached as a problem for the couple. Nobody chooses to have fertility difficulties.)

- "I'm fed up with this treatment. I'm not doing it anymore." (You have a right to be frustrated. *Better:* "Some days I feel like giving up, but I know I wouldn't really want to do that. Do you ever feel that way?")

- "I don't want to discuss this." (Couples need to find a mix of talking together and having some personal space. *Better:* "I'm not in the mood to talk. Can we talk tomorrow? I just need to concentrate on other things right now.")

- "It's because of me we can't have children. I've ruined your life." (Secretly, you want reassurance that you are loved and that your partner won't hold it against you that you cannot have children together. *Better:* "I feel badly that I can't provide you with a child. I know it would have meant a lot to each of us if it could be different.")

Miscarriage

52

Carol and Joe spend the morning at a craft fair. It is a bright autumn day. Carol is two months pregnant, expecting their first child. Joe heads straight for the table where hand-woven baby clothes are sold and selects a yellow infant's sweater. It is their first purchase for the new baby and makes the morning complete.

But the next day Carol feels something is wrong. She notices some spotting and immediately phones her doctor.

Several days later Joe places the yellow sweater in his bottom dresser drawer. The miscarriage has taken them both by surprise. They still hope to use the sweater someday, but right now all they can think about are the dreams that will have to be set aside.

Have You Heard?

～ Even one year after a miscarriage, a woman can have a clinically significant depression. Those at the highest risk for depression lacked social support and did very little to try to cope with the loss.

～ Men are more troubled by miscarriage than is sometimes obvious. They cope by worrying about their partners or trying to ignore the issue. Men often find comfort in staying busy and often resist crying. They may wish to avoid discussing the loss for fear of further upsetting their wives. Women are more likely to seek spiritual counseling and talk to other women who have had miscarriages. Women also tend to blame themselves for what happened and become easily irritated. Little things can bring on tears or anger.

〜 A major source of grief for men and women was abandoning their fantasies, dreams, and hopes for their unborn child. Over time, husbands feel helpless and burdened by their wives' depression.

〜 Strong differences in coping styles between men and women (one wants to talk, the other wants to forget) can add to depression in women. This in turn makes men reluctant to discuss the loss, fearing it will add to the women's pain. Understanding and cooperation on both sides is necessary.

How to Say It

First, talk about the loss. Recognize that while you each may have different coping methods, it is important to discuss your loss together. Be understanding if your partner wants to talk more (or less) often than you do.

- "I keep thinking about what the baby might have looked like."
- "How are you holding up?"
- "Sometimes I don't talk about it because I don't want to upset you. What would you like me to do when I feel that way?" (Point out your assumptions. They may be incorrect.)
- "The baby would have been born in August. I imagine we'll be thinking about that when the time comes."
- "It must be particularly hard for you since you carried the baby inside you."
- "Sometimes I think you are insensitive because you go to work every day and you only cried once. But I know you are very sad. You are just trying to handle it differently from the way I do."
- "The last thing I think of when I fall asleep is the baby."
- "Do you think the baby is in heaven?"

Some people view a miscarriage as a sad but random event. Others try to find meaning in the loss, believing that everything happens for a reason. Don't debate the issue and don't force your viewpoint on your partner. Whichever way your partner sees it, respect that viewpoint.

- "I like to think that we have an angel in heaven looking out for us. Maybe that's a reason it happened."

- "I think God has a plan for our lives that is good. Even though we didn't want this to happen, there are still good things in our future."
- "These things happen. I don't like to figure out the reasons why because I can never know those reasons absolutely. I just have to accept it."
- "Even though it has been a few months since the miscarriage, I still think about what might have been. Do you ever think like that?" (Bring up the topic periodically. Chances are your partner is thinking about it too. There is no reason to be alone in your thoughts.)

Encouragement and words of hope are fine and important, but not if they replace discussions about the pain of loss. Both are needed.

- "At least the doctor told us there is no reason we can't get pregnant again and have a healthy baby."
- "When we finally become parents I'm sure we'll have some crises to deal with. We've handled this one pretty well. Maybe that's an indication we can get through hard times together."

If your partner says things like:

- *"I don't want to talk about it. There's nothing we can do. We have to forget about it and move on."*
- *"You're avoiding the issue. You have to discuss this; otherwise, you'll get depressed. It's not fair to me that you won't talk."*
- *"Next time I'm pregnant I'll worry that another miscarriage will happen."*

You reply:

- *"I know you prefer not to talk about it. But I need to talk about it sometimes. I'm willing to talk to others but I also need to discuss it with you once in awhile. I won't insist that you must talk, but please don't insist that we never talk. Let's meet each other halfway."*
- *"Talking isn't easy for me. Maybe I'm wrong, but I cope best by trying to put things out of my mind that I can do nothing about. But you're right, it's not fair to you."*
- *"I imagine that everyone worries it could happen again. Let's talk to some people who have had miscarriages and let's talk to the doctors. On the other hand, worrying is good practice for when we do become parents. Don't all parents worry?"*

How Not to Say It

- "You never bring up the topic. How can you be so cold?" (Some people—usually men—cope by keeping in their feelings. Husbands also worry about upsetting their wives by bringing up painful topics. Chances are the man is not "cold" but worried and helpless. He needs guidance, not criticism. *Better:* "My guess is you don't talk about the miscarriage because you don't want to upset me or yourself. But I need to talk about it from time to time. Please just listen to how I feel. That helps enormously.")

- "It's over and done with. There's nothing we can do to change the past. So why talk about it?" (When a loss occurs, people need time to integrate what happened into their personal reality. Talking helps achieve that. When a person is in emotional shock, talking lets the person accept the reality of what happened. *Better:* "I guess I feel helpless when we talk about it because I can't change the past. But I know it is important for us to talk.")

- "It's been four months since the miscarriage. You should be over it by now." (It can take longer than several months to grieve. The best way to forget is to remember. Show more empathy and a willingness to listen and your partner may make more progress. *Better:* "I wish you were feeling better by now but I understand why you are still grieving. How about we go for a walk and discuss it?")

- "You're not the only person who's ever miscarried."

Death of a Child

53

"It was my fault. I was driving the car and I never saw the other car run the red light. I've replayed that moment a thousand times in my head. If only I'd reacted sooner I could have prevented the accident and my little girl's death. If only . . ."

"Our baby was stillborn. It felt like my world had shattered that day. Some people told us we'd get over it sooner because it wasn't the same as losing an older child. They are wrong."

"After the death, I could see how much pain my wife was in and I knew there was nothing I could do. I felt helpless. I tried to stay focused on my work but I was in a fog."

No conversation a couple ever has will be more needed or more painful than talking about the death of their child.

Have You Heard?

~ The grief experience of a loss in the womb, an infant loss, or the loss of an older child can be similar.

~ Typically, the grief reactions of one parent are somewhat different from the reactions of the other—although there are many similarities. This is due, in part, to personality differences. Criticizing these differences is never helpful.

~ Common issues after a child's death include the husband's frustration and helplessness over his wife's grief, a temporary halt in communication, and irritability between the spouses.

∼ In order to make sense of a senseless tragedy, people look for answers to *why* the death had to happen. In an effort to maintain the belief that the world is predictable, couples sometimes come up with blaming answers. *"If only I didn't take him in the car with me . . . If only we had him checked by a doctor sooner . . . If only I rested more during my pregnancy . . . If only I paid more attention to the warning signs . . ."* These kinds of thoughts are common but must eventually be put aside.

∼ It is common for parents to regret moments during the child's life when they were angry at the child or when they chose not to play with the child. All parents need to remember that raising a child involves the full spectrum of emotions, that cross words are sometimes required, and parents cannot always be available at all times to their children.

∼ Let your partner grieve at his or her own pace and in his or her own way. There is no timeline for grief that must be followed. In a study of parents who lost a child in a car accident, the parents routinely thought about the sequence of events that led to the accident even seven years afterward.

∼ If a baby is stillborn or dies shortly after birth, mothers sometimes have a more intense grief than fathers because they had bonded with the baby inside them, according to Maribeth Wilder Doerr, author of *For Better or Worse: A Handbook for Couples Whose Child Has Died.*

∼ It is not unusual for grieving fathers to hold their feelings in and to resist discussing the subject. In contrast, mothers are more likely to let out their feelings and will want to talk about what happened many times.

∼ Religious participation is associated with greater well-being and less distress 18 months after a sudden infant death.

∼ In a study of parents whose children died of cancer, the mothers were two and a half times as likely to become pregnant within a year after the death, compared with similar families where no death had occurred.

How to Say It

- "Remember when . . . ?" (Memories of everyday events or special moments with your child can be mentioned anytime. These comments need not lead to in-depth discussions. They are simply tender thoughts spoken aloud.)

- "I'd like to do something special as a memorial. Can we talk about possibilities?" (A memorial can be a wonderful idea that also continues to bring the rest of the family closer in a common cause. A memorial can be simple, such as planting a tree, or it can be a gift to a charity in the child's name. Some couples begin support groups or give speeches as a way to bring something good out of what happened. Others may talk to the legislature about passing laws that will help prevent future similar deaths.)

- "I find myself wanting to look at the photo album and pushing it away at the same time. If I'm looking at pictures and I want to show you one, it's okay if you aren't ready to look at it just yet."

- "I'm in a bind. There are times I want to talk and yet I know you'd rather not. I don't know what to do in those moments. Can we find a way to offer support to each other? Otherwise, we'll each be grieving on our own."

- "Whenever you talk about Jennifer I just want the conversation over with. It's too painful. But I know you want to talk. Please bear with me. I'm trying to be as supportive as I can. Some days I can't talk the way you want, however."

- "I can't get the last few days of his life out of my mind. Do you ever feel like that?" (Shock and disbelief are common. Preoccupation with the loss is a way for us to finally come to terms with the awful truth. Eventually, the preoccupations lessen and hopefully will be replaced by happy memories of the deceased.)

- "Let's hold hands in the mall. It won't be easy seeing all those people with their children." (Tender affection is very important. Try to show it frequently.)

How Not to Say It*

- "You never cry. Don't you care?" (People grieve in different ways. Some people try to hide their grief, especially if they wish to appear strong for their family. A gentler approach is called for. *Better:* "I know you are suffering, too. I want to be more connected to you and I'm not sure of the best way to do that.")

- "There is more to life than being depressed." (This comment is often motivated by a sense of helplessness in making a partner feel better.

---

*I am grateful to Joy Johnson of the Centering Corporation for her wise comments. The Centering Corporation is a not-for-profit organization with a vast assortment of books and tapes on how people of all ages can cope with loss. Call 402-553-1200 for a free catalogue.

However, it can make the partner feel misunderstood and alienated from you. *Better:* "I feel helpless when you are depressed. I know I can't make you feel better, but I want to remind you that I love you.")

- "My grief is deeper than yours." (Don't make comparisons.)
- "This wouldn't have happened if you hadn't . . ." (This kind of comment can kill a relationship. Even if a parent had made a mistake that cost a child his or her life, the parent did not intend that to happen. Besides, it is faulty logic. The death would never have happened if a multitude of choices hadn't been made. If you had never married, the child would never have been born. Also, you never know the countless small decisions that were made that may have avoided accidents and prevented an untimely death. If you are angry with your partner, don't blame him or her unfairly for the child's death.)
- "I'm not going to talk about it. I'm trying to deal with this in my own way. Stop forcing your way onto me." (If your partner wants to talk and you refuse, then you are forcing your way on him or her. It's okay to not want to talk but you must find a way—each of you—to support one another even if it is hard for you. *Better:* "I can talk once in awhile. But it is extremely difficult for me and I know I won't be able to talk as often as you'd like. But let's try and see what happens.")

Nothing may seem normal anymore after a child dies. Making love may seem impossible due to depression and it may be a reminder of how the child was created. Feeling joy and seeking pleasure may seem the wrong thing to do. Yet, a couple can miss the special closeness that sexual intimacy can bring. If there had been strong disagreements about lovemaking before, the issue may be particularly divisive now. It is neither wrong to want to make love nor wrong to feel turned off by the idea. What's needed is gentle talk, understanding, and an agreed-upon goal. It is perhaps best to start out with a lot of tender affection, followed over time by sexual intimacies that need not result in intercourse. The message when you do make love should be one of "I love you."

If you aren't ready for lovemaking, tell your partner:

- *"I want to make love soon but I'm not ready yet. Thank you for understanding."*
- *"You are very important to me. Don't forget that. I just need more time."*
- *"It's hard to imagine I can enjoy anything. I know that won't always be how I feel. Affection and holding mean a lot to me right now. Can we stay with just that for awhile?"*

Child Hospitalized
with Serious Injury

54

Six-year-old Anna and her parents watch as Anna's brother, Luke, comes to bat. It is the last Little League game of the season. Anna's parents sit on the bleachers while Anna plays with friends on the sidelines. A loud commotion distracts the parents from the ballgame. When Anna's dad looks in her direction, he sees Anna on the ground, her head covered in blood. Apparently, a young boy was practicing his swings and struck Anna squarely on her forehead with a baseball bat.

An ambulance is called and Anna's father accompanies her to the hospital. Her mother and brother follow in their car. It is a frightening experience for both Anna and her dad.

Anna is home from the hospital the next day. Her head injury leaves her face black-and-blue and swollen, but the physical trauma is not extensive. The psychological trauma is more severe—particularly for Anna's dad.

Have You Heard?

~ Studies show that children who are hospitalized for serious physical injury can recover with few psychological scars. However, up to 12 percent of children may have symptoms consistent with post-traumatic stress disorder one month after the injury.

~ Parents are at risk for post-traumatic stress after a child has been severely injured. Parents may make sure that their child is comforted and given treatment, but they pay little attention to their own stress symptoms.

~ Parents may have more symptoms after the child is out of danger and is safe at home. That is a time when the enormity of what happened may finally register.

How to Say It

In addition to offering support and comfort to the injured child, conversation between parents must address two areas: emotional support for each other and decisions about practical matters such as the running of the household. Often, one partner feels a need to discuss the emotional impact of what has happened, while the other needs to make sure that necessary day-to-day tasks are being taken care of.

- "I can't let our child stay alone in the hospital. One of us should be with her. The other one can take care of the other kids at home. What are your thoughts?"
- "Let's think about what questions we need to ask the doctor. Otherwise, I know we'll forget to ask something important."
- "After she gets out of the hospital, we'll have to rearrange our work schedules for a little while."
- "How are you holding up?"
- "Even though everything is fine now, I can't stop thinking about what happened. I know I'm going to want to talk about this some more. Are you up for that?"
- "You were really comforting to our daughter. I know she felt reassured."
- "I'm glad you're with me now."
- "I find myself being overprotective of all our kids now. Do you feel that way, too?"
- "I sometimes need to get away for an hour or so and just do something to take my mind off this. But I want to be available to you too."
- "Even though I snapped at you earlier, I really don't blame you for the accident. I'm just worried."

How Not to Say It

- "How can you think about going to work at a time like this?" (Often, one partner tries to cope with a frightening child's injury by distracting himself or by putting his energy into something he can control. It is not a sign of coldness or indifference on his part. *Better:* "I'm sure that going to work will get your mind off things but I need you here with me.")

- "It's over and she's out of danger. Try not to worry anymore." (That's a nice sentiment but unrealistic. If the injury was potentially life threatening, a parent can suffer from stress and obsessive worry even when matters have improved. *Better:* "I can understand why you still think about it. I'm glad it's over.")

- "Everything's okay now. Stop making too much out of what happened." (Show some empathy and reassurance. Otherwise, you will push your partner away at a crucial moment in your life together. *Better:* "It was scary, I know. I'm glad things are improving though. Soon this will be a distant memory.")

- "If you had been more observant, the accident would never have happened." (Such blaming is poisonous. Parents can't prevent all children's injuries no matter how hard they might try. *Better:* "I know you blame yourself but I don't blame you. Accidents happen under the best of circumstances.")

- "You're not as upset as I am. Don't you care?" (Some people cope best by keeping their emotions in check. You may not like that, but it doesn't mean they don't care.)

Let's Talk

A recent study showed that family environment can predict recovery in children with traumatic brain injury. Children were between the ages of 6 and 12. In families where there was more dysfunction and where parents were more psychologically distressed, children with the most severe injury scored more poorly one year after the injury on perceptual–motor skills and adaptive behaviors. Families that are already stressed by strained relationships or parental distress are less adept at coping with serious injury to a child.

Parents in such situations might do well to seek as much support from others as possible and do what they can to strike a balance between providing emotional support and practical support (doing more chores, taking the kids out to give a burdened parent a break, cutting back on expenses if money is tight, and so on). A simple "What can I do today that would make your day go easier?" may make a difference to a beleaguered partner.

Death of a Spouse's Parent

55

Camille always felt close to her mother. She spoke to her often and they would see each other at least once a week. When the woman dies unexpectedly, Camille is heartbroken. Her mom wasn't that old, only 64. Camille's dad seems lost in the weeks that follow his wife's sudden passing. Camille does her best to comfort her father although their relationship has always been mildly strained. Her husband, Stan, tries to assure Camille that her dad will eventually overcome his grief. Camille is grateful for her husband's support but is simply too stunned and lost in her own grief to take any of his words to heart. Stan tries to look at the bigger picture but has more questions than he has answers. Will Camille's grief linger? Will Camille's father spend more time with them? How will the kids handle the death of their grandmother? What can he say to Camille that might ease her suffering?

Have You Heard?

~ Studies show that compared with nonbereaved adults, people grieving from the loss of a parent suffer a decline in health status. There is also a slight increase in alcohol consumption.

~ The impact of a parent's death on a marriage depends upon the quality of the marriage and the quality of the relationship between the adult and the deceased. People who are every close to a parent but dissatisfied with their partner will experience more marital conflict after the parent's death.

~ There is a slight increase in the divorce rate in the years following a parent's death.

∾ If you didn't get along with your deceased in-law, you can anticipate some anger from your partner.

How to Say It

Say something nice about the deceased.

- "I'm really going to miss your father. I always liked his company."
- "Your mom and I had our differences but were in agreement on one thing: We both loved you."
- "If it wasn't for your mom and dad, you wouldn't be here. I'll always be grateful to them for that."

Keep in mind that your partner needs two kinds of support—emotional and practical. Try to do both.

- "Don't worry about cooking. I'll take care of all that." (If your grieving partner insists on doing some chores so she can keep busy, let her do them.)
- "I'll arrange for one of the neighbors to look after the baby when we go to the funeral home."
- "It's been a few weeks since your dad died. I know you're still sad and pre-occupied. Is there something else I could be doing that might help your day go easier?"
- "Today would have been your mom's birthday. How are you doing?"
- "I don't know what to say other than I love you."
- "This will be the first Christmas (special holiday) without your dad. I wonder if there is something we could do to remember him by?"
- "Every day feels kind of surreal, doesn't it? . . . It's hard to get it through my head that your mom is gone . . . Some days it must feel like you are living in a fog . . ." (This type of comment helps to normalize your partner's inner experience.)

If there has been a history of ill will, your partner may not be appreciative of your efforts to offer support. If your partner says:

- *"You never really liked my mother anyway. It seems hypocritical to say nice things about her now."*

- *"I was closer to my parent than I ever was to you."*
- *"You don't understand what it's like."*

You reply:

- *"You're right. Your mom and I didn't get along as well as I would have liked. I don't blame you for thinking I'm being hypocritical. But she did have many good qualities and I'll miss her."*
- *"So I can imagine just how hard his death must be for you. But I'd like to think you and I could get closer over time."*
- *"I guess I don't understand, but I'm trying. What do you want me to understand better?"*

How Not to Say It

- "Death is part of life . . . We all have to die someday . . . At least she didn't suffer . . . It was God's will . . . Her memory will be with you always . . ." (Clichés may be well-meaning but they often miss the mark. They tend to disqualify a person's emotions by implying it is wrong or unnecessary to feel sad. Better to say nothing or simply show some tender affection.)
- "You've been moping around ever since your mother died. When are you going to get over it?" (Your lack of sensitivity is probably adding to your partner's grief and making it hard for her to find moments of contentment. *Better:* "I've noticed you're still very sad. Want to talk about it? Is there anything I could do that would help?")
- "You had six months to prepare for your father's death but you act like you're still in shock." (Death, even when anticipated, can still be hard to accept. A ritual can help, such as planting a tree in the loved one's memory.)
- "I haven't spoken about your mom's death because I thought it would upset you." (*Better:* "Sometimes I want to ask how you are doing but I don't want to make you feel badly. Is it okay if I ask anyway?")
- "The kids will get depressed if you don't snap out of it." (It's okay for children to see a parent grieving. Grief is a natural emotion. Kids simply need to know that their home life can continue normally over time.)

Caring for a Chronically Ill/Disabled Child

56

Maria and Carlos have just returned from the hospital. Their son, Miguel, had lapsed into a hypoglycemic coma but is now doing well. The boy has juvenile diabetes. Daily insulin shots and food restrictions are accepted as part of the routine, but on rare occasions more serious complications occur. Miguel will be fine soon, but his parents will not stop worrying.

Jill and Mike's daughter has asthma and multiple allergies. Environmental toxins and numerous foods make her break out in hives and sometimes make it difficult for her to breathe. Jill has to cut back on her work hours so she can be home when her daughter arrives from school. Eventually she stops work altogether because she needs to be home during school vacation days. The financial cutback is an additional strain to the family.

Bill and Donna's child has Down syndrome. The girl is a treasure to her parents, but her developmental delays and need for surgeries weigh heavily on their minds.

Chronic illnesses and disabilities can be mild, but some can be serious and life threatening. About 15 percent of kids have some kind of chronic illness that can add to parents' stress and strain.

Have You Heard?

～ Despite role strain, many couples improve their relationship quality when they have a chronically ill or disabled child. Although estimates vary, the divorce rate for such couples is no higher than the rate for other couples. In fact, there is much evidence that these couples have a lower divorce rate.

～ Family and friends often give extra support for the child. That serves as a protective buffer for parents, too.

~ Couples with a chronically ill child or a child with a birth defect or disability must find time for each other. Husbands, in particular, seem more dissatisfied when their wives have little or no time for them.

~ Women are most dissatisfied when the men don't help out enough with the medical care of the child. Overburdened, these women pull away from the men. The men, in turn, spend more hours working to earn extra money and to take their mind off their family worries.

How to Say It

Partners need practical help and supportive comments. One without the other is insufficient.

- "Let me take my coat off, then I want to hear all about your day." (Frequent, informal talks help maintain your connection with your partner.)
- "I like these quiet moments together. I miss them when we don't find the time for them."
- "On days like this, I'm glad we're a team."
- "Some days I don't know what's needed more—for me to work more hours so we have money to pay all our bills, or to stay home and help you out more. What are your thoughts?"
- "I'm not blaming you when I say this, but some days I resent that you get to go to work while I have to deal with all of the doctors' appointments and the frustrations at home. I wish I could see other people once in awhile."
- "Let's find a way for you to have more free time. You need a regular chance to take a break."
- "What could we do differently that would help make your days go easier?"
- "Sometimes I just need to talk about my frustrations with caring for our child. I know you feel that talking accomplishes very little. But feeling heard makes me feel better and makes me feel more connected to you."
- "Some days are very hard. Some days I hate being here. But I'm glad we're a team."
- "I know you are tired and stressed. We both are. But sometimes I need to see you happy and upbeat. Can we try to be that way for one another once in awhile?"

How Not to Say It

- "I go to work. It's your job to take care of the children."
- "We can't go to a movie. Who will look after the kids?" (It is important to find someone who is knowledgeable and qualified to look after your child once in awhile. You and your partner need time alone together.)
- "Why do you still need to talk about the problems with having a disabled child? Aren't you used to it by now?" (As the child gets older, new issues may emerge as a result of the illness or disability. Knowing you can talk to your partner about your frustrations and concerns is a big help. *Better:* "I guess I don't like to discuss it. But I know it's important to do that.")
- "You're always so tired and unhappy! Can't you look at the bright side? Can't you try to enjoy life as best as you can instead of wallowing in misery?" (If your partner is that unhappy—and depression is possible when caring for a chronically ill child—he or she is probably not getting enough emotional support and not enough time away. Do something about that.)
- "You're uncaring! You don't spend enough time with me." (Tone down the accusation. *Better:* "I know we have a lot of responsibilities, but we don't have enough time for each other. Can we find some way to improve the situation?")

If your partner responds critically and says things like:

- *"If you would help out more, maybe we'd have more time."*
- *"What more do you want from me?"*
- *"You only think about yourself."*

Don't respond defensively. Don't say:

- *"I do help out. You don't appreciate all the other responsibilities I have."*
- *"Never mind. Forget I even asked."*
- *"That's because you never think about me."*

Instead, reply with some understanding (one of you has to say the right thing):

- *"I thought I was doing all I could. But let's reevaluate the situation and find ways I can be even more helpful."*

- "*I know you're exhausted. I just want us to find a way to spend a little more quality time together. What can I do that will help make that happen?*"
- "*I don't intend to come across that way. I'm worried that we have so little time together. Let's talk about this, okay?*"

Depression

57

Sal became clinically depressed when his business failed. Owning a restaurant was a dream that had finally come true two years ago. But after a huge investment of money and time, he realized he had to shut down the business. He feels like a failure and believes he has disappointed his wife and children who are counting on him to provide for their welfare. Even though his wife is supportive and optimistic, Sal cannot be consoled. He keeps to himself, has lost interest in applying for work, and rejects his wife's attempts to offer solace and reassurances. His doctor finally prescribes antidepressants.

Have You Heard?

~ Depression can be triggered by loss of status or job failure, especially among men. For women, depression is more often associated with cutoffs from close relationships.

~ A common complaint of depressed wives about their husbands: "We don't talk."

~ People with marital dissatisfaction are 25 times more likely to get depressed than people in satisfying relationships. A good marriage serves as a buffer to many of the stresses and injustices of life.

~ Depressed husbands do not reach out to their wives for support, although they cope better when they do.

~ When one partner is depressed, the relationship becomes emotionally deprived over time. These couples show less affection, disagree more often, are less able to understand one another, and listen poorly.

~ Improving the marriage (especially the ability to communicate) can reduce depression. Good communication improves intimacy and reduces the buildup of resentments, both of which make the couple more likely to withstand any external stresses.

How to Say It

Partners of depressed people often feel frustrated that they cannot help their partner "snap out of it." They may therefore blame themselves or their partner for the ongoing depression—an attitude that only fuels misery. Assuming a very depressed person is receiving some kind of therapy or medication, the goals of the couple are to reduce blaming, increase intimate dialogue, and increase positive and fun activities.

- "I get frustrated that things haven't improved. I'm not blaming you. I just wish the situation were different. I can imagine you must feel even more frustrated." (If a depressed partner can respond to such a comment with understanding, intimacy will improve.)

- "I know you don't feel like going to dinner with us, but I also know depression makes you lose interest in most things. It would mean a lot if you could come with us for a couple of hours. I think you know it's important to push yourself a bit."

- "I get confused on how best to talk to you. I want to hear how you are feeling, but I don't want to come away feeling discouraged. Maybe we can agree to talk every day about your depression for a little while, but then agree to talk about our day-to-day lives and plans for the future. How does that sound?"

- "I sometimes think you should deal with your depression by plowing ahead despite how you feel. But from what you're telling me, it would mean a lot to you if you and I had more intimate moments together. I wonder if we could do both?"

- "I'm depressed and you want me to push myself and act like I'm not depressed. But when I ask you to show more affection and to spend more time talking to me, you refuse. I think both of us need to push ourselves to do more. If we support each other, maybe we can accomplish more."

- "The most frustrating part of your depression for me is when you seem helpless. Then I get mad that you are giving up. Is there something I could say or do that would help encourage you to feel less helpless?"
- "Even though you are depressed, let's try to go to a movie every week or let's just go out for a cup of coffee together."
- "I love you and I have faith that we'll get past this."
- "You went out and worked in the garden today even though I'm sure you didn't feel up to it. Thank you. I feel wonderful when I know you are doing your best."

How Not to Say It

- "You're always so negative and pessimistic. How do you expect to feel better if you always look at the dark side of things?" (*Better:* "You sound very discouraged. Would you like me to help you think of other ways to look at this situation that are more optimistic?")
- "Everybody gets depressed. Why are you making such a big deal out of it?" (Clinical depression is not simply feeling blue.)
- "Finally you're doing something positive for a change!" (There is a tendency for the nondepressed partner to make critical comments when the depressed partner is feeling more energetic. *Better:* "You must be feeling better today. How wonderful!")

If you are depressed, avoid criticizing yourself to your partner. It won't make your partner feel better and will add to his or her troubles.

- "You must hate me that I'm so depressed." (*Better:* "I'm so grateful that you are here for me. My depression hasn't made your life easy.")
- "How do you put up with me?"
- "I wouldn't blame you if you left me some day."

How to Say It to Yourself

If you are depressed:

- "The fact that I'm feeling hopeless doesn't make it true. Depression is treatable and most people overcome it."

- "All problems are temporary."
- "There was a time when I wasn't feeling this way. There will be a time again when I don't feel this way."
- "I don't have much of an interest in anything. Still, I can force myself to do a few things or to ask my family about their day."
- "I don't have to fully enjoy doing something in order to decide to do it. Depression makes many things unenjoyable, but I might feel better knowing I've accomplished some things by the day's end."

If your partner is depressed:

- "Instead of focusing on the depression only, let me look at ways I know I could be a better husband (or wife)."
- "I can take some time every day and spend it with my partner. I can still show affection."
- "I can find ways to show appreciation and enthusiasm for the things my partner does do. Now is not the time to take her (him) for granted."

Anxiety and Phobias

58

Janet suffers from panic attacks. They began out of the blue one day while she was driving. The first episode was so frightening that Janet thought she was having a heart attack. She sought medical help but was told her heart was fine. Her panic attacks have continued and soon Janet avoids places where she doesn't feel safe. Over time, she can drive only within a short radius of her home. Checkout lines, restaurants, and malls all trigger intense anxiety because she worries she won't be able to get out of those places quickly should another panic attack occur.

Art, Janet's husband, doesn't understand why she is so frightened. He is accommodating at first, and doesn't mind that he has to accompany her to places she used to go to by herself. But over time he grows impatient and annoyed. Now Janet feels much more alone.

Have You Heard?

∿ About 15 million Americans currently suffer from an anxiety disorder.

∿ Between 1 and 2 percent of Americans will have a panic disorder. In most cases, these people restrict their activities and limit where they travel so as to avoid more panic episodes, especially in public. That avoidance is called agoraphobia.

∿ Women are twice as likely to be diagnosed with panic disorder than men.

∿ Anxiety disorders are among the most readily treated, often by a combination of medication and psychotherapy.

～ Couples where one person has a diagnosed anxiety disorder tend to report greater discord. Phobic people tend to be unassertive and greatly concerned about what others think of them.

How to Say It

A nonphobic partner has a difficult job. He or she should not be too accommodating because that doesn't help the phobic person overcome the problem. But a partner cannot be indifferent, hostile, or pushy. Nonphobic people should assist their partners in small ways but encourage independent functioning.

- "I'll go shopping with you. But from time to time I'll go off for a few minutes by myself. That will give you an opportunity to practice coping."
- "You've been doing much better driving with me as a passenger. How about next time you drive alone and I'll follow?"
- "Remember, you are not having a heart attack. You are fine. Your body is simply acting as if you are being threatened. You'll start to feel calmer in a few minutes."
- "Let's break down your goal into smaller steps. If your goal is to go inside the mall and shop, the first step might be standing inside the doorway for a few minutes. The next step might be walking fifty feet into the mall, and so on."
- "Remember, anxiety is a signal to relax."
- "You can call me on your cell phone when you get to the store."
- "I'm proud of you for working so hard to overcome this problem."
- "Apart from your anxiety problem, what parts of your daily life—including our marriage—might be adding stress and strain?" (Often, communication problems exist when a partner has a phobia or anxiety problem. Correcting relationship problems can have a beneficial effect on anxiety.)

If a phobic partner says:

- *"You have to come with me to the store. I can't go alone."*
- *"I'm afraid I'll die."*
- *"My anxiety attack was horrible."*

You respond:

- *"I'll accompany you, but some of the time you'll have to be by yourself even if just for a few minutes. We'll go at a pace that's challenging but not overwhelming."*
- *"I know you are scared but anxiety won't kill you. It's just a feeling."*
- *"Your anxiety attack was very uncomfortable, not horrible."*

How Not to Say It

- "You just want attention." (People with anxiety problems want them to go away. Panic attacks can be very frightening. If your anxious partner thinks you don't care or don't want to understand, your relationship will suffer even if the anxiety improves.)
- "Don't worry. I can do it for you." (Your partner won't overcome the problem unless she challenges herself. Offer occasional help but no pampering.)
- While driving together or while accompanying a partner to a social event asking: "How are you feeling? Are you getting panicky yet?" (Usually, a phobic person doesn't find such comments helpful. It is best to have an arranged signal that the anxious partner can give when she or he wants some assistance or support.)
- "I'm sick of your anxiety. Everybody gets nervous. Just learn to deal with it." (No doubt it can be frustrating when a partner has unrealistic fears. But this approach doesn't help. In fact, it worsens the anxiety. *Better:* "Yes, it is frustrating for me at times. I'll be glad when you feel less afraid and can do more.")
- "Now that you are feeling better, how about we take that plane trip to Florida?" (A phobic person does best taking smaller, incremental steps. A plane trip is usually a big step.)

Let's Talk

Anxiety causes the body to become physiologically aroused: heart rate increases, blood pressure increases, dizziness may occur, as well as trembling, breathing difficulties, and excessive sweating. Anxious people breathe more rapidly and shallowly—a process that perpetuates the anxiety state. If anxious people learn to breathe the way they would if they were completely relaxed, they can trick the body into calming down sooner.

Abdominal breathing is the appropriate method. When you inhale, your stomach should puff out. You need not take deep breaths. A normal intake of air is sufficient. Breathing this way for several minutes helps trigger the parasympathetic nervous system, which helps calm you down. Gentle reminders from a supportive partner to "Breathe" can make an anxious situation a calmer one.

Happy Reunions:
When Career/Business
Keeps You Apart

59

Hal is an interstate truck driver. He is often away from home for days at a time. His wife, Helen, has never quite grown accustomed to their on-again, off-again lifestyle. "Sometimes it feels like emotional whiplash," she says. "When he comes home after many days on the road, he expects to jump right into family life. But I've been in charge while he's been away. It isn't easy for me to shift gears."

Kate is a business executive. Her business trips are less frequent but she can expect to be away from home at least a few days a month. She and her partner, Steve, have no children and don't want to have children as long as their careers keep them so busy. "The hard part," Kate says, "is finding time for each other. We're each so accustomed to taking care of ourselves, we don't rely on each other so much emotionally."

Couples separated by career demands have a unique problem. They must learn to detach from one another in order to cope with frequent separations. But detachment makes reunions less exciting. Sometimes it takes couples a few days to adjust to having each other around.

Have You Heard?

~ Frequent short separations due to business or career demands create loneliness in the home-based partner and make it difficult to establish agreed-upon child-rearing strategies.

~ Reunions tend to be less happy than expected. The home-based partner carries a lot of mixed feelings—wanting attention and affection and yet resenting the partner's absence.

～ Wives of seamen and truck drivers view reunions as disruptive to the family routine. The men arrive home feeling unwanted or unneeded as their partners have learned to get by without them.

～ In one military base after the Persian Gulf War, the number of divorces filed by reunited couples was double the amount prior to the war.

～ Telephone conversations don't make up for absences.

How to Say It

It helps when each partner understands that frequent separations are disruptive—even though they may be necessary. It is normal for couples to have mixed feelings during a reunion, including some anger or detachment.

- "I'm sure you get angry at times after I've been away from home. I understand. We need to make the most of the time we do have."

- "It's weird being back home. In order to not feel lonely, I have to try to focus on my job when I'm away. But once I get back it isn't easy to automatically feel intimate. I guess we each need some time to decompress."

- "I'm not trying to undermine your authority with the kids. It's just that I have to make all the decisions by myself when you're away. It's easier for me to stay in charge while you're here. But I know that makes you feel left out. Let's discuss ways you can feel more a part of things."

- "Even though it takes us awhile to get used to being together, when I'm away I always miss you and dream about the next time I'll see you."

- "It's normal for us to feel uncomfortable at reunions, at least some of the time. So I'm just going to try not to feel uncomfortable about feeling uncomfortable."

- "Yes, I'm happy to see you and I hate it when you leave. But I also feel angry that you have to be away so much. I'll feel better soon. I always do."

If your partner says:

- *"You know I have to be on the road a lot. Why can't you get used to it?"*

- *"I don't like it when you don't let me have authority after I come home."*

- *"We're growing apart."*

You reply:

- *"If I could get used to it, it would mean I don't miss you. I don't think there's a way I can ever truly get used to it."*
- *"I'm glad you're home but I need you to ease into your role. I'm too accustomed to making all the decisions while you're away. We need time to get used to being with each other again, okay?"*
- *"If we're growing apart, then we have to do something. We don't have enough time together. We need to discuss all of our options."*

How Not to Say It

- "My job requires me to be away a lot. Get used to it." (Divorce rates are higher for couples who see little of one another. Don't add to that likelihood by taking a hard line. Empathy and understanding can help. *Better:* "I guess it bothers me when I see you upset over my job hours because I feel helpless to change them. But it's not fair to expect you to like the situation.")
- "Don't think you can take over and start barking out orders just because you've arrived home." (*Better:* "I know you want to feel like part of the family again but it will help me if you try to ease back into that role. Let's start by spending some nice, fun family time together.")
- "I know I just got back after being away for a week, but I have chores to do here and mail to catch up on." (Family comes first. Keep chores to a minimum no matter how necessary those chores may seem.)
- "Now that you're home, you take care of the kids. I need some time for myself." (You may need time for yourself, but a gentle transition is better than a harsh one. Get reacquainted with each other for awhile and then make it known that you might need some time for yourself.)
- "If you don't quit your job, I'm leaving you." (Giving ultimatums should come only as a last resort, especially if you knew what you were getting when you established a relationship with your partner. Some jobs can be changed more easily than others. Military careers cannot end abruptly and at will. *Better:* "Your career is causing me to grow apart from you and that scares me. I need some hope that things can change for the better in the future. Let's discuss options.")

Healing Words:
Increasing Trust

Nothing undermines a relationship more than mistrust. Betrayal is a destructive offense. The injured partner's shock and hurt cascades into anger, bitterness, withdrawal, desperateness, and an overriding grief. When a sexual affair is uncovered, it is often not the sex per se that creates the most difficulty for the betrayed spouse. It is the deceit. Affairs always involve deceit. Once a spouse discovers that his or her partner lied and can no longer be believed, the entire history of the relationship goes under scrutiny. *Who is this person I married? I don't know him anymore* is a common sentiment.

But trust can be undermined in lesser ways. Flirting with members of the opposite sex can make a partner feel insecure. Reading or watching a great deal of pornographic material can make a partner feel inadequate. Sex is the number-one topic researched online with about 300 million "hits" registered each month on the various sites. People who would never cheat on their partners find themselves exploring chat rooms and sex Web sites (usually in secrecy). Many couples argue over what constitutes "cheating."

When a person has reason to mistrust his or her partner, conversations become heated and frustrating. A partner may feel unfairly accused; the other, betrayed. Even when a person admits he or she cheated or lied and wants to reconcile, and even if he or she remains honest and faithful thereafter, doubts and accusations will arise. That is what happens when trust has been betrayed. Knowing how to handle these conversations becomes essential if the couple is to ever get past the hurt and move toward forgiveness and reconciliation.

Cybersex

60

Marge doesn't know what to do. Her husband has been spending an increasing amount of hours at online sex sites. She never liked the habit; in fact, it makes her feel inadequate. But lately he has spent several hours a night, often after she has fallen asleep, on the Web. He denies making use of any chat rooms, but Marge isn't sure he is telling the truth. In the past two months he has shown less interest in having sex with her. On weekends when she comes home with the children after an outing, she makes sure she makes enough noise coming up the steps to alert her husband. The last thing she wants is for her children to surprise their father while he is glued to the computer screen watching sex acts.

Have You Heard?

~ The majority of people who use the Internet for sexual stimulation do so for an hour a week or less. A significant minority does so for 10 hours a week or less. Users addicted to the Internet for sex may spend 15 hours a week online, with 25–40 hours not uncommon.

~ Chatting with a person online for the purpose of sexual stimulation is cheating on your partner, even if it's for five minutes a week.

~ Addicted individuals may be suffering from depression.

~ Nonaddicted users are often white-collar, educated males.

~ Partners of online users often feel ignored, unimportant, angry, and humiliated. Children are often ignored as well.

〜 A cybersex affair—even if the couple never meets in person—is just as devastating as an old-fashioned affair. The more online chatting there is, the more likely the messages sent are increasingly sexually graphic.

〜 The online cybersex user often reduces his interest in sex with his at-home partner.

〜 Marital problems can result, but these problems are often harder to discuss with friends or family due to embarrassment.

〜 ACE—Accessibility, Convenience, and Escape—are the three powerful reasons people get hooked. Use of Web servers that block pornographic material will help, but they are not foolproof.

〜 Evidence that there may be a cybersex problem include:

— *Caught in a lie about Internet use.*
— *Up late at night using the Internet.*
— *Reduction in carrying out home responsibilities.*
— *Hiding telephone bills.*
— *Moving the computer to a more secluded area of the house.*
— *Frequent attempts (failed) to reduce the time online or to quit altogether.*
— *Reduced interest in sex with one's partner/reduced involvement with partner.*

How to Say It

Even if your partner goes online for brief periods, and even if he or she says that the chat rooms are innocent and just for fun, you have a right to be concerned. Be firm, not wishy-washy.

• "I don't like you using chat rooms. It is a form of flirting and shows disrespect to me. I won't tolerate it."

• "You are taking time away from me and the kids so you can spend it with a stranger. That is unfair and wrong."

• "I feel neglected when you spend all that time on the computer."

• "We haven't made love nearly as often since you've been using the chat rooms. That's a problem. Things are just getting worse between us."

If your partner says:

- *"Everybody does this. It's innocent fun."*
- *"If you'd have more sex, then maybe I wouldn't need to find other people."*
- *"I'm at home the entire time."*
- *"I've cut back some already. What more do you want?"*
- *"You're just too insecure."*
- *"It's not a real affair."*

You reply:

- *"Most people don't do this. It's not innocent. It's hurting me."*
- *"You stop the cybersex and then you and I can look at our relationship. I'm not interested in having sex when I don't feel respected."*
- *"You are spending intimate, sexual time with someone other than me. That's an affair. I won't put up with it."*
- *"Cutting back is a sign that the person knows it is a problem. Besides, even one hour a week feels like a betrayal."*
- *"I don't entirely trust you. You've lied, you've spent time online with another person talking sex, and you insult me when I ask you to stop. Our relationship does not feel secure. If I were truly insecure, I'd do nothing about it for fear of offending you."*
- *"It involves lying, deceit, sex, and escape from intimacy within our marriage. If it's not an affair, it is every bit as damaging."*

Talking Point: A partner who cares about you and is not addicted to online sex will take your concerns seriously. If your partner expresses legitimate relationship concerns as a reason for the Internet use (*"You never have time for me . . . You're always working . . . You never listen to me like this other person does . . ."*), do not dismiss those issues. Take the complaints seriously and do what is needed to improve the quality of your relationship. However, the cybersex must stop. Marital problems are no excuse for cybersex.

How Not to Say It

- "How much time did you spend online yesterday? What time did you get to bed? Were you in a chat room again?" (An interrogation is a sign that the problem is getting out of hand. Whatever the answers, you will not be satisfied, at least not for long. *Better:* "I'm getting to the point where I cannot tolerate your being online for sex. If you won't stop, I have to reconsider if I can stay in this relationship.")

- "You're a pervert." (Your partner will disagree and tune you out. *Better:* "What you are doing is not something I can respect or tolerate.")

- "Just limit your time. You do it too much." (You are naive. It is not a mild form of entertainment if it affects your esteem and the quality of your marriage.)

If you are the one who enjoys Internet porn or sex chat rooms, you will most likely defend your habit. Any statement by you other than an honest recognition that you have let personal gratification take precedence over your relationship is self-serving.

Emotional Affairs

61

"We're just friends!" Nancy claims. "I work with the guy so what am I supposed to do when he wants to talk, say no?"

"You've been spending too many lunch hours with him," Nick says, "and lately when the phone rings somebody keeps hanging up on me when I answer it. I think it's him."

"Oh, you're sounding so juvenile. He's a nice guy, I like talking to him. You could learn some things from him in the conversation department."

Nick sighs. "And in what other department has he taught you things?"

"For Pete's sake, Nick. I keep telling you he's just a friend. Adult women can have adult male friends. This is the twenty-first century."

"I don't want you talking to him any more."

"Is that an order?"

Some male–female friendships are just that. Some start out innocently but become romanticized. If your partner doesn't want you having friends of the opposite sex, he or she may be a bit controlling. But you have to be honest with yourself. Do you flirt? Do you and your friend have frequent, intimate discussions that stir your passions even a little? Do you spend more quality time with your friend than you do with your partner? If so, you may be having an emotional affair.

Have You Heard?

〜 Secrecy and lying are the hallmarks of affairs. If your relationship with a "friend" has become secretive in some ways, watch out.

~ If your partner has a close friendship with a member of the opposite sex, don't automatically think betrayal. If you are uneasy, first examine how you have been as a partner. Improving your own relationship is the best protection.

~ Partners who tend to be harsh and controlling are easily jealous and misinterpret male–female friendships as threatening.

~ Warning signs that the friendship may really be an emotional affair:

- — *You spend more time talking with your friend about your marriage than you talk about it with your spouse.*
- — *You lie to your partner about meeting this person. Or you fail to mention that you saw this person because you don't want your partner to know about it.*
- — *You start withdrawing emotionally and physically from your partner and fantasizing more about your friend.*
- — *You hide your cell phone bills.*

How to Say It

If you are uneasy about your partner's friendship but have no basis for disproving it, it's okay to express your concerns. But don't sound accusatory.

- "It seems to me that you really enjoy your time with ____. I guess I feel a little jealous. I wish we had more enjoyable time together."

- "I may be wrong to say this, but it's beginning to bother me that your friend calls here when I'm not around. Should I be concerned?"

- "I want you to discuss with me the kinds of things you discuss with him (her)."

- "I notice you are always friendly and smiling when you talk to ____ on the phone. But you don't seem so happy to be with me when you get off the phone."

If you feel your partner's friendship is interfering in your marriage, or if you have reasons to believe your partner may be developing romantic feelings for the friend, you need to speak up. Anticipate defensiveness.

- "When I called you at work they said you were having lunch with Phil. But you never told me about that when I asked you about your day. I'm worried that you and Phil might be developing feelings for one another."

If your partner responds:

- "*You're letting your imagination get to you.*"
- "*How dare you check up on me.*" (Your partner sounds defensive here and may be hiding something.)
- "*I can have friends. You have no right to run my life.*"

You reply:

- "*Then I need some reassurance that you are happy in our relationship and that there is no one else. Can you do that?*"
- "*I've noticed that you are more detached from me lately. Frankly, I'm worried that you are developing feelings for someone else. If that is so, I want to know about it. I also want us to improve our relationship.*"
- "*I'm expressing a concern, I am not running your life. I need an honest answer about your feelings toward your friend.*"

If there is clear evidence that a friendship is blossoming into something more, or if your partner admits that romantic feelings have started to develop (but there is no sexual affair), you have to discuss how to rebuild trust and how to improve your relationship.

- "I need to know that the relationship is over. It is important to me that you no longer see this person. I know you started out as friends but I cannot trust you if I know you are continuing to talk to this person even casually. Maybe I'll feel differently over time."

- "I just want you to know that it isn't easy for me when you go to work and I know you will see your friend. I believe you when you tell me you don't speak to him anymore, but it's hard for me still." (Let your partner know that you will periodically *report* your uncomfortable feelings—to report is not to accuse but to inform. If your partner can be understanding and not defensive at those times, you will move past this issue more quickly.)

- "What could have prevented this from happening?"

- "It's important that we take a hard look at our relationship and make improvements where necessary."
- "Please do me a favor and several times a day please put yourself in my shoes. Imagine that I have had an emotional relationship with someone. Imagine what you would think and feel every time I left the house or came home later than expected."

How Not to Say It

Keep in mind that your partner did not have sex with another person and that emotional affairs usually begin innocently. Overblown accusations and cries of being victimized by your partner won't help.

- "I don't want you having friends of the opposite sex. It will always lead to trouble." (Opposite-sex friendships can be just that—friendships. But a controlling or overly-jealous spouse is hard to put up with.)
- "Your friend is only after one thing." (Your partner will dismiss this argument or view you as pathologically jealous. Point to reasonable evidence.)
- "I can never trust you again after what you did." (An emotional affair can be devastating. However, if a couple wants to remain together and improve their relationship, a willingness to trust again is essential. *Better:* "It's hard for me to completely trust you. But I'm hoping over time I can.")
- "Yes, I cared about this person and I looked forward to being with her. But I did not have an affair!" (Don't get caught up in semantics. Affairs can be nonsexual if romantic feelings develop and a person starts to close doors to their partner while opening doors to their friend. *Better:* "Since we never had sex, I always told myself there was nothing wrong with this relationship. I can see where I was wrong.")
- "Even though we won't have any secret meetings, I still intend to be good friends with this person." (Be careful. You have to decide if you are more loyal to your partner or to your friend. You may resent the idea of giving up a friendship, but you need to examine the ways that friendship was keeping you emotionally detached from your partner. A true friend will not want to interfere with your relationship. *Better:* "I want to be polite if I see her at work or on the street. But I won't talk to her like I did before.")

- "My friendship is over. Are you happy? Now let's move on with our lives and forget what happened." (Your partner cannot forget. Tender, romantic feelings and intimacies that should have been shared within the confines of your marriage were offered to another person. *Better:* "I can't blame you for feeling hurt and worried. I guess I'd like us to spend more time together and make our relationship the best it can be.")

- "It's been months since it happened. Won't you just forget about it?" (Sorry, but when trust has been compromised, it takes a forgiving partner a long time to feel at ease. Your attitude is making it harder for your partner to forget. *Better:* "I wish I could make the pain go away. I know you'll still worry from time to time, but I know that I am devoted to you.")

After the Affair

62

It has been three weeks since Ted's affair ended. His wife, Marie, found out the truth after finding Ted's cell phone bill and confronting the other woman. While Ted admits he has feelings for the other woman, he wants to stay married. He has been dissatisfied in his personal life for over a year—he is never clear whether he is unhappy with Marie or with himself. But he knows in his heart that the relationship with his mistress would never have succeeded. *

"What did you tell her when she called you at work? I thought you already insisted that she never call you again. Or was that another lie?"

Ted rolls his eyes. "I told her I couldn't talk to her. Then I politely hung up."

"That you couldn't talk to her?" Marie says. "You make it sound like it's not your choice. And why were you polite? I think you care more about not hurting her feelings than you care about not hurting mine."

"That's not fair, Marie. I blame myself for the affair, not her. I'm not going to be mean to her."

"Don't tell me she's an innocent victim. I'm more of a victim than she'll ever be."

Ted and Marie's conversations go on like that. Ted wants to forget the affair as quickly as possible and Marie insists she can't forget so easily. They both want the situation to improve. Neither of them know how to make that happen.

---

*It is estimated that in less than 10 percent of cases do couples having an affair end up happily together. This is discussed in my book *25 Stupid Mistakes Couples Make.*

Have You Heard?

~ Don't believe the myth that infidelity is rampant. More than 80 percent of women and about 75 percent of men are always faithful once they are married.

~ While the sexual aspect of an affair is difficult for an offended partner to cope with, it is the lies and secrecy that are most corrosive to trust.

~ There are many kinds of affairs and many more reasons for affairs. A one-night stand is different from a series of affairs by a philanderer. Some people have affairs due to relationship problems; others, because of personal problems or deficits in character.

~ Some people respond "I don't know" when asked why they had the affair. That can be an honest answer, especially if the person has a history of poor communication and is not prone to introspection. However, such a response will not be believed.

~ Some offended partners want to know all the graphic details of an affair. Where did they have sex? Did they perform oral sex? How attractive and sexually talented was the other person? These questions can haunt the offended partners. As much as they might hate hearing the answers, they find that their imagination can be worse than the truth. It is best that such questions are answered truthfully, however painful they are to hear.

~ Most offended partners need to ask and reask questions. Months after the affair has been revealed, the same questions may be repeated to an exhausted, increasingly frustrated partner. It is a mistake to refuse to answer the questions. The best demeanor of the guilty partner should be one of admitting guilt, showing remorse, and trying to be as honest as possible in answering (repeatedly) the questions.

~ Complete, up-front honesty when admitting the affair is best. However, the guilty partner often leaves out details that could be embarrassing or cause further damage to the relationship. A persistent partner usually gets more information over time. But since it required so much effort, he or she wonders what else has been kept hidden and so the questions and doubts continue.

~ Regaining trust takes a lot of time. The untrusting partner may notice that about 90 percent of trust might be regained within one or two years.

～ It is helpful for the guilty partner to realize that small events—arriving home 20 minutes late, driving by a certain restaurant, hang-up phone calls, and so on—will arouse suspicion or bad memories in one's partner. Complaining about it shows you are insensitive to your partner's pain.

How to Say It

If your partner had the affair:

- "I know I've asked you some of these questions before but I need to ask them again. Let's set a time limit, say, thirty minutes." (This can be a helpful strategy as opposed to asking questions at random, often inopportune, times. Plan on a day and time every week where questions can be asked. But stick to that schedule. If new questions arise, write them down and save them for the scheduled meeting.)

- "What aspects of our relationship were you dissatisfied with?"

- "If your girlfriend should contact you in any way, I'd like you to tell me about it. I promise I won't criticize you for it. I understand you can't control her behavior. I simply need to believe that you can be honest with me about what happens."

- "I'm finding that on some days I feel good and on other days I feel bitter. Some days I want to make passionate love with you, and on other days that repulses me."

- "I'm afraid to have a nice weekend with you (to make love, and so on) because you might take that as a sign that I'm doing better with this. If I can believe that you do understand the depth of my pain, I might be able to allow myself to enjoy some time together."

- "I'm not comfortable having sex with you until you've been examined by a doctor for a possible disease."

- "I can try to forgive but I cannot forget."

- "I will trust you a day at a time, then a week at a time. Nothing you did today has made me question your trustworthiness."

- "Even though it has been many months since we've tried to get past your affair, there are still days when I'm in pain, such as when I drive by the restaurant in which you and your friend had lunch. I need you to care about that."

- "I'm trusting you more and more. I feel I'm ready to look ahead to our future instead of focusing on the past." (Let your partner know when you feel better.)

If your partner is angry at repeated questions, show some understanding and make an in-flight repair.

- "You're right, it must be frustrating to not be believed. But I don't fully trust you just yet. That is why I'm asking the same questions."
- "You look disheartened. I know you worry that I'll never get over this. But I'll be more hopeful if I know you can put up with my questions and bad moods."
- "It means a lot to me when you can cooperate. I know you want this all to be in the past. We're getting there."

How Not to Say It

If your partner had an affair, you are entitled to say many things and in angry, uncooperative ways. You are not expected to always be polite and understanding. But if you want to repair the relationship, you must eventually say things in ways that will help heal the relationship, not cause further harm.

- "But why? Why did you have the affair? How could you really love me if you had an affair?" (There is no answer to "Why?" that will suffice. No matter what personal or relationship issues your partner had, you can always claim he had no good reason to have an affair. But since he did have an affair, you are left thinking he is hiding more of the truth from you. Your partner may still love you, hard as that is to believe right now. Look for other evidence of your partner's love.)
- "You're a whore."

Talking Point: Don't avoid the topic if you had the affair. Occasionally ask your partner "How are you doing?" If you are watching a movie and a character has an affair, take your partner's hand and tell her you are sorry. Even if she pulls away, she'll be grateful that you are trying to show compassion. Don't always wait for her to bring up the topic of your affair.

If you are the one who had the affair, you need to show frequent remorse and be understanding of your partner's moods and her difficulty getting close to you. Irritation that your partner is not forgiving or irritation at being asked repeated questions will not help your situation. Any of the following comments should be avoided:

- "Can't you forget what happened? Why do you have to live in the past?" (That shows a lack of understanding of the impact your affair had on your partner. *Better:* "I can't blame you for feeling that way. I'll be glad when you don't feel a need to bring up the topic.")
- "I've told you all that I intend to tell you. The rest is private." (Bad move. It appears that you care more about protecting yourself or the other person than you do about helping your partner heal. *Better:* "There are more details that don't change what happened but will only make you feel worse (such as the affair happened earlier than you think). But I will tell you if you really want to know them.")
- "I know that what I did was wrong but I think I paid the price. It's time that we stop talking about it and move on with our lives." (You haven't paid the price, trust me. *Better:* "I can't blame you for still wanting little to do with me. But I'm looking forward to the day when we can find closeness again.")
- "Why do *you* think I had the affair? When do *you* think the affair started?" (Throwing questions back to your partner is an attempt to hedge. Be upfront. There are already a lot of issues between you. Don't add to them by making wisecrack comments.)
- "I never would have had the affair if you had only done _____." (Don't even try to go there.)
- "I had too much to drink . . . She came on to me . . . A lot of people have affairs . . . " (Stop sounding like a teenager. Own up to your mistake.)
- "Are you going to let something like an affair ruin twenty years together?" (You need to be more sensitive to how your partner is feeling. *Better:* "It scares me that this might cause you to want to end our marriage. I never wanted that.")

Partner Still Has Some Love for the Ex

63

"Jean told me she was buying a new car," Dan says to his wife, Ellen.

"Oh? When did you see Jean?" Jean is Dan's former girlfriend. They had lived together for three years before breaking up.

"Didn't I tell you? I saw her in the mall yesterday so we had a bite to eat."

"No, you didn't tell me," Ellen says. "Seems like a strange thing to forget."

Dan sighs. "How many times do I have to tell you? I care about Jean but not like I used to. It's over between us. I chose to marry you."

"I'm not so sure it's over. I think you still carry a torch for her. If I wasn't in the picture right now, I bet you'd call her up today and ask for a date."

Dan doesn't know what to say. He is tired of Ellen's insinuations. But she is right about one thing—he does still hold some love for Jean. He simply knows it would never have worked out between them so that is why he married Ellen instead. But if he tells that to Ellen, she'd flip.

Have You Heard?

∿ The more attached one is to a former partner, the more distress there is in the new relationship. Wives are especially troubled if their husbands hold feelings toward their ex-wives.

∿ Relationships between former partners tend to be more positive when there are no children involved.

∿ In one study, about one-third of participants had feelings of attachment to their ex-spouses one year after the breakup.

~ Feelings of love or caring do not imply commitment. Don't hold your partner hostage to the fact that he or she was in love with someone else before you.

How to Say It

If your partner's relationship with an ex makes you insecure, speak up. But don't accuse. Using the GIFTS mnemonic, be sure to start gently, find underlying issues (if they exist) that might be fueling your insecurity, and remember teamwork.

- "Sometimes when you talk about ____ I feel a little jealous and insecure."
- "I guess I'm a little jealous. But I'd rather you get along with your ex than fight with him."
- "I know you still care about your ex-wife and I know you are committed to me. Still, I feel uneasy at times when the two of you talk or get together. I guess I need an extra hug on those days."

If your partner says:

- *"I wish you'd stop mistrusting me."*
- *"Yes, I care about her. But not like I used to."*
- *"I shouldn't have to always defend myself. You're just jealous and insecure."*

You reply:

- *"You're right, I'm sure it's annoying. But what bothers me about it is ____. Maybe I just need a little more reassurance."*
- *"Thanks for saying that. I'm sure over time it will bother me less."*
- *"You're probably right. Perhaps I would feel better if we changed a few things in our relationship. Can we discuss that?"*

How Not to Say It

- "If you loved me, you wouldn't have anything to do with her." (That's not fair. Better for you and your partner to improve your relationship rather than focus on his or her past relationship.)

- "You still love him, don't you!" (Stated as an accusation, this will add more tension than necessary. Your partner cannot help how she feels. She can control her behavior, however. *Better:* "I feel uneasy knowing you still love him, but I know you are committed to me. Bear with me if I sound too insecure.")

- "There is no need for you to talk to your ex-wife except about the children." (Your partner and his ex should not be keeping secrets from you. But his children are better off the more he and his former wife can get along. Cut them some slack.)

- "Do you ever fantasize about making love to him?" (Don't go there. You have probably fantasized about others. Fantasies are common. Make sure you are showing love to your partner and that she is showing it to you. If you do that, her feelings about her ex won't matter.)

If your partner is uneasy about your relationship with your ex and you know you are devoted to your partner, you can show some compassion without compromising your viewpoint.

- "I wish you didn't feel the way you do. But I do love you and I am committed to you."

- "Maybe I'd feel a little squeamish if you were friendly with your old boyfriend. I can understand how you might feel. But I know I am trustworthy and I appreciate it when you trust me."

How to Say It to Yourself

The goal is to look for alternative interpretations to your partner's feelings toward his or her ex that won't add to your insecurity.

- "He still cares about her. But that's a quality I can love about him. His concern for others isn't superficial."

- "I guess if we were to break up, I'd want him to think well of me and act kindly to me if we ran into each other."

- "My partner is fully committed to me. There are many people she could have chosen but she chose me."

- "I've always been a little insecure. It's not fair blaming my partner for that."

- "I guess what's really bothering me is that she hasn't been treating me very well of late. I've felt ignored. Maybe that's why it annoyed me when she was so cordial to her ex. I need to talk with her about my feelings of being neglected."

Partner Has Grown Cold and Distant

64

Paul is a trial attorney with a busy practice. He and Leslie have raised three children and have had their share of misunderstandings. Once Paul left for several days, saying he needed time to think about his life. Leslie was more angry than shocked. In her view, Paul tends to focus on his needs and problems more than hers. Still, they have had many years together and seem to love each other. But Paul's tendency to grow distant is a sore spot for Leslie. Recently, Paul seems more detached than usual. When she approaches and asks what is wrong, he politely says nothing is wrong. When she persists, he barks that she should leave him alone. Leslie's imagination takes over. Are there business problems? Is he having an affair? All she wants is to draw him out. But he is in his own world.

Have You Heard?

~ Partners who grow cold and distant are usually angry about perceived (but often unspoken) injustices.

~ A pattern develops whereby they will not say what's on their minds when asked, but instead will take out their anger passively by sulking or withdrawing or giving the cold shoulder.

~ The angry and distant partner feeds his (her) anger by negative self-talk about his (her) partner.

~ The GIFTS are in short supply. Refusing to talk about what's wrong while remaining cold and distant shows an unwillingness to make in-flight repairs, to look for underlying issues, to operate as a team, and to show support.

How to Say It

If your partner is angry and uncommunicative (and this is a repeated pattern), your best approach is to acknowledge the anger without cajoling him or her to open up.

- "I think you are upset about something. If you are, you can talk to me about it whenever you want."
- "When you act withdrawn, it usually means you are angry at me about something. I know you don't feel comfortable expressing your anger, but I'll listen."
- "I'll talk with you about it when you're ready."
- If your partner does speak up, express gratitude. "Thanks for talking to me. It means a lot to me when you do that."

When things are calm, you need to discuss the larger issue: How your partner holds grudges and holds you hostage to his anger while not being open about what's bothering him.

- "Please tell me what's bothering you at the time you are upset. I have a hard time sympathizing with you when you bring up something weeks later. Can you do that?"
- "If you bring up complaints sooner and don't give me the cold shoulder, I promise I'll be receptive to your concerns."
- "Sometimes what you get mad about is really a misunderstanding on your part. If we discuss it sooner, it can eliminate a lot of unnecessary anger."

A common but *ineffective* dialogue might go like this:

"Is there something I could do differently that would make it easier for you to bring up your complaints sooner?"

"Yes. You could stop getting defensive or critical. Whenever I make a complaint, you tell me I'm wrong, so I figure 'Why bother talking?'"

(Mildly defensive) *"I'm not criticizing, I'm just giving my point of view. You just take it as a criticism. Then you shut down."*

(Accusatory) *"No, you don't realize how critical you can get. You may think you are offering an opinion but you're really telling me I have no right to feel the way I do."*

(Defensive) *"That's not true!"*

(Accusatory) *"See? You did it again."*

An *effective* dialogue might go like this:

"Is there something I could do differently that would make it easier for you to bring up your complaints sooner?"

"Yes. You could stop getting defensive or critical. Whenever I make a complaint, you tell me I'm wrong, so I figure 'Why bother talking?'"

(Nondefensive; Teamwork) *"That's where we get stuck. You think I'm being critical, I think I'm just giving an opinion and don't intend to sound critical. We need to find a way around that."*

(Nondefensive; Teamwork) *"Well, if I think you are being critical, I could tell you that. Then you could rephrase what you said."*

"Okay. I'll do that if you hang in there with me and don't withdraw. Deal?"

"Deal."

How Not to Say It

- "You're giving me the cold shoulder again. What's wrong with you, huh? Speak to me!" (Don't demand. Acknowledge that your partner is standoffish, offer to talk, then go about your business until your partner speaks up.)

- "If that's the way you want to be, fine. See if I care." (It's frustrating when an angry partner refuses to say what he's (she's) angry about. But this response will only add to your partner's view that you are a difficult person.)

If you have a tendency to give cold shoulders, you need to work on reporting your feelings instead of acting on them.

How to Say It

- "I have something on my mind. Ordinarily I'd keep it to myself and stew about it. I don't want to do that anymore."
- Be direct without being sharply critical. "I'd really like it if you wouldn't . . . I have a problem with . . . It bothers me when . . . I'm uncomfortable speaking about this but . . . Please hear me out, this isn't easy for me . . . I'd appreciate it if . . . Something has been on my mind and I should have mentioned it sooner . . . "
- Be willing to make in-flight repairs. Don't let a partner's critical comment or defensiveness be your excuse to shut down. "You're right, it isn't easy for you when I shut down . . . I can see why this upsets you . . . You have a point . . . "

How to Say It to Yourself

If you tend to hold grudges and give the cold shoulder, you need to change your negative self-talk. Instead of saying this to yourself:

- *"He'll never understand. I'll just ignore him."*
- *"Why did I even marry her? I just wish she'd leave me alone."*
- *"I'll show her. I'll just refuse to talk to her."*

Say this:

- *"I have to give him a chance to understand. That can only happen if I speak up."*
- *"The more I withdraw from her, the less close I'll feel. I need to talk to her even if I find that hard to do."*
- *"I'm just trying to get even. But maybe she didn't hurt me the way I thought she did. Maybe I'm overreacting. I need to talk things over with her."*

Partner Won't Commit

65

Phyllis and Sam have been living together for over two years. Phyllis wants an engagement ring. Sam keeps saying he isn't ready for marriage. Phyllis isn't willing to end the relationship, but the possibility that she could be unmarried and still living with Sam two years from now horrifies her.

Leslie is 29. An attractive career woman, her relationships with men tend to fizzle. She is reluctant to make a full commitment to a relationship in part because career advancement is important to her.

Like many young adults these days, Leslie views a relationship without strings as the perfect way to have closeness and companionship without a binding commitment. Unfortunately, a relationship is likely to fail without commitment. That can make a person reluctant to make a commitment the next time around for fear of getting hurt all over again.

Have You Heard?

~ Men and women whose parents had divorced have a higher chance of fearing commitment.

~ Common reasons cited include fear of losing one's identity, fear of financial loss, fear of loss of control over one's life, and fear of taking on adult responsibilities.

~ There are three types of commitment. The first is based on attraction and love: "I'm committed to you because I love you." The second type is moral. It is a commitment to marriage as a sacred institution, a commitment to one's vows: "I'm committed to you because my vows meant something to me and our marriage is important." The third type is due to fearing the consequences of a breakup and is empty of love: "I'm committed to you because I don't want to be alone . . . I can't afford to be single . . . My parents would disown me . . ."

～ While the second and third types of commitment seem less romantic, they are nonetheless essential. It is precisely when feelings of love fade or problems arise that a couple must rely on more than just their tender feelings to get them through. Staying together for the sake of the children or because you take your vows seriously can provide the time needed to make necessary repairs and hopefully allow the feelings of love to reemerge.

～ In my book *25 Stupid Mistakes Couples Make*, I discuss research that shows how living together before marriage does not improve a couple's compatibility. In fact, the divorce rate for couples who cohabited before marriage is twice as high as couples who did not live together.

～ The sooner you have sex when dating, the less likely the relationship will last. If you want a committed relationship, postpone having sex.

～ The longer you remain in an uncommitted relationship, the less likely there will be a commitment.

How to Say It

If you truly want a commitment but your partner is avoiding it, you have to be willing to ultimately end the relationship. Your job is not to make threats, but to clearly identify and state your wishes and goals.

- "We've been together for almost two years. As much as I love you, I want a lifelong, committed relationship. I cannot continue in this relationship if you are unable to make a commitment."

- "We've been living together for a year. Our intention was to plan a wedding if we made it through the first year. I want us to get married. I can't stay in this relationship if we won't get married."

If your partner says:

- *"That sounds like an ultimatum."*
- *"I haven't made up my mind yet."*
- *"If you loved me, you'd give me more time."*

You reply:

- *"It isn't a threat. I'm simply telling you what I believe. I love you and want us to get married. I can't stay with you much longer if we don't have a goal to get married."*
- *"You're entitled to take your time. All I'm saying is that the longer we go on without a commitment, the more I may have to move on. I want to marry you, not just live with you."*
- *"I do love you. Take the time you need. I certainly want you to be sure of what you want. But I have to look after my needs, too. If I believe you won't want to get married, I won't stay with you."*

Examine some of the reasons for lack of commitment.

- "What could happen that would make you more eager to commit?"
- "Have you felt this way in other relationships?"
- "What changes would you like to see that would help you want to make a commitment?"

Examine your own motivations for remaining in an uncommitted relationship.

- "What could happen that would make me say it's time to move on?"
- "Have I put up with a low-committed partner in the past?"
- "Am I afraid to move on?"

How Not to Say It

- "Maybe we should live together first. That will help us decide if we're compatible." (Cohabitation does not improve relationship quality, does not help a couple determine if they are compatible, and diminishes one's attitude toward the value of marriage.)
- "It's been three years. How much longer before you decide you want to get married?" (You should take a stand, not wait for your partner to take a stand. *Better:* "Unless you can make an honest commitment to marriage, I won't stay with you.")

- "Don't you think marriage is a good idea?" (Talking like this shows that you have been passive and submissive regarding the issue of commitment. The more passive you are, the more likely your partner will take his or her sweet time making a commitment. *Better:* "I come as a package deal: me and marriage.")

Flirting

66

Corrine and Elliot have been dating for a year. She works as an administrative assistant. Elliot sometimes comes by her office after work to take her to dinner—and sometimes he doesn't like what he sees.

"Don't you think you're being just a tad friendly to those executives?" he accuses. "Half of those guys would hit on you if you gave them the smallest hint of interest."

Corrine dislikes the insinuation. Yes, she is friendly. She enjoys bantering with the people in the office—men and women. What is wrong with that? If some co-worker gets the wrong idea, she'd disabuse him of that notion quickly.

"What are you accusing me of?" she asks Elliot.

"I'm not accusing—Oh, all right. I think you enjoy flirting and frankly it bothers me. How would you feel if I flirted with your friends or with some of the teachers I work with?"

"If it were just a form of friendliness, I wouldn't mind at all. That's your problem. You confuse friendliness with flirting."

Have You Heard?

~ Men are more upset about a partner's flirting if they view their rival as having a dominating demeanor. Women are more upset by a partner's flirting if they view their rivals as sexually attractive.

~ Socially shy women may be more animated, self-disclosing, and flirtatious after drinking alcohol. People with higher social confidence are not as affected by alcohol in that way. Thus, if your partner seems to flirt only after drinking, it may be that he or she is simply shy to begin with and is not hitting on someone else.

~ In a study of married, obese individuals who had stomach bypass surgery to lose weight, they became more friendly and playful in social interactions and liked to flirt. Their spouses felt threatened and jealous.

~ Flirting with someone other than your partner is risky. If you love your partner and do not desire to hurt him or her, be friendly toward others but don't flirt. At best, your partner will think you are immature or rude. At worst, she (he) will think you are lacking in devotion.

How to Say It

- "I don't like it when you flirt. Please stop it."
- "I felt mildly humiliated when you were flirting. Would you stop doing that?"
- "I know you are just being friendly and I think I am probably overreacting. But I guess what I need is more reassurance from you about your love for me. I think because I don't have that, I get uneasy when I see you being very friendly with other men (women)."
- "My last boyfriend (girlfriend) cheated on me. So I am a little skittish when I think you are flirting. It's my problem, bear with me."
- "Thanks for paying attention to me at the party. That meant a lot."
- "I'm not sure if you are intentionally flirting or not, but when you say _____ and when you _____, it looks like flirting to me and it bothers me."

If your partner says:

- *"I wasn't flirting!"*
- *"You're overreacting!"*
- *"You know I didn't mean anything by it. I was just having some fun."*
- *"You don't trust me."*

You reply:

- *"What I saw you do was _____. Maybe that isn't flirting, maybe it is. But I know I don't like it. Is it something you'd be willing to stop?"*
- *"Maybe I am overreacting. I just get uncomfortable when I see you do _____. I guess I'm a bit insecure."*

- *"You probably didn't mean anything by it but it really hurts my feelings. You can be friendly. Just don't _____ ."*
- *"I simply don't want to have reasons to doubt how you feel about me. When you flirt like that it doesn't make me feel secure in our relationship."*

How Not to Say It

- "Why were you hitting on that person? Why did you lead that man (woman) on?" (These comments are more accusatory and likely to invite defensiveness. Asking "why?" questions when you are hurt or angry usually sounds like an accusation more than a request for information. *Better:* "It looked to me like you were leading that man (woman) on. It really bothered me. Were you?")
- "Where were you at the party when I couldn't find you? Flirting again?"
- "If you loved me, you wouldn't talk to certain people." (That's unrealistic. Your jealousy is out of hand.)

If you have been accused of flirting but believe that the accusation is unfair, it's okay to speak your mind.

How to Say It

- "I wasn't flirting, I was simply talking to that person. It worries me that you think I'm doing something wrong when I'm not."
- "If you want me to pay more attention to you, I will. But I'm not going to ignore others just so you can be reassured I'm not flirting. That isn't fair."
- "You've often accused me of flirting when I wasn't. It concerns me that you don't trust me. Have I done something to cause that mistrust or are you oversensitive?"

How Not to Say It

- "If it will make you feel better, I won't talk to certain people at the party." (If the flirting accusation is unfair, it is a mistake to significantly change your behavior. The problem is your partner's insecurity. You will resent him or her over time as your life becomes more restricted.)

- "I can talk to whomever I want. You can't tell me what to do." (Tone it down. *Better:* "If I knew that I was wrong I would certainly make some changes. But I'm not doing anything wrong. I'll be happy to pay more attention to you when we are out in public, but I can't stop talking to certain people just because you think I'm flirting.")

Talking Point: A jealous or insecure partner will misread friendliness as flirting. If you withdraw from social interactions in order to please your insecure partner, you are making a mistake. An insecure partner can always find something to feel insecure about. Unless your partner is willing to change his or her pattern of thinking, there is little you can do that will help.

Soul Mates:
Encouraging Dreams
and Spiritual Longings

Love must be sacrificial; otherwise, it is superficial.

Without sacrifice, love is fondness and attraction. That means that when your partner has dreams and spiritual longings, you are obligated out of love to help your partner evaluate the legitimacy of those dreams and pursue them, if possible. Pursuing them may be difficult because the laundry must still get done, the children must be bathed and fed, and the groceries must be put away. But when your partner has a dream, a dream that won't easily die and that makes her glow whenever she talks about it, you should try to help her achieve it.

Some dreams are about career changes or learning some new skill. Some dreams have a clear spiritual focus to them, such as when a person wants to rediscover his spiritual roots, return to worship services, modify his lifestyle to reflect new soulful pursuits, or forgive a deep hurt. Conversations about dreams and spiritual longings require a willingness to hear each other out before reaching a conclusion. Challenging your partner's ideas the moment you hear something you don't agree with may turn the discussion into a debate instead of what it should be—an exploration.

When you and your partner can talk freely about dreams and spiritual longings, you are not just connecting mind to mind or heart to heart. You are connecting your souls.

You Want Your Partner to Attend Church

Hillary and Gerry are part of the 95 percent of Americans who believe in God. They try to lead good lives but are never regular churchgoers. When their children were toddlers, attending church services was even more of a hassle. It was a lot easier just to stay home on a Sunday morning.

Now their children are in grade school. Hillary feels a growing obligation to attend church with her children. Gerry doesn't feel so strongly as she does.

"You don't need to go to church to have faith in God," he says. "Besides, many people who attend church are hypocrites and organized religion is divisive. Everyone thinks their way is the right way. It leaves a bad taste in my mouth."

"But our children should have some religious identity. Otherwise, they may have none when they get older, " Hillary argues. "It won't hurt them to attend services. But it would be so much easier to show them how important it is if you would come with us. Otherwise, they'll think they don't have to go if they don't feel like it."

Have You Heard?

〜 Couples who pray together and attend church regularly are much less likely to divorce than couples who do not attend church. These couples are not just staying together out of a grim sense of obligation. They are genuinely happy.

〜 Couples who believe their marriage is sacred are far less likely to have aggressive verbal arguments.

〜 Attending services together allows a couple to share in meaningful rituals and to develop or enhance shared values.

301

〜 Frequency of joint prayer is a better predictor of marital happiness than frequency of sexual intercourse.

〜 People abused as children seem to suffer a spiritual injury as well as a physical one. Their religious beliefs wax and wane but they show an increase in prayer life over time. This suggests that while adults abused as children struggle with religion, they have strong spiritual longings.

How to Say It

Don't try to persuade your partner using flawless logic. Instead, discuss why attending services is important to you.

- "I know many people don't agree that attending church is necessary. But it reminds me of my obligation to God, it allows me an hour a week of meditation, and it shows our children that we don't just believe in God but want to worship Him."

- "I fear the longer we go on without attending synagogue, our children will believe it is not important. Twenty years from now I want to believe we did the right thing as parents, regardless of what our children choose to believe about religion."

- "It is important to me to become more spiritual. I don't want that side of me to be something you cannot appreciate."

If you meet resistance, try to validate some of your partner's viewpoints.

- "I can see why you feel that way . . . It makes sense that you think some churchgoers are hypocrites . . . You're right that this represents a shift in my thinking . . . "

- "I understand you don't feel the same way I do. But I'm wondering if you can accompany me to church (synagogue, mosque) anyway."

- "It has always meant a lot to me when you did go to services with me."

- "I know I intend to go to services regularly. I guess I'm hoping you will be willing to try it for a few months. After that, if it really is something you feel you can't do, I'll know that you made an effort."

- If you believe there are hidden reasons for your partner's refusal to attend services, inquire about them. "I've noticed you don't seem that enthusiastic about many things lately. Is it possible something is on your mind that you're not talking about?"

How Not to Say It

- "Don't you think going to worship services is something we should do?" (Asking "Don't you think?" questions ["Don't you care about God? . . . Don't you care what your children will think? . . .] is a mistake. You are really telling your partner he [she] is wrong and forcing him [her] to defend his [her] position.)
- "If you're not going, then I won't go." (If you are sincere in your desire to attend, you should go even if your partner refuses. Walk the walk, don't just talk the talk.)
- "You never do anything I want." (If you have complaints that go beyond this issue, try to separate them out. If you throw the kitchen sink at your partner, he or she may never be open-minded about going to services.)
- "What should I tell the pastor when he asks where you are?" (This will only irritate your partner. Attend services by yourself and occasionally make requests for your partner to attend with you. Be willing to take "No" for an answer. You can always pray that your partner will change his or her mind.)

Discussing in Which Religion to Raise Your Children

68

Pauline and Frank are about six months away from getting married. Frank is a Catholic and Pauline is a Presbyterian. Neither is especially devoted to his or her religious faith, but they each feel more comfortable attending services in his or her own religion. Still, they will often attend services at each other's church. The main difficulty surfaces when they have to decide who will officiate at the wedding ceremony. Frank speaks to a priest and is told he could receive a special dispensation that would allow his marriage to be registered in the Catholic Church even if a minister married them. However, Frank has to agree to raise his children as Catholics. He isn't sure Pauline will agree to that.

Have You Heard?

～ Interfaith marriages are common. Interfaith couples have a slightly higher divorce rate than same-faith couples.

～ On measures of happiness, same-faith couples report a slightly higher happiness level than interfaith couples, who are happier than couples where one or both have no religious faith.

～ In a 1991 study, children of Jewish–Christian couples were psychologically healthier if raised in the religion of one parent than in both faiths (or in none at all).

～ Interfaith couples should teach children to honor and respect their dual heritage. However, the children should be provided with a single religious identity.

⤳ It is beneficial for couples of different faiths to decide in which faith to raise the children *before* there is a pregnancy.

⤳ If you and your partner do not have children and you *strongly* disagree with one another about religious education, you should consider ending the relationship.

How to Say It

Remember the GIFTS. Begin comments gently.

- "It is important to me in which religious faith our children are raised. May we discuss this?"
- "This may be a difficult topic but we should come to an agreement. When is a good time to talk?"
- "I know your religious faith has some importance to you, as does mine. We need to discuss in which faith the children should be brought up. What are your expectations?"

Your goal is not to cajole or browbeat your partner. If you and your partner disagree about the religious education of your children, you must be prepared to not get your way. Since the decision has long-lasting consequences for the children and perhaps for the quality of your marriage, you want to make sure the "loser" of the discussion can be supportive, not resentful.

Discuss the dream behind your desire to have your children raised in your religion.

- "While I haven't been the most devoted person, I do love my religion. I remember growing up and attending church with my parents. It is something I look forward to repeating with our kids."

If there are flare-ups in the discussion, make in-flight repairs and supportive comments.

- "You're right. Your family is very religious and our decision will affect them."
- "I can't blame you for feeling strange at the prospect of raising the kids in a different religion."

- "It makes sense that you would want the kids involved in some of the religious rituals with which you're familiar."
- "Your religion is important to me too."
- "Whatever we decide, the children will learn respect for both religions."
- "I understand why your faith is important to you."

Yield to some of your partner's ideas, if at all possible. The "December Dilemma"—deciding which religious rituals to follow—need not be a dilemma at all.

- "I don't mind having a Christmas tree."
- "Sure, we can give gifts at Hanukkah too."
- "Yes, the kids may attend services at your church."
- "I'm sure it would be wonderful to teach the kids the history of some of your religious traditions."

Find some ways to meet each other's concerns.

- "If we raised the children according to my religion, what could we do that would help you to not resent it?"
- "What could happen that would make it easier for you to agree to go along more with my wishes?"
- "If the kids were not raised in my faith, I would probably feel better if
  _____."

> *Talking Point:* How a couple handles this problem is an indication of how they are likely to handle other disagreements. Disagreements about religious upbringing must be handled with sensitivity, sacrifice, respect, and an ability to keep one's promises over time.

How Not to Say It

- "My parents would be so upset if the kids were raised in your religion." (Perhaps they would, but that is not a justification. Your religious faith should be important to *you*, not only your parents.)

- "There is no way I'd have the kids raised in your religion." (There is no need to be disrespectful.)

- "We won't raise the children according to any religion. Instead, we can let them make up their own minds when they are older." (If religion is important to you, it should be important enough that you raise your children with religious principles and beliefs. If it is not that important to you, yield to your partner's wishes.)

- "We'll raise them in both religions." (Not a good idea. Children should have a clear religious identity. You can let them participate in various religious rituals if you like, and you can teach them various aspects of both religions. But they should be clear about which religious faith they are members of.)

- "We can do it your way, but don't expect any help from me." (You don't want a religious war in your house. You don't have to agree with your partner's beliefs, but it is okay to show some interest in the faith for your children's sake. Even teaching the kids why your faith is different is perfectly reasonable.)

- "If we're raising the children according to my faith, it will be less confusing for them if we did not teach them any aspects of your faith." (Both faiths should be honored and respected. All faiths have beautiful and meaningful traditions. Let the kids know about them.)

- "You're not that religious anyway. So we should go to my church (synagogue), instead." (People may get out of the habit of attending services but still may be reluctant to abandon their faith altogether. Often, people become more religious and spiritual once they have children. *Better:* "Up until now your religion has not been an important and regular part of your life. If the children were to attend your church, I would feel better if you were a regular churchgoer and were willing to teach the kids about your faith.")

Loving the Eternal Pessimist

69

Dave's outlook on life has always been pessimistic. He walks through life as a victim, especially after he suffers some permanent injuries in a car accident. When his wife, Clara, tries to cheer him up, he criticizes her for being a Pollyanna. When she speaks about future goals, he complains that she always has her head in the clouds. When his doctor recommends special physical exercises that might help him, he declares them worthless after only a few attempts.

Clara always has an idea or new suggestion for Dave—most of them sound. But Dave pooh-poohs them and insists that life is not as simple as she makes it out. As a result of his pessimism, Dave has no goals for himself. With no goals, he has little to look forward to. But Clara has no idea how to help him. All of her attempts to encourage him and offer him hope have failed.

Have You Heard?

~ Some people are "help-rejecting complainers." They always have a gripe and, when you try to advise or help them, they reject your ideas and continue to complain.

~ Pessimism can lead to depression. Pessimistic people have a hard time imagining a positive outcome. When putting forth effort to achieve something, they will give up early at the first signs of difficulty and create a self-fulfilling prophecy.

~ If you are more invested in a pessimist changing than he or she is invested in changing, you will always be frustrated and aggravated. Trying to "fix" somebody who refuses to be fixed is a recipe for misery.

How to Say It

Well-intended, upbeat suggestions won't work if your partner has been pessimistic for a year or more. If you are frustrated by your partner's pessimism, you've probably fluctuated between giving advice or withdrawing in a huff. Neither approach will help your partner to change if he or she hasn't changed yet, but will only make you feel ineffective and drained.

Stop trying to make your partner an optimist. Instead, do the opposite of what he or she expects. Practice making empathetic and supportive comments when your partner expresses a pessimistic idea. Never challenge him or her. Pessimists like to complain about being misunderstood, but your supportive comments will give him or her less to complain about.

- "You must be feeling sad."
- "It must be discouraging for you when there is nothing to look forward to."
- "You sound disappointed."
- "It must be hard for you day after day."
- "There doesn't seem to be an answer to your concerns."
- "You must suffer silently a lot, too."
- "It probably frustrates you when I try to make you look at the bright side. If I understood you better, maybe I wouldn't be so quick to give advice."
- "Life certainly hasn't been kind to you."

If your partner is making a string of complaints about his or her life, make brief comments that show you are listening.

- "I don't blame you."
- "I see."
- "Keep talking. I'm listening."
- "Tell me more about that."
- "Uh-huh."
- "Maybe you're right."

If your partner questions your new attitude, say:

- "I want to accept you for who you are, not try to change you."
- "Maybe I've been too optimistic over the years."

- "What right do I have to tell you how you should act?"

It will be important for you to have outside interests or good friends to keep you from feeling drained. If your partner criticizes your activities or complains that you are not around that much, do not get defensive. These criticisms are setups designed to make you say harsh things so your partner can once again feel misunderstood and victimized. If your partner criticizes your schedule of activities, say:

- "You sound lonesome."
- "I'd be happy to have you join me."
- "I'm sorry you feel that way. But I really need to do this for me. I'll be back soon."
- "If I'm happier, I can be a better spouse."

How Not to Say It

- "Life has been hard for you. But if you'd just . . ." (Never give advice to an eternal pessimist. Show empathy or support and that's all.)
- "I'm not going to talk to you if you never listen to my advice." (*Better:* "I notice that when I give you advice, you don't find it helpful. That must be frustrating for you.")
- "You're such a pessimist! You should talk to a professional!" (You are correct, but these comments won't accomplish anything. Your partner will just get annoyed.)
- "Your problem is your attitude!"
- "Snap out of it!" (It isn't that simple.)
- "How many times have I told you what you should do, but do you listen?"
- "I have to find new hobbies. Don't you know how depressing it is to be with you?"

How to Say It to Yourself

Be careful. While a pessimist's self-talk is negative, your own self-talk can become negative as you feel drained from trying to perk up your partner's enthusiasm for life. If you say to yourself things like, *"I can't stand this!"* or *"How can I live with someone who is so negative all the time?"* you need to improve your self-talk.

- "I can find peace in my life."
- "Since trying to cheer him (her) up doesn't work, I can simply try to show some empathy without trying to get him (her) to change."
- "There are many things I can do and people I can talk to who will bring joy."
- "My partner needs my prayers."
- "I can find the good in all of this."

Staying Upbeat When Your Partner Wants to Change Careers

70

Felicity wants to go back to school and become a veterinarian. The youngest of her three children is a junior in high school and she thinks it is time to put her life on a different career path. Her husband, Vince, agrees. Although their income will drop while she attends school—and they will have to get used to having a little less time for one another while she is busy studying—they believe it is important for Felicity to make her dream come true.

Mid-life is a time when many people rethink their life's goals (although dreams and yearnings happen at any age). They see themselves as young enough for a new career and past the age of raising children. Ironically, just as many husbands are ready to settle into home life and stop trying to climb the career ladder, their wives are looking outside the home for a new direction.

Whether it is changing careers or learning to play a musical instrument or growing a fabulous garden, people search for meaning in their lives. They want their lives to stand for something and their days to be eventful. They want a reason to get up in the morning. They want a sense of achievement or a deep intimacy with others.

Have You Heard?

~ In a study of women from Radcliffe who graduated in 1964, two-thirds had made a major change in education or career between the ages of 37 and 43.

312

~ Of these women, those who regretted earlier life decisions but had not made any subsequent changes had a more negative outlook on life by age 43.

How to Say It

Let your partner know you are aware of the impact your life changes may have on the relationship. It will be easier for your partner to support your needs if you show some empathy.

- "It might mean less income for us. What are your thoughts?"
- "I imagine I'll be spending some of my weekends studying instead of spending them with you. What can we do to help make up for that?"

If your partner has misgivings, don't automatically defend your position. Your partner may not be saying "No" but simply raising questions. Yield to some of your partner's more legitimate concerns.

- "You're right. We will have less time together and that is a drawback."
- "I can see why you might be uneasy. You had imagined we'd have more time to travel and be together and now I'm planning on returning to school."
- "I don't blame you for not being excited. I'm springing this on you rather suddenly."
- "Maybe we should just think about it for awhile and discuss it again in a few days."

Discuss why this change has particular meaning for you, especially if your partner has some concerns.

- "I guess I look at our life together and realize we still have about thirty or more years left. I'd feel I was wasting some of those years if I didn't try something new. I want to learn as much as I can and feel a sense of accomplishment. And I want our children to see me as a role model. They should know that it's never too late to do something you believe in."

If your partner says:

- *"You never spoke of this before."*
- *"You're just going through a mid-life crisis. It will pass."*
- *"What about us?"*

You reply:

- *"I guess I waited until the time was right for me to make some changes. Now the time is right. But I still want to spend the rest of my life with you."*
- *"Perhaps, but I don't think so. Anyway, I want to try. I fear that if I keep postponing it I may never do it."*
- *"You sound worried. You are still my priority. I just think I can also pursue this other interest. I think it will make our life together even more interesting and give us more things to talk about."*

How Not to Say It

- "I can do what I want to do." (*Better:* "I really feel strongly about doing this, but I'd like to hear any concerns you have. I will need your support during this.")
- "You don't have a right to disagree. I went along with everything you wanted over the years regarding your career." (He or she still has a right to disagree. *Better:* "I was happy to go along with your career wishes when the kids were younger. Now it is just the two of us and I feel a strong need to take on a new challenge.")
- "I'd like to learn a new skill or take on a really challenging hobby. But maybe I'm kidding myself. I should be content with what I have." (Don't be so quick to discourage your dreams. Think them through and find the courage.)

If your partner is eager to make a career change, try to become a cheerleader for the cause. You certainly should express any concerns you have and such things as the financial impact of the change must be discussed. But overall, show enthusiasm.

- "I know you've been wanting to do this for a long time. Let's do our best to make it happen."

- "I love you and I want you to be happy. If you think this is important to you, I'll back you up."
- "It won't always be easy for me but I'm willing to make this sacrifice for you. I want you to feel fulfilled."
- "I really support the idea in general. I just need to get used to it. But if it's that important to you to do this, I think we should give it our best shot."

Helping Your Partner to Forgive

Hal is estranged from his father. He has good reasons, for his father had rarely been involved in his upbringing and had made Hal's mother's life unnecessarily hard. Now his father is critically ill. Hal wants to put aside his bitterness, but he isn't sure his father deserves forgiveness.

The longer we live, the more likely we will encounter someone who will hurt us deeply. If our anger or fear over having been hurt is strong, our current relationships can suffer from the fallout. Forgiveness may be the only legitimate path to overcoming resentment.

If your partner wants to forgive someone else, you can be helpful in the process.

Have You Heard?

∼ Forgiveness starts as a decision, not a feeling. You do not have to feel forgiving for you to choose the path of forgiveness.

∼ Forgiveness does not overlook the harm that was caused. It does not minimize the pain or make excuses for the offender. In its truest form, forgiveness is not mere letting go of anger or hurt. It also includes a willingness to treat the wrongdoer with some form of generosity or love—which the wrongdoer does not deserve.

∼ Forgiveness is not reconciliation. To truly reconcile with a person and continue a relationship with someone who has deeply hurt you, there must be

316

forgiveness. But you can forgive without choosing to reconcile. Some wrong-doers are not remorseful and would continue to be hurtful. There is no moral obligation to reconcile with that person.

~ Fundamentally, there are four phases to the forgiveness process.* The *Uncovering Phase* involves identifying the nature of the hurts and the awareness that they have caused significant, perhaps life-altering, pain. The *Decision Phase* involves insight that the old methods of coping with one's anger have not worked and a willingness to consider forgiveness as an option. The *Work Phase* involves developing compassion and empathy for the wrongdoer and absorbing the pain (rather than seeking vengeance). The *Deepening Phase* occurs when a greater meaning to one's suffering is discovered and one's life takes on a greater purpose.

How to Say It

Help your partner make his or her way through the four phases of forgiveness listed above. Always validate your partner's hurt or anger. Don't suggest that it is wrong not to forgive. Give your partner time to sort through all options without pressuring him or her.

- "He was wrong to do what he did to you."
- "You have a right to be angry."
- "I can't blame you for wanting little to do with that person."
- "If you want to try to forgive her, I will support you any way I can."
- "It is hard to forgive something like that."
- "You can choose to forgive without feeling love for that person."
- "By choosing to forgive, you don't have to have a relationship with that person if you don't want to."
- "By choosing to forgive, you are not minimizing what was done to you. In fact, you are acknowledging that it was wrong and hurtful."

---

*Dr. Robert Enright and his colleagues have conducted groundbreaking research into the forgiveness process at the University of Wisconsin. He is also the founder of the nonprofit International Forgiveness Institute. The quarterly publication is available by writing to the International Forgiveness Institute at 6313 Landfall Drive, Madison, Wisconsin 53705.

- "Forgiveness is not a sign of weakness. It takes strength and compassion to forgive, especially when the person who hurt you has never apologized."
- "Thinking about how you have been hurt helps you to examine all that needs forgiving."
- "As a result of the hurt against you, how have you treated other people?"
- "If you want to show some compassion for the person who hurt you, you can always pray for her . . . or even just wish her well."
- "There really isn't a way to get even. If you forgive, you must absorb the pain. It has to stop with you."
- "Even though you've forgiven him, it can take time for the pain to go away."
- "Some hurts and losses are permanent. But the negative effects of them don't have to be."
- "You're doing the right thing, even though it's hard."
- "You want to forgive that person but it is obviously hard for you. Sometimes, thinking about that person in more sympathetic ways can help. Do you believe that person is a child of God? Do you know anything about his or her upbringing? Do you have a sense of what he was experiencing in life at the time he hurt you?"
- "Maybe in the future, something good will come out of this for you."
- "You are showing our children the value of forgiveness."

If you think your partner's hurt and resentment toward another has interfered in your marriage, raise the issue gently. (People usually dislike being psychoanalyzed by their partners.)

- "I'd like to bring up a point with which you might disagree. But I'd appreciate it if you would think about it before responding. You've told me how your father mistreated you. Well, sometimes I get the feeling that you react to me as if I were your father. You assume I do things with malice when my intent is never to hurt you."
- "I know you have a right to mistrust people after what happened to you. But I think I've earned the right to be trusted."
- "Is it possible that when you get mad at me for certain things, you are really reacting to some past hurt that I had nothing to do with?"

How Not to Say It

- "Forgiveness is for weaklings." (Actually, it is very hard to forgive a deep hurt. If your partner wants to forgive, don't criticize him or her. Besides, you may have to be forgiven someday, too.)

- "It's been such a long time, you should have forgiven him by now ... How can you refuse to forgive a member of your family? ... It's wrong to withhold forgiveness ..." (Instead of lecturing or giving well-intended advice, take time to listen to your partner's story and show some compassion. When a person knows that his or her feelings of hurt and betrayal are understood, it is a little easier to work toward forgiveness. *Better:* "He must have really hurt you if you can't forgive your own father ... Forgiveness is a wonderful goal, but it is understandably difficult.")

- "If you're still angry, you obviously haven't forgiven." (Not true. According to psychiatrist and forgiveness expert Richard Fitzgibbons, a person can decide to forgive without feeling forgiving. Forgiveness allows the "victim," who likely could not control the hurt against him (her), to take some control over his (her) response to what has happened. If a person chooses to forgive and tries to offer compassion toward the wrongdoer, the forgiveness process is underway even if painful feelings linger.)

- "Forgive and forget." (It's not that simple—and forgetting does not usually occur.)

- "I'm not your father. Stop treating me as if I were the enemy." (This may be a good point to make. Make it with more compassion.)

- "I wouldn't forgive if I were you." (Withholding forgiveness comes with a cost. Let your partner make up his or her own mind. *Better:* "I wouldn't blame you if you chose not to forgive. I'm not sure I could be forgiving. But it might be an option to consider.")

Talking Point: Keep in mind your own issues with forgiveness when you are trying to assist your partner. If you are a champion of forgiveness, you may come on too strong at first and give your partner the message that it is not okay to withhold forgiveness. If you have not forgiven someone else for a deep hurt, you may try to persuade your partner to not forgive either. Separate your needs from your partner's.

Having (More) Children

72

"I've changed my mind," Nicole says. "I think two kids are plenty. I don't have the energy to deal with another baby."

"But we agreed before we got married that we would have three children at least," Mike answers.

"I know," Nicole says. "Let me try to explain . . . "

Andrew and Kate have each been previously divorced and are about to be married. Andrew has three kids and Kate has two. All the kids are in their late teens. Kate is nearing 40 years of age and wants one more chance at motherhood. Andrew is 46 and looking forward to retiring at age 55. Starting a new family is not in his plans.

These two couples have a serious decision to make. It is particularly difficult because one person in each couple will have to go along with a decision they don't agree with. It is quite a sacrifice, no matter which way it turns out.

Have You Heard?

~ If you are not married and you and your potential partner disagree about having children, you should not commit to a life together unless you can agree.

~ If you married with an understanding about whether or not to have children and your partner has changed his or her mind, you have reason to consider ending the marriage. But you also have an obligation to one another to try and make the marriage work.

~ If you have any religious faith, this is certainly an issue to pray about. The decision you make has far-reaching implications for your future. The best prayers? Pray that God's will be done. Ask God what He wants you to do. Ask God to help you cope with the decision.

How to Say It

Be prepared to discuss this topic many times. Strong emotions are to be expected, but try to speak with an even temper, or your partner may refuse to have future conversations. Your goal is to truly understand your partner's position and to speak so that your partner understands yours. Put aside coercive efforts—they always lead to resentment. Begin gently.

- "I have something to say that isn't easy. I've changed my mind about having children. I no longer feel I can stand by our agreement."
- "I know you still may feel differently from the way I do. But we'll need to talk this over."
- "I feel like I'm betraying you a bit. I know we decided we never wanted to have children. But for quite some time I've been rethinking my position. Now I'm convinced that it would be a mistake for me not to be a parent. But I do love you and hope we can discuss this honestly."
- "I guess you've noticed that I've been reluctant for us to get pregnant. I truly believed I wanted to be a parent. Now I'm really unsure. I know I'm letting you down. Let's talk this through."

If your partner responds with hurt and anger and says things like:

- *"That's not fair! You promised! We had an agreement!"*

You reply:

- *"I can't blame you for being upset. I wish I didn't feel this way, obviously it would make our lives so much easier if I didn't. What I'd like to do is discuss why I feel the way I do."*

If your partner has just told you that he (she) changed his (her) mind about parenthood and you disagree with his (her) position, you have a right to express hurt and anger. Do so without maligning your partner.

- "I'm stunned. I can't imagine not having children and I always wanted to have children with you. I need to hear your explanation because I sure don't understand why you changed your mind."
- "Yes, I'm angry with you. I feel betrayed. I may not have married you if I knew you felt this way."

You also want to know if there is any reasonable chance that your partner may change his or her mind.

- "Can you imagine a scenario where you would go back to our original agreement?"
- "Delaying having children is something I could agree with. But only if I knew we would have a child eventually."
- "Religion is important to both of us. God knows our situation. What would God want us to do?"

Talking Point: Don't give impulsive ultimatums. But be very honest with yourself. Can you *truly* live a life as a parent when you have no desire to? Or, can you *truly* live life without being a parent (or without more children) when you've always expected to? Defining your deepest, truest position on this matter is essential. That will only occur if each side stops trying to persuade and instead tries to listen with understanding.

- "As much as I love you, my reason for being with someone is to become parents together. I can't imagine myself not being a parent. If you truly cannot be a parent with me, I cannot stay with you."
- "As much as being a parent means to me, I know I could be happy with you even if we remain childless. It isn't my dream and it would be a major sacrifice, but it is something I believe I can do."
- "As much as I'd prefer that we remain childless, I know how important having children is to you. I'm sure we'll make great parents."

If the debate is about whether or not to have *more* children, it is an opportunity to discuss the issues that might be unresolved from prior parenting experiences. Usually, the main concern is financial, followed by an unwillingness to make the kinds of daily sacrifices that are necessary when young children are around. Sometimes, a partner can readily be persuaded to go along with a differing viewpoint. But much empathy and sensitivity is required since that partner may be giving up a dream.

- "I can agree to not have any more children. But I think I'll always regret that we didn't. I won't hold it against you. But don't hold it against me if years from now I express regret."
- "I can agree to have another child, and I'm sure I will be forever grateful once the child comes along. But I'll probably never be able to retire early and we won't be able to afford some things we'd hoped to have. Years from now if I sigh about money being tight, please cut me some slack."

Check to see if other, hidden issues are lurking.

- "Is it possible that one of us is being more stubborn because of past disagreements we've had?"
- "If we had cooperated more often on other issues, would we be debating this topic now?"
- "One way or another, one of us will not get what we want. What would need to happen so that resentment doesn't last?"
- "We have to figure out which one of us is capable of making the bigger sacrifice."

How Not to Say It

- "I changed my mind about having children. I'm sorry. What else do you want me to say?" (This is cold and insensitive. Have a genuine concern for the impact your change of heart can have on your partner.)
- "The world is overpopulated as it is." (Weak excuse. If overpopulation is a genuine concern of yours, adoption may be a reasonable course of action.)
- "I want a child. If you won't go along with it, I'll find someone else who will." (You have a right to end your relationship if need be. But take some time to understand one another's concerns and let the matter rest a bit. There may be a change of heart.)
- "I'm not discussing this anymore. You know my position." (*Better:* "We can talk but I don't think I'll change my mind. Is there something about the way you feel that you don't think I fully understand?")

The Daily Grind:
Handling Everyday
Occurrences and
Misunderstandings

When you can handle the little things that can go wrong in a relationship, the big things may never get that big. Any committed relationship, especially marriage, is not made strong by big events—the first house, the first baby, and the big career advancement—but by braided strands of little events. These day-to-day occurrences take on a flavor and tone that define your life and are a measure of the strength of love in your marriage. When the winds of adversity blow, it is these common daily experiences that can anchor you in place—the kiss when you arrive home, the baby's diapers that need changing, the school concert that must be watched and applauded, the sore shoulder that needs rubbing. So much of your relationship with your partner is spent doing small things that have the potential to mean so much—good or bad. That is why these events should be paid attention to. For example, if you often come home at the end of the day in a grouchy mood, it's possible that your family anticipates your arrival with dread or anxiety rather than eager anticipation. Such a momentary thing—your mood as you walk in the door—but it can make a world of difference to a waiting family.

This final section will help you talk to your partner about the little things that often aren't so little—the bad habits, the petty comments, the annoying attitudes, and the daily hassles. Done the right way, these conversations can make the home atmosphere brighter and more loving.

Chores

73

Clarissa married Ken because he was a kind person and they shared common goals. What she didn't realize was that he is a lousy housekeeper.

"He's not a slob," she says. "He just doesn't have any initiative when it comes to cleaning up. I have to get on his back. He'll cooperate, but why do I have to be the one to give orders? Why can't he just look around, see what needs cleaning, and clean it without being asked?"

A couple can be very happy even if one person does most of the chores. But for that to happen, the relationship must feel fair overall. If one partner works two jobs while the other stays at home with the kids, the stay-at-home parent might not mind having to take the brunt of household chores. Still, especially with dual-career couples, an uneven split on chores can feel very unfair very quickly. Since a certain amount of cleaning must occur, one partner can resent it when both are sharing the benefits of a kept-up home but only one is taking responsibility for cleaning it.

Have You Heard?

∿ Inequities in housework and child-care profoundly affect women (who usually are the ones doing the work). When unfairness persists, women grow increasingly unhappy and marital satisfaction can drop sharply.

∿ Wives who work are more likely to experience role overload than husbands who work.

~ Studies repeatedly show that husbands whose wives work outside the home are fully aware that household responsibilities must be shared more equitably. Yet these men spend an average of four minutes a day more on household tasks than men whose wives are not employed.

~ Men who do their fair share of housework are also more involved in the emotional life of the family.

~ Some men (women too, but mostly men) particularly resist legitimate efforts to get them to help out more—and their relationship inevitably suffers. Regardless of whatever positive things these men might be doing for the relationship, if they resist requests for help with housework or child rearing, their wives view them less favorably over time and the marriage quality declines. These women do not feel cherished by their husbands and often withdraw from intimacy.

How to Say It

Speak up early and often if allocation of housework seems unfair. If you put up with the unfairness with the hope that your partner will change for the better, you may be in for a surprise. Lifestyles tend to become more entrenched over time.

- "The situation with housework feels unfair to me. I'd like to discuss a more equitable way to share the chores."

- "I know I like the house to be tidier than you do and maybe I'm a fanatic. But there are a few things you could do that would really make my days go easier. May we discuss them?"

- "What percentage of the household chores do you think you do? What percentage do you think you should do?"

- "It seems that no matter how much we talk about housework, you don't always do what you agree to do. That frustrates me. Is there something you would like me to understand about this issue that I don't understand?"

- "How can I approach this issue in a manner that you will find helpful?"

- "I don't expect you to change your attitude about doing housework, just as I won't change mine. But we do live together and we do have to get along. What would seem to be a fair allocation of housework from your viewpoint?"

- Look for hidden issues. "Sometimes I get the idea that you drag your feet with housework because you are annoyed with me. Is that so?"
- "I get resentful when I do more than my share of housework. I don't want to feel that way. What do you think gets in our way of making the housework more fair?"

If your partner says:

- *"Whenever I do help out, it's never good enough for you."*
- *"I do help out. You aren't always aware of what I do."*
- *"Tell me what to do and I'll do it."*
- *"I'm in charge of the outside of the house, and you're responsible for the inside."*
- *"Housework just isn't as important to me as it is to you."*
- *"I'm too busy!"*

You reply:

- *"I didn't realize I was that critical. Let's discuss how to make this seem fairer to you and to me."*
- *"I guess we're not being clear with each other just what it is we are doing when it comes to housework. Let's figure out a way to do housework so that I don't have to complain and you don't have to feel unappreciated."*
- *"I really appreciate your offer. But you're asking me to be in charge. I'd like you to look around the house once in awhile and clean what needs cleaning without my having to ask."*
- *"The fact that you are in charge of the outside helps me. But day in and day out I think I have more responsibilities. They wear me out. We need to talk about a fairer system."*
- *"It's probably true that having a clean and tidy house is more important to me. I'm not asking you to have the same attitude that I do. But I think you can make my job easier without going out of your way too much."*
- *"We're both busy. I can't continue to do the work myself."*

Talking Point: A spouse who feels overburdened by housework may "get even" by not cooperating with her partner in some other issue. She may overspend, knowing that he hates bills. Or she may lose some of her interest in sex. Regardless, if a couple cannot negotiate issues in a fair way, the scales of justice will get balanced—but in a manner that adds to a couple's frustration.

How Not to Say It

- "I need you to help out more with housework." (This sounds like a reasonable request. However, it implies that housework is primarily your responsibility and that your partner is only "helping out." The same goes for child-care responsibilities. One parent shouldn't ask the other to "baby-sit." Raising a child is the responsibility of each parent. *Better:* "I need to discuss how we've allocated the household chores.")

- "Would you clean up around here while I'm out shopping?" (Be specific. Your partner may clean up but may not do what you want. You'll get annoyed and he'll feel unfairly criticized.)

- "If you want sex, then you have to do more work around here." (Some women will actually trade sex for housework—and some men will oblige. While it might work for some couples, it degrades the relationship. *Better:* "If I have too much to do around the house, I'm too tired when it comes to spending time with you. Let's talk about a fair way to do chores. Then I'll have more time for you.")

Partner Swears
Too Much

74

Rick is horrified. His fiancée, Michelle, is meeting his family for the first time. He overhears her talking to his sisters and telling an off-color joke. To make matters worse, she uses a profanity. He has heard her swear before. He never likes it but always imagined she'd use good judgment and not swear in situations that could be embarrassing.

Angela is married to Mel. She doesn't mind that he swears on occasion (particularly when he is trying in vain to do any plumbing work in their house). But he will often swear in front of the kids, which bothers her. When they argue, well, his language is downright crude. She asks him to stop swearing, but he always responds by saying that swearing is commonplace and she should lighten up.

Have You Heard?

〜 Depending upon the context, swearing can promote bonding or be divisive. Close, longtime friends may swear during conversation and it will be well received. Even swearing in the presence of one's partner *might* be an indication of comfort with one another. Crude language in the company of strangers is usually frowned upon.

〜 Swearing is common. Studies show that from 4 to 13 percent of everyday language consists of swear words, depending upon the situation. On average, one out of every fourteenth word uttered socially is a swear word.

〜 Swear words tend to fall into one of three categories: sexual, religious, or bodily functions.

〜 The motive for swearing must be taken into account. The most common motive is to express anger or emphasize feelings. The next most frequent

331

motive is to get attention or to make a connection to the listener. Finally, some people swear more out of habit than anything else.

∿ On average, men swear more often than women—up to twice as much. Women are more offended by swearing than are men.

∿ Most people who swear will admit that they control their language in the presence of people who might be offended, such as children, parents, church members, strangers, or members of the opposite sex.

∿ Swearing is most likely to be perceived negatively when the listener cannot justify the use of swearing in the context. When a listener believes "There was no need for him to talk like that," he or she is likely to think less of the speaker.

How to Say It

If your relationship is strong, your partner will probably go along with your request and try to control his swearing. If he swears out of habit, it may take longer but his intent will be to cooperate. In such a situation, a straightforward, nonharsh approach will work best.

- "I'd really like it if you would cut down on your swearing. Would you mind?"
- "I've noticed that you occasionally swear when the kids can hear you. That bothers me. Is that something you can pay more attention to?"
- "I know people swear all the time but it really offends me, and it would really bother me if you swore in front of my parents or friends. Would you please control your swearing, at least when I'm around?"
- "I don't like hearing you swear. It isn't something I can ever find pleasing. Would you mind trying to cut back? I'd really appreciate it."

How Not to Say It

If your partner is likely to cooperate, don't attack him for swearing. He'll likely get defensive.

- "Only rude people swear. Stop it."
- "Where did you learn such language? Didn't your parents raise you properly?"

- "Everybody looks down at you when you swear like that."
- "How do you expect to be a good parent if you swear in front of the kids?" (Your partner will argue that he can be a good parent in other ways.)

If swearing has become a bone of contention between you and your partner, there is more going on than just rude language. Perhaps the two of you frequently get into power struggles, and his use of swear words is just one of many things you do battle over. Maybe he has a tendency to be controlling or verbally abusive. If so, his use of language can be one way to exert power. Or, he might believe you have unjustly criticized him for his swearing and he resents it. If so, he may be willing to cooperate but not if you are showing disrespect in your criticisms of him.

How to Say It

If your partner isn't cooperating as well as you'd like, remember the GIFTS and try these comments:

- (Gentle approach, try to find common ground) "We seem to be butting heads. I don't want us to be like that. Is there something about the way I'm asking you to stop swearing that you dislike?"
- "You're right. Swearing is common and I don't mean to be so critical. It's simply something I cannot get used to, so I'm asking you not to do it when I'm around or when the kids are near. Is that reasonable?"
- "Is there something about your point of view that you don't think I understand? If so, tell me again and I promise I'll listen."
- "Is there something I do that bothers you a lot? If so, maybe I can work on changing that while you try to cut back on swearing."

If your partner says:

- *"You're acting like my mother, always telling me what to do."*
- *"Your parents (friends, and so on) have heard me swear before and they don't seem to mind. Only you are bothered by it."*
- *"I can do what I want."* (This is a bad sign. A comment like this suggests contempt by your partner for you. Contempt is poisonous to a relationship.)

You reply:

- *"Then please tell me how else I can ask you not to do something that bothers me. I'm not trying to be parental. I simply dislike it when you swear, and I'm asking you out of respect for me to please not swear in my presence."*
- *"How my family feels is not the issue. It troubles me when you swear and it bothers me more that you won't try to cut back on it for my sake."*
- *"Yes, you can do what you want. But for us to be a couple we have to make sacrifices for one another and find common ground. Is this something you will do for me or not?"* (If the answer is "No," it is likely that your partner won't cooperate much about anything. If that has proven true, you may have to reconsider whether you can remain in this relationship.)

Partner Takes You for Granted

75

Frank watches television while his wife, Cindy, chats on the phone. She enjoys talking with her friends, but Frank wishes she had just a little time for him once in awhile. He doesn't begrudge her the time she spends doing other things—but when he wants her attention or if he looks forward to perhaps seeing a new movie with her, more often than not she is too tired or preoccupied. He feels like he is far down on her list of things to do.

Have You Heard?

~ Every couple takes one another for granted at times. It isn't fatal but it is a problem that needs correcting.

~ If you feel taken for granted, you may argue over small things that really aren't important. You will do that in an effort to get your partner to do things your way so that you won't feel ignored.

~ It isn't enough to know you are loved. You have to be shown that love from time to time. If your partner doesn't show you much love, you will feel taken for granted.

~ On the positive side, if your partner takes you for granted, then he or she probably feels very comfortable with you and probably trusts you. The two of you may simply be in a rut.

How to Say It

Don't make yourself out to be a victim. Don't whine. State the issue and try to come up with a plan of action.

- "I think we're in a rut. I'd like us to spend more time together. Any ideas?"
- "I was thinking back to when we dated and how we paid more attention to each other. I miss that time of our lives."
- "I know we're both busy but we're not spending so much time together as we should. What could I do that would help?"
- "Do you think I'm neglecting you or taking you for granted? Sometimes I feel that we're ships passing in the night."
- "Let's brainstorm ten things we could do that would help us not take each other for granted. For example, I could call you during the day, I could write an occasional love note and post it on your dashboard, you could rub my back before bed and ask me how my day went . . . "

If your partner says:

- *"I don't take you for granted!"*
- *"We've just been too busy. We'll have time for each other when our schedules lighten up."*
- *"Well, you take me for granted too!"*

You respond:

- *"Well, I can't read your mind so it's very possible you aren't taking me for granted. But because I can't read your mind, I need you to show me in ways I can see. Let's come up with some small things we can do for one another that might help."*
- *"Yes, we have been busy. That's all the more reason to get out of the rut. Probably, just a few small gestures or thoughtful words will make the difference."*
- *"Then we both need to make some small changes."*

How Not to Say It

- "Don't you love me anymore?" (Unless you really question your partner's love for you, don't use this line. Your partner will see you as overreacting and may not take the more legitimate issue—taking you for granted— seriously. *Better:* "I know you love me, but I think we've gotten so busy that we take each other for granted.")
- "You obviously don't care about me."
- "I shouldn't have to tell you what to do to not take me for granted. You should be able to figure that out for yourself." (Do each of you a favor and give some suggestions.)

Happy Anniversary!

76

Elliot snuggles up to his wife in bed. He tries to read the digital clock on the night-stand. Two in the morning. Jill stirs as he places his arm around her. "Happy anniversary, my love," he whispers. Jill hears him and gives him a warm, tender kiss. "Happy anniversary to you too," she murmurs. They hold each other tighter and fall back asleep within minutes. The new day is barely two hours old but it has started out beautifully.

Have You Heard?

～ Anniversary greetings needn't be elaborate but they need to be sincere. Casual greetings with little enthusiasm diminish the meaning of the day and can be a cause for hurt feelings.

～ Greg Godek's book *1001 Ways to Be Romantic* is a handy guide that all men (in particular) should browse through before anniversaries or birthdays. Men often need ideas on how to be romantic.

～ Every once in awhile do something memorable on your anniversary. Go on a special vacation, have a party, plant a tree in your backyard, write a song, or begin a scrapbook that will hold your anniversary pictures from year to year.

How to Say It

- "I'm so happy I married you."
- "You are the best thing that ever happened to me."
- "I love you more and more each year."

337

- "You're still my beautiful, young bride (handsome bridegroom)."
- "Marrying you was the best thing I ever did."
- "I'm glad we have anniversaries to celebrate how much I love you."
- "Let's discuss how we might spend the day . . . do something special . . . "
- "Yes, it's raining (cold) outside but it's still a great day. It's our anniversary!"
- "I wanted to get you something special but wasn't sure what to get. Let's go to the store together and pick something out."

How Not to Say It

- "Oh, yeah, I almost forgot. Happy anniversary to you too."
- "Let's just relax today. I'm tired."
- "I didn't know what to get you. Here's some money. Go pick out something."
- "I don't like to make a big deal out of anniversaries." (But you should at least express your love sincerely and be in an upbeat mood.)
- "It's just another day, really. We don't need a special day." (It is unlikely that you have shown as much devotion as you think you have over the years. Use the day as a reminder of the commitment you made to one another and find a way to celebrate and convey a genuine feeling of love.)

Breaking the Ice
After an Argument

"*What do you want for dinner?*" *Noah asks Marilyn. It is his first words to her since their argument the day before. He is trying to break the ice and resume some sort of normal relationship.*

Marilyn just stares off into space. He can't tell if she didn't hear him or if she just isn't answering.

"*I said what do you want for dinner?*" *he repeats.*

Marilyn sighs. "I'm not that hungry."

Once again Noah isn't sure what she means. Is she saying she is still too angry to want to eat with him? Or is she simply not hungry?

"*You should eat something,*" *he says.*

Marilyn doesn't answer. Noah senses that she is still hurt by their argument. Part of him wants to tell her he is sorry. The other part wants her to apologize.

"*I'll make enough for the two of us,*" *he says. "If you don't want any, I can wrap it up and put it in the fridge for later."*

He reaches for the meat in the freezer and takes it to the microwave for defrosting. If only relationships could thaw out so quickly, he thinks to himself.

Have You Heard

~ Break the ice as soon as possible after an argument. The longer the delay, the harder it can be for one of you to offer an olive branch.

~ If there is a long delay, each partner will fill his or her head with a lot of negative thoughts about the other. Even if you make up later on, those negative thoughts can linger and spark another argument in the future.

〜 Find ways to apologize. Even if you didn't start the argument, did you mishandle it? Did you say something you shouldn't have? Look for *any* merit to your partner's complaint against you, even if you disagree with most of what was said.

How to Say It

You have three goals: Admit where you were wrong; look for unstated issues that may have fueled the argument; and come up with a plan on how to handle the discussion differently next time.

Admit it when you are wrong:

- "Can we start over? I'm not handling this very well."
- "You were right when you said ____. I guess I needed time to think about it."
- "I'm sorry for saying ____."
- "I hate it when we argue."
- "I've been oversensitive lately and I probably overreacted."
- "I haven't been a good listener during our conversations."
- "I was wrong to have said ____."
- "I never should have done that during our argument. It was hurtful."
- "I shouldn't have waited this long to apologize."

Find alternative reasons for why you had the argument:

- "I guess what was really bothering me when we argued about the car was ____. Maybe it had nothing to do with the car after all."
- "I don't think I was really upset about what we argued about. I was more upset about ____."
- "I was upset with you because our disagreement touched on a basic fear I have. That fear is ____."
- "I was upset with you because our argument touched on some dreams I've had that don't seem to be coming true. Those dreams are about ____."

- "I think that when we argued it reminded me of the time when I was a child and ____."
- "After thinking about it, I was upset this time because I was still angry over an argument we had last week that never got settled."

Plan ways to handle the conversation differently next time:

- "What is something I could have said or done differently during our argument that would have made you feel more supported?"
- "It would have made a big difference to me during the argument if you had said ____ instead of ____."
- "What part of your viewpoint did you not think I understood? How could we have handled things differently so that I did understand?"
- "Next time, let's agree to do the following: We'll sit down during the discussion and if the tone gets intense we will hold hands. Agreed?"

Apologizing and admitting mistakes will not always be well received. Be prepared that your partner may still strike back verbally after you try to make peace. Find ways to make in-flight repairs (remember the GIFTS) and don't get sidetracked from your goal.

If you break the ice and admit some wrongdoing but your partner says:

- *"Don't think you can apologize and make everything okay again!"*
- *"You damn well better apologize! You had no right to . . . "*
- *"You always apologize later and expect me to be forgiving. Well, I'm not going to be forgiving this time."*

You reply:

- *"I don't expect to make it all okay. I just want to begin the process. I was wrong to have said ____ and I want you to know that. I'm willing to see what we can do so it doesn't happen again."*
- (Find something to agree with, even though your partner is clearly resuming the argument. If you challenge your partner, the discussion will stall.) *"You're right. I shouldn't have said ____. It's also clear to me that you don't think I've understood your viewpoint. I'll listen, but you don't need to shout or get critical."*

- *"I guess the real problem is that we still hurt each other even after we apologize, so the apologies don't seem sincere. We need to come up with a plan on how to avoid hurting each other during arguments."*

How Not to Say It

- "It's about time you apologized."

- "I'm not going to apologize. I did nothing wrong." (This is theoretically possible, especially if you are living with someone who argues when he or she gets drunk, or if your partner is abusive. Then you shouldn't apologize. In most cases, however, each side contributed in some way to the argument. If you truly think you did nothing wrong, say, "I don't know what I did that was hurtful. Please tell me what it was.")

- Never give nonverbal signs of rejection that last more than a couple of hours. Withdrawing, giving the cold shoulder, icy stares, and so on are perhaps understandable but rarely helpful. If you are very angry and do not wish to talk about the argument, say so. "I'm still upset about our argument. I'll calm down in awhile. In the meantime, I just need time to think.")

- "I don't accept your apology. It's too late. You waited too long." (It is frustrating when a partner doesn't apologize in a timely way. You can accept the apology but still address your concern about the long delay. "Thank you for saying you're sorry—that means a lot. I'm sorry too about ____. I don't know about you, but it bothered me that we took so long to mend fences. What can we do so that next time we apologize sooner?")

- "It's over and done with, let's forget about it." (Not so fast. Avoidance of the issues will always backfire. As arduous as it may seem, try to go back and solve the argument, if possible. At least, you should acknowledge what was said or done during the argument that was unfair or hurtful, and make a plan to prevent that from happening in the future.)

- "I'm not going to apologize if you won't." (You are not in elementary school. Rise above the situation and do the right thing even if your partner does not. After, you can always address your concern that your partner did not apologize.)

How to Say It to Yourself

Breaking the ice after an argument can make you feel like you are "giving in." This is especially true if you and your partner are competitors—one of you must be right and try to make the other person wrong.

Breaking the ice often requires you to pay attention to your self-talk after an argument and change those thoughts that perpetuate your anger to thoughts that soften it.

- "She had no right to say those things!" *"Yes, she was wrong. But she was frustrated with me and didn't think I was truly listening. Everybody has said things in the heat of the moment that they regret. I should give her the benefit of the doubt."*

- "It's his turn to apologize!" *"I can ask to resume our discussion and this time I'll be careful not to be so critical. I can ask him what it is that he wants me to understand. Then I can talk about the things we each said that were hurtful and give him a chance to say he's sorry."*

- "I have a right to be angry!" *"Yes, I do. But my goal is not to stay angry but to have a happy relationship. I know I'll feel better if I can break the ice and help get our relationship back on track."*

- "Why do I always have to be the one to say I'm sorry! Why do I have to break the ice?" *"It is frustrating that he can be stubborn. Although I'd like him to apologize more often, I don't want to get in a battle of wills. This is a fault of his but one I may have to accept. He has other fine qualities. I'm sure he has to accept things about me."*

Partner Is Moody and Irritable

78

Mike arrives home and finds his wife, Pam, in a grumpy mood. He asks what is the matter and she mumbles something incomprehensible before leaving the room to scold the kids who are arguing in the next room. Mike assumes she's had a rough afternoon with the children and makes a mental note to put on a pleasant face and stay out of Pam's way until she feels better. It is the wrong move, but he doesn't know any better.

A few days later, Pam comes in the house and finds Mike in a grumpy mood. She asks what is the matter and he mumbles something incomprehensible before turning up the volume on the television.

"Did something happen at work?" she asks. Mike says nothing. Pam checks on the kids and a few minutes later returns to Mike. "Did you have a conversation with your sister again? She always upsets you."

"It's nothing," Mike says. He never looks at Pam, just at the TV.

"Well it must be something," Pam persists.

Mike gets up and tosses the remote control on the couch. "I said it's nothing!" Then he walks into the other room.

Pam is annoyed. She is only trying to help. Can't he see that? She makes a mental note to give him the cold shoulder for awhile. If he wants his space, he can have it. It is the wrong move, but she doesn't know any better.

Often, one partner (usually the man but not always) prefers to mull over personal problems before he talks about them. If he solves the problem on his own, he may never even mention it. The other partner (usually the woman, but not always) wants to discuss her personal problems as a way to find a solution. When Mike arrived home and saw that Pam was in a grumpy mood, he assumed (wrongly) that she wanted some time to herself to think things over.

So he didn't persist when she told him nothing was the matter. But Pam wanted to talk. She only told him nothing was the matter because she sensed that he wasn't in the mood to talk.

When Pam arrived home a few days later and saw that Mike was in a grumpy mood, she approached him the way she would want to be approached if she were in a bad mood: She persisted in her efforts to find out what was wrong. But Mike really wanted to mull things over by himself. He got annoyed when she kept it up. He tried to be polite when he said nothing was wrong. Now he had to be firm so she'd let him be. He hated it that she put him in the position of being a grouch when all he wanted was time alone for awhile.

Have You Heard?

〜 A man should gently probe for what's wrong when a woman is in a grumpy mood. He should persist a little even if the woman doesn't seem to want to talk.

〜 A woman should back off if told "I don't want to talk about it" or "Nothing is wrong" when she knows something is wrong.

〜 Men, in particular, are apt to assume they are to blame if they arrive home and their partners are in a bad mood. Because they feel responsible but do not know what the crime was, they sometimes feel the wiser thing to do is lay low. However, the best thing they can do is try to find out what's wrong and—if they are to blame—admit their mistakes.

How to Say It

If you are a man (or, regardless of your gender, if your partner usually wants to discuss feelings and problems), persist—gently—in finding out what's wrong.

- "You seem upset. What's wrong?"
- "You don't have to discuss it if you don't want to, but I'd like to know what's bothering you. Maybe I can help."
- "Last time you said nothing was wrong you were upset about something. I'd be happy to talk if something is on your mind."
- "Earlier you said nothing was wrong, but you still seem preoccupied. Is there anything you'd like me to do?"

- "Okay, I get the message. You don't want to talk. If you change your mind, just let me know."

If you are a woman (or if your partner usually is uneasy discussing feelings and personal problems), back off if your partner doesn't want to talk. Don't hold it against him.

- "It looks like something is bothering you. I'll be happy to listen whenever you decide you want to discuss it."

- "I know something is on your mind. But I also know you like to mull things over by yourself. I won't bother you. Let me know if you want to fill me in."

- "Whatever it is that's troubling you, I have faith that you'll work it out. If you want my input, just let me know."

- "You look like you have a lot on your mind. What can I do for you? Would you like some time for yourself? How about a hot shower?"

How Not to Say It

- "I insist that you tell me what's wrong and I'm not leaving this room until you open up!" (If your partner really wants to talk, you don't need to be this insistent. If your partner doesn't want to talk, you are being too pushy and your partner may feel smothered. Don't be surprised if *he* leaves the room.)

- "Fine! If you don't want to talk, I'll leave you the hell alone!" (Don't punish your partner for wanting some alone time. Your partner is more likely to come to you if he feels you respect his wishes.)

Partner Not Always Home When He Says He Will Be

79

"You said you'd be home an hour ago!" Carol cries. *"I've been waiting to take my shower so I can go out later. Why didn't you call me?"*

"I told you I'd be home around *six o'clock,"* Jerry says. *"You know that with my job I can never be precise. I'm expected to stay late with no warning."*

"That's always your excuse—"

"It's not an excuse! I'm a restaurant manager. Some days I can't leave exactly when I want because there's a problem in the kitchen or a waiter is late for work. You know how it is."

"Well, the other day you went to the gym and you said you'd be about two hours. It took you over three hours."

"So? I was talking with the guys. It was my day off. I asked you before I left that morning what was on the agenda for today and you said 'Not much.' So I figured I didn't have to rush."

"That's not the point. You could have called me. What if I needed to do something and was counting on you to be home on time to watch the kids?"

And so on and so on. Partners rely on each other to be reliable when it comes to time management. But it isn't always that easy.

Have You Heard?

～ The more hectic a couple's life, the less understanding partners can be when one is too casual about time management.

～ If this type of argument persists even when one partner has legitimate reasons for being late (job requirements, bad weather, and so forth), then there is more to the problem than meets the eye. The frustrated spouse may understand that her partner cannot always arrive home on time, but she may also believe that her partner is not taking her concerns seriously enough. She believes he could be taking steps to minimize the problem but that he is not doing so. It is also possible that a larger issue exists—the frustrated spouse feels taken for granted or believes the relationship is unfair—and she is using this topic as a stand-in for the larger issue.

How to Say It

The goal is to assess the situation and determine if there are ways to reduce the frequency of the problem. It is also likely that the problem may continue to exist to some extent and must therefore be accepted. Keep the GIFTS in mind: Use a gentle start-up, make in-flight repairs, find hidden problems, remain a team by yielding to valid viewpoints, and offer supportive praise and encouragement when possible.

- "You're right. Your job does make it difficult for you to be on time. I guess what bothers me is that I don't think you are doing what you can to make it less frustrating for me. Phone calls would help a lot. So would helping me out when you come home late instead of wanting to take time to relax. What do you think of those ideas?"

- "I'd rather you tell me ahead of time that you'll be home an hour later—and then surprise me by coming home earlier—than tell me you'll be home on time and arrive late."

- "I imagine it puts pressure on you to try to leave your job on time when you really should stay there longer."

- "I guess I put pressure on myself when you are late. I tell myself I still should spend time with you, eat dinner with you, give you time to relax or take a shower—and yet the later you are, the harder it is to do all those things for you because the kids demand my attention. I'll take the pressure off of you to be home on time, if you can understand that I may have little time to spend with you on nights you come home late."

- "I understand you have to be late. I guess what's really bothering me is that I feel taken for granted. Maybe if we talked about other things that could happen that would make me feel appreciated, I wouldn't be so bothered when you are running late."

If you are the one who tends to be late:

- "It is a real inconvenience for you when I'm home later than expected."
- "Thanks for putting up with me."
- "I really appreciate it that you understand when I'm late. I wish it could be different but I don't know what to do to make it better."
- "If I come home late, I'll take care of the kids as soon as I come in the door. That way, you can have some free time for yourself."
- "Sometimes I don't call you because I think I'll only be a few minutes late. Then it takes longer than I thought it would and I'm in such a rush to leave I forget to call. What would you like me to do in that situation?"

How Not to Say It

- "Be home on time. No excuses!" (That may be unreasonable. Better to find ways to make it more palatable for you if your partner is late.)
- "I'll be home when I get there. You should understand that." (If your job really is one where you cannot punch a clock, your partner will be more understanding if you show some compassion for her situation. *Better:* "I wish I could tell you when I'll get home. It's not easy for you when you can't count on me being there by a certain time. I'll call when I'm ready to come home. I love you.")
- "You're not even trying to get home on time." (Unless your partner cares little about you, he or she probably is trying—but in ways you don't know about. At a minimum, your partner may feel a lot of internal pressure as the workday progresses and he or she worries about making it home on time. Assume that your partner is trying. *Better:* "I'm sure you are doing your best to be home on time more often. Is it possible you've overlooked some idea?")

Talking Point: If the problem cannot be resolved but only managed, make it work for you. Have an agreement with your partner that every time he or she is more than 15 minutes late you get a bonus point. The bonus points can be collected and cashed in at a later date to do something special for yourself or the two of you. For example, 10 points might earn you an extra night out together. Use your imagination. Try to include things your partner will enjoy, too. It can take the tartness out of tardiness.

Out-of-the-Blue Arguments

80

"What are you doing?" Hank asks Julie.

"It's a new exercise routine," Julie says. "I bought the tapes yesterday. I really think these will help me lose some weight."

"But you're not even breathing hard. You won't lose weight that way."

"Trust me, I'm breathing hard."

"It's a waste of money if you ask me. You won't be using these tapes after next week. And you are not breathing hard. You don't even know how to exercise."

Julie stops her workout. "What's your problem? I was doing just fine until you came in here and started criticizing me."

"There is no problem because I'm leaving now. You'll have the whole afternoon to exercise all you want, for all the good it will do you."

Hank opens the front door and leaves.

What was that all about? Julie wonders.

Have You Heard?

∽ Out-of-the-blue arguments are usually not about what the current argument is about. Something else is bothering the person.

∽ If the outbursts happen infrequently and the couple is generally happy, the underlying problem can be detected and discussed with little or no repercussions.

How to Say It

The goal is to get your partner to talk about what's really bothering him (her) since the topic at hand is probably a smoke screen. However, you might be put into a bind: If you respond to the content of your partner's complaint, you are discussing something that isn't the real issue. But, if you tell your partner that there must be some other problem that he's not telling you about, he may get even angrier. (After all, he may truly be unaware that there is an underlying issue even when one exists.) Your best bet is to find something you can agree with about his complaint, then veer off the topic and try to get to the underlying issue.

- "Maybe I did waste money on these exercise tapes. But you usually don't get that upset about this kind of issue. I'm wondering what else might be on your mind."
- "This is not something you would get angry over. Are you angry at me for something else?"
- "You probably are right about some of what you're saying. But the intensity of your anger concerns me. If you think there may be some underlying issue, feel free to talk to me about it."

If your partner says:

- *"There is no underlying issue. You're just avoiding the topic."*
- *"If there is an underlying problem, I have no idea what it is."*
- *"Well, now that you ask, maybe I'm really upset about _____."*

You reply:

- *"If you want to discuss this topic, I will. But please let's sit down and talk and try to hear each other out without yelling. Okay?"*
- *"All I know is that you seem to be angrier than you ordinarily would be over something like this. Does this issue remind you of some other issue that bothers you? I'll be happy to help you sort through the possibilities if you want. It's up to you."*
- *"Okay, let's discuss that."*

If your partner routinely *explodes* about little things, you are better off avoiding a discussion about whatever he's (she's) upset about because that is not the issue. Neither is the issue any underlying/unstated problems he might have. The issue is his explosiveness. Until he gets control over that, no other conversations are likely to be productive. Therefore, ignore the content of his complaint. It is irrelevant.

Patricia Evans, in her immensely helpful book *The Verbally Abusive Relationship*, suggests that you not think of your often-angry partner as your boyfriend or husband, but as a petulant, tantrum-throwing child. With that image in mind, say things like:

- "You may not raise your voice to me!"
- "I will not talk to you when you speak to me that way."
- "Calm down and I'll talk."
- "That used to work before but it won't anymore. I will not be intimidated by your abuse."
- "That's enough!"
- "Stop that! Don't you ever speak to me in that tone of voice."

If your partner is generally considerate and you are content in the relationship, but he still has a tendency to get easily angered over small things, he is probably open to helpful suggestions and does feel badly about his impulsive ways.

- "We agreed before that when I think you are too angry I will point it out and you will speak more calmly. Please do that now, thanks."
- "Take a breath and relax for a minute. Then let's sit down on the couch and you can calmly tell me what's on your mind."
- "Let's rewind this tape. Begin the conversation again, but this time speak more gently."

How Not to Say It

- Your partner snaps at you for no good reason over something you've done. "Okay, I won't do that again." (Even if his complaint is legitimate, he is wrong to be so angry. *Better:* "You're right. I shouldn't have done that. But we have a second problem and that is your degree of anger. I need you to make complaints more respectfully. Can you agree to do that?")
- Don't sit quietly while your partner is angrily exploding about a small issue. As soon as you can, Patricia Evans suggests you yell "Hold it!" and see if your partner stops the outburst. If he does not, then walk away.

How to Maintain Happiness Over the Long Haul

81

Ever try to lose weight? If you succeeded, you probably had trouble keeping the weight off. Maintaining progress is usually more difficult than initiating change. That's just as true in overcoming conversational bad habits as it is in weight management. As you and your partner improve your conversational know-how, backslides will occur. They are inevitable. That is why Chapter 2 on making in-flight repairs is crucial to your communication success. Without that ability, predictable backslides and snafus will snowball into communication standoffs and breakdowns.

To maintain happiness, discuss your communication progress occasionally and call attention to any backslides that are happening. Then get back on track without delay.

Have You Heard?

~ Fifty percent of couples who made positive changes in counseling will relapse within a year unless they adhere to a follow-up plan. Regular progress checks can be a marriage saver.

~ Setbacks happen for many reasons. The most common include:

— *Lack of stick-to-it-iveness.* Couples focus on their communication problems long enough to make progress, then they coast.

— *Lack of faith.* Doubting that the changes made will be permanent, one or both partners slow down, anticipating a setback, and unwittingly set the tone for failure.

— *Failure to take outside sources of stress into account.* People regress under stress. They abandon new ways of coping and fall back to more familiar (but less helpful) patterns. If a couple experiences an unexpected health or financial crisis, for example, they might go back to old habits. It can be helpful to understand that, not criticize it, and make an effort to reapply the new communication skills.

— *Depletion of the supply of goodwill.* Acting with less thoughtfulness or spending less time with one another causes crankiness. The inevitable conversational errors will then be more bothersome.

— *Pretending that lack of arguments or disagreements means all has been fine.* In fact, one partner may simply be unwilling to make complaints for fear of an argument.

How to Say It

- Be clear about what backsliding means to you. "Not every communication mistake means we're backsliding. I would think we're backsliding when . . . "
- "I'd like us to figure out a plan of what we'll do when one of us thinks we're backsliding. Okay?"
- "What foreseeable events might throw us off track?" (Overtime hours on the job, a new baby, a busy time of the year, and so on)
- "The communication rule I have the hardest time following is . . . "
- "The rule I can follow no matter what is . . . "
- "It would be hardest for me to handle the conversation if you broke this communication rule . . . "
- "I'm likely to avoid stating a complaint if . . . "
- "I think having more fun together as a couple and making sure we act thoughtfully will make it easier for me to have effective conversations."
- "I think we've been communicating just fine this past month. What do you think? I particularly liked it when . . . "

How Not to Say It

- "If we start to backslide, we'll know." (Not necessarily. It is easy to excuse an unsatisfying dialogue as the exception to the rule. It might be, but it might be the beginning of a setback. Don't clang the alarm bell at the first conversation problem, but don't wait for matters to get ugly before you correct them.)

- "We shouldn't get upset during conversations. If we do, we're doing something wrong." (That's not true. Even conversations where you each get angry and raise your voice at each other can be fine—perfectly acceptable—if you are able to avoid nasty criticisms and arrive at some mutual understanding. You and your partner are human. Don't expect calmness and emotional restraint at every turn.)

Let's Talk

TESTING YOUR SKILLS

Satisfied couples who are likely to remain together succeed in two fundamental ways: Their day-to-day interactions (about nonconflict topics) are usually positive, and their conversations about areas of conflict contain much more positive actions (showing support, interest, compliments, empathy, in-flight repairs, affection) than negative actions (criticisms, defensiveness, belligerence, withdrawal).

Using a scale from 0–100 where 0 equals "0-percent confidence" and 100 equals "100-percent confidence," rate your level of confidence in performing the following behaviors:

1. I have reasonably pleasant conversations with my partner about the events of the day or plans for the week. _____%
2. I can start conversations about neutral topics in a pleasant, nonharsh way. _____%
3. I can start conversations about an unpleasant (but nonrelationship) topic in a nonjarring, nonharsh way. _____%
4. I can start conversations about an unpleasant relationship issue in a nonjarring, nonharsh way. _____%
5. When my partner accuses me of something or is upset with me about something, I don't automatically disagree and defend myself. _____%
6. When my partner accuses me of something or is upset with me about something, somewhere in my response I try to agree with my partner—even in a small way—about his or her complaint. _____%
7. When my partner accuses me of something or is upset with me about something, I want to hear more details instead of cutting him or her off. _____%
8. I initiate meaningful conversation with my partner fairly often. _____%
9. If a conversation starts to get frustrating, I can find the right words to help put us back on track. _____%
10. If a conversation starts to get frustrating, I won't walk away or shut down. _____%
11. I avoid the use of harsh criticisms or put-downs. _____%
12. I try to stay emotionally in touch with my partner every day using small but effective words and actions. _____%
13. I am genuinely fond of my partner and show that by thoughtful words or gestures. _____%
14. If I make an assumption about my partner's motivations or intentions, I will check out that assumption—especially if it is a negative view. _____%
15. If we make some progress in our communication, I can make regular progress checks with my partner so we'll stay on course. _____%

Any items that you (or your partner) rated below the 80-percent confidence level are areas that need work. Retake this test periodically to assess your overall progress.

20 Quickie Comments and Comebacks for 20 Situations

82

This entire book has been dedicated to the idea that the words we use in our daily conversations with our partner can make the difference between getting along or getting a lawyer. You can't expect every conversation with your partner to run smoothly, but you can make overall improvements so that most discussions will turn out well.

Most conversations are not about major issues. Rather, they are run-of-the-mill, off-the-cuff, here-one-minute-and-gone-the-next discussions that nevertheless set a tone for the relationship. If you and your partner can learn to respond to these situations with thoughtfulness and a willingness to find common ground in areas of disagreement, then relationship satisfaction will inevitably rise.

One key for having productive discussions is getting off to a good start. Unhappy couples are notorious for their tendency to escalate the fighting once an argument has begun. Happy couples, on the other hand, have gentle start-ups, especially to difficult discussions. If the start-ups are harsh, happy couples find ways to quickly make an in-flight correction and de-escalate the argument. Just as important, happy couples are more invested in being friends than they are in being right.

Quickie 1

You arrive home, exhausted after a hard and crazy day at work. You hear the kids fighting and your spouse screaming the minute you open the door. Your spouse sees you and immediately starts to complain.

SAY ───

❧ "Okay, I'm here to help. Tell me what you need."

❧ "I'll take over, honey. Looks like you need a break."

❧ "Sweetheart, I'm happy to help out. Please stop shouting and tell me what you'd like me to do."

❧ (Smiling) "I love these warm welcomes. Kids, I'm coming in. You have three seconds to stop fighting. Dear, I expect a kiss when this is all over."

DON'T SAY ───

❧ "Can't you control those kids?"

❧ "I'm not doing a damn thing until I take my shower."

❧ "I hate coming home to this house." (Any negativity on your part will just add to the misery. Even if things calm down, you won't be perceived as having helped.)

Quickie 2

Your spouse complains that you left the lights on. He then states that you never care about the cost of electricity and he's asked you before to be more attentive—but still you leave lights on when you could just as easily turn them off. You know he has a point, but you view him as being too fastidious and unreasonable. (This is likely a repetitive problem based on personality differences. Thus, it may never get solved permanently.)

SAY ───

❧ "You have a point. But you and I don't see eye to eye on this. I promise I'll be more careful if you promise not to scold me whenever I leave a light on. Okay?"

❧ "I did agree to turn off all the lights when I leave a room. The problem is that I agreed to something that I know I can't do all the time. Plus, I don't like it when you treat me like a child. I will do my best but it won't be perfect. I need you to promise not to have a bad attitude when you see a light on."

❧ "You are saying that if I loved you I'd turn off all the lights when I leave a room. I'm saying that if you loved me you'd cut me some slack and not be so rigid about this. The truth is we both love each other and we need to accept quirks in our personalities."

❧ "Most of the time I do turn out lights. Show some appreciation instead of always criticizing me."

DON'T SAY

❧ "Screw that. I can do what I want with the lights."

❧ "I'm sorry. I'll try to get it right next time." (You don't live in a prison. If you've been careless about lights, pay more attention. But don't act like a scolded child who is trying to please a stern parent.)

Quickie 3

You dislike your partner's driving.

SAY

❧ Absolutely nothing unless you really are worried about safety.

❧ "Most of the time I am comfortable when you drive. But I get nervous when you _____. Would you mind not doing that when I'm in the car with you?"

❧ "Back-seat drivers can be a pain in the neck. But I'd really like it if you would _____. Thanks."

❧ "I know you've been driving for years with no problems, but I get very uncomfortable when you drive fast on snowy roads. Would you humor me and slow down a little?"

DON'T SAY

❧ "You drive like a maniac!"

❧ "Who the hell taught you to drive?"

❧ "You're going to get us killed!"

Quickie 4

Your spouse just criticized your driving. You are annoyed.

SAY ────────────────────────────────────

- ❧ "Please don't criticize me as being wrong when it is just something that makes you uncomfortable."
- ❧ "If you would *ask* me to slow down instead of *tell* me, I'd feel less annoyed."
- ❧ "I'd be happy to do as you wish if you would ask me instead of criticize me."
- ❧ "Let's make a deal: I won't criticize your driving habits if you don't criticize mine."

DON'T SAY ────────────────────────────────

- ❧ "If you don't like it, you can leave."
- ❧ "Do *you* want to drive?" (If what's bothering you is that your partner could have used a softer touch when commenting on your driving, say that instead.)
- ❧ "I was *not* going too fast . . . I did *not* take that corner too sharply . . . I was *not* following that guy too closely . . . " (This isn't a debate. It's a matter of personal preference and perception. *Better:* "I wasn't concerned about my driving. But if it makes you feel better, I'll slow down."

Quickie 5

Your partner gives you a gift and you really don't like it.

SAY ────────────────────────────────────

- ❧ "I love that you gave it to me but it's not my favorite style. Would you mind if I exchanged it?"
- ❧ Nothing about your dislike for the gift. If the gift is not returnable or is simply too unique or homemade, do the right thing and express gratitude. If it's something to wear, wear it once in awhile. It won't kill you.

❦ "I'm so glad I married you. This is a nice gift but the wrong color (style, size). Want to come with me when I return it? We can have lunch together."

DON'T SAY

❦ "You should know what to get me after all these years."

❦ "I hate it, send it back."

❦ "It's nice but I'll never wear it (read it, use it, display it, find a place for it)."

❦ "You obviously don't know my tastes."

❦ "Is this the best you could do?"

Quickie 6

Your partner gets a promotion/pay raise.

SAY

❦ "I'm very proud of you!"

❦ "You deserve it!"

❦ "It's good for the kids to see that hard work pays off."

❦ "That must make you feel appreciated."

❦ "I'm so excited for you! I'm also concerned how it will affect your schedule and the time you get to spend at home. Let's make sure we make the most of our time at home."

DON'T SAY

❦ "Now you'll be so busy I'll never see you."

❦ "Everybody gets a raise eventually. You should have gotten one last year."

❦ "You still don't make as much money as I wish you would."

❦ "Don't let it go to your head. You didn't win the Nobel Prize, you know."

Quickie 7

Your partner fails to get a promotion and feels very discouraged.

SAY ——————————————————————————

❥ "You worked hard for that promotion."

❥ "I hope your boss recognizes your worth soon."

❥ "Does this change your mind about your future plans with the company?"

❥ "I still love you."

DON'T SAY ——————————————————————

❥ "Try not to feel so bad. Not everybody can get a promotion." (You mean well but your partner feels what she feels. Telling her not to feel that way can make her believe you don't understand.)

❥ "That reminds me of the time I didn't get a raise . . . " (This is not the time to discuss your story. Focus on your partner.)

❥ "I told you to prepare for the possibility that you might not get it."

❥ "We were counting on that promotion! Now what are we going to do!"

Quickie 8

You've had a hectic day with the kids. Your partner arrives home and sees that certain chores were not accomplished. He says, "What have you been doing all day!"

SAY ——————————————————————————

❥ (If your partner's comment is not typical) "You're not usually so grumpy. Is something bothering you?"

❥ (If your partner often makes this kind of remark) "I resent your attitude. If you want to discuss how we can make sure some chores get done, I'll discuss that. But I don't like being micromanaged."

❧ "Your criticism is unfair and I don't appreciate it. I don't like being judged when you have no idea what my day was like. Give me the benefit of the doubt from now on."

❧ "I know you prefer the house be in order but it isn't always possible. I do what I can. Some days you'll get your wish but some days you won't. I hope you can accept that."

❧ "I'm willing to hire a maid."

DON'T SAY

❧ "You're right. I'm sorry." (Assuming you did what you could to manage the household and the children, you have nothing to apologize for.)

❧ "You have no right to complain." (Yes, he has a right and will quibble with you about that. *Better:* "I know it bothers you but I need you to understand that I'm doing all I can. Some days I have to make a choice between spending more time with the kids or more time housecleaning.")

Quickie 9

Your partner's hair is getting gray and you'd like him or her to darken it.

SAY

❧ "I don't think I'm ready for either of us to have gray hair. What do you think about using a hair color?"

❧ "If you think I'm being unreasonable, just say so. But I'd like it if you got rid of some of the gray in your hair."

❧ "I'm not ready to grow old gracefully just yet. What do you think about each of us getting rid of some of our gray hair?"

❧ "How about getting rid of the gray for a month and see how you like it. If it's too much of a bother to keep it that way, you can let the gray return. I'll still think you are sexy. Gray, but sexy."

DON'T SAY

❧ "Your gray hair makes you less attractive."

❧ "For some people, gray hair makes them look distinguished. On you it makes you look old."

❥ "People will think I'm married to an old person."

❥ "Don't you care about your appearance?"

Quickie 10

You know you and your partner should do more fun things together but you have no common interests.

SAY

❥ "Even though I don't enjoy skiing I'll be happy to go with you. We can have wonderful evenings together and I'll find something enjoyable to do during the day."

❥ "We can take turns making a decision on what to do and where to go. The other one of us will agree to go along and make the most of it."

❥ "We're in a rut. Let's do something even if neither of us thinks it will be terrific fun. If we give it our best shot, we just may enjoy ourselves after all."

❥ "Once a month we'll go somewhere or do something a little different. How does that sound? We need to break out of our slump."

DON'T SAY

❥ "That event doesn't sound exciting." (Do it anyway. You're in a rut.)

❥ "If one of us doesn't enjoy the activity, we shouldn't do it." (Yes, you should do it.)

❥ "One of these days we should . . . " (One of these days may never arrive. Be firm and decisive. Do some activities that sound even modestly enjoyable and make the most out of them. Be spontaneous if need be.)

Quickie 11

You really want to go someplace special but you know your partner will hate it.

SAY

❥ "I rarely ask you to do this but I'm asking now."

❥ "I usually give up doing these things because you don't want to go. But I'm asking you to go with me this time. It would mean a lot."

❧ "I could find someone else to go with but my first choice is you."

❧ "Please do this for my sake. And try to have some fun. I appreciate it."

❧ " I know you don't enjoy these things so I don't ask often. But I'd love it if you would join me."

❧ "You'll go? Terrific! You've made my day!"

❧ "Some of my fondest memories are those rare moments of you and me dancing together."

DON'T SAY

❧ "You should do what I want to do for a change!" (If this works, you'll probably have a grump on your hands. Try a gentler approach.)

❧ "Finally, you agree to go! Up until now you've always been such a stick in the mud." (If your partner agrees to go with you, show enthusiasm. Don't criticize.)

❧ "I'm sure you'll say 'no' so I don't know why I even bother asking."

❧ "What did I ever see in you?"

Quickie 12

Your beloved enjoys calling you at work "just to hear your voice" and to briefly chat. While you appreciate the sentiment, you are usually busy when the calls come and feel irritated that your partner expects you to drop everything for a few minutes and talk. You want to tell her to ease up on the phone calls but you don't want to hurt her feelings.

SAY

❧ (Blame it on the boss) "Sweetheart, my boss is cracking down on personal phone calls. You'll have to call less often."

❧ "I love talking with you but I can't do that very well when I'm so busy. How about if I call you once in awhile when I'm free?" (This is a good strategy. If you do the calling, you can call on your terms ["I only have a minute, honey, but I wanted to say hi."]. It also tells your partner that you like hearing her voice, too.)

❧ "I'm not the kind of person who can be hard at work and attentive to the person I love—both at the same time. It's just not a good idea to call me a lot at work. But I do love you for trying."

DON'T SAY ————————————————————————

- "Why are you calling me at work when you have nothing important to say?"
- "I really don't appreciate it when you call me at work."
- "You're embarrassing me."
- "I don't call you at work just to say hi. Why do you always have to call me?"

Quickie 13

Your partner seems to be ignoring you at a party made up of his or her friends and co-workers.

SAY ————————————————————————

- "I can introduce myself to people once in awhile, but I'd prefer it if you stayed by my side when you can."
- "Please don't walk away without telling me. I don't know many people here."
- "I know you like to mingle, but I'm feeling a bit ignored. Would you mind staying by me until I get to know these people better?"
- "Is this what you intended? You've paid little attention to me so far."

DON'T SAY ————————————————————————

- "You are being rude to me."
- "Your friends must think you don't like me that much."
- "I'm never coming to any of these events again if you intend to ignore me all night."
- "You shouldn't leave my side the entire night."
- "Look at that man over there. He stayed by his date all evening long. Why couldn't you do that?"

Quickie 14

Your partner likes to gossip. You find it rude. (Indeed, gossip can be hurtful to people. However, it does tend to help some people bond as they share stories.)

SAY ————————————————————————

❧ "I know a lot of people enjoy hearing gossip, but I don't. Would you mind not gossiping when I'm around?"

❧ "That sounds like gossip. I'd rather not hear about it."

❧ "You know, it's not nice saying those things about people. You're a better person than that."

❧ "I don't like hearing all those details. I wouldn't want people talking about you like that."

❧ "I understand that you and your friends like to gossip sometimes. That's fine. I just don't like hearing it."

DON'T SAY ————————————————————

❧ "I told you not to gossip. Why do you keep doing it?" (Asking your partner to tone down the gossiping is sufficient. If you really don't like hearing it, leave the room.)

❧ "Haven't you got anything good to say about people?" (Your partner will take offense and may miss the merit of your point. *Better:* "I like it better when I hear you say nice things about people.")

Quickie 15

You are very proficient at some tasks—fixing a broken pipe, painting, sculpting, making a special casserole, gardening, changing the oil in the car—and your partner, who is not an expert, questions your judgment. He or she says, "Why did you use *that* pipe fitting? . . . You're not putting *that* spice in the casserole, are you? . . . Make sure you stir the paint . . . Plant those rows of seeds at least eight inches apart . . . "

SAY ————————————————————————

❧ "I know what I'm doing. Do you have an opinion to offer?"

❧ "You make it sound like I don't know how to do this. Is that what you mean to say?"

❧ "You sound critical. Is that your intent?"

❧ "Do you think I've forgotten how to do this?"

❧ "Can you say that in a way that doesn't sound so critical?"

❥ "Who the heck made you the expert all of a sudden?"

❥ "You're such a know-it-all!"

❥ "Everybody hates it when you act like this."

❥ "Don't ever question my judgment when you don't know what you're talking about!"

Quickie 16

Your partner doesn't seem to appreciate the demands of your job. You get very little sympathy when job demands are high and you get criticized if your job interferes with home life. (It's possible that your job is not the issue for your partner. Perhaps he or she is feeling neglected or overburdened by home responsibilities.)

SAY ————————————————————

❥ "You're right. Some days my job demands get in the way of our home life. I do my best trying to juggle home and work. But it hurts me when you criticize my job. I enjoy my work and feel good about it. What could I do differently that might help this situation?"

❥ "You don't have to like my job but what bothers me is that I don't feel you respect me for the work I do."

❥ "Sometimes it feels like we're competing for who has it tougher."

❥ "If you are feeling neglected, we can try to come up with ways to correct that. But I love my job, too. It would help me if you understood that."

❥ "You're right. It is hard for you when my job requires that I work late. But quitting isn't an option. What else can we do to deal with this problem?"

DON'T SAY ————————————————————

❥ "Tough. My job is my job. You knew that when you met me."

❥ "My job must come first. How else can I provide for the family?" (Your job may indeed be demanding and important to you. But this comment reveals that you are not trying to address the deeper concerns of neglect that your partner feels.)

❥ "It has nothing to do with my job. You're just unhappy with yourself."
(Don't psychoanalyze. If you think there is truth to the idea, say it with a
gentler tone. *Better:* "Sometimes I think you are also unhappy about
other things, maybe even things about yourself. Is that possible?")

Quickie 17

You feel your partner wastes time on the computer, watching TV, or reading
magazines. He or she says it's a form of relaxation.

SAY

❥ "You should relax. But I get the impression that you're simply bored. I
guess I'm worried you are bored with our life."

❥ "It concerns me that you spend so much time on those things."

❥ "Maybe now is the time to consider a hobby, or to join the gym again."

❥ "The problem for me is that you say you don't have time to help the kids
with their homework or paint the garage, but you spend hours on the
computer. Even when you do it late at night, I'd rather have you in bed
with me. Can you try to cut back on TV and computer time?"

❥ "How about we do an experiment. Let's not use the TV or computer for
two weeks."

DON'T SAY

❥ "You're lazy. Do something productive."

❥ "What you're doing is a complete waste of time."

❥ "You care more about the computer than you do your family."

❥ "You're teaching the kids that it's okay to be lazy."

Quickie 18

Your partner dented the car. It was his or her fault.

SAY

❥ "Are you all right?"

❥ "How did it happen?"

❥ "I'm glad you weren't hurt."

❥ "How was the other driver?"

DON'T SAY ────────────────────────────────

❥ "You just had to have an accident with a new car, didn't you."

❥ "I've told you not to follow cars too closely." (There is no need to say "I told you so.")

❥ "Since it was *your* accident, you take it to the body shop and find a rental." (Remember that you're a team.)

❥ "You're so careless. What were you doing, chatting on your cell phone while trying to drive?"

Quickie 19

Your partner doesn't abuse alcohol but you feel he or she is drinking a bit more than necessary.*

SAY ────────────────────────────────

❥ "I've noticed you are drinking more often. I'm not saying it's a problem, I'm just saying you're drinking more than you have in the past. Do you plan to keep drinking this much?"

❥ "You're drinking more at night. Is something troubling you?"

❥ "Since you usually don't drink this often, I'm concerned that something is bothering you."

❥ "I know you enjoy wine at night lately but I'm a bit uneasy about that. Would you mind if you had only one glass?"

❥ "For my sake would you not keep a supply of alcohol on hand? I know you aren't abusing alcohol, but when you drink I feel like you are in your own world."

─────────────

*Some key signs of alcoholism or alcohol abuse include a preoccupation with drinking, gulping drinks, drinking alone, an increased tolerance to the effects of alcohol, needing an "eye opener" in the morning, using alcohol regularly to reduce stress or as a nightcap, difficulty stopping once drinking has started, and failed attempts to cut down on drinking.

❥ "I won't say any more about it. But if I continue to worry, I'll have to talk about it again."

DON'T SAY ———————————————————————————

❥ "I think you might be an alcoholic." (Taking an extreme position will invite defensiveness. A person without a drinking problem is likely to recognize when he or she is drinking to excess and will stop or cut back.)

❥ "You should talk to a counselor about this." (This may be premature.)

❥ "I'll keep bugging you until you stop."

❥ "You should know better."

Quickie 20

Your partner wants to have sex after an argument. You don't.

SAY ————————————————————————————

❥ "Maybe later. I can't have sex after an argument. I need to feel closer to you first."

❥ "I'm not punishing you. I just can't have sex when I'm aggravated."

❥ "My body doesn't work that way. As soon as we're getting along better, I'll be in the mood."

❥ "If you want to cuddle and try to resolve our argument, I'd be up for that."

❥ "I know from reading all the books that men sometimes want to have sex as a way of making up after an argument. I can't do that. Let's make up some other way."

DON'T SAY ———————————————————————————

❥ "You're such a pervert!"

❥ "I wouldn't have sex with you now if my life depended on it."

❥ "That's all you ever think about!"

Resources

Take This Test and Open the GIFTS

Coleman, Paul. *The 30 Secrets of Happily Married Couples.* Holbrook, MA: Adams Media, 1992.

Margolin, G. & Wampold, B. Sequential analysis of conflict and accord in distressed and nondistressed marital partners. *Journal of Consulting and Clinical Psychology* (1981) 49:554–567.

Chapter 1: How to Start a Conversation Without Starting an Argument

Gottman, John. *What Predicts Divorce?: The Relationship Between Marital Processes and Marital Outcomes.* Hillsdale, NJ: Lawrence Erlbaum Associates, 1994.

Chapter 2: How to Make In-Flight Repairs and Deflate Anger

Gottman, J., Coan, J., Carrere, S., & Swanson, C. Predicting marital happiness and stability from newlyweds' interactions. *Journal of Marriage and the Family* (1998) 60:5–22.

Chapter 3: How to Find the Hidden Issues in Conversations

Wile, Daniel B. *After the Honeymoon: How Conflict Can Improve Your Relationship.* New York: John Wiley & Sons, 1988.

Chapter 4: How to Remain a Team and Slip Out of the "I'm Right/You're Wrong" Knot

Coleman, Paul. *25 Stupid Mistakes Couples Make.* Chicago: Contemporary Books Roxbury Park, 2001.

Chapter 6: How to Make Chitchat Charming

Holtzworth-Munroe, A. & Jacobson, N. Causal attributions of married couples: When do they search for causes? What do they conclude when they do? *Journal of Personality and Social Psychology* (1985) 48:1398-1412.

Holtzworth-Munroe, A., Jacobson, N., Deklyon, M., & Whisman, M. Relationship between behavioral marital therapy outcome and process variables. *Journal of Consulting and Clinical Psychology* (1989) 57:658-662.

Jacobson, N., Follette, V., & McDonald, D. Reactivity to positive and negative behavior in distressed and nondistressed married couples. *Journal of Consulting and Clinical Psychology* (1982) 50:706-714.

Noller, P., Beach, S., & Osgarby, S. Cognitive and affective processes in marriage. In W.K. Halford and H.J. Markman (Eds.), *Clinical Handbook of Marriage and Couples Interventions (pp. 43-72)*. Chichester, England: Wiley, 1997.

Wile, Daniel. *After the Honeymoon: How Conflict Can Improve Your Relationship.* New York: John Wiley, 1988.

Chapter 7: How to Solve Common Problems with Uncommon Effectiveness

Bolger, N., DeLongis, R., & Wethington, E. The contagion of stress across multiple roles. *Journal of Marriage and the Family* (1989) 51:175-183.

Butler, M., Gardner, B., & Bird, M. Not just a time-out: Changing dynamics of prayer for religious couples in conflict situations. *Family Process* (1998) 37:451-475.

Cohan, C. & Bradbury, T. Negative life events, marital interaction, and the longitudinal course of newlywed marriages. *Journal of Personality and Social Psychology* (1997) 73:114-128.

Conger, R., Rueter, M., & Elder, G. Couples' resilience to economic pressure. *Journal of Personality and Social Psychology* (1999) 76:54-71.

Chapter 8: How to Respond When Past Mistakes Are Thrown in Your Face

Coleman, Paul. *Getting to the Heart of the Matter: How to Resolve Ongoing Conflicts in Your Marriage Once and for All.* Holbrook, MA: Adams Media, 1994.

Chapter 9: How to Encourage More Conversation

Christensen, A. & Heavey, C. Gender and social structure in the demand/withdraw pattern of marital conflict. *Journal of Personality and Social Psychology* (1990) 59:73-81.

Richmond, Virginia. Amount of communication in marital dyads as a function of dyad and individual marital satisfaction. *Communication Research Reports* (1995) 12:152-159.

Ross, Joellyn. Conversational pitchbacks: Helping couples bat 1000 in the game of communication. *Journal of Family Psychology* (1995) 6:83-86.

Sher, T. & Baucom, D. Marital communication: Differences among maritally distressed, depressed, and nondistressed-nondepressed couples. *Journal of Family Psychology* (1993) 7:148-153.

Walsh, V., Baucom, D., Tyler, S., & Sayers, S. Impact of message valence, focus, expressive style, and gender on communication patterns among maritally distressed couples. *Journal of Family Psychology* (1993) 7:163-175.

Chapter 12: How to Listen with Love

Coleman, Paul. *25 Stupid Mistakes Couples Make.* Chicago: Contemporary Books Roxbury Park, 2001.

Nichols, Michael P. *The Lost Art of Listening.* New York: Guilford, 1995, p.177.

Chapter 13: Celebrating Pregnancy

Chapman, H., Hobfall, S., and Ritter, C. Partners underestimate women's distress in a study of pregnant inner-city women. *Journal of Personality and Social Psychology* (1997) 2:418–425.

Kurdek, Laura. Marital stability and changes in marital quality in newlywed couples: A test of the contextual model. *Journal of Social and Personal Relationships* (1991) 8:27–48.

Chapter 14: You Dislike Your Partner's Friends

Voss. K., Markiewicz, D., & Doyle, A. Friendship, marriage, and sex roles. *Journal of Social and Personal Relationships* (1999) 16:103–122.

Chapter 15: You Aren't Fond of Your Partner's Children

Fine, M., Coleman, M., & Ganong, L. Consistency in perceptions of the stepparent role among stepparents, parents, and stepchildren. *Journal of Social and Personal Relationships* (1998) 15:810–828.

Fine, M. & Kurdel, L. The relationship between marital quality and (step)parent–child relationship quality for parents and stepparents in families. *Journal of Family Psychology* (1995) 9:216–223.

Fine, M., Voydanoff, P., & Donnelly, B. The relationship between parental control and warmth and child well being in stepfamilies. *Journal of Family Psychology* (1993) 2:222–232.

Ganong, L., Coleman, M., Fine, M., & Martin, P. Stepparents' affinity seeking and affinity maintaining strategies with stepchildren. *Journal of Family Issues* (1999) 20:299–327.

Chapter 18: Partner Is Too Gruff With the Kids

Coleman, Paul. *How to Say It to Your Kids: The Right Words to Solve Problems, Soothe Feelings, and Teach Values.* Paramus, NJ: Prentice Hall, 2000.

Chapter 20: Thoughtful Attention After the First Baby Arrives

Cowan, C. & Cowan, P. Interventions to ease the transition to parenthood: Why they are needed and what they can do. *Family Relations* (1995) 44:412–423.

Gottman, J., Coan, J., Carrere, S., & Swanson, C. Predicting marital happiness and stability from newlyweds. *Journal of Marriage and the Family* (1998) 60:5–22.

Shapiro, A., Gottman, J., & Carrere, S. The baby and the marriage: Identifying factors that buffer against decline in marital satisfaction after the first baby arrives. *Journal of Family Psychology* (2000) 14:59–70.

Chapter 21: Your New Partner Wants You to Relocate Away from Your Children

Amato, P. & Keith, B. Parental divorce and the well being of children: A meta-analysis. *Psychological Bulletin* (1991) 110:26–46.

Wallerstein, J. & Lewis, J. The long-term impact of divorce on children: A first report from a 25-year study. *Family and Conciliation Courts Review* (1998) 36:368–383.

Whiteside, M. & Becker, B. Parenting factors and the young child's post-divorce adjustment: A meta-analysis with implications for parenting arrangements. *Journal of Family Psychology* (2000) 14:5–26.

Chapter 22: How to Happily Agree about Holiday Traditions

Clamor, Aphrodite. Interfaith marriage: Defining the issues, treating the problems. *Psychotherapy in Private Practice* (1991) 9:79–83.

Horowitz, June. Negotiating couplehood: The process of resolving the December dilemma among interfaith couples. *Family Process* (1999) 38:303–323.

Chapter 25: Needing Time for Yourself

White, L. & Keith, B. The effect of shift work on the quality and stability of marital relationships. *Journal of Marriage and the Family* (1990) 52:453–462.

Chapter 26: Cherishing One Another When the Nest Is Empty

Heidemann, B., Suhomlinova, O., O'Rand, A. Economic independence, economic status, and the empty nest in mid-life marital disruptions. *Journal of Marriage and the Family* (1998) 60:219–231.

Chapter 27: The "Accept Me as I Am" Conversation

Swindle, R., Heller, K., Pescosalido, B., & Kikuzawa, S. Responses to nervous breakdowns in America over a forty-year period: Mental health policy implications. *American Psychologist* (July 2000) 55:740–749.

Chapter 28: Rigid versus Flexible Personalities

Strazdins, L., Galligan, R., & Scannell, E. Gender depressive symptoms: Parents' sharing of instrumental and expressive tasks when their children are young. *Journal of Family Psychology* (1997) 11:222–233.

Chapter 29: Rejection-Sensitive Partner

Downey, G. & Feldman, S. Implications of rejection sensitivity for intimate relationships. *Journal of Personality and Social Psychology* (1996) 70:1327–1343.

Rabines, D. & Coie, J. Effects of expectancy induction on rejected children's acceptance by unfamiliar peers. *Developmental Psychology* (1989) 25:45–57.

Chapter 30: Spenders versus Savers

Coleman, Paul. *Getting to the Heart of the Matter.* Holbrook, MA: Adams Media, 1994.

Chapter 31: Partner Not Ambitious Enough/Too Ambitious

Feingold, A. Gender differences in mate selection preferences: A test of the parental investment model. *Psychological Bulletin* (1992) 112:125–139.

Chapter 34: Partner Is Boring

Aron, A., Norman, C., Aron, E., McKenna, C., & Heyman, R. Couples' shared participation in novel and arousing activities and experienced relationship quality. *Journal of Personality and Social Psychology* (2000) 78:273–284.

Gigy, L. & Kelly, J. Reasons for divorce: Perspectives of divorcing men and women. *Journal of Divorce and Remarriage* (1992) 18:169–187.

Reisman, C., Aron, A., & Bergen, M. Shared activities and marital satisfaction: Causal direction and self-expansion versus boredom. *Journal of Social and Personal Relationships* (1993) 10:243–254.

Rupp, D. & Vodanovich, S. The role of boredom proneness in self-reported anger and aggression. *Journal of Social Behavior and Personality* (1997) 12:925–936.

Chapter 35: Partner Is Too Shy

Larsen, R. & Ketelaar, T. Personality and susceptibility to positive and negative emotional states. *Journal of Personality and Social Psychology* (1991) 61:132–140.

Chapter 37: Low Sexual Desire

Barrett, G., Pendry, E., Peacock, J., Victor, C. Women's sexuality after childbirth: A pilot study. *Archives of Sexual Behavior* (1995) 28:179–191.

Beck, J.G. Hypoactive sexual desire: An overview. *Journal of Consulting and Clinical Psychology* (1995) 63:919–927.

Ferroni, P. & Taffe, J. Women's emotional well-being: The importance of communicating sexual needs. *Sexual and Marital Therapy* (1997) 12:127–138.

Larson, J., Anderson, S., Holman, T., & Neimann, B. A longitudinal study of the effects of premarital communication, relationship stability, and self-esteem on sexual satisfaction in the first year of marriage. *Journal of Sex and Marital Therapy* (1998) 24:193–206.

Meston, C. & Gorzalka, B. Differential effects of sympathetic activation on sexual arousal in sexually functional and dysfunctional women. *Journal of Abnormal Psychology* (1996) 105:582–591.

Trudell, G., Landry, L., & Larose, Y. Low sexual desire: The role of anxiety, depression, and marital adjustment. *Sexual and Marital Therapy* (1997) 12:95–99.

Chapter 39: Discussing Sexual History and Safe Sex

Edgar, T., Freimuth, V., Hammond, S., & McDonald, D. Strategic sexual communication: Condom use resistance and response. *Health Communications* (1992) 4:83–104.

Einon, D. Are men more promiscuous than women? *Ethology and Sociobiology* (1994) 15:131–143.

Krull, C. Level of education, sexual promiscuity, and AIDS. *Alberta Journal of Educational Research* (1994) 40:7–20.

Michael, R., Gagnon, J., Laumann, E., & Kolata, G. *Sex in America: A Definitive Survey.* New York: Warner Books, 1995, pp. 185–198.

Sheahan, S., Coons, S., Seabolt, J., & Churchill, L. Sexual behavior, communication, and chlamydial infections among college women. *Health Care for Women International* (1994) 15:275–286.

Walsh, A. Parental attachment, drug use, and facilitative sexual strategies. *Social Biology* (1995) 42:95–107.

Chapter 40: Mismatched Desire

Frank, E., Anderson, C., & Rubinstein, D. Frequency of sexual dysfunction in "normal" couples. *New England Journal of Medicine* (1978) 299:111–115.

Greeley, A. *Faithful Attraction: Discovering Intimacy, Love, and Fidelity in American Marriages.* New York: Tor, 1991, pp. 119–120.

Michael, R., Gagnon, J., Laumann, E., & Kolata, G. *Sex in America: A Definitive Survey.* New York: Warner Books, 1995, pp. 111–131.

Chapter 41: Fun and Positive Sexual Coaching

Michael, R., Gagnon, J., Laumann, E., & Kolata, G. *Sex in America: A Definitive Survey.* New York: Warner Books, 1995, pp. 132–154.

Chapter 44: When You Don't Want the Relationship to Become Sexual—Yet

Cohen, L. & Shotland, R. Timing of first sexual intercourse in relationships. *Journal of Sex Research* (1996) 33:291–299.

Hirsch, L. & Paul, L. Human male mating strategies: I. Courtship tactics of the "quality" and "quantity" attitudes. *Ethology and Social Behavior* (1996) 17:55–70.

Hynie, M., Lydon, J., & Taradash, A. Commitment, intimacy, and women's perception of premarital sex and contraceptive readiness. *Psychology of Women Quarterly* (1997) 21:447–464.

Laumann, E., Gagnon, J., Michael, R., & Michaels, S. *The Social Organization of Sexuality: Sexual Practices in the United States.* Chicago: University of Chicago Press, 1994, pp. 240, 507.

Sawyer, R. & Smith, N. A survey of situational factors at first intercourse among college students. *Journal of Health & Behavior* (1996) 20:208–217.

Chapter 45: Erectile Problems

Althof, S. Erectile dysfunction: Psychotherapy with men and couples. In S. Leiblum and R. Rosen (Eds.), *Principles and Practice of Sex Therapy.* New York: Guilford, 2000.

LoPiccolo, J. Postmodern sex therapy for erectile failure. In R. Rosen and S. Leiblum (Eds.), *Erectile Disorders: Assessment and Treatment.* New York: Guilford, 1992, 171–197.

Zilbergeld, B. *The New Male Sexuality.* New York: Bantam, 1992.

Chapter 46: PMS

Coughlin, P. Premenstrual syndrome: How marital satisfaction and role choice affect subjective severity. *Social Work* (1990) 35:351–355.

Frank, B., Dixon, D., & Grosz, H. Conjoint monitoring of symptoms of premenstrual syndrome: impact on marital satisfaction. *Journal of Counseling Psychology* (1993) 80:109–114.

Ryser, R. & Feinauer, L. PMS and the marital relationship. *American Journal of Family Therapy* (1992) 20:179–190.

Siegel, J. Marital dynamics of wives with premenstrual tension syndrome. *Family Systems Medicine* (1986) 4:358–366.

Chapter 47: You Dislike Aspects of Your Partner's Appearance

Keller, M. & Young, R. Mate assortment in dating and married couples. *Personality and Individual Differences* (1996) 21:217–221.

Chapter 49: Coping with Chronic Pain

Schwartz, L. & Ehde, D. Couples and chronic pain. In K. Schmalling and T. Sher (Eds.), *The Psychology of Couples and Illness*. Washington, D.C.: American Psychological Association, 2000, pp. 191–216.

Chapter 50: Cancer

Clay, Rebecca. Survivors are slow to seek help for sexual problems. *APA Monitor* (June, 1999) 32.

Coyne, J. & Anderson, K. Marital status, marital satisfaction, and support processes among women at high risk for breast cancer. *Journal of Family Psychology* (1999) 13:629–641.

Halford, W., Scott, J., & Smythe, J. Couples and coping with cancer: Helping each other through the night. In K. Schmalling and T. Sher (Eds.), *The Psychology of Couples and Illness*. Washington, D.C.: American Psychological Association, 2000, pp. 135-170.

Weihs, K., Enright, T., Howe, G., & Simmens, S. Marital satisfaction and emotional adjustment after breast cancer. *Journal of Psychosocial Oncology* (1999) 17:33–49.

Chapter 51: Infertility

Band, D., Edelmann, R., Avery, S., & Brinsden, P. Correlates of psychological distress in relation to male infertility. *British Journal of Health Psychology* (1998) 3:245–256.

Cooper-Hilbert, B. Helping couples through the crisis of infertility. *Clinical Update* (January, 2001) 3. Published by the American Association for Marriage and Family Therapy, Washington, D.C.

Levin, J., Sher, T., & Theodos, V. The effect of intracouple coping concordance on psychological and marital distress in infertility patients. *Journal of Clinical Psychology in Medical Settings* (1997) 4:361–372.

Pasch, L. & Christensen, A. Couples facing fertility problems. In K. Schmalling and T. Sher (Eds.), *The Psychology of Couples and Illness*. Washington, D.C.: American Psychological Association, 2000, pp. 241–268.

Chapter 52: Miscarriage

Butel, M., Willner, H., Deckard, R., & Von Red, M. Similarities and differences in couple's grief reactions following miscarriage: Results of a longitudinal study. *Journal of Psychosomatic Research* (1996) 40:245–253.

Lister, M. & Lovell, S. *Healing Together: For Couples Whose Baby Dies*. Omaha: Centering Corporation, 1991.

Stirtzinger, R., Robinson, G., Stewart, D., & Ralevski, E. Parameters of grieving in spontaneous abortion. *International Journal of Psychiatry in Medicine* (1999) 29:235–249.

Swanson, K. Predicting depressive symptoms after miscarriage: A path analysis based on the Lazarus paradigm. *Journal of Women's Health and Gender-Based Medicine* (2000) 9:191–206.

Chapter 53: Death of a Child

Cherico, A., Ragni, G., Antim, A., & Minori, A. Behavior after cancer death in offspring: Coping attitudes and replacement dynamics. *New Trends in Experimental and Clinical Psychology*. (1995) 11:87–89.

Doerr, Maribeth Wilder. *For Better or Worse: A Handbook for Couples Whose Child Has Died*. Omaha: Centering Corporation, 1992.

Lister, Marcie & Lovell, Sandra. *Healing Together: For Couples Whose Baby Dies.* Omaha: Centering Corporation, 1991.

McIntosh, D., Silver, R., & Wortman, C. Religion's role in adjustment to a negative life event: Coping with the loss of a child. *Journal of Personality and Social Psychology* (1993) 65:812–821.

Schwab, R. Effects of a child's death on the marital relationship: A preliminary study. *Death Studies* (1992) 16:141–154.

Chapter 54: Child Hospitalized with Serious Injury

Daviss, W., Mooney, D., Racusin, R., Ford, J., Fleischer, A., & McHugo, G. Predicting post-traumatic stress after hospitalization for pediatric injury. *Journal of the American Academy of Child and Adolescent Psychiatry* (2000) 39:576–583.

Taylor, H., Yeates, K., Wade, S., Drotar, D., Klein, S., & Stancin, T. Influences on first-year recovery from traumatic brain injury in children. *Neuropsychology* (1999) 13:76–89.

Chapter 55: Death of a Spouse's Parent

Guttman, H. Parental death as a precipitant of marital conflict in middle age. *Journal of Marriage and Marital Therapy* (1991) 17:81–87.

Umberson, D. & Chen, M. Effects of a parent's death on adult children: Relationship salience and reaction to loss. *American Sociological Review* (1994) 59:152–168.

Chapter 56: Caring for a Chronically Ill/Disabled Child

Gaither, R., Bingen, K., & Hopkins, J. When the bough breaks: The relationship between chronic illness in children and couple functioning. In K. Schmalling and T. Sher (Eds.), *The Psychology of Couples and Illness.* Washington, D.C.: American Psychological Association, 2000, pp. 337–365.

Chapter 57: Depression

Goldberg, J. Papp illuminate depression with gender role analyses. *Family Therapy News* (December, 1994) 25.

Johnson, S. & Jacob, T. Sequential interactions in the marital communications of depressed men and women. *Journal of Clinical and Counseling Psychology* (2000) 68:4–12.

Prigerson, H., Maciejewski, P., & Rosenheck, R. The effects of marital dissolution and marital quality on health and health services among women. *Medical Care* (1999) 37:858–873.

Chapter 59: Happy Reunions When Career/Business Keeps You Apart

Vormbrock, Julia. Attachment theory as applied to wartime and job-related marital separation. *Psychological Bulletin* (1993) 114:122–144.

Chapter 60: Cybersex

Cooper, A. , Delmonico, D., & Burg, R. Cybersex users, abusers, and compulsives: New findings and implications. In Al Cooper (Ed.), *Cybersex: The Dark Side of the Force.* Philadelphia: Brunner-Routledge, 2000, 5–30.

Schneider, J. Effects of cybersex addiction on the family: Results of a survey. In Al Cooper (Ed.), *Cybersex: The Dark Side of the Force.* Philadelphia: Brunner-Routledge, 2000, 31–58.

Young, K., Griffin-Shelley, E., Cooper, A., O'Mara, J., & Buchanan, J. Online infidelity: A new dimension in couple relationships with implications for evaluation and treatment. In Al Cooper (Ed.), *Cybersex: The Dark Side of the Force.* Philadelphia: Brunner-Routledge, 2000, 59–74.

Chapter 62: After the Affair

Lusterman, Don-David. *Infidelity: A Survival Guide.* Oakland, CA: New Harbinger, 1998.

Michael, R., Gagnon, J., Laumann, E., & Kolata, G. *Sex in America: A Definitive Survey.* New York: Warner Books, 1995, 105.

Chapter 63: Partner Still Has Some Love for the Ex

Buunk, B. & Matsaers, W. The nature of the relationship between remarried and former spouses and its impact on marital satisfaction. *Journal of Family Psychology* (1999) 13:165–174.

Goldsmith, J. Relationships between former spouses: Descriptive findings. *Journal of Divorce* (1980) 14:1–19.

Chapter 65: Partner Won't Commit

Adams, J. & Jones, W. The conceptualization of marital commitment: An integrative analysis. *Journal of Personality and Social Psychology* (1997) 72:1177–1196.

Curtis, J. & Susman, V. Factors related to fear of marriage. *Psychological Reports* (1994) 74:859–863.

Chapter 66: Flirting

Dijkstra, P. & Buunk, B. Jealousy as a function of rival characteristics: An evolutionary perspective. *Personality and Social Psychology Bulletin* (1998) 24:1158–1166.

Marshall, J. & Neill, J. The removal of a psychosomatic symptom: Effects on marriage. *Family Process* (1977) 16:273–280.

Chapter 67: You Want Your Partner to Attend Church

Coleman, Paul. *25 Stupid Mistakes Couples Make.* Chicago, IL: Contemporary Books, Roxbury Park, 2001.

Mahoney, A., Pargament, K., et al. Marriage and the spiritual realm: The role of proximal and distal religious constructs in marital functioning. *Journal of Family Psychology* (1999) 13:321–338.

Chapter 68: Discussing in Which Religion to Raise Your Children

Clamor, A. Interfaith marriage: Defining the issues, treating the problem. *Psychotherapy in Private Practice* (1991) 9:79–83.

Glenn, N. Interreligious marriages in the U.S.: Patterns and recent trends. *Journal of Marriage and the Family* (1982) 44:555–568.

Horowitz, J. Negotiating couplehood: The process of resolving the December dilemma among interfaith couples. *Family Process* (1999) 38:303–323.

Chapter 70: Staying Upbeat When Your Partner Wants to Change Careers

Stewart, A. & Ostrove, J. Women's personalities in middle age: Gender, history, and mid-course corrections. *American Psychologist* (1998) 53:1165–1194.

Chapter 71: Helping Your Partner to Forgive

Enright, R. & Fitzgibbons, R. *Helping Clients Forgive: An Empirical Guide for Resolving Anger and Restoring Hope.* Washington, D.C.: *American Psychological Association,* 2000.

Chapter 72: Having (More) Children

Baumeister, Roy. *Meanings of Life.* New York: Guilford, 1991, p. 166.

Chapter 73: Chores

Gottman, John. *What Predicts Divorce?: The Relationship Between Marital Processes and Marital Outcomes.* Hillsdale, NJ: Lawrence Erlbaum Associates, 1994, pp. 269–270.

Chapter 74: Partner Swears Too Much

Winters, A. & Duck, S. You ***!: Swearing as an aversive and a relational activity. In Robin Kowalski (Ed.), *Behaving Badly: Aversive Behaviors in Interpersonal Relationships.* Washington, D.C.: American Psychological Association, 2001, 54–77.

Chapter 81: How to Maintain Happiness Over the Long Haul

Carlson, J., Sperry, L., & Dinkmeyer, D. Marriage maintenance: How to stay healthy. *Topics in Family Psychology and Counseling* (1992) 1:84–90.

Jacobson, N., Schmaling, K., & Holtzworth-Munroe, A. Component analysis of behavioral marital therapy: Two-year follow-up and prediction of relapse. *Journal of Marital and Family Therapy* (1987) 13:187–195.

Index

from
The Heart

JACK GRIFFIN

Dedication

For Anita—from the heart.

Why This Book Is for You

"The heart has its reasons, which reason does not know."

—*Blaise Pascal (1623–1662)*

"Say what you mean and mean what you say."

How often have you been given that advice? Probably about as often as you have given it yourself. And why not? Advice just doesn't get much better than this. Saying what you mean and meaning what you say is all about saying it from the heart. Simple, yes?

You bet.

But, like most truly simple concepts, putting it into practice is, for most of us, devilishly difficult.

The Head-Heart Disconnect

We all believe that sincerity, genuine expression, and emotional truth are vital to our relationships with family, friends, loved ones, and also with the people with whom we work. Yet if you have trouble connecting heart with head with words, you are not alone. Getting these three variables to come out equal is the great equation of life. It is an equation we try each and every day to solve. For most of us, the calculation is hit-or-miss. For some of us, the results just never balance out. For the truly successful among us—those who get full pleasure and satisfaction from living and working with and among families, friends, colleagues, customers, subordinates, and bosses—the equation almost always comes out just right. For these fortunate folk, the line from heart to head to words runs straight and true and sure.

But what about the rest of us?

- We want to say what we mean, but we sometimes speak before we know what we mean.

- We mean one thing but end up saying another.

391

- The "right" words just don't come.
- The "right" words come—but much too late.
- We feel strong emotion, which we cannot put into words.
- Words just get in the way of what we feel.
- What we feel just gets in the way of words.
- We feel the "right" things, but we say the "wrong" things.

Love, anger, fear: No emotions are more basic or more universal— more heartfelt—than these. Yet no emotions are more difficult to communicate, to manage, to put into words. This book will show you how.

More Words for More Feelings

If love, anger, and fear are not major problems for you, that still leaves plenty of other challenging matters of the heart to tackle. For example:

- Making meaningful announcements
- Apologizing from the heart
- Expressing heartfelt thanks and appreciation
- Providing real encouragement
- Extending congratulations from the heart
- Asking favors
- Making invitations more inviting
- Making a persuasive case
- Providing genuine sympathy
- And just keeping in touch

Saying It from the Heart—to Your Kids

You'll also find helpful how-to advice on talking with children about such emotionally difficult subjects as

- Anger
- Caring

- Death
- Divorce
- Drugs
- Feelings
- Manners
- Sex

Learning the Language of Love

Then there's the life arena in which absolutely nothing is more important than saying it from the heart: love.

In love, we find it most essential—and most difficult—to say what we mean and mean what we say. This book will help you identify and overcome the obstacles that stubbornly interfere with heartfelt expression just when we need it most.

- You'll learn about the body language of love, about what to say when you want to get acquainted, and about what to say on a date.
- A special chapter is devoted to the enduring romance of the love letter in the 21st century.
- There are chapters on getting a date, on what to say during a date, on writing love letters via e-mail, and on how to use words to patch up the rough patches in any relationship.

The Heart of the Job

Anybody who thinks saying it from the heart has nothing to do with saying it on the job must be in a pretty dreary line of work. The truth is that the workplace is filled with intense emotion and populated by fragile egos. As for the stakes, they are the very highest—your future and that of your firm. Work time is the right time to say it from the heart. You'll find guidance on:

- Making announcements
- Turning occasions of apology into opportunities for strengthening business relationships

- Expressing thanks with sincerity
- Creating inclusive celebrations and congratulations
- Criticizing creatively, precisely, and without leaving scars
- Complaining effectively
- Reaching out with sympathy and condolence
- Motivating from the heart
- Asking favors
- Making invitations more inviting
- Promoting yourself and promoting your projects

The Heartline Concept

If all this information in one book seems a bit overwhelming, the fact is that saying it from the heart is saying it from the heart, regardless of whom you're communicating with. The concept that unifies the approach to all of the diverse people and situations included in this book is what we call the heartline: the most direct route from heart to head to words. Truly effective communication begins with discovering the heartline for a particular time, place, and person.

> Each situation we explore in *How to Say It® from the Heart* identifies the heartline for that particular situation and tells you how to get onto it and use it to journey to your goal without detours, without stalling, and without getting lost.

Learning Your Lines

It is natural to think the following:

1. My feelings are unique. No one can know what I'm really feeling.

2. Feelings in general are unpredictable; therefore, speaking from the heart has to be spontaneous. It either happens, or it doesn't. Hit or miss. Lucky or unlucky.

It is natural to think this way, but it is neither accurate nor useful. Sure, your feelings are your feelings, but that doesn't mean you are alone in having them. This book will help you identify your feelings with those of others, and, once you do that, we'll look together for the words that connect you most directly not only with what your heart says, but what the hearts of others need and want to hear.

And you'll learn something else, too: Saying it from the heart is too important to leave to chance. In any important communication, the last thing you want to do is wing it. This book will show you how to rehearse and prepare for meaningful emotional communication.

Keys to Understanding

"The heart," the great French philosopher Pascal wrote, "has its reasons, which reason cannot know." Learning to say it from the heart will help you to know those reasons, to understand them, and to communicate them. I promise you this: *How to Say It® from the Heart* will help you to communicate effectively, powerfully, and successfully, to the people and in the situations that matter most to you.

Part 1

Getting Ready
to Say It
from the Heart

*T*his part introduces you to the concepts
and techniques of communicating from the heart.

1

Find Your *Heartline*

*J*ust be yourself! Don't think so much! Just say whatever comes into your head! Let it all hang out! Don't censor yourself! Let your feelings be your guide! When the time comes, the words will come to you!

Our world is filled with bad advice, and this is some of the worst. Not that it is motivated by anything malicious; all of these pronouncements are founded on the belief that our society and our culture value spontaneity above all else. We take it for granted that spontaneous expression is the most direct form of communication and that the most direct communication is necessarily the most honest. In effect, we equate thoughtless speech with honest speech. If we take this to the next step, that the most honest speech is necessarily the best speech, then we must conclude that the best speech is the least thoughtful speech—and, indeed, the less thought given to what we say, the better!

Language, many biologists, anthropologists, and philosophers tell us, is what finally distinguishes human beings from the other subjects of the animal kingdom. Language is certainly the medium through which we make most of our needs known and, largely, through which we obtain satisfaction of those needs. Language, any way we look at it, is central to everything we are and hope to be. Should we, then, be so willing to disavow responsibility for it and control over it?

There is no need to waste your time answering what is obviously a rhetorical question. The point is this: Honest, effective language—speaking from the heart—does not require abandonment of thought. Quite the contrary: The more thought, the more imagination that goes into what you say, the more honest, effective, and heartfelt it can be.

399

What Is the Heartline, Anyway?

But why should we have to give more than a passing thought to expressing what we feel? Shouldn't this just come naturally?

Maybe it should. It would be nice if it did. But, then, it would also be nice if we all played golf like Tiger Woods, played guitar like Eric Clapton, and played the stock market like Warren Buffett.

The Declaration of Independence notwithstanding, we aren't all created equal, and life ain't necessarily fair. To a Woods, a Clapton, or a Buffett, excellence in their particular fields seems natural. We know, however, that their skills are not simply inborn, but are a combination of natural ability, hard work, and, probably, some other elements thrown in along the way. Yet when we listen to an eloquent, persuasive speaker, we assume that the right words just come naturally to her, and we bemoan the fact that we don't share her eloquence.

The *bad* news is that sports prowess, musical virtuosity, and financial genius are not birthrights. Nor is the ability to speak from the heart. Like a skillful golf swing, a perfect command of the guitar, or an insightful grasp of investment strategy, creating honest, clear, persuasive speech is too complex a process to be entirely natural and native to us. The *good* news is that all of us, if we want, can learn to play golf or play it better, pick out a chord or two on the guitar, and even invest with a degree of sound judgment. We can also learn to speak from the heart. The steps in this learning process follow.

Step One. Give up the notion that speaking from the heart is speaking without thought. This entails abandoning the lie that motives of the heart and the head are incompatible and necessarily in conflict.

Step Two. Give up the notion that spontaneous speech is the best speech. Not only is it okay to prepare, it is the best way to ensure that you really will. And, above all else, speaking from the heart is saying what you want to say.

Step Three. Give up the notion that you naturally know what you want to say, but just have trouble putting it into words. The fact is that an important initial process in speaking from the heart is to determine just what it is you need to say. Often, we have to devote some time and thought to figuring out what is in our hearts. Just because something is important to us, we can't assume that we are fully aware of it. You need to determine what you want to express before you begin to put it into words.

Step Four. Give up the notion that once you know what you want and need to say, the words will just come. It doesn't necessarily work that way. Certainly, you can't count on it. How many times have you felt strong, urgent emotion—only to find yourself tongue tied: so angry you couldn't speak, so happy you couldn't speak, so sad, so moved, so frustrated? As often as strong emotion drives speech, it also inhibits it or trips it up. Motivated by powerful feelings, we all too often say things we later—or even instantly—regret.

Now, having abandoned the preceding four obstacles to speaking from the heart, you can take the following positive steps:

Step Five. Discover what is in your heart. Determine what you want and what you need to say. We begin to discuss this step in detail in Chapter 3, but it is also a theme throughout the book.

Step Six. Find your *heartline*—the most direct route from heart to head to words. Not only do you need to determine what it is you want and need to say, you need to say it most efficiently and directly. Communication, like a radio or television signal, is subject to interference from various sources. Some of the most common sources of interference include:

- Conflicting emotions, competing motives. We aren't always sin-gleminded. Sometimes we feel more than one strong emotion about a given issue.
- Fear of embarrassment
- Fear of causing embarrassment
- Fear of incurring criticism
- Fear of what the other person will think or feel
- Imperfect understanding of the situation at issue
- Inadequate command of the range of language options available

Many of the chapters in this book will help you focus on overcoming interference, the obstacles that sometimes block the heartline, the route from heart to head to expression.

All About Janus

The heartline is not a bodily organ or physiological structure. It is, rather, a strategy for communication. As such, it changes, depending on the time, place, and people involved. By definition, communication cannot be a solo endeavor. At minimum, it is a dialogue. "If a tree falls in the forest," the familiar philosophical question goes, "and no one is there to hear, does it make a sound?" Similarly, without someone with whom to communicate, is there communication? The search for the heartline in any given instance depends as much on who the other person is as it does on your own feelings, needs, and desires.

The communication strategies presented in this book always look two ways, toward yourself and toward others. Think of the Roman god Janus, the mythic guardian of gates. He is a god with two faces, one that looks inward, to the space within the gate, and one that looks outward, beyond the gate. Keep the image of Janus in mind when you set out to say it from the heart. Your task is to focus on yourself and your needs while simultaneously directing your attention to the recipient of your communication—to what you know about him, about his interests, his needs, his concerns. Saying it from the heart is as much about other people as it is about you.

Imagination Is the Key

It doesn't take the genius of a rocket scientist to figure out that those we celebrate as the great users of language—the famous poets and novelists, the great historians and orators—are also great users of the imagination. Indeed, it is the imagination that we most treasure in our great writers. But why reserve this faculty for the great writers? What about us more ordinary folk?

Whether you set out to write the great American novel or a note of congratulations to a friend who's just gotten a plum job, an exercise of imagination will make the communication more effective.

- Never try to communicate to a void. Use your imagination to visualize your audience, your reader, your conversation partner, the recipient of your message. Imagine writing as conversation, face to face.

- Imagine how the other person feels *now* and how you would like him to feel *after* he reads or listens to your message.
- Imagine yourself out of yourself. That is, focus on the other person.
- Imagine the dialogue before you even utter a word. When you have something really important to say, preview the conversation in your imagination. Rehearse it. Play the scene for yourself, like a movie.
- Imagine the outcome of the communication. What issues will it resolve? What will things be like *after* you've written that all-important letter or had the conversation you know is necessary but you've been dreading?

The Best Policy

It's been said many times: *Honesty is the best policy.* But it is also true that honesty is not the *only* policy—just the best.

If you can communicate with absolute truthfulness and objectivity, you are in the best possible position. Take that as your starting point. Begin with the truth, the whole truth, and nothing but the truth.

But honesty is not always simply equivalent to the truth. Your best friend is a Sunday painter, an art amateur who takes a lot of pleasure in the little canvases he creates. He's modest about them, but it's clear to you that he is very proud of his work. He's just completed a new portrait of his son and daughter, a picture he's been laboring at, off and on, for months now. He shows it to you . . . and it's a dreadful mess. The poor kids look like they've been playing in heavy traffic.

You gaze, slack-jawed, at the painting. Your friend beams.

Is honesty the best policy here?

Yes—but not the truth. In this case, an honest response takes into account the following:

- *What you feel about your friend.* You like him, and you don't want to hurt him. These are the feelings and this is the goal closest to your heart.

- *How you imagine your friend feels.* In this case, only a very slight exercise of the imagination is required. Obviously, he's proud of what he has done. He wants you to share his opinion of the painting.

- *The purpose—the objective—of this communication.* You are not an art critic, and, although you have been asked your opinion of this painting, the true purpose of this conversation is not art criticism. It is letting your friend feel good about what he has done.

The response that is most honest in this case, truest to your feelings, truest to what you conceive as your friend's feelings, and truest to the purpose of this particular communication, does not fully adhere to what you perceive as absolute, objective truth.

"You really see your kids in a unique, loving way. That certainly shows in this portrait!"

It is an honest, if not fully truthful, response.

15 Ways to Begin to Say It from the Heart

Every fugitive from high school physics is familiar with the principle of inertia: the tendency of a body in motion to remain in motion or a body at rest to remain at rest unless acted upon by an external force. This law of physics also translates nicely into a law of human psychology. Many of us just naturally have trouble getting started. The first words are the hardest to get out, and sometimes the prospect of communication seems just too daunting even to begin. Here are some tactics for overcoming the inertia that may keep us from saying it from the heart.

1. *What's your hurry?* There is no law against thinking before you speak or write. Take the time to sort out your thoughts, to identify the purpose of your communication. Think about what you are feeling, and what you want to accomplish by communicating on this occasion.

2. *Don't put yourself on the hot seat.* We are conditioned to believe that dialogue or conversation should be a rapid-fire give and take. Many of us are made uncomfortable by silences of even a few seconds between question and response. Don't feel obliged to come back with a fast answer. Take the time you need. If necessary, buy time with phrases such as, "That's an important question. Give me a moment to think about that."

3. *Mentally review what you feel, think, and want.* Then formulate what to say.

4. *Rehearse spontaneity.* If you envy the quick, suave wit of Hollywood leading men and ladies, just remember: They're all following scripts. But be aware that real life can be scripted, too. It is not dishonest to plan what you are going to say in a particular situation, and it is also a good idea to exercise your imagination in order to anticipate what the others involved in the situation are likely to say. Mentally rehearse all important upcoming exchanges.

5. *Do your homework.* The most convincing, persuasive communication is not filled with flowery phrases and lovely language, but with useful, relevant facts. If you feel strongly about a certain issue, learn all you can about it before you sit down to write or get up to speak.

6. *Select your audience.* Be certain that you direct your important communications to the right people. Often, this is obvious—but not always. For example, if you have prepared a heartfelt appeal in an effort to get hired for a new job, be sure that you identify the person who has the power to hire you. Talk to her, rather than to her assistant or associate.

7. *Communicate at the right time.* Too many of us speak up whenever the spirit moves us. Sometimes this is necessary; but whenever possible, give careful consideration to selecting the most advantageous time to speak or write. For example:

   • You really want a raise. Bring up the subject after you have successfully completed a project, not following some disappointing result.

   • You know that your spouse has good and bad days, or that he/she is most decidedly not a morning person. Broach critical subjects on the good days and never in the morning.

   • Your workplace has a rhythm all its own. Mornings are hectic, afternoons generally quiet. Bring up important issues when they are likely to receive extended, cool, calm attention.

   • In any workplace, Mondays are typically bad days to raise issues that can be put off until Tuesday.

   • At work, come Friday, many people find it difficult to focus.

- All other things being equal, the high-energy time for most people is late in the morning, between about ten and eleven. A high energy level typically correlates with positive emotions and higher levels of optimism. Often, this is a good time to present issues that matter to you.

- For most people, late afternoon is a dull, low-energy time, especially between two and four.

8. *Give up the idea that there are "good" versus "bad" feelings.* Accept the idea that there are "right" and "wrong" feelings. This distinction has nothing to do with morality. "Right" feelings are those you want your listener or reader to have as a result of your communication. In contrast, "wrong" feelings are those that will prompt your listener or reader to act in a way contrary to what you want. Exercise your imagination to determine which feelings are the "right" ones in a given situation, and shape your communication in ways you believe will produce those feelings.

9. *Don't ask for what you want.* Instead, go into the communication focused on what the other person wants. This does not require you to commit to a life of ceaseless self-denial and self-sacrifice. It does require a change of perspective. Let's say you are an auto salesperson. What you want is to sell the customer a car. You want this not so much because you have a strong desire to see the customer happily driving a car, but because you need to earn this month's mortgage money. If you were absolutely honest, you might approach the customer in the showroom with a remark like this: "You really *have* to buy this car. If you do, I won't have to worry about this month's mortgage payment." Of course, this approach is not likely to produce a sale. Instead, try focusing not on your needs and wants, but on those of the customer: "This car is a great value because . . ."

10. *Deal with your fears.* Fear—anxiety about potential embarrassment, about eliciting an angry response, about possible rejection, and so on—can certainly block or distort important communication. Don't try to ignore your anxious feelings. The surest way to intensify a negative emotion is to *try* to ignore it. This only forces you to focus on the feeling. Instead, try the following:

- Recognize and acknowledge the negative feelings that you have. Don't try to ignore or run away from them.

- Deliberately try to imagine the worst things that can happen to you as a result of the communication you are about to make. Develop a full scenario. Play it out. Experience the emotions *before* the conversation or before you send the letter; don't wait for the fears to sneak up on you.

- Having played out the worst that can happen, imagine the best outcome. How will you feel? What will it be like to succeed in this encounter? Play out this scenario, too. Will this exercise cure your case of nerves? Probably not, but it will make the emotions associated with a high-stakes communication more familiar and, therefore, less threatening. To this extent, it *will* reduce your anxiety and help you get in touch with your heart-line in this particular situation.

11. *Look like you're saying it from the heart.* Chapter 2 is all about how you can use body language to communicate persuasively.

12. *Don't just "speak" effective body language, learn how to "read" it, too.* Chapter 2 will also help you to become sensitive to the body language cues your listener gives you. Observe the effect of your words on the other person.

13. *Persuade with your ears.* Those who speak most successfully from the heart are those who listen most acutely and sensitively. Chapter 4 will help you become the best listener you can be.

14. *Never beg, but be prepared to bargain.* Persuasive speech establishes a certain rhythm of give and take. You can create this rhythm by not *asking* for what you want but by negotiating for it instead. What's the difference? Asking is taking; negotiating is trading one valuable commodity for another. It is taking *and* giving. Most persuasive communication is based on negotiation. For one thing, negotiation keeps issues alive. If you simply ask, "Can I get a raise?" and the answer is "No," the conversation grinds to a dead halt. If, however, you approach this issue as a negotiation, it tends to become a living thing—or at least a request that invites a creative response. For instance:

- Since I took over management of Project X, we've seen a 15 percent increase in profit margin, and we've added two new territories. Best of all, the year's not over. You've given me a lot of creative freedom, for which I'm grateful. However, I now feel that it is time for my salary level to catch up to the level of my responsibilities, qualifications, and, most of all, achievements.

15. *Create a pleasant climate.* It is easier to speak sincerely and persuasively in a friendly, receptive context than in a climate that feels cold or even hostile. Among family and friends or in the workplace, cultivate the habit of creative small talk. Not all communication needs to be profoundly heartfelt. Get into the habit of asking people how their day is going, or how they enjoyed that recent vacation, or how that new car is working out. Ask your kid what kind of day he had at school. Ask your friend for recommendations of must-see movies. Whatever you ask, focus on the interests of the other person—but keep it light and good natured.

Here's a final tip for overcoming the inertia that holds you back from saying it from the heart: Dig into the rest of this book. You'll get the most out of it if you read all the chapters in Part 1 and consult the rest as your needs dictate.

2

Not Another Word!

$\mathcal{I}$n 1971, psychologist Albert Mehrabian concluded a study of the nature of persuasion. He found that when listeners judge the emotional content of a speech, they give the most weight to the speaker's facial expressions and body movement—his "body language." Mehrabian was able to quantify just how much weight: 55 percent. That is, he found that 55 percent of a speech's power of persuasion—its effectiveness—depends on visual, not verbal, cues.

This is a powerful conclusion. So we find that only 45 percent of the effectiveness of a speech comes from the words?

No.

Actually, Mehrabian found that the *next* most important factors in determining the persuasive power of a speech, after visual cues, were "vocal qualities"—not words, but tone of voice, voice pitch, and the pace of delivery. These accounted for 38 percent of the speech's effectiveness. Adding 55 and 38 percent gives us 93 percent. According to Mehrabian's study, 93 percent of the effectiveness of a speech—ostensibly a *verbal* presentation—has nothing to do with the meaning of the words used. The words themselves account for a mere 7 percent of the effectiveness of a speech.

The Body's Language

The lesson of Mehrabian's study is that anyone who would communicate from the heart—convey important matters in a sincere and persuasive way—must always address the nonverbal aspects of verbal communication. Movement, expression, and tone speak volumes, regardless of the words that are used or not used.

Space Invaders

In his popular 1970 classic, *Body Language,* Julius Fast explains that human beings, like other animals, stake out and defend a certain territory, or personal space. Among nonhuman animals, defense of territory is carried out through a combination of symbolic gestures—a cat will arch its back, a dog will snarl and bare its teeth—and out-and-out violence. Among people, however, the defenses are purely symbolic. They are sufficiently subtle that we aren't always consciously aware of the defensive gestures and postures, but they are effective nonetheless.

The Masking Defense

Fast speaks of our masking behavior, the face we present to the outer world, which is rarely our real face. Indeed, it is often considered inappropriate, even outrageous and "antisocial" to allow our face to express what we really feel. From a very early age, we are conditioned to mask our feelings through certain facial expressions and other bodily gestures. In effect, we are taught to employ a body language that lies and that, most of the time, disguises more than it reveals about what we have in our hearts. The ultimate motive of this masking behavior, Fast argues, is the defense of personal space. The trouble is, however, that such a defense not only is often unnecessary—a kind of outmoded artifact of our biological and cultural evolution—but can be downright destructive. It can make us appear insincere, nervous, afraid, evasive, or even treacherous. It blocks the heartline, and it often contradicts visually and subconsciously what we are saying verbally and deliberately.

Some of the common masks include the following:

* *The forced smile.* The smile can be one of the most powerful means of nonverbal communication. It can be the ultimate ice-breaker, a surefire messenger of sincerity, pleasure, trust, and good humor. Yet it can also be a powerful mask. We smile when we are happy, to be sure, but also when we are embarrassed, when we apologize, and when we suffer a minor mishap. Often the smile masks annoyance, impatience, even anger.

- *The forced scowl.* The great World War II general George S. Patton spoke of putting on his "war face," a stern scowl, rigid and immobile, which he used to practice daily in front of a mirror. Many of us adopt similar masks.

- *Closed gestures.* The way we fold our arms across our chest or cross our legs is often a defense against the invasion of our space.

These and similar masks are not all bad. In crowded urban societies we couldn't get along without them. They make day-to-day casual contact with any number of strangers and near-strangers easier. Doubtless, they avert much unpleasantness, ranging from harsh words to fistfights. We do not want to let the whole world into our most intimate range. Our social, cultural, and psychological well-being demands the maintenance of a certain zone of personal space.

But the masks we wear can also interfere with important communication, sabotaging the messages we want to convey.

- We may subconsciously telegraph unfriendliness.

- We may subconsciously tell the world we are insincere, uncertain, fearful, or out-and-out lying.

- We may convey anger and impatience.

- We may convey boredom.

Is there any way to control when and where we put on our masks? And is there any way to shed the masks we don't want?

Body language is truly a language in that it is a symbolic means of communication and it can be learned. Because it can be learned, we can control and regulate the way we use it. We can indeed become aware of the language we use in given situations, and we can alter it to a significant degree. The next section has some suggestions for how to do this.

Body Language: 15 Key "Phrases"

1. *Make a forthright entrance.* We've all known a man or a woman on whom all eyes focus when he or she enters a room. It is not necessarily that this person is particularly attractive, but, as the cliché goes, he or she "really knows how to make an entrance."

The problem with clichés is that we become so familiar with them that we stop thinking about what they really mean. The fact is that how you enter a room makes a very powerful statement about who you are and, perhaps even more important, who you think you are. To some lucky people, making a powerful positive first impression comes naturally and easily. For others, hard work and practice are required to overcome a natural tendency to awkwardness. Even if you are one of the latter, the extra effort is worth it. Why? Uncomfortable though it may be, it's a lot easier to put the effort into a positive first impression than it is to attempt to undo the negative effects of an unfavorable impression. Sometimes, you never get the opportunity even to try.

2. *Walk tall.* Life, our parents tell us and tell us more than once, ain't always fair. If you're on the short side, you won't like to hear that tall people have a built-in body language advantage. We tend naturally to invest more authority in tall people. We find them "naturally" more commanding, maybe we even think they are more sincere or trustworthy. The good news is that, even if you aren't tall, you can *walk tall.* Begin by dressing in ways that emphasize whatever height you have.

- Avoid boxy-looking tailoring.
- Avoid horizontally striped patterns.
- Shorter men should avoid baggy, loosely cut pants, and shorter women should favor longer hemlines.

Even more important than dressing to accent stature is to avoid entering a room or approaching another person in a cringing, stooped, or slouching manner. Concentrate on maintaining an erect posture as you make your entrance, and do so forthrightly, without hesitation, and with a purposeful stride.

How do you acquire a "purposeful stride"? Move with a purpose, and know where you are going.

- Try always to approach any communication situation having already formulated the purpose and the objective of the communication.
- If you have to do your thinking as you make your entrance, chances are that you'll appear hesitant or absent-minded. Work out as much as you can beforehand.

3. *Show a sincere smile.* Have you ever had the misfortune to face a grim, closed-mouthed loan officer? It gives you a sinking feeling, with cartoon visions of winged money bags flying anywhere but toward you. A scowling negotiator won't cut you much slack, you believe, just as a frowning salesperson probably won't make the sale. In contrast, a sincere smile is an invitation. Anything less than this sends the message that you intend to offer little or nothing and that you are receptive to little or nothing. If you come on like a tough nut to crack, many of the people you approach will decide that you just aren't worth dealing with.

If you find it easy and natural to smile, good for you! But some of us have to work harder at it.

- Begin by relaxing. Before you make your entrance, glance downward, move your jaw around, then move your tongue around the inside of your mouth. Inhale deeply, hold it, then let out your breath forcefully. Repeat this exercise a few times.

- When your facial muscles feel relaxed, think about something, someone, or some place you enjoy. Imagine pleasurable times, people, and places. Chances are that the combination of facial relaxation and a pleasant frame of mind will bring the easy, welcoming smile that is a tremendous communication facilitator.

4. *Make and maintain eye contact.* The one body language "phrase" that just about everyone knows about is *eye contact.* We all know and accept that looking someone in the eye conveys openness and honesty. It also transmits powerful energy. We've all heard people speak about the "sparkle" in someone's eye, as if that sparkle were an unusual thing, a thing that made the person in question seem special. Actually, *all* of us have a sparkle in our eyes, but it is rarely noticed. Why? Because, even though we all recognize the importance of eye contact, few of us actually make full eye contact when we meet or speak.

To exploit the sparkle in your eyes, to convey honesty and transmit energy, make eye contact—immediately, before the first words are spoken. For some people, this is not easy. Many of us learn to be shy. We are afraid of seeming to stare. We are, in fact, fearful of "invading" another person's space with our gaze. Working to overcome these inhibitions, these obstacles to making and maintaining eye contact, is well worth the effort of practice. Eye contact is a highly charged form of communication.

5. *Develop a memorable handshake.* Back in that amorphously undefined time known only as the good old days, diligent fathers took their sons aside and solemnly explained the great importance of a good, solid handshake. The handshake was seen as the deal maker and the deal closer. It conveyed a world of confidence, trust, and strength. The power of a hearty handshake was regarded as very nearly mystical.

Maybe this seems corny nowadays, but the fact remains that physical touch and physical warmth cut through the veneer of techno-sophistication and antiseptic business practices to make a compelling *human* impression.

And it is an impression that lasts far longer than the moment occupied by the gesture. A warm, hearty handshake not only conveys openness and a willingness to communicate, it creates a physical association with your presence that tends to fix you that much more vividly in the other person's memory.

Here are the steps to a memorable handshake:

First: Deliver a dry-palm handshake. Keep a handkerchief with you to wipe your hands dry before entering a meeting or conference where there will be handshakes all around. A sweaty, clammy palm is physically unpleasant—and it conveys your anxiety rather than your confidence and the pleasure you take in this meeting.

Second: Grasp the other person's hand fully, at the palm rather than by the fingers.

Third: Deliver a *moderately* tight grip. A firm handshake does not require a bone-crushing grip, but you should not offer a passive dead fish, either.

Fourth: Hold the other person's hand a few fractions of a second longer than you are naturally inclined to do. This conveys additional sincerity and truly "holds" the other person's attention while greetings are exchanged.

Fifth: While giving the handshake, resist the urge to look down at the clasped hands. Instead, look into the other person's eyes.

Sixth: Be sure to start talking *before* you let go. A simple phrase like "It's great to meet you" or "Glad to be here," spoken while hands are still clasped, becomes a powerfully effective greeting.

6. *Don't rush to take a seat.* You enter a room. What comes next? Often, the next action is taking a seat in an office, at a conference table, or in a living room. How you do this tells those present something about your attitude and approach to them. You need to be aware that the people already in the room cannot help but watch you sit. We always tend to look intently at anyone who enters "our" territory. When you enter the room and take a seat, you are—at least for the moment—the center of attention.

- Don't rush to sit. Doing so will make you appear anxious. More important, if others in the room are already seated, your standing will give you a few moments to be looked up to. Remember: Height has its advantages. If everyone in the room is sitting and you are standing, then you are the tallest person in the room—at least for the time being. This gives you an aura of authority, however temporary.

- Think about where you will sit. If you have a choice, choose a firm chair rather than a sofa or a very soft chair. You want a chair that keeps you upright and that allows you to maintain an erect posture, not a chair that swallows you whole.

- If you are to be seated at a table, it is not appropriate for you to usurp the seat at the head of the table—unless, of course, you are running the meeting. Beyond this, be aware that there is a psychological power geography at work around any conference table. The greatest power position is at the head of the table. The second most dominant position is at the other end of the table. Perhaps surprisingly, the seats to either side of the head of the table are the weakest positions at the table and should be avoided, if possible.

7. *Transmit a feeling of relaxed energy.* Personal energy is a positive quality conveyed largely through nonverbal signals. Avoid confusing energy with restlessness or nervousness; instead, strive to convey a feeling of relaxed energy, a combination of enthusiasm and confidence that may be summed up in the word *poise.*

8. *Breathing is an important aspect of nonverbal communication.* Obviously, you don't need a book to teach you how to breathe—but by becoming conscious of how you breathe, you can gain a further measure of control over your body language. Most of the time, we give no thought to how we breathe. The process is, as it should be, completely automatic. However, when you become upset, nervous, or scared, breathing typically becomes shallower, shorter, and faster. Under these circumstances you probably become quite conscious of the change in breathing pattern. More important, the change is also noticeable to others who observe you.

Being perceived as short of breath and anxious is not a positive body language message. Fortunately, it is possible to train yourself to breathe slowly and deeply, even when you are nervous. This requires some thought, but it can be done, and doing so will benefit you in two ways. Learning to control your breathing will not only keep your nervousness from being communicated, it will also actually cause you to feel less nervous. Fear creates certain physical sensations and symptoms; then, as we become aware of these sensations and symptoms, we become even more anxious, which, in turn, intensifies the sensations and symptoms. It is an all-too-familiar vicious cycle.

When you feel anxious, focus on your breathing. Force yourself to slow down, to breathe deeply and regularly. The task of directing your attention to your breathing will, in and of itself, help reduce your anxiety. Regulating your breathing will reduce anxiety as well.

9. *Nothing "speaks" body language more eloquently than the head and face.* The head tilted to one side indicates interest and close listening. This is a positive, desirable gesture, which always engages your conversation counterpart. Just make certain to vary the gesture. No body language gesture is positive if it is held statically.

10. *A slightly out-thrust chin conveys confidence.* Be careful with this one, however. Don't exaggerate. Boldly thrust out your chin, and you will probably be perceived as arrogant—or as someone with a most peculiar knack for impersonating Mussolini.

11. *Nodding the head up and down conveys agreement, while shaking the head from side to side conveys disagreement.* This is obvious, of course. But it is quite common to fall into the trap of sending mixed signals. We've all talked with people who *say* yes even as

they—ever so slightly—shake their head *no*. It is very important to become sufficiently conscious of your body language to prevent garbled transmissions such as this.

12. *Use your hands.* Next to the head and face, the hands are the most fluent speakers of body language; however, many people worry about "what to do with" their hands. Stop worrying. Instead, feel free to gesture with your hands to help drive home your verbal points. Here are some tips:

- Open hands, palms up, suggest honesty and openness.
- Rubbing the hands together communicates positive expectancy.
- Putting the fingertips together steeple-fashion conveys confidence.

13. *When you're on stage . . .* The body-language basics that apply in everyday communications are also useful in more formal public speaking situations. Here are some ideas:

- Maintain eye contact with your audience. This is not always easy when you have to look down at your typescript; therefore, rehearse the speech and practice looking up frequently. Each time you look up from your typescript, try to make contact with a specific person in the audience. Don't stare out blankly. Vary the targets of your gaze, but do pick a specific target each time.
- Insofar as it is appropriate to your subject matter, smile as often as possible.
- Use hand gestures to underscore key points. Choreograph and practice useful, expressive gestures as required.
- Adopt a firm, upright, but comfortable stance at the podium. Soldiers required to stand at attention for extended periods quickly learn to appear rigid without actually standing rigidly. Do not lock your knees, but, instead, flex them slightly. This will have the effect of relaxing you without leading to a slouch position.

14. *Extend your nonverbal message with the clothes you wear.* You don't need this book to tell you how important clothing is in our culture. Here are some general rules for achieving solid, positive nonverbal communication through clothing:

- Be sensitive to the manner of dress that prevails in the group you work with. Dress appropriately for this context.

- Among sales professionals, a rule of thumb is to dress "a notch above" the customer. This is a safe, conservative guideline for most business situations.

15. *Adjust your tone of voice.* Remember, Albert Mehrabian's study of the sources of the persuasiveness of a speech concluded that 38 percent of the power of a speech is the result of "vocal qualities," especially tone of voice. Here are some suggestions for developing vocal qualities that help you to speak from the heart:

- Much as tall people tend to command more authority than shorter folk, people with deep voices are generally perceived as more persuasive than those whose voices are relatively high pitched. This is true of women as well as men. If your voice is pitched in the higher registers, consider consciously trying to speak in a lower pitch. Practice until you are comfortable with the level you have achieved.

- Consciously pitching your voice lower has the added benefit of slowing you down, which enhances the articulation of each word. Slower, more precise speech tends to add value to each word. Whether in conversation or in a formal speaking situation, most speakers can benefit from making a deliberate effort to slow down. For public speakers, the rule of thumb is not to exceed 150 words per minute, which means that it should take you a full two minutes to read a double-spaced, typewritten page of text. The 150 WPM rule is too slow for most casual conversation, which usually proceeds at about 200 words per minute.

- Lowering pitch also tends to minimize any nasal vocal quality, which many listeners find annoying. (If you suffer from persistent allergies or chronic breathing problems, the state of your health as well as the effectiveness of your communication may benefit from a visit to the doctor.)

- Especially in formal speaking situations, be sure to speak loudly enough. Don't strain, but be aware that a speaker can do absolutely nothing more annoying than fail to make herself heard.

25 Moves to Avoid

Just as body language can be an asset to effective, persuasive communication, it can also undercut and sabotage your message. Many conversations are compromised before a single word is spoken. Here are some moves to become aware of and to avoid:

1. *Avoid the tentative entrance.* When you decide to enter a room, a meeting, a conference, or even when you approach someone with whom you want to speak, carry the action through smoothly and forthrightly. Approach with the knowledge of what it is you want. This will help you move with confidence.

2. *Do not fail to establish eye contact.* Avoidance of eye contact will be interpreted as fear, indecisiveness, weakness, dishonesty, or any number of other negative things.

3. *Avoid the "dead fish" handshake.* A weak, limp handshake is an instant disappointment. People anticipate pleasure in a warm, firm grip. If you fail to deliver this, you will begin communications with a failure of expectation.

4. *Avoid the bone-crushing handshake.* You don't have to prove your strength or assert your dominance by making someone else uncomfortable. This is not impressive. It kicks off communication with resentment.

5. *Men should avoid offering women a loose, overly delicate handshake.* Men should use the same *moderately* firm grip they would deliver to another man.

6. *Avoid displaying what is generally called "nervous energy."* Remember, your object is to convey relaxed energy. This is *not* transmitted through tapping feet, darting eyes, drumming fingers, and fingers that fiddle with necktie, jewelry, or hair.

7. *Don't lose control of your breathing.* The rapid, shallow breathing associated with anxiety will only increase your anxiety—thereby creating a vicious cycle that will tend to make your breathing even more rapid and shallow—and will communicate nervousness to others. This will compromise your credibility. Practice breathing deeply and regularly.

8. *Avoid sighing.* This is a bad habit in most communication contexts because it is usually interpreted either as a sign of distress or of boredom.

9. *Avoid yawning.* If you must yawn—and, after all, you're only human—disguise it as best you can. If the yawn becomes obvious, apologize and explain: "Please excuse me. My neighbor pulled in the driveway at three this morning, his car alarm went off, and I just couldn't get back to sleep."

10. *Avoid scratching your head.* This is a classic signal of confusion or disbelief.

11. *Don't bite your lip.* People who are scared chew their lip. Don't transmit this signal.

12. *Keep your hands away from the back of your head or neck.* People often rub the back of the head or neck when they are frustrated or feeling impatient.

13. *Don't let your chin hang down.* The familiar expression "keep your chin up" is good advice in most communication situations. A lowered chin conveys defensiveness or insecurity.

14. *Don't squint.* Narrowing the eyes communicates disagreement, resentment, anger, or disapproval. A pronounced squint suggests utter puzzlement.

15. *Don't look down or otherwise avoid eye contact.* If you can't look the other person in the eye, she will assume that you are hiding something.

16. *Don't stare.* Eye contact is crucial, but a steady stare suggests at the very least an arrogant need to control, intimidate, and dominate. At its worst, vacant staring just seems weird and will alienate the person or persons with whom you are speaking.

17. *Be careful about raising your eyebrows.* Raising the eyebrows indicates surprise. Nothing wrong with that, if you want to communicate surprise, but, in some contexts, raised eyebrows suggest disbelief. You may inadvertently offend the speaker.

18. *If you wear eyeglasses, look through them, not over the top of them.* This gesture communicates doubt and disbelief. It may also be interpreted as a not-so-subtle put-down.

19. *Don't cross your arms.* Crossing your arms in front of your chest is a powerful signal of defiance, defensiveness, resistance, aggressiveness, or a closed mind.

20. *Don't rub your eyes, ears, or the side of your nose.* These gestures always communicate a degree of doubt that can seriously sabotage your verbal message.

21. *Get out of the habit of wringing your hands.* Few gestures more strongly communicate anxiety—even something verging on terror.

22. *Avoid holding head position and facial expressions for a long time or repeating any single gesture over and over.* Look alive and lively, not embalmed.

23. *Avoid assorted tics and nervous habits.* Here's what to watch for and avoid: continuous hand motions, rubbing your face, putting your hands anywhere near your mouth, repeatedly shrugging your shoulders. If you do such things, work to wean yourself away from them. The first step is awareness.

24. *In formal speaking situations, beware of nervously shifting your weight from side to side.* This is highly distracting to your listeners.

25. *Avoid ending declarative sentences on a rising note.* This is a verbal habit more common to women than men. It makes a statement sound tentative, even doubtful, as if the speaker were continually seeking approval.

Simple awareness of the positive and negative nonverbal body language "phrases" we all use is a major step toward taking control of these gestures and using them to advantage.

3

Plain Talk

On November 19, 1863, the president of the United States delivered a speech at the dedication of the Soldiers' National Cemetery at Gettysburg, the scene of what, even in the midst of the bloody conflict, seemed the turning-point battle of the Civil War. Abraham Lincoln had been invited to speak at the last minute. His appearance was an afterthought; for the *featured* speaker of the afternoon was Edward Everett, widely regarded as the greatest orator of his age. Indeed, Everett's ringing remarks consumed a full two hours, whereas Lincoln's speech was concluded in two minutes. Today, no one remembers a word of Everett's flowery oration, but the brief, simple, straightforward utterance of Lincoln, *The Gettysburg Address,* is beyond doubt the most profound verbal monument ever erected to military achievement and human sacrifice.

If ever a political leader spoke from the heart, it was Lincoln at Gettysburg. At 271 words, it takes little enough space to reproduce here:

> Fourscore and seven years ago our fathers brought forth on this continent a new nation, conceived in Liberty, and dedicated to the proposition that all men are created equal.
>
> Now we are engaged in a great civil war, testing whether that nation or any nation so conceived and so dedicated, can long endure. We are met on a great battle-field of that war. We have come to dedicate a portion of that field, as a final resting place for those who here gave their lives that that nation might live. It is altogether fitting and proper that we should do this.
>
> But, in a larger sense, we can not dedicate—we can not consecrate—we can not hallow—this ground. The brave men, living and dead, who struggled

here, have consecrated it, far above our poor power to add or detract. The world will little note, nor long remember what we say here, but it can never forget what they did here. It is for us the living, rather, to be dedicated here to the unfinished work which they who fought here have thus far so nobly advanced. It is rather for us to be here dedicated to the great task remaining before us—that from these honored dead we take increased devotion to that cause for which they gave the last full measure of devotion—that we here highly resolve that these dead shall not have died in vain—that this nation, under God, shall have a new birth of freedom—and that government of the people, by the people, for the people, shall not perish from the earth.

Don't skip over it. Do yourself the favor of reading once again these very familiar words. What is so moving about this speech?

- The language is elegant, to be sure, but hardly ornate or flowery—certainly not by the leaden Victorian oratorical standards of the day.

- The language is straightforward, with a preponderance of nouns and verbs rather than adjectives and adverbs.

- The speech concerns certain abstract principles such as liberty and equality, but it focuses on concrete manifestations of those principles: the sacrifice of those who fought and fell at Gettysburg.

- The speech is not a lecture. It is a kind of conversation. That is, Lincoln emphasizes communion with his audience. He does not say "I" or "you," but "we." He focuses on what "we" are doing, here at this new cemetery at Gettysburg, and in this "great civil war."

- The speech has vigorous, very clear direction. It begins by evoking the American Revolution, which created a nation conceived in liberty and dedicated to the proposition that all men are created equal. It then explains that we are engaged in a civil war to test whether a nation so conceived and so dedicated can endure. It then explains what the dedication of the cemetery has to do with this struggle. But then it concludes by magnifying the achievement of those who fought and died at Gettysburg. The movement is simple, direct, and swift. The result is that both the battle and the ceremony are given the greatest possible meaning, and the audience is swept up in that meaning.

Lincoln wasn't just a gifted orator. He was a man who knew what he had to say, and then he found the most direct, most sincere way to say it. At Gettysburg in particular, he found his heartline. There are no oratorical tricks; no fancy metaphors; no evasions. There is a thorough understanding of the facts, a firm grasp of what this speech must accomplish, and an unwavering drive to accomplish it.

Many of the most profound, most consequential of human utterances are the simplest. It takes work and hard thought to achieve this level of *effective* simplicity. The architect Ludwig Mies Van Der Rohe understood this when he summed up his aesthetic philosophy in the famous phrase "Less is more." Or just consider one of the most advanced expressions of human thought ever produced, Einstein's statement of the equivalence of mass and energy. An expression of the foundation of reality itself, it consists of only three terms: $E = mc^2$. The income tax return that the most humble earner among us files yearly is far more complex than this—but hardly of equivalent consequence.

The real work of Einstein's equation was not in the writing of an *E*, an equals sign, an *m*, a *c*, and a superscript 2. As with Lincoln's speech—so brief that it was written on the back of an envelope—the real work was in all the preparation toward knowing what to say, then distilling that information to its most direct form. The major work of saying it from the heart begins before a word is said or written.

Finding Out What You *Really* Want to Say

Fans of the original 1960s television show *Star Trek* are familiar with the pointy-eared Vulcan, Mr. Spock. The product of a mixed marriage—Vulcan father, earthling mother—Spock was perpetually torn between his thoroughly logical Vulcan heritage and his highly emotional earthling heritage. Viewers had no difficulty accepting this conflict, since they took for granted that logic and emotion are naturally and inevitably incompatible.

This, in fact, is one of the many myths that guide our lives. For the purpose of persuasive communication, it is not a useful myth and should be discarded. Communicating on an emotionally effective level requires thoughtful preparation and logical presentation. Think about *The Gettysburg Address*. Certainly, it is an example of emotionally powerful communication. In its directness, simplicity, and utter clarity, it is also a model of logical presentation.

Your first step, then, in preparing to speak or write from the heart is to discard the erroneous notion that the heart and the head are incompatible. On the contrary, determining the logic of what you *want* to say will make communication on an emotionally potent level possible.

Once you accept this, you can proceed to the next step: the Inventory.

THE INVENTORY METHOD

This can be as simple as drawing up a list of the points you wish to make about a particular subject, issue, or problem:

Point A

Point B

Point C

Then take a sheet of paper and write your Point A on the top. Below this, make another heading: *What I know*. Now list the facts you know about Point A. When you have finished this, make another heading: *What I need to know*. Write down the items you need to learn more about in order to discuss Point A more effectively.

Repeat this procedure for each of the points you have listed in your inventory. When this is completed, take out another piece of paper and head it, *Objections*. Here you may jot down arguments against any or all of the points you intend to make. Study this list, then head another piece of paper, *Answers*. Sketch out responses to the items you have listed on your *Objections* page.

Once this inventory is complete, you will find that you have a blueprint from which you can construct your speech, your letter, your memo—whatever item of communication you are creating. In short, you will know what it is you *want* to say, as well as what it is you *need* to say.

The inventory method works well when you need to focus on some particular subject or set of issues that you wish to discuss or write about. This is not particularly surprising. You can also use a version of the inventory method to help plan your workday so that you can employ the time more effectively as a period in which your communications will be meaningful and most effective.

Try thinking of your workday in an entirely new way—not as a series of hours or a series of projects, customers, or tasks, but as a series of equations.

Let's hold on to this idea for a moment or two.

Equations consist of known and unknown variables. The fewer unknowns, the easier it is to solve the equation. From the perspective of six o'clock in the morning, as you turn on the tap of the shower, the impending workday seems to be filled with variables. After all, you're not a soothsayer who sees into the future. But consider this: However many other variables there may be in a particular workday equation, *you* are always one of them. And you have a choice: You can enter the equation as a known or an unknown variable.

It's easy to nail yourself down.

Before you leave for the office, jot down a short list of objectives and issues for that day: things you want to accomplish and issues or problems that you believe you will confront. Once you've made this list, your next step is to review it, item by item, and ask yourself what your position is relative to each item:

- How you feel about the item
- What kind of outcome you want to obtain in dealing with the item
- What the item means to you
- What you need to do in order to deal with the item
- What you need from others in order to deal with it

Here's an example of a list of items a person might address on a certain day:

1. Estimate costs for Smith project.
2. Speak to boss about the Jones & Jones proposal.
3. Talk to Claire about expediting shipments to Mr. Barney, one of our top customers.

Next, take these one by one and jot down what they mean to you:

1. *Estimate costs for Smith project.* I'll need to talk to Pete to get figures. I need for him to make this a priority. If I can get these costs estimated today, I can get to my customer before the competition does. It's important to me to make this sale.
2. *Speak to boss about Jones & Jones proposal.* She's resistant to this, but I think this is a good idea, and it would do my career good to take charge of a project like this—if it works. I think this is a

good idea, but I'm not sure. I need more information on the demographics of the proposed territory.

3. *Barney is giving me hell about shipping delays.* I'm worried about losing this customer. It is important that this issue get resolved. How can I motivate Claire?

Now you have outlined not only your objectives for the day, but also what each one means to you, and, at least in a general way, what you have to do to achieve them.

The second objective, talking to your boss about the Jones & Jones proposal, looks like it needs to be put on hold so that you can get more information. No use talking about it today, then. So you reduce its priority to last place. Although the original objective number 3 is pressing, number 1 probably needs to get underway first. So, now you have your day's priorities mapped out:

1. *Estimate costs for Smith project.* I'll need to talk to Pete to get figures. I need him to make this a high priority, because, if I can get these costs estimated today, I can get to my customer before the competition does. It's important to me to make this sale.

2. *Mr. Barney is giving me hell about shipping delays.* It makes me look bad—makes the company look bad, too. It is important that this issue get resolved. How can I motivate Claire to expedite?

3. *Get more information on the demographics* of the proposed territory for the Jones & Jones proposal before talking to the boss about it.

THE K.I.S.S. FORMULA

Many people who are fond of acronyms reserve particular affection for this rather rude one: *K.I.S.S.*—Keep It Simple, Stupid. It's just abrasive enough to be memorable, and the advice it embodies is valuable, if we add to it a dash of thought.

As you outline just what it is you want to say, keep the outline as simple as possible. The "as possible" part is important. What you *decide* to say should be no more complicated than what you *have* to say—but it shouldn't be any simpler, either. Both complicating and oversimplifying distort expression. Keep it as simple as it can be, but no simpler than that.

You can apply the K.I.S.S. formula to specific subjects, problems, and issues, of course, but you can also apply it more generally to your workday.

If you've ever envied the way a Hollywood star walks through a film role, knowing how it will all turn out, knowing just what to do and just what to say, consider giving yourself the Hollywood advantage: a script.

Terrific idea! The only problem is that this is *real* life. Real life doesn't come with a script.

True enough. But this doesn't mean you can't create one.

- Focus on the most important and difficult of your day's objectives, and plot out your approaches to them. This might take the form of a few quick notes, or it might be a genuine script, with your lines written out.

- Look at what is now your number-one objective for the day: Estimate costs for the Smith project. I'll need to talk to Pete to get figures. I need for him to make this a priority. If I can get these costs estimated today, I can get to my customer before the competition does.

How will you go about motivating Pete? Give some thought to this now, before you approach him. You decide that you know two important facts:

1. The most powerful motive is self-interest.
2. Pete takes pride in doing the best job he knows how.

The first fact, while not specific to Pete, is certainly a safe assumption. The second, which relates more directly to what you happen to know about Pete, is also important. Now, write a script that exploits both of these facts about what motivates Pete.

You: Pete, can I speak with you a moment? We have an opportunity to hook up with a very major customer. To do this, we'll need to give him the most competitive bid possible—our very best shot. And you, my friend, are the only one who can get us the figures we need to present our leanest and meanest bid.

You've sketched out an opening that plays on Pete's self-interest (he'll be given a key role in this big deal) and on his pride in workmanship (he's the only one who can furnish what's needed). But you're not home yet. Having scripted a good approach, keep preparing. The next step is to anticipate potential resistance:

Pete: I'll get to it just as soon as I can, but I'm swamped right now.

Don't back down. Your mission is to keep your project on the front burner.

You: I sure know that feeling! The thing is, this is such a high-profile deal that I'm sure you'll want to be part of it. And, right now, our priority has to be to take an aggressive stance. We don't want to let it slip.

Here is a secret of saying it from the heart, which you will encounter repeatedly in this book: Never *tell* the other person what to do. Telling is not persuasive. Instead, arrange reality so that he'll decide for himself to do what you want him to do.

How do you pull this off?

The easiest way is to imitate what top-notch sales professionals do. Focus on the "customer's" needs, not on yours. How will complying with your request benefit Pete? That is the question you must answer. Remember, the car salesman is almost certainly more concerned about making his next mortgage payment than he is about seeing to it that you drive away happy. The benefit he derives from selling you a car is the ability to pay his mortgage this month. Nevertheless, he makes no mention of his mortgage payment. To make the sale, he focuses on the benefits you will derive from the purchase.

Having prepared a script for your number-one priority, you can go on to sketch out another script for the number-two priority: motivating Claire in Shipping to expedite shipments to your customer, Mr. Barney.

You understand what you need from Claire, but you also understand that, for the purposes of persuading her, you must focus on her needs. There is nothing wrong about beginning with the assumption of her self-interest. But what else do you know about Claire, more specifically? From past experience, you've found that she's a bit touchy, defensive about her turf. This is important to know, because you realize that she isn't likely to respond positively if you imply that her department is not up to snuff where Mr. Barney's shipments are concerned. So, you decide not to go there. A better strategy is to paint her a picture.

> **You:** Claire, I've been getting some flak from one of our major cus-
> tomers, Barney. You know him, don't you?
>
> **Claire:** Yes, sure. I know Mr. Barney.

Put the burden on Mr. Barney, not on yourself and not on Claire. Start to define the problem not as *yours* or *hers,* but *ours:* "one of our major customers."

> **You:** Well, Barney's been complaining about lead times for shipping. Now, my first reaction to this is, well, everybody's worried about shipping time. But take a look at this . . .

You decide that you'll show Claire log entries that demonstrate the gap between request date and ship date. Let her draw her own conclusions. Let the decision to improve be *her* decision, *her* idea, not *yours.*

10 SIMPLE GADGETS OF PLAIN TALK

Gadgets are simple devices to make work a little easier. Here are some gadgets to help you to speak plainly, directly, and as simply as the subject and issues will allow:

1. Ask yourself what you want.
2. Ask yourself what you need.
3. Ask yourself how you feel.
4. Sketch a verbal plan to help you communicate with others to achieve your objectives.
5. Use words that unite (*we, us, our*) rather than divide (*I, you*).
6. Beware of setting *I* against *you.*
7. Focus on how what you want will benefit the other person.
8. Avoid defining a winner versus a loser.
9. Use language that emphasizes potential rather than limits.
10. Use many nouns and verbs, but few adjectives and adverbs.

50 Words from the Heart

One of the many advantages of living in modern times is indoor plumbing. Turn a tap, and water flows. In the old days, people resorted to a pump, and to get the pump working, you often had to prime it by adding a bit of water from a bucket. Modern water delivery systems have improved, but our verbal pumps can still benefit from priming. Here are some words and phrases that will help you get started speaking from the heart:

admire	extraordinary	learning
advice	foundation	love
advise	generous	loyalty
benefit	genius	marvel
best	grateful	mentor
celebrate	guidance	model
congratulate	guide	perform
contribute	help	praise
create	honor	progress
dedicate	hope	resourceful
enhance	humanity	succeed
enterprise	improve	thanks
ethics	ingenious	understanding
example	innovative	valuable
excellence	inspiration	willingness
exceptional	invaluable	wisdom
experience	inventive	

50 Words to Avoid

Try to avoid these downers. They tend to cast activity and enterprise in a negative light:

absolute	bitter	dead
accident	cheated	dire
against	clueless	disaster
angry	company policy	doom
annihilate	cornered	dreary
beat	crush	dumb

escape	mediocre	robbed
exclude	minor	shocked
exhausted	mistake	showdown
exploit	must	status quo
fail	obey	strict
gut	obligatory	tired
hardship	quit	trouble
hopeless	retire	ultimatum
humiliate	retreat	unchanging
luck	retrench	unfair
maul	rid	

4

Speaking with
Your Ears

$\mathcal{I}$n the previous chapter, we talked about actually scripting your key verbal encounters as a way of ensuring that you deliver your message as simply, directly, and fully as possible. Thinking about speaking from the heart as a kind of scripted performance is a good thing.

At least, mostly.

The benefits such an approach offers include giving you a feeling of greater control and permitting you to prepare, to rehearse, and to set specific goals concerning just what it is you wish to communicate. Nevertheless, it is not useful to carry the idea of performance to the extreme, causing you to neglect the interactive aspect of all meaningful communication.

Perhaps we just need to think about the idea of performance more deeply. The great stage actors do not simply follow a script, "broadcasting" their part to the audience. Instead, they learn to "read the house," to pick up on the signals the audience sends their way. For them, a performance is, in large measure, a give-and-take proposition. For the actor, this faculty of give and take is an extraordinary skill, a kind of sixth sense. For those of us, however, who just want to speak persuasively, sincerely, and effectively, it is a much simpler matter. The skill we must develop is the ability to listen and to hear. Do you want to persuade others? Use your ears.

The Two-Way Street

When you enter into a conversation or rise to speak, you naturally feel a certain burden. You take upon your shoulders the responsibility for

433

creating meaning, for putting yourself across. This is an important responsibility, and it can be a weighty burden. It is easy to forget that it is actually a shared burden. Your listener also has a responsibility to interpret what you say, to listen to it, to hear it, to understand it. If you've ever spoken to someone who refuses to hear—or who is simply, well, rather dense—you know how much heavier your load becomes. Communication is like moving a massive piece of furniture. It really is a two-person job. If one of the people gets lazy or just isn't strong enough, more of the burden falls on the other. Sometimes, the load is just too great, and the piece tumbles to the ground. The coffee table is broken; the message fails to get across.

Carrying your heavy load, you are grateful for all the help you get. You are resentful if that help isn't there.

Communication is much the same. If you are blessed with a good listener, your task is easier and much more gratifying. You feel good about yourself, and you naturally feel grateful to the other person.

Now, you can't always choose your listeners. With luck, you'll find yourself communicating with someone who hears you, who understands you, who carries her share of the load. Then, again, you might not be so fortunate. What you *can* control, however, is your own ability to listen. The benefits of this are great:

- The mere presence of a listener helps the speaker direct his communication toward a goal.

- The more effectively the speaker communicates, the greater value you *and* the speaker receive from the communication.

- The more effectively the speaker communicates, the more positive will be his feelings about you.

- The more positive the other person feels toward you, the more readily you'll be able to put your message across when it is your turn to speak. You will be more persuasive.

Many people needlessly mystify communication, seeing it as a kind of black art practiced most effectively by people with a special gift for spellbinding genius. Actually, the essence of effective communication is information. The more useful information you load into a package of communication, the more effective, persuasive, and dynamic that communication will be.

There are, of course, many sources of useful information. But one of the richest—a surefire source, in fact—is the person with whom you are speaking. The more you know about what that person feels, thinks, wants, and needs, the more background you will have at your disposal to help you pack your words with information that is useful to him.

How do you gather this information? You listen. You listen to the other person.

The Pronoun Equation

You enter a conversation as the personal pronoun "I" confronting another personal pronoun, "you." How can you tell if the conversation is successful, the communication effective? The sum of "I" and "you" comes to equal "we." This is the equation of persuasion. There is no winner or loser. Neither the "I" nor the "you" is greater. Together, however, they come out as "we." This will not happen without effective speaking as well as listening. Do not focus so intensely on the one that you neglect the other.

10 Ways to Become a Better Listener

1. *Practice creative self-restraint.* Remember the kid in the fifth grade who somehow couldn't resist raising her hand to answer each and every question? When you are in an intense conversation, a high-stakes exchange, it is very easy to start acting like that fifth grader. In your eagerness to keep the conversation going, to parade before the other person everything you know, to answer questions before the other person's mouth is even closed, you may well find yourself nearly unable to sit still, be quiet, and just listen. Be careful not to hog the conversation. *Listen.*

2. *Make a conscious effort to appear as if you are enjoying the conversation.* The message you want to convey is that you are intensely interested in what the other person is saying to you. Keep your self-restraint lively. Smile. Nod when appropriate. React.

3. *Use verbal mirrors: echoing.* Let the other person know that you are hearing and understanding her. You may do this by repeating—echoing—key phrases she uses.

| **Other person:** | I need to get this project moving. |
| **You:** | I understand. It's critical for you to get the project moving. |

4. *Use verbal mirrors: rephrasing.* Another way to reassure the other person that you understand what she is telling you is to rephrase key points of her message:

| **Other person:** | I need to get this project moving. |
| **You:** | You want to get off the dime on this project. |

5. *Tell the other person that you understand.* This is obvious, but often neglected:

| **Other person:** | I need to get this project moving. |
| **You:** | I understand you. |

6. *Don't neglect your response, but suspend it long enough to hear out the other person.* Be sure to learn what interests and concerns the other person, what he needs and what he wants, before responding by introducing your opinions, ideas, and needs. To the extent possible, create a foundation of common interest before offering any differing opinion or point of view.

Let's say you enter a conversation believing that Task A is important and that the best approach to Task A is through Methods 1 and 2. The conversation turns to Task A. Like you, the other person thinks this task is highly important; however, she believes that the best approach to it is through Methods 2 and 3. Now, what's your best move?

- Choose not to express your opinion, but just agree.
- Choose to disagree.
- Choose to agree as much as possible, then, taking off from this common ground, explain how and where your opinions differ.

The last alternative is probably the most productive.

| **Other person:** | Task A is crucial to our operation. The approach I favor is Methods 2 and 3. |
| **You:** | I certainly agree with you that Task A is extremely important to achieving our goals, and I also like Method 2, but have you considered using Method 1 instead of Method 3? |

Other person: Why should I?

You: Well, these are the benefits I've found . . .

7. *Listen, so that you can focus on the other person's needs.* The goal of a conversation is not to come off as mindless and selfless, but always to express yourself in a way that exhibits your interest in the other person—*his* needs, *his* concerns—even when you are discussing your own point of view. Listening is a gift you exchange with the other person in the conversation. It provides benefits to both of you. By listening carefully, you ensure that the ideas and opinions you express are relevant to the needs and concerns the other person expresses.

8. *Stalk the main thought.* Think back to how your high school English teacher struggled to get you to put some focus and direction in the essays you wrote. "Begin with a topic sentence!" she'd plead. "State your theme and develop it."

This is simple, sound advice. Starting with a clear, strong statement of theme keeps your writing focused and makes your essay far more persuasive. Nobody enjoys reading a pointless, meandering essay. It's frustrating and a waste of time.

You can apply the same principle to verbal communication. State your topic clearly. You can also apply the principle to *listening* to someone else's verbal communication. Try to identify the "topic sentence" in what the other person says, then underscore it verbally. For example, your friend John, who is struggling with the decision over which new car to buy, is meandering generally about automobiles. Suddenly, he remarks that "Safety is my biggest concern." You recognize this as a "topic sentence." Don't let it pass you by. "John, it sounds to me like you really want to begin your shopping around by focusing on the cars with the best safety features. Maybe that will help you narrow down the field." Now the conversation will have a sharper, more definite direction.

9. *Pounce on and develop what interests you.* Perhaps this has happened to you: You're riding to work on the same old bus or commuter train. The man seated beside you strikes up a conversation. You'd just as soon keep reading your paper, but, to be polite, you respond. Suddenly, he says something that actually interests you. Suddenly, the conversation takes on direction and purpose. It has acquired a theme, a main thought, and you're almost sorry when your stop rolls by.

Be on the alert for anything that strikes a chord. Stay alert for a main thought that sparks and fuels the conversation. When you find it, jump on board.

10. *Connect with your own interests.* Focus on the other person's needs, feelings, and interests, but bring them home to yourself. When the other person expresses the need to "move the project along," think about how that need feels to you. Get in touch with the feeling created by a sense of urgency. Strong feelings are the basis not just of a conversation, but of a relationship. Connect with those feelings and let them drive your remarks.

You: I know what it's like to get excited about the possibilities of a project. You really want to move it along, keep that energy flowing, and maintain the momentum.

Other person: Exactly. That's exactly how I feel.

Body Language: How to Hear More Than Words

One of the most excruciating spectacles one may witness is the agony of a failed stand-up comic. He drops joke after joke, punch line after punch line, only to be met by silence.

"I *died* up there tonight," the poor man moans to the bartender after his performance. "I just *died*."

You probably can sympathize with this feeling. All of us have, from time to time, said something in the anticipation of eliciting a certain response, only to receive nothing but a stone face and silence. Imagine, then, how your partner in conversation will feel if you fail to react to what he says. Don't let him die.

Of course, you should avoid phonying up an exaggerated response to each and everything said. But do demonstrate that you are listening—listening with interest, comprehension, and pleasure—by mirroring the speaker's message:

- If the speaker is excited about something, get excited, too.

- If the speaker expresses delight, smile in return.

- If the speaker raises an issue that is clearly of critical importance to him, narrow your gaze, bring your hand thoughtfully to your chin—*show* that the subject is of critical importance to you, too.

Body language works two ways. You can broadcast it, and you can receive it. The more sensitive your "receiver," the more fully you will comprehend the other person and the more accurately and effectively you will be able to tailor your remarks to the needs, desires, and interests of the other person. Look for the following signals from your conversation partner:

- *Head tilted to one side.* Assume that she is listening intently to what you are saying and is interested. Astute sales professionals call such a gesture a "buy signal." It is a nonverbal cue that the other person is intrigued by what you are offering. Keep going. Pursue this line of conversation.

- *Scratches head.* A signal of confusion or disbelief. Don't panic when you encounter this. Instead, pause, and ask a question: "Am I making myself clear enough here?" Or: "I'm not sure I'm making myself clear. Let me put it another way. . . ." Respond to the need that is being transmitted to you.

- *Lip biting.* An indication of anxiety. This may suggest that an issue you've brought up has touched a nerve. It may also signal concern about something that has come up in the conversation. If you are aware that an area is sensitive, you will have to exercise judgment as to whether to move on quickly to another topic or express your understanding of the sensitive nature of the issue: "I realize that this is an area that causes anxiety, but I think it's an important issue to explore."

- *Rubbing the back of the head or neck.* A signal of frustration and impatience. When you pick up on this cue, it is probably best to move on to another topic. Practice a graceful transition: "But, of course, that's not nearly so important as XYZ." Alternatively, you can pause and ask the interviewer where *he* wants to go: "Maybe you'd rather talk about ABC."

- *Chin lowers markedly.* This is a token of defensiveness. It is possible that something you've said has been interpreted as a criticism. Insert a soothing remark: "Of course, I recognize that each department has its own management style. I am wide open and prepared to be flexible."

- *Nodding up and down.* A major buy signal. Keep the conversation going in the current vein. You are eliciting agreement.

- *Shaking head from side to side.* What you have said is being rejected. Respond directly. "It seems that you don't agree with me on this point. What part of my position gives you trouble?" Don't offer a challenge. Instead, ask a question like this, which will keep the conversation from grinding to a halt.

- *Eyes narrow.* Much like a head shake from side to side, this indicates rejection of what you have said. Respond directly: "I feel that we're not in agreement on this point. Can you tell me what disturbs you about what I've said?"

- *Squinting or very marked narrowing of the eyes.* This does not signal rejection so much as puzzlement. Pause, take a breath, then offer: "I want to be very clear on this point. Let me put what I've said another way."

- *Raised eyebrows.* A signal of surprise or disbelief. Meet this situation head on: "I know this is hard to believe, but . . ."

- *Peers over the top of his/her glasses.* Another signal of disbelief.

- *Avoidance of eye contact.* If eye contact has been tenuous or nonexistent from the start of the conversation, it is likely that you are simply speaking with a shy person. Go out of your way to be friendly. Take the lead in this dance. Note, however, that if eye contact drops off during the interview, you may be losing the interviewer's interest. Move quickly in response: "Shall we move on to a different topic?"

A more subtle nonverbal signal to look for is the way the other person breathes. Don't strain yourself looking for this sign. If you notice nothing unusual, there is no message being conveyed. However, if the other person's breathing pattern changes noticeably, you can assume that something you have said has struck a chord.

- *Breathlessness or shallow, rapid breathing.* This indicates anxiety. Respond with reassurance: "Well, don't worry. This is a problem we can certainly solve."

- *Sudden intake of breath.* Indicates the eagerness to say something. Pause. Let the other person speak—now.

- *Sigh.* This is a powerful indication of frustration or boredom. It is a signal that you should move on to another topic.

Words and Phrases to Promote Active Listening

Don't become so focused on listening that you let your end of the conversation lapse. This might well kill the conversation. Punctuate your listening with words and phrases such as the following. These are calculated to keep the conversation moving as well as on track:

accurate	extraordinary	positive
additional	fertile	productive
agree	further	right
Can you explain that further?	I agree	take into account
	I appreciate that	tell me more
Can we pursue that further?	I hadn't thought about it that way	that's a concern of mine, too
consider	I see	that's interesting
correct	I understand	thought
discuss further	It's an issue we face	we should discuss
evaluate	opportunity	yes

Just as certain words and phrases can keep things lively, others tend to bring the dialogue to a premature halt. Avoid such negative expressions as the following:

absolutely not	that can't be done	wrongheaded
couldn't possibly	that's not the way I do it	you're mistaken
no		you're wrong
no way	that's settled	

Part 2

Among Family and Friends

*N*owhere is saying it from the heart more important than when you speak or write to family and friends.

5

Announcements

$\mathcal{S}$hakespeare's Macbeth expresses what is perhaps the most chilling, dismal view of life to be found in all literature. "Tomorrow, and tomorrow, and tomorrow," he says,

> Creeps in this petty pace from day to day,
> To the last syllable of recorded time;
> And all our yesterdays have lighted fools
> The way to dusty death. . . .

Macbeth goes on to conclude that life is "a tale / Told by an idiot, full of sound and fury, / Signifying nothing."

Fortunately, most of us don't feel quite this low. We see our lives as meaningful, filled with friends and family; filled, too, with events that are milestones, crossroads, and turning points, which make life no tedious, idiotic tale, but an exciting story to be shared with those who matter to us. That's where announcements come in. They are a sharing of the news—good, bad, and always important.

Finding the Heartline

The essence of the announcement is news, and the essence of news is fact. If you were ever on the staff of your high school newspaper, you doubtless recall the faculty adviser drumming the "five W's" into your head. Every good news story answers these five questions: Who? What? When? Where? Why?

While all good announcements should incorporate the five W's, you'll want to move beyond the facts to the feelings. In doing so, recall that the announcement may be about you and your family, but its purpose is to include others in the recognition and celebration of the event.

Sidestepping the Pitfalls

Announcements typically risk problems in three areas:

1. They fail to be sufficiently inclusive.
2. They fail to convey your feelings.
3. They fail to include all of the relevant facts.

1. Keep your audience in mind when you compose an announcement. How much does the reader or listener know about you and your family? Obviously, if you are speaking or writing to a close friend or family member, you don't have to fill in a lot of background information. But if you are sending an announcement to your outer circle of acquaintances, the reader may need more background material: names, dates, occupations, activities, achievements, and so on.

2. For certain events and to certain people, you may want to send a simple commercial card to carry your announcement. There's nothing wrong with that, but when you want to say it from the heart, take the time and effort to express your feelings—not just about the event, but about sharing the news of the event with the other person.

3. Double check to make certain that your announcement is a good "news story" in that it includes the five *W's*.

Saying It: To Family

A BIRTH—PHONE CALL TO THE NEW GRANDPARENTS

Hi, Mom and Dad. It's finally happened! Three-thirty-five this morning. She's a girl, Claire Rose, beautiful of course, 8 pounds, 4 ounces, head full of jet black hair. Sally and I are both tired, but incredibly happy. It all went so well that we'll be coming home tomorrow. So, congratulations, Grandma and Grandpa!

It's okay to sound excited about exciting things! Just remember to pack in all the essential data.

CAREER MOVE—PHONE CALL TO SISTER

Hey, sis. I've got big news, and I wanted you to be the first to know. I'm leaving Ajax and moving to Smith and Johnson. I'll be an account executive—a big move up from account associate—and while the money is good, $7,500 more per year, it's the opportunity that I'm really excited about. I'll be handling at least three major accounts myself and filling in on others as needed. This will be what I've always wanted: a chance to develop business from the ground up.

Let me give you my new address, phone, fax, and e-mail. All of this is effective on May 15.

The key phrase here is "I wanted you to be the first to know." Those closest to you get a substantial kick from the knowledge that you thought of them first. Be sure to let this fact be known.

If you feel comfortable discussing money with the person on the other end of the phone, there is nothing wrong with doing so. It's an important component of the news. Note here, however, that the speaker is careful to distinguish the money from what excites him most about the new job. This information also provides material for the other person to respond to. The subject of money does not open up the conversation as the subject of opportunity does.

AN ENGAGEMENT—PHONE CALL TO PARENTS

Mom, Dad, there's one less question you'll have to ask me: "When are you two going to tie the knot?" We're looking at June! Bill proposed yesterday—at dinner—with the most beautiful ring I've ever seen. Right before the dessert course!

I suppose you're wondering where we're planning to live. Bill's been offered a terrific job in Hendersonville. So we'll be no more than an hour from you guys.

A person certainly can be forgiven a self-centered focus in an announcement like this one, but note that this daughter makes the effort to shift the focus to her folks, telling them, with delight, that she and her husband plan to live nearby.

DIVORCE—PHONE CALL TO BROTHER

Well, Ted, I'm sorry to have to tell you that it's final. Sheila and I signed the divorce papers this morning. I know this disappoints you and hurts you, because you always worked so hard to help us try to patch things up. Both Sheila and I appreciate that, you know, but we just couldn't make it work.

Ted, both of us feel this is best for us, and I know Sheila will be giving you a call soon. She loves you like a brother, and she doesn't want to lose your affection or drift out of touch.

I'm sure you understand this is hard for us, but we're both going to be okay.

Even if it's not entirely unexpected, an announcement like this is bound to come as something of a shock. It is a mistake to attempt to sugarcoat bad news or hard truth, but that doesn't mean you can't present it in its best light and with whatever reassurances are possible under the circumstances. A divorce affects more than the two people most directly involved. It sends ripples through a whole matrix of relationships. Here the speaker does his best to contain the damage by reassuring his brother that no one is falling apart—life will go on—and that the brother's relationship with his sister-in-law does not have to end.

Saying It: To Friends

A BIRTH—PHONE CALL TO A CLOSE FRIEND

Hi, Sweetie. Congratulations! You are an aunt!

He's a boy, Thomas William, 9 pounds, 4 ounces, and he came into the world at 9:44 this morning. And he is a real loud one!

I feel terrific—tired, but very happy. Bill took it all harder than I did. He's sound asleep!

Look, you can come by the hospital tonight, if you want. We plan to be home day after tomorrow.

The best "news stories" are those that hit home. This new mother focuses her announcement on her friend—a brand-new honorary "aunt"—before going on to the all-important details concerning the baby, herself, and her husband.

CAREER MOVE—PHONE CALL TO A BUSINESS ACQUAINTANCE

Mr. Mackinson, this is Ed Walters. I'm calling to thank you for our conversation two months ago, in which you gave me some very helpful advice and information concerning positions at Smith and Johnson. I followed up on our conversation, applied, and interviewed, and, as of March 3, I'll be working at Smith and Johnson as a sales associate in aftermarket services.

This is an exciting opportunity for me, and I just wanted to share the news with you—since you were so instrumental in helping me to make the move. I would like to stay in touch. My new phone number is 555-555-1234 and the e-mail is edwalters@internet.com.

It is important to keep your acquaintances and business associates informed of career moves you make. In this case, the speaker also wants to acknowledge the role his acquaintance played in landing him a new job. Those who help you deserve to be thanked, of course, but putting it in the form of an announcement call adds an additional dimension to the thanks. It gives the other person a certain proprietary stake in the caller's success. Thus the caller has added to his network of business contacts—an important step in a developing career.

AN ENGAGEMENT—PHONE CALL TO A FRIEND

Ellie, I hope you're sitting down. Big news. The biggest. As of yesterday, I am engaged to Howard Wallace. You met him last year, at Cindy's party. Tall, very good looking, works as a financial analyst, drives a '57 Chevy. You remember him, right?

We haven't set the date yet, but it looks like no more than six months. We don't want to wait forever.

Gauge your audience. In this case, the speaker is not certain that her friend remembers her fiancé, so she is careful to jog her memory, to give his full name, some background, then place him in time. Finally, she asks for feedback: "You remember him, right?" Sharing exciting news is not fun if you leave the other person in the dark.

DIVORCE—PHONE CALL TO A FRIEND

Helen, I'm sorry to have to tell you that Bob and I are now divorced. It is official as of Friday. It's really hard for me to give you this news, because I know how much effort you put into helping us try to work things out. Bob and I are both very grateful, and you certainly enabled us to go through this with a lot more civility and understanding than would have been the case without your concern and help.

Bob, I know, is very worried that our split up will end his friendship with you and Clark. I hope that isn't the case. I hope that we will all be able to maintain our friendship. You mean a lot to me—and to Bob, too. I really need your support.

The speaker fully understands and appreciates that her divorce has effects that reach beyond her and her former husband. This announcement takes her friend's feelings into account and serves to reassure her that the divorce does not include divorce from the friends she and her former husband have in common. An announcement should convey more than completed fact. It is also an opportunity to look toward the future.

Writing It: To Family

A BIRTH—NOTE TO A BROTHER WHO LIVES FAR AWAY

Hey, Bro—

You're always on my case about never writing to you. Well, now I've actually got something to write about. You now have a nephew, Sean Graham, 8 pounds, 11 ounces. He came into this world at precisely 5:45 this morning—a regular little commuter! Sally, Sean, and I are doing just fine, and we'll all be home by the time you get this.

I'm going to try to get some sleep now—while I can. Next letter will include some snapshots.

All the best,

Pete

Strike a tone appropriate to the person you're writing to. The kind of banter present here conveys the warmth of an easy, loving relationship. Writing a letter like this is easier if you visualize your correspondent. Think of the letter as a conversation, face to face, except that the face is in your mind's eye.

AN ENGAGEMENT—A NOTE HOME

Dear Mom, Dad, and Sis,

If my handwriting is hard to read, I apologize. I'm writing as fast as I can to keep up with my excitement. I'm getting married!

Her name is Cheryl Young. We met just a month ago, and, well, it's just one of those things, as they say. Everything about us just clicks. We know we're made for each other. We met at an environmental rally—like me, Cheryl's a believer in living in harmony with the planet—and we just can't get enough of each other.

I can't say that *I* asked her to marry me. The subject came up, we talked, and we came out wanting to get married. So there we are.

We haven't set a date yet, but Cheryl and I will be coming home for the Christmas holiday, and we'll all have a chance to sit down and make our plans. See you in a few weeks.

Can't wait to see you,

Simon

Sudden announcements can be fun—or more than a trifle terrifying. The writer acknowledges the suddenness of the decision to get married, and he explains the circumstances as best he can. Recognizing that the surprise announcement may make some family members feel as if they've been left out of a crucial life decision, the writer is especially careful to ensure that the family is included in the planning for the wedding. To the degree that it is possible to do so, an announcement from the heart should reach out to others and draw them into the impending event.

CAREER MOVE—LETTER TO DAD

Dear Dad,

As of June 5, you may address your daughter as Marybeth Koslow, Branch Manager, Garner and Yost.

You know that promotion I'd been waiting for? It never came. So I made a move to a firm that agreed to hire me at the level I was bidding for at Smith and Johnson. I'll be leaving a lot of great people, but I just couldn't keep my career on hold any longer.

My new firm is Garner and Yost, at 1234 West Peter Lane, same Zip as the old place, 00056. The phone number there is 555-000-9999. I'll call you with my direct line as soon as I get started there.

Dad, I'm very excited by the new responsibility. The pay raise is welcome, too, although it is about 10 percent less than I would have gotten at Smith and Johnson. But, then, that promotion seemed to be a ship that just wasn't coming in—and you know what 10 percent of nothing is. I'm just proud of myself that I was able to make this move and get what I wanted. You, Dad, taught me that—to decide on what you want, then aim for it and don't give up until you've reached your target. That's what I was thinking about when I made the move. Thanks. Thanks for everything.

Love,

Marybeth

This announcement does double duty as a heartfelt expression of gratitude. Always look for ways to include your correspondent in your message. Sometimes, you have news to share that is all about you, period. That's fine. But, often, you will discover that you can expand *your* news to take in others, including the person to whom you are writing. If you can do this, you ensure a meaningful communication that will generate much warmth.

DIVORCE—A LETTER HOME

Mom, Dad—

This is the hardest letter I've ever had to write. Carla and I finalized our divorce Tuesday. The papers are all signed.

Hard as it has been on us, I know it is, in many ways, even harder on you. You were always so hopeful that things would work out, and you were helpful, too, in trying to guide us through these past several months. From the bottom of my heart, I thank you for your support and kindness. It's just that Carla and I both realized that our marriage had gone beyond fixing. We are both convinced that the divorce, hard as it is, is for the best.

Mom, Dad, I'll be home for the Thanksgiving holiday. I really look forward to seeing you both. I need to spend some time with you—at home.

Love,

George

The letter does not ask for sympathy but, instead, offers it. Here is a good example of a writer getting his message across without dwelling on himself. Note also that while the subject of the letter concerns the severing of one bond, it closes by reaffirming another: the bond between a child and his parents.

Writing It: To Friends

A BIRTH—LETTER TO MULTIPLE FRIENDS

Dear Friends:

Ken and I are thrilled to announce the arrival of our first baby, Cindy Marie, who made her debut on April 15, at 3:55 p.m. She's a perfect 10. (Actually, she weighs 8 pounds, 3 ounces, and measures 21 inches long.)

All three of us are healthy and happy—though two of us are pretty tired just now!

Please give us a call at 555-453-9000, and we'll fill you in some more.

Love,

Ken and Patty

Many announcements can be more or less mass produced and sent out in multiple copies to your friends. If you want to use the news as an occasion to get in touch, why not invite a phone call? Such an invitation is particularly important here, since some people might assume that the new parents are too busy to be bothered. If you want to invite contact, do so.

AN ENGAGEMENT—NOTE TO A GROUP OF FRIENDS

Dear Sally, Penny, Gina, and Brenda:

Roger and I are engaged!

It took place Friday at Chez Maurice.

"I know you don't usually have dessert," he said, "but after a meal that good, I thought you should have *something.*"

And he takes this gorgeous diamond ring out of his pocket. He didn't even say anything. I just looked at the ring, and I said, "Yes. Yes, I will."

We haven't set an exact date yet, but June has always looked good to me. I'm counting on you guys as bridesmaids. I'll let you know as soon as we've set a date.

Love to all of you,

Patti

In these days of word processing, there is nothing wrong with sending out multiple copies of the same announcement. The letter can still be personalized, like this one to a group of friends. There is also no rule dictating that a letter can do nothing more than report and describe. When you have an exciting event to talk about, consider giving your account more immediate impact by including actual dialogue. Step into the role of novelist—even if only for a moment or two.

CAREER MOVE—NOTE TO A FRIEND WHO HAS BEEN OUT OF TOUCH

Dear Fred:

How long has it been since we were last in touch? Two years? Three? Anyway, I've got big news, and it seemed that sharing it was a really good excuse to write.

As you know, I've been with Stein Company for years now, working in Customer Service. Recently, I started investigating another track, in sales, and found a position with Youngblood, here in Dayton. I'll be starting on March 3 as an account executive. It's a major move for me—and I have to tell you that your advice and support when I was just starting out helped me get to this position.

Fred, thanks, and I hope that we can get together next time you come
through Dayton. Or why not give me a call at 555-555-0003. We have a lot
of catching up to do. What's up with your life and work?

All the best,

Frank

Sharing news makes an excellent occasion for reestablishing old
connections and getting back in touch with old friends.

A DIVORCE—LETTER TO A FRIEND

Dear Meg,

I am sorry to have to tell you that Ben and I are now divorced. The decree
became final last week. As you can imagine, it's been a rough several
months, but, finally, it is what both Ben and I want and need, and it is for
the best—hard as it is.

I am writing to you in particular to tell you how much I have come to value
your friendship over the years. Ben gave me many wonderful things during
our marriage, and your friendship is one of these. I truly hope that, even
though Ben and I are no longer together, you and I can stay in touch and
remain friends.

Meg, I'll call in a few days. I'm still at the old address and number.

Hoping you will understand,

Emma

Divorce is painful for the couple directly involved, of course, but
it is also awkward and difficult for others, especially friends of the couple. This announcement also serves as an opportunity for the writer to
express her wish that the change in her circumstances does not end a
friendship. Look for opportunities to leverage your communications, to
make letters and conversations serve multiple purposes.

E-Mailing It: To Family

A BIRTH—E-MAIL SENT TO MULTIPLE FAMILY MEMBERS

Hi, Everybody!

With all of us online these days, e-mail seems the fastest way to get the big
news out. The big news? We have a boy! He came into this world at 2:19 on

the morning of December 3 after a wonderful natural childbirth delivery—well, wonderful for me, since it was Sarah who did most of the work! Little Sam—Samuel Patrick—was 8 pounds, 4 ounces, and he measured just over 20 inches in length. All of us are happy and healthy and eager to get out of this hospital and back home.

As you can appreciate, we're all a bit exhausted just now, but we'd love to hear from all of you, at our home number (555-009-3492) anytime after Saturday.

Gary and Sarah

E-mail is the perfect tool for sending quick, informal announcements to groups of family, friends, and others. A big part of communicating from the heart includes inviting further contact—but be sure to make it convenient for you. This new family wants some time to itself before fielding a lot of phone calls.

ENGAGEMENT—E-MAIL TO THE FAMILY CIRCLE

Attention all!

Well, I've finally gone and done it. I asked Carol to marry me—and, shocking though it may be, she said yes. We haven't set the date yet, but stay tuned.

Mom, Dad—Carol and I plan to visit you for the holidays. I'll call with the details.

This quick, lighthearted announcement was sent to the family members who are online. Because it was sent to multiple recipients, the sender is careful to address a special aside to his mother and father, who are just two of many recipients.

CAREER MOVE—E-MAIL TO DAD

Dad:

I wanted you to know right away that I am leaving Acme Tire for a new position in sales at Supreme Automotive. The money's quite a bit better—25 percent increase—but it's the increased opportunity and challenge that really excite me, Dad. I have a half dozen salespeople reporting to me.

I start on the 15th, and I'll call you then from my new office to give you my new numbers and fill you in on all the details.

Best to Mom,

Jerry

The writer understands what his father wants to hear: an increase in salary and responsibility. The other details are secondary and can wait for a subsequent phone conversation.

E-Mailing It: To Friends

A BIRTH—E-MAIL TO MULTIPLE RECIPIENTS

Howdy, Friends:

Please join Carol and me in welcoming John Peter into our family and into this world. He arrived—three weeks early, I might add—at 6:30 p.m. yesterday, and despite the early arrival, he's just fine, perfect in every way. Birth weight was 7 pounds, 2 ounces, and he's almost 20 inches long. Carol is tired and very, very happy.

We'll be sticking around the hospital through today and tomorrow, but we expect to be home by Friday. We'd welcome your calls on the weekend.

Ed Porter

25 Words and Phrases to Use

announcement	friends	please call
big news	get together	proud
delighted	gratitude	share
event	happy	stay in touch
excited	include you	thanks
exciting news for you	major change	thrilled
first to know	milestone	understanding
for the best	news	your help
	opportunity	

15 Words and Phrases to Avoid

bad news	no time	regret
bore you	nothing much to say	same old routine
bored	nothing new	too busy
disaster	nothing exciting	won't want to hear this
dull	owe you an explanation	
I won't go into that		

6

Apology and Forgiveness

$\mathcal{M}$ost of us look at apologizing as an act of damage control. We don't like to do it, but we all know it's sometimes necessary. That's a pretty dreary way to look at the subject, so maybe it's high time to change our thinking about apology.

Recall the last time you were on the receiving end of somebody's error. Absent an apology, it was undoubtedly a completely negative experience. But what happened when an effective apology followed?

Some months ago I purchased an attache case. Within days, the latch on the right side broke. I trotted it back to the store, and they gave me a new case. Less than a week later, the latch broke off that one as well.

This time, I was pretty steamed. I didn't just go back to the store, I called the manufacturer.

"Mr. Griffin," the customer service person I spoke with began, "I am very sorry to hear about the problem you've had—not once, but twice. The fact is that we have recently become aware of a manufacturing defect in some of our units. We'll make it right. You don't need to go back to the store a second time. We'll send you an improved attache, and you can return the defective one in the same shipping carton. You won't have a problem with the new case—but if you do have any questions, please call. We are very sorry for the inconvenience we caused you, and we want you to be delighted with our product."

I can't say that this phone call made me deliriously happy about my purchase, but I did feel pretty good about the manufacturer. They hadn't left me hanging, they took responsibility, they expressed concern, and I believed that they were determined to make things right.

457

But there was more to how I felt. After this apology, I was willing to forgive—and that felt good.

I'm no saint, but my feeling of forgiveness and even gratitude was not unusual. It does feel good to be able to forgive. In forgiveness we have the power to relieve someone of bad feelings, perhaps even of anxiety. Forgiveness empowers us.

So try thinking of the apology you have to say or write not as an onerous chore, an embarrassment, and a grim necessity, but as an opportunity to empower someone, to make someone feel good. Think of the act of apology in a positive light, as an opportunity to please and to create satisfaction, to give somebody an occasion for good feelings.

Finding the Heartline

Before you embark on an apology, it is important to address an area of frequent misunderstanding.

We apologize because we feel bad. This is normal; however, it is not a motive that makes for a truly effective apology. Instead of apologizing because you feel bad, consider apologizing to make the other person feel good—or, at least, better. As always, a crucial step toward effective communication is moving the focus from yourself and training it on the other person. This does not mean that you must deny your needs or your objectives; rather, it implies that the most effective way of getting what you want is to focus on what the other person needs. You apologize because you feel bad and want to feel better. In order to feel better, communicate in a way that addresses the other person's feelings, that makes him feel good. The effect your communication has on him will work wonders on you.

The heartline here—the most direct route from your feelings to effective expression—is via your sympathetic imagination of how the other person feels now, how you would like him to feel after you have apologized, and what you can say to create that feeling. Imagine beyond yourself.

Sidestepping the Pitfalls

Apologies tend to falter and fail for one or more of the following three reasons:

1. *The speaker/writer focuses on himself rather than on the feelings and needs of the other person.* As just stated, the most effective apologies are those that remove the focus from your own feelings and address the feelings, needs, and concerns of the other person. Insofar as the apology succeeds in making the other person feel better, it will succeed in making you feel better as well.

2. *The speaker/writer mistakes excuse for apology.* It is all too natural to become defensive when we apologize and offer excuses in the guise of apology. There is nothing wrong with a valid excuse; that is, a *valid* excuse is an explanation—information—and information is almost always valuable and helpful. The problem is when we set out to apologize and end up offering excuses instead. This creates disappointment, augmenting the bad feelings created by the error in the first place. Separate the apology from the explanation or excuse. You may deliver both, but, whatever you do, do not fail to deliver the apology— and deliver it first.

3. *The speaker/writer tells the other person how to feel.* "You must hate me for this," one mortified soul exclaims. Or: "You must think I'm a real idiot."

Statements such as these do not make anyone feel better about whatever problem has occurred. By making such declarations, you are telling the other person that he *should* hate you and he *should* think you are an idiot. You are prompting, even daring, him to think as poorly of you as possible.

A dependable rule of thumb in offering any apology is never to tell the other person what to think or how to feel.

Saying It: To Family

TARDINESS OR MISSED APPOINTMENT

Dad, I'm sorry I'm late. I really appreciate your having waited. I got caught in traffic, and my cell phone wouldn't work. I kept expecting the traffic to open up, but it just got worse and worse. I hope this hasn't put too big a dent in your day. Anyway, I can drop you off at the store when we're finished here, so that should save you some time.

The speaker knows his father well, and nothing formal or elaborate is required by way of apology. He begins, as most apologies should begin, by saying that he is sorry, then goes on to express appreciation for his father's patience. Only after apologizing and expressing appreciation does the speaker offer an explanation. He then expresses the hope that his tardiness has not wasted too much of his father's time; again, note that the emphasis is on the other person's needs. Finally, the speaker finishes the apology by offering something in the way of reparation. No matter how sincerely and persuasively you express your regrets, the most effective part of any apology is the offer of a solution—of some act or gesture or step to make the situation better.

MISINFORMATION—TO A SON

A 12-year-old boy has been told by his mother that the video store down the block is having a big sale on video games today. The boy took some allowance he had saved and went to the store, only to discover that his mother had given him the wrong information. The sale was yesterday. He returns angry and disappointed.

> Billy, I'm very sorry I gave you the wrong information. I don't know how I made that mistake. I must have misread the ad in the newspaper. I wish I could undo it. Maybe we can make some phone calls together and see if other shops have on sale any of the games you are interested in.

The parent should not dismiss the child's anger and disappointment, but she needn't make lavish amends, either. It would certainly be possible for the mother to give her son enough cash to buy what he wants, even if it isn't at a sale price. But, in the so-called real world, it is seldom possible to undo mistakes in this fashion. Instead, the mother thinks of another alternative, which more realistically reflects the way things occur in the adult world.

BAD BEHAVIOR/RUDE TREATMENT—BROTHER TO SISTER

> Sis, I'm sorry I teased you yesterday. I was in a bad mood, and I acted like a jerk. I'll do the dishes tonight—if you say you forgive me.

Minor friction is part of everyday family life. Acknowledging it, apologizing for it, then offering a modest penance is usually all that's required to clear the air.

CARELESS REMARK—APOLOGY TO WIFE

Sweetheart, I'm sorry I let the cat out of the bag with Mark and Terri. I should have known you wanted to surprise them with the news, and I went ahead and spoiled it. I know that disappointed you—but at least I've learned my lesson. Next time, I'll think before I start running my mouth.

Most acts that merit apology are the product of a moment's thoughtlessness. Apologize, express understanding of the thoughtless mistake you made, empathize with the other person's feelings, promise it won't happen again—then move on.

Acknowledge your errors, but don't dwell on them or blow them out of proportion. Remember, you do not want to tell the other person how to feel—especially if your message is that she should feel worse than she does.

DELAYED THANK YOU—FOR A BIRTHDAY GIFT

Tom, I don't deserve such a thoughtful brother as you are. Your wonderful gift arrived almost a week ago, and here I am just picking up the phone now. Things have been incredibly hectic around here, with the children home from school. But that, of course, is no excuse. I really love the gift, and I use it all the time. Thanks so much for it!

With a close family member, a sentence like the one that begins this apology is appropriate. Be careful, however, about delivering such stern self-criticism to friends or acquaintances. Note that, after the opening sentence, the speaker does not dwell on her sin of omission but instead focuses on the "wonderful gift" and how much she enjoys it. The point of the apology is not to demonstrate how bad you feel about your own oversight, but how grateful you are for the other person's thoughtfulness—even though your expression of gratitude is tardy.

ACCIDENT—BROKEN HEIRLOOM

Mom, I just wanted to tell you again how sorry I am about the figurine. I know how much that piece meant to you. I am happy I found a place that can repair it, but I also know that it just won't be quite the same. I wish I could undo my clumsiness, but, instead, I'd like to take you out to dinner this evening. Maybe you can watch me knock over the dessert trolley at Chez Pierre.

Accidents happen, and it won't do anybody any good if you beat yourself up over a relatively minor mishap. Make your first priority damage control. What can be done? What can be fixed? Attend to that first, rather than lavish a lot of words on regret. A little self-deprecating humor, as in the closing line of this example, may lighten the tone of the episode. Just make certain that you don't make light of the other person's feelings or imply that she has no right to be upset.

Saying It: To Friends

TARDINESS OR MISSED APPOINTMENT—PHONE CALL: RUNNING LATE

> John, this is Ted. I'm very sorry, but I just got out of a client meeting that ran late. Can you stand to wait for me another twenty minutes? With crosstown traffic, it will take me at least that long. I really appreciate it. Thanks, buddy.

The best time for an apology is before the harm is done. Try to inform the other person of a problem either before it occurs or even while it is occurring. Provide the essential information only. Note that the speaker does not waste time with excuses. After first apologizing, he gives a simple explanation. It is always best to *ask* the other person for patience, not demand patience of him. There is a big difference between "Can you stand to wait for me another twenty minutes?" and "You'll have to wait twenty minutes." You have already inconvenienced the other person; now is not the time to back him into a corner, too.

Do not make promises you can't keep. If you know it will take you 40 minutes to get where you are going, don't promise 20. Note here that the speaker provides a basis for his estimate of 20 minutes—crosstown traffic—and mentions this figure as a base ("at least").

End by thanking the other person for his understanding.

MISINFORMATION—WRONG PHONE NUMBER GIVEN

> Hi, Tom. I heard from Ed that the phone number I gave you for that customer was wrong. I am very sorry. I double-checked the number I have, and I just must have written down the wrong number. I hope my mistake didn't mess you up too badly. Were you able to get all the contact numbers you need?

This is what might be called a preemptive apology. Tom didn't call the speaker to tell him about the error; the speaker heard about it from Ed, a third party. To salvage some part of an impression that, despite the mistake, he's on top of the situation, the speaker did not wait for Tom to complain, nor did he just let the incident pass. Instead, he took the initiative and called Tom to apologize.

Don't make trouble for yourself, but it is generally a useful move to go out of your way to own up to your errors. Note here that, besides the apology, the speaker takes the opportunity to ask Tom if he needs any more information.

BAD BEHAVIOR/RUDE TREATMENT—TOO MUCH TO DRINK

> Mary, I am very sorry if I was out of line last night. I want you to know that being boorish like that is just not my style—at least not without three martinis in me. I used just terrible judgment, and I value your friendship and opinion so much that—well, I just want to say I'm sorry. I hope I didn't cause you any embarrassment. If I did, I hope that you will be frank with me, and I hope that you will let me try to make it right.

Apologies for irresponsible behavior are difficult to make, because we—quite appropriately—feel ashamed. The best approach is to own up to what you did, apologize for it, and invite a response from the other person. Do not carry on about the incident, however, accusing yourself of a multitude of sins. Do not burden the other person with your guilt. Your object is not to make the other person feel sorry for you or feel that *she* has caused *you* embarrassment. Your object is to take responsibility for your actions and to apologize for them, period.

CARELESS REMARK—REVEALED PRIVILEGED INFORMATION

> Patti, I hope my remark to Darren at lunch today hasn't put you in hot water. I should *not* have mentioned those wholesale figures. Of course, I wouldn't have, had I known that Darren is a client of yours. But, in any case, I shouldn't have been broadcasting that kind of information indiscriminately. I am truly sorry. Is there anything I can do that would help with damage control?

Making a careless remark is like breaking an egg. Once it's done, it's done. All that's left for you to do is apologize sincerely, express the hope that you have not caused much harm, and ask if there is anything you can do to repair the situation. If you have any suggestions for a remedy, you should mention them. If not, just offer your help. Do not, however, make any promises you cannot keep.

DELAYED THANK YOU

> Harry, I have been meaning to thank you for putting me in touch with Max
> Goberman. He and I talked, and it looks like we'll be doing some business
> together. I should have called you right away to thank you, but—well, I have
> no excuse. I was just thoughtless. So, better late than never. I'd like to take
> you to lunch, if you're free later in the week or next.

Sometimes we slight our friends or commit a minor sin of omission without any good reason at all. In these cases, don't fabricate an excuse. Just deliver the apology and, if possible, make amends—here, a lunch invitation.

ACCIDENT—CONVERSATION WITH A NEIGHBOR

> Molly, I can't tell you how sorry I am about what our dog did to your rose bed.
> This isn't like her at all, but let me assure you that she'll be confined to our
> yard from now on. I just won't let something like this happen again, and I
> really do appreciate your being so understanding and forgiving. I know how
> much your beautiful roses mean to you. Now, what can I do to help you get
> your roses back in order?

The principal object of an effective apology is not to let the other person know that you are sorry—although you should make that clear. Instead, your primary object should be to assure the other person that you will act responsibly and that you will do whatever can be done to make things right. In this case, two courses of action are called for: First, something to ensure that the accident won't be repeated and, second, an offer to help repair the present damage.

Note that the speaker does not blame his dog, but takes the responsibility on himself. Note also, that he does not go overboard and wallow in self-castigation; however, he does sympathize with the other person, letting her know that he understands how important the roses are to her. Someone who has suffered a loss or injury because of your error or oversight not only wants the damage repaired, but also has the need for understanding. Feelings are very much involved.

A very effective way to salvage something quite positive from an accident is to praise and thank the other person for her patience, understanding, and generosity. Yes, it would be better if the accident hadn't happened, but the aftermath of the accident does give the injured party an opportunity to be magnanimous and forgiving. Acknowledging such emotional generosity builds good feelings.

Writing It: To Family

TARDINESS OR MISSED APPOINTMENT—ARRIVED LATE AT BROTHER'S GRADUATION CEREMONY

Dear Gary,

Thank you for being so understanding about my late arrival on your big day. I felt terrible about being so late, but your understanding made me feel much better. I guess my little brother really has grown up—and grown up to be just a great guy.

Anyway, late or not, I was thrilled by the ceremony, and I had a great time at your party. I'll see you at the Fourth of July get-together!

Love,

Mary

Some of life's most significant moments come once and once only. It is very appropriate to make a big deal about them. The writer had certainly apologized on the occasion of her lateness, but she feels that an event so important merits a follow-up letter to underscore just how proud she is of her brother. The writer goes out of her way to praise, admire, and thank her brother for his understanding. The goal of a good apology is to create positive feelings, not just to patch up hurt ones.

MISINFORMATION—WRONG DIRECTIONS

Dear Mom and Dad,

Little brother let the cat out of the bag and told me what you were too polite and considerate to tell me: that the directions I had given you to the big outlet mall were all wrong and that the two of you drove all over Creation for two hours before finally calling it quits and coming back home.

Your patience and understanding amaze me. *I* would have been on the phone the minute I got home. Thanks for going so easy on me.

I am very sorry I steered you wrong. I don't know how I got the wrong directions, but I wish I hadn't passed them on to you. I called my friend Elise, who gave me the *right* directions (she swears it!), and I'd like to drive you guys out to the mall on the weekend of the 23rd. I'll be able to get into town then. Please call if it's a date.

Love and apologies,

Cindy

With family members, a lighthearted but sincere tone is often best. You want to affirm the bond between you by showing that, where your loving and understanding family is concerned, you do not live in fear of the consequences of a mistake. At the same time, you do not want to make too light of the inconvenience your error has caused.

The two positive steps taken here include praise for the kindly, loving character of the parents and an offer to turn this frustrating incident into an occasion for a family excursion.

BAD BEHAVIOR/RUDE TREATMENT—LOST TEMPER

Dear Dad:

I'd give anything if I could take back the harsh words I spoke yesterday. I know I apologized over the phone earlier, but I wanted you to have something in writing, something you could look at to see how I really feel.

I've been under a lot of pressure on the job. That's not an excuse for my outburst, but it is an explanation. I'm just sorry you got in the way of my temporary seizure of immaturity. I am happy, though, that you did not return my angry tone in kind and that, as always, you were the voice of sanity, wisdom, and love.

Sorry, Dad.

Love,

Ned

A note of apology following up on a verbal apology underscores your earnest desire to patch things up. Often, we can say more emotionally meaningful things in writing than in speaking. That is the case here. Note, by the way, how the writer shifts the focus from himself to his father in the closing sentence. The best apologies do not dwell on oneself.

CARELESS REMARK—NOTE TO BROTHER-IN-LAW

Dear Bob,

I hope my remark didn't get you in trouble with June. My sister and I are accustomed to speaking frankly, but then it occurred to me that you might not have wanted to share all that information with her at this time. Of course, this fit of discretion came upon me only *after* I had opened my big mouth.

> Please let me know if my remarks have upset anything, and, if you wish, I will have a talk with June.
>
> Regards,
>
> Clyde

If you are not sure that you have done something wrong, it may still be a good idea to write a note that clears the air. Just be careful not to create trouble unnecessarily.

DELAYED THANK YOU

> Dear Aunt Beth:
>
> I have been wearing the wonderful sweater you sent me for three days straight, and it suddenly occurs to me that I haven't so much as thanked you for it. What a thoughtful gift! And how thoughtless of me not to have thanked you the moment I had unwrapped it.
>
> I love the sweater. The very best thing about it is that, every time I wear it, I think of my favorite aunt.
>
> Love,
>
> Louisa

Never write a belated thank-you note that reads as if it were the product of a painful sense of duty. This one looks as if it had been a heartfelt pleasure to write. Certainly, it would be a delight to read.

ACCIDENT

> Dear Dad:
>
> I am very relieved that insurance will cover the damage I did to your car. Thanks for letting me know. Again, I can't tell you how sorry I am for my carelessness. If there is anything the insurance doesn't cover, please, please, *please* let me know, so that I can take care of the shortfall. My reason is selfish: It would make me feel better.
>
> Love—and thanks for your understanding,
>
> Danny

This note addresses the aftermath of a minor fender bender. Despite the insurance payment, it accepts continued responsibility for the accident—without, however, magnifying the incident out of proportion.

Writing It: To Friends

TARDINESS OR MISSED APPOINTMENT

Dear Martha and Crawford:

Sam and I are so very sorry that we missed your party. We had been looking forward to it for weeks, but a family emergency came up at the last minute, and we really had no choice—nor did we have any time to get word to you.

I'm sure the evening was a tremendous success and great delight. Please keep us in mind for next time!

Sincerely,

May Morgan

You owe some acknowledgment and an expression of regret when you fail to attend a party after having accepted the invitation. You need not, however, go into a detailed explanation of what prevented your attending. "Family emergency" communicates urgency without compromising your privacy.

MISINFORMATION

Dear Roy:

You're right: I was wrong. The information I had received concerning the availability of the new equipment was not accurate. I am very happy that you chose not to act on what I insisted was correct, but I certainly regret having given you a hard time about it. It *must* have been very frustrating for you—but you certainly had the great good grace not to show it.

Next time, I'll try to keep a more open mind. I apologize for trying your patience.

Yours,

Ed

When you're right, you're right, and when you're wrong—well, don't evade it. Step up to the plate and acknowledge your error. In this case, no lasting harm was done, but the writer does not emphasize this or use it to excuse himself. Instead, he expresses gratitude that the other person did not lose his temper, despite being put in a frustrating situation.

BAD BEHAVIOR/RUDE TREATMENT

Dear Mary:

Something's been bothering me since Friday. You came into the store and were looking for something special for your friend. I was so busy—so rushed—that I just did not treat you very politely. Certainly, I did not offer you the time and courtesy that you deserve.

I regret this very much, and I hope that you can see your way clear to forgiving me for this lapse. Next time you come in, please expect the kind of treatment you certainly deserve.

Sincerely,

Martin Overman

A timely note can do much to repair an oversight or lapse in courtesy. In situations such as this, a written note is more effective than a phone call because it suggests that you have devoted more time and effort to the gesture of apology.

E-Mailing It: To Family

CARELESS REMARK

Max:

I just realized that I mentioned to Mom that she would be seeing you in May. Of course, she doesn't know about the surprise anniversary party you're planning for her and Dad. I don't think I spilled the beans—or that she suspects anything. But she may mention you're coming out in May, so be prepared with an alibi.

I'm sorry I put my foot in it, Max. But I think we'll be all right.

A quick attempt at damage control can often minimize the consequences of a careless remark.

DELAYED THANK YOU

Hey, Cuz—

E-mail seemed the quickest, surest way to get hold of you. I forgot to thank you over the phone yesterday for the help you gave my friend Ted in putting together his resume. He was just full of praise for everything you did. He's a good guy, who deserves all the breaks he can get. Thanks—and sorry for the delay in acknowledging your timely help.

E-mail is such an easy, ready-to-hand, casual medium of communication that it sometimes seems necessary to justify using it in place of a letter or phone call. Don't apologize for sending an e-mail. This suggests that you are knowingly doing something inappropriate or taking the easy way out. However, if you feel you need to explain your choice of medium, do so.

E-Mailing It: To Friends

TARDINESS OR MISSED APPOINTMENT—TO A WORKGROUP

Everyone:

I've decided that the two saddest words in the English language are "flight" and "cancelled." Imagine my surprise when I got to the airport yesterday morning and found that my flight had dematerialized. Next one was a three-hour wait—and even that was delayed on the ground. So my absence yesterday was not due to lack of interest or will—just the whim of the airlines. Please accept my apologies.

Folks, can we get together Wednesday at 8:30 for a quick fill-in session for yours truly?

If you've got an ironclad, bullet-proof excuse, use it. Note that this explanation/apology ends not with a "too bad," but a proposal for positive action.

BAD BEHAVIOR/RUDE TREATMENT

Al:

I'm sitting at my keyboard feeling like a real jerk. I wish I could just rewind the tape and erase the rude remark I made to you this morning. I was way out of line. I have absolutely no excuse to offer, but will you accept my sincere apology?

In the heat of the moment, we sometimes say things we instantly regret. E-mail is a handy means of instant communication and can be the best route to a quick apology. Note the frank, straightforward approach here—an appeal to accept the offered apology.

ACCIDENT—TO CO-WORKERS IN AN OFFICE

To the Person With the Broken Souvenir Mug:

You know who you are. Now I'll own up to who I am. I am the person who broke your 1965 New York World's Fair souvenir mug. I was admiring it in the coffee room, and it slipped out of my hand. I left the pieces there, but, alas, it looks to me beyond repair.

I am very sorry for this accident, and I hope that the owner of the mug will approach me—kindly and gently—to discuss some form of reparation.

Ed McGraw

This is lighthearted, but it does not make light of the loss. It is also an opportunity for the writer to demonstrate to the entire office his willingness to take responsibility for what he has accidentally done.

25 Words to Use

accept	discuss	negotiate
acknowledge	effective	plan
agree	generous	prepared
apologize	goodwill	resolve
appreciate	help	responsibility
appropriate	hope	thank
care	improve	willing
concerned	investigate	
correct	judgment	

25 Words and Phrases to Avoid

afraid	fault	refuse
blame	hopeless	reject
can't do anymore	impossible	too late
cannot	incapable	unfair
catastrophe	insist	unworkable
crisis	mess	waste
demand	nonnegotiable	worthless
disaster	not my fault	
fail	panic	

7

Appreciation and Thanks

*C*ommunicating thanks and appreciation should be easy. For one thing, it is an inherently pleasant task. We enjoy expressing gratitude, and we enjoy receiving such expressions. It is pretty hard to go seriously wrong when you thank someone. Just uttering the word "thanks" does wonders. Yet, like almost any other communication endeavor, this one can be improved on. There are three potential problems with communicating thanks:

1. *Failure to do it at all.* This is the most serious problem. In the rush of our day-to-day affairs, we often fail to take the time to thank others for what they have done. Get into the habit of expressing gratitude. Everyone wants to be appreciated. Everyone wants to have their work recognized.

2. *Failure to do it in a timely fashion.* It is important to communicate your thanks as soon as possible. Don't put off that thank-you note you've been meaning to write.

3. *Failure to be specific.* This last point deserves further discussion. Many expressions of thanks seem insincere or, at least, unsatisfying, not because the person expressing gratitude is actually ungrateful, but because the expression is vague, general, and abstract. There is a big difference between saying "Thanks very much" and "Thank you very much for mailing those letters. It saved me enough time to get to the drugstore before it closed, and my poor kid really needed his cough syrup."

To be sure, the short expression is much better than none at all, but the longer, highly specific expression is far more valuable.

- It fully acknowledges the favor or service that was done.
- It lets the other person know the beneficial effect of what he has done.

We all like acknowledgment—the more specific, the better. Even more, we derive satisfaction from seeing the impact of our work. This, at minimum, is what a fully developed thank-you communication should furnish: specific acknowledgment and an assessment of impact. You don't need flowery adjectives and adverbs to do this. You don't need blissful outcries of eternal gratitude. What you need are the facts, nouns and verbs mostly, simply and straightforwardly expressed.

Finding the Heartline

Take two preliminary steps:

1. Identify the person or persons to thank. This may be self-evident, but if it requires asking some questions, take the time to do so.
2. Put aside what you are doing and make the thank-you call, write the thank-you note, or send the thank-you e-mail. Do it now.

A note on the second step. Be prepared to follow up with additional thanks once the full impact of the favor or service performed is known. For example, you ask a friend for permission to be listed as a credit reference on a loan application. He says yes, and you thank him, explaining what this loan will enable you to do. A few days later you get word that the loan has come through. You call your friend to tell him the news, to thank him, and to let him know that the full amount was approved and at a favorable rate. "Thanks. I know that including your name as a reference really helped."

Beyond these preliminaries, energize your thank you by getting in touch with your gratitude. Take the time to appreciate what is being done for you. Next, assess the effect of the favor or service and communicate that effect to the other person. Remember, if he cares enough to do what you ask, he cares enough to want to know the beneficial effect of the effort he is making. It really is that simple.

Sidestepping the Pitfalls

Avoid lavish, but hollow expressions of thanks. You don't have to repeat the thanks. Just make it specific. If appropriate, follow up your initial thanks with a report on results, but don't drown the other person in your gratitude. In and of itself, this is annoying. Beyond this, it also suggests your disbelief that this person could act decently.

Avoid tardy expressions of thanks. To be effective, a thank you should be timely.

Avoid ill-advised attempts at wit that make light of the service or favor that is being performed. Bantering when sincere gratitude is called for can be highly damaging to a relationship:

> "I was able to get you 25 cents more per hour," said the assistant manager.
>
> "Great! Now I can buy that yacht I've had my eye on," quips the grocery clerk.
>
> "Go to hell," concludes the assistant manager.

Saying It: To Family

FOR A GIFT—PHONE CALL FROM A COLLEGE STUDENT

> Hi, Dad. The Super-X Calculator just arrived today. What a fabulous tool! It is just what I need. I mean this is really a thoughtful gift. The best thing about it is that I can take it with me to the lab. I don't have to drag out the laptop. This is faster, more efficient. Just what I need. Thanks.

This is a good example of a thank you with a high degree of specificity. The speaker vividly explains the benefit he will derive from the gift.

FOR A FAVOR—PHONE CALL FROM SISTER TO BROTHER

> Bob, hi. I just wanted to thank you, Big Brother, for taking my car to the mechanic. I know I'm supposed to be a liberated woman and all, but I'm convinced that mechanics take men more seriously than women, and, anyway, I've been all over the place with that car, trying to find someone who'll believe me about the squeaks and rattles. I don't know what you said to this mechanic, but I just picked up the car—and it runs perfectly. No squeaks. Not a single rattle. Whatever you did really produced results. I knew I could depend on you—as always. Thanks, Bob.

Share the successful outcome. Did the brother's intervention really help to resolve the problem? Who knows? The point is that he did what his sister asked and the result was positive. She doesn't speculate in her thanks, but simply gives him credit for the good work.

FOR FINANCIAL SUPPORT—PHONE CALL FROM A STRUGGLING STUDENT

Aunt Esther, hi. I just picked up the money you wired. You are a real lifesaver! What a time for my computer to go down! I have reports due in three classes, and these professors are not kindhearted like you. Tell them your computer's on the fritz, and you might as well tell them the dog ate your homework.

This cash will get me up and running right away. My grades are saved—and so is my scholarship. I just can't thank you enough for being there when I really needed you.

In part, this phone call lets the student's aunt know that the money has been wired safely and successfully. Beyond this, she is treated to a vivid picture of what her generosity has accomplished: nothing less than the salvation of her nephew!

FOR ENCOURAGEMENT

Mom, Dad, I just got word. The job is mine! I still can't believe it. But the important thing is that *you* both believed it, from the beginning, and your encouragement was really important to me—especially, Dad, when you told me about your experience with the architectural firm. That helped me hold my head up high and make a good impression. Thanks for everything you've done and said.

Letting loved ones share in a victory is an intense experience. What makes this a moment to remember is the degree to which the caller is specific, citing a particular episode his father shared with him.

Saying It: To Friends

FOR A GIFT

Martin, I've just begun reading the novel you gave me. It really is beautiful—and I just laid it aside long enough to call you to tell you what a thoughtful gift it is. Thanks. It means a lot to me.

The sooner you convey your thanks the better. You don't wait to finish the dinner before you begin to compliment your host. So why wait until you're through with the novel?

FOR A FAVOR

Dan, just calling to thank you for the loan of the pickup truck. I couldn't have rented anything in time, and, without the truck, I would have been late on this contract. And this was one customer I didn't want to tick off. Thanks to you, he's happy. Great truck you've got there, too!

The added compliment sweetens the thanks.

FOR FINANCIAL SUPPORT

Ellen, your check just arrived in the mail. I can't tell you how much I appreciate this loan. It will get me through until my internship kicks in. I really don't know what I would have done without your help. This goes above and beyond friendship. Thanks so much.

In addition to letting the lender know how much her generosity means, the speaker offers a gauge of the magnitude of the good deed: something "above and beyond."

FOR ENCOURAGEMENT

Tom, thanks for putting up with me yesterday. I know I was pretty down in the mouth—and certainly no fun to be around. Your kind words were just what I needed. I can always count on you to provide perspective on the hardest problems. Thanks to you and our talk, I feel much better, and I will proceed with the plan we discussed.

Advice and encouragement are delicate commodities. Those who offer them are rarely 100 percent sure of their effectiveness. Positive feedback, in the form of heartfelt thanks, is most welcome.

Writing It: To Family

FOR ADVICE

Dear Dad,

I am now 15 percent richer than I was yesterday. I got the raise you and I talked about. And I sure am glad we talked about it. Your advice about letting

Mr. Perkins be the first to mention an actual figure was perfect. I would have angled for 7 percent, 10 at the most. By doing what you suggested and letting him propose a number, I did much better. He offered 12, I countered with 18, and we settled on 15. I couldn't have done it without you, Dad. Thanks.

Best to Mom,

Sandy

The more you can tell the advice giver about the successful effect of his advice, the more delighted he will be. Here the writer provides a concise blow-by-blow description. She's careful also to compare and contrast what she would have done without the advice versus what she did armed with it.

FOR FINANCIAL SUPPORT

Dear Mom and Dad:

Your wonderful check arrived today. Thanks so much. I know it is a sacrifice for you both, and Sally and I deeply appreciate it. This will get us over the hump until my first paycheck from the new job. Most of all, it represents relief from worry. That's the greatest gift of all, and I am very, very thankful for it.

Love,

Eddy

Demonstrate that you take no gift for granted; however, do not dwell on any hardship you may be causing. Acknowledge the sacrifice, but don't rub it in!

FOR A GET TOGETHER—NOTE TO BROTHER AND SISTER-IN-LAW

Dear Ken and Lynn,

It was just great seeing you again—and the food, well, it's hard for a Texan to vote for a Georgia barbecue, but you've won me over. It was sloppy and delicious. Just the way it should be.

The talk was equally appetizing and satisfying. I haven't had an opportunity to relive old times like that since the old times weren't that old! The occasion has given me wonderful memories, more than enough to last until the next time we're together.

All my love,

Jake

Hit the highlights. Choose a detail or two to throw into relief. This will reawaken some of the original pleasure of the event itself.

Writing It: To Friends

FOR FRIENDSHIP

Dear Clark,

Like most other reasonably happy people, I take a lot for granted. One thing I do not want to take for granted is your friendship. I've been around long enough to have learned that it is rare to find a friend as loyal, entertaining, and kind as you. True, we've been out of touch from time to time, but, mostly, we've shared a lot of key life experiences—and we also shared our notes to American History 101 way back when, which was my only A that semester.

Clark, you are a wonderful friend. I want you to know that. And I want you to know that *I* know it, too.

All the best,

Phil

You don't have to restrict your thank-you correspondence to notes in acknowledgment of some particular gift, favor, or service. Why not thank a friend for being a friend? This kind of letter makes both the writer and the recipient feel great, and it is the kind of letter that is saved and treasured for years—a cherished gift.

FOR A GIFT

Dear Mary:

I could begin, "How did you know I wanted a toaster oven?" But the fact that I've been talking about buying one for the past, oh, three or four years probably makes the question unnecessary. You *knew* it was just what I wanted, and I am so thrilled that you bought it for me. I love it!

Your friend,

Selma

A little humor at your own expense is always welcome. Do be careful with humor in letters of thanks, however. Humor should never be allowed to undercut the sincerity of the sentiment. It should certainly not belittle the gift or the deed.

FOR A BUSINESS REFERRAL

Dear Perry:

Many thanks for referring Mr. Thornton to me. We had a meeting yesterday, and we will be doing business together. He is a delightful person, which comes as no surprise inasmuch as he is a good friend of yours.

Perry, I not only appreciate the business you have sent my way, but, even more, the vote of confidence you have given me in making the referral. Your good opinion means the world to me.

Thank you, my friend,

Ben

Acknowledging and giving thanks for all business referrals is an absolute must, and it should be done promptly. It is also highly effective to put such thanks in the form of a letter, rather than with a phone call or even an e-mail. The traditional formality of a letter underscores the value you place on the referral.

Go beyond thanks. The essence of a referral is a vote of confidence for you. Acknowledge this by saying how much you value your friend's good opinion of you.

E-Mailing It: To Family

FOR BIRTHDAY GIFT—E-MAIL TO BROTHER

Frank:

The golf clubs just arrived. I can't believe it! These aren't golf clubs. They're monuments to engineering. Just beautiful. I will use them, and I will treasure them.

Why did I say "I can't believe it"? I should have expected nothing less than first-class, top-drawer thoughtfulness from you.

Love,

Max

Ideally, an e-mail message to family or friends should embody a feeling of spontaneous intimacy and informality. In a thank you for a gift, try to set down your initial reactions to the gift. The use of e-mail suggests immediacy, even urgency. It shows how impatient you were to convey your gratitude. Take advantage of this by sending e-mail thanks without delay.

FOR ADVICE

Mom: Thanks for the advice on what to serve at my dinner party. I intend to follow it to the letter. With a menu like the one you've laid out, I don't see how I can miss. I was very nervous when I spoke to you about this. Thanks to you, I am confidently looking forward to the evening. I'll give you a full report.

You don't have to wait for final results to express your thanks for advice. Even without the *final* results, however, note that the writer does communicate *a* result: Thanks to her mother's help, she no longer feels anxious about the impending dinner party, but is looking forward to it with pleasure. Moreover, she ends by promising to keep her mother in the loop.

FOR UNDERSTANDING

Dear Mom and Dad:

A quick e-mail to thank you for your understanding. I was looking forward to seeing you both for dinner—but I couldn't say no to this client. And much as it hurt me to change our plans, I just knew that you would understand and forgive me. Thanks for making my life easier!

Can we reset the date for next Saturday?

This is a follow-up e-mail message to reinforce an expression of gratitude for understanding in a difficult situation. Thanking people for understanding in such situations reassures them that they are not taken for granted or relegated to a secondary priority.

E-Mailing It: To Friends

FOR HOSPITALITY

Dear Martha:

What a pleasure—what a kick—it was, staying with you! And I can't tell you how grateful I am that you were able to put me up on such short notice. My trip was so sudden that a hotel was out of the question. I don't know what I would have done without your wonderful hospitality.

Please take this as an open invitation to stay with me next time you get up to Baltimore. I don't know that I dare claim that I will be as gracious a hostess to you as you were to me, but I'll sure give it my best.

Thanks again, Martha.

Love,

Cindy

The best hospitality thank you's include a reciprocal invitation. If you make the invitation, be absolutely prepared to make good on it.

Note that the writer emphasizes two principal points: the pleasure of the stay, and the fact that her friend responded so generously on short notice. A thank you is most effective if the writer identifies one or two specific highlights. This keeps the message from sounding "canned."

FOR A FAVOR

John:

Thanks for covering for me yesterday. You were a real lifesaver! It was the first time I ever made conflicting appointments—and, boy, I sure picked two top-drawer clients to double book like that. Thanks to you, I didn't end up disappointing and alienating one of them.

Thanks, Buddy. I knew I could count on you, and I owe you one.

And I *mean* it, too. Just ask whenever you need this favor returned. Consider it done.

Best,

RJ

"A friend in need . . ." It is a great feeling when your friend proves his friendship by bailing you out of a tight spot. Render recognition and thanks as soon as possible. Put muscle behind the thank you by promising a quid pro quo—and make certain to live up to what you promise.

FOR A DINNER INVITATION

Dear Edna—

I wanted to thank you again for thinking of me and including me among the guests for your big dinner. It sounds like the social event of the season, and I am thrilled to be a part of it. Your friendship means the world to me.

Tammi

Just because you have already accepted the invitation does not mean that you can't offer a quick, casual note of thanks—or of added thanks. Notes like this are truly life's grace notes. They enhance the experience of friendship.

25 Words to Use

achieve	grateful	sacrifice
accomplish	gratitude	selfless
acknowledge	heartfelt	sincere
appreciate	invaluable	succeed
commitment	opportunity	thanks
contribution	pleasure	thoughtful
dedication	priceless	tremendous
generous	privilege	
goal	profound	

15 Words and Phrases to Avoid

blame	made the effort	thanks a million
debt	must	tried your best
eternally indebted	old college try	
greatest in the world	shocked	
have to	sorry I had to ask	
how can I ever repay you?	surprised	
	thanks a bunch	

8

Cheers and Encouragement

$\mathcal{S}$orrow, misfortune, and tragedy can create powerful emotional bonds among people, especially if accompanied by effective communication. This is an area addressed in Chapter 12. It is also true that occasions of positive enterprise and great expectation call for communicating from the heart, both before and during the event. This is what we'll cover in this chapter. After the successful completion of a project, it is time to convey heartfelt congratulations, which reinforce and celebrate the achievement. This is the subject of Chapter 9.

Finding the Heartline

Actions, begins a well-worn cliché, speak louder than words. Yet think of some of the most momentous actions the world has known. Take, for example, the American Revolution. Is it possible to think of this event without the words of the *Declaration of Independence?* Or the Civil War: Lincoln's *Gettysburg Address* comes to mind. World War II? Perhaps it is President Roosevelt's stirring request to Congress for a declaration of war following the attack on Pearl Harbor, a "date that will live in infamy," or Winston Churchill's promise to offer the British people nothing but blood, tears, and sweat.

The fact is that actions without words are often events without meaning or, at least, with compromised and diminished meaning. Words—the right words—shape, ennoble, intensify, guide, and elevate action. Often, they make the difference between the success and failure of an enterprise.

Finding the heartline in the midst of such an enterprise depends on using words that build, reinforce, and affirm the self-confidence of everyone involved. How is this done?

- By demonstrating knowledge, awareness, and appreciation of the realities involved in the enterprise.

- By drawing on experiences that demonstrate past success in similar situations.

- By showing that the experience and skills of those involved in the enterprise are adequate to achieving success.

- By reminding all involved of the objectives and goals of the enterprise.

- By ensuring that all involved in the enterprise understand the benefits of achieving the objectives and goals.

Sidestepping the Pitfalls

The most common error made by those who would cheer and encourage is a failure to demonstrate a grasp of the realities of the situation in question. People readily see through fantasy and empty rhetoric. Instead of finding encouragement in hollow words, they find reason to doubt the feasibility and outcome of the enterprise.

- Avoid empty rhetoric, including such meaningless expressions as "You can do it," "We can do anything," and the like.

- Avoid hollow predictions of success that are not based on facts, experience, or reasonable expectations.

Just as it is important to avoid empty, groundless, inflated enthusiasm, it is even more critical to avoid projecting negativity or pessimism. In planning a project, it is essential that you express any doubts and reservations you may have. The planning stage is no time for thoughtless optimism. Once you and your group are committed to a course of action, however, you should keep all doubts to yourself—unless you are thoroughly persuaded that a radical change of course is required. That is, if you are burdened by doubt, be prepared to propose a change of plan. If, on the other hand, you are committed to the plan, do not share your doubts and fears. Keep the tone and climate thoroughly positive.

Negativity to be avoided includes the following:

- Expressions of doubt.
- Predictions of disaster and doom.
- Complaints about objectives, goals, and the people involved in the project or enterprise.

Perhaps the greatest mistake people make in situations where morale-lifting encouragement is called for is a failure to know and to marshal the facts of the enterprise.

- Know what you and your group are about.
- Know the objectives and the goals of the project.
- Know the dangers.
- Know the benefits.
- Know the risks and the rewards.
- Know what means are necessary to achieve the ends that the group agreed on.

Those you work with have an uncanny ability to penetrate even the thickest layers of baloney. Know the facts—and use them.

Saying It: To Family

ENTERING COLLEGE—WORDS TO A SON OR DAUGHTER

I'm very proud of you, and I'm very excited for you. College was one of the very greatest experiences of my life, and I bet you'll find it the same for you. What you've done in high school—the study skills you've learned and already demonstrated—will really get a workout in college. It feels good to stretch. That's what college did for me. It gave me a chance to realize just how much I could achieve, and, let me tell you, you find out that you can do a lot more than you think. That's really what it's all about: Finding out what you can do and always pushing the envelope. But that's a way of working and living you're already very familiar with. I think you'll do great in college. You'll find it challenging and different from anything that came before—but you'll also find it, well, comfortable. What can I say? Have fun!

Although it may not always seem to be the case, children at the threshold of adulthood want their parents to share experience with them—and not just experience, but the feelings associated with experience. This need is especially acute as the young man or woman is about to embark on a milestone event such as entry into college. Here the speaker combines two approaches to encouragement:

1. He shares his assessment of the positive feelings associated with the experience.
2. He creates a context for success by reminding the young person of her record of high school achievement.

Both of these steps create continuity with past experience while simultaneously acknowledging the newness of the impending adventure. Yes, this is a new, challenging, exciting, even somewhat frightening episode of life, but I have been through it—with great feelings and positive results—and you have already demonstrated many of the skills you'll need to get you through the experience successfully.

A NEW BUSINESS VENTURE—PHONE CALL TO A SISTER

Hi, sis. I heard the exciting news about the franchise you and Dave just bought. From what I've heard, it sounds great. I've seen these businesses blossom here in Cleveland, and I would think the demand would be even greater in a place like Pine Bluff. People need a one-stop-shopping center for the kind of service you'll be offering. Seems to me you'll have plenty of opportunity for growth down the line.

So, when do you close on the deal, and when do you open your doors?

Notice the absence of *empty* enthusiasm here. There are no exclamations of "Congratulations!" or "I know you can do it!" Instead, the speaker conveys her sense of excitement for her sister, and she offers the genuinely encouraging example of similar enterprises with which she is familiar. That is, the speaker is careful to base her prediction of success on a precedent, not on mere wishful thinking.

Two additional features of this little speech are worth noting:

1. The comments do not remain focused on the past or the present, but turn toward the future. Encouragement is about what one has done and is doing, to be sure, but, most of all, it is about the great things yet to come. This speaker talks about the potential for future growth.

2. The speaker ends by inviting her sister's comments and conversation. She shifts the focus to her sister. Nothing is more encouraging than showing genuine interest in the other person's enterprise. The way to show this interest is to invite the other person to talk about what she is doing.

MATURE CAREER CHANGE—PHONE CALL TO A PARENT

So, Dad, Mom tells me you've finally decided to pursue your dream. I'd like to tell you that I admire your guts, leaving the firm to go off on your own. But, in your case, I don't think the move takes a great deal of courage. You've got everything it takes to make a huge splash with your own agency. If ever there was betting on a sure thing, this is it. Growing up, I saw how you carried promotional operations for the firm, and, sometimes, I also saw how frustrated you were by the dumb decisions of others. Well, it's about time you were in a position to call the shots. I'm really excited by this move. The industry is going to sit up and take notice.

The speaker immediately identifies with his father's motivation: pursuing his dream, following his own direction. This is a very effective strategy for communicating encouragement—provided that you know the other person well enough to understand his motivation. Don't guess. Don't put yourself in the position of trying to tell another person what he is thinking or feeling. This does not create encouragement, but, rather, frustration and, perhaps, a degree of anxiety, since the other person feels misunderstood.

It is often difficult to avoid falling back on hollow words of encouragement. Here, the speaker stays away from this by recalling the perception he has had of his father. Basing encouragement on shared experience is highly effective. Nothing is more heartening than the evocation of a positive track record, a continuity with a successful past combined with the prospect of improving on that past.

Saying It: To Friends

ON A BUSINESS VENTURE—PHONE CALL

Gene, I just received your mailer announcing your new business. What a great idea!

It's going to be exciting watching you grow. And based on my work with you when you were with Acme, Inc., I know that you *will* grow. You have the brains, you have the experience, and you have the contacts. You can count me among your customers from day one.

News from a friend concerning a new venture is your cue to make a phone call, write a note, or send an e-mail to express your best wishes and to provide encouragement and a vote of confidence. The most powerful expression of confidence you can make is based on your experience with your friend. Invoke your past together. Use this as the foundation for voicing your excitement and enthusiasm.

CAREER CHANGE—CONVERSATION

No, Bob, I don't think you're crazy to leave Benson & Goulding for an entry-level position in something you really love. You owe it to yourself to be the best—and I'm inclined to agree with you: You can't be your best at Benson & Goulding, doing what you're doing now.

You know, Bob, you're not alone in making a move like this. I read somewhere that, according to the Bureau of Labor Statistics, the average worker changes employers seven times in his working life—and changes *careers* at least three times!

So, I know it's scary. But you've made the decision, and I'm confident you will make a go of it. Just to hear the way you talk about the new field convinces me that you'll do great things.

A large part of encouragement is providing reinforcement for decisions that have already been made. Base that reinforcement on whatever facts you can muster. Remember, facts—not fancy words— are the most powerful instruments of persuasion.

TO A DISCOURAGED STUDENT

John, I really am sorry that the scholarship didn't come through for you. It's bad enough that you won't be getting the money, now don't beat yourself up over what you think this disappointment says about you. You know your record, and so do I. You are at the very top of you class, and nothing can change that. No one's denying that   scholarship would have made this coming year easier for you. But you ᵥₐn get along without it very nicely, too. Keep your eye on the prize. Don't let this distract you.

I don't mean to sound preachy, but you know that a big part of study is independence from outside reward and pats on the back. You need to just keep doing what you've been doing: achieving excellence for the sake of excellence—and to satisfy yourself. And if you do need some outside approval, well, just to turn to me.

Providing encouragement when the chips are down is a vital service, but it is not easy. "Feel good" speeches are not always appreciated by someone who has just suffered a disappointment. Your words of encouragement should, first and foremost, put the setback into perspective. This is a crucial first step toward refloating a sinking morale. Part of this process of maintaining perspective is to offer a mirror to your friend. Let his achievements be reflected in you. Remind him of what he has done and what he is capable of doing. Provide him with the means of seeing past a temporary problem. Finally, it is *always* a good idea to end on a note that reaffirms your friendship and the esteem with which you regard your friend. Don't let him feel diminished, let alone abandoned, by you.

Writing It: To Family

BUSINESS VENTURE—LETTER TO SON OR DAUGHTER

Dear Pat,

I'm writing because I am so thrilled about your plans for the store. You have done a magnificent job lining up the financing, and your knowledge of the industry and the retail picture is so thorough that I see nothing but success in your future. I am very excited about the location you have chosen, which, I agree, is both a high-demand area and one with remarkably little competition.

You know better than I do the nature of the challenges you will be facing, but I know—maybe even better than you do—how well equipped you are to handle those challenges and to turn them into opportunities.

Pat, dear, I can hardly wait to see the grand opening next month. This is going to be big for you, and it makes me very proud.

Love,

Dad

For something as momentous as a new business venture, a letter from father to child is highly appropriate and most welcome. In this age of rapid, casual communication, there is something ennobling and even ceremonial about a written, mailed letter. The document does not have to be profound, but if it is written in sincerity, it will be meaningful the moment it is read, and it will be preserved and treasured over the years.

In this letter, the father avoids preaching or dishing out advice. He gives a realistic, encouraging assessment of the child's skills and knowledge—the complete competence that will virtually ensure success. He does not deny that challenges lie ahead, but, again, he expresses confidence in the ability of his son or daughter not only to meet the challenges, but to capitalize on them.

While keeping the focus on the recipient of the letter, the writer also expresses his own love and enthusiasm.

CAREER DECISION—LETTER TO A DAUGHTER

Dear Meg,

I'm so happy we spoke yesterday about your decision to enroll in graduate school to continue your studies in anthropology. It is something you love, and so few people have the courage and determination to pursue what they love. I am very proud of you for having that courage.

The course work you've described to me does sound challenging, but also deeply fascinating. I believe it will expand and enrich your life, and I am also convinced that whatever the field of anthropology gives you, you will return to it a hundred-fold in terms of advancing knowledge and understanding.

I am eager to follow your adventure for the next few years.

Love,

Mom

This is a letter to a young adult daughter, and it recognizes and respects the woman's maturity. There is no debating or second guessing the young woman's choice. There is no discussion of possible financial hardships that a career in anthropology may present. Instead, the writer focuses exclusively on the positive aspects of the decision: The daughter is embarking on a career in a field she obviously feels passionately about.

REMARRIAGE PLANS—FATHER

Dear Dad,

It was great seeing you this weekend! I was thrilled by the news about Mary. You've been alone so long since Mom died that I was beginning to think you had given up on looking for someone. And Mary isn't just someone. She really seems to be *the* one. She is a lovely, funny, sweet lady. I liked her instantly.

Dad, I know the two of you will be very happy together. The chemistry is very apparent and very positive. I loved seeing the two of you together, and I absolutely believe you will be great for each other.

Love,

Sarah Ann

This letter not only provides important affirmation of the father's choice in remarriage, but also signals to him in unequivocal terms that the choice creates no conflicts. The single most encouraging thing the daughter can do in this case is to let her father know that she supports his plans and that she is happy for him. Why convey this in a letter instead of a conversation? In truth, it is best to do both; the letter should reinforce the conversation.

Writing It: To Friends

NEW BUSINESS VENTURE

Dear Max,

I greatly enjoyed talking with you about the new Internet business you are starting up. We both know how competitive the field is, but the more I've thought about your approach, as you explained it to me, the more I am convinced that you've really taken hold of something sensationally promising. If anything, I think that your projections are conservative. I'm just speaking from my own perceptions and business needs, of course, but if my case is at all representative, you should do very well indeed.

My confidence and enthusiasm are based on even more than my perception of the field. They are also founded on my experience with you, both as a friend and as a business associate. You have a way of making things work—and work very well.

All the best,

Sam

CAREER CHANGE

Dear Jane,

I was surprised by your announcement the other day about your radical shift in career direction. But, of course, I should not have been surprised at all. You have always been both adventurous and imaginative. In this context, your upcoming career move seems perfectly logical.

Naturally, I cannot tell you whether or not I think you are making the "right" move. I do believe, however, that it is a bad idea to fail to follow your dream, and I support your decision to set off in a new direction. I think this is important for you. And if anyone can pull off this kind of career move, I know that you can.

Best of luck,

Bill

Providing encouragement does not require you to generate false confidence in a positive outcome. Just don't dwell on your doubts. Instead, identify the most positive approach to the subject and pursue that course. Hollow encouragement or fabricated optimism is highly transparent and instantly discovered. The result is a loss rather than a building of confidence.

RETIREMENT PLANS

Dear Pat,

I envy you. The ideas you have for your upcoming retirement are simply remarkable. It's as if you've decided to "retire" into a whole new career. I certainly enjoyed discussing your plans, which are very inventive and highly worthwhile. You've managed to turn retirement into a whole new beginning.

The very best to you,

Ben

This brief letter is effective because it focuses on the most valuable and important aspect of the recipient's retirement plans—a retirement that really amounts to a second career. The most effective encouragement identifies special strengths or unique features of a plan, enterprise, or course of action and acknowledges as well as praises these.

E-Mailing It: To Family

CHANGE OF COLLEGE MAJOR—E-MAIL TO A SISTER

Joan:

I'm excited by your decision to change from pre-med to pre-law. I've always pictured you in a public-speaking role more than as a scientist, so I really do think that you are finding your groove by making the switch. I have known you to achieve nothing short of excellence, and I have every reason to believe that you will continue to do so in your new field.

Love—and have fun!

Pete

Be cautious when you offer an opinion on the wisdom of a course of action. However, if you really do approve of the choices that have been made, say so—and give your reasons. This is the most effective vote of confidence you can give. Does it assure the other person that she has made the right decision? Of course not; but it does let her know that you, at least, agree with the decision—and that, furthermore, your agreement is based on sound, well-thought-out reasons.

VACATION PLANS—E-MAIL TO PARENTS

Dear Mom and Dad:

So you're finally taking that world cruise you've been talking about since I was old enough to understand what you were talking about! I think it's a great idea. You deserve it—nobody deserves it more than you do. And, even more important, nobody will get more from it or appreciate it more than the two of you. Every trip, every vacation we ever took as a family you made special by your appreciation and understanding of each new site. I learned a great deal, and I had a wonderful experience. Now it is about time to do the same for yourselves. Bon voyage! I'm eager to see your pictures and hear your stories.

Love, Ned

The core of the encouragement here is assurance to the parents that this "extravagance"—a world cruise—is fully justified. They deserve to indulge themselves. This approval and affirmation, coming from a son or daughter, is bound to enhance the parents' experience of the cruise. Notice that the writer focuses exclusively on the positive:

The parents deserve the trip. He does not bring up any counter-position, such as "I know some people might think a cruise like this is extravagant and a waste of money, but . . ." When you provide encouragement, the cons are usually present by implication. Most of the time, it is better to avoid trotting them out explicitly. Instead, focus exclusively on the pros. This, of course, does not apply if you are actively helping another person to make a decision. In that case, it is essential to enumerate and to weigh the pros as well as the cons. But the essence of encouragement is reinforcement of a decision already made, not an occasion to raise doubts.

FACING SURGERY

Dear Mom—

Just a quick note to tell you what you already know, that we love you, and we are sending you all good thoughts. I am very impressed with Dr. Goodson and would have no qualms about putting myself in his very skilled hands. As for you, having been raised by you and loved by you, I know how very strong you are. That strength will get you through this, as it got Cindy and me through so much.

Mom, I'll see you after you come out of the recovery room tomorrow. You know that we'll be there to help you in every way.

Love,

Matt

If you know that your correspondent regularly reads his or her e-mail, this form of communication is ideal for quick, informal, even intimate messages. No occasion cries out more loudly for encouraging words than when your correspondent is facing a challenging, frightening ordeal such as surgery. Try to base your encouraging words as firmly on reality as possible. Usually, it is not necessary or advisable to discuss the details of diagnosis, prognosis, or procedure. These are matters between the doctor and her patient. However, if you are familiar with the reputation of the physician or the hospital, state your high opinion of these. Also draw on your experience of the patient. In this case, the writer assures his mother that he has experienced her strength and that this proven strength will carry her through.

At moments like this, it may be difficult to avoid expressing your own anxiety. Difficult though it is, do avoid it. Keep the focus on the correspondent, the patient. Address her situation and feelings, rather than your own. As you focus on the other person, maintain a thoroughly positive tone.

E-Mailing It: To Friends

NEW PROJECT IDEA

Danny:

I'm glad we talked this morning about the new software. I like the idea. I like it a lot. Based on my own experience with off-the-shelf accounting software, I'm convinced that your "custom modular" approach will be greeted with high enthusiasm.

I hope that you will contact Jim and Karen about venture capital. They love ideas like this.

Keep the faith and stick with it. This seems to me a real winner.

Cynthia

You don't have to be an expert to base your enthusiasm on facts. Just point out that you are drawing on your own experience. Do this, and your words of encouragement will not ring hollow. Note also here that the writer uses the terminology her correspondent has given her: "custom modular." This suggests that there is depth of comprehension, not just wishful thinking, involved in the assessment of the idea and the prediction of its success. Finally, the writer reiterates the item of practical aid she has offered—the names of potential investors. Repeating this information adds substance to the good wishes offered.

COPING WITH AN ILLNESS

Dear Penny,

Mike told me about your diagnosis. I was shocked, of course, and frightened, as I know you must have been. But, almost immediately, I remembered how strong you are, how resourceful, and how wise. When Mike told me about the medical team you had assembled, I realized that you were not about to let this thing get the best of you. You were fighting, and you were fighting intelligently.

And, of course, you're not in this alone. Your family, like you, is strong and loving and supportive. I know you have a horde of friends who are behind you, rooting and praying. I am one of them. Penny, if there is anything I can do to help you during this time, please, please, please don't hesitate to call.

I am thinking of you.

Love,

Marcia

Responding to a friend's illness generally calls for three things:

1. An expression of sympathy and fellow feeling
2. Encouragement and hope
3. A realistic offer of help

In expressing sympathy, take care. Do not tell the other person how horrible the situation is. Do not intensify a sense of calamity. Do not convey hopelessness. Do not paint a dark picture. Just let her know that you understand the situation is painful, difficult, and frightening. Make it clear that you do not take it lightly.

Base your offer of encouragement on what you know about the person—her strength, her supportive family, the level of medical care she is receiving. Do not offer false hope. Do not simply say, "I'm sure it's nothing" or "You'll come through this just fine." Do not offer medical opinions—unless you are a physician. Offer realistic encouragement only, but *do* offer it. Focus on the positive.

Finally, to the extent that you are able to do so, offer realistic help. Be prepared to act on this offer.

25 Words and Phrases to Use

ability	knowledge	thoughtful
adventure	optimistic	timely
calculated	planned	understanding
confident	prospects	venture
enterprise	right time	well-equipped
enthusiastic	skills	wisdom
exciting	smart	wise
experience	strength	
future	support	

25 Words and Phrases to Avoid

a breeze	luck	terrible
cinch	mistake	tough
crap shoot	no problem	tragic
dangerous	no sweat	trouble
don't worry	piece of cake	what will be will be
easy	risky	you'll be fine
failure	simple	you'll do fine
hopeless	sudden	
impossible	sure thing	

9

Celebration and Congratulation

Communicating celebration and congratulation is, if anything, easier than conveying encouragement (Chapter 8). The reason is that the success of the enterprise or project has already been achieved, so there is less risk of saying the wrong thing—of instilling doubt or worry instead of confidence, or of providing false confidence when this is not warranted. Nevertheless, inept or ineffective congratulations can create hard feelings, ill will, or disappointment. The same is true in the absence of any congratulation or celebration at all. In contrast, effective, heartfelt congratulation and celebration is a reward that makes everyone involved in the enterprise feel great. Even more, an effective congratulation contributes to the climate and conditions that may promote future success.

Finding the Heartline

The secret of effective expression of congratulation and celebration is to develop a dual perspective. Look backward, at what has been accomplished and achieved, but also look forward, to what the achievement predicts about the future. Too many congratulations are one sided, looking to the past only. This neglects the opportunity to make the achievement enduring and dynamic by applying it to the future. Congratulations are not just about history. They are also about the future.

As with so many other acts of communication at momentous times, it is important to begin by identifying the facts of the event and focusing on them.

- Focus on the facts; recount them.
- Identify the significance of the facts. What does the accomplishment mean? What effects does it have?

  After dealing with the facts, celebrate those who achieved them.

- Name names. Who did what?
- If appropriate, celebrate the teamwork involved.
- Finally, express your feelings and your appreciation.

Sidestepping the Pitfalls

The biggest mistake that is made where congratulations are called for is simply to fail to offer them. Any acknowledgment is better than none at all. Beyond this, avoid the following:

- *Empty, inflated praise.* When your friend makes employee of the month, don't tell him that it is "without a doubt" the greatest accomplishment in human history.

- *Faint praise.* Unless you can deliver heartfelt, unqualified congratulations, don't bother. Do not qualify your praise: "This is a great accomplishment for someone like you."

- *Uncomprehending congratulations.* Be certain that you understand what you are praising or celebrating. If your son graduated summa cum laude, don't congratulate him on graduating magna cum laude.

- *Pinning the person to the past.* Too often, well-meaning offers of congratulations are delivered as epitaphs. They imply that the achievement is over and done and that the achiever will never do better: "This is your masterpiece!" A statement like this is counterproductive. An effective congratulation celebrates achievement, but it also inspires new achievement. Look to the future as well as the past.

Saying It: To Family

WEDDING ANNIVERSARY—TO PARENTS

Are you both on the phone? Mom, Dad, I just wanted to congratulate you on loving—and deserving—one another for thirty years. In lesser people, this would be a remarkable achievement, but for a couple like you, loving and loyal, it must have come naturally. Your marriage is a lesson I have learned much from, and will always look to in my own life.

Too often, anniversary congratulations put such emphasis on the longevity of the relationship that the union comes off sounding like an epic ordeal or even a prison sentence. This phone call seeks both to recognize the achievement, but also to lighten the tone and ensure that the message is entirely celebratory. Note also the self reference—the "lesson" the son or daughter has learned. This both personalizes the congratulation and orients it toward the future.

HIGH SCHOOL GRADUATION—WORDS TO A SON OR DAUGHTER

Pat, this is a great day for you—and for your mother and me. What you have achieved no one can take away from you, and you are now ready to take the next step—into college—with real, solid, fullydeserved confidence. We are very proud, and you should be, too.

Let the achiever know that what she has accomplished not only enriches her life, but the lives of those close to her. There is nothing selfish about sharing in the achievement of another.

Note that these comments "define" the achievement of graduating from high school. That is, the speaker tells his daughter that she can legitimately derive confidence from the achievement. Congratulations should build confidence, and defining the achievement in this way does just that. Be careful, however, to avoid telling the achiever what to think and what to feel. Don't let your words pigeonhole the achievement by defining it too narrowly.

ON A SUCCESSFUL BUSINESS VENTURE—PHONE CALL TO A BROTHER

Max, it's Tom. Dad just told me that you closed the Anderson deal. I know how hard you've worked for it, and I'm just so happy that Anderson saw the light and chose you. That firm will be glad it did, and I'm thrilled that your hard work paid off. This should mean a great deal for your business and will open up a whole new market for you. It is very exciting.

Effective congratulations recognize that good things don't just happen. They're *earned* and *achieved* through hard work. By acknowledging this, you ensure that your words will not inadvertently diminish an achievement.

Saying It: To Friends

PURCHASE OF A NEW HOUSE

Hey, Buddy. Sally just told me the great news. You've closed on the house! This is wonderful. That house sounds like a dream, and I know the neighborhood well. It is a wonderful place to live. I know how tense a closing can be, but you guys handled it beautifully. I can hardly wait for you to get moved in so that Betty and I can visit!

Closing on a new house is an important achievement that deserves congratulations. This is an occasion for 100 percent celebration. Do not debate the pros and cons of the house or the location. Be fully positive. To the extent that you can, draw on your personal experience and knowledge.

AWARD RECEIVED

Jane, I can't say I'm surprised, but I sure am thrilled for you! If any project ever deserved the Smith Prize, yours certainly did. I think that was apparent to everyone. Your approach is so innovative and exciting that the jury really had no choice. Add to that the quality of the execution of the project, and it was a no brainer.

Jane, I have some idea of just how prestigious the award is, but what, exactly, will it mean for you?

You don't need to know everything to deliver heartfelt and persuasive congratulations. The speaker here provides several good reasons why the recipient deserved the award, and he acknowledges its importance; however, he also asks the recipient to tell him more. There is nothing at all wrong with this approach. Just make certain that your remarks in no way diminish the importance of the achievement.

BUSINESS DEAL

Well, Joe, you've bagged the whale! The Young account is quite a prize, and no one has worked harder or more intelligently than you to get it. The campaign you mounted was brilliant. I have to confess that it taught me a thing or two. Best of all, the people at Young will not be disappointed. Brilliant as the campaign was, the fact is that you can also deliver on what you promise. Congratulations!

Take care to avoid implying that an achievement was the product of good fortune, accident, hype, or that in any other way it was undeserved. Here, for example, the speaker praises the campaign that earned her friend the business he sought, but then is careful to point out that the campaign was based on solid achievement and ability.

Writing It: To Family

WEDDING ANNIVERSARY

Dear Mom and Dad,

A note for you on a very special day—your fortieth anniversary! I want you to know that, all my life, you have been for me an example of love, strength, and understanding. My family has benefited from your achievement in ways that make us all very, very grateful.

The very best to you today!

Love, Ted

BUSINESS ANNIVERSARY—NOTE TO AN IN-LAW

Dear Karen,

Your first year, come and gone already! And what a splash you've made! I don't personally know of any shop that has done so much in so short a time. In this past year, you've built a reputation that should propel you to ever greater heights. Press coverage has been tremendous, and word of mouth— well, let's just say that I hear an awful lot about you.

All of this is richly deserved, Karen. Your shop is a delight and a pleasure. I look forward to the next year and the next and the next . . .

All the best,

Stan

Anniversaries are such natural times for celebration and congratulations that it can be difficult to sound enthusiastic, let alone original. Don't strain yourself. Just identify the facts and address them. In this case, the writer begins with the fact that a year has passed and then continues with some details of the excellent reception the enterprise has received. The writer ends on a personal note, with the opinion that the shop is a delight.

COMPLETION OF MEDICAL DEGREE—TO A SISTER

Dear Doctor Sis,

I am so very, very proud of you. Of course, I knew you'd do it. All of our lives, you would set your mind to do something, figure out how to do it, plan how to do it, then you did it. This was no different—just longer and harder.

I realize you've got a lot of hard work ahead of you, a long, demanding, and very exciting residency. But you'll come out of it what you are destined to be: a great physician. It will be a terrific life for you, and you will, I believe, give a great, great deal to so many others.

Congratulations and love,

Ben

A truly significant achievement deserves a thoughtful letter written from the heart. People love to share good feelings, especially on occasions of achievement. Be generous with your feelings on such occasions. Here the writer recalls the childhood experience the two shared. Personalize your communications with facts, events, memories rather than mere words or prefabricated emotion.

Writing It: To Friends

ENGAGEMENT—TWO FRIENDS

Dear Sally and Gary,

It's about time! Mary and I have been biting our nails in suspense for almost a year now, wondering when the two of you would realize what all of us could see from the first time you guys met. You are made for each other. You—as a pair—are meant to be. I can't tell you how relieved we are now that you've finally recognized your destiny.

We know the two of you so well. We know what wonderful people you are. You deserve each other and will have a life of love together that will, I predict, be the stuff of legend.

Congratulations, best wishes, and love,

Frank and Mary

When you write to a good friend, visualize him or her. Hold a conversation. Writing to friends does not have to be very different from talking to them. Good-natured kidding is appropriate and welcome. Just make certain that it is good-natured and not belittling. Share good feelings good naturedly.

CAREER PROMOTION

Dear John:

Great news yesterday! Your firm is getting a great associate director. You will take your department to record heights. The fact that the firm realized who you are and what you can do speaks volumes for its wisdom. It knows it's lucky to have you on the team.

John, congratulations!

Carrie

Try a new approach to congratulations on a career-building promotion. Instead of patting the promotee on the back, reverse the situation by congratulating the company that did the promoting. The lucky one here is not your friend, but the firm that has hired and promoted him. There can be no higher or more genuine praise than this.

AWARD

Dear Janet,

Let me add my voice to the swelling chorus of congratulations on the recognition and honor you've received. Your moving and generous acceptance speech told the truth: The competition was extraordinary and extraordinarily worthy. But you were also too modest. I think it was clear to the membership from the moment the first reports on your project came in: You had achieved something memorable and remarkable, something well beyond any competitor.

I am thrilled for you, and I'm honored to be your friend.

Congratulations,

Sarah

An award is public recognition for an achievement. Even when communicating congratulations to a close friend, acknowledge the public nature of the award. Here the writer "adds" her voice to the "swelling chorus of congratulations"; she recognizes that hers is not the only congratulatory message that will be received, and, indeed, she celebrates that fact.

E-Mailing It: To Family

BIRTH—CONGRATULATIONS TO SISTER AND BROTHER-IN-LAW

Em and Ted,

If you're anything like Bill and me, you're thrilled, tired, and a little scared just now. Let me tell you, the thrill never really ends, and you will be tired more than a few times, and, more than a few times, you will be a little scared, but, all in all, you really have just begun the most rewarding years of your lives together. And you'll have a lot of fun, too!

Congratulations, you two—or, rather, you three. Kiss little Jenny for me.

Love,

Marcia

A birth is such a momentous event that many of us feel inadequate to find suitable words, words that are profound enough for the occasion. The best approach is not to try to make a great oration or launch into a flight of poetry. This is a time to summon up your own experience and to share it. Birth is the beginning of a voyage, and the novice voyagers will greatly appreciate any wisdom and knowing emotion you can share with them. Do, however, avoid reeling off a list of advice items, and do not tell the couple how they *should* feel.

BIRTHDAY GREETING—TO A BROTHER

Ken,

Welcome to the ranks of the "real" adults—those of us who have reached 30! I know it's a shock, but, believe me, life goes on and, as I have discovered, continues to be a lot of fun.

Speaking of fun, I'm sorry I can't be at your party today, but I wish you much happiness as you celebrate today.

Love, Sandi

Too often we forget that birthdays are occasions of celebration and congratulations. Consider a quick, personal e-mail as an alternative to a store-bought card—especially when the birthday involved is a milestone, such as turning thirty. Emphasize celebration and the future rather than the inevitable passage of time.

PROMOTION—TO A DAUGHTER

Cindy, Dear—

Your dad just told me the great news about your promotion. I can't say I'm surprised, but I am thrilled for you—and very proud. You were wise to choose to work for a company that obviously recognizes your talent and is willing to reward it. I know that you will continue to excel, and I hope that, through all the challenges you will face, you will find increased fulfillment and satisfaction.

Congratulations and love, Mom

In offering congratulations on a career promotion, take care to avoid implying that the promotion is in any way overdue: "Well, they've *finally* given you what you deserve." Your tone should be 100 percent positive. Here, the writer ensures that her daughter will not only feel good about herself and her achievement, but will also have good feelings about the company that has recognized her talent and ability.

PUBLICATION OF A MAGAZINE ARTICLE

Uncle Ed,

I just read your article in *Fishing Life* magazine. What a stunner! I particularly enjoyed the careful explanation of your spin-casting technique, something I've always admired. Now I feel as if I can emulate it, if not duplicate it. I'm so happy that *Fishing Life* published the piece, and I hope it will be the first of many more. It was an informative pleasure to read.

The one thing you can be sure a writer appreciates is being read. When you convey congratulations on a publication, show your genuine interest by saying something meaningful about the piece. If possible, don't just tell the author that you enjoyed what he wrote; tell him what you especially liked about the work. Flowery language, hyperbole, or lavish praise are not required. Solid, fact-based praise is far more welcome.

E-Mailing It: To Friends

CONTRIBUTION TO THE COMMUNITY

Gary:

A word of congratulation on your fine presentation to the Neighborhood Board meeting last night. Your report on crime prevention in the community was extraordinarily detailed and insightful. Most important, it was filled with ideas that are perfectly feasible and well within our capability as a community organization. We all appreciate your hard work, and I am delighted that you are on our team.

Best,

Hannah Cohen

An achievement does not have to be epoch-making to deserve congratulations. The ready availability of e-mail communication makes it easy and convenient to acknowledge contributions of all kinds. Timeliness is of the essence in such informal communications. Compose and transmit them as soon as possible after the occasion in question.

BIRTHDAY

Terri,

As always, today is starred on my calendar: Your birthday! I'm sorry I'm not in town to celebrate it with you, but I trust your many (other) friends will make it a happy occasion.

Here's to a great year!

Tom

Never let a birthday greeting come across as an obligation. Note the detail the writer includes here: "today is starred on my calendar." A deft touch like this is bound to make the recipient feel special—and that is what birthday congratulations are all about.

AWARD

Dear Fred,

I just read in *Marketing News* that the Grainger Prize was awarded to— who?—*you!* If it had been given to me, I'd have been on the phone to you in a New York minute. But you, you're so modest that you didn't even mention it when we spoke the other day.

Winning the Grainger is a great achievement, and you richly deserve it. As you know, you join a very distinguished roster of recipients. I've always been honored to call you my friend, now I'm even more proud to do so.

All the best,

Ray

If you hear of your friends' achievements indirectly, through a third party or in the media, dash off a timely congratulations. Let your friends and associates know that you are thinking of them and that you are always interested in what they are doing.

25 Words and Phrases to Use

accomplishment	fulfilling	skilled
achievement	hard work	success
award	news	successful
congratulations	pleased	thought
contribution	praise	triumph
delighted	proud	value
deserve	recognition	wise
distinguished	rewarding	
enduring	satisfying	

6 Words and Phrases to Avoid

it's about time	luck of the draw	surprising
luck	lucked out	unexpected

10

Asking Favors

$\mathcal{N}$obody likes asking for a favor, right? After all, from childhood, most of us are trained "not to impose" and not to expect "something for nothing." Well, it's true: Imposing on others and angling to get something for nothing are not attractive options. Fortunately, there is another option. Rethink the definition of *favor*.

Instead of thinking of your request as a bid to get something for nothing, look at it as *giving* someone an opportunity to help you. The key word here is *opportunity*. Why? Because the fact is that most people actually enjoy helping others.

- Being asked to help empowers the helper.
- Being asked to help is a compliment and a vote of confidence.
- Being asked to help provides an opportunity to feel good about oneself.

Most of the world's religions include a tenet of faith that is similar to the concept of karma found in Hinduism and Buddhism. Karma is the total effect of a person's actions in the world. As popularly and informally conceived, karma is the notion that what goes around comes around. That is, doing someone a favor creates goodwill that will ultimately benefit the doer of the good deed as much as it does the recipient of the favor.

The bottom line? The world is actually ready and willing to help you out.

Finding the Heartline

To find the heartline when you request a favor, transform your request into an opportunity to help.

Begin by providing a basis for the request. This will get you past what most people find most difficult about asking for a favor: simply broaching the subject. Try some of these approaches:

- "We've been friends so long that I feel comfortable asking you for a favor."

- "You know so much about computers that I'd like to ask you for some help."

- "Dad, I need your help."

After establishing the basis for asking for help, describe what you want. Be clear and specific. Be realistic in your request. Tell the truth— but don't stop there. Continue by explaining how the favor will benefit you. This is important, because it will give the other person a way to gauge just how much he or she can help.

Sidestepping the Pitfalls

In a letter or e-mail, conclude with an expression of appreciation, but do not make the mistake of using such phrases as "thanking you in advance." This implies that you take your correspondent's compliance for granted. It is offensive, and it may be embarrassing for both of you. In a direct conversation, be certain to express your thanks only *after* you have secured the favor. Never take compliance for granted.

Here are other all-too-common pitfalls to avoid:

- Telling the other person how much you "hate to ask" for a favor. This sends a number of negative messages. It suggests that the favor will be unpleasant or difficult to perform. It also suggests that you doubt the other person's generosity.

- Telling the other person how to feel. "I know that you must hate being asked for favors, but . . ." Why plant a negative response?

- Minimizing the extent of the favor requested. If, for example, you know that performing the favor will require an hour of time, don't tell the other person that you only need a "minute or two."

- Making promises you cannot keep. "If you help me, I'll use my influence to get you such-and-such." Such quid pro quo promises are, in fact, not requests for favors at all, but, rather, business propositions. Made honestly, there is nothing wrong with such a deal. Just be aware that it is not a request for a favor, which requires no explicit quid pro quo.

Saying It: To Family

REQUEST TO BOARD A PET

> Mom, I have a favor to ask you. Jenny and I are going out of town next month. We'll be gone for a week. I hate to board Fido in a kennel for that time. He loves you, loves Dad, and he loves your backyard. It would be great for all of us if you could take him for six days, from July 2 through the 7th.

The request is forthright and factual, with the focus on what the dog needs and loves, rather than on what the requester wants. The basis for the favor is how the dog "feels" about Mom, Dad, and their backyard. Who could resist such a request?

FINANCIAL HELP

> Hi, Dad. My old beater finally gave up the ghost—blew a head gasket—and I need a new car. As you know, the car's the only way I can get from school to my job. Dad, I found a good used (MAKE, MODEL, YEAR) for just under $10,000. I can get financing, but I need help with the down payment. Can you loan me $1,000? It would really help me out. I didn't expect to have to buy a car at this time.

Don't prey on your relatives. Don't plead. Don't whine. Don't try to make them feel guilty. State your need and all the relevant facts. Give the other person the data he needs to make the decision you want. Don't try to make the decision for him. Here, the speaker clearly states the need: A new car, because the old one is beyond repair. He goes on to detail the urgency of the need: A car is essential transportation between school and work. The speaker does not ask for a vague sum to cover a vague expense, but gives the particulars—make, model, year, and price. He then asks for exactly what he needs, then closes by telling his father that the loan will *help* him. Remember, most people derive satisfaction from helping. To help another person is an empowering and, therefore, fulfilling and satisfying experience.

ADVICE

> Mom, you and Dad have bought three houses, which, as far as I'm concerned, makes you real estate experts. As you know, we've just started looking at houses, and, before we get too far into the process, I'd like to come by with Ed to get some advice from the two of you. Any evening this week would be great for us.

Many people enjoy giving advice, but, make no mistake, to ask for advice is still to ask for a favor. Don't take advice for granted. Ask for it in a way that shows how much you value the advice and how much you appreciate the effort that will be made in giving it.

Saying It: To Friends

RESCHEDULE A PLANNED DINNER

> Harry, I'm beginning to think that everything our parents told us is wrong. For example: "Plan ahead." We planned our dinner Tuesday a month back. My schedule was clear, and so was yours. Now, suddenly, my boss needs me to go out of town to troubleshoot a major crisis with one of our top accounts. I know this is awfully short notice, but can we reschedule? I know how hard it is to rejuggle your schedule, but Dan and I really want to get together with the two of you, and I just cannot get out of this trip.

Changing carefully made plans can be very upsetting. This speaker prepares for it with mild humor followed by a clear explanation of the scheduling problem she faces. Although you should never tell the other person how to feel or discourage him by implying that the favor requested is difficult or troublesome, in a case like this, it is necessary to acknowledge that what is being requested requires effort and does cause inconvenience. Don't add to the other person's feeling of burden, but do acknowledge the effort required.

BUSINESS REFERRAL—TELEPHONE CALL

Hi, Pete. It's Sarah. I ran into a friend of yours yesterday, Eunice Williams, who, it turns out, is in the market for a new widget. I'd sure like to sell her one. Of course, I gave her our literature and discussed some of the options with her, but nothing would be more valuable or helpful than a good word from you. Would you be able to give her a call today to say one or two kind things about me? What she's particularly concerned about is after-sale customer service, so if you could speak up about our "never-on-hold" policy, I think she'll do business with us. She's a nice lady, and I would enjoy doing business with her.

Here is a good example of the straightforward approach. There is no dramatic buildup to the favor. The other person is not kept in suspense. Instead, the facts are presented:

1. I met a friend of yours.
2. I want to sell her something.
3. Your help would be valuable.

Notice that the caller is careful to indicate that Eunice Williams is genuinely interested in buying the widget. It is important for the other person to know that, in calling Eunice, he will not only be helping the person requesting the favor, but will also help his other friend, Eunice Williams. That is, he is being of assistance to the seller as well as the customer.

The caller in this case is also careful to follow an important rule when asking for a recommendation or referral: Give the other person something to say. Don't just ask for a referral or recommendation; supply an item or two to be discussed—in this instance, a mention of the "never-on-hold" customer service policy.

Finally, note how the caller shows regard for Eunice Williams, who is, after all, a friend of the person from whom she is requesting a favor. She is not just a customer, but a "nice lady" with whom it would be a pleasure to do business. Take every opportunity to present yourself as unselfish. Focus on the needs and feelings of others—especially when you are asking for a favor for yourself.

MOVING HELP

Ben, you are a good friend and a strong man, which are the two reasons for my call. I've just bought a sofa from the elderly woman who lives down the block. She's pushing 80, weighs maybe 90 pounds, and I think you'll appreciate my reluctance to ask her to help me heft the sofa out of her apartment. So, would *you* be able to give me a hand? I've got the loan of a pickup truck for tomorrow afternoon, if you could get away . . .

This caller begins, half humorously, with the basis for his favor. His friend is both a friend and a "strong man." This good-natured touch of flattery paves the way for the request. The caller builds on the humor by explaining why the little old lady can't give him a hand. Again, this serves to keep the tone of the request light, but it also signals that no one else is available, so underscores the need for the help of a friend. Finally, the caller makes it clear that he has already attended to a key transportation issue, which not only allays any anxiety the friend may have about being called on to provide transportation, but gives added urgency to the request: The job needs to be done tomorrow afternoon. In asking for a favor, it is important to eliminate vagueness. Make clear what you need and when you need it, but avoid making this information come across as a demand. Be certain to supply a reason for any deadlines.

Writing It: To Family

FINANCIAL HELP—LETTER TO SISTER

Dear Marge,

The good news is that I'm starting a new job next week, at the Acme plant, and at 15 percent more than I was making at the old job. The bad news is that the credit card people are breathing down my neck, and I won't have my first paycheck for another three weeks. Could you float me a loan of $1,250 until the 30th? I can pay you in full at that time, plus $125 interest.

Marge, this isn't a matter of life or death, but the loan will keep my credit rating intact. It would be a very great help to me. You can call me at home.

Love,

Tom

Asking for a loan can be hard, and some people find it easier to write rather than call. The writer leads off with the positive news, which directly addresses his ability to repay the loan he is about to ask for. He then makes clear the short-term nature of the loan he is requesting, but also its urgency. The writer is very specific about why he needs the money, how much he needs, how long he needs it for, and when, how, and how much he will repay. Such detail is critical when requesting a loan. Finally, the writer presents his need realistically: His life won't end if his sister doesn't lend him the money, but his standing with the credit card company will be damaged. Do not apply false or misleading pressure to the person from whom you are asking a favor. Present your case fully and honestly. Neither minimize nor inflate your needs.

EXTENSION OF LOAN REPAYMENT DEADLINE— LETTER TO SISTER

Dear Marge,

This month, I have had some unexpected expenses, including the sudden need to get my car's transmission rebuilt. If it is at all possible, can you extend the due date on my loan repayment by thirty days? If it will help, I can pay half now and the balance by the 30th of next month.

I imagine you were counting on being paid in full by the end of this month, but if you can hold out for another thirty days, it would be a very great help to me.

You can reach me at the home number or at the office, 555-555-5555.

Love,

Tom

If asking for a loan is difficult, asking for an extension of a repayment deadline can be even harder. Don't dwell on your embarrassment or guilty feelings. Doing so will only make the other person feel bad or, even worse, resentful of being emotionally pressured. The best approach is to express yourself in more emotionally neutral terms. Provide the facts, including the problem or problems that prevent you from meeting the original deadline and a proposed alternative to the original deadline. Providing alternative options to nonpayment or late payment allows the other person to avoid feeling as if she has been deceived or cornered.

SPEAK AT A MEETING

Dear Aunt Ida,

You are a natural storyteller. You know it, I know it, and our whole family knows it. I'd like to ask you to share your gift with a little wider audience—the members of my Travel Club.

We are a group of about fifty men and women—mostly women—who get together once a month to swap travel recommendations and stories. It suddenly occurred to me that *you* have some of the best travel stories of anybody I've ever heard or, for that matter, *read*.

Would you be willing to talk to us for about forty minutes? It would be fun for you, I think, and I know it would be a hoot for our club members. The meeting after next—that's on November 8—is wide open just now. Please give me a call and say you'll come and talk to us.

Love,

Betty

Flattery, when it is sincerely delivered and genuinely deserved, is a great persuader. The writer has good reasons for inviting her aunt to talk to her club, and expressing these reasons involves sincere tribute to the woman's talent as a teller of tales. The writer does not plead and does not beg, but wisely lets her reasons do the persuading for her. She merely asks her aunt to do what she is good at doing.

Writing It: To Friends

JOB FOR A RELATIVE

Dear Mary,

I swore I would never do what I am about to do: Ask a friend to interview a member of my family for a job. Well, we can both stop groaning, because the pleasant surprise is that my nephew, Gary Unger, is a bright, eager, thoroughly delightful young man who is about to graduate from State with a major in accounting and a 3.8 GPA. He interned for two summers at Acme, Inc., whose general manager, Clara Weeks, will furnish any references you require.

In all, Mary, I guess I don't feel too guilty about breaking my pledge. If you are at all inclined to interview Gary, you can call him directly at 555-555-5555 or, if you prefer, give me a call first at 555-555-4444. We both appreciate your consideration.

All the best,

Mike

Asking a friend to consider a relative for a job is a major request. It should be presented in a friendly but businesslike manner, with the emphasis on what the job candidate has to offer. Underscore the value of the referral rather than the fact of friendship.

Note that this writer recognizes that prevailing on a friend to interview a relative may put the friend on the defensive. After all, the referral does not come from an unbiased source. For this reason, the writer begins by light-heartedly addressing the issue of people who recommend relatives for jobs. Sometimes, it is best to begin a request for a favor by clearing the air.

RECOMMENDATION

Dear Carla,

Can you help me?

I interviewed at Smith and Son for the position of assistant manager in one of their best branch stores. Understandably, they're looking for a 100 percent dependable person with good people skills. I have a slew of business references, but I thought it would also be great to let these folks talk to one of my closest friends.

Could you give Jane Clark—she's director of Human Resources—a call at 555-5555? You might fill her in on our friendship and, in particular, on the work we've done together for the Community Chest. Your good words would mean a lot to me.

With thanks,

Amos

Business recommendations from friends are often useful supplements to recommendations from colleagues and professional associates. Be sure to provide all the necessary contact information. Don't try to dictate what the person should say, but do feel free to make some recommendations or outline a subject or two.

PLACE TO STAY

Dear Fran and Dan,

I will be coming through Detroit at the end of the month for the widget convention and would love to mix business with pleasure by staying with you instead of at a hotel. Can you put me up—and put up with me—for three days, from the 29th through the 31st? My days will be occupied with the convention, but I'll have the evenings free, and it would be great to get together with the two of you.

Please give me a call at 555-555-5555. Don't worry if you can't accommodate me, but it *would* be great to spend some time together, and I really want to see your new house.

Best to you both,

Paul

This writer makes it clear that he very much wants to stay with his friends, but he is also careful to avoid applying undue pressure. He closes by letting his friends know that, if they cannot accommodate him, it will not create any great problem. It is always most desirable to frame requests for favors as positively as possible.

E-Mailing It: To Family

MAKE A PURCHASE

Janey—

One of the few things I don't like about living in Smallville is the absence of anything even remotely resembling a fine food store. I need a really nice Gouda cheese, and you, dear sister, are the only person I can trust to buy some for me. You know what's good, and you know what I like.

Please buy a half-pound of the best. Have the store send it directly to me, and have them bill me directly, too. There's no big rush, but I need the cheese for a party on the 25th. People out here have never tasted great cheese, so your mission of mercy is bound to change some lives.

Madeleine

Sometimes it is fun to couch routine, even mundane requests in colorful language. Let your sense of fun convey your affection for your correspondent.

LOCATE A FORGOTTEN ITEM

Mom,

Yesterday, I was looking for my high school yearbook. I looked for a good hour or so before I realized that I never took it with me and that it is at the house, somewhere up in the attic. I'm trying to get in touch with some old friends, and I'd really like to get at the yearbook. Could I trouble you to rummage in the attic for it before I come out to visit on Sunday? You know that attic a lot better than I do.

Love,

Glenn

A quick e-mail is a convenient means of communicating a request for a simple favor to be performed in a timely manner. Because you don't want a request to come across as a command or a demand, consider framing it as a question: "Could I trouble you to rummage in the attic for it before I come out to visit on Sunday?" This naturally softens the tone.

BORROW AN ITEM

Patty,

I am so happy that you will be coming to the party Friday night. Could I borrow your big, beautiful punch bowl for the event? I know how much you value it, but I promise that I will guard it with my life. I could pick it up Thursday afternoon or evening.

Doris

The writer paves the way for her simple request by bringing up the impending party and reminding Patty that she will be a part of the festivities. Note that the writer signals her appreciation of the value of the item she asks to borrow. A prospective lender likes to know that her treasure will be safeguarded and treated with care.

E-Mailing It: To Friends

HOUSE SIT

Dear Ed,

Maggie and I are planning a three-week vacation this summer during August, and it occurred to us both that we would be much more comfortable leaving if we knew our house was being watched by a trusted friend.

Can you house sit for us, Ed, during August? We know that there's no place like home, but it's also good to get a change of scene once in a while, and you'd be welcome to use our membership in the neighborhood swimming pool while we're gone. As far as guests go, invite whomever you want. Our house will be yours. We want you to be comfortable—because we want you to say *yes*. How about it?

Yours, Nat

A lightly bantering tone is appropriate between good friends. Here the writer applies a little good-natured pressure at the end: "we want you to say *yes*." With your very close friends, you should feel free to express forthrightly what you want.

ADVICE

Jack,

I need the advice of someone with taste and expertise in home decorating. Since your house is the most beautiful of any I have ever been in, you're my nominee. Would you be able to accompany me to Home Showcase on Friday or Saturday to help me choose some wallpaper? I really just cannot make a decision about such things, and I need all the intelligent advice I can get. I'll take you out to lunch afterward. Is it a date?

Yvonne

Honor the person from whom you seek advice. Prove how much you value his opinion.

Generally, it is best to keep a request for a favor distinct from a quid pro quo business proposal ("You do this for me, and I'll do this for you."); however, there is nothing wrong with incorporating a modest token of gratitude into the request you make. Here, for example, the writer includes an invitation to lunch, thereby transforming the request for a favor into something of a social event ("Is it a date?").

25 Words and Phrases to Use

accommodate	caring	counsel
advice	considerate	friend
appreciate	consideration	grateful
assistance	could you	great

help	need	thought
important	permission	valuable time
judgment	please	valuable
make a big	request	wisdom
difference	thanks	

18 Words and Phrases to Avoid

a drag	must
chance of a lifetime	pain in the neck
deadline	require
demand	rush
don't say no	this will be easy
I hate to ask	you can't refuse
I'll never bother you again	you can't turn me down
I'll scratch your back if you scratch mine	you must
insist	you won't want to do this, but

11

Invitation and Welcome

*J*nvitations simultaneously ask a favor and bestow a compliment. They request the presence of someone's company, even as they extend the great compliment of offering to share your valuable time with another. If you approach invitations from this dual perspective, you will make them effective and heartfelt.

Closely associated with an invitation is the act of welcoming. Welcoming is, in fact, a broad invitation to a newcomer to join your team, your community, your circle of friends. Approach welcoming from the same dual perspective that governs invitations. To welcome someone is a profound act of generosity, the extension of your hand toward a newcomer, but it is also a request for the favor of that person's acceptance of you and what you and your circle have to offer.

Finding the Heartline

Invitations are a balancing act. Not only do you need to combine a message of compliment with a request for the favor of the correspondent's company, you must also convey a sincere, warm tone without neglecting the nitty-gritty of the invitation as a communication of clear and specific information. Remember the journalist's all-important five questions: *Who? What? When? Where? Why?* Each of these five questions must be answered in an effective invitation. Miss any one of these, and the invitation, no matter how warm and sincere, will be a failure. Let's take a closer look:

- The *who* is the person or persons you are inviting. Be clear about this. Is the spouse or significant other welcome? What about children?
- The *what* is, first and foremost, the occasion. Be clear about the purpose of the event—a birthday party, a dinner party, a holiday celebration, whatever. Your invitation should also specify *what* type of response you want. If you want the invitee to call and tell you whether or not he can attend, be sure to ask for a reply. If the invitation is at all formal, you can write R.S.V.P. (*Répondez s'il vous plaît*) or the phrase "Please Respond" somewhere on the invitation, followed by your phone number and, if necessary, a date by which you need the reply. An alternative to the request for a response is your promise that you will call to confirm. If you make such a promise, be sure that you do, indeed, call. If you are inviting a large number of people to an event, consider substituting the phrase "regrets only" for R.S.V.P. This way, only those who cannot attend need call you.

Before we leave the *What?* question, be sure to include in the invitation any other special "whats." For example, you might specify what to wear—"black tie optional," "come as you are," "bring your swimsuit," whatever is appropriate. You might ask invitees to contribute their favorite food or drink.

- The *when* should specify the date and time of the event. Be specific.
- The *where* is the place. Again, be specific and avoid confusion. Supply an accurate address. If the event is to take place in a restaurant, get the name right and include an address. This is especially important if the restaurant is part of a chain with multiple locations. Be certain to furnish clear and accurate directions to the location.
- The *why* is the purpose of the occasion. This does not mean that all parties have to focus on a specific occasion—a birthday, an anniversary, and such. But you can make even a nonspecific event special: "Please come to my 'It's-Been-Ages-Since-We've-Seen-Each-Other' party." Specify such details as a cocktail party, a pool party, a Super Bowl party (a get-together to watch the big game on TV), a dinner party.

Remember, communicating a message of welcome is similar to an invitation in that it is an extension of your hospitality and generosity even as it is simultaneously a request that the newcomer accept your offer of friendliness. Effective gestures of welcome also recognize that the recipient of the message, as a newcomer, is in the midst of change. Most of us find some aspects of change refreshing and exciting, but also unnerving and anxiety-provoking, perhaps even traumatic. The warmth of your welcome can go a long way toward heightening the excitement of change while reducing the anxiety associated with it. Extending a message of welcome is more than a polite act; it is an opportunity to make another person feel good—about himself, about the group or community he is about to join, and about you.

Sidestepping the Pitfalls

The most common and most serious problem with many invitations is a failure to answer fully, adequately, and clearly the five questions, *Who? What? When? Where? Why?* Invitations should bring pleasure and pleasure only. Failure to present all the relevant information and to present it clearly creates not pleasure, but frustration, irritation, and even anxiety.

Another invitation pitfall is neglecting to take full advantage of an excellent opportunity for communication. While all invitations must include answers to the five *W* questions, an invitation truly conveyed from the heart should include even more. Take the opportunity to convey something of your feelings about the person you are inviting.

Gestures of welcome, fortunately, present few pitfalls. Just about any expression of welcome will be accepted with gratitude. Nevertheless, do avoid the following:

- *Pushing or forcing yourself on the newcomer.* It may take weeks or months or even longer for a newcomer to feel fully comfortable in new surroundings. This is natural. Don't force the process by claims that you want to be the person's "best friend" or that you intend to introduce her to "absolutely everybody."

- *Making the newcomer feel anxious about fitting in.* Don't imply that the new situation is fraught with dangers. That is, avoid such statements as "You need someone to show you the ropes.

Things can be very complicated here," or "Let me guide you through this minefield." Always accent the positive. It may be true that the newcomer needs guidance, but the negative aspects of this message should be avoided in an initial communication of welcome.

Saying It: To Family

LUNCH—PHONE CALL TO MOTHER

Hi, Mom. Can I take you to lunch Wednesday? I was thinking of Fabio's at, say, one. You know where Fabio's is, on the corner of Main and Fifth. It's been so long since we just went out together, relaxed, and talked. I really miss talking with you—and, with my new job, I have a lot to talk with you about.

This brief phone call says it all. In a few words, it includes all of the information an effective invitation should have. In addition, it conveys genuine warmth, the unmistakable message of love.

SURPRISE PARTY FOR SPOUSE—PHONE CALL TO SISTER

Cheryl, I'm planning a surprise birthday party for Sam on the 23rd. I'm taking him to dinner at Jason's Place. Do you know where that is? Good. And you and Ben can make it? Great!

You should get there by 6:30—no later. Go to the back room. About a dozen people have been invited. I'll be by with Sam at 7. You know the drill: Everyone yells *Surprise!*

Dinner will be catered, and the drinks are on me. Sam will be thrilled that you're there, and I'm so glad that you can make it! And, *please*, let's keep this a surprise. Be sure to tell Ben not to let the cat out of the bag.

This informal invitation covers all the informational bases, with emphasis on the surprise aspect of the party. Always be sure to include any special instructions that may be necessary; in this case, a reminder to be careful to avoid spoiling the surprise.

WELCOME TO A NEW TOWN—PHONE CALL TO A COUSIN

Hi, Cousin! Welcome to Plainville. You have no idea how thrilled I am to have you in town. It will be like old times, when we used to visit each other's houses. Like being kids again.

Listen, let me give you a day or two to get settled, then I'd like to drive you around downtown to show you my favorite places to shop and eat. There are a lot of very nice shops and restaurants in town. I think you'll be very pleasantly surprised. I'll call you on Wednesday. In the meantime, if there is anything I can do to help you find your way or settle in, just give me a call.

The caller clearly understands that a message of welcome should help allay the anxiety of change. She immediately summons up the past, remarking that her cousin's "new" experience will be like "old times." The caller goes on to offer guidance and to make the new town sound inviting; however, she is also careful not to intrude herself on the newcomer. She recognizes the need for a day or two to "settle in." Finally, the caller sets a specific day for the next contact. A message of emotional warmth need not be fuzzy and vague. Clear information and specific plans are by no means incompatible with friendly, informal, heartfelt communication.

Saying It: To Friends

DINNER INVITATION

Larry, I'm so happy I ran into you. I was about to call you this evening to invite you and Pat to dinner at our house. Sarah and I were just talking about how much we enjoyed getting together with you last month—we have so much in common—and we thought it would be a great idea to have the two of you over. We were thinking about a week from Friday—that's the 5th—say, 7 o'clock. We could start with drinks.

Why don't you talk it over with Pat, and I'll call you this evening, around nine. We would love to get together with the two of you.

Don't expect an off-the-cuff and on-the-spot invitation to elicit a final, definitive response. Here the speaker conveys his enthusiasm for the couple he is inviting, but he also recognizes that a response to the invitation will require Larry's consulting with Pat. Instead of putting the burden of the response on the invitee, the speaker makes a clear arrangement for a follow-up call. This is a good strategy, but it requires the host to ensure that he does indeed make the follow-up call as promised and when promised.

WELCOME TO MEMBERSHIP IN A SOCIAL ORGANIZATION— PHONE CALL

Marty, your first meeting is tomorrow evening! This is exciting for all of us. I can't wait to introduce you around. We have a great organization, with interesting and very friendly members. I'm so happy you joined us, and I know you'll be pleased, too. The organization is a great way to make business as well as social contacts, but it's also just plain fun being with a group of people who enjoy getting together with each other.

Do you have all the information you need? Time and place? Do you need directions to the restaurant?

The caller takes care to reinforce his friend's decision to join the organization, assuring him that membership offers valuable business and social benefits and is "just plain fun" as well. The caller's purpose is to ensure that his friend feels good about what he is doing. Notice that he emphasizes the excitement he and the other members feel about the new member. He is careful to avoid implications of exclusivity or that the new member will be judged or evaluated in any way. Nor does he imply that his friend is lucky to have been chosen. Instead, the focus is put on making him feel welcome.

Writing It: To Family

INVITATION TO A WEDDING—NOTE TO BROTHER

Dear Hank,

Tyrone and I are getting married on Saturday, June 23. The ceremony will be held at 2 P.M. at First Christian, 1234 Young Street, here in Thornton. The reception will begin at 5, at Davidson's, 5678 Brewster Lane.

Hank, as you can imagine, I am very excited, and I would be even more thrilled if you could be here. Please try. I especially want you to meet Ty, and having you share the day will make it absolutely perfect for me. Please call me at 555-555-5555 to let me know if you can make it. And, please, bring a friend!

Not all wedding invitations have to be store bought and formally engraved. For special people or in special circumstances, consider sending a personal note, in which you can express yourself fully. Just remember to include all the basic and essential information, along with your personal message.

This is an example of a strongly worded invitation. The writer wants to make clear how much she wants her brother to attend the wedding; note, however, that she stops well short of pleading. The intention here is unmistakable, but the tone is thoroughly positive and upbeat.

INVITATION TO A FAMILY REUNION

Dear Carlson Family Member:

For the first time ever, we are trying to assemble as many Carlsons as we can find for a mammoth Family Reunion.

The place is Grinder Park, Picnic Ground C, in Mason City, Utah. Please see the attached map for detailed directions.

The date is June 14.

The hour is 10 A.M. until well after dark.

The goal is fun, fellowship, and a great time. We will settle for nothing less.

Please, move heaven and earth to attend. I'd appreciate a call at 555-555-5555 to let us know if we can look forward to your being there. I've also attached a list of the Carlsons I've invited. If any of you know of anyone who is not on the list, please call me with the information. We want to reach everyone!

Love to all,

Edna Carlson
1234 Gary Street
Penn, UT 12345

When inviting a large group of people, a generic invitation can be useful. Not only does it save time and effort, it can actually create a sense of community and togetherness. This invitation spells out all of the necessary information and introduces a lighthearted tone in its statement of the "goal" of the reunion. It also focuses on inclusiveness. Where family reunions are concerned, the more truly is the merrier, so the writer leaves no doubt as to her intention to reach as many Carlsons as possible. Thus the invitation becomes something more than personal and individual. It is an invitation to participate in a group effort, a collective, a collaboration.

Writing It: To Friends

INVITATION TO JOIN A CLUB

Dear Joan,

I know that you've heard me talk about our Saturday Evening Book Club and how much I enjoy it. We're a small group—we like it that way—and so the opportunity to invite a new member does not come up often. I'm happy to tell you that we have room for a new member, and I cannot think of anyone I would rather have join us than you. Nor can I think of anyone who would enjoy membership more than you, an avid reader, a great conversationalist, and someone who enjoys the company of kind and interesting people. So, you and the Book Club seem to me, beyond question, a natural fit.

Joan, please consider this letter a formal invitation to our next meeting, Saturday evening, the 15th, at 8:30. We meet at one another's homes, on a rotating basis. This Saturday, the meeting is at Chris Jenson's house, 568 West Adams. If you like, you can come over to my house first, about 7:30, and we can go to Chris's together. The book we're discussing is *How Deep Is My Ocean* by Eunice Carver—but you don't have to read it prior to the meeting. The idea is just to sit in and see how you like the group.

Please give me a call by Friday evening, Joan, to let me know if you would like to attend—or if you have any questions. It would be wonderful to have you as a member.

Yours,

Paula

When inviting a friend to join a club, remember that such an invitation is a two-way street. The effective invitation conveys that the club is right for your friend and your friend is right for the club. You might want to think of yourself as a kind of matchmaker, someone who represents the interests both of the organization and of the prospective new member.

Note that the writer here is careful to provide all necessary information, and she thoughtfully suggests that the newcomer accompany her to the first meeting, something that might make her friend more comfortable.

WELCOME TO THE COMPANY

Pete—

Thanks for the great news! You've taken the job here at Perkins. I'm thrilled for you, and I'm excited for our firm. Most of all, I look forward to working with such a good friend.

Pete, I firmly predict that you will love working here. You are joining a great group of people, who will welcome and reward your contributions. I've arranged with Bill Williams and Clara Foley, the heads of advertising and marketing, to have lunch with you and me on your first day. They're people you should meet right away, and I want them to get to know you. I'll pick you up at your office just before noon on the 15th.

Welcome aboard!

Ann

This letter is designed to make a friend feel at home in a new job. It is 100 percent positive, and it creates the impression that the writer is determined to help her friend hit the ground running. The writer also understands that the essence of communicating welcome is to convey the *mutual* benefits of the new situation. In this case, the company is right for the new recruit, and the recruit is just right for the new company.

E-Mailing It: To Family

INVITATION TO A CHRISTMAS PARTY—MULTIPLE E-MAIL

Dear Children,

Dad and I are giving our annual Christmas Party on the 23rd, here at the house. This year, we've decided to start an hour earlier, at 7 p.m. instead of 8, for one reason and one reason only: to start having a good time an hour sooner.

There will be the usual drinks and food, and everyone gets a Christmas stocking. The sing-along, as always, is mandatory. No excuses.

Please reply to this message only if you *can't* attend.

Love to all,

Mom

E-mail is a great way to communicate to a set group of recipients quickly and with a minimum of effort. This invitation to an annual event requires little in the way of information, except to announce the new starting hour. The invitation hits the highlights—presumably treasured family traditions—and pokes fun at one tradition in particular, the sing-along. Used wisely, humor reinforces bonds among a group. Just be careful to avoid using it to belittle or diminish any aspect of the upcoming event.

INVITATION TO LUNCH

Cal,

What about lunch? Tomorrow, 12:30, at Luigi's. Dutch treat. Hit the reply button.

Hal

The closer you are to your brother, the fewer words you require. Indeed, communicating this way expresses the intimacy of family members who feel they can almost read one another's minds. An invitation can be as economical as this one, especially if it is sent via e-mail.

WELCOME HOME

Benny,

Mom just told me you're coming home for a visit. Welcome, stranger! It's been almost a year!

Benny, I can hardly wait to see you. I want to take you to the new CD store that's opened on Warren Street. This place is great and definitely raises the culture quotient of our little town. We'll have a blast.

See you soon,

Demi

A timely communication can serve as a welcome to a familiar place as well as a new place. Here a sister expresses her affection for her brother by choosing to focus on a new favorite place she wants to share. Emotions may be expressed in words, but they do lose something in the translation. It can be more effective to convey your feelings with real things, by sharing events, places, and other favorite things. Such an act of sharing is a warm welcome, which goes far beyond merely telling the family member how eager you are to see him. Reality—real places, real events—almost always speaks more clearly and tenderly than abstract words.

E-Mailing It: To Friends

TO A CONCERT—DUTCH TREAT

Terri,

I have an opportunity to buy a pair of tickets for the Big Tomato concert, which, as you know, has been sold out for months. It would be great if we could go together. The ticket is $35, and the concert starts at 8 on April 4, at the Paradise Dome.

This is *the* event of the year, Terri. I hope you can go with me. Please let me know right away.

Sonny

Some people are made uncomfortable by the prospect of sending out a "Dutch treat" invitation, an invitation to an event in which each person pays his own way. There is no need to feel any embarrassment, provided that the invitation is to an event you believe of genuine value and interest to the other person. Two rules to observe:

1. Do not apologize for requiring that the invitee pay his own way. Present this as a fact, period. Do not say such things as "I wish I could pay for you" or "I wish I could get you in for free." Payment is a condition of the invitation, and that is all there is to it.

2. State the amount of the payment as clearly as possible. If you know what a ticket costs, specify the price. If the event has a range of costs, nail down this range. The invitee needs to know what he is committing to.

GROUP ACTIVITY

Daryl,

John, Ken, Rich, Mark, and I are going to see *Curl Up and Die* at the Cineplexis tomorrow afternoon. We're going to meet at the Burger Palace around 3, then catch the 3:45 show. Come on and join us!

Danny

E-mail is ideal for short-notice, informal invitations. When you invite someone along on a group activity, be sure to mention who the other participants will be. Avoid phrases that make it sound as if the invitation is an afterthought or in any way halfhearted: "Do you want to tag along?" or "We don't want to leave you out." Close with a simple, enthusiastic phrase of invitation, as here. Since this is an e-mail, the writer reasonably assumes that the recipient will reply one way or another.

WELCOME TO MY HOME

Dear Janice,

Ron and I are eagerly looking forward to your arrival Wednesday. Ron will pick you up at the airport, Terminal Y, Gate N, when your flight gets in at noon. We have the guest room ready for you, and I've laid in a supply of your favorite breakfast food, Pop Tarts in assorted flavors. There is also a small army of your old friends standing in line to see you. We will make sure that you feel at home.

Denise

There are many ways to tell a guest that she is welcome in your home. The most effective way of making a guest welcome, however, is not to *tell* her, but to *do* things that make her feel welcome. In this case, the writer reminds the guest that she will be picked up at the airport, that she will have a comfortable room, and that her desires (Pop Tarts and friends) will be catered to.

25 Words and Phrases to Use

comfortable	include you	pleasure of your company
delighted	interesting	
eager	join	R.S.V.P.
excited	let us know	Regrets Only
fascinating	like old times	see you again
friendly	miss you	thrilled
fun	opportunity	welcome
get together	please reply	your company
honored	pleasure	

10 Words and Phrases to Avoid

come if you want	must
don't be left out	must attend
don't fail	snooty
exclusive	sorry to have to ask you to pay
lucky to be invited	tag along

12

Sympathy and Condolence

*O*ccasions calling for sympathy and condolence are, universally, occasions of loss: loss of a loved one, loss of health, loss of property, loss of a job. And when it falls to us to communicate in such situations, we, too, often find that we have suffered a loss, a loss of words. It is not just that we do not know what to say—and are afraid of saying the wrong thing—but that, in times of grief, words seem hollow, inadequate, even profane or offensive. The most intelligent and articulate among us sometimes find it hard to say the right things on occasions of death, serious illness, or other loss. Yet it is precisely at such moments that saying it from the heart is vitally important, not just because it is the polite and caring thing to do, but because it is the *healing* thing to do. Make no mistake, your words will not work magic, but they will *work*. Even if you feel that anything you have to say will be inadequate, anything you *do* say will be more adequate than saying nothing. At the very least, loss demands acknowledgment. Without it, the loss is compounded, magnified, and made more miserable.

Finding the Heartline

Knowing the right things to say in a sad or traumatic situation requires, first and foremost, a leap of imagination. Put yourself in your correspondent's position. Under these circumstances, what would *you* like to hear? What would help *you* most? The most direct way to make this leap is to look into yourself in order to express your own grief.

Your neighbor's husband dies suddenly of a heart attack. You liked the man. You spoke with him almost daily. You lent each other garden implements and shop tools. He was not a close friend, but his passing saddens you. Of course, your grief is far less intense than that of his family, but it is still real. Begin by expressing that grief.

Once you have accepted the importance of saying something, even knowing that it will not take away all of the pain, and once you have gotten in touch with your own feelings about the loss, bear in mind the following five steps:

1. Express your own sorrow at hearing of the death or loss.
2. Sympathize by acknowledging the emotional pain of loss.
3. If the loss is a death, say something good, something positive about the deceased. If possible, share a memory.
4. It is often helpful gently to remind your correspondent of the healing power of time.
5. To the extent possible and appropriate, offer your help and support. Try to offer to do something specific that you know will be helpful. Perhaps you can offer to take the kids to school. Perhaps you can offer a visit. Identify something appropriate, then offer to do it.

All effective communicators get in sync with the person they address. Strike the emotional tone appropriate to your correspondent. You will, doubtless, communicate with a family member on a different level than you communicate with a personal friend or a business friend. Think about the nature of your relationship with your correspondent.

Sidestepping the Pitfalls

The deepest and most common pitfall is the paralysis of silence. We may feel so inadequate to speak or write on this occasion, that we fail to say anything, fail even to acknowledge the loss.

- Don't expect too much of your words. No matter what you say, you will not magically erase the grief.
- Nevertheless, expect much of your words. Whatever you say is likely to help. Inadequate as your words may be, they are far more adequate than silence. Words heal. They may not cure, but they do heal.

Although you should not worry much about making the situation worse by your words, do avoid the following:

- Adjectives and nouns that may magnify the loss, for example— "your *terrible* loss," "your *horrible tragedy*," and so on. Your correspondent does not need help feeling bad.

- Minimizing the loss. Don't tell the person that "things aren't so bad" or "you'll feel better" or "it could be worse" or "it's all for the best." Acknowledge the loss simply, and with sympathy and understanding.

Saying It: To Family

DEATH OF FATHER—TALKING WITH MOTHER

Mom, I'm so sorry. Right now, I have to tell you, it's hard to think of a world without Dad. It's hard for me, and I know it must be even harder for you. But Dad knew this was coming, and he did his best to prepare us for this. That's how much he loved us all. He loved us so much that he found the courage, sick as he was, to make his leaving easier for us. I miss Dad so much, but his generosity, selflessness, and courage are still with us, still a part of us.

Mom, I'm going to be coming out to see you every week for as long as you need me. I can help you with the grocery shopping. Dad left his affairs in such good order that there's not much to do about that, but I'll be here to help you in any way I can.

You know, Mom, we'll never "get over" this. We wouldn't want to if we could. But we will live through it. Dad has seen to that.

Never deny the loss, but do seek to emphasize whatever remains. In this case, the husband/father, suffering an illness, had taken great pains to provide for his family after his passing. The speaker, recognizing this, builds on it in his remarks to his mother. The message is that the man's presence remains strong, despite his death. Note also that the speaker concludes with offers of specific, practical help.

DEATH OF FATHER'S MOTHER

Dad, this is a shock. I thought Grandma would go on forever, and I know that whatever loss I feel is even more intense for you. I hope, Dad, that you can take some comfort in knowing that you made Grandma very proud, and whatever she taught you about being a parent—well, I couldn't have been raised by a better father. Grandma's life meant a lot to all of us. She's made us all better sons and daughters and mothers and fathers.

If there is anything I can do to help you and Mom over the next few days and weeks, please don't hesitate a moment about calling. I'm going to be staying in town for the next four days. I can take even more time off of work, if you need me.

The speaker expresses his own feelings, then acknowledges that the loss must be even more intense for his father. He then shifts to the living legacy of his grandmother. This is important, for part of the pain of loss is the feeling that much has been left unsaid. It may be possible for you to say some of those things. In this case, the speaker lets his father know that his mother—the speaker's grandmother—had every reason to be proud of his dad. The implication is that the grandmother/mother's spirit continues to live through the father/son as well as the son/grandson. Once again, the speaker ends with an offer of practical help.

DEATH OF SISTER'S CHILD

Jane, I hardly know what to say. Knowing and loving Ronnie was such a blessing and a joy. We all need to take some consolation in the time we had with him, but I know it's easy to say this and very hard to accept it.

I have to be selfish, Jane, and tell you that I look to you, my big sister, for strength at this time. I'll share with you what little strength I have, but I need to hold you and feel your strength. You do know that I will be here for you, to help with anything you ask.

Right now, we just have to believe—together—that time will ease this pain and leave us with memories of the joy Ronnie brought to our little world.

It is all right to confess the poverty of your words, the feeling that your power to make things better is very limited. Without minimizing this terrible loss, the speaker strives to put emphasis not on what has been lost, but on the meaning, influence, and joyful effect of the young life that has been lived.

HURRICANE DAMAGE TO IN-LAW'S HOME—PHONE CALL

Frank, I just heard about what Hurricane Maurice did to your house. I know you well enough to realize that what you're mostly feeling right now is thankfulness that Louise and the kids came through safely. Nobody's been hurt. But I also know how much that house meant to you, and I'm very, very sorry.

People tell you at times like this that "Things can always be replaced." Well, that's a lot easier said than done, but it's also true—hard, but true. You guys are a very strong family, and I know that, step by step, you'll not only get through this, but you'll rebuild even better than before. What I mean is that you'll all come through this even stronger and closer than ever before. I have confidence in you.

In the meantime, if you need a place to get away from it all for a while—to step back from it all—please come up here to Northville. Alice and I would love to have you, and we have plenty of room.

After the loss of physical possessions, it is common for well-meaning consolers to remark that "Things can always be replaced." This is very true, but, stated glibly, the cliché is not very helpful. The speaker expresses this common sentiment in a way that recognizes its truth as well as its inadequacy. He then shifts the focus to where it more properly belongs: to his confidence in the strength and ability of his friend and his friend's family to come through the ordeal. In a situation like this, it is necessary to acknowledge the loss, but it is most helpful to turn toward the future, toward repair and recovery. Also, remember to offer as much practical and specific assistance as you are in a position to offer.

Saying It: To Friends

DEATH OF A FRIEND'S MOTHER

Karen, we were all saddened this morning when news of your mother's heart attack came. As you know, I lost my mother suddenly two years ago, and I think I understand what you must be going through and feeling right now. It is a shock that is alternately painful and numbing and confusing. I don't know if it helps much to hear this now, but you *will* get through these feelings in time.

Your mother meant a lot to me—and not just because she was the mother of my best friend. She was always so kind and cheerful, and she took time to give me advice whenever I asked for it—and sometimes even when I *didn't* ask for it! Do you remember that long discussion we had about my first boyfriend? That was a riot! She was a great lady.

Karen, if there is anything at all I can do for you, please call. I want to do whatever I can to make this time a little easier for you.

Sympathy requires understanding the feelings of another, and a good way of getting in touch with your ability to sympathize is to look inward, into your own range of experience. This is how this speaker begins, after first registering her own shock and grief. The next step is to extend and deepen your sympathy by recalling experiences in common. Karen lost a mother, but the speaker lost a friend. True, the magnitude of these losses differs, but the losses have more in common than not. Recalling her own relationship with Karen's mother, the speaker can express herself more fully from the heart and with greater meaning.

DEATH OF A FRIEND'S DOG

> Tom, I am very sad to hear about Fido. He was such a part of the family, and I loved the way he greeted me at the door whenever I came to visit. A really sweet, gentle dog.
>
> I know how difficult a decision it was to put him to sleep, but he was very sick, and, certainly, no one could have done more for him than you did. I have to tell you that I think it took a lot of courage and character on your part to make the decision that he had suffered enough and to let go.
>
> I know that no dog can replace Fido, but I hope that you and the kids will adopt another pet soon. You're all just so good with animals. It is a delight to see.

The loss of a family pet is not to be dismissed or taken lightly. Cats, dogs, and other animals readily become part of the family, and their loss produces grief similar to the death of a human family member.

The speaker expresses his sadness and shares a memory as well as kind words about Fido. He also expresses informed sympathy about the manner of the animal's death, euthanasia, taking care to affirm the wisdom of this difficult decision. Finally, the speaker looks toward the future. He does not want to imply that a new animal can replace the old, but he does suggest that a new life will help fill the void left by the passing of the family pet.

LOSS OF A JOB

> Tom, I just heard about the shake-up at B&R. I know getting laid off, after 15 years with the firm, must have been the last thing you expected just now. It's the unexpected aspect of the whole thing that makes it such a sharp, deep blow. That's just the way it is, a Sunday punch. But I know you. You may not

feel much like one at the moment, but you are a real fighter, and you have built a record in the industry that few can match.

Tom, if you want a suggestion from me, take a few days off, just to breathe, then let's get together for lunch. I have some ideas for you. You may not think so right now, but you are in big demand in this industry. We just have to get the word out. Let me help.

The loss of a longtime job can be every bit as traumatic as a death in the family. Losing a job attacks our self-confidence and, sometimes, our entire sense of who we are. Typically, it creates immediate and direct anxiety about paying bills in the short term and earning a living in the long term. If the job loss is sudden and unexpected, confusion compounds the anxiety. The danger is that feelings of worthlessness and depression will sap the strength, will, and wit required to get a new and fulfilling position. In responding to someone who has just lost his job, don't just try to assure him that "something else will come along"; instead, after acknowledging the blow suffered, do what you can to bolster his self-confidence and his sense of self.

Jobs are lost and found all the time. Inner strength, morale, and resilience, once lost, are much more difficult to restore. Focus your remarks on maintaining and rebuilding these. If you are in a position to help—even with nothing more than a brainstorming session—offer help; however, don't add to a sense of panic by implying too much urgency. Here, the speaker advises his friend to take a few days off, to let the air clear, to settle down, to "breathe." Advising an emotional interval like this is a good idea, since it may allow the other person to see his situation from a clearer, cooler, less anxious perspective.

Writing It: To Family

SERIOUS CAR ACCIDENT—LETTER TO COUSIN

Dear Jerry,

I have hardly slept since your midnight call. I am so sorry about the loss of Kathy. How hard it is, how shocking. My heart is filled with sympathy for you.

I did not know Kathy well, but I didn't have to spend much time with her to know that she was loving, intelligent, and lovely. I can only begin to imagine what her loss means to you, and the only comfort I can offer is that, difficult as it may be to feel this now, time will ease the pain.

Jerry, you have a large number of friends, and you need to turn to them for help and support. You know that you can call on me if I can be helpful to you in any way.

Love,

Tammi

The sudden loss of a loved one through accident is an especially cruel blow because it is unexpected. Accidents, by their nature, are senseless and random, a fact that often adds bewilderment and bitterness to the bereaved's grief. If you are a religious person, you may feel moved to share the comfort of your faith with the bereaved. This is best done, however, if you also know something of this person's religious beliefs; for now is not the time to raise religious issues with a person who may not be inclined toward faith in general or toward your faith in particular.

In the absence of religion, what comfort can you offer? First and foremost, you can share your sympathy, your own grief, and your concern. Second, you can remind the bereaved of the healing power of time. These things may provide small comfort, but, modest as it is, such comfort will be welcomed.

DEATH OF FATHER—LETTER TO MOTHER

Dear Mom,

We knew this day would come, with Dad so sick for so long, but I can't say that I was ready for it. Thank God, you are stronger than I am. I saw how you cared for Dad, even in the worst of his illness. It has made you stronger and stronger, and now I look to you as an example and source of strength.

I look to Dad, too. He was a man who truly lived his faith, and now, more than ever, I see the great value of that. His example of faith I have taken to heart, and I know that he has gone to a better place.

Mom, it would help me now if I could help you. I'd like to come back home for a week or two to help you out with day-to-day things, shopping, putting Dad's things in order, and so on. Please let me know when my coming out would be best for you. My boss is very understanding, and I can easily get time off from work.

Love,

Manny

Expressing your condolences does not require that you present yourself as a tower of strength. In this case, the writer recognizes the intensity of his own grief and, while seeking to comfort his mother, also asks her for help. It is a remarkable thing that seeking help from another tends to make that other person feel stronger and more emotionally capable. Asking for help empowers the other person. This does not mean that the expression of sympathy and fellow feeling is an invitation to fall apart emotionally, but, under the circumstances, it is an opportunity to create mutual reliance, an emotionally supportive situation for both people.

Note that, in this letter, the writer acknowledges his father's religious faith. If you know that the others involved in the grieving situation possess religious conviction, it may be helpful and healing to make meaningful reference to religious belief. Let your own convictions and your knowledge of the others involved be your guide in this respect.

BUSINESS LOSS—LETTER TO BROTHER

Dear Ron,

I've been thinking about what happened with your big investor. On the phone, I called his backing out of the deal a "serious blow," but, as I think about it now, the word that comes to mind is not "blow," but "setback."

Look, there's no way around the fact that Smith's bailing out is *not* a good thing; however, I am convinced that you can recover from it. The project is such a good one that I believe you will readily find a new backer—more than one, if you need to.

I wish I could offer you a list of prospects, but I don't have the contacts. If there is anything else I can do to help, however, please don't hesitate to call.

Keep the faith, brother—in yourself and in this project. You will prevail.

Yours,

Sid

Nobody's perfect. In this case, the writer sends a follow-up letter to modify a remark he made in haste on the telephone, when his brother first reported a financial reverse. A sudden loss can provoke panic or, at least, a hasty conclusion. A letter, written in greater leisure and after some thought, can reassess the original conclusion. Here the writer modifies his response from an expression connoting near hopelessness to one that allows more latitude for positive action. The writer seeks to restore his brother's confidence, without, however, denying the seriousness of the problem. Effective letters of condolence can serve one, or perhaps two functions:

- They can provide a measure of comfort and consolation in a painful situation.

- They can look toward and encourage and even guide positive action for the future.

It is not always possible to perform both of these functions, but, at the very least, a communication of condolence should avoid intensifying the negative feelings associated with the event.

Writing It: To Friends

SERIOUS INJURY

Dear Claire,

I just heard from Sarah about your terrible accident. You are in my thoughts and prayers and hopes for as speedy a recovery as possible. I know that injuries of the kind you have suffered require a good deal of time for healing and a lot of effort from you in physical therapy. Effort, however, you have never shied away from. Achieving all that you have in the professional and business worlds does not come automatically or easily. You have faced, met, and surmounted one challenge after another, and I have no reason to believe that you'll turn away from the new challenges that now face you.

And you'll have help. You know far better than I do how thoroughly supportive your family is. As for me, if there is anything I can do to help you during the challenging days to come, please don't hesitate to lean on me.

My love to you,

Nell

Serious injury is a form of loss and, like other losses, creates sadness, depression, and feelings of despair. Communication in response to such an event should acknowledge the seriousness of the injury, but should avoid medical diagnosis or speculation. Note that the writer expresses a hope for "as speedy a recovery *as possible*," thereby acknowledging that recovery will, indeed, take time. She also express-es her understanding that the process of physical therapy required will not be an easy one. Even so, the writer expresses this in terms of chal-lenge rather than difficulty, and she defines challenge as something with which her friend is quite familiar and in dealing with which she has been quite successful. At times like this, encouragement is most welcome, provided that it is based on some plausible interpretation of reality. In this case, that reality is the writer's knowledge of her friend's personal history.

BURGLARY LOSS

Dear Tom and Martha,

I was very shocked and sorry to hear about the break-in at your house. I know that insurance covers much of the loss, but it can't erase that feeling of hav-ing been violated. I know, because I also experienced a break-in, about two years ago. It's just a terrible feeling. So, I'm writing to sympathize, but also to assure you that you will get past this thing. You'll replace the missing stuff, you'll change the locks, you'll install a security system, and you'll get on with your lives. That spooky feeling you have now does fade in time. Just hold out and be patient. Don't let whoever robbed you get hold of your peace of mind, too.

If you want somebody to talk to about this, please don't hesitate to give me a ring.

All the best,

Pete

Sometimes something bad happens to a friend, and you have spe-cial knowledge, insight, or experience that may help. This letter deals with one such case. The writer is careful to confine his remarks to his personal experience. He does not present himself as an expert on home security, but he does have something valuable to say about what burglary victims generally feel, and he shares this insight with his friends. The object is not just to make them feel better, but to help them see beyond the immediate trauma and loss. The most effective communications of sympathy and condolence share useful experience and feelings. This makes whatever has happened more understandable and, therefore, less frightening.

E-Mailing It: To Family

CANCELLATION OF VACATION PLANS

Dear Dad,

Sorry to hear that Mom's hurt foot has torpedoed your vacation plans. I know how much the two of you were looking forward to getting away to Europe. Although it's hard to find a bright spot in this, at least you can be thankful that the accident didn't happen while you were already abroad. Let's get Mom back on her feet and then reschedule. I know it's a hassle, but I'm happy to help you make new reservations and arrangements when you're ready.

Love,

Nan

It is not terrible traumas and tragedies alone that warrant a note of consolation. Sympathy and understanding are also welcome in lesser instances of life's tribulations. Here the emphasis is put on placing the incident in a larger perspective and in the offer of assistance in the rescheduling of the postponed vacation.

LOSS IN A CONTEST OR COMPETITION—E-MAIL TO SON

Billy,

Your project looked just great at the Science Fair, and I was proud to see it there. I was also proud of the original approach you took to the experiment you presented. Science fairs often exhibit a lot of ingenuity, but are typically short on original thought.

I understand you're disappointed that you didn't get a prize this time around, but the prizes represent the judgment of a small handful of people, nothing more, nothing less. What I am so pleased with and proud of is that you took a problem, tackled it, and approached it in such an inventive, original way. Well done!

Love,

Dad

We all enjoy sending congratulations to a loved one who has won a contest, but we also need to be there when the results are more disappointing. The object of the consolation is not to dismiss the loss, as if the contest weren't important in the first place, nor is it to dispute the judges' decision, but, rather, to demonstrate the writer's undiminished love for and pride in the family member. The writer here realizes that this does *not* mean communicating a message to the effect that "You lost, but *I* still love you." Instead, he focuses on the project and points out what he most admires about it. Indeed, the writer makes only secondary reference to his son's disappointment. His primary focus is on achievement, as if to point out that the absence of a prize cannot negate what has been achieved.

E-Mailing It: To Friends

ILLNESS

> Karl,
>
> We missed you at the party. I understand that you're down with the flu—big time. Well, don't try to fight it. Just stay in bed, drink plenty of fluids, get as much sleep as you can, and try to keep from going crazy with boredom. Hard as it may be to believe at the moment, you will feel better soon.
>
> Mary

A note to a friend absent on account of illness is a very welcome morale booster. You can buy a "get well" card in a store or, even better, dash off a few lines of your own. In the case of minor illness, it is helpful to convey the message that the misery will soon pass.

LOST LUGGAGE

> Jen!
>
> Sorry to hear that you went one way and your luggage another. Unfortunately, this is something that happens all the time. As I understand it, such mix ups are usually resolved pretty quickly. I hope the airline is being reasonably helpful. In the meantime, try to relax. You know, Jen, we're about the same size, so if there's anything you need to borrow in the meantime, please let me know. You're more than welcome.
>
> Stay cool,
>
> Pat

Showing your concern in a minor disaster like this helps put the problem in a perspective that should help your friend to feel better. Any practical help you can render is also greatly appreciated.

25 Words and Phrases to Use

adjust	express	share
aid	feel better	shock
assist	heal	sorry
celebrate	help	surprise
condolences	hope	sympathy
cope	joy	take time
delight	patience	time
emotion	recover	
endure	remember	

15 Words and Phrases to Avoid

bounce back	forget it	shake it off
could be worse	hopeless	snap out of it
despair	it's nothing	terrible
disastrous	miserable	tragedy
don't worry	no big deal	you'll be all right

13

Just to Keep
in Touch

No law binds us to wait for special occasions, for times of joy and celebration, or for moments of crisis and sorrow, to speak or write—from the heart—to family or friends. Sometimes we just want to keep in touch.

Now, keeping in touch means different things to different people and in different situations. Some of us want to say or write something special to a family member or friend virtually every day. In other cases, keeping in touch is what we do with family or friends who have gone their own way. Perhaps a son is off at college. Perhaps a friend has found work in Tucson, and you live in Chicago. In still other instances, it is not just miles that separate us, but years as well. We may wish to get in touch with a friend or even a family member we've not seen or communicated with for years.

Any of these situations offer ample reason to reach out.

Finding the Heartline

But what do we say? If someone graduates, gets married, has a child, or, alas, dies, we have news, a subject. But what is the subject of "keeping in touch"?

Keeping in touch. The phrase is so familiar that we hardly give it thought anymore. It's just a phrase, a figure of speech, after all. We take it for granted. But think about the phrase for a moment or two. *Touch* describes both a most vital human sense and a most intimate gesture. It is all about closeness, and "keeping in touch" is an effort to maintain closeness.

Now, what things maintain closeness between people? Each of us could readily draw up his or her own list, but here's a generic one:

- Shared thoughts
- Shared feelings
- Meaningful experiences, shared
- News of mutual friends and acquaintances

The most effective attempts at keeping in touch combine items from all four of these categories. Keep this in mind when you pick up the phone or sit down to write. And here are some other rules of thumb for keeping in touch:

- *Communicate with enjoyment.* If you set about the task of keeping in touch as if it were a chore, the result will be disappointing both for you and your correspondent. If you approach the task with pleasure, that feeling will illuminate whatever you have to say.

- *Be personal.* This does not mean confessing your innermost secrets. But it does require you to go beyond simply reeling off a list of things you have done lately. Talking about interesting things you've done or are doing is great, but animate this material by including what you've been thinking and feeling, too.

- *Zero in.* You don't have to deliver a novel-length account of the last decade or so. Instead, choose one event (or two) and tell a story about it. It is always more interesting to hear in detail about a specific event than it is to plow through a laundry list of one event after another. Good writing or speaking shares sensations, sights, sounds, and it shares emotions. When the American writer Stephen Crane wanted to write a realistic novel about the Civil War, he didn't summarize one battle after another, but, instead, focused on the experience of a small group of men in a single engagement. He explored this in detail, and while *The Red Badge of Courage* is certainly not a comprehensive history of the Civil War, it communicates far more about the nature and reality of that war—and war in general—than any number of dry-as-dust chronicles. You, too, can make your experience vivid by focusing on a small aspect of it and delivering the information in detail. After all, it is always more fun to read or hear a story than it is to read or hear a list.

- *Yield to the adventure.* A good storyteller lets her story lead her as well as her listeners. Select a subject, focus on it, and start talking or writing about it. See where the tale takes you.

Sidestepping the Pitfalls

The most common pitfall where keeping in touch is concerned is simply this: failing to keep in touch. Remember your high school physics—and the principle of inertia. The relevant part of this natural law goes something like this: If a body is at rest, it's difficult to get it moving. A similar principle applies to keeping in touch. We may think about doing it. We may say, *I really ought to write my cousin* or *I should give Bill a call*, but actually doing these things is another matter. The hardest part about keeping in touch is getting started.

Once you overcome the inertia, you face at least three more pitfalls:

1. *What do I say?* As mentioned earlier, occasions of great joy or deep tragedy automatically give you a subject. The subject is less apparent when you simply decide to get in touch with someone. Reread the pointers given in the previous section for some topic ideas.

2. *Forgetting to be human.* For most people, this is more of a problem when writing than when speaking. We tend to forget that writing or speaking from the heart is the communication of one person to another. The result is that we slip into a dull, dry, impersonal, artificial kind of speech. The most effective way to avoid this, to keep from forgetting that you are a human being communicating with another human being, is to use your imagination. When you are on the phone or—even more important—when you sit down to write, imagine your correspondent sitting in the next chair or across the table. Imagine that you are having a conversation with him or her. When we learn to read, we are taught to avoid moving our lips. When you write to a friend or a family member, it's okay to let your lips move as you write. *Talk* to the other person.

3. *Biting off too much.* Even if you've not communicated with your old buddy for a decade, two decades, or longer, you need not feel obligated to do all of your catching up in a single phone call, let-

ter, or e-mail. Be selective. The first attempt at keeping in touch can trigger a whole series of letters or calls over the years. Don't worry, you'll cover a lot of territory—by and by.

Saying It: To Family

MISS YOU, MOM

Hi, Mom. No, nothing's wrong. I'm just calling because I miss you. This morning, I was scrambling some eggs, just the way you used to, with olive oil, and I thought about the million or so breakfasts you made me on those chilly mornings before school. I just remembered how great it all was, and then it occurred to me that I hadn't called for a while.

What's new with you?

The caller zeros in on the homiest of memories to share with his mother. The act of scrambling eggs is pretty simple, but contained within that act is a wealth of feeling and memory. Keeping in touch is touching precisely such moments, such gestures, such actions, then sharing them.

One of the keys to a satisfying keep-in-touch phone call is to invite the other person to talk. Don't feel obliged to deliver a monologue.

MISS YOU, MOTHER TO DAUGHTER

Hello, Mary. I know I dropped you off at State just two days ago, but, a minute ago, I walked into your room to put some things away, and there was your bed—neatly made! So it hit me: You are indeed away. And I missed you, so I just wanted to see how you're settling in.

Is there anything I can send you? What's your new roommate like?

Sending a child off to college is an intensely emotional experience for many parents. This mother conveys her feelings not with gushy, strongly weighted emotional words, but with gentle humor. The girl's bed is neatly made, so the mother *knows* she is no longer at home.

There are some other important things the caller does *not* do in this conversation:

- She does not scold her daughter for failing to call. Too many efforts to keep in touch are spoiled by words aimed at making the other person feel guilty for letting the relationship lapse in some way.

- She is careful to avoid giving the impression that she is overprotective or prying. The questions this mother asks focus on her daughter's needs and her surroundings. They are not intrusive.

- She doesn't smother her daughter in sage advice. By all means, share your wisdom with your children, but recognize their need for independence, too.

WHY I HAVEN'T CALLED—SON TO FATHER/MOTHER

Hi, Dad (Mom). Maybe you've forgotten the sound of my voice. This is Ted, Ted Williams, your son. Before you bawl me out for not having called in so long, let me tell you my excuse: I'm a lazy bum. I was going to run down the list of what I've been doing, studying for midterms, working day and night on my chem lab project, and all the rest. But the fact is that I was just too lazy to pick up the phone.

So, let me tell you about what's been happening here. The big news is that I've gotten a research grant for next year . . .

It's a vicious cycle. For one reason or another, you put off making the call you've been meaning to make. Then, the longer you put it off, the more difficult it is to make the call. After all, how do you explain why you've stayed out of touch for so long? Pretty soon, you actively look for reasons not to call.

How do you break this cycle of inaction?

Just make the call. If you want, you can begin with the reasons for not having called. You may have very good ones. Avoid outpourings of guilt, however, because these will only make the person on the other end of line feel bad. He or she does not want to be the cause of your guilty conscience. The caller in this case uses gentle humor and frankly admits that he has no good excuse for having failed to call— although he does manage to alert his parents to the fact that he has been very busy indeed.

Once the caller has cleared the hurdle of excusing his failure to keep in touch, he goes on to some real news, focusing on his research grant rather than including it in a list of lesser, and less significant, activities and events.

Saying It: To Friends

MISS YOU

Jane, you've been on my mind a lot lately. It's just not the same around here since you left. I miss talking to you, of course, and I miss the sound of your kids playing up and down the block. Our new neighbors are very nice people, don't get me wrong, but it's not the same as having someone you just feel so comfortable with, to sit down with and solve the world's problems.

Speaking of problems, the town still has not put in a traffic light on our corner. There have been at least three wrecks since you left. Remember how we worked together on all those petitions? We put in a lot of time together on them, and I haven't given up hope that they'll ultimately have an effect.

So, how are you settling in? The kids adjusting to the new school yet? And what about *your* new neighbors? What are they like?

Telling an absent friend that you think about her and that you miss her may sound like a cliché, but it is really a valuable gift from you to her. It is a moving—a most touching—sentiment, especially if you add a few specific details, former conversations, the sound of the children playing, and so on.

Note that the item of news the caller chooses to focus on is one she knows is of common interest to her and her friend. Emphasizing shared experience is a way of reestablishing the familiar connections from which the fabric of a friendship is woven.

COMING TO TOWN

Hey, Max! The Candy Convention is coming to Chicago during the last week in August. I'm going to attend, and it sure would be great to see you while I'm in town. I'll be tied up at the convention until about noon on the 23rd, but I'm free after that. I could come by and spend the afternoon and evening, then take the late flight. It would be a lot of fun to get together, if this will work out for you.

Perhaps you feel self-conscious about inviting yourself to a distant friend's house. This is understandable, but it's best to avoid betraying any reluctance when you want to call on an old friend. Present the circumstances clearly, be specific about time, and express your enthusiasm for a reunion. Just be sure to leave your friend an out—"if this will work out for you."

PLEASE VISIT

Karen, Larry told Jane and me that you were going to be coming out to Jacksonville on business next week. I don't know what your schedule's going to be like, but it would be a lot of fun for all of us if we could get together. We could pick you up from wherever you're going to be and bring you back here. Maybe you could arrange a Sunday flight, and, that way, we could have you as a weekend guest. It would be wonderful to revisit old times together.

A spur-of-the-moment invitation to a friend who just happens to be coming through town can be most welcome. Of course, you must also be prepared for the possibility that your friend won't be able to accept, and you must never present this form of keeping in touch in any way that seems coercive. Be enthusiastic, be specific, and offer whatever you can to make it easy and convenient for the other person to accept, but also express your understanding that she may not be able to accept. This does not mean saying, "I know this might be impossible for you," which might be read as a lack of enthusiasm on your part, as if the invitation were extended half-heartedly; however, do include an acknowledgment of the possible difficulties of getting together: "I don't know what your schedule's going to be like."

Writing It: To Family

MISS YOU, LETTER FROM FATHER TO DAUGHTER

Dear Cindy,

Your mother and I were so happy to hear from you last night, and we are thrilled by the news of your success at college. We sat up much of the night talking about you, not so much about where you are now—though we're so very proud of that!—but about our old times together, how we used to sit together and read or watch TV, those great road trips we took together, the first time we went to the Grand Canyon. Cindy, believe it or not, it's not easy for old folks like us to get accustomed to not having you around every day!

Anyway, Cind, please keep calling. We love to hear from you—and often. And we are very excited for you and your success.

Love,

Dad

Psychologists have long known about positive reinforcement. If your child's action pleases you, reward it, reinforce it. If you want your daughter to stay in touch, respond positively and enthusiastically. A sweet, thoughtful letter is such a response.

Note that while the writer recalls the "old times," he does not wallow in them, and he by no means denies the value and accomplishments of his daughter in the present. Still, he communicates about shared experience, and he is able to admit that it is difficult for parents to let go. Letters have always been ideal vehicles for expressing feelings, and this is precisely what the writer does here.

WHY HAVEN'T YOU WRITTEN? LETTER TO BROTHER

Dear John,

The guy who runs the newsstand on the corner thinks I've gone wacko. You see, I've started buying up all the supermarket tabloids he has on sale—you know, the ones with the headlines about TWO-HEADED BABY BORN TO 80-YEAR-OLD GRANDMOTHER. I keep looking in them for a story about how *you* have been abducted by aliens and taken to Venus. How else to explain the fact that you've apparently left this planet?

John, you haven't written in ages! I'm starting to get concerned. And if this desperate attempt at humor doesn't get a few lines from you in return, I'm really going to start to worry.

I'd love to hear from you!

Love,

Barbara

Never scold another person into writing, but a letter asking for a response is perfectly reasonable, polite, and even welcome. It shows your concern and caring without, however, making any insistent demands. Mild humor is an effective means of ensuring that your request for correspondence doesn't sound too insistent or even indignant.

TO A HOMESICK SON

Dear Daryl,

It was good talking to you last night. Your Dad and I are so sorry that you're feeling homesick. I know it's painful—I know, because I've been through it myself. The bad news is that it makes you feel pretty low, but the good news is that it's strictly a temporary problem. It doesn't *feel* temporary now, I realize, but, trust me, you'll feel better soon. In the meantime, call us as often as you want. We love to talk to you—anytime. After all, Daryl, we miss you, too—very much!

Love,

Mom

Homesickness is a common complaint, and it hits some kids hard. Your response should be understanding and sympathetic. Don't deny or minimize your child's feelings, but do what you can to persuade him that the problem, though intense and real, is temporary. Few things are more convincing than sharing personal experience, as the writer does here. While you should avoid minimizing the problem, don't allow your response to magnify it out of proportion, either.

Conclude as positively as possible. The most positive step you can take is to offer a reasonable means of relief, namely an open and warm invitation to call home—often. Finally, note that the writer turns the tables on her son by confessing that the feelings he has are in some ways reciprocal. She and her husband miss their boy.

Writing It: To Friends

TO AN OLD FRIEND

Dear Ron,

It was great seeing you again, buddy, after much too long. Too long, yes, but it was oh so easy to get back in the groove with you. It was like old times. It was as if all those years hadn't passed by at all. The feeling, Ron, was very special, and I wouldn't like to lose it in another long silence. So let me fill you in on what's been happening since you left.

The big thing, which has us really fired up, is Jenny's success in the local band. She just got promoted to first clarinet—this after only a year marching with the band. We're thrilled, and I just love to see Jenny enjoying something so much, taking such satisfaction in a hard-won accomplishment.

As for me, I mentioned while you were here that it looked as if I'd be stepping up to assistant manager for the district, and, thank goodness, that's just what happened. It means I have to work longer hours, unfortunately, but the challenge is a welcome one—and so is the extra money.

Ron, my friend, what's been happening with you since we parted? I'd love to hear all about it.

Yours,

Ben

Friendships don't just happen. They require a certain amount of work. Call it maintenance, if you like. Neglected, a friendship fades away. Take positive action by following up on a pleasant visit with a phone call or letter. Make clear your desire and intention to stay in touch, and reinforce this message by sharing choice current personal events with your friend. Close by inviting him to share likewise.

MISS YOU

Dear Kathy,

Last night, I was cleaning out the bureau drawer and ran across a packet of snapshots from a dozen years ago. They were photos of that trip you, Dave, Martin, and I took together to Yosemite. Suddenly, the smell of the cool, crisp air, the sounds of the birds, the deep green of the forest, all of this came back to me in a flood. And so did memories of the great pleasure we had there together and all the fun we've had over the years. That, I realized, was the secret formula of our friendship: that we always enlarged and amplified the enjoyment we took in whatever we did together.

So, my dear friend, I'm writing to say how much I miss you—how happy I am for the times we had together, but how much I wish we could be together much more often. Let's plan a new trip together. We're open to vacation plans any time in August. What about it? Life's too short to spend so much of it apart.

Love,

Ella

Time and distance are formidable obstacles and undeniable facts of life, but a good letter to an absent friend can do much to overcome these barriers. Feelings of friendship, after all, live in the heart and mind, places in which time and distance can be compressed.

The writer evokes strong emotion here not through the use of flowery language, but by recalling and sharing specific moments from the past, including sights, sounds, smells, and feelings. If you can awaken the senses of your correspondent, you can be confident that your letter will come across as real, vivid, and touching. A key to communicating from the heart is to tie your language to the real world, to real events, to actual experiences, and to vivid emotions.

WHY I HAVEN'T WRITTEN

Dear Jack,

No, I have not dropped off the end of the Earth. Even more important, the fact that I haven't written in so long is no indication that I've stopped thinking about you.

My excuse?

Well, there is no adequate *excuse* for my not having made the time to write a few lines. I do have an *explanation*, however. I have been swamped, what with starting up my own business—it's what we always talked about, a specialty CD shop—and attending to my aunt, who is in the hospital again. Swamped, yes, but I could have found a few moments to drop a line or two. It's just that I never feel I can say what I want when I dash off a note.

So, please take this brief letter as my promissory note to you—an IOU on a much longer letter, which I promise to write as soon as I can. In the meantime, how about letting me know what's happening on your end?

All the best to you,

Patti

The writer hits on an important truth here. Often, we fail to make time to write to those we care about not because we have absolutely *no* time, but because we feel we have insufficient time to do full justice to what we want to say. The result? Neither a long nor a short letter, but no letter at all. If you find yourself in this bind, you owe it to yourself to do at least one of two things:

- Find time now to write the letter you want to write.

- Write a short letter now, promising more later.

Don't burden your correspondent with a long, guilt-ridden explanation of why you haven't written. Acknowledge that you have not written, offer a brief explanation, but point out that you regret having been out of touch and that you want to reach out now, to make up for lost time.

E-Mailing It: To Family

WHAT'S HAPPENING?—E-MAIL TO SISTER

Hi, Sis—

Been thinking about you. It's been weeks since we've spoken. What's been happening? In particular, how's the job search going? Anything interesting come up? Have you thought about contacting Mary Williams at Union Company? If not, she's someone you probably should talk to. She knows the market in your town pretty well. Maybe she can provide some leads.

Anyway, how about a call or e-mail to get me up to date on your life and times?

Love,

Mike

Prodding someone to call or write should never come across as a demand. Instead, express interest by asking for news. If you can be specific in your request, so much the better. Note that this message also adds an offer of help.

MISS YOU—MOTHER'S E-MAIL TO SON AT COLLEGE

Dear Matt,

I'm getting to love e-mail. I can just sit down and fire off a few lines to you whenever I miss you—which, Matt, is pretty often. I know that you'll take off like a rocket in college, but I hope that you won't accelerate so fast that we'll lose touch with you. You know, all you have to do is click on the reply button to send a message back to me. Tell me a little bit about your classes, about your professors, and about your roommate. And is the food decent?

Love,

Mom

E-mail invites reply, because technology has made it so very easy to respond to messages. Exploit this when you want a response. But don't depend on the technology to prompt a busy, lazy, or otherwise reluctant correspondent. Try *telling* him what to write about. This makes his job that much easier, and it improves the odds of your getting the reply you seek.

PARENTS TO WORRIED DAUGHTER

Dear Meg,

I have been thinking about your phone call. I'm not going to tell you to stop worrying about your grades. Look, they're important, but you and I both know that they don't always accurately reflect your performance or your ability. Don't be discouraged. You have a lot of time to pull those grades up. Take some positive steps: Organize your study time more efficiently, and *talk* to the professors. When you are studying, jot down every question you have, then take these to your professors. Remember, your success is *their* success, too. They want to feel that they are doing a good job. They want to help. Once you realize that you do not have to go this alone, I think you'll feel better—and your grades will improve.

Please, Meg, call us anytime you need to talk.

Love,

Dad

E-mail is an ideal medium for quick afterthoughts, following a conversation or phone call.

It is painful to see a loved one wracked by worry. The natural impulse is to assure her that "everything will be just fine." The impulse is natural, but it isn't necessarily helpful. In the first place, such reassurances usually come across as hollow, a denial of reality. In the second place, it is quite possible that your correspondent's worry has a legitimate basis in the real world. It is not helpful to encourage ignoring it. Instead, admit the problem, sympathize with the bad feelings it is causing, then try to offer some genuine help and advice, if at all possible. Do not say anything that either reinforces or magnifies the bad feelings that already exist, but try to advise a course of action that may improve the situation that is causing distress.

E-Mailing It: To Friends

COMING TO TOWN

Jim:

Marilyn and I will be passing through Middletown next week on our way to New York. We haven't seen you and Cynthia for over a year—and that's a year too long. Are you guys going to be home and open to a pair of wayfarers on the 6th? I expect we'll be in the neighborhood by three in the afternoon. We'd love to take you out to dinner and chew over old times.

Click on reply. Say yes, if you can.

Best from both of us,

Dan

E-mail is fast and easy, which makes it a good medium for arranging impromptu visits. Give as much specific information as you can, and communicate your enthusiasm while also allowing for the possibility that your friends may not be available.

GREAT TO SEE YOU AGAIN

Dear Ralph and Eunice,

It was so wonderful seeing you again after way too many years. Tom and I have talked about practically nothing else since. We've both remarked how the two of you have hardly changed, but how "little" Mike has grown into a fine young man. It is so inspiring—I can't think of another word—to see your family, solid, sane, fun, and loving people, all of you.

Let's make a vow to stay in touch and to try to see more of each other.

Love,

Nancy

A note acknowledging the pleasure of a visit after long absence is more than a polite gesture. It is an effort to reach out, to ensure that the visit will help reestablish a lapsed friendship. It is a gesture of reconnecting.

Don't be shy about expressing your genuine admiration for a friend. Don't be shy, but do try to be specific, as the writer is here. She makes the effort not just to express her affection and admiration, but to explain why she feels the way she does. She also makes it clear that she speaks for her husband's feelings as well.

25 Words and Phrases to Use

admire	embrace	faith
affection	encourage	friendship
delight	exciting	fun

get together	miss you	share
great time	news	too long
hear all about it	old times	too many years
hear from you	please reply	wonderful
keep in touch	pleasure	
memories	reach out	

10 Words and Phrases to Avoid

ashamed of yourself	must reply
don't know what to say	no time to write
everything will be fine	shame on you
get together sometime or other	snap out of it
have to hear from you	why haven't you called?

Part 3

Talking with Children About . . .

*E*ffective, loving communication with our children
is the subject of this section.

14

Anger

"*I* hate my brother!"

It's an exclamation at least as old as Cain and Abel, and what parent has not heard it? Or its equivalent:

"I hate my sister!"

"I hate my teacher!"

"I hate Tommy!"

"I hate you!"

How do you respond?

Whatever else it is, anger is the verbal expression of energy. Energy is difficult to control or contain. Set off an explosion, and it affects everything in the vicinity—usually adversely. Thus you may find it difficult to respond to your child's anger with anything other than anger. As energy begets energy, so anger begets anger.

But you *are* an adult, and you have learned to exercise adult-level restraint. Instead of responding to your child's provocations with anger—which will only escalate the prevailing rage—you respond calmly: "Oh, you know you don't mean that!"

Does this restraint, admirable though it may be, resolve the problem?

Hardly.

Responding to anger with anger is as effective a means of dealing with rage as throwing gasoline on a blaze to put out the fire. However, simply denying the child's feelings is equally ineffective. It may even be more destructive.

Yet it is understandable. Looking around at present-day popular culture, at our songs and TV shows, it may be hard to believe that our society sets any value at all on courtesy. More often than not, it defines courtesy simply as avoiding—or ignoring, if necessary—unpleasant emotions and the expressions to which those give rise. Therefore, if we manage to avoid a knee-jerk response to anger—that is, expressing anger in return—our next automatic choice is to deny the anger altogether.

Denying feelings does not deal with feelings. It only cuts off communication.

What's wrong with this? Well, let's pause here to discuss the reasons why communication is so important. It is a daunting subject to which vast volumes have been devoted, books by eminent philosophers, scientists, psychologists, and even theologians. *How to Say It from the Heart* is a humble handbook aimed at helping you to write and speak more effectively. So allow me to boil down the discussion to a mere three points.

1. *Verbal expressions of anger are intimately related to physical expressions of anger.* Verbal violence and physical violence are both forms of violence. Most outbursts of physical violence begin with verbal violence. Cope effectively with verbal violence, and you will reduce the incidence of physical violence. Denying verbal violence—ignoring or rejecting the expression of anger—is not an effective way to cope with anger and, therefore, will do nothing to forestall the physical expression of anger.

2. *Effective communication, especially where strong emotions are involved, is essential to future success.* What parent does not want a bright future for his or her child? We spend hours at parent–teacher conferences, we willingly pay for tutors, we buy books, we drag the kids to museums. Yet too many of us fail to realize that the denominator common to most success is a highly developed ability to communicate. Your conversations with your kids, from a very early age and until they grow into young adulthood and leave home, are the chief vehicles by which children arrive at their communication skills. To turn away from an emotion is to forsake an opportunity for communication, and to miss such an opportunity is to fail to build your child's communication skills. This, in turn, diminishes his or her chances for future success.

3. *Communication contributes to good health.* We all know people who "bottle up" their emotions. They are flushed of face and tight

of lip. They walk through life stiff, complaining of their aching backs, their high blood pressure, their sour stomachs. The ability to express emotion verbally—including strong and painful emotion—is essential to physical well-being. To help a child develop effective ways to talk about his feelings, including (and especially!) anger, is as important to his future health as the good food you feed him.

Finding the Heartline

Find the heartline in talking to a child about anger, and you have a key to effective communication with children on virtually any subject and in any circumstance.

The first principle to bear in mind is the necessity of recognizing and maintaining the connection between feelings and words. In the case of anger, this means accepting the child's feelings and dealing with them in words. When a child says he hates his sister or he hates his teacher or he hates you, don't tell him he can't mean or doesn't mean what he has just said. Hard as it is, accept the fact that, right now, at this moment, in these circumstances, this is precisely what he means. Be prepared to use words to deal with this.

In addition to this prime directive of communication with kids, this overriding truth, consider the following when you speak to your child about any powerful emotion:

- *Theories of language aside, the only meaning a communication has in the real world is whatever the listener understands it to have.* This is true whether you, an adult, are speaking to another adult or whether you are speaking to a child. The problem is that when you speak to a child, her understanding may be quite different from your intention, because, as a child, her experience, her frame of reference, is different from yours. Try to understand the child's frame of reference before you speak.

- *Communication is developed through feedback.* Exasperated, we sometimes feel that communicating with our children is like putting a message in a bottle and sending it out to sea. The communication is one way, and there is a very little guarantee that it will reach its intended recipient. While this image may accurately reflect our frustration, especially when trying to communicate in situations of intense emotion, it is not a good model of communication. All conversation is based on the model of the feedback loop.

Let's pause a moment to look at the feedback loop. Here is a snatch of conversation:

You: I went to the store.

Him: What did you buy at the store?

You: I bought a new dress.

Him: How much did the dress cost?

It would be easy—if, perhaps, a trifle tedious—for you to continue this dialogue from this point. And you don't have to possess the imagination of a Charles Dickens or a Stephen King to do so. Why not? Because of the feedback loop. The first words "*Him*" utters are feedback to the first words of "*You.*" They don't come out of thin air, but directly from "*You's*" statement. For one thing, they share a word in common, "store." Because "*Him*" knows what one does in a store, the natural feedback to "*You*" is "*What did you* buy?" Similarly, this question prompts feedback relating immediately and directly to the content of the question. "*You's*" response employs the past tense of the verb in the question "*Him*" asks:

Him: What did you *buy* at the store?

You: I *bought* a new dress.

Now, the fact that this conversation runs on a feedback loop does not mean that "*Him*" has no choice in his next response. He could have asked what color the dress is, what it is made out of, where the hemline falls, and so on, depending on what most interests him. In this case, the question concerns cost. It is one response out of many that are possible—but the important point here is contained in the phrase *that are possible*. The content of the statement "I bought a new dress" does not dictate what "*Him*" says next, but it does narrow the relevant possibilities. That is, "*Him*" might next have said, "Louis XIV was called the Sun King," but, then, we would no longer have a conversation. But, "*Him*" does say something that constitutes feedback, and this leads us to the next heartline principle:

- *Your child bases what he says on what you say.* If you speak accusingly or angrily or disparagingly to your child, you will be paid back in kind. This applies not only to a particular conversation, but to the context of communication you build up over the years.

Let's take time out again. Your child, playing recklessly after you told him not to play in the living room, knocks over your favorite vase, which shatters on the floor.

You:　　　What's the matter with you? You are so clumsy!

Your child:　You shouldn't have put that there if I'm so clumsy.

There's only one direction the conversation can go from here: to a place of greater and greater anger. Clearly, the child misbehaved. Clearly, it is his fault that the vase is shattered. Clearly, both of you would be best served if the kid would sincerely apologize.

Why doesn't he?

One reason is that you have not provided the right words to elicit that feedback. By verbally attacking the child, you invite defensive—not contrite—feedback. Such feedback, in turn, provokes even angrier feedback from you, and you have the makings of a vicious cycle of escalating emotion.

Let's not leave this point without exploring an alternative to verbally attacking your child. The shattered vase is a bad thing. It is no wonder that it makes you angry, especially after you told your child not to play in the living room. Don't deny your feelings about the incident, but do focus your remarks on the incident, the event, the issue, rather than on your child, his character, or his abilities.

You:　　　Oh, Max! That was my favorite vase! I feel terrible about it!

Your child:　I'm sorry . . .

And, from here, the conversation can take a more constructive turn, aimed at controlling anger without ignoring it. Another heartline principle, then:

- *Focus on issues, not personalities.* This is a principle to apply to all communication, especially those involving strong negative feelings. If the child breaks the vase, talk about your feelings concerning the loss of the vase. Do not focus on how you feel about your child at this particular moment. Do not use the event as a lever to pry open the child's character flaws. Events, like feelings, are often quickly past, over and done with; but character, self-image, self-esteem, and personality endure. Do not allow momentary feelings born of particular incidents to label enduring qualities of self. Separate events—and the feelings elicited by events—from the person that is your child and how you feel about him or her.

- *Look to language for the cause of communication problems before you blame your child.*

Let's give this principle some thought. Even people who don't care much for classical music generally agree that Beethoven's *Fifth Symphony* is a great piece of music. But what if you had never heard it played by a full symphony orchestra and instead heard a novice kazoo player struggle through it?

"Who *is* this guy Beethoven? His music is incredibly lame!"

Of course, we *have* heard the *Fifth Symphony* played by an orchestra and, hearing a kazoo rendition—a bad one at that—we understand that the fault lies not in Beethoven's music, but in this particular expression of it. Similarly, we need to recognize that many of the problems we experience in communication, including negative feelings that may result from certain exchanges, are due not to the person talking to us, but to language itself. Understand that not everyone is a great communicator with a virtuoso command of language. This is especially true of your child. As a speaker, Sir Winston Churchill possessed a philharmonic orchestra of eloquence. Your six-year-old is still learning the kazoo.

- *You don't have to be a child psychologist to talk effectively with your child.* Understand that your child probably will see most issues from a different perspective than you. Understand, too, that, depending on his age, your child's vocabulary is less extensive than yours. But, aside from this, you may speak with a child *essentially* as you speak with an adult. More precisely, you may speak with a child the way you might speak to a respected subordinate at work. This means expecting *and giving* courtesy and attention. It means not talking down to the child. It means listening to him without interruption—anymore than you would cut off or interrupt an adult partner in conversation.

Sidestepping the Pitfalls

The pitfalls in communicating with children are many, and they are yet more numerous and deeper when strong emotions, especially anger, are involved. The major pitfalls may be expressed as negative versions of the heartline advice just given. That is, parents should look out for and avoid the following:

- *Denial of feelings.* This is both the biggest and the most common pitfall in talking with kids about anger. If a child expresses anger, do not reply that he "doesn't really mean it." Accept the feeling. Engage it. Discuss it.

- *Focusing on the child instead of the issues.* Focusing the discussion on your child—his personality, his "attitude," his character, his skills (or lack of them)—almost always intensifies anger, making both you and your child feel worse. Point the conversation at the particular event in question and about the feelings you and your child have about the event.

- *Sending out angry messages.* In communication, you really do reap what you sow. If you habitually speak to your child—or other family members—in angry tones and with angry content, you will get anger in return. On a smaller scale, if you respond to your child's anger with anger, you will only intensify his anger.

- *Blaming the child instead of his language.* You have no right to expect great eloquence from your child at any time, but especially not when he's angry. Recognize that much of what he says— or fails to say—is a product of his limited command of the instrument of language.

- *Talking down to the child.* Children, of course, are not "little adults." Nevertheless, you are better off talking with them as adults who are subordinate to you than you are talking down to them. Expect and deliver the same courtesy and attention in your conversations with children as in those with adults.

Angry Scenarios

The following three scenarios call for different responses, but it is important to make two basic responses to all three—and, indeed, to any conversation with your child about feelings:

1. *Pay attention.* Stop whatever you're doing, turn to your child, pause, make eye contact.

2. *Do not avoid, evade, or otherwise ignore your child's feelings.* This does *not* mean that you have to understand exactly what your child feels. Just acknowledge the fact of the feelings with a phrase such as, "I see you're very angry" or "I see you're upset."

If your child is having difficulty putting angry feelings into words, you might try to help: "When your brother did that to you, it must have made you very angry." Or: "I bet that was embarrassing, huh?" Or: "That probably hurt your feelings."

LITTLE BROTHER SNOOPS IN BIG SISTER'S ROOM

Child: I hate Billy! He's always messing up my stuff. Next time, I'm going to go into his room and break one of his toys!

The temptation is to "correct" this threat, because the behavior it mentions is definitely out of bounds, against the rules, and unacceptable. But replying with a "You'll do no such thing, young lady" ignores feelings and will only escalate the anger. Here is an alternative:

Parent: Oh, Debbie. I'm sorry. Nobody likes their stuff getting snooped into. I can understand why you're so upset. Let's talk about what we can say to Billy.

The parent neither denies her child's feelings nor condones her proposed action. Instead, she offers justification as well as sympathy for the feelings, and she proposes an alternative course of action—communication with Billy rather than vengeance against him. Moreover, she offers her help in resolving the situation that caused the anger. This is especially important because frustration—a feeling of powerlessness—fuels anger. Children see themselves as low on the family totem pole. They often feel powerless, frustrated, and therefore, angry. Demonstrating to them that what they say to you can produce a desirable and positive effect does much to relieve the frustration. Also important is the shift in focus here from the character of Billy to the issue at hand, invasion of privacy. Issues are always easier to deal with than people.

"IT WAS BORING AND I HATED IT!"

Dad took time off work and spent more than a few dollars to take his two sons to a baseball game. John loved it, but Mike squirmed and complained through much of the game. When it was over, he screamed out: "It was boring and I hated it!"

The temptation is for Dad to say something like, "What's wrong with you? Look at John. *He* had a good time—just like everyone else!" Instead, Dad bites his lip, swallows his own disappointment, and addresses his son's feelings: "I'm sorry you were bored. That must have been very disappointing. Tell me, what was boring about the game?"

This may spark a conversation. It acknowledges Mike's feelings, and it reinforces his willingness to share those feelings with his father. Perhaps the conversation can be led to a practical question: "What would you like to do next time? Where would you like me to take you?"

"MY MATH TEACHER IS A JERK!"

Your house rule is that children must not be disrespectful to an adult. Furthermore, you want your child to respect adult authority, especially the authority of teachers. Naturally, therefore, the temptation is to jump in and "correct" the child:

> Sarah, you can't call your teacher a jerk. That is not allowed. Period. And what do you expect if you spend so little time on your math homework? In this life, you get the treatment you earn. Work hard, and you will be rewarded. Goof off, and you'll suffer the consequences.

All of the above is perfectly logical, but such reasoning won't help Sarah cope with her anger just now. Feelings are like a house afire. You could stand next to the homeowner and watch the flames, remarking to him about the consequences of smoking in bed or overloading an electrical outlet or piling up oily rags next to the kindling stored in the basement. Alternatively, you could call 911 and, in the meantime, get your garden hose going. It is always best to begin by fighting the fire.

Dad might reply to Sarah:

When Mrs. Smith criticized you, that must have made you angry. I always hated being chewed out in class, especially in front of everybody.

Or:

You used to like Mrs. Smith, didn't you? Sounds like you're pretty angry with her just now.

Or:

It does hurt to be criticized like that. I know how it feels.

From here, father and daughter can talk more about her feelings. Once the girl's anger has been acknowledged, Dad can direct the conversation toward ways in which the *cause* of the anger might be eliminated in the future:

It sounds to me as if Mrs. Smith was disappointed in your answers to the problems, because she's used to your doing better work. Can I help you with your math homework?

Note that not all anger scenarios will result in "creative" solutions or practical plans for remedying an unpleasant situation. Such is life. Resolving an underlying issue is desirable, but it is less important than addressing feelings rather than ignoring or denying them.

25 Words and Phrases to Use

angry	must have hurt
appreciate	next time
feelings	say
frustrating	sympathize with
help	tell me
How did it make you feel?	think about
I see	together
it's okay	understand
let's talk about it	use words
mad	we
made you feel bad	What can I do?
make better	What would you like to do
must have been difficult for you	about it?

25 Words and Phrases to Avoid

ashamed of yourself
bad
behave
don't say that
don't talk to me like that
get away with it
I don't want to hear that
it's wrong to feel that way
nasty
naughty
nice girls (boys) don't say that
nobody says things like that
see it logically

shut up
stop crying
stop whining
straighten up
suffer the consequences
that's not nice
that's what you get
that's the way it is
You don't mean that!
you'd better
your fault
you're wrong

15

Death and Divorce

Young parents buy their first home. They want a safe neighborhood for their new little son or daughter. They want a location on a cul de sac, away from speeding traffic. They want good, safe schools nearby. They "babyproof" the home, putting special latches on drawers, plastic inserts into electrical outlets, spring-loaded gates at the top and bottom of the stairs, and moving household cleaners out from under the sink. They dote. They worry. They want to protect their precious child. It's only natural.

It's only natural to want to protect children from harm and hurt. That is why it's so difficult to talk with kids about the biggest hurt of all, death—death and that other major loss, divorce.

But death itself is natural, and, like it or not, divorce is also a fact of life, with one of every two marriages ending in legal dissolution. We cannot protect, cannot insulate our children from such losses. We have to deal with them and, even more important, help our children to deal with them.

Is this, then, the grim reality?

There's no denying, it *is* reality. But it doesn't have to be grim.

Why not? What's the alternative?

First, here's what the alternative is *not*. It's not making light of the loss. It's not telling the child that "he'll get over it" or "it's not so bad." The alternative to *grim* is not *denial*. Never minimize or deny a child's feelings.

The true, valid, productive, and positive alternative to *grim reality* is *opportunity*. Death and loss are universal. There's no escaping them. Your child sees death on television and in the movies, and she

578

sees death when the daisy in the window box droops and withers and when you swat a fly. When this reality is experienced close to home, close to the heart, the opportunity is for understanding, accepting, and moving beyond. The opportunity is for learning to deal with a most basic condition of existence. As parents, as caring adults, we wouldn't dream of denying our responsibility to equip children for life: to feed, to clothe, to educate them. In matters of death and loss, we have both the responsibility and the opportunity to help children learn and grow and gain productive, healthy understanding.

Finding the Heartline

Death and divorce create powerful emotions for adults as well as children. The drive to protect our children is natural, and so are the facts of death and other loss. It is natural also to assume that dealing with death or divorce is all about feeling. The assumption is natural, but misleading. Dealing with serious, painful loss involves feelings, to be sure, but it most directly requires work toward achieving four goals:

Goal 1: Understanding

Goal 2: Mourning

Goal 3: Remembering

Goal 4: Continuing

In talking with children about death—or about divorce—the way to the heartline is via these four goals. To shortcut any of them is to deny the child the opportunity to realize from the experience of loss something more than mere pain and emptiness—and to realize something much greater. Achieving all four goals not only helps the child to cope with the loss, but also to gather from it something positive for now and for the rest of her life.

GOAL 1: UNDERSTANDING

Too often, in dealing with a crisis or any occasion associated with strong emotions, we separate feeling from understanding, as if the two were incompatible. In truth, they are not only compatible, but inseparable and seamless. One of the elements that produces fear in a child confronting death or other loss is bewilderment. It is a cliché to say that we fear the unknown, but it is a cliché precisely because it is so true. Understanding reduces fear. Thus, the first goal in helping a child deal with death and loss is understanding. This is a priority item.

But how do you explain death to a child?

Begin by focusing on the needs of the child, not on your own need to soften the facts of death. In our culture, death is treated very nearly as an obscenity. Many of us go through our entire lives without ever seeing a dead person—other than portrayed on television or in movies. We indulge in euphemisms for *death* and *die*. Mother "passed on" or "passed away." Or: "I lost my mother years ago." Or: "My father's deceased."

Before we can speak frankly with children about death, we must reject for ourselves the attitude that approaches death as impolite or even obscene.

Grandma died. That is the fact. Do not, therefore, tell your child that "Grandma passed away" or that "Grandma is sleeping now." Tell her that "Grandma died."

For young children—preschoolers and early primary schoolchildren—it is not enough to state this fact. The child wants to know what happens physically to the person who died. Tell her the facts, not in clinical detail, but straightforwardly:

Grandma's body stopped working. A dead person can't eat or talk or walk or breathe. A dead person doesn't feel anything or do anything.

Depending on the child's age and level of understanding, she may or may not accept your explanation of the physical facts of death. Preschoolers, for example, may insist that Grandma is coming back or that she's simply in another place, perhaps living underground, where she was buried.

- Don't argue with these interpretations.

- Listen to what the child says. You need not comment, agree, or disagree. Just listen.

- If the child specifically asks if Grandma is coming back, tell her the truth—gently and calmly: "No. She isn't."

Preschoolers have not reached the stage of cognitive development at which they understand death as a concept. Don't be concerned if the child does not understand. At this age, the lack of understanding of the concept of death is natural. However, you do not have to reinforce or play along with this absence of understanding. Explain quietly. Listen attentively. Do not argue or debate.

School-age children may have a very literal-minded response to death. In contrast to preschoolers, they may be fascinated with the physical facts of death and may closely question you about what happens to the body after death. They may dwell on decay and other things that most of us find disturbing. Disturbing or not, however, we should not evade the questions. Instead, answer them as honestly and positively as possible:

Child: Will Grandma rot in the ground?

You: Her body is sealed in a special coffin, so I think it will stay preserved for a long time. But, you know, she can't feel what happens to her body now. So it doesn't matter to her.

More urgently, school-age children will worry about themselves and their families.

Child: Your mommy died, Dad. What if my mommy dies?

You cannot deny the reality of death. Everyone dies. But reality isn't only about white, black, yes, no, and other absolutes. It's also about degree and probability:

You: Sally, Grandma was 78 and she had been sick for a long time. Mommy is only 34, and she is very healthy. Everyone dies someday, but most people live a long time. Your mother and I are young—and you are even younger!

Religion and Understanding Death

For some adults, religious belief is all that is needed to explain death and to make it acceptable. For children, especially young children, it is not sufficient. If religion plays an important role in your family, it should also figure importantly in how you explain death to your child; however, do not expect religious or spiritual belief to satisfy the child as it may satisfy you.

As adults, *we* may take comfort in explaining that "God called Grandma to heaven to be with Him." Because such an explanation gives us comfort, we may assume that it does the same for the child. This, however, is not necessarily the case.

- The child may resent God for taking his Grandma away. God may seem mean and selfish.

- If God can take Grandma whenever He wants, what's to stop Him from taking Daddy or Mommy or even the child himself? Instead of providing comfort, the religious explanation may increase anxiety.

The best approach, especially with preschool and early school-age children, is to combine the physical explanation of death with any religious beliefs you may have—in the expectation, however, that the child will not fully comprehend the religious explanation:

> Danny, Grandma was very, very old, and her body stopped working. But, in our family, we believe that there is a part inside Grandma, the part that made her happy and that made her love us, that we call the spirit. And even though Grandma's body stopped working and is now in the ground, her spirit is in heaven with God. I don't know if you understand how that works, but I can tell you that you'll understand more about it when you get older.

GOAL 2: MOURNING

Achieving Goal 1, Understanding, does not prevent the painful feelings associated with death or loss. Such feelings are normal and natural. In fact, experiencing them—mourning—is a second goal of dealing with death or other loss. We need to recognize this not only in our children, but in ourselves.

A death in the family will produce mourning and grief not only in your child, but in you. Do not feel that you need to put up a "strong front" and hide your grief from your child. On the contrary, it is important for your child to see that you are sad—but that, sad as you are, you will continue to care for your child and will in no way abandon her. Showing and sharing your grief is also important as an example to your child. She needs to know that it is okay to feel sad about the loss. If you hide your grief, she may well get the message that her feelings are somehow bad, and this will short-circuit the emotional processes by which she deals with death.

Showing your grief does not mean moping about in silence. Talk about how you feel:

> Pam, I'm feeling sad about Grandma. Thinking about her makes me cry sometimes. I'll feel better soon, but right now I feel sad. How do you feel?

Beyond sharing their own grief, adults need to recognize that children often feel—and show—their grief differently from adults. Preschoolers and early school-age children do not simply feel sad when someone close to them dies, they feel anxious, even frightened.

Young children thrive on the security of certain routines, and the mere fact of change—let alone change brought about by death—is enough to create a profound disturbance. The response to this may not be an obvious demonstration of sadness, but, rather, what we consider misbehavior—disruptive behavior, angry actions, unruliness. Such a response can be especially trying during a time when the parents' energies are at an especially low ebb. It takes a special effort to understand that this disruptiveness is the child's way of expressing grief. There is no magic way of communicating with the child during times like this, but communication is important:

- Share your grief.
- Check in with the child. Ask her how she feels.
- Offer extra love and comforting. You may not feel like embracing an obstreperous child, but now is the time to do just that.

Few experiences in life are more painful than witnessing the pain of a child. Our natural impulse is to try to hasten the grieving process. Alas, nothing we do will shorten this process, which may last for weeks, months, even years. We *can* do the following, however:

- We can share our own grief.
- We can give the child the message that what he's feeling is normal and okay.
- We can listen to the child.
- We can offer realistic assurance of our continued love.
- We can tell the child that, as time goes by, he will feel better.

GOAL 3: REMEMBERING

Remembering and commemorating the dead is an activity common to every culture. It is almost certainly a basic human need. In our culture, remembering the dead is done in both formal, highly ritualized ways, and in informal ways.

Funerals

Think of the first funeral you attended. If you were a child, chances are that the memory is hardly a pleasant one. For most children, especially preschool and early school-age children, funerals combine anxiety with boredom, and both of these feelings are born of bewilderment.

Should children attend funerals? Better put the question this way: Should *your child* attend a funeral? For there is no generally "correct" answer. You should decide based on the child's relationship to the dead person, the circumstances of the death, and the child's age and his ability to understand the rituals he'll be a part of. Often neglected entirely is this very important criterion: The child's own willingness and desire to attend.

If you decide that the child should attend the funeral, you can make the experience less anxiety provoking and more meaningful if you discuss beforehand what will happen and what you want the child to do:

- To the best of your ability, outline the proceedings.
- Define unfamiliar terms, such as *casket, wake, shiva, coffin, funeral home,* and so on.
- If the body will be displayed, explain this.
- Encourage questions.

Do not give the child detailed instructions concerning behavior, but do explain that she will meet a lot of people who are sorry Grandma died and who want to spend some time with all of us to remember Grandma. Let your child know that she may see people talking and even crying, and that this is all normal and okay.

Never try to coerce the child into being on his "best behavior." Many children, especially those of school age, feel anxious about how they should behave during the funeral, and threats, even gentle threats, will only serve to increase anxiety.

Formal funeral rituals are important. They are more important to some people and families than they are to others. But the formal commemoration is only one way in which most families remember the dead. We remember loved ones personally, and there is great pleasure, comfort, and relief in sharing those memories. Children should be counted in on these informal commemorations. Let them participate in conversations. Invite them to share a memory:

Parent: Honey, what did you like about going to Grandma's house?

Child: I liked the chocolate cake she gave me.

Parent: That *was* good, wasn't it? She always had delicious chocolate cake for you. That was fun, wasn't it?

GOAL 4: CONTINUING

Do not rush or deny the process of grieving, but it is helpful, from time to time, to share with children two important truths:

- The pain of loss—the sadness—diminishes with time. You *will* feel less sad.

- Your grandma, your father, your sister, your friend may die, but the people we love remain in our memories.

The fourth goal of coping with death is, simply, carrying on, continuing with life. From time to time, your child will bring up the subject of the dead person. These are important occasions, and you should always make time to listen, and to listen sympathetically. To the degree that you can, share feelings on these occasions:

Child: *(three years after her brother died)* I was eating a Hershey bar, and I remembered how Howie loved Hershey bars, and I almost cried.

Mother: Sarah, sometimes, when I make hamburgers I remember how much Howie loved to drown the hamburger in ketchup, and I remember how much fun we had with him. I miss him. Do you miss him?

Child: Yes, I do.

Mother: But I'm also so very glad and grateful I have you and we have each other!

Divorce

In many ways, talking with a child about divorce resembles talking with him about death. For the child, death and divorce are both losses. Both are a kind of death in—and of—the family. In some respects, divorce may be an even crueler loss than death:

- Whereas death is final, divorce tends to feed children's fantasies about eventual reunion. This makes it harder for the child to accept the finality of divorce.

- Whereas death may be blamed on accident, illness, or age, divorce is blamed on the parents.

Communication during a divorce may be made more difficult by mother's and father's feelings about themselves and about each other. Because of the complexity and intensity of the emotions involved, it is all too easy to get confused and to give out confused and confusing messages. Such confusion increases children's anxieties. The best course is to keep your messages as simple as possible:

- In simple language, explain what's happening. In particular, explain what will happen with living arrangements and with school. Emphasize what will change *as well as what will* not *change.*

- Make it crystal clear that both mom and dad love their children, and that the kids will be taken care of. Nothing bad will happen to them.

One of the great, grave, and often unspoken fears of children whose parents are divorcing is that they, the kids, are somehow at fault. Perhaps they weren't well-enough behaved. Perhaps if their schoolwork had been better, Mom and Dad would have stayed together.

- Make it clear that the children in no way caused the divorce. Repeat this. Repeat this often.

- Make it clear that your love for your children has not changed and never will change.

Communicating during a divorce is not a one-way process. Keep your children informed, but don't forget to listen to them. Encourage them to express their feelings. This sounds easier than it is, because the feelings you may hear expressed are not always pleasant, and your children's expression of their emotions may make you feel guilty, offended, hurt, angry, and depressed. However painful, take the heat. Listen to them. Never preempt or deny their feelings.

Sidestepping the Pitfalls

In helping your child cope with loss, whether death or divorce, it is difficult to go far wrong if you listen to your children and respond honestly to what they tell you. On the other hand, the most destructive course is failure to listen and the denial of feelings.

- Do not tell your children how they should feel.
- Do not tell your children to "snap out of it."
- Do not criticize feelings.
- Do not lie. In the case of death, do not encourage fantasies of return. Do not tell your child that "Grandma is sleeping now." In the case of divorce, do not encourage false hopes of a reconciliation.

25 Words and Phrases to Use

always love you	fun times	sad
cry	good times	scary
dead	help	share
death	life	spirit
divorce	love	take care of you
everyone	memory	talk
explain	normal	tell
feelings	not alone	
frightening	remember	

25 Words and Phrases to Avoid

act grown up	blame
act like a big boy/girl	don't want to hear you say that
asleep	don't think about it
bad	don't be sad
better behave yourself	don't cry

don't disappoint me   passed away
fault   passed on
gone to sleep   snap out of it
gone away   taken away
hate to hear you talk that way   taken from us
have to be quiet   you don't mean that
it's not so bad   you'll feel better soon
must behave

16

Drugs and Alcohol

The most recent (2000) federally approved statistic is this: 16 percent of boys and girls, ages 12 to 17, use drugs. The most generally accepted statistic on underage drinking is that more than 50 percent of high school seniors drink alcohol more than once a month.

Most people find statistics boring. So stop thinking about numbers. Instead, close your eyes. In your imagination, line up a hundred kids. Throw your own children into that line. Now, mentally herd 16 of the hundred to one side, and ask 50 at random to step forward. The chances are pretty good that your kid—or kids—are among the 16 who use drugs, the 50 who drink, or even belong to both groups.

The next step is neither to panic nor to shake your head and do nothing. The next step is to talk to your kids about drugs and alcohol.

Finding the Heartline

Talk to your kids. That's a good idea, but the advice is incomplete. Talk freely *and* really listen. The object is to create a dialogue, not to deliver a monologue. The single most important thing you can do to protect your child against drug use and alcohol abuse is to know what's going on in your child's world. The way to gain this information is not by spying or prying, but by talking and *listening*.

Begin, then, by opening up a two-way channel of communication. When it is your turn to talk, keep the conversation free of threats and drama. Rely on facts:

- Let your child know that you love him and that, because you love him, you want him to be happy and healthy. The focus of the conversation should be on the child, not on you, and not even on the "rules."

- Tell your child that you find alcohol and illegal drugs unacceptable. Astoundingly, many parents never make this simple statement. To a surprising degree, kids are willing to abide by the house and family rules—provided they know what those rules are.

Let's pause a moment. Illegal drugs are illegal and should have no place in the family. The use of alcohol, however, has a long tradition in our culture. Can you tell your children that you find alcohol unacceptable if you, in fact, drink? The answer is yes—you find it unacceptable for anyone who is not an adult to drink alcohol. Make this clear: The decision to drink is an adult decision, period.

- Explain the health risks of drug and alcohol abuse. You need not go into clinical detail, and you need not exaggerate. Do mention, however, the great danger of contracting AIDS and other blood-borne infections from shared needles in the use of injectable drugs; slowed growth caused by drugs and alcohol; brain damage; impaired judgment; impaired coordination; impaired thinking; impaired memory; learning difficulties; the greatly increased likelihood of accidents; emotional problems; the problems of addiction; organ damage; death.

- Explain the legal issues. Conviction for a drug offense can result in jail time and a criminal record. Driving under the influence of alcohol can result in jail time. At the least, convictions for drug use or drinking while driving may cause you to lose a job, a driver's license, a college loan.

- Explain the dangers of association. The drug world is a world intimately connected to criminality. Criminals are dangerous people. People get killed dealing in drugs, including buying them.

- Explain the moral issues. This does not mean preaching that drugs are "wrong," but do point out that the purchase and use of drugs supports criminals, people who hurt and kill other people.

- Set clear limits. "In this family, we don't do drugs—and we do not spend time around people who do drugs."

What you say, then, can be quite straightforward. How you express yourself is as important as what you say. Fortunately, it is not difficult to speak effectively about drugs:

- Keep the conversation calm and soft. There is no need to exaggerate. Let the facts do the persuading.
- Don't just hand your child a pamphlet or two. Speak to him face to face.
- Invite response. Listen. Don't preach.
- Use TV shows, news stories, and the like as occasions to discuss drug use.
- Don't make "The Speech" and then drop the subject. Talking about drugs and alcohol is a perennial part of parenting. It is ongoing, a conversation that continues over a period of years. A good rule of thumb is to spend a half hour each month discussing the subject.
- Set an example. You cannot dodge this issue with the *do-as-I-say-not-as-I-do* ploy. Do not use illegal drugs. If you have a substance abuse problem, get help. If you drink socially, be sure that you drink responsibly. This includes never drinking and driving.

Help Your Kids Say No

As parents, speaking from the heart includes establishing rules, setting limits, and giving instruction. It also requires communicating in ways that *help* our children obey those rules, respect those limits, and follow those instructions.

- Do something practical: Make it easy for your child to leave a party where drugs or alcohol are being used. Discuss with her how you will come to pick her up if she feels uncomfortable—for *any* reason. Do not put your child in a position of dependency on other kids for transportation.
- Encourage sound decision making and good choices. Reinforce your child's positive choices. Tell her that you're proud that she

chose to go out for the school band or get on the swim team. Build her confidence in decision making. Help her make difficult decisions. Talk about how to weigh the pros and cons of a given decision.

• Try role playing: "You're going over to Dave's after school. Dave digs a beer out of his parents' refrigerator. Kids don't drink alcohol in our family, right? What do you say to Dave?"

Listen to your child's response. Play Dave: "Oh, come on. Your folks will never know!"

If your child can't come up with effective responses, suggest some: "No, thanks. I don't drink. I want to stay in shape for the swim team." Or: "No, I don't want any beer. Let's play Nintendo instead."

In general, communicate in ways that build your child's self-esteem. Kids who feel good about themselves are much less likely to abuse drugs and alcohol than kids with low self-esteem, who feel the need for illegal substances to make them feel good.

• Take every opportunity to offer lavish praise for jobs and chores that are well done.

• Spend "quality time" with your child. Listen to him.

• Give your child chores and assignments that he can do and do well. Praise him when he does them.

• When you need to criticize your child, focus on actions and issues, not on the child. Looking over your kid's math homework, you find a lot of mistakes in addition. Instead of saying what you may be feeling—"You've got to stop being so lazy about your homework!"—focus on the *immediate* issue: "There are a number of mistakes in addition here. Check your work and try again."

What to Watch Out For

Be alert to your child, your child's world, her friends, and her activities. Be especially alert for the following indicators of drug use or alcohol abuse:

- Mood changes, especially irritability, secretiveness, sudden withdrawal, inappropriate outbursts of anger, euphoria

- Irresponsible behavior, including lateness coming home or getting to class

- Lying

- A significant change in friends or lifestyle

- Unexplained influx of cash

- Physical changes, especially difficulty in concentration, loss of coordination, unexplained weight loss, unhealthy appearance

- Decline in grades, loss of interest in school or extracurricular activities

Sidestepping the Pitfalls

This is an area of parenting and communication in which the stakes are the highest imaginable. It is natural to feel uneasy over talking to your children about drugs. What if you make a mistake? What if you say the wrong thing?

The *real* danger lies in saying nothing—saying nothing, and failing to listen to what your kids say. For the truth is that almost *any* communication about drugs and alcohol is better than none. Nevertheless, try to avoid the following:

- Preaching and lecturing. Drug and alcohol conversations should be *conversations*, not parental rants.

- Failing to listen.

- Delivering "The Speech," then turning away. Remember: Speaking from the heart about drugs and alcohol abuse is a continual process. Make it your business to devote at least a half an hour each month to the topic.

- Failing to set the desired example. Words are only one vehicle by which we communicate to our children. Our actions also convey a message—the most powerful of all. If you use illegal drugs or abuse alcohol, you can expect your child to do likewise.

25 Words and Phrases to Use

addiction
alternatives
choice
confidence
crime
criminals
danger
decision
facts
harm
health
help
hurt

information
love
love you
no
prison
rely on you
sickness
success
talk to me
think
trust
want you to be happy and
    healthy

15 Words and Phrases to Avoid

ashamed of you
can't help you
disappoint me
disown you
don't bother me
don't come to me about it
fail
I don't want to know about it

I'll talk, you listen
ignorant
it's your business
lazy
must
shame
worst thing you can do

17

Manners

$\mathcal{M}$anners are a gift. They are a gift you give your children, and, when your children possess good manners, they are a gift they give to you. For the child, good manners open many doors:

- Manners are as important to getting along in a civilized world as motor oil is to the functioning of your car. Manners aren't the fuel that drives society, but they are the lubricant that keeps it from breaking down on a daily basis.
- Good manners are essential to coping day to day.
- Good manners give the child confidence that he can get along in the world.
- Good manners help the child get what she wants. Ask an adult for something *politely*, and you're far more likely to get it than if you shouted, whined, and demanded.

For the parent—and other adults—good manners in children come as a delightful surprise.

- They make our lives easier on a day-to-day basis.
- They contribute to our serenity.
- They give us confidence in our children. Children who know how to ask for things and how to behave in the world are far less helpless and vulnerable than children who are ill at ease and bewildered.

- Good manners in our children reflect well on us. They show that we care about our kids—and about the rest of the world.

Talking to your child about manners is saying it from the heart, because manners are not just the superficial trappings of behavior. Nor—despite what many people think—are they designed to hide our true feelings. They are positive expressions of how we feel about ourselves and others. Help your child learn such positive expressions, and she will be happier, you will be happier, and the circle of adults and other children around her will be happier.

Finding the Heartline

Manners are taught. In large part, they are taught through clear explanation. In even larger part, however, they are taught through modeling—through your own example. This makes the acquisition of manners a long-term project.

- Act as you would like your child to act. Explain your actions.

- Treat your children as courteously as you would like them to treat you and others.

- Introduce new habits gradually and at the appropriate time. Dinnertime is the right time to introduce table manners.

- Explain in a loving voice. Don't bark out instructions.

- Praise your child's demonstration of good manners. When your child finally starts saying "please," praise her: "Thank you for saying 'please.' It makes me feel good to hear that word."

- Talk about how certain behavior makes you feel. Rude behavior is painful, whereas courteous behavior produces pleasing feelings.

- Be consistent. If, for example, you want your child to ask for things politely, always remind him to say please. Don't let it slide with certain groups, only to demand it with others.

- Prompt—courteously—the behavior you want. "Please remember to hold the door for mommy. Thank you."

Sidestepping the Pitfalls

Teaching manners should be a gentle process. Too often, however, it is strident and filled with stern threats and name calling. In short, it exhibits anything but good manners. *Request good manners.* Don't demand them. Provide instruction so that your request can be met.

You will also find it difficult to teach the behavior you want if you do not model such behavior yourself. If you shout, make imperious demands, and use foul language, these are the modes of behavior your child will learn—your verbal instructions to the contrary notwithstanding. Actions always speak louder than words.

Remember that teaching manners is a long-term process, which should span much of childhood. Don't expect overnight miracles. Do look for small, incremental victories and modest successes. Reward these with praise.

Meeting People

Even very young children—preschoolers—can and should be instructed in the basics of what to do when they are introduced to adults. Most basic of all is teaching the child to acknowledge others.

- With very young children, it is enough to remind them to say hello or hi. The idea is for the child to acknowledge the other person verbally.

- Ask older children to attach a name to the "hello": "Hello, Mrs. Smith."

- Teach older children to introduce others: "John, when we meet one of your friends, tell me his name—like this, 'Mom, this is Gary.'"

- Conversely, teach older children to introduce you to their friends: "Dad, this is Ben. Ben, this is my dad." If you like, you may ask your child to do it this way: "Ben, this is my dad, Mr. Roberts."

Early on, children should be made aware of the nonverbal as well as the verbal components of meeting people. From an early age, encourage your child to look the other person in the eye. This is a habit that serves lifelong. Looking another person in the eye communicates warmth, sincerity, and trustworthiness. Also from an early age, teach the child the mutual pleasure of a firm (but not crushing) handshake.

At the Table

Here is the venue in which manners are most critically on display. A surprising number of families can hardly bear to eat together because of fidgeting children, impatience, and short tempers. Before you begin to instruct your child in good table manners, take steps to ensure that the family dining table is an enjoyable place:

- Tell your children how much you enjoy and value their company at dinner.

- Make dining pleasant by encouraging interesting discussions, swapping news about family members' experiences during the day, and absolutely avoiding any heavy discussions, debates, or criticism.

- Focus on the present activity. Don't betray impatience. Don't convey the impression that you'd rather be somewhere else or doing something else—such as watching TV.

The family dining experience should be a daily haven.

Having done what you can to create a pleasant, positive dinnertime climate, begin with the basics, which even young children can understand:

- Explain to children that they are to sit during meals and remain seated. This single rule will make dining more pleasant for everyone. Enforce it not with threats and punishment, but with natural consequences: "Billy, if you leave the table, you will not be permitted to return—which means that you'll miss dessert tonight."

- Most people consider it important to refrain from eating until all have been served; therefore, this is a good habit to instill in your child. With very young children, such restraint may be difficult to enforce. You might have fruit or raw vegetables available on the table for children to nibble on before the main meal is served.

- Another hallmark of good table manners is chewing with the mouth closed. The only way to instill this habit is by repeated, gentle reminders. Watch your tone of voice. Keep it kind, soft, and gentle. But be consistent and persistent.

- Related to chewing with the mouth closed is refraining from talking with the mouth full. This is a habit that must be modeled by the adults in the house, and that may be difficult for many of us. As with chewing with the mouth closed, gentle and repeated reminders are effective. Add an element of cause and effect: "Chew and swallow before you speak, sweetie. I can't understand what you're saying."

- Utensil manners require a good bit of parental judgment. Small children have to learn how to use utensils, and that takes practice. In the meantime, fingers help. When you think the child is ready, gently encourage the use of the appropriate utensil: "Why don't you try using your fork on that piece, the way Daddy does?" Gradually, patiently initiate the child into the world of adult table manners. When he uses a utensil, praise him, emphasizing how grown up he is acting: "You handled that just like a grown-up!"

- Most adults have a short fuse when it comes to "playing with food." Play is a natural and healthy part of childhood, of course, but you do want to communicate that there is a time and a place to play and a time and a place to get down to business. Don't lash out at the child, but do quietly ask him not to play with the food. If you discover that the child has a favorite food for playing with, try omitting that from the table next time. Explain: "Cathy, you'll notice there are no carrot sticks tonight. If you'd like them back on the table, you'll have to promise to stop using them as swords."

- Thank the chef. Model this behavior by praising and thanking the cook. "Sam, you made marvelous fried chicken tonight. I really enjoyed it. Thanks!" Then prompt the child: "Did you like the chicken, Eddie?" If the answer is yes, suggest that Eddie thank mom or dad for preparing it. "Everyone feels good when they're thanked. It's nice to make other people feel good."

- Discourage expressions of disgust. Present a child with broccoli, and you may get a simple "Yuck!" or an elaborate improvisation on the sounds of gagging, retching, and puking. Don't laugh. This reinforces the behavior. Don't scold. Instead, instill a quiet take-it-or-leave-it attitude: "Tom, you don't have to eat that if you don't like it, but I don't want to hear those noises."

- Use your napkin, not your clothing. When the child sits, instruct her to put the napkin on her lap. "That way, it catches any food you might drop, and it's always ready when you need it. If your fingers feel sticky, just wipe them on the napkin. Don't wipe them on anything else." You can also, at intervals, prompt the child to wipe his mouth: "John, dear, wipe your mouth with your napkin."

- Ask to be excused. In our culture, dining is a highly social event. It is very rude and disturbing to get up suddenly from the table and leave. Make it a rule that the child must ask before getting up from the table. Teach her the magic words: "May I please be excused?" To reinforce this behavior, grant the request. You want the child to learn that asking permission in this case almost always produces the desired response. If you feel that the request is premature, explain: "Honey, we haven't had dessert yet." If the child stays at the table, fine. If she is insistent—"But I don't want any more"—give her permission to leave, but add: "Okay. But dinner is over for you. You can't come back to the table."

- When you feel that your child is old enough to carry his plate and utensils from the table to the sink or counter, instruct him to clear his place at the end of dinner. Be sure that the adults and older children model this behavior. "Pete, please clear your place. Carry your plate and utensils to the sink. It's a big help to me."

As your child gets older, you can work on refining her table manners. Approach this task as a favor you do for your child. It will help her get along with others and, ultimately, increase popularity.

Speaking Manners

Today's parents may sometimes long for the days in which the common wisdom was "children should be seen and not heard"; however, few parents seriously believe this really is a good approach to child rearing. They understand that children should be encouraged to use words, to express themselves, and to develop sophisticated communication skills. Therefore, any rules you make concerning talking should be made in a context that, above all, encourages communication and expression. You do not want to bully your child into silence.

Early on, you can begin to instill an awareness of the basic rhythm of conversation. Don't interrupt. Wait for the other person to finish before speaking. This is not so difficult a habit to instill as you may think. Children rapidly become accustomed to the idea of taking turns. This concept becomes a cornerstone of their perception of fairness. "Everyone gets their turn. Please wait for your sister to finish speaking before you say what you want to say."

Don't be foolishly rigid. Of course, there are times when interruption is necessary. Talk to your child about when this may be appropriate—somebody is at the door, say, or the bathtub is about to overflow—and give him the magic formula for interrupting: "Excuse me."

Instill the habit of "please" and "thank you." This is also easier than it sounds, especially if you model the behavior. Explain that these words make people feel good.

Preschoolers begin to appreciate the power of words, especially when they see the impact of certain "bathroom words." The most effective way to curb the use of objectionable words is to avoid reacting emotionally to them. Don't get angry. Don't act surprised. Above all, don't laugh. If the language persists, consider this action: "Sheila, those are bathroom words. Please go to the bathroom to use those words."

Older children can be taught greater sophistication of speech. Rules you might consider include:

- No whispering. People don't like to feel they're being talked about behind their backs.

- Respond when spoken to. Explain the pain you cause by ignoring people. Make it clear that you don't always have to have the right answer to a question, but you should at least acknowledge the question. Q: "Do you know what time it is?" A: "No, I'm sorry. I left my watch at home."

- Don't be a smart mouth. When your child responds sarcastically, try to restrain your own urge to lash out in return. Instead, *without emotion*, point out that "nobody likes a smart aleck."

25 Words and Phrases to Use

acknowledge

apologize

attitude

best way

better way

communicate

courtesy

delightful

don't like

enjoy

eye contact

feel good

fun

get what you want

hurtful

may I

May I be excused?

nice

pleasant

please

pleasure

polite

shake hands

sorry

thank you

15 Words and Phrases to Avoid

ashamed of yourself

bad boy/girl

be quiet

brat

disgraceful

Do as I say, not as I do.

go away

keep your mouth closed

little monster

nasty

people won't like you

punishment

shut your mouth

shut up

Who cares?

18

Sex

$\mathcal{I}$t would be hard to find a parent who'll tell you that the "Big Talk"—birds and bees, the facts of life, sex—isn't important. It's even harder to find a parent who will tell you that the Big Talk is easy. In fact, it's so difficult that most parents put it off or hand the child a book ("Here, read this."). Some parents simply avoid the topic altogether. If you are one of these parents, you're hardly in the minority.

- Most of us are more or less inhibited when it comes to talking with our children about sex.

- We lack a clear idea of what we should say.

- We aren't really sure how we ourselves feel about sex and about how we would like our children to feel about it.

The first problem can be dealt with straightforwardly: Just accept the fact that you may feel somewhat embarrassed about the subject. Parents make a great many sacrifices and endure any number of uncomfortable situations for the sake of their children. If the subject of sex makes you uncomfortable, well, just chalk it up to one more trial of parenthood.

The second two problems require more work to solve.

It is beyond the scope of this book to tell you how you should feel about sex and how you should guide your children toward feeling about sex. Arguably, it is beyond the scope of any book to attempt these things. What this book *can* do, however, is tell you that effective communication requires, first and foremost, knowing what you want to say. Based on this, you can create a plan for saying it. Saying it from the heart requires knowing what is in your heart.

Step one, the step you take before you speak with your child, is to explore your own feelings and beliefs about sex, and how these relate to what you would like for your child. Without going into detail that may be either impertinent or irrelevant to your particular cultural, spiritual, and personal attitude, suffice it to say that you will probably want to focus your thought and planning on the objective of conveying sex in a way that is positive, exciting, joyful, and inextricably linked to family, to commitment, and to love. Along with this sense of the power and joy of sex, you will want to provide information and guidance that will enhance the child's capacity to protect himself from the physical as well as emotional dangers of sex.

Finding the Heartline

First, then, decide how you feel and what you would *like* to convey. If you cannot decide, you may wish to speak with your child's pediatrician or you may wish to consult any of a vast number of books either devoted to the subject or containing chapters on the subject. This, however, is a bewildering array. Worth seeking out is Linda and Richard Eyre's *How to Talk to Your Child about Sex* (Golden Books, 1998). If you have a close relationship with a clergyman or clergywoman, you may wish to talk to him or her. Your own parents are yet another possible source. Ultimately, you will have to make your own decisions about what to say, but don't be hesitant about looking for guidance.

Once you feel prepared to speak, you need to consider the matter of timing. When is the right time to talk to a child about sex? How old should he or she be? How much can he or she understand? Can you tell too much?

Many experts believe that children are ready to talk about sex by about eight years old—certainly between the ages of eight and twelve. In this age range, the focus of the talk is on *knowing*. Beyond this age range, the focus begins to shift to behavior, from *knowing* to *doing*.

Probably the best idea of all is to make talk about sexually related matters a part of regular communication with a child, even before he is eight. This does *not* mean getting down to the nitty gritty of sex and sexuality, but, rather, talking about such issues as the following:

- The body
- "Modesty"—based on respect
- Family commitment
- Loyalty and friendship
- Love

Talking about such issues with your child from an early age—say three or four—creates a context of positive, loving understanding that makes talking later more specifically about sex that much easier and more effective.

Getting Into It

When you decide the time is right for a talk more specifically focused on sexuality, the most natural approach is the time-honored discussion of where babies come from. You might begin the discussion by asking your child a question:

Where do you think babies come from?

Answers vary. Often, the response is "from the hospital." In this case, ask another question:

True, but how do they get there?

This may be met with bewilderment or such answers as "a little seed," "from God," or even "from mommy's tummy."

At some point, you may be tempted just to start a lecture. Instead, consider asking more questions. Don't do so in the manner of a school marm or a police interrogator. Put some joy and excitement into your voice. Make these sound like questions about things that really fascinate you. This should not come across to your child sounding like a test.

Mommy's tummy? Wow! Good answer. But how did that little baby get in there?

It is likely that the child's responses will become much more vague at this point. Let them become vague. As they do, let go of the subject and shift the focus:

Who should have babies? What kind of parents should have babies?

Steer the response to something like this: *People who like kids and who like taking care of kids. People who love children.* The idea is to put the physical explanation of procreation on hold while you introduce the more familiar concept of love. Go ahead and discuss love and caring. After you've discussed this subject for a time, ask your child how people show one another love. Responses will probably include doing nice things for each other, buying presents, doing favors. Perhaps the child will also talk about hugging and kissing. Great! If not, prompt her:

How do people show love with their bodies? What do you do with your arms and lips?

Then open your arms so that you and your child can hug. Now continue the discussion:

Do you know what? There is a bigger kind of hug that a husband and wife do. This kind of hug feels wonderful, and it is the kind of hug that starts a baby growing inside the mom.

From this point, you need to decide how much detail you want to explore. In large part, take your cue from your child's curiosity. This is a good time to share an age-appropriate illustrated book with your child. Don't just offer the book to read on his or her own. Go through it with the child. Some good books for children aged about eight include the following:

* Peter Mayle, *Where Did I Come From?*
* Sheila Kutzinger, *Being Born*
* Lennart Nilsson and Lena Swanberg, *How Was I Born?*

Following Up

Depending on the age and interest of the child, the follow-up discussion of sex may be part of a first "real" talk about the "facts of life" or you may discuss the following matters as and when you feel they are necessary.

One thing you should do as you discuss sex with your child is touch base with her to assess what she's already heard. You can ask,

"What have you heard about sex?" Then listen. Don't concentrate on correcting particular misconceptions, but do put yourself in the fore-front of information providers about sexual matters:

> A lot of kids don't learn much about sex from their parents. They talk to their friends or they hear stuff on TV. They joke about it. That's because they don't know the whole story. After the talk we just had, you probably know more about sex than most of your friends. But if you want to know more—or if you hear something that you don't understand or that interests you or that bothers you—come to me. Okay?

An effective way to get into a follow-up discussion about sex, after you've had the basic discussion about the "special hug," is to ask your child another question:

> How old do you think a person has to be to have sex?

Listen to the response, then explain what puberty is: "a time when people's bodies get ready to have babies."

> It is a time when girls start to become women and boys start to become men. You know, a fourteen- or fifteen-year-old boy and girl might be old enough to make a baby. Did you know that? Just because they can make a baby, should they?

Most likely, the response from your child will be no. Ask why not, and the reply will probably be remarkably sensible:

> They are too young to take care of the baby. Too young to be a good mom and dad.

Reinforce such a response:

> That's right! You have to be all grown up before you can really take care of a baby. But, before you're grown up, you're going to hear a lot about sex and even about having babies. A lot of what you hear is going to be pretty strange and confusing and mixed up. Remember, not everybody's parents talk to their kids about what we've been talking about. When you're confused, come to me or Mom.

"Dirty" Talk

The June 15, 1998 issue of *Time* magazine reported the results of a poll in which 7 percent of children said they learn about sex mostly from their parents. The remainder—93 percent—said they get their information from the media and from other kids. Perhaps the greatest gulf that separates what that 7 percent hears from what that 93 percent hears is language, the words associated with sex and the sex act. Parents can't ignore the "dirty words" floating around out there. Most of us don't want our children using such language, of course. It is rude, and it reflects badly on your child and you. But the fallout from dirty talk is even more serious, because it confuses the child, not just intellectually, but emotionally. At some point, talking to your kid about sex should probably address "dirty" talk:

> Remember when we talked about the "special hug" between a husband and wife? People have made up a lot of names for it. My favorite is "making love," because that's really what it is all about: love, loving each other. Some people just call it "having sex." But I've heard a lot of other words for it, some of them stupid and silly and some pretty nasty. Do you know what I mean?

Your child may reply that he does, and he may come up with a number of words you didn't dream he had learned. If he doesn't, prompt him.

> Well, there's "screwing," and there's the "f" word—a word so unpleasant that we just call it the "f" word, because we don't like to repeat it. Can I tell you something? People who like to use these words probably don't know much about "making love." They think the words make them sound grown up. But they're just faking it. People who use these words don't know as much as you do. I bet their parents haven't talked to them the way I've talked with you.

> So, anyway, don't let these nasty words bother you. People who use them aren't really thinking about what the words mean. Or maybe they don't even know what they mean.

Responsibility

Talking about "dirty words" can be a good lead-in to the subject of responsibility. When you are ready for this discussion, point out that "making love" or "having sex" doesn't always produce a baby, but it always should show how much a man and woman love each other.

> When they are old enough, people make love to show that they are committed to each other, that they really care about each other, and that they will be loyal to each other. We've talked about some nasty words, well, what about some really great words? What do you think "committed" means? What does it mean to "care about" another person? What do we mean by being "loyal"?

A discussion focused on key words can be the solid foundation of valuable talks about responsibility and self-control.

Making love should be special, something that adults can do when they feel loyal and committed and loving to one another. People who have sex with just anyone—without feeling loyalty or love or commitment—spoil the great feelings that go along with making love.

And there are other important reasons why people shouldn't just go around having sex with just anybody. You've heard a lot about HIV, right? AIDS? . . .

At this point, you can explain whatever you feel is appropriate about AIDS and other sexually transmitted diseases. Don't frighten your child, however. Emphasize that people can learn to protect themselves from diseases, especially if they keep sex special, something shared between two people who love each other and who feel loyalty toward one another and who are caring about one another.

Talking Puberty

The discussions we've just outlined are intended to take place between parents and preadolescent children. With the onset of puberty, the discussion becomes both more objective and more personal. It becomes more objective because your responsibility as a parent is to share more information—facts—with your child. It becomes more personal, because you now must reinforce whatever values you and your family decides to uphold.

The facts can be acquired from books; the values are drawn from your own experience, upbringing, spiritual background, feelings, and beliefs.

Facts that you will probably want to cover for children just entering puberty (approximately ages nine to twelve) include:

- what "puberty" is
- body changes
- new feelings
- acne
- menstruation
- wet dreams
- masturbation

As puberty progresses, you will also want to cover some harder topics. These might include:

- abortion
- rape
- abuse
- prostitution
- homosexuality
- sexually transmitted diseases
- pornography

Part of your discussion of topics such as these needs to be purely factual and unemotional. The discussion will lead into issues that grow out of your own system of belief and morality. This is as it should be. The important thing to remember is to provide reliable information without an edge of threat, panic, or hysteria.

Where to From Here?

What we have presented here is a starting point for discussing sexuality with your child in an informative as well as loving way. Where you take the discussion from here depends on many things, including:

- Your child's needs
- Your child's questions
- Your own beliefs and values

It is also a good idea to become thoroughly familiar with any sex education curriculum your child's school offers. Programs vary widely. If you are fortunate, your school will have a sensitive program that dovetails well with your own beliefs and values. If you are less lucky, you may find the school's program poor or even objectionable. Just what you discuss with your child may well be influenced by material learned in school.

Sidestepping the Pitfalls

Most of us find it difficult to talk to our children about sex. Even if we aren't embarrassed by the subject, we fear that we'll say the wrong things. These feelings and fears are normal.

To avoid saying the wrong things, take the time and effort to get your facts straight. Then take additional time and effort to decide what values you want to impart to your children. Sexual behavior, after all, like other aspects of behavior, is in large part an expression of the values we hold. Those values are ours to give our children.

The deepest and most dangerous pitfall is also the most common. It is the mistake of never speaking to your child about sex. No one avoids sex. (Even a choice to remain celibate is a sexual choice, a choice made in response to sex.) And the world around us does not lack for models of sexual behavior. Do we, as parents, want our children to choose whatever model is presented most appealingly on TV or in films, or by a friend, a boyfriend, or a girlfriend? Or do *we* want to guide our children? Absent parental communication about sex, we relinquish our children to whatever models of behavior happen along at the "right" time and place.

About Words to Use and Words to Avoid

Most of the chapters in this book conclude with a list of words and phrases to use and words and phrases to avoid in saying it from the heart. Talking to your kids about sex is not a topic that lends itself to such word lists. Instead, here are some rules of thumb for finding language appropriate to this subject:

- *Use the real words.* It is best—least confusing—to call things by their real names. A penis is a penis, a vagina a vagina. However, for young children, you may have family or "private" names for sex organs. If so, there is no reason to reject these, but you might point out that the "grown-up name for pee-pee is penis."

- *Don't use vulgar terms or four-letter words.* If your child asks you about one of these terms, do *not* punish, criticize, or admonish him! Instead, reply with gratitude: "Tim, I'm glad you asked me about that word. It's not a word we use in this family, because it is a word used by people who don't think about what it means. It's not a word most people like to hear."

- *Avoid hushed tones.* Speak about sexuality in a normal, open voice.

- *Be prepared to define terms.* Pause frequently to ask your child if she understands what you are saying. If not, be sure to avoid any hint of frustration on your part. Talking about new things takes patience.

Approach your conversations with your child not as a difficult duty, but as a pleasure and a joy. *This is an opportunity to teach and to share.*

Part 4

The Languages of Love

*H*eartfelt and crystal clear communication builds, enhances, and preserves romance and relationships with those we love.

19

Getting Acquainted

$\mathcal{W}$ho isn't interested in love? Grounded in the species' drive to survive, love also rises to spiritual heights that tower far above basic biology. Love is the engine that drives much of what we do, it is the focus of much music, art, and literature, and most movies. It surrounds us. A universal presence, it is free to all. Love, and all that leads up to it, is the most natural thing in the world—thoughtlessly easy.

Not!

For many of us, love, with all its pleasures and urgencies, is complicated, frustrating, even bewildering. It should be as effortless as breathing, but, instead, when it arrives, it hits most of us like a crisis— a crisis we crave, but a crisis nonetheless.

Whatever else we feel and excitedly anticipate when we meet what the cheesy greeting cards call "that special someone," we are, most of us, also profoundly puzzled:

- What should I say?
- How should I say what I should say?
- When should I say what I should say?

However positive we feel at the moment, somewhere at the back of our minds are worries about saying the wrong things, things that will hurt us, hurt the other person, and blast the budding relationship.

Turn to a friend to ask advice about these feelings and fears, and, most likely, the reply will be something like "Oh, don't be silly!" Or: "Don't worry about it!" Or: "Just let nature take its course."

Well-meaning though such responses may be, helpful they are not. They are non-responses. They are evasions. And what they evade is not a set of imaginary problems, but very realistic concerns that are central to the commencement and continuance of any loving relationship. Look at those questions again:

- What should I say?
- How should I say what I should say?
- When should I say what I should say?

What they have in common is the word *say*. It is no coincidence that these three central questions concern communication.

In matters of love, communication is central. In matters of love, communication is driven by the heart, but it is guided by the head. Don't yield to your friends' well-meaning advice to "let nature take its course" or to just "act naturally." All this really means is that you should stop thinking. Now, when you have found what just may be "that special someone," is definitely *not* the time to stop thinking, to abandon will, to just give up and drift. This occasion, this moment of contact is too important. Effective communication at this point in your life can mean the difference between—

- Getting together or not getting together
- A love that grows or love that never has a chance
- A satisfying, enriching relationship or a disappointing one
- A relationship built on and enhanced by shared feelings and values or one that is hollow and incomplete

Any successfully married couple will tell you, whether after a year or after fifty years, marriage is about communication. So is the failure of marriage. Or, rather, it is about the failure of communication. Often, that failure is a gradual process, but it generally begins with the very first encounter. Fail to communicate successfully early on, and the relationship may simply end—or it may go on, failing a little more with each passing day and month and year. Launch the relationship with a full, positive communication from the heart, and the chances for a fulfilling experience, perhaps of lifelong duration, are increased exponentially.

Finding the Heartline

In love, as in every other important aspect of our lives, communication consists of two elements:

- Speaking
- Listening

The first element, speaking, is built on the second, listening. Where love is concerned, finding the heartline depends on careful, sensitive listening, which allows you to respond in a meaningful way. How you listen determines what you say, but you, of course, shape your speech. For now, the one rule you need to know about speaking to someone you love—or feel you may love—is to shape that speech in positive terms. Find positive, affirmative things to say. For example, a man or woman who interests you says, "It's a beautiful day!" Your choice of replies is broad:

- Yes, it is.
- I love days like this.
- I love days like this, with the air so crisp and clear.
- I love days like this, with the air so crisp and clear. They make me want to get up and *do* something.
- A bit cold, if you ask me.
- I prefer it warmer.
- Well, it's fall. The beautiful summer will soon be over, and the lousy winter is just around the corner.
- Do you really think so?
- Actually, I like rainy, gloomy weather.
- It won't last.

All of these responses are triggered by listening. The first four are positive. The others are, in varying degrees, negative. Put yourself in the place of the person who remarked, "It's a beautiful day!" How is he or she likely to think about each of these responses?

- *Yes, it is.* (Pretty noncommital. Perhaps I should say something else.)

- *I love days like this.* (Wow! We seem to be on the same wavelength!)

- *I love days like this, with the air so crisp and clear.* (Great! This is someone who feels the way I do!)

- *I love days like this, with the air so crisp and clear. They make me want to get up and do something.* (Well, well! I guess I should suggest that we go out and do something!)

- *A bit cold, if you ask me.* (Oh. To each his own, I guess.)

- *I prefer it warmer.* (Mmm. A fussy one.)

- *Well, it's fall. The beautiful summer will soon be over, and the lousy winter is just around the corner.* (I don't like pessimists.)

- *Do you really think so?* (I'd better be careful what I say around him/her.)

- *Actually, I like rainy, gloomy weather.* (That's kind of creepy. She/he probably thinks that's sophisticated.)

- *It won't last.* (Why not just shoot yourself now and get it over with?)

The point is this: Most of us respond positively to positive communication. Positive language launches things. Negative language stops things.

Sidestepping the Pitfalls

Okay, so you are already acquainted with one major pitfall in the language of love: negativity. How do you avoid it? Focus on the positive as much as possible.

In just a moment, we'll go on to talk more about listening. The other major pitfalls in communicating with someone you want to get to know all involve problems with listening.

This is the principal pitfall: *You hear, but you do not listen.* It is a pitfall that comes in several varieties:

- You don't give the other person a chance to be heard. Perhaps you monopolize the conversation, delivering a monologue instead of engaging in a dialogue. Or perhaps you rush through the conversation, without inviting meaningful reply: "You like fall days? Great! So do I. Gotta go now!"

- You draw conclusions and make assumptions—without really listening. You attribute motives or feelings or attitudes to the other person that he or she may not have. She was fifteen minutes late meeting you. "I don't care what her excuse is, she just doesn't care enough about me to be on time."

- You read between the lines. The other person says, "I like American automobiles." You conclude that what he is *really* saying is that he doesn't plan to spend a lot of money on this date, because he's telling you he can't afford an expensive import.

- You are quick to come to negative conclusions. She was fifteen minutes late meeting you. "Well, she's a person who just can't get it together. Obviously totally disorganized."

- You play amateur shrink. She was fifteen minutes late meeting you. "She's afraid of men and subconsciously wants to avoid them."

Communicating with Your Ears

The really serious pitfalls in communicating interest in another person can all be avoided by careful, sensitive listening. Eloquence depends less on a good set of vocal cords than on a good pair of ears—with plenty in between them.

Effective listening is *not* a passive process. You have to work at it.

- You have to focus on the other person, on what he/she needs, feels, wants.

- You have to set as your goal understanding what the other person is saying.

- You have to suspend your own opinions, interpretations, and judgments while the other person is speaking. On a temporary basis, you need to become selfless.

- You have to stop thinking about what you're going to say.
- You have to stop thinking about your own opinions.
- You have to resist being overtaken by anger or other negative emotions, even if you don't like what you are hearing.
- You have to resist preparing a rebuttal while listening.
- You have to get rid of the attitude of waiting for the other person to stop talking so that you can say what you want to say.

Most of these objectives are accomplished internally, inside your mind. They are a form of *self*-discipline. However, you can aid the process of active listening by deliberately reflecting what the other person says.

- From time to time as you listen, pause, and repeat to the person the nub or essence of what he or she has said.
- A good time to pause and reflect is when you have heard just about all you can remember.
- Don't elaborate or "correct" what the other person has said. Distill, paraphrase what was said.
- Confirm your understanding. After reflecting what the other person has said, ask: "Do I understand you?" If the answer is yes, great! You *have* understood. What is more, you have demonstrated to the other person that you are indeed focused on him or her. If the answer is no, then ask the other person to repeat what he or she has said.

Active listening can serve as the foundation of a strong relationship right from the very first encounter, and it can continue to serve the relationship lifelong.

Making the Connection

We've begun by talking about the foundation of effective communication so that you'll be ready to get a potential relationship started in the best way possible. But before you can get a relationship started, you have to meet someone who interests you—and you need to make a connection. You don't have to become a denizen of singles bars or take out an ad in the local newspaper's personals pages to meet others. Take a look at the opportunities that abound around you—and make the most of them.

ON THE JOB

Most people meet girlfriends, boyfriends, and future spouses at work or in the context of work. This is not an astounding revelation. Let's say you work an 8-hour day (probably even longer!). That is one-third of your day. Another third is occupied in sleep. So the time you spend at work, at least five days out of the week, represents at least half the time you have available for meeting people. You can enhance the opportunities for such meetings by considering any of the following:

- Join volunteer or service groups that may be sponsored or organized by your firm.
- Make small talk in the hall, in the elevator, at the water cooler, at the fax machine.
- Ask people out to lunch.
- Participate in any after-work social activities that appeal to you.
- Attend office parties.
- Attend industry or trade functions.
- Carpool.

AROUND THE HOUSE

A well-worn song from the 1930s tells us:

> You'll find your happiness lies
> Right under your eyes,
> Back in your own backyard.

Make yourself visible and accessible around the neighborhood:

- Read a book on your front porch.
- If your apartment complex has a pool, use it.
- Do yard work and talk to folks.
- Wash your car and talk to folks.
- Throw a party. Invite singles, or ask couples to bring single people along with them.

AROUND TOWN

Running errands and going shopping are fine activities for meeting people.

- Ask for advice on a purchase.
- Offer advice on a purchase.
- Hang out in the local bookstore café.
- Frequent coffee bars and the like.
- In line—at the bank, at the cleaners, at the motor vehicle bureau, wherever—strike up a conversation.

RECREATIONAL ACTIVITIES

Consider some of the following:

- Join a health/fitness club.
- Join a bowling league.
- Take dance classes.
- Go to concerts, sporting events, theatrical performances.
- Go to pleasant city parks.

OTHER ACTIVITIES

Expand your horizons and your opportunities by considering some of the following:

- Take adult education classes or craft classes.
- Join a worthwhile, stimulating organization, such as the Sierra Club, Habitat for Humanity, or a political organization. Get involved in community work.
- Volunteer to support a political candidate.
- Join a church, mosque, or synagogue.

SINGLES-FOCUSED ACTIVITIES

Selectively choose from among the wealth of singles-focused activities available in many places, especially in larger towns and cities. For example:

- Singles tours or cruises
- Music clubs
- Religious, social, and charity events oriented toward singles

Of course, it is one thing to put yourself out there and yet another to spark conversation. You may have to devote some conscious effort to opening yourself up to the possibilities of conversation with a stranger:

- *Smile.* A smile invites response. All other facial expressions discourage response.
- *Slow down.* Allow yourself time to meet others.
- *Look up and look around.* Take in the people around you.
- *Expect contact.* Be optimistic. Most people do not live out their lives in solitary confinement. There is a natural urge to meet others, to get together, and even to fall in love.

Remember this: You're not in it alone. Not only do others want to meet you, but you have friends and acquaintances who can help you expand your network of potential mates. If you are looking for a man or woman to date, tell your friends. Talk about it. People love bringing other people together.

The Inertia of Fear

Okay. Let's say you are aware—or become aware—of the many possibilities out there for making contact. What do you do now?

Nothing.

Why nothing?

You are afraid.

In some situations, such as finding yourself in a burning building, fear prompts you to run for your life. This is healthy self-preservation. In such instances, fear is a most valuable emotion. In other cases, however, fear merely creates inaction. You don't run away from the person who catches your eye, but you don't approach him or her, either.

What are you afraid of?

The catalogue of things to fear is endless, but, for most of us, the overriding fear, the one that creates the strongest inertia, is fear of rejection.

This is a book about communication, not a hefty tome on psychology. For you, there may be no quick fix for fear of rejection. Maybe it's something you need to work on long term. On the other hand, perhaps there *is* a quick fix. Consider the following propositions:

- Fear of rejection is natural. You don't have a monopoly on it. Fear of rejection, doubtless, is born in infancy, when rejection means death. If our parents fail to care for us, fail to feed us, fail to shelter us, we don't survive. It's a fact of biology. Therefore, we crave nurture, and, at some level of our being, we harbor a fear that this nurture will be denied. In infancy, such fears have a very real basis, but they are irrational—that is, not the product of rational thought. Irrational though they are, these fears become part of the psychological baggage most of us carry into adulthood. Some of us travel light—just a carry-on bag, perhaps—others of us are burdened with lumpy suit bags, bulging suitcases, and massive steamer trunks.

- Since fear of rejection is natural, accept your feelings. Fear of rejection is not a brick wall topped with razor wire. It's a feeling. Accept the feeling and try to work around it.

- Try to adopt an adult perspective. Remember, feelings of rejection are rooted in infancy. You are now an adult. You have much more power now than you had as an infant, a child, or even a teenager.

- Spend some time inventorying your assets. Think about what you have to offer, what makes you attractive. Go ahead, draw up a list.

A major premise of this book is that you can use your feelings and emotions to make communication more effective, to say what you want to say and to say it from the heart. As powerful as this concept is, it does have limits. Although effective communication can greatly enhance any relationship, from the very beginning and throughout life, attraction is by no means 100 percent conscious, deliberate, and rational. That is, while poor communication can torpedo almost any relationship, effective communication does not guarantee a successful relationship. Nor is it a foolproof means of sparking attraction. We are attracted to others for a variety of reasons, including many that are beyond our conscious control. In short, sometimes the flame is there, and sometimes it is not.

|| Sometimes you feel the flame, but the other person's pilot light is out.

Such instances can be very frustrating, even heartbreaking. You may blame yourself, you may blame the other person, you may blame both, or you may not know who to blame. The fact is that no one's to blame. Do you blame yourself for not having been born with blue eyes? There would be no point to that. Your eye color is a fact of nature. Many factors behind attraction are also rooted in facts of nature—or aspects of upbringing or personal history. They are beyond your control, and beyond that of the other person.

This realization does set a limit to what you can consciously achieve in romance, but it is also liberating. Once you accept that attraction is not always mutual—*and* that nothing you can do will *make* it mutual—you no longer need to drag along so much fear of rejection baggage or fear of failure baggage. You are free to go on to the next potential partner.

Here is another possibility:

|| Someone may be attracted to you, but is incapable of igniting your flame.

You need feel no guilt. Even if you recognize that this other person is a fine human being, beautiful or handsome, kind, successful, you need not conclude that something is "wrong" with you—even if your well-meaning friends suggest that there is. ("What's wrong with you? Are you crazy? He drives a BMW!")

Openers

Poke around any bookstore or leaf through any number of magazines, and you will find books and articles offering lists of "surefire" opening lines.

If it were only that easy! You could just memorize a few lines and get a good shot at pairing up with whomever you set your sights on.

Why doesn't this approach work in real life?

For one thing, we communicate with a lot more than words. In the next chapter, we'll talk about the importance of body language, especially in the first encounter. But even more important than body language is the fact that what you say is less significant than what is *behind* what you say. Get in touch with your feelings and your positive emotional and intellectual attributes. Get in touch with these and speak from them. They will energize your opening line. Get in touch with or develop:

- A positive attitude
- Warmth
- Interest in others
- A gentle sense of humor
- A sense of general well-being

Get in touch, too, with your life experiences. Be ready to share them.

Okay. Good. Fine. But *what* do you *say* to someone you want to meet and get to know?

It's ridiculously simple, really. Here it is—

Hello, my name is Alice.

There's your opening line. Of course, you'll want to substitute your own name. But simply walking up to someone and simply introducing yourself is the single most powerful thing you can do to express your interest in that other person.

Now, where to from here?

There are two schools of thought on this. Both are based on the very sound assumption that what most interests people is themselves. Therefore, one school of thought teaches that you should ask questions that focus on the other person:

She: Hello, my name is Alice. You are?

He: Ted.

She: Nice to meet you, Ted. Do you come to these conventions every year?

He: No. This is my first one.

She: Is that so! What firm are you with?

And so on. This can generate a conversation. After all, no rhythm of dialogue is more natural than the pattern of question and answer. But this approach can also lead to an early breakdown of the conversation.

- What if the other person doesn't want to answer one of your questions? Where do you go from there?
- What if the other person feels that you are prying?
- What if some of the answers are unpleasant? ("What firm do you work for?" "Oh, I've just been fired . . .")

The second school of thought, still founded on the assumption that people are interested in themselves, makes the questions implicit rather than explicit. Begin by introducing yourself:

She: Hello, my name is Alice.

Then stop. Make eye contact, hold it, and be silent. Silence is one of the most powerful tools of communication. It is both an invitation and a spur. Few people will allow a silence to endure for long. The response you'll get, most likely, is something like this:

He: Hi, Alice. My name is Ted.

You might get even more. The important thing is that Ted is not responding to your explicit question, but to the question your silence implies. This is a much less mechanical and rigid pattern of conversation. It allows for more spontaneity.

You might continue:

She: Very nice to meet you, Ted. Let me tell you something about me. I just *love* this city.

Make it a statement about yourself—nothing deliberately provocative or controversial. And don't ask a question, such as, "I just *love* this city. Don't you?" Instead, stop talking. Let the silence lie there for a time, if necessary. Very soon, you'll get a response—one that involves a piece of personal information:

He: Well, I like it, too. I am a city person, I guess. This place is nice, but I really love New York. That's my home town.

And so on. One statement prompts another, yet neither of you is locked into a question-and-answer format, which is vulnerable to breakdown. Moreover, the conversation you're now having is spontaneous and natural. The result may or may not be the development of mutual attraction. Sometimes this happens immediately, sometimes it develops over time. What *will* develop is a rapport that allows the two of you to feel whatever feelings being together may produce.

The next chapter will explore nonverbal communication in matters of meeting and developing romance, and the chapter after that will delve into the world of dating.

20

The Body Language
of Love

*I*n Chapter 2, we mentioned the results of a 1971 study conducted by the psychologist Albert Mehrabian. He wanted to explore the mechanics of persuasion. What makes one speaker persuasive and another less so? As you may recall, Mehrabian discovered that when listeners judge the emotional content of a speech, they give the most weight to the speaker's facial expressions and body movement—that is, "body language."

How much weight?

55 percent.

That is, substantially more than half the power of a speaker to persuade us depends on visual rather than verbal cues.

You approach another person. Even before you utter a word, you begin to communicate. You begin to communicate powerfully and, for better or worse, persuasively. This is body language.

And there is more.

Even after you begin talking, a parallel communication proceeds in your gestures, your glance, your stance. In truly effective communication, this nonverbal component enhances, emphasizes, underscores, and, if you will, *sells* the verbal component. In less effective communication, the body language does little or nothing to sell the verbal message. In downright ineffective communication, it may actually conflict with and work against the verbal component: "Are you telling me the truth?" the parent asks her misbehaving little boy. "Yes, Mommy, I am," the kid replies—while shaking his head from side to side!

The Eyes Have It

Take a piece of paper and make a quick list of what is most important about a person's appearance. Chances are that your list includes some or all of the following:

Height

Body shape

Weight

Fitness

Hairstyle

Fashion sense—clothing, shoes, accessories

General facial features

All of these things are important, but most important of all is the face. That is usually what we look at first, and it is certainly what we focus on most intently. Within the facial focus is an even more intense focus: the eyes.

Through the eyes you send important messages:

- About how you feel

- About your energy level

- About your emotional state—happy, sad, and so on

- About your level of interest in the other person

The single most important nonverbal message you can send is interest, and the most powerful way of sending this is by making eye contact. Some people find this easy and natural, while others must make a self-conscious effort to keep their eyes from drifting aside.

- Eye contact always signals interest.

- Failure to make or maintain eye contact suggests avoidance, lack of interest, or even evasiveness—an absence of trustworthiness and sincerity.

While simply making and maintaining eye contact is a powerful signal, you can speak even more eloquently with your eyes.

- Men convey power by making eye contact with a woman and then holding their gaze longer than what feels like "normal." This may be given added power by slightly narrowing the eyes.
- Women may engage in "flirty" eye contact. They incline the entire head slightly downward, then look up at the other person, using only the eyes—not moving the head.

When you are on the receiving end of eye contact, look for the following signals of interest: Pupils slightly dilated, and eyebrows slightly lifted.

We want to *see* the person to whom we are attracted, so, involuntarily, the pupils dilate and the eyes widen to admit more light. This provides a clearer picture of the other person.

Facing Reality

As to the rest of the face, express interest and openness with gestures such as these:

- Smiling. Nothing is simpler to do, and nothing is more inviting, reassuring, and encouraging.
- Nodding the head.
- Tilting the head slightly to one side from time to time.
- Turning the face toward the other person attentively.

Taking a Stance

It is no accident that we talk about "taking a stand" on some issue or asking a politician about "her stance on" such and such a topic. This metaphor embodies the intuitive understanding that how we feel about things is reflected in the physical postures we adopt. Talk to a dyed-in-the-wool Republican about the latest Democratic taxation proposal and, chances are, you'll be speaking to a man whose arms are folded across his chest. Without having to say a word, his stance has made his "stance" clear. He's opposed.

When you meet another person for the first time, your posture reveals your "stance" toward that other person. Consider the following:

- Crossed arms indicate closedness, defensiveness, a desire not to be approached. *Stay away*, this says.

- Open gestures are inviting. Arms loosely hanging at one's sides or elevated slightly in a gesture with the palms up and outward suggest interest, openness. The same is true of hands behind the back.

- Arms akimbo is a provocative gesture. This may suggest either boldness or defiance. Most people find this stance intimidating.

- The trunk turned away from the other person conveys an absence of interest.

- The trunk turned toward the other person suggests interest.

- Leaning slightly toward someone is a strong signal of interest.

- Generally focusing on the person in front of you to the exclusion of others in the room signals interest.

- Standing *a little* closer than what feels "normal" or "natural" strongly signals interest. Standing *too* close, however, makes most people quite uncomfortable and may even brand you as creepy.

Touch

We readily label some people as "touchy feely." They like to clap others on the back, they embrace readily, they like to touch. Many people are put off by "touchy feely" folk. Touch is a very potent signal of interest, but like all powerful agents, it needs to be applied with delicacy and care during initial encounters. Touching should never come across as groping or grabbing.

- Punctuating the initial conversation with a touch on the forearm of the other person is a very strong signal of interest.

- During a handshake, holding the other person's hand a little longer than what feels "normal" is another potent signal. While shaking hands (and do so gently, but not limply), make and hold eye contact, say your greeting ("Hi, my name is Elmo."), then hold the other person's hand for just a beat or two *after* you have stopped speaking. That is, the physical handshake should last a second or two longer than the spoken greeting.

- Consider a two-handed handshake. Beginning with the right hand, then bringing the left up to gently clasp the other person's hand.

15 Signals to Give

1. Make and hold eye contact.
2. Open your eyes wide.
3. Smile.
4. Nod to communicate interest and understanding.
5. Keep your head turned toward the other person.
6. Focus on the person in front of you. Don't let your glance stray to others in the room.
7. Turn your entire body toward the other person.
8. Lean slightly toward the other person.
9. Stand a little closer than "normal."
10. Use open gestures.
11. Gesture with palms up.
12. Keep your arms generally at your sides.
13. Shake hands gently.
14. Hold your handshake a little longer than "normal"; don't release the other person's hand until *after* you have spoken your initial greeting. Consider a two-handed handshake.
15. At some point during the conversation, touch the other person gently on the forearm.

10 Signals to Avoid

1. Averted eyes
2. Frowning

3. Crossed arms

4. Eyes scanning the room

5. Face turned away

6. Body turned away

7. Fidgeting behavior

8. If seated, nervously pumping your leg or legs, or shuffling your feet (These signal a desire to get up and run away.)

9. Putting your hand across or near your mouth (This signals insincerity or evasion.)

10. Rubbing your brow, temples, or the back of your neck (These are strong signals of discomfort, displeasure, and frustration.)

21

Ungaming the Dating Game

$\mathcal{T}$he Date: Some manage to approach it easily, even casually. For others, however, it is an event shrouded in mystery, charged with powerful significance, and a source of great anxiety. It is foolish to deny that a date could—as the Steve Allen lyric goes—be the start of something big. But it is also true that even the most casual encounter, a glance, the exchange of a friendly word, can also be the start of something big. Dating has no monopoly on opportunity.

Perhaps the most realistic—and least anxiety-provoking—way to look at a date is to see it as an extension of that casual encounter or friendly word, to see it as an elaboration of an interesting, exciting, and pleasing conversation. It is not a mysterious and momentous event, but the development of an everyday exchange or series of exchanges. This doesn't mean it's not important, but it does mean that the date is no act of extraordinary genius or heroism. It is normal. It is ordinary. And it is no less wonderful for being that.

Finding the Heartline

Nothing kills romance faster than cynicism. So, don't get me wrong when I make what is bound to sound like a cynical statement. Here goes: Getting a date means making a sale.

The "merchandise"?

Your company and time.

The price asked?

The other person's company and time.

Experienced, effective sales professionals follow a time-tested formula for approaching and engaging a prospect and then closing the sale. This formula is often expressed in an acronym, AIDA.

- A—Attention. The first step in making the sale is to get the prospect's attention.
- I—Interest. The next step is to develop his or her interest.
- D—Desire. Now is the time to escalate interest into desire for the merchandise.
- A—Action. The sale is closed by moving the prospect to action.

ATTENTION

Let's see how AIDA translates into getting a date. First the A, *Attention*. This is largely addressed in chapters 19 and 20. Someone commands your attention, and you respond by taking steps to get his or her attention. This is the purpose of conversation.

INTEREST

The conversation may develop from attention into I, *Interest*. To promote this development, try guiding the conversation with some open-ended questions or statements that invite comment. Any successful sales professional knows the value of questions. They involve the prospect in the merchandise. They prompt the prospect to invest time in considering a purchase.

You can get your "prospect" to invest time in you by asking questions—or making statements—that call for more than a simple yes or no answer. Ask someone, "Do you like movies?" and you do not set up the conditions that create conversation. The question calls for nothing more elaborate than a yes or no—a minimal investment, indeed. An open-ended question requires a larger investment: "What kind of movies do you like?"

This is similar to the difference between the dopey true-or-false exams you were given in high school and the more challenging, engaging, and creative essay exams handed out in college. Open-ended questions invite creativity, thought, and engagement with the subject *and with you*. They open up whole areas of discussion.

Most closed-ended, yes-or-no questions can easily be transformed into open-ended "essay" questions:

- Not: "Do you like Japanese food?" But: "What's your favorite Japanese restaurant in town?"
- Not: "Do you like jazz?" But: "What kind of music do you like?"
- Not: "I haven't seen you here before. Is this the first time you've come to this club?" But: "How did you find out about this place?"

When you are on the receiving end of a question, give as full and conversational an answer as you can:

Her: What kind of music do you like?

Him: I enjoy all kinds, but I really love jazz, especially Swing and Be-bop. I can't get enough of Charlie Parker. What musicians are you passionate about?

Notice that the "close" to this answer is open ended. It invites more conversation.

There is another way to open up your questions. Begin with a personal revelation, *then* go on to the question:

I have a confession to make. I'm *really* into jazz—and all kinds of other music, too. What kind of music do you like?

DESIRE

"Desire" in the romantic sense may or may not be driving you—or the other person—at this point, but the "desire" you *do* need to develop now is the desire to continue the conversation. At this point, it is probably premature to ask for a date. Instead, set up nothing more than the potential for a date. This is as simple as an exchange of phone numbers:

I have really enjoyed talking to you. Can we continue this later? Let me give you my phone number—and, if you're comfortable with the idea, would you give me your number?

SAYING NO

If you are on the receiving end of the dating "sales pitch," and you don't want to go further, you can decline abruptly or gracefully.

The abrupt approach. This is appropriate if you are quite certain that you have no interest in the other person. Use body language (Chapter 20) to exhibit your lack of interest. If this fails to clue the other person in, do not respond openly to his or her open-ended questions. Deliver curt, monosyllabic answers. If this fails, just say "I don't want to talk," and walk away. It is important that you move on, make an exit, or at least walk away. You want to communicate that no means no.

The graceful approach. This is appropriate if you have been enjoyably conversing, but you do not wish to continue the conversation elsewhere, much less go out on a date. When the other person asks if he/she can continue the conversation later or asks you out for coffee, reply politely, but honestly: "Thanks for the invitation, but I'm not available to go out." You do not need to launch into an explanation.

ACTION

Assuming that you have exchanged phone numbers, the next step is to make a date. For quite some time now, it has been socially acceptable for women as well as men to do the asking; however, even today, women are more often on the receiving end.

- When to ask? Ideally, you should ask the other person out two or three days after the exchange of phone numbers. This is not a hard and fast rule, of course, but if you wait longer than a week, the other person may have assumed you aren't interested and may now be lukewarm to your invitation. If you ask sooner, you probably haven't given him or her sufficient time to think about his or her level of interest in you.

- Sales professionals learn that once you've made the sale, it's time to shut your mouth. The invitation to a date is not the time to carry on a get-to-know-you conversation. This is material for the date itself. Keep the conversation brief . . .

- . . . but not *too* brief! Don't just pop the question. Make a little light small talk first. Ask about the other person's day. Reminisce briefly about the circumstances of your meeting.

- Keep the conversation positive. Don't complain about your day, your job, your life.

- Be aware that this is a call to *action*. Sales professionals know that closing a sale requires providing the prospect with a specific course of action—for example, exactly how to order the merchandise.

Following this analogy, be certain to call with a specific invitation, not just a "we really should get together sometime." You might suggest something like this: "I'd like to meet you for lunch, any day next week. Noon would be nice. I'm thinking about Fredo's, that Italian place on 10th and Market." Obviously, you need to be flexible. If he or she can't make it at a certain time, be open to an alternative.

CAN—*SHOULD*—THIS "SALE" BE SAVED?

Flexibility is one thing, but what if the response to your proposed plans is something like "Oh, I just don't know. I'm not sure what my plans are for next week."

There are several possible reasons for such a response:

- He/she really *is* unsure of his/her plans.

- He/she is uncertain about whether to accept your invitation.

- He/she doesn't want to accept, but has a hard time saying no.

None of these reasons bodes very well for getting a date. If the person were really interested, but unsure of his/her schedule, the reply would be something like: "Oh, look. I'd love to go, but I'm not sure of my plans for next week. Can I call you back tomorrow?" As for the other possible reasons, you are faced with either trying to save the "sale" or deciding that it is not worth doing.

One advantage to the uncertain or put-off response is that it gives you an opportunity to assess just how enthusiastic *you* are about the prospect of a date. If a lukewarm or cool response quickly dashes your interest, then you are best off dropping the invitation. If, however, you find that you are still interested, you may choose one of two courses:

1. Propose an alternative time to call. "Kathy, what if I call you again at the end of the week?"

2. Find out what's *really* going on. "Kathy, I want to be sure that I'm not being a pain. Are you really interested in going out? Or would you rather not? I'd love to go out with you, but if you don't want to, I'll understand. The last thing I want is to make you uncomfortable." Be certain to deliver this speech gently and without a trace of sarcasm or bitterness. Don't *dare* the other person to say no, but do give him or her permission to do so.

ACCEPTING NO

If the answer to your invitation is no, accept the answer with grace.

- It's the right, decent, and mature thing to do.
- He or she may have friends. You want to leave a favorable impression on him/her and his/her circle of friends.
- Minds do change. Don't slam the door as you leave.

One thing is critically important. Take no as no. If he or she is playing a mind game, saying no only to invite pursuit, that is not *your* problem. Dishonest games are never a good foundation for a relationship.

How do you keep the possibilities open for the future? Accept the no gracefully and as positively as possible:

Ed, thanks for your honesty. I understand that you're involved just now.

Then invite future reconsideration:

If things change for you or you change your mind, why not give me a call? I'd love to hear from you.

On the Receiving End

When you're asked out—and you want to reply with a yes—do so!

- Reply honestly and with enthusiasm. Don't play hard to get.
- Don't protract the acceptance. The invitation call is not the time to get into a long heart-to-heart. You can do that during the date itself.
- Keep the conversation positive. Don't start complaining about your hard day or your hard life.
- If you like, set limits when you accept. If you are invited to what is obviously intended as a romantic dinner and you are not ready for that on a first date, suggest an alternative: "I'd love to meet you. But I'd really like to get to know you better before we do the whole dinner thing. Can we get together for a cup of coffee later in the week?"

Should you move heaven and earth to accept a date that conflicts with other plans? That's up to you. Nothing wrong with taking a raincheck, however, just as long as you make it clear that you truly are interested in going out.

- Express your disappointment.
- Explain the conflict—briefly.
- Offer or invite an alternative time.

John, I would love to see you again. But next week I'm going downstate to visit my folks. I'll be back on the 23rd. Can we set something up for that week?

Sidestepping the Pitfalls

The pitfalls of dating are many, but, really, they are all variations on one major error: Thinking of dating as a kind of game, the object of which is to outwit your opponent. Many of us are brought up to believe that acting coy or cool on the one hand and trying hard to be impressive on the other are what is expected on a date. The antidote advice to this, to "just be yourself," is well intended, but not very helpful.

Avoid the major pitfalls by thinking of the events leading up to a date and the date itself as an occasion for saying it from the heart. This requires, first and foremost, listening from the heart, hearing the other person and responding to what you hear. A great date is one of life's most wonderful self-indulgences. Paradoxically, however, the more *selflessly* you approach the date, the more gratifying you will find it. Focus on the other person.

The Conversation Begins

Remember the lesson of Chapter 19: The greatest secret of eloquence lies in your ears. Listening is the most important component of effective communication, especially when the knowledge you are trying to arrive at is knowledge of the heart.

A knowledge of the heart, the understanding of your own feelings and those of another, is what the dating ritual is really all about. It is communication on a most tender and important level.

This book can't tell you what to say on *your* date, but there are rules of thumb that can guide the dating dialogue and make it more satisfying:

- Listen, so that you can focus on the needs, wants, desires, and anxieties of the other person.

- Although you should respond to the feelings the other person expresses, never speak for him/her. You can avoid this by censoring yourself when you feel yourself about to begin a sentence with *you*. This usually means you are about to project a feeling or motive or intention on the other person. Ultimately, such projections erode a relationship. Speak for yourself. Address the feelings of the other person, but speak from your own feelings.

- Own your feelings. The other person will trigger in you feelings both pleasant and painful. Remember that they are *your* feelings. Talk about your feelings, but don't attribute them to the other person. That is, avoid sentences beginning with "You make me feel . . ."

- Focus on the present. There is nothing wrong with pleasant reminiscence, but blame and complaints for bygone affronts and injuries kill relationships.

- Accent the positive. Resolve to focus on the positive pleasures, not negative complaints.

- Focus on one another, not others. Avoid comparing your behavior or that of the other person to anyone else or to other couples.

- Use words. Express your feelings rather than act them out.

25 Words and Phrases to Use

accept	cannot accept	express
alternative plan	eager	feelings
appreciate	excited	fun
ask	explain	grateful

great	look forward to	would love to
happy	no	would love to, but
I have plans	pleasure	yes
interesting	thank you	
invitation	wonderful time	

15 Words and Phrases to Avoid

blame	maybe, maybe not
boring	never forgive
can't stand	no (when yes is meant)
depressed	yes (when no is meant)
don't like	you always do . . .
fault	you make me feel
feel bad	your fault
hate	

22

The Romance
of the Love Letter

$\mathcal{I}$n the late 1970s and early 1980s, with the advent and early development of personal computers, technology gurus everywhere predicted the coming of a "paperless world." With digital electronic communication, they said, paper would be rendered all but obsolete.

Wrong!

At the dawn of the 21st century, with the digital revolution over and won, somebody estimated that American business was actually using far more paper than ever before in history: 775 billion pages of paper per year, enough to make a stack 48,900 miles high.

Yet in this avalanche of paper, how many *personal* letters do you get each week? Each month? Each year?

If the answer makes you feel lonely, well, you're not alone. Although our mailboxes are jammed with more paper than ever, fewer of those envelopes contain personal messages.

The most personal message of all is, of course, the love letter. If you write one in this day and age, does that mean you're bucking the trend?

Decidedly.

Does it mean you're hopelessly romantic and old fashioned?

Let's hope so.

In an age of phone calls, e-mailed notes, and junk mail, a love letter, on paper, in an envelope, with a stamp, is greeted as something rare and valuable, precious as a lovely antique. It is a very powerful medium for saying it from the heart when saying it from the heart matters more than anything else.

644

Finding the Heartline

"Love," that song lyric from the 1960s goes, "makes the world go 'round." Certainly, it powers prodigies of achievement. For love, the Trojan War was fought. For love, the Taj Mahal was built. For love, men and women risk and sacrifice their lives for one another. And so the force of love should make our words not just flow, but gush in a torrent of eloquence.

Right?

Not for most of us. Most of us find it highly daunting to express love in writing.

- We feel inadequate to the task.

- The emotions of love are pleasant to feel, but don't always look "right" on paper.

- Love seems to engage the part of the brain that is least verbal.

- We're afraid of sounding corny.

- We're afraid of causing or experiencing embarrassment.

These are all real and legitimate obstacles, but they come from the fundamental error of expecting too much of a love letter. Remember this: The very fact that you have taken the time and necessary thoughtfulness to *write* a letter in the first place is a powerful statement of love in and of itself. Whatever you may actually say in the letter simply amplifies the gesture.

- Anyone qualifies to write a love letter. You do not have to be a poet or novelist.

- Try to write what you feel.

- Share memories of experiences the two of you have had.

- Don't reach for high-flown rhetoric and flowery language. Use simple words.

- Picture the other person in front of you. *Talk* to him or her. Make your writing conversational.

- Keep it real. Don't talk about abstract ideas. Focus on real events and real things.

The last point is especially important when saying it from the heart. Human beings are capable of very elaborate abstract thought, but they respond most vividly and intensely to concrete, physical reality. Think about the last novel you read and enjoyed. Did it speculate about *ideas* of pain and pleasure and adventure? Or did it present *scenes* and *stories* of pain and pleasure and adventure? If the answer to the first question were yes, there would be little market for fiction. The fact is that novels are appealing because they appeal to the senses, to our *sense* of reality. Good letters—especially letters to someone you love—also appeal to reality.

- Instead of "You're so sweet," think of *why* he/she is this way—then write about it: "I love the way you took my side when I told you about that argument I had with my boss."

- Instead of "You're so thoughtful," try: "I am amazed that you remembered how much I love *white* roses. They were so lovely."

Sidestepping the Pitfalls

The great pitfall in writing love letters is intimidation. You may feel inadequate to the task of expressing the depth and breadth of your love. You may feel that your letter will somehow undercut or belittle your feelings. The result of this intimidation? You don't ever get around to writing the love letter, or you adopt a stilted, high-flown language that is not your own. The more you think of the love letter as a conversation, the easier it will be to avoid intimidation.

In the Beginning

Here are two ideas for the first love letters of a relationship:

Dear Cindy,

I *said* it to you yesterday, and now I want to set it down on paper: *I love you!*

There it is, in black and white—for me to see, for you to see, for everyone to see. Because it's the wonderful truth. And because it is the truth and so wonderful, I intend to say it and write it repeatedly to you now and forever.

I love you,

Ned

Dear Alex,

The concert last night was wonderful—but even more wonderful was what I felt after I left your house. I felt—simultaneously—complete and incomplete. I felt complete because I had been with you, and incomplete because I was not with you at the moment. That's when I realized that you are part of my life. The phrase sounds a little cold to me. But it's what I mean: You are *part of my life* now.

I want to share with you whatever I do and whatever I feel. That makes me feel complete.

I love you, Alex—

Wanda

Sharing

Dearest Joan,

The concert last night was fantastic!

I know, you're about to say I'm crazy, because, last night, you were raving about how great the concert was, and I was complaining about the songs as well as the band.

But that is the fantastic part. You and I are so much alike in so many ways. I mean, we're both fanatics about the environment, we're both stubborn as— what?—whatever animal is really, *really* stubborn, we both love the poetry of John Donne and W. B. Yeats, and we sure do feel the same way about sunsets—as well as sunrises. But we're also very different. Last night was an example. You loved the concert, and I did not. And here's the fantastic part: It is okay.

We love being alike, and we love being different.

No matter how bad that concert was (to me), I loved it because I heard it with you. I was there with you. I also love the fact that you so enjoyed the concert and that you could tell me how much you enjoyed it, and I could tell you how much I didn't enjoy it, and we *still* love each other!

I love being free together—so alike and so different.

Love a million times over,

Benny

Dear Mike,

We walked in the woods for hours—I don't know how many—but I wished the walk would go on and on. It was so very, very lovely.

The trees, the colors of the fall leaves, the smell of the moist earth, the pines, the crisp cool of the autumn air—all of this was multiplied, amplified by your being there to breathe it all in with me.

Mike, this is what love must be! Think about it. It's seeing, hearing, feeling, *breathing* the world differently because you're with the person who means most to you and makes everything else mean more than it ever meant before. I feel as if I never really looked at a wildflower before, now that I've seen it with you beside me.

I love you very much,

Sally

Missing You

Dear Nadia,

So here I am in Santa Fe at the medical conference. Yesterday evening, I attended a cocktail reception out in the desert, at a place overlooking the Sangre de Christo Mountains. The sunset paints the peaks a salmon red, a glowing red. You must think it was very beautiful. I'm sure it *was* beautiful. Half listening to a conversation, I stared at the glowing mountains, and all I could think was *This must be beautiful*. But I couldn't really feel the beauty of it.

That's when I realized how much I miss you.

Without you here to see this with me, the best I can do is know that there is beauty here, but *feel* it, really *feel* it? No.

Without you, the world is incomplete. It's that simple. Thank goodness this conference will be over in two more days, and I'll be on my way back home to you.

Love,

Stan

Dear Tom,

I look at myself in the mirror, and I'm the same woman. Same face, same eyes, same hair. I walk down the same stairs I walked down yesterday and last week and last year. I go to the office I've been going to for three years now. Same job, same nice people.

But it's all so much better because I am in love with you. The feeling I carry around with me makes everything brighter. Yet, with you gone for the rest of the summer, the world also seems emptier, unfinished, waiting to be completed. Tom, I miss you very much, and I count the days until we'll be back together again.

Love,

Frieda

25 Words and Phrases to Use

adore	I miss you	see you again
better	I love you	share
delight	intense	together
dream	kiss	understand
embrace	love	us
experience	my life	we
fantastic	my world	wonderful
feeling	our	
great	realize	

Words and Phrases to Avoid

The vocabulary of love is virtually without limit. Avoid words that do not feel like your own.

23

You Have Mail

$\mathcal{E}$-mail may lack the old-fashioned charm of the envelope-and-paper love letter, but it does have the advantage of spontaneous immediacy and a casual quality that is both friendly and intimate. The e-mail love note is not a substitute for the snail-mail letter, but, these days, it is a natural supplement to it and can be a great way to stay connected.

The Heartline Online

The same general principles that govern love letters (see Chapter 22) also apply to e-mail notes. But be aware that the digital medium invites spontaneity, an off-the-cuff approach, and is also best suited to brevity. There is nothing to stop you from writing a long letter and sending it via e-mail, but most people don't like to read extended amounts of text on a computer screen. It is also true that an envelope-and-paper letter generally delivers richer emotion. It is perceived as more romantic, more substantial, if you will, more *real*—and less virtual. This being the case, you may not want to "waste" your more fully developed thoughts and sentiments on a digital transmission when you can commit them to paper instead.

We said in the previous chapter that the best love letters are conversational, written as if the addressee were sitting beside the writer. If anything, this is even more true of e-mail. E-mail invites a conversational tone. When you sit down to write, imagine the other person there before you. Don't be afraid to speak aloud as you type.

Sidestepping the Pitfalls

E-mail offers some unique—and uniquely serious—pitfalls.

As of the beginning of the 21st century, at least one of every two households owns a personal computer. If the number of PCs has exploded, even more explosive is the growth of Internet access. A majority of home computers is now connected to the Internet, and these ranks swell daily, hourly, and even by the minute. Many people regularly use e-mail to communicate with one another, from one home to another. Of course, e-mail made its first inroads in corporate settings, as business communication, and one would be hard pressed these days to find a business that does not use e-mail communication at least to some extent. In many firms, e-mail is the chief form of communication, outstripping the telephone and even face-to-face meetings. This said, please consider the following advice carefully:

> E-mailing love notes should be a home-PC-to-home-PC activity. It is very, very risky to send personal correspondence of any kind via corporate e-mail systems!

Recent court cases have repeatedly upheld the principle that e-mailed messages sent via corporate e-mail systems are the property of the corporation. This means that your employer has the right to read all of the e-mail you send—or that is sent *to* you—via the employer's e-mail system, network, and computers. You have no right to privacy when you transmit or receive e-mail via the company's network.

At the very least, then, intercepted love notes can be embarrassing, but there is even greater risk. Your employer may—

- disapprove of your using the company's equipment and time to send and receive personal messages

- consider sending personal messages unprofessional

- interpret personal messages as forms of inappropriate sexual behavior or even harassment

The result of this may be censure or other disciplinary action, up to and including dismissal.

The moral of the tale is this: E-mail invites casual communication and has the aura of intimacy, but, in a corporate setting, e-mail is public and fully open to scrutiny by any number of people. Corporate e-mail systems are not appropriate vehicles for transmitting or receiving personal communications.

Developing Digital Style

It is truly remarkable how quickly e-mail has become a part of our lives. Most of us now use it as naturally as we do the telephone; however, some of us take to the keyboard *more* naturally than others.

- For some, typing out an e-mail is a very conversational activity. The language is casual and natural.

- For some, typing out an e-mail is a careless activity. The writing is so casual that it is difficult to read.

- For some, the digital style is a kind of shorthand. Incomplete sentences are dashed off. Fragments. Words. Abbreviations. Capitalization and punctuation are abandoned.

- For some, the digital style is less like a conversation between two people facing one another in comfortable surroundings than it is like walkie-talkie communication from one besieged foxhole to another.

For personal communication, the best approach to e-mail is conversational. This is made easier if you are an adept typist. If you plan to use e-mail extensively for day-to-day correspondence, and you are not comfortable at the keyboard, you might invest in one of the several typing instructional software packages currently on the market. It is by creating a conversational style that your personality will come across most vividly in digital form.

In the early days of e-mail communication (which means only a few years ago), correspondents had nothing at their disposal beyond words. To enliven e-mail communication and broaden its emotional range, e-mailers developed a set of symbols called *emoticons*.

The idea behind emoticons was to bring to e-mail communication something of the physical immediacy of face-to-face conversation. When you talk face to face, you gesture, smile, frown—in short, express emotion. Since e-mail is often recruited to stand in for such conversation, a visual vocabulary for adding emotional expression to e-mail messages may be of some use. Hence the *emoticon*. Combining "emotion" with "icon," *emoticon* describes a symbol developed as shorthand to express via e-mail the emotions that are otherwise conveyed face to face. Reflecting the technology of early e-mail systems, emoticons use nothing more than the basic, so-called ASCII characters found on your keyboard. No fancy graphics are required. The chief limitation of the emoticons is that the "emotions" they express must be interpreted by viewing the icons at a 90-degree angle—that is, sideways. Just tilt your head to the side and start reading:

:-)	Humor (smile face)
:-) :-) :-)	Ha, ha, ha!
:/)	Not funny
'-)	Wink
(@ @)	You're kidding!
:-"	Pursed lips
:-V	Shouting
:-W	Sticking tongue out
:-p	Smirking
:-O	Eeeeeeeek!
:-*	Oops! (Covering mouth with hand)
:-T	Keeping a straight face
:-D	Said with a smile
=|:-)=	Uncle Sam
:-#	Censored (or Expletive deleted)
:-x	Kiss, kiss
:-(	Unhappy
:-c	Very unhappy
:-	Desperately unhappy
(:-(	Even sadder
:-C	Jaw dropped in disbelief
:-|	Disgusted
:-?	Licking your lips
:-J	Tongue in cheek remark

:-8	Speaking out of both sides of your mouth
(:-&	Angry
||*(	Handshake offered . . .
||*)	. . . and accepted
(-_-)	Secretly smiling
@%&$%&	Curses!

Emoticons can perk up your e-mail message—though like any other good thing, they can be overused. Take care not to transform a light, witty message into something cutesy and childish.

In any case, most e-mailers no longer need to work exclusively within the confines of ASCII text. Most e-mail systems today allow you to attach pictures, sounds, and even video clips to your messages. Are you far from your loved one? Why not send him/her a photo of yourself, or a recording of your voice, or even a video clip? Nor are you limited to sound or graphic material you create yourself. The Internet is filled with Web sites that feature interesting pictures, sounds, music, and video clips you might like to share. You are limited only by your imagination. But the point is this:

- Face to face is generally the best way to communicate.

- A love letter usually offers more emotional value than an e-mail or even a phone call.

- Despite these first two points, e-mail does offer certain advantages: It is convenient and immediate. Transmitted from *personal* computer to *personal* computer, it is, in a word, *personal*. Nowadays, e-mails can carry more than just typewritten words; they may also convey pictures, videos, and sound.

Editing Yourself

Spontaneity is the name of the game with e-mail. What could be wrong with this? The trouble is that composing and sending an e-mail is so easy that we are tempted to do it with little thought. The typical approach is *ready! shoot! aim!* We dash off the message, click on the send button—and *then* we happen to read over what we have just irretrievably committed to the digital ether. Invariably, we find it riddled with dumb mistakes, typos, spelling errors, and, much worse, a couple or three things we regret having said.

Just because e-mail invites spontaneity and enables haste, you are not obligated to be totally spontaneous and hasty. You can compose messages that have the feel of spontaneous conversation, but, since you aren't communicating in real time, you *do* have the opportunity to review your work, to edit yourself.

Pause a moment before clicking on "send." Reread the message, correct glaring errors, and make certain that what you've said is what you want to say, because once you do click, the message is no longer yours.

6 Digital Love Letters

The following are examples of love "letters" tuned appropriately to the digital vehicle. Remember: Personal e-mails should be sent from *home* PC to *home* PC and *not* on your employer's computer over your company's network. Nor should you send, from your home, a personal message to someone at work. Once an e-mail enters a corporate network, it becomes the property of that corporation.

FIRST NOTE

Hi, Rhonda—

I sat down at my computer to catch up on some work at home, but all I can think about is you or, to tell the truth, *us*. I've never felt so happy, excited, and comfortable—all at the same time—with anyone else. You are wonderful.

I love you—

Pete

Dear Tod,

The flowers you sent just arrived. I woke up this morning thinking *roses*. You sent *roses*. This *must* mean something—and it must be something pretty great!

If you truly can read my mind, Tod, I guess I don't have to tell you that I love you.

Sarah

SHARING MOMENTS

Terri—

I was out the door on my way to work, then I looked up at the sky, and at the big crepe myrtle in blossom at the front door. A beautiful morning, I thought, and, thinking of beauty, I thought of you. So I rushed back inside the house, turned on the computer, and wrote you this note, my love.

Sam

Bill, Dear—

They just showed *Casablanca* on TV, and I watched it for the millionth time, give or take. But, this time, I thought: Bogart and Bergman don't have a tenth of the romance in their lives that we've found in ours.

I can't wait to see you again Friday.

Beth

MISS YOU

Hello, Dear Nora—

This convention is dull, dull, dull. But I could be in a tropical paradise, on the beach, and, without you, it, too, would be dull, dull, dull. Anyplace I go, anything I do is the poorer for our not being there together. I will be very happy when I am back in good old Anytown with you.

Love,

Marv

Dear Daryl,

I'm sitting at my little brother's computer. Mom is about to call us all in for Thanksgiving dinner. I love being home for the holiday, but I'm also learning an important thing: I miss you. I wish you were with me here.

Got to go, dear. See you soon—Claire

25 Words and Phrases to Use

a few words

adore you

be with you again

blissful

can't wait to see you again

dash off a few words

embrace you

fun

hug you

I love you

in love with you

joy

love

marvelous

miss you

need you

quick note for you

reach out to you

romance

romantic

share a few minutes

thrill

together

wish we were together

wonderful

Words and Phrases to Avoid

The vocabulary of love is virtually without limit. Avoid words that do not feel like your own. Always be sensitive to the fact that others may have access to your correspondent's computer.

24

Understanding Misunderstanding

"*M*isunderstanding" is among the most misunderstood words in our common vocabulary. We often use it as a euphemism, a polite, emotionally neutral way of describing any argument, dispute, or even break-up. It is a fact that many arguments, disputes, and break-ups are the product of genuine misunderstanding. Person A says something that means something to him, and Person B hears it, but interprets it as meaning something else. It is also a fact, however, that some so-called misunderstandings are really arguments, disputes, and break-ups caused not by faulty understanding, but by all too accurate understanding. Person A says what he means, and Person B doesn't like it.

Relationships are full of arguments and disputes—sometimes leading to break-up. These are sometimes the product of serious, critical issues that each member of the couple understands, but cannot reconcile or resolve. Honest, open, sensitive communication generally provides the best chance of resolving these problems, but there is no guarantee that saying it from the heart will patch up all the wounds and cure all the ills. What honest, open, sensitive communication *can*—almost always—fix is genuine misunderstanding: arguments and disputes that are triggered by and perhaps exacerbated by Person A failing to make himself clear to Person B or expressing himself in such a way as to aggravate a situation instead of clarifying it so that it can be addressed and worked through.

Finding the Heartline

Communicating to avoid misunderstanding requires, first and foremost, disciplined listening. This is listening that is governed by three broad principles:

1. *Assume honesty and no hidden agenda.* Enter into the communication in good faith, with the intention of being honest and the assumption that the other person is also being honest.

2. *Hold your tongue—and your judgment.* Remember that your first objective is to listen and hear. You cannot do this while shouting. Give the other person the time, space, and silence he/she needs to say what needs to be said.

3. *Keep an open mind.* Before a trial, lawyers spend a good deal of time questioning prospective jurors to ensure that they are not sitting in judgment with their minds already made up. Listen with your mind open. Leave your agenda at the door.

When it is your turn to speak, the path of the heartline goes through the following points:

- Respect—for yourself and for the other person.

- Rules of engagement: Resolve not to allow the discussion to escalate to harsh words, name calling, or violence of any kind.

- Refusal to project: Recognize that it is potentially destructive to assume that the other person sees and feels the situation the same way that you do.

- Refusal to blame or accuse: Don't deny your feelings, but don't automatically blame them on the other person. Instead of "You make me angry," try "I feel angry with you."

- Separating behavior from the person: Instead of criticizing the other person for being bad or stupid or insensitive, criticize a specific action for being bad or stupid or insensitive. Not "You're just an insensitive person," but "Bringing up that old issue was insensitive."

Sidestepping the Pitfalls

The great pitfall that creates misunderstanding is the failure to pass conversation through the points just outlined. This failure often comes from an initial loss of perspective. When a conversation becomes a confrontation, it is very easy to lose sight of the desirable outcome of the encounter: a resolution that satisfies both people and that strengthens the relationship. Instead, you may see the only desirable outcome as your emerging the winner—no matter who gets hurt. And remember, if you get hurt, you get hurt; if the other person in the relationship gets hurt, you also get hurt. Give up the need to win for the sake of winning. Give up the need to be "right" even when being "right" makes you feel wrong. Instead, work—struggle—to retain your focus on the truly desirable outcome.

How to Stay in It Together

While effective, positive habits of communication cannot guarantee a loving, enduring, and rewarding relationship, you can be pretty certain that poor communication habits will contribute to the degradation and even the destruction of any relationship. The good habits tend to bridge the distances between individuals, while the bad habits tend to emphasize or even widen these distances.

THE SELF CONVERSATION

Conversing with yourself: The two of you are together, but you are talking to yourself. What could be less constructive than this? And yet it happens all the time. You assume and insist that you know what the other person is thinking and feeling. The result is that you carry on a conversation with yourself: "You say you want to go to the concert with me, but you'd rather be playing cards with the boys." Pretty soon, the other person ceases to exist. There is only you and *your* impression, your version of the other person.

Avoid the self-conversation. By all means, express your feelings and your fears to the other person, but then let him/her respond to them. Stop talking. Listen.

EXPECTING MIRACULOUS UNDERSTANDING

The flipside of the self conversation is the expectation that the other person in the relationship must know what you are feeling and thinking. Why? Because he/she loves you, of course, and people who love each other can read each other's mind.

There is a grain of truth in this myth. People who have lived together twenty, thirty years or more would have to be dense indeed if they did not pick up on one another's habits and habits of thought. But love does not confer the power of mental telepathy, and it is a big mistake to assume that it does and an even bigger error to assume that a failure of mind reading indicates the absence of love. It is *your* responsibility to express *your* feelings, *your* needs, and *your* desires.

PASSIVE AGGRESSION

This alternative to communication is an all too common feature of many relationships. Failing to express feelings does not magically make the feelings go away. If the unexpressed feelings are sufficiently significant to you, you're likely to express them in some nonverbal way.

"Sure, I'll drop those off at the cleaners. I *know* it's important for tomorrow."

Tomorrow comes, and . . .

"Hon, did you get my suit back from the cleaners?"
"What suit?"

Don't leave important issues undiscussed.

STONEWALLING

Feeling low, you may benefit most from a good talk. But, feeling low, you may not want to talk. The same is true when something your partner has done upsets or offends you. This is precisely the time when communication is most important, but it is also when you may feel least like talking.

Stonewalling invites the other person to carry on a self-conversation, to project his/her feelings onto you. The result, at the very least, is misunderstanding and a consequent failure to resolve whatever issue is troublesome. In the worst case, the result is that your partner magnifies whatever it is that is bothering you, making it seem—or just plain making it—worse than it is.

NAME CALLING AND RIDICULE

Not much to say about this, except don't do it. It is very hurtful, particularly because it denies adult-level dignity to both partners. Be aware that ridicule is often disguised, thinly, as "kidding": "Can't you take a joke?" Far from lightening the tone of a put-down, the fiction that it is all in good fun just adds insult to injury.

LYING

Lying tears down any relationship. The same goes for simply withholding the truth. You have to figure out a constructive way to tell the truth so that it can be dealt with.

Anger

Anger is not bad for relationships. Anger is not good for relationships. Anger is simply a part of relationships, because it is a part of emotional life. Deal with it.

- Identify the real source of anger. Anger is a threat, so we often displace it. You're in a difficult position with your boss at work. He makes you angry, but you can't afford to lash out at him. You need the job. You go home and yell at your wife instead. This is displaced anger.

- You get angry when you get hurt. By getting angry at the person who hurt you, you defend yourself against further injury.

- You get angry when you are frustrated—including frustrated by your own failures or perceived failures. This leads you to lash out at others, often with blame and accusation.

You can't ignore or simply get rid of anger, but you can recognize it in its many forms and disguises, and you can take steps to deal with it in a healthy way.

Begin by recognizing that anger is not a thing, but a feeling and that the only person responsible for your feelings is you. If you are responsible for your feelings, you are also responsible for managing them. If you feel overwhelmed by your feelings, manage them before talking to the other person about them:

- Take a walk around the block—or maybe a run.
- Count to ten. Breathe deeply.

Commit yourself to absolutely avoiding violence—to yourself or to anyone else.

If you still feel that you cannot talk about the anger without making the situation worse, consider writing down your thoughts. You might even compose a letter to the other person in the relationship. Put the letter away for at least a day, then look at it. Decide what parts of the letter you still feel like talking about.

When you are finally ready to talk, make sure that you do not relinquish responsibility for your feelings. Instead of saying "You make me furious," explain: "When you discussed our personal finances with Joe Williams, it made me very angry." This may still be a hard pill for the other person to swallow, but at least it does the following:

- It retains ownership of the anger.
- It does not directly attack the other person, but instead focuses on a particular action.
- It defines precisely the source of the anger, fixing it in time and attaching it to a particular event.

This last point is especially important, because it offers real, practical hope for a solution to the problem. If you simply tell someone that he/she makes you angry, few desirable solutions present themselves: Either the person must somehow "fix" himself/herself— or leave. If, however, you focus on a particular behavior, action, or event, you have identified something much easier to fix than a person. Try to choose a time when you can talk—*really* talk, without interruption.

Apology

Apologizing is not just saying you're sorry or expressing regret over an incident or an outburst, but is an act of accepting responsibility for the action.

The first step in a meaningful apology is not speaking, however, but listening.

- Listen without preconception or prejudice.

- Use positive body language to show that you are receptive to whatever complaints or criticisms your partner expresses.

- Express your understanding of what the other person is saying, even if you don't agree with it. It is perfectly possible to understand a point or a concept without agreeing to its truth or accuracy: "I can understand why you feel the way that you do."

- Reflect the other person's words. "You're saying that I don't respect your opinions about financial matters. Am I understanding you so far?"

- Exercise as much restraint as possible to ensure that the other person gets to talk first and express herself/himself fully. Try not to interrupt. Do not break in to defend yourself.

Once you begin to speak, you may need to decide whether you are apologizing—accepting responsibility and expressing regret—for something you purposely did to be hurtful or something you did unconsciously, even accidentally. In either case, it is up to you to claim responsibility. That is step 1 of the apology:

- Accept responsibility.

Step 2?

- Express regret. "I'm sorry what I did hurt your feelings."

Go to step 3:

- Propose a remedy. Sometimes there is some specific action that can be taken to repair damage. Sometimes it is a promise to take steps to prevent the damage from happening again: "From now on, I'll be sure to talk over any financial decisions with you. We'll work together and make the decisions together."

Apology does not occur in a vacuum. It is completed by forgiveness. If you are on the receiving end of an apology, it is up to you to decide whether to forgive or not. The decision may be made more easily if you stop to consider what forgiveness is—and is *not*.

- Forgiveness is accepting that the other person has made a mistake, regrets it, and still deserves your love.
- Forgiveness is not the same as forgetting what happened.
- Forgiveness is not the same as saying what happened is okay.
- Forgiveness is not guaranteed for life. It is important for both people to realize that you may sincerely forgive someone today, only to become angry again tomorrow. This is *not* the same as going against your word.

Disposing of the Past

Apology does not erase error or the hurt caused by error. Forgiveness is not forgetting. Yet the past must be overcome, because it is a reality that cannot be changed or affected in any way. Against the past we are powerless. To get beyond the past, we must focus on the present and create a plan for the future. When you do something hurtful, apologize. As part of the apology, offer a remedy. But don't leave it as a unilateral solution. Have a conversation about what you will do, together, to avoid a repetition of the problem. The more specific you can be together, the better. Without a plan, you can both become prisoners of the past.

25 Words and Phrases to Use

agree	help me	quiet discussion
apologize	help you	regret
as much time as we need	hurt	sorry
	in the future	talk
ask your forgiveness	listen to you	together
feel	move forward	understand
forgive	next	work it out
get past this	plan	work out a plan together
hear you	promise	

16 Words and Phrases to Avoid

bad

blame

can't change

did it on purpose

evil

fault

forever

impossible

incapable

incompetent

never be the same

no good

permanent

ruined

you made me

your fault

On the
Job

*T*he workplace engages the head as well as the heart.
This section will help you to speak and write
more effectively on the job.

25

Turning Apology into Opportunity

"Say you're sorry."

Remember your mother telling you this? Remember how hard it was to squeeze the words out? For many of us, it doesn't get much easier when we grow up. In fact, the stakes of adult actions are generally higher than they are for kid's stuff, so, all grown up now, it can be even more difficult, embarrassing, and painful to apologize. Nobody likes doing damage control, but we all know it's necessary sometimes. Things go wrong. Mistakes are made. Stuff happens.

Think for a moment about the last time you were on the receiving end of somebody's error.

You're a do-it-yourselfer, a real tool freak. Down at the home improvement store your eyes went wide when you saw that fancy cordless drill. You bought it. You brought it home. You took it ever so gently out of the box, waited hours for its first charge-up, then, at long last, you put it to work.

No sooner did the bit bite into the wood than it ground down, slowed down, and stopped dead.

Steeped in chagrin, you are steamed. Certainly, you don't feel very good right now about Drill-O-Matic, Inc.

But the story's not over.

You get on the phone and call Drill-O-Matic's customer service department. The call is answered promptly, and somebody in charge apologizes to you and promises you that the company will stand behind the product and will ship you out a new Drill-O-Matic immediately and at no cost to you.

How do you feel now?

Chances are that you are still disappointed, but at least you're feeling better about Drill-O-Matic. Those people haven't abandoned you. They've taken responsibility. They are determined to help you.

In the world of business, errors, failures, and disappointments are not good things, and they never will be. But an effective apology can take these disasters and turn them into opportunities for creating a positive relationship between customer and company. No matter what your business, you don't just sell a product, you also sell yourself and your firm. If a particular product should happen to fail or a service fall short, you still have an opportunity to sell yourself and your firm by sending the message that you will make things right. You can turn damage control into relationship building.

Finding the Heartline

The heartline, the quickest route to effective communication in response to a customer complaint about your company's error, is *not* just about finding a slick way to say "We're sorry." It is about communicating a willingness to help the client or customer. Focusing on fixing things is what builds a positive relationship between you and that customer. Take it step by step:

1. Acknowledge the complaint.

2. Express sympathy for the customer and concern for his situation and his feelings. *Briefly* apologize.

3. Be sure to get all relevant facts. Do not grill or challenge the customer. Frame your questions in ways that make it clear that you need the information in order to make things right: "You say the unit isn't operating correctly. Can you tell me a little more about just what is going wrong? This will help me diagnose the problem and get you up and running again."

4. If possible, provide an immediate solution to the customer's problem. For example: "Please take the widget to the nearest authorized dealer, who will repair it at no cost to you." If you require additional information or some other action on the part of the customer, explain it here: "So that I can get this problem corrected as quickly as possible, I need to know . . ." If possible and appro-

priate, give your customer choices as to remedies and solutions. Choice confers a sense of empowerment, which makes a disappointed customer feel less like a victim—less like *your* victim.

5. After you have proposed a helping action, close with an apology. "I am sorry for this problem."

6. Offer ongoing assistance: "I'm sure that this problem won't be repeated, but if you have any questions or concerns, don't hesitate to call us at this number."

Sidestepping the Pitfalls

Whatever else goes into a business, business success is built on creating customer satisfaction. Errors, malfunctions, disappointing performance all threaten satisfaction and, therefore, threaten the basis of your business. In responding to a complaint or making an apology, you have the opportunity to restore lost satisfaction; therefore, avoid the following pitfalls:

- *Dwelling on the apology.* The customer is far less interested in hearing how sorry *you* are and how bad *you* feel than in what you will do to help *him.*

- *Bad mouthing the product, the company, or other employees.* Never respond to a complaint in ways that undermine the customer's confidence in the product or the firm.

- *Being defensive.* It is not true that the "customer is always right." What is true, in the case of a complaint, is that the customer is unhappy. You cannot argue with that. Instead, focus on doing whatever can fairly be done to make the customer happy. Do not defend the product by criticizing the customer's feelings about it.

- *Arguing.* If the customer is mistaken or misinformed, if he is misusing the product, or if he is using the product for an inappropriate application, do not argue with him. Instead, educate him. Work with him. Remember, your goal is not to defend your product or service, but to create customer satisfaction with that product or service. This may require helping your customer to use the product or service correctly or more effectively.

- *Lying.* Don't do it. And don't promise any solutions you cannot deliver.

3 Model Letters

OFFERING CHOICES

Dear Mr. Jackson:

I was very sorry to learn that the X unit on your Widget is defective. I can work with you in two ways to resolve the problem:

1. While the X unit certainly failed prematurely, it is a "wear part" that must be replaced from time to time. It is designed to be replaced by the customer. Therefore, I can send you a new unit, with instructions on how to replace it.

2. If you prefer, you may return the entire unit to us, and we will replace the part, then return the unit to you, together with reimbursement of your shipping costs.

The first alternative is faster, but if you really don't like to use a screwdriver, just pack the unit in its original carton and return it to us. Follow the warranty return instructions in your Owner's Manual.

Be assured that, whatever option you choose, we will make every effort to get you up and running with a minimum of delay. If you would like us to send a replacement X unit, just call me at 555-555-5555. You may leave a message on my voice answering system.

I apologize for the inconvenience and disappointment, and I thank you for your patience and understanding.

Sincerely,

William Johnson
Customer Service

Do not fail to thank your customer for patience and understanding. Not only is this an act of common courtesy, it strengthens the bond between you and the customer by reminding him that he has made an emotional investment in you by giving you his patience and understanding.

SPEEDY ACTION

Dear Ms. Smith:

I am very sorry that the Widget is not performing to your expectations, and I am eager to resolve the problem as quickly as possible. For that reason, I ask that you bring the unit to your nearest authorized Widget service center, which is located at 1234 East Huron Street in Brunswick. The technician there will diagnose the problem and take whatever steps are necessary to insure that it will operate to its optimum specifications. If the service center is unable to repair the problem within twenty-four hours, I have authorized that you be given a replacement unit. In either case, there will be no cost to you.

We want you to be 100 percent satisfied, and we will ensure that this is the case. Thanks for your patience and understanding.

Sincerely,

Benito Guiterrez
Customer Service Associate

GETTING THE FACTS SO YOU CAN HELP

Dear Ms. Perkins:

I was deeply concerned by your letter of October 4, in which you mention that you were very unhappy with the work of one of our sales representatives, Patty Smith.

I have discussed the matter with Ms. Smith, but before I meet with her again to discuss an appropriate course of action, I would like to have as much information as possible from you regarding the difficulty you experienced. Your comments on the following questions will help me—as well as Ms. Smith—understand the situation more fully and resolve it to your complete satisfaction:

1. In what way(s) was Ms. Smith "rude" to you?

2. Your impression was that Ms. Smith "deliberately delayed" action on your order. Can you explain what created that impression?

Ms. Perkins, I don't want to put you to the trouble of writing down formal responses to these questions. You might just jot down a few points and call me at 555-555-5555 with your comments.

We at Jones Company are proud of the level of service we offer. You can understand, then, how concerned I am that you were dissatisfied. Both Ms. Smith and I are eager to turn this situation around and create your complete satisfaction.

Sincerely,

Helen Smithers
Sales Manager

3 Model Memos

The essence of an effective memo is economy. Give all the pertinent facts and nothing more. Sell your message. Remember, many business organizations are flooded with daily memos. They come to be regarded as a species of office junk mail. Be sure that you state your point quickly and sharply, so that your communication stands out from the rest of the flood.

INCORRECT INFORMATION

Date: 00/00/00
To: Shipping Group
From: Pete Hackney
Subject: Contact numbers for George Youngblood

The phone contact numbers I gave you last week for George Youngblood were incorrect. Sorry for the error, but my database was not up to date. I am in the process of updating it now, and I expect to have the correct numbers tomorrow. Sorry for the inconvenience. You can be sure that the next batch of contact numbers will be up to date and correct.

ERRORS IN REPORT

Date: 00/00/00
To: Frank Peterson
From: Ellen Corwin
Subject: Problem with the Flash Reports

Frank, I've looked into the problems you pointed out in the Flash Reports. I'm pleased to say that I've located the source of the problems, but I'm not so pleased to tell you that the source is me.

I used figures from April instead of May, and the result was, to say the least, misleading. The good news here is that *you* caught my mistake before we put anything into action. Thanks for your vigilance—and thanks, too, for your patience and understanding.

I am currently rerunning the numbers, using figures from May. The report will be ready for you before the end of the day. I'll run it down to your office personally.

Frank, I'm really sorry for this.

WE'RE LATE

Date: 00/00/00
To: All employees
From: Hal Dean, Cafeteria Manager
Subject: Cafeteria closed for the rest of the week

I am sorry to report that the cafeteria will be closed for the remainder of this week, Wednesday through Saturday. Necessary renovations are taking longer than anticipated because of a delay in shipping some building materials. I have been assured that the work will be completed over the weekend and that we *will* be ready to serve you on Monday.

In the meantime, the cafeteria staff and I apologize for the inconvenience. We have installed two additional vending machines in the third-floor break room and another two machines on the second-floor break room. I know these are a poor substitute for the cafeteria, but I hope they'll help. The best solution for now might be good old-fashioned home cooking!

3 Model Phone Calls

Your number-one priority in responding to calls concerning problems with a product, service, billing, or delivery is to arrive at an action that resolves the issue. Just *how* you arrive at that action says a lot about you and your company.

Build rapport with the caller. You need to discover the facts of the matter. However, be careful to avoid asking for this information with words that convey command or demand. For example, do not demand "What is your account number?" but inquire: "Do you have your account number handy?" or "Do you happen to have your account number with you?" Be careful to request, rather than demand, information.

Guide the conversation so that the words "you" and "I" become "we." You could say something like, "I need to get some information from you." But it is far more effective to say, "Let's fill in some information together." If a customer has a problem, and you can fix it, you might be tempted to declare—heroically—"I can fix that for you." Still, it is better to say something like, "We can work that out together without any difficulty at all."

Remember, few customers call to *complain*. What they really want
is *help*. If you can give them the help they want and need, you become
a hero and your company becomes a source of satisfaction rather than
failure or irritation.

SHIPPING DELAY

Hello, Bert. This is Frank Muir at Dextron. We've run into a scheduling glitch
with one of our suppliers. He has manufacturing delays, which, unfortunately,
will mean that we can't ship your order before the 30th.

I'm sorry that this delay is unavoidable. However, I'm putting extra people on
the job at our end, so we will minimize the delay. You'll get your shipment no
later than the 5th. In the meantime, is there anything you would like me to
do to help you accommodate to the revised ship date?

SHIPPING ERROR

Miss Smith, hello, this is Jay Norwood at Acme Limited.

Having to apologize for a mistake isn't something I enjoy doing, but I wanted
to make sure that you received a personal apology for our having shipped the
wrong item to you. I know that this caused you a certain amount of inconvenience.

I wish I could come up with some spectacular excuse for the mistake. But,
the fact is, we goofed. Period. So, instead of offering you an excuse, I'll make
you a promise: I won't let this happen again.

Thanks for all of your understanding and patience.

DAMAGED GOODS

Ed, it's Beth Cosgrove at Murray Hill. I just heard that your Widget arrived
damaged. I'm very sorry about that. I want to take care of this problem as
quickly as possible and without any hassle for you. So, let me offer two good
choices: Either return the damaged item to me by Unique Express, and I will
immediately trans-ship a replacement and will reimburse you for freight. Or,
if you prefer, I will send one of my staff out to your location with a replacement on Friday. He will also pick up the damaged unit. Which way do you
want to go on this?

3 E-Mail Messages

PRODUCT FAILED

Ms. Smiley:

Thank you for e-mail concerning your experience with the Model 234 Widget. I am very sorry that the unit failed. I realize that it comforts you little to learn that such failures are very rare. We make every effort to ensure that our products are free from defects. But, sometimes, even the best efforts are not always adequate.

A replacement unit has been sent to you and should arrive at your location by the 5th. I am confident that it will give you years of trouble-free service.

Ms. Smiley, I apologize for the inconvenience you were caused, and I sincerely thank you for your patience and understanding. Please e-mail or call me at 555-555-5555 if you have any questions concerning the unit.

Peter Hawkins,
Sales Manager

REPAIR FAILED

Mr. Thomas:

We don't like to hear that one of our products does not perform as expected, but on the rare occasions when we fail to service the product adequately the first time we're called out, we are acutely aware that we have really let you down. That's why I was concerned when I learned that the service we provided on April 15 didn't take care of the problem, and it is why I sent our service supervisor to your plant to ensure that our fix would work once and for all.

Mr. Thomas, I am very sorry for any inconvenience the problems with the unit and with the subsequent servicing may have created. I am sincerely grateful for the patience and understanding you have shown. I hope that you will believe me when I assure you that such problems—both with the product and with the service—are rare indeed.

If you have any questions at all, please phone me directly at 555-555-5555 or send me an e-mail message.

Eunice Smith
Customer Service Manager

BILLING ERROR

Frank:

I'm very sorry that you had to go to the trouble of helping us to resolve an error we made in billing your account. I understand, Frank, that the problem is now resolved, and that your account has been properly and fully credited. You know that we will make every effort to prevent something like this from happening again, Thanks a lot, Frank, for your patience and understanding. We appreciate it.

Ted

25 Words and Phrases to Use

alternatives	grateful	rush
apologize	help	service
assurance	immediate	solution
assure	make good	sorry
choice	patience	thanks
excellence	prevent	understanding
explain	problem	urgent
fix	put right	
future	repair	

15 Words and Phrases to Avoid

against company policy	not our fault	to be expected
cannot be true	not our problem	you're wrong
don't count on it	nothing we can do	you've made a mistake
excuse	nothing wrong	
hands are tied	problems with our company	
no choice	stupid	

26

Heartfelt Appreciation
and Thanks

*E*xpressing thanks is not just an act of courtesy—although it certainly is that—it is also a means of reinforcing positive action and building a cohesive organization. Behavioral psychologists have long known that praise and thanks are more effective means of reinforcing desired action than using punishment or threats of punishment. The memo expressing thanks is a powerful vehicle of positive reinforcement.

Finding the Heartline

What spells the difference between a pro-forma, perfunctory thank you and a meaningful expression of thanks? In a word, *specificity*. State exactly what you are thanking the other person for, and be sure to say something about the positive effect that person's suggestion, action, good deed, or whatever has had on you or your organization.

Keep the communication straightforward. Instead of lavishing adjectives upon the recipient, get specific with nouns and verbs that describe positive consequences. The sincerity and effectiveness of your thanks are directly proportionate to the degree of specificity you include in the thank-you message.

Sidestepping the Pitfalls

It is hard to make a mistake when you thank someone, but the biggest mistake is putting off the thank you or, even worse, neglecting it altogether.

- Deliver your thanks as soon after the event or deed as possible.
- Do not put off delivering thanks.
- Do not fail to write that thank-you note or make that thank-you call.

Any thanks are better than no thanks at all; however, the best, most sincere-sounding thanks get specific. Devote a little time and thought to your thank-you communications. People love to see the *effect* of their good deeds. So, show 'em.

3 Model Letters

THANKS FOR YOUR BUSINESS

Dear Jane:

Just a note to thank you for your recent order and to express my appreciation for your continued confidence in us. When a customer remains loyal for more than five years, as you have done, it gives me great pride in my organization.

Jane, it is always a pleasure to serve you. And please be assured that we are well aware that there is plenty of competition out there. I promise that we will continue to work for you every day to make certain that you continue to be happy with the choice you have made.

Sincerely,

Gary Thomas
Sales Director

FOR A FAVOR

Dear Pete:

Many, many thanks for giving John Young a demonstration of the Wonder Widget System we installed in your plant. There's nothing that sells this product more effectively than seeing it in action, for real, at a real location. Let me tell you: You made the sale for us. Mr. Young called this morning to place his order.

By way of thanks, please let us perform your next scheduled maintenance for free. Just call me when you're ready for our technician to come by.

With great appreciation,

Ben Hilldreth
Sales Manager

FOR A RECOMMENDATION/REFERRAL

Dear Mary:

Absolutely the greatest feeling I get in this job is when I do my work so well that one of my customers recommends my services to a valued colleague.

Based on your good word, Harry Hopkins hired our firm to do his inventory. You know that we won't let him down. We'll make sure he has every reason to thank you for the recommendation.

Sincerely,

Arnold Blatz
Account Representative

3 Model Memos

THANKS FOR THE GOOD IDEA

DATE: 00/00/00
TO: Jenny Gerhardt
FROM: Joan Sullivan
RE: Your upgrade idea

Your idea about an upgrade incentive program has stimulated a lot of lively and productive discussion in our department. It looks like we will indeed introduce a high-profile program along the lines you have suggested. I also believe that this will significantly improve our bottom line.

Speaking on behalf of the department's management team, I am very grateful for your stimulating idea and for the initiative you have shown.

QUICK THINKING, TIMELY ACTION

DATE: 00/00/00
TO: Len Owens
FROM: Juan Bautista
SUBJECT: Saving our hides

You became the man of the hour when you managed to expedite shipment of the Smith order. We came very close to losing a major customer, but, thanks to your quick and skillful action, we ended up by strengthening the relationship.

You acted professionally and with great initiative. The entire sales team is proud of you—and grateful, too.

PITCHING IN

DATE: 00/00/00
TO: Ken Rolfs
FROM: Moira Murphy
SUBJECT: Working the weekend

Thanks to your extra effort, we completed the Smith job on time, delivering it this morning. Giving up your weekend, I know, was a big sacrifice for you, but it did mean the difference between totally satisfying this customer and failing to deliver on time. Your dedication is greatly appreciated. Thanks, Ken.

3 Model Phone Calls

FOR YOUR ORDER

Mr. Jackson, this is Larry Larson at Peptalk, Inc. I was calling to thank you for your order and to confirm that the full order will ship on Monday.

Your business means a lot to us, Mr. Jackson, so I want to encourage you to give us a call if you have any questions at all after you receive your order.

It's a pleasure working with you.

FOR LENDING EQUIPMENT

Dan, Ray Miller at RayCom. I want to thank you again for lending us that D-100. You were a real lifesaver. Without that piece of equipment, we would never have gotten our big order out on time—and that would have really hurt one of our major customers.

You made a big difference, Dan, and I want you to know I won't forget it. Thanks so much.

FOR A BUSINESS LEAD

Penny, this is Lee. I want to thank you for sending Mr. Sawyer our way. On your good word, I contacted him yesterday, and it looks like we'll be doing business. That makes me feel good, of course, but what really gives me a thrill is when we earn the confidence of customers like you, Penny. Your vote of confidence means the world to us. Thanks again.

3 E-Mail Messages

ATTENDING MEETING

Joe, John, Ben, and Gail:

Thanks to you all for taking the time to attend yesterday's last-minute meeting. I know short-notice events are a pain, especially on the subject of asset allocation—but you were ungrumbling, thoroughly professional, and super helpful. Thanks to your input, I was able to secure the additional funds we need to complete Project X. This will mean a lot to our firm—and to our department.

Way to go!

Carl

FAVOR

Tom,

Many thanks for picking me up at the airport yesterday. My schedule was as tight as it gets, but, thanks to you, I made the meeting on time—good thing, too, since developments with the new technology are unfolding faster than any of us thought they would.

Thanks for being there.

Jena

GOOD ADVICE

Kathy:

Your advice about the word processing software was right on. I bought the product you recommended, and it is exactly what I needed. So easy to use, too! You're always so well informed and thoughtful. Thanks for taking the time to help me out.

Sandra

25 Words and Phrases to Use

accept my thanks

appreciate

couldn't have been better

couldn't have done it without
    you

count on you

generosity

godsend

good advice

grateful

helpful

invaluable

just what I needed

lifesaver

making the effort

on target

perfect

sharing

splendid

successful

taking the time

thanks

very useful

worked out fine

you were right

your contribution

5 Words and Phrases to Avoid

did the best you could

good enough

nice try

owed it to me

thanks anyway

27

Celebration and Congratulation

$\mathcal{T}$he most shopworn of clichés have an annoying way of often being quite true. Take this one, for instance: *Nothing succeeds like success.*

Sharing congratulations is a way of celebrating success that also builds a climate of success in your business, office, or department. Such a climate is likely to produce even more success. Acknowledging and celebrating achievement builds morale and reinforces a winning attitude and approach.

Don't limit congratulations to the circle within your own organization. Congratulations transmitted to associates, colleagues, and customers in the outside world can serve as a way to acquire new business while building goodwill. Make it a habit to keep your ear to the ground in order to learn of promotions and appointments in your industry. Write letters of congratulations to promotees and new appointees. Before long, you'll find yourself with a full-fledged network.

Finding the Heartline

Congratulating achievement should be straightforward.

- Begin simply with the congratulation itself.
- Describe the achievement.
- Assess its beneficial effect on the organization.

Remember, although the immediate purpose of a congratulation is to celebrate achievement and make the recipient of the praise feel

685

good, it also functions to "raise the bar" of achievement for the entire organization. Everyone should acknowledge the creation of a new standard.

When you send a congratulatory message outside of your organization, be certain to do the following:

- Emphasize your business relationship with your correspondent.

- Use the occasion of congratulation as a springboard to further business; for example, if you are congratulating a client on a promotion within his organization, you might briefly suggest how the services or products you offer can be of assistance in your correspondent's new position.

- Express the desire to continue a successful business alliance.

- Repeat the congratulations; this is especially important if you are introducing yourself—lest the letter seem wholly self-serving.

- Be generous. Never qualify your congratulations.

- Take the opportunity to reinforce existing business relationships and to establish new ones.

- Make it a habit to keep abreast of promotions and appointments in your industry. Congratulating a new appointee is an opportunity to enlarge your network and your customer base.

Sidestepping the Pitfalls

Congratulating others is one of the pleasures of business life. Too often, however, it is a pleasure we deny ourselves. The biggest mistake people make with regard to congratulations is never getting around to them. It is also a mistake to delay congratulations. The handshakes and pats on the back should come as soon after the event as possible. Finally, do not stint. Congratulations should never be stingy or qualified. The best congratulations are specific—they specify the achievement and its benefits—yet they are also extravagant: They are liberal with praise. This is not a time for careful evaluation, but for the most open-handed generosity.

3 Model Letters

CAREER ADVANCEMENT

Dear Sophie:

Congratulations on your promotion to district sales manager. I'm not going to tell you that you don't deserve all the credit for your great success—but, well, I'd like to think that we at Wonderful World helped by always supplying you with prompt, personal service and terrific value. I trust we helped make you look as good as you are.

I wish you all the best in your new position, and I look forward to continuing our partnership and raising it to even greater heights.

Sincerely,

Devon Phillips

SALES ACHIEVEMENT

Dear Ben:

What a year this has been for you! Nobody has moved so much product so well.

Ben, it's a lot of fun working with a winner, and I look forward to many more years of continued success as your supplier of high-quality widgets.

Congratulations and warmest personal regards,

Tony Pastor

NEWS OF A CLIENT'S ENGAGEMENT

Dear Ned:

Word is that you're about to leave the bachelor ranks and join the rest of us in married life. I extend my hand in welcome. Well done!

You know, marriage changes everything. For the better. And, Ned, you'll find that includes your professional life as well as your personal life. It gives you added focus and motivation.

I'm happy for you. Congratulations.

Best regards,

Norm Hollings

3 Model Memos

JOB WELL DONE

DATE: 00/00/00
TO: Helen
FROM: Ron
RE: Well Done!

Wow!

Your work organizing the recent convention was nothing less than miraculous. You made us all look very, very good. The display of the new line was especially effective and sparked a lot of conversation. I have no doubt that it will also bring us a good deal of new business.

I am looking forward to next year's convention. With you organizing the show, it will be another great event.

On behalf of the entire department, I congratulate and thank you.

EXCELLENCE ACHIEVED

DATE: 00/00/00
TO: Quality Team
FROM: Sarah Goodheart, Quality Assurance Manager
SUBJECT: Error-Free Achievement

Industry standard: 97.5 percent error-free average. A lofty goal for a healthy industry.

It was not good enough for us. And when we told the industry it wasn't, a lot of people shook their heads and wagged their fingers. Better than 97.5 is not possible, they said.

Your team proved otherwise.

Thanks to your great work, we now enjoy a 98.9 error-free rate. It is the best in the business. Maybe the best in *any* business.

Well done, ladies and gentlemen! You inspire us all.

BIRTH ANNOUNCEMENT

DATE: 00/00/00
TO: All
FROM: Tammi Coles
SUBJECT: New Life

On Friday, June 19, at 5:36 a.m., Philip Gray Doane, 8 pounds, 6 ounces, came into the world. He is the first son of Susie Doane, our assistant controller, and her husband, Benton Doane, who is associate sales manager for the Tompkins Group. Mother and son are doing fine.

Susie will be home from the hospital by Wednesday. Please join me in signing the attached card, which I will deliver to her personally.

3 Model Phone Calls

PROMOTION—POTENTIAL CLIENT

Hello, Mr. Benson. This is Peter Pryor at Do-It Fast. I just read in *News Now* that you've been named production head at Acme. I want to extend my congratulations. I've always admired Acme, and your new position should be both challenging and rewarding. I also wanted to let you know that my firm offers a wide variety of printing services, and I'd like to help you get off to a great start in your new position by getting together with you to explain some of what we have to offer.

PROMOTION—BUSINESS FRIEND

Gail, this is Herb. I just heard the great news! What a terrific move Gelbart made in bringing you on board the management team. You bring incredible talent to that group and real savvy. Congratulations to them—and to you, too!

As soon as you're settled in, I'd love to get together for lunch. I'll call in about a week to set something up, okay?

AWARD

Fred, it's Cole. Man, you are *too* modest. Why weren't you on the phone about the Lowman Prize? I had to read about it in *Carpet News*. This is a great achievement, and no one deserves it more than you. I really am thrilled for you. If I'm surprised by one thing, it's that it took the committee so long to wake up, do the right thing, and present you with the award. Well, better late than never. If you're half as excited as I am about this, you must be floating right now. Congratulations and well done, Fred!

3 E-Mail Messages

BIRTH IN CLIENT'S FAMILY

Roberta!

Ed told me the great news. An addition to your family! Wow!

Please accept the congratulations and very best wishes of all of us here at Acme Widgets.

Pam

SALES TARGET EXCEEDED

To: Everyone in Sales

From: Tom Woodworth, CEO

I'm not known for going easy on people. I don't encourage settling into a familiar, comfortable groove. I have always set high goals for all of us— and, time and again, all of you have not only achieved, but exceeded those goals.

Now you've done it again.

For First Quarter, we were looking to move 30,000 units. Your team has pushed through 41,000.

Your achievement is a testament to the excellence of our product—let's not forget that—but it is also a testament to your commitment to that product, to this company, and to the customers we serve. You work hard, and you work smart.

Thanks. Congratulations. This is *your* victory.

PROJECT COMPLETED

Tom, I just saw your report on Project X. Congratulations on bringing it in on deadline and under budget! What an achievement! This will mean a big jump in our bottom line. I am thrilled for you—and for all of us.

You should be very proud. I know I'm proud to be working with you.

Ben

25 Words and Phrases to Use

accomplishment	perspective
achievement	pride
acknowledge	proud
all of us	recognition
celebrate	share in your triumph
congratulations	smart
deserve	success
exceed	superb
excellence	triumph
goal	victory
great work	well done
great impact	wise
happy	

10 Words and Phrases to Avoid

at long last	good enough
best you could	it's about time
finally done	lucky
finally over	okay
glad that's behind us	pretty good

28

Sympathy and
Condolence

$\mathcal{B}$usiness can be a hard, harsh world. Yet the world of business is also a community. You may be competitive, you may insist on keeping your business associates separate from your friends and family, but, nevertheless, you and the people you work with, both inside and outside of your company, are a community. One of the standards by which a community should be judged is how its members respond to one another in times of loss, stress, and sadness. Yet even the most intelligent and articulate people sometimes find it hard to say the right things on occasions of death, serious illness, or other loss. If this is the case when we communicate to friends and family, it is even truer when we reach out to business associates, colleagues, and even competitors. We are not accustomed to thinking of these people as fully dimensional human beings. We are not used to addressing the full range of their emotions. Difficult as it may be, humanizing those we work with serves to enhance and deepen the work experience. It is a good *business* move, and it is the right *human* move.

Finding the Heartline

Knowing the right thing to say in a sad or traumatic situation requires a deliberate exercise of the imagination. Put yourself in the other person's place. Under the current circumstances of loss or sorrow, ask yourself: What would *you* like to hear? What would help *you* most?

Now that you have put yourself in the mind and heart of another, return to yourself. As you sit down to write that note or to make that phone call, be yourself. Express what is in your heart and imagination.

Emotions can be difficult to contain. Do you need to find an appropriate form for your expression of sympathy? Think of it as having five parts:

First: Express your sorrow at hearing of the death or loss.

Second: Sympathize by acknowledging the emotional pain of loss.

Third: Say something good about the deceased. If possible, share a memory.

Fourth: It is often helpful gently to remind the other person of the healing power of time.

Fifth: To the extent possible and appropriate, offer your help and support.

Find the emotional tone appropriate to the situation. You may be writing or talking to a business associate on the death of one of her valued employees or you may be writing or talking to that person about the death of a mutual business friend. Another circumstance involves communicating condolence to the decedent's family. Pitch your tone to what you see as the nature and the level of the loss.

Sidestepping the Pitfalls

It's odd, and not a little frustrating, that at precisely those moments when others need our kind words most, we often feel least able to communicate. Death, serious illness, or other loss erects barriers. We *want* to say the "right thing," but we are fearful of intruding on another's grief, or we fear that what we say will only cause more pain. This leads us into the single most common and most serious pitfall of communicating condolence and sympathy: The failure to speak or write.

The fact is, all other things being equal, a person who has suffered a loss craves comfort and kind words. How do you get started? As just mentioned, begin by imagining what *you* would like to hear in the current situation. Think about your feelings, and try to speak or write from these.

What you write or say need not be a bouquet of flowery words or profound pronouncements on grief and faith. In fact, avoid vivid adjectives and nouns that may even magnify the loss: "your *terrible* loss," "your *horrible tragedy*," and so on. Your correspondent does not need help feeling bad. Beyond simply saying how sorry you are, you may share a memory or two with the grieving person. Perhaps you believe that bringing up a common memory will only increase the other's pain. This is not the case. Demonstrating that the deceased still lives in memory brings comfort.

Don't be afraid that what you say will somehow intensify the other person's grief. Do not deliberately attempt to trivialize or minimize the feelings of grief. You may give comfort by suggesting that the passage of time will salve the hurt, but do not imply that the person who has suffered the loss will soon forget all about it.

3 Model Letters

DEATH OF A BUSINESS ASSOCIATE

Dear Jenny,

I was very sorry to learn of the passing of your president, Hank Morton. As you know, I've done business with Hank for the past five or six years, and it was always a great pleasure. You know even better than I that Hank was a brilliant, generous, and honorable man. You'll miss him, I know, not just as a leader, but as a friend. I feel for your loss.

Jenny, if there is anything I can do to help during what will be a difficult time for you, please don't hesitate to call.

Sincerely,

Irv Schneider

DEATH OF A BUSINESS FRIEND

Dear Marcy:

You know all too well that Ben Goring was more to me than a business associate. He was a great friend, and I miss him very much. Believe me, I feel for your grief—because I feel your grief as well. For you, the loss is double: a good friend is gone, and so is a valued member of your management team.

But, Marcy, you have to believe that Ben will live on—through his legacy of leadership, a legacy entrusted to people like you. And he has also left us great memories of personal friendship.

If there is anything you need from me—any service I can render—please don't hesitate to call.

Sincerely,

John Sebastian

TO THE FAMILY OF A BUSINESS ASSOCIATE

Dear Mrs. Hawks:

I was saddened to hear of the death of your husband, Howard. As a business associate, it was impossible not to respect him and not to like him. He was a strong person. I can only imagine how wonderful a husband and father he must have been. I'm truly sorry for your loss.

Mrs. Hawks, you don't need many words from someone who's almost a stranger to you. Take heart in the knowledge that time will at least soothe your pain. And, please, if I can be of any assistance to you, don't hesitate to call me.

Sincerely,

Kathy Norton

3 Model Memos

DEATH OF A COWORKER

Date: 00/00/00
To: Billing Department staff
From: Pam Isham, Manager
Subject: Karen Spencer

Some of you have already heard the tragic news: Karen Spencer, one of our billing associates, was killed in an automobile accident over the weekend.

The accident occurred on I-10 at about 7 o'clock on Sunday evening. I understand that Karen was involved in a head-on collision. No one else was in her car, and I am told that she died instantly, so—small mercy—she did not suffer. I have no information about the driver or passengers in the other vehicle.

Folks, as soon as I have information from Karen's family concerning funeral and wake arrangements, I will distribute another memo. At that time, I will have information on how to contact Karen's family to express condolences.

We were all Karen's friends, and we will miss her kind words and energetic presence, as well as the high level of professionalism she represented.

SERIOUS ILLNESS OF A CO-WORKER

Date: 00/00/00
To: Shipping Department staff
From: Porter Waylon, Supervisor
Subject: Illness of Ben Thompson

Yesterday, at about 4 o'clock, Ben Thompson, warehouse foreman, was taken ill. An ambulance was summoned, and he was transported to Holy Cross Hospital, where he is being treated for a heart attack. The latest word on Ben is that he is in fair condition. At the moment, he is still in the cardiac intensive care unit, so he's not seeing visitors just now. I am in frequent contact with the hospital and with Ben's family, and please be assured that I will keep all of you informed of his condition, and you'll be the first to know when Ben is ready for visitors.

In the meantime, I know that you will join me in sending Ben our good thoughts and best wishes for a speedy recovery.

CATASTROPHIC MISFORTUNE

Date: 00/00/00
To: Editorial Staff
From: Otis Mack, Editor in Chief
Subject: Tornado hits home

As we all know, Harrisville was hit and hit hard by a series of tornadoes over the weekend. I am greatly relieved and happy to report that all of us here at Rex Publishing survived the catastrophe, but it gives me great pain to tell you that Edna Perkins, chief of the Proofreading Section, lost her house. It was completely destroyed. Thankfully, Edna and her family are fine—but, as you can imagine, they are reeling from their loss and struggling to pick up what pieces they can.

Edna and her family are staying with her sister and brother-in-law, Sarah and Peter Coughlin. Edna, trooper that she is, expects to be at work on Monday. In the meantime, I know that she can use help sorting through the remains of her home. If anyone wishes to lend Edna a hand, Rex Publishing can lend you the time. Please see me.

3 Model Phone Calls

DEATH OF A BUSINESS ASSOCIATE AT ANOTHER COMPANY

Caller:	Hello, Pete. It's Sam. I just heard about Larry Miles. It was a shock to me, and I can only imagine what a blow it must be to you. He was not only your top manager, but a close, close friend.
Callee:	Yes. It's very hard . . .
Caller:	I know it doesn't seem like it at the moment, Pete, but you—you and your company—will get through this. Larry, above all things, would not want the company to falter. That's the kind of person he was. Remember when he broke his leg skiing? He was out of the hospital and behind his desk in record time. The company meant the world to him—and, if he could, he'd be telling you to get on with it.
Callee:	That was Larry, all right.
Caller:	You know, he's still there with you—in the company the two of you built. Remember that. And, Pete, if there is anything I can do to help right now, let me know. Don't hesitate to call.

TO THE SPOUSE OF A BUSINESS ASSOCIATE

Iris, this is Bob Kean. I just heard about Paul. I am so, so sorry. He and I did a lot of work together, and I not only enjoyed working with him, but I learned a great deal from him. I feel the loss deeply, and I can only imagine how you feel. But I know that Paul would want you to be strong for your children. So, hang in. Iris, if there is anything I can do to help you, please call me.

FOLLOWING CATASTROPHE

Len, I just heard about the fire in your building. It's a shock, I know, but I've also known you long enough to be confident that you will come out of this quickly and even stronger than before. Have no fear.

If there is anything I can do to help you out—including lend you some office space and the use of our phones—let me know. I'd like to be of help to you.

3 E-Mail Messages

DEATH OF A BUSINESS ASSOCIATE

Owen:

Gail was such a good friend to us both that I am painfully aware of how deeply you feel her loss. I also know that, hard as her passing is on me, it's even more of a trial for you, who have lost not only a dear friend, but a key member of your management team.

Owen, nothing can replace our friend, but I know how much confidence and trust she placed in you. She always spoke of you as a full partner. She relied on you. She shared her knowledge and judgment with you. Gail was savvy about people. She knew how well you could manage the company, and we all believe you will do just that, not only *carry* on, but *move* on—to even greater success.

Owen, please know that I am here to help in any way I can. Don't hesitate to call or e-mail.

Tom

BELATED CONDOLENCES

Max:

Just in from a two-week vacation and was given the sad news that Jake died last week. I wanted to send these condolences—belated though they are—as soon as possible. I feel for the loss to you and to your firm.

You know better than I do that Jake was a great pleasure to work with. He was a fine and generous man.

If there is anything I can do to be of assistance during this painful time, please don't hesitate to call.

Arnie

OTHER LOSS

Ted, I just ran across the news in *Industry Tabloid* about SmithCo going out of business. I know that this firm is one of your biggest accounts, and I'm sure its passing did not come as welcome news to you.

You have a great company, Ted, and I have no doubt that you'll weather this loss and emerge stronger than ever.

Let's get together over lunch to discuss some strategies and ideas for the future. I'd really like to see you. Why don't you give me a call?

Dan Miller

25 Words and Phrases to Use

admired	help	painful
anything I can do	here for you	please call
assist you	invaluable contribu-	respected
blow	tion	serious
condolences	just heard	shock
feel for you	just learned	sorry
future	let's get together	sympathy
grieve with you	loved	time will help
grieve	news	

12 Words and Phrases to Avoid

despair	passed away
gone to a better place	shake it off
hopeless	What will you do now?
How can you go on?	worst thing that could have
never recover	happened
not that bad	you'll get over it
nothing I can do	

29

Encouragement and Motivation

$\mathcal{A}$ll supervisors and managers agree: A key to effective leadership is the ability to motivate others to achieve excellence. Agreement quickly breaks down, however, over just how to go about the task of motivation. The truth is that few of us are comfortable either with giving pep talks when things go well or with rendering "constructive criticism" when things don't go so well. We find ourselves falling into generalities and platitudes, sounding off the way a high school sports coach might.

Why do most of us come up so lame when it's time to motivate the group?

We fail to be specific. Most motivating communication is made not from the heart, but in a vacuum, without reference to specific circumstances. Want to make an effective motivating speech or memo? Then dig into what's happening now. Dive into the present situation. Talk about a real problem or a current triumph or a genuine opportunity—something specific and immediately relevant to your "audience." Focus on what the problem, triumph, or opportunity means to that audience.

Finding the Heartline

Motivation is selling. You sell the idea of excellence and achievement. As in any other selling situation, success, making the sale, depends on your ability to shift the focus from your own needs and concerns and onto those of your "prospects"—in this case, the people you want to motivate.

Such salesmanship does not come out of context. One or two memos or pep talks isn't going to do the trick. To cultivate the best in your group requires developing and nurturing enthusiasm. This is not done in an instant, but over the long term. The inspired manager circulates among her team, infusing it with enthusiasm. She makes the following part of her daily routine:

- Talking with staff and subordinates
- Working closely with the group
- Suggesting new approaches to stubborn problems
- Expressing empathy in difficult situations
- Consulting and coaching on a continual basis

Communication is the soul of motivational management. The motivating leader tirelessly does the following:

- Shares observations.
- Reinforces positive achievements and attitudes.
- Continually corrects the team's direction and focus as required.

Praise, specific and sincere, is essential to ongoing motivation. Consider convening regular reinforcement meetings:

- Such meetings should be positive and upbeat; their objective is to reward, refresh, and, if necessary, refocus.
- Invite staffers to bring up their concerns, but defer full discussion of these to separate meetings, if they threaten the upbeat tenor of the reinforcement meeting.
- Introduce an element of pleasure into each meeting. Serve refreshments, perhaps, or share a funny story.
- Greet group members with kind and pleasant words: "You guys, as usual, look great!"
- Keep the tone of the reinforcement meeting light, warm, and friendly.
- Be specific in your positive reinforcement. Invite the staffers you single out for praise to talk about their success.

- Spend less than an hour in the meeting—enough time to cite, in detail, several positive examples. Allow ample time for questions, discussion, and clarification.

Don't depend solely on meetings to keep the motivational dialogue going. Supply vigorous and continual feedback designed to reassure subordinates that you have confidence in their skills and abilities.

- Make feedback specific.
- To the degree that it is possible to do so, stress the positive.
- Practice delivering feedback in a sincere tone.
- When you have to deliver critical feedback, always suggest alternatives. Never simply criticize an employee or reject his work.
- Put some *fun* in your instructions and directives. Don't turn them into jokes, but feel free to use imagination when you give directions, discuss ideas, or deliver feedback.

Motivation is not exclusively about praise. Excellence also requires correction and guidance—in other words, criticism. The heartline to effective criticism is to be generous in giving it. Consider the following rules of thumb:

- Communicate criticism in the manner of a mentor or a coach.
- Make it clear that you are committed not just to your department's or company's bottom line, but to the development of the employee as a long-term member of the team.
- Before you criticize, *be certain of your need to criticize*. Avoid using criticism merely to vent frustration, anger, or irritation.
- Ask permission to criticize. Asking permission to criticize will actually enhance the effectiveness of your remarks. Instead of starting out with something like, "You're not doing an effective job with so-and so," begin with "We have a problem with so-and-so, which I would like to discuss with you. Is now a good time?"
- Be certain that the cure will not be worse than the disease. Even sensitively expressed criticism can damage a fragile ego. Use judgment to decide whether the problem or issue is worth the risk that critical words entail.

- Do not criticize subordinates in front of others. Take the person aside—subtly. "Mary, I need to speak to you about an important matter. When is a good time for us to get together for a few minutes of uninterrupted time?"

- As far as possible, quantify your criticism objectively: "Turnaround time in your area is a good 10 percent more than we need it to be."

- Maintain your perspective. You are both on the same team; therefore, approach the subordinate not just as an employee, but as a member of *your* team. Be friendly.

- Always address issues, never personalities. Resist the temptation to tell an errant employee what you think of him. Focus on the issue.

- Combine as much praise as possible with the criticism. You might observe that, in general, you are pleased with the subordinate's work, but that, as regards issue A, an improvement needs to be made.

- Limit your criticism to what can be changed. It does no good—and may do great harm—to criticize a subordinate for something over which she has little or no control.

- Address one issue at a time. Avoid bombarding the subordinate with a cluster of faults and problems.

Sidestepping the Pitfalls

The main reason motivation fails is that it fails to be clear and specific. Always outline specific problems or goals. Avoid issuing blanket criticism or generalized criticism. Cite specific issues and incidents. Also be sure to take the following steps:

- Resist the temptation to yell at people. Focus on problems and issues, not on personalities. It is far more feasible to fix things than to try to fix people.

- Censor yourself. If your remarks are not likely to improve the situation, don't make them.

- Reinforcement meetings should not be lectures. Make them interactive.

- Avoid criticism first thing in the morning or at quitting time. Criticism is not a good way to start or end the day.

3 Model Memos

DATE: 00/00/00
TO: Sales Department
FROM: Jim
SUBJECT: Attitude

So I'm in the hall yesterday, and I hear one of you complaining: "I missed the sale because EXPLETIVE DELETED John Doe didn't get me the right EXPLETIVE DELETED numbers until it was too late!"

Okay. We all get angry. But there are two things wrong with just fuming about a bad situation.

Number 1: It doesn't pay to get angry at people. Get angry at the situation. Don't try to fix people. Fix the situation.

Number 2: When you start blaming others—even when they do screw up— you can forget about achieving your goals.

Look, the fact is that any sale can be saved, even if we don't always have all the information at our fingertips. It takes extra effort, but it can be done. Don't panic. Don't swear. Just work the problem.

You have all shown me that you are not only capable, but also superb sales-people. I am proud of all that you have accomplished. But I don't want you to get the idea that it should always be so easy. Make the sale, if you can. Save the sale, if you must. By all means, lean on the team—but depend on yourself, and take responsibility for what you do and for what you fail to do.

REINFORCING SUCCESS WITH A GOOD STORY

DATE: 00/00/00
TO: Customer Support Division
FROM: Don Ibsen
SUBJECT: Above and Beyond

What makes a good news story?
Disaster.
What makes a great news story?

A disaster that didn't happen.

Last week, we shipped one of our best customers, M&N, a bad TVX circuit board. M&N called Dora Donbey, the customer service rep assigned to the account, who moved heaven and earth to get a new board out there.

Guess what? The new board failed.

You can bet there was another call to Dora. She scrambled to get yet another board. Nothing doing. The cupboard was bare.

End of story. Disaster—for the customer, and for us. Right?

Dauntless Dora got on the phone and called a list of her other customers until she was able to find one who was willing to lend a TVX unit to M&N. We picked up the tab for the loaner, and Dora personally ran the board over to M&N.

That, ladies and gentlemen, is motivation. Not just doing everything that's expected of you, but more—committing yourself to each and every customer, becoming that customer's partner, and refusing to give up, even when the "normal" options are exhausted.

Well done, Dora. You not only saved an important client, but you taught us all a valuable lesson. Thanks!

GETTING THINGS DONE

Date: 00/00/00
To: Billing Department
From: Iris Berman, Billing Manager
Subject: Procrastination

Inertia, any high school physics teacher will tell you, is the property of a body by virtue of which it opposes any agency that attempts to put it in motion or, if it is moving, to change the magnitude or direction of its velocity. In other words, inertia opposes action or change.

Physical objects have no monopoly on inertia. It is also a property of human beings. Many, many of us have trouble starting projects that need to be started. Call this procrastination, if you like, but it's inertia all the same.

As with physical inertia, mental inertia often requires the application of an outside force to get moving: A client screams; a boss threatens; your kids clamor for food, clothing, shelter, and a college education. These are all highly effective outside forces.

But you cannot always depend on the timely application of outside forces. Besides, if you're kicked hard enough, you'll bruise. The better answer to procrastination is to formulate ways in which you yourself can overcome inertia and break free of the procrastination pattern. Now, this does not mean simply telling yourself to "work harder" or to "get going." Procrastination has little or nothing to do with laziness. It's about structure—or, rather, lack of it. Without structure and direction, it is very difficult to get things started—and, conversely, very easy to find excuses to put things off.

Your most powerful weapon in the war against procrastination, then, is creating a schedule. Do you have trouble keeping to a schedule? Well, maybe that is because you don't create a daily or weekly or monthly schedule. The fact is that making and keeping schedules is vital to getting ahead and staying ahead in business.

Let's start with the most basic schedule for the typical work day. Plan what you're going to do for the day at the *beginning* of each day. Plan what you're going to accomplish during the week at the beginning of the week. Here's how to get started:

- Take out a piece of paper and write down the projects you are working on.
- Number them in priority order, starting with the most critical projects and working your way down.
- Now, take out your calendar—or fire up your desk-top computer calendar program—and begin plugging in time slots for the most important projects at the beginning of the week.
- If you prefer, divide the time for each project each day, but always give proportionately more time to the critical tasks.
- Next, set firm deadlines.

Let's pause on this last point. Remember when you were in college and you knew you were going to be tested on a chunk of material—but you didn't know when? I bet you cracked those books right away!

Sure.

The truth is that only when a firm date for the exam was set did you start to study. Let's face it, given a choice, we wander down the path of least resistance. With a firm deadline and a little discipline, however, you'd be surprised at all that you can accomplish. Set personal deadlines, write them down, and plan your work to meet them.

Procrastination begins at the start of the day. Well, you say, you're just not a morning person? You simply can't get your work going at 9 a.m. sharp? Then try getting into the office just a little earlier, say 8:45. By the time you've had you're first cup of coffee, checked your e-mail, and shot the breeze with everyone, you're ready to go—and, wonder of wonders, it's 9:00, or just a bit past the hour.

When you plan your schedule, do be realistic. Don't expect to produce in a half hour an hour-long presentation on a subject you don't know much about. And don't schedule for yourself more time to work on something you really enjoy, but that you know you could complete in a matter of minutes. Schedule according to needs, not desires.

Intelligent, thoughtful scheduling provides the framework you need to help you climb out of the pit called procrastination. I urge you to try it.

3 Model Speeches

INCREASING PRODUCTIVITY

Acme Industries is not the kind of place where you have bosses breathing down the necks of their staff or cracking the whip and bellowing for more "productivity." Here we pride ourselves on being self-starters, and if anyone is dissatisfied with the level of productivity generated, it's each of us ourselves. We self-starters are our own harshest critics. It seems that no matter how hard we work, most of the time we feel that we just don't get enough accomplished.

I think it is a mistake to talk about productivity in the abstract. It certainly doesn't help to tell yourself to "work harder." No, increasing personal productivity is a matter of working on the little things in your life to make them more convenient and efficient. It's about time management.

Let's begin at the best place to begin: the beginning. Begin by asking yourself: "Are you efficient?" Answer this question by making a private list. Divide the page in half. In the lefthand column, write tasks you ordinarily perform during a typical day. In the righthand column, assess how well you do them. For example, in the lefthand column you write: "Finishing projects on time," and in the righthand column: "I usually only finish the projects I'm interested in first, then get around to the others." That's an honest start. Now keep going. You'll end up with a snapshot of your level of efficiency.

Since, in essence, productivity is a matter of time management, work toward getting a handle on your time. Keeping time sheets or using a computer program that tracks the hours you spend on specific tasks is a concrete method of managing your time and gauging your productivity. You may discover, for example, that you've spent eight hours on a relatively trivial project that should have been done in no time, and yet, in that same month, you spent only three hours on a project that is critical both to your career and to the company. Einstein told us that time is relative. Who are we to argue with Einstein? But that eight hours spent on trivial tasks is still five hours more than you spent on the really important work. Don't just record your time; *track* it. Look for the important patterns by studying time sheets from several months.

Now let's talk about "free time."

If the concept of "free time" makes you laugh because you're constantly bringing home work, you're either just extremely busy or not being productive enough during regular working hours. Is there something wrong with you? Do you have colleagues who seem always to get their work done on time and at work rather than at home? What is it about their work habits that makes this possible? Do they get to work early? Do they take work home with them? Do they take shorter lunch breaks? Make a list of what you feel gives them the advantage. Study the list. Is there something you should be doing differently?

One thing you may do differently is to plan out your day. Start the morning by making a schedule of what you have to accomplish before leaving the office that day. Write down how long you think it should take to complete each individual task. Don't cheat! As you go through the day, mark down the start and stop times for each task. How did you do? Did some tasks take longer than expected? This is a sign that there may be a better way to get the task done. You just haven't thought of it yet. You can take a high-tech approach to this exercise by using your contact manager PC or Mac program. Set start and stop points for each task. You can set the alarm on your program to sound when it's time to start wrapping things up. Be sure to record how well you keep to your original schedule as you go through each task. Be sure to keep a record of all of your starts and stops. This will help you diagnose problem areas.

Now, we've been talking about managing time at the office. But who said travel time has to be "down time"? If you commute to work on the bus or subway, bring something work-related to read. Create a "traveling folder" in which you keep all the papers you're working on at the moment. This way, they stay in one place and are easily accessible, ready for you to grab for the commute to and from the office. You might also use the morning commute to plan your day. If you manage to grab a seat on the subway, bus, or train, open up your planner (you do have a planner, don't you?) and jot down what you need to get done today. You might also use your evening commute to take stock of what needs to be done the next day.

Now for those of you who drive to work, don't try to read while you're driving. However, you can still use driving time for more than just driving. If a great idea comes to you while you're driving, don't let it pass. As soon as you can stop—at a traffic light, say—jot down a note or two. Most auto parts and accessories stores sell paper pads that can be mounted on your dash. It is even a better idea to invest in a small hand-held microchip recorder. Speak your ideas into one of these.

While we're on the subject of the commute, give some thought to whether or not you're really taking the shortest route to work. Plan it carefully, taking into account traffic as well as distance. For a variety of good reasons, you might also consider car pooling. Now this won't save commuting time, but it may buy work time, including early-morning discussions with your colleagues and co-workers. You know, if nothing else, car-pool conversation gets out of the way a lot of the small talk that often adds to first-thing-in-the-morning office inertia.

Speaking of colleagues, you might start thinking of ways to coax others—not just yourself—to greater personal productivity. Begin by communicating your expectations clearly. For example: "I'm going to need that report by 4 p.m. tomorrow. If we don't have it ready by then, we risk losing this account. If you have any questions or concerns, please talk to me while we can still do something about them. Thanks."

In addition to open, clear communication, remember to plan the work, and work the plan. Sit down with those you work with and plan for the month, the week, or even just the day ahead. Be certain that you're all agreed on which projects have priority, what the deadlines are, and just how the tasks should be executed.

Just as you hold yourself accountable, don't be afraid to hold others accountable as well. While you shouldn't point fingers, browbeat, or terrorize, you don't have to be overly eager to express understanding and to accept excuses. React honestly and helpfully if you receive work that is just not up to par. Remember, though, address the issues of the work, *not* the personality of the worker. Separate the person from the problem. Then attack the problem, not the person.

Don't be reluctant to criticize constructively, but don't just criticize, either. Suggest solutions. As a manager or colleague, it is your responsibility to offer constructive solutions to the problems you detect.

Remember that information is the single most valuable driver of productivity. Get people to feel closer to what you are doing by empowering them with information: copies of important memos and other documents. Keep them "in the loop," even the memos that are only FYI.

Folks, these are all small things—small, real, concrete things. You can do them, and they will add up. Their sum will be greater than the parts. You *will* be more productive, and, almost even better, you will *feel* more productive.

LEADERSHIP—ADDRESS TO MANAGERS AND SUPERVISORS

As managers, you are the leaders at Acme Corporation. I want to speak with you, in practical, down-to-earth terms, about what leadership means.

If you are looking for a nutshell definition of what a manager is expected to do in our organization, it is that he or she is not expected to do anything, but, rather, to ensure that whatever needs to be done gets done.

Is a manager a leader or a boss?

Truly effective managers are leaders, not bosses. Bosses bark out orders, whereas leaders give direction—not just "directions," but direction. Bosses, naturally, are always right, whereas leaders are willing to admit that others may have good ideas. Bosses bully, but leaders motivate. Bosses intimidate, whereas leaders educate. The boss is a driver, the leader a coach. The boss stands upon the principle of authority, the leader on good will. The boss inspires fear, the leader enthusiasm. Whereas the boss commands "go," the leader says, "let's go."

That's all well and good—inspiring people, leading rather than bossing. But management is not only about inspiration. Effective management is about controlling time, money, and people. "Administrative management" is what we call the time and money part of the job. It includes budgets, policies, and procedures. The people part includes hiring, training, coaching, setting goals, motivating, counseling, and, when necessary, terminating.

Now, as a manager, you will be judged chiefly—almost exclusively—on the basis of how well your people do. An effective leader, therefore, devotes most of his or her time to developing and improving staff members. Spend at least three-quarters of your time working the "people" side of the management job and only about a quarter of your time on "administrative management." If you spend more time than that on administration, you may be managing, but you are not leading.

Now let's talk about leadership style. There's more than one right way to lead. You might pick and choose your favored methods from the following menu:

- *You may lead through example.* This means working harder than anyone else in the office and knowing more about the product line than anyone else. Leading by example is incredibly hard work. It's also one of the most consistently successful leadership styles.

- *You may lead through encouragement.* Since the early days of scientific psychology, tests and studies have repeatedly shown that people respond more favorably to positive rather than negative reinforcement. They learn faster, and they comply more willingly and readily. Learn to take genuine and generous pleasure in the accomplishments of your staff. Always have something positive to say. Stimulate and inspire.

* *You may lead through teaching.* This requires a high level of technical expertise and a tireless willingness to share your knowledge. You need to cultivate within yourself a passion for solving problems.

* *You may lead through motivation,* through tirelessly encouraging individual staff members to improve themselves, to work harder, and to work smarter. This style of leadership requires frequent and crystal-clear goal setting. Make rewards visible, tangible, and available. Cultivate top people. Groom them for promotion.

I've removed one highly popular leadership style from the menu I just offered. Many, many managers try to lead through intimidation. This isn't really leading at all. It's pushing. You lead from the front, not the rear. Your organization is like spaghetti. It is much easier to pull than it is to push!

An effective leader creates loyalty. This is a quality that cannot be bought or bullied. Loyalty must be earned, and managers who earn it generally do the following:

* They treat people fairly.

* They are always accessible.

* They listen well.

* They recognize achievement.

* They praise achievement.

* They reward achievement.

* They themselves are loyal. When appropriate, an effective manager stands up for his staff, defending them to senior management and, when necessary, to customers.

* They are helpful and expedite important matters with other areas of the company.

* They ensure that credit is given where credit is due.

* They are dependably knowledgeable.

* They are great coaches, mentors, teachers.

* They have and they communicate a clear sense of purpose.

This is the last leadership point I will leave you with: An effective leader has—and communicates—a clear sense of purpose. When all is said and done, this is the single most important aspect of leadership. On this, all the rest depends.

OPTIMISM—ADDRESS TO A MANAGERS' GROUP

On July 2, 1862, the Union army was about to lose the Battle of Gettysburg. With the loss of Gettysburg, very likely, would come an end not only to the Civil War, but to the United States as a single, unified nation. The northern United States would have a slave-holding neighbor on its southern border. All the Confederates had to do was take the high ground, and the Union forces wouldn't have had a prayer.

The end of the Union's line of troops—its flank, its most vulnerable point— was occupied by a badly weakened regiment from Maine, whose colonel, Joshua Chamberlain, had been a professor of rhetoric at Bowdoin College. The rebels charged repeatedly, but, somehow, Chamberlain and his men held firm.

Finally, there came a massive charge. Chamberlain's regiment, exhausted, was also out of ammunition. The proper thing to do was to surrender.

But Chamberlain knew that to surrender the flank would mean losing the battle and, quite probably, the war. In a desperate, depressing, no-win situation, Chamberlain, trained as a teacher and not as a military commander, chose the road of optimism.

He ordered his men to attack, to charge—using bayonets in the absence of ammunition.

The Confederates, shocked, retreated, then surrendered.

The tide of Gettysburg turned, and, on the next day, the Union won a victory that effectively sealed the doom of the Confederacy and ensured the resurrection of the Union.

By all reports, Chamberlain was a soft-spoken, scholarly man. He did not lead by terrorizing his troops, but by inspiring them with confidence and optimism. His optimism outlasted his ammunition and, in the end, was far more effective. Deeply felt, that optimism was contagious.

Most contagions, of course, are not so positive. Gloom, doubt, and defeatism are, if anything, even more contagious than optimism. If we allow these feelings to dominate us, we will create defeat. Now it is true that, just because we are driven by optimism, it doesn't necessarily follow that victory will be ours. However, it is far more likely that a defeatist attitude will spread and will bring disaster than it is that an optimistic attitude will create anything negative. With defeatism, then, we have everything to lose, whereas, with optimism, we have nothing to lose and, perhaps, much to gain.

To be sure, both defeatism and optimism are only feelings. But feelings are fuel. They do not *determine,* but they do *drive* our success—or our failure. So how do we "spread" optimism?

The answer is most definitely *not* to deny the reality of setbacks, challenges, problems, and disasters. However, we must embrace and broadcast a faith in our ability to cope with and even profit from setbacks, challenges, problems, and disasters.

When Thomas Alva Edison was laboring away at inventing the electric light, he told a newspaper reporter that he had tested some 1,600 substances as potential filaments for his lamp, all of which had failed.

"You must be very disappointed at the waste of time and labor," the reporter remarked.

"Not at all. Nothing was wasted," Edison replied. "Now I know of 1,600 things that will not work."

Edison had found a positive—and true—way of looking at his experience. This drove him, of course, to ultimate success.

Our task, as managers, is to help our employees look at their experience as positive. Is a customer calling to complain about a problem with a widget? Look at this as an opportunity to satisfy this customer by making that problem right. Cultivate this attitude in yourselves, and it will be broadcast to your staff.

25 Words to Use

advice	discuss	learn
advise	evaluate	lesson
analyze	expedite	manage
assist	formulate	navigate
consider	future	plan
control	glitch	reconsider
cope	help	rethink
counsel	invest	
determine	lead	

25 Words and Phrases to Avoid

better shape up	fault
blame	figure it out yourself
can't do it	force
catastrophe	foul-up
crisis	hell to pay
demand	hopeless
destroyed	idiotic
disaster	impossible
don't ask	mess
don't come to me about it	misguided
don't want to hear it	must
don't worry about it	snafu
exploded	

30

Asking Favors

If you look forward to asking for a favor about as much as you look forward to root canal dentistry, you are decidedly in the majority. Root canal is hard to endure, and so is begging: asking for something in return for nothing.

That's the way most of us think about requesting a favor.

Want to make it easier to get what you need? Begin by rethinking your definition of *favor*. Erase the definition of it as a bid to get something for nothing, and substitute this: Asking for a favor is providing somebody with an opportunity to help you.

And this *is* an opportunity. Most people enjoy helping others. Being asked to help empowers the helper. It is a compliment and a vote of confidence. It is an opportunity to feel good about oneself. Asking for a favor provides an opportunity to make someone feel good.

And there is more. The business community is not all about cutting throats and pummeling the competition. Hard as it is to believe sometimes, business operates according to a kind of corporate karma—the belief that what goes around comes around. Doing a colleague a favor creates good will. Most of your colleagues recognize that and are eager for the opportunity to create good corporate karma.

Finding the Heartline

Get to the heartline by putting yourself in the right frame of mind. Purge from your head that outworn notion of the favor as freeloading.

715

Think of it as an offer of opportunity. Next, overcome the inertia that preceded that first difficult step: broaching the subject.

Begin by furnishing a basis for the request—"We've worked together for so long that I feel comfortable asking you for a favor." That done, state what you want:

- Be clear and specific about what you want.
- Explain how the favor will benefit you. This gives the other person a way to gauge just how much he can help.
- Express gratitude.

Remember also to express yourself in positive terms, and if you *can* offer a quid pro quo, do so—just don't try to disguise a request for a favor as a business deal.

Sidestepping the Pitfalls

The biggest mistake most people make when they ask for a favor is to apologize for doing so: "I'm sorry to ask . . ." This is the equivalent of warning the other person that you are about to make his life miserable. It also puts him on his guard, suggesting that you are about to make an unreasonable demand.

- Do not apologize.
- Do not tell the other person how he should feel about your request: "I know this is annoying . . ." Or: "I hate to ask you . . ."

Do not attempt to soften the request by minimizing it: "Joe, this will take a half-hour of your time at most." That's a fine thing to say— if it is a true assessment of the effort required. Joe will be justifiably annoyed, however, if the favor consumes two or three hours or more. Don't minimize the request. Don't lie.

Always express your gratitude, but avoid such phrases as "thanking you in advance." This implies that you take the other person's compliance for granted—and that is always offensive. It may also end by embarrassing both of you.

3 Model Letters

ASKING FOR A RECOMMENDATION

Dear Ed:

We've had such a great working relationship that I actually look forward to asking you for a favor.

I need a brief letter of recommendation to the Waldorf Company to help us secure a major contract with them.

We've been asked to bid on supplying them with widgets and widget-maintenance services. I don't have to tell you that this represents major business for us. It would be very, very helpful if, in addition to whatever else you feel inclined to comment on, you could make the following points about your experience with us as a supplier:

- We supply high value.
- We furnish a high level of client support.
- We offer three-hour emergency response.

Ed, we're working on a tight schedule to make Waldorf's tight schedule, so I would appreciate your sending out the letter before April 3. You'll be writing to:

> Mr. Frank Miller
> President
> The Waldorf Company
> 444 23rd Street
> Warrentown, NH 00013

Please call me if you have any questions, and, as always, I appreciate your time and attention.

Sincerely,

Sam Korn

CHANGE IN MEETING TIME

Dear Tom:

I am looking forward to meeting with you about Project X. In the past day or two, I discovered three new marketing venues relevant to the project, and it would be a benefit to both of us if I could have a little more time to explore these venues.

Specifically, I could use four more days to do some legwork. Can we push the meeting back to February 4?

Please call or fax with your response. The investment of a little extra time will pay off, I believe.

Sincerely,

Ron Sheldon

EXTEND DEADLINE

Dear Ms. Schultz:

I thought this would be a good time to give you a progress report on Project X.

We have completed the first three phases of the project, but we are finding that research for phase 4 is consuming more time than we had anticipated. I know that you do not want any corners cut on this crucially important project, especially not at this culminating stage. I ask, therefore, that you agree to extend the deadline for completion of the entire project to March 16.

I am confident that the improved results will justify the additional time invested at this point.

Please give me a call to confirm the new deadline or to discuss the proposed adjustment to the schedule.

Sincerely,

Robert Bennet
General Manager

3 Model Memos

CALL FOR VOLUNTEERS

Date: 00/00/00
To: Customer Service Staff
From: Tod Pointer, Manager
Subject: Volunteers Needed

Next weekend (September 23-24), we will be working with the Build-A-Home organization to help in the construction of affordable homes for needy families. Our department has been given the opportunity of contributing to this valuable and highly rewarding enterprise. Accordingly, I am calling for volunteers for the weekend.

No special skills are required. Volunteers will be fully supervised. What *is* required is a willingness to pitch in and make life better for a family in our community.

Those of us who pitched in last year remember this weekend not as a sacrifice, but as a fulfilling time spent with other good people. To join us, please call me at extension 123 by Thursday afternoon.

CHANGE MEETING TIME

Date: 00/00/00
To: Bill Williams and Gail Storch
From: Ted Matthews
Subject: Change Meeting Time

In view of the new technical developments bearing directly on the widget rollout, Bill and Gail, I think we should postpone the launch meeting for at least one week, which should allow us sufficient time to get a fresh report from Engineering.

I know we're under the gun in terms of deadline, but we can't afford to ignore the changes that are about to happen. If we don't wait for the new information, there is a good chance we will have to revise the rollout anyway—and lose even more time.

Can we meet on the 14th, then? Please let me know.

USE OF OFFICE

Date: 00/00/00
To: Ben Marks
From: Celia Randolph
Subject: Borrow Your Office

Jim Matthews from AccountTech is scheduled to come in for a meeting on Friday. I've just learned that the conference room is booked up that day. My office, as you know, is a cubicle. That leaves us without anyplace to sit Mr. Matthews down for a major strategy meeting. Can you bail me out with the loan of your office? We would need the space for three hours, from 9 to noon, on the 14th. You are, of course, welcome to my humble cube during that time.

Ben, if you can spare the space for that morning, it would really help me out of a jam. Just give me a buzz to let me know.

3 Model Phone Calls

REQUEST FOR REFERRAL

Caller: Hello, Jack. This is Pat Smith at R&T. I'm calling to ask a favor.

Callee: Oh? You are?

Caller: XYZ Company has just asked us to bid on an installation of a widget, which is quite similar to the kind of work we did for you last year. From our point of view, that project was a great success, and I believe you think of it the same way.

Callee: We were pleased.

Caller: I also believe that you know Sam Maxwell at XYZ. Am I right?

Callee: Yes, I know him very well.

Caller: That's what I thought. It seemed to me that you would make an ideal reference. What I'd like to ask is for you to make a quick phone call to Mr. Maxwell and tell him something about the kind of job we did for you. Could you do that?

Callee: Yes, sure.

Caller: It would be very helpful if you could stress the efficiency of the installation and the minimal impact the work had on your routine. XYZ is particularly concerned about down time. You have Mr. Maxwell's number?

Callee: I do.

Caller: Is it possible for you to make the call today?

Callee: As soon as that?

Caller: I would really appreciate it. This would be a major contract for us. It means a great deal.

Callee: Okay. I'll call this morning.

Caller: That would be wonderful. We would be very grateful for whatever kind words you could pass along. I hope you'll call on me some time to return the favor.

CHANGE IN MEETING PLANS

Mark, this is Kelly Pressler. I've a favor to ask you. Jack Green, from Youngblood & Youngblood, is going to be in town on Monday. He's an expert on the kind of work we plan to be doing with Project X. I'd really like to take advantage of his being in town. I know we want to keep our meeting low key, but could you see your way clear to make room for Jack? His perspective would be well worth having.

ALTER PAYMENT SCHEDULE

Ben, this is Murphy. I've got a problem I'm hoping you can help me with. As you know, when we set up the payment for our last order, I was counting on our schedule meshing with the one we'd worked out with our client, Singer and Son. Well, they got underway with the project three weeks late. Accordingly, for our cash flow, it would be great if we could reschedule our last two payments to you—namely from September 3 to September 20, and from December 5 to December 28. Would this work for you? It would do wonders for us.

25 Words and Phrases to Use

advantage	convenient	please
appreciate	do the same for you	rely on
ask	emergency	request
assist	favor	thank you
bail out	grateful	urgent
benefit	help	valuable
big help	last minute	volunteer
call on me	mutual friend	
comfortable	need	

15 Words and Phrases to Avoid

don't like to ask you	no problem for you
easy for you	no time at all
hate to ask	owe it to me
have to	pain in the neck
I know I can count on you	piece of cake
must	sorry to ask
my last hope	you can't turn me down
no choice	

31

Invitations that Invite

$\mathcal{I}$nvitations are acts of both asking and giving. They ask for a person's presence, participation, time, and sometimes, talent, even as they offer that person one's own time, as well as hospitality, perhaps, or, depending on the occasion, even opportunity and honor. The tone of the invitation should reflect its dual nature. The idea is to be respectful and grateful, but also to "sell" the value of what is being offered.

Finding the Heartline

Invitations, even in a business context, are intensely social documents. The emphasis should be on courtesy and sincerity.

- Make it clear that the invitee's presence or participation is genuinely desired.

- "Sell" the event. Be certain that the invitee understands what he is being asked to do and what benefit he will derive from doing it.

Underpinning these two messages is information. Whatever else an invitation is, it is a vehicle of some simple but crucially important items of information—the five *W*'s so familiar to journalists and news reports:

- *Who?* Be sure the invitation makes clear who, exactly, is being invited. Names must be double checked for accurate spelling. Are spouses included in the invitation? Others from the invitee's firm?

722

- *What?* What—exactly—is the event in question? What is included in the event? (Dinner? Lunch?) What, if anything, is the invitee expected to do at the event? (Give a speech? Participate in a panel discussion?)
- *When?* Date and time.
- *Where?* Place. Be sure to include directions, if it is likely the invitee is unfamiliar with the location.
- *Why?* What is the purpose of the event or occasion? Be certain that this is clear, especially if you are asking the invitee to prepare a speech or presentation.

Also essential are the names and phone numbers of people to contact if the invitee has questions or requires clarification. Specify, too, a response due date, together with an address or phone number for making the response.

Sidestepping the Pitfalls

Business invitations are plagued by two common problems:

1. *Unclear, incomplete, garbled, or erroneous information.* Make sure all five *W*'s are present in your invitation. Be certain the information is correct.

2. *Inappropriate tone.* Some business invitations sound like command performances. A more common fault is the invitation that is couched in apologetic terms: "I hate to ask you to come to another one of these rubber-chicken banquets, but I don't have much choice." If you cannot offer an enthusiastic invitation, it is best to rethink the invitee, the event, or both.

3 Model Letters

TO SPEAK AT BUSINESS MEETING

Dear Ms. Lawrence:

One of my most pleasant business memories is of the speech you made in Chicago last year. What you said was not only enlightening and lucid, it was also delightful. When I met with the Speakers' Committee yesterday to plan our annual XYZ Convention, I mentioned to the group how great it would be to get someone like Sarah Lawrence to speak.

"Hey, Mike," one of the committee members said, "why don't you just ask her?"

What an idea!

I would be doing a great service to my firm and our organization if I succeed in persuading you to speak. I've enclosed a flier describing the event and giving the time and place. You will have an opportunity to address—and to meet—the top people in the wholesale textile industry. The choice of topic is entirely up to you, although I might mention that computerizing inventory is a hot-button issue in our industry just now.

In addition to offering you access to industry leaders, we also serve a pretty good meal at the event. The speaker's honorarium is $500, plus your expenses.

Please think over this opportunity, and kindly call me at 555-555-5555 no later than September 5.

Sincerely yours,

Michael Wall
Vice President

TO JOIN A TRADE ORGANIZATION

Dear Frank Williams:

It was a great pleasure speaking with you the other day about our organization, Trade Focus Association. It is a great group of people who wield significant influence in our industry.

I was delighted to learn from you that you are interested in joining us, and I immediately discussed the matter with the membership at our most recent meeting. They enthusiastically agreed to extend this invitation to you.

We would be delighted if you would attend our next meeting on Monday, November 3, at 8 p.m., in the Wonder Room of the Grand Hotel, 1234 East Pell Street. You'll have the opportunity to sit in on one of our meetings, and you'll be given a full presentation on membership, including benefits, responsibilities, and dues.

I look forward to seeing you there. If you have any questions beforehand, please call me at 555-555-5555.

Sincerely,

Jan Baker

TO ACCEPT AN AWARD

Dear Ms. Standish:

Each year The Service Club presents its Milhous Award to individuals who have demonstrated an extraordinary commitment to community service. It is my pleasure to inform you that the Awards Committee has voted to confer this year's Milhous Award on you in recognition of your long and distinguished record of service.

We would be greatly honored if you would consent to accept the award and to attend the annual Awards Dinner, which will be held on December 3 at 8 p.m. at the Grand Hotel, 12324 Downtown Street.

I ask that you telephone me at 555-555-5555 to indicate your acceptance of the award and your availability for the dinner and presentation ceremony.

Congratulations and thanks.

Sincerely,

Peter Wald
Chairman, Awards Committee

3 Model Memos

MEETING—SHORT FORM

DATE: 00/00/00
TO: Marketing Staff
FROM: Arnold Booth, Marketing Manager
SUBJECT: Market Plan software meeting

Those of you who currently use or plan to use the new Market Plan software package will want to attend a tutorial meeting on Friday, May 3, at 3 p.m. in the third-floor conference room. A representative from the Market Plan firm will be present to answer any questions you may have about the software.

MEETING—LONG FORM

DATE: 00/00/00
TO: Marketing Staff
FROM: Arnold Booth, Marketing Manager
SUBJECT: Market Plan software meeting

We are currently evaluating a new software system, which, we hope, will allow us all to evaluate more effectively and more quickly the performance of our products in the marketplace.

This software promises to limber up the organization, making us more flexible, more responsive to the market, and, even more important, more capable of making accurate *proactive* decisions.

In short, Market Plan promises to make your lives easier and more profitable. That is, *if—*

1. You know how to use it.
2. It actually works for you.

On Friday, May 3, at 3 p.m. in the third-floor conference room, you will have an opportunity to explore the software, find out how it works and if it will work for you. A representative from Market Plan will be here to demonstrate the product and to answer all of your questions.

This could be a very important tool for us. Attending this meeting will be your opportunity to hit the ground running with this new technology.

GOING-AWAY PARTY

Date: 00/00/00
To: Accounting Staff
From: Pam Deaner, Manager
Re: Going-Away Party for Ed Meeks

As you all know, Ed Meeks is retiring after more than twenty years with Bold & Bolder. Whether you've been here for most of those years or for just a few months, you've doubtless come to admire and respect Ed and will want to give him a hearty send-off.

You'll have that opportunity on Friday, May 5, at 4 p.m. in the dining room. We'll celebrate Ed's twenty years with us and give him our thanks as well as our best wishes. Food and drink will be abundant.

Please join us.

3 Model Phone Calls

INFORMATIONAL MEETING

Caller: Good morning, Otis. This is Perry. Ben Karlson, Claire Toombs, Ed Spiro, and I are getting together to discuss implementation of the new accounting program. I know that you don't work with accounting software every day, but it occurred to me that you would find information on the software useful, since you do work with us quite a bit. Would you like to join us on Tuesday?

Callee: Yes. It sounds worthwhile.

Caller: Great! I thought you'd be interested. We're getting together on Tuesday, at 3, in my office. See you then.

LUNCH

Ken, this is Sam Weinstein at Benton and Hart. It's been quite a while since we last touched base. Certainly I haven't had the opportunity to meet with you since my company introduced its new line of widgets. I think you'll want to know about their new features, and I thought the most pleasant way to introduce the line to you would be over lunch. Can I take you? Say, 12:30 on Tuesday or Thursday of next week?

SURPRISE PARTY FOR EMPLOYEE OF THE MONTH

Caller: Larry, this is Marla. Ted Williams has just been named employee of the month. A number of us—Mike Jones, Billy Taylor, Ron Shelton, Patty Lease, and I—thought we'd make something special of it by giving Ted a surprise party. You're such a good friend of Ted's that we didn't want to throw this shindig without you.

Can you make it on Friday, at 4, in the conference room?

Callee: Sure. Sounds great.

Caller: Okay. We've got funding from petty cash, so no donations are necessary. The only requirements, then, are that you be there—4 P.M., Friday, conference room—and that you do *not* tell Ted! It *is* a surprise party. You know Ted. He'd never agree to this kind of thing if he knew about it.

Callee: Your secret's safe with me.

Caller: Great. See you then.

3 E-Mail Messages

AFTER-WORK PARTY

Jim, Jack, Jane, and Harold:

The Smith project is safely launched—after three solid weeks of 14-hour days. Won't you join me in a little celebration after work on Friday?

The Time: 5:30 sharp, May 3
The Place: Ivan's
The Purpose: Pleasure

Hit the reply button, please, and let me know if we're on.

Simon

INFORMATIONAL SEMINAR

John:

Our department is holding a seminar on the new mailing software Tuesday, March 6, at 10:30 in the main conference room. Ordinarily, it's just our department folks who attend, but since you are involved in a project that requires a mass mailing, I thought you would be interested in an overview of the software.

No need to reply. If you're interested, just drop in on Tuesday.

Parker

POWER BREAKFAST

Terri,

Ned, Frank, Earl, and I are getting together before the presentations on Tuesday to review our position on the new projects. We figured the most efficient way to do this was at breakfast. Your input would be very helpful to us, and I suspect you'd be eager for the opportunity to get your views known to us before the big meeting.

Our plan is to meet at Nelson's, the coffee shop downstairs, at 8 a.m. on the 23rd. It would be great if you could make it.

Sam

25 Words and Phrases to Use

any questions	hash out	invite
ask	help	meet
benefit	helpful	offer
brainstorm	honored	opportunity
eager	invest your time	overview
get together	investigate	participate in

plan   share   welcome
proud   valuable   worthwhile
review

12 Words and Phrases to Avoid

boring   probably not interested, but
don't be left out   show up
feel obligated to ask you   sorry to ask
fight it out   spend your time
have to ask you   you could come
if you really want to come
probably don't want to come,
   but

Index

to encourage leadership, 710-11
for favors asked, 718-19
to increase productivity, 707-09
of motivation, 704-07
to set meetings, 725-26
Minor mishaps, 547
Misinformation
apology for, 460, 462
written apology, 465, 468
Missed appointment
apology for, 459, 462
e-mailed apology, 470
written apology, 465, 468
Missing loved one, 648-49
Modeling behavior, 596
Motivation, 700-04
of others, 428-30
Mourning, 582. *See also* Death

Name-calling, 662
Negativity, 484-85
in asking for favors, 510-11
in love relationship, 618
Negotiation, 407-08
Nervousness, and body language, 419-21
News, announcing to family, 445-46
Nodding, 440
Nonverbal communication, 409-21, 629

Objections, 425
Objectives, 425-27
Obscenity, 607-08
Obstacles
to expression, 400-01
overcoming, 404-08
Opening lines, 625-28
Optimism, encouraging, 712-13
Organizing, *see* Preparation, methods for
Outcomes, fear of, 509

Party invitation, 522-24
business, 726, 727-28
Passive aggression, 661
Past hurts, 665
Personal love notes, 644-47
Personal space, 410
Persuasion, 409
Phone calls
of appreciation, 682

to ask a favor, 720-21
of condolence, 697
of congratulation, 689-90
from customers, 675-76
Pitch, voice, 409, 418
Plain talk, 430
Poise, 415
Posture, 412, 632
Praise, 499
Preparation
for effective speech, 400-01, 404-08
methods for, 424-30
Priorities, 427
Procrastination, 706
Productivity, encouraging, 707-09
Promotion, 504, 506. *See also* Career move, Success
Puberty, 609-10
Public speaking, 417

R.S.V.P., 523
Rage, *see* Anger
Rejection
accepting, 640
fear of, 624
graceful approach, 638
Relationships
communication in, 617-20, 624
misunderstandings, 658
Religion, 581-82
Remarriage, encouragement for, 491
Remembering the dead, 583-84
Repairs, failed, 677
Response, and body language, 438-41
Responsibility, 608-09
accepting, 664
Ridicule, 662
Rules, 591

Sadness, 535-37
Sales, applied to dating, 636-39
Sarcasm, 601
Saying No, 637
Scenarios of anger, 574-75
Scowl, 411
Scripting, 428-30
Self-conversation, 660
Self-esteem, 592
Self-interest, as motivator, 428, 429